THE BALFOUR DECLARATION

LEONARD STEIN

NEW YORK
SIMON AND SCHUSTER

PRINTED AND BOUND IN GREAT BRITAIN BY
TONBRIDGE PRINTERS LTD
TONBRIDGE · KENT

CONTENTS

v

CONTENTS

PART III

THE YEAR OF DECISION, 1917

PART IV

EPILOGUE

THE DECLARATION, NOVEMBER 1917 – SAN REMO, APRIL 1920

CONTENTS

Acknowledgments

The names of those to whom I am indebted for access to, and permission to quote from, unpublished documentary material are mentioned in the list of sources on pages 665–670. To all of them I offer my grateful thanks.

I owe much to the friendly interest of some of those who were, in various capacities, personally concerned with the events leading up to the Balfour Declaration, including, in particular, Viscount Samuel, the late Leopold Amery, Justice Felix Frankfurter, Lord Hankey, Viscount Harlech, Sir Harold Nicolson, Mr. Harry Sacher, Sir Leon Simon and Sir Charles Webster. I desire also gratefully to acknowledge the help I have received in collecting material and in other ways from Frances, Countess Lloyd George of Dwyfor, Lord Beaverbrook, Colonel Richard Meinertzhagen, c.b.e., d.s.o., Mr. Florian Sokolow, Mr. Christopher Sykes, and Mrs. Chaim Weizmann.

As explained in the body of this work (see pages 206, 504), I have benefited greatly by the use of information generously made available to me by Mr. Richard Lichtheim and Professor Selig Adler. I am indebted to Mr. F. S. Stambrook for valuable material derived from the archives of the German Ministry of Foreign Affairs and to Dr. Oskar Rabinowicz for drawing my attention to various sources of information and giving me access to his collection of books and papers bearing on my subject.

To Mr. Boris Guriel (Director of the Weizmann Archives) and to Dr. Alex Bein (Director of the Central Zionist Archives) I am under a special debt of gratitude, not only for their invaluable assistance in dealing with the documents in their charge, but also for the infinite pains they have taken in replying to my enquiries on questions arising in the preparation of this book.

ACKNOWLEDGMENTS

For permission to quote from published works my thanks are due to the following publishers and owners of copyright:

THE CONTROLLER OF H.M.S.O.:

British Documents on the Origins of the War, 1898-1914, Vols. IX and X, ed. G. P. Gooch and H. W. V. Temperley.

Documents on British Foreign Policy, 1919-39, First Series, Vols. IV, VII and VIII.

Syria and Palestine (Handbooks prepared under the direction of the Historical Section of the Foreign Office).

Letter of 2nd November 1917 from A. J. Balfour to Lord Rothschild (The Balfour Declaration).

GEORGE ALLEN & UNWIN, LTD.:

Napoleon and Palestine, by Philip Guedalla.

W. H. ALLEN & CO. LTD.:

A Piece of My Mind, by Edmund Wilson.

EDWARD ARNOLD, LTD.:

Social and Diplomatic Memories, by Sir Rennell Rodd.

ANSCOMBE:

Fifty Years of Zionism, by Dr. Oskar Rabinowicz.

G. BELL & SONS, LTD.:

The Foreign Policy of Palmerston, 1830-1841, by Sir Charles Webster.

The Jews of Today, by A. Ruppin.

JONATHAN CAPE, LTD.:

The Letters of T. E. Lawrence, ed. E. Garnett.

The Land of Three Faiths, by Philip Graves.

CASSELL & CO., LTD.:

The Second World War, by Winston Churchill.

Mark Sykes—His Life and Letters, by Shane Leslie.

Memoirs and Reflections, by Lord Oxford and Asquith.

ACKNOWLEDGMENTS

CONSTABLE & CO., LTD.:
Heading for the Abyss, by Prince Lichnowsky.
The Hapsburg Monarchy, by H. Wickham Steed.
Letters and Friendships of Sir Cecil Spring-Rice, ed. S. Gwynn.

THE CRESSET PRESS, LTD.:
Memoirs, by Viscount Samuel.
Middle East Diary, by Colonel R. Meinertzhagen.

EAST AND WEST LIBRARY:
Judah L. Magnes, by Norman Bentwich.

EYRE & SPOTTISWOODE, LTD.:
The Unknown Prime Minister, by Robert Blake.

FABER AND FABER, LTD.:
Some Recollections of C. G. Montefiore, by Lucy Cohen.

VICTOR GOLLANCZ, LTD.:
The Truth About the Peace Treaties, by D. Lloyd George.

HAMISH HAMILTON, LTD.:
Trial and Error, by Chaim Weizmann.

WILLIAM HEINEMANN, LTD.:
The Life and Letters of Walter H. Page, ed. B. J. Hendrick.
Jacob Schiff, by Cyrus Adler.
An Indian Diary, by Edwin Montagu.
The Memoirs of Count Bernstorff.
The Life and Letters of Woodrow Wilson, by R. S. Baker.

THE HUTCHINSON GROUP:
Life of Lord Oxford and Asquith, by A. J. Spender and Cyril Asquith.
An Ambassador's Memoirs, by M. Paléologue.
Tempestuous Journey, by Frank Owen.
Arthur James Balfour, by Blanche Dugdale.
My Political Life, by L. S. Amery.

ACKNOWLEDGMENTS

JEWISH HISTORICAL SOCIETY:
Nation or Religious Community, by C. G. Montefiore.
Notes on the Diplomatic History of the Jewish Question, by Lucien Wolf.

MACMILLAN & CO., LTD.:
Outlines of Liberal Judaism, by C. G. Montefiore.
The War and Democracy, by R. W. Seton-Watson.
The Caliph's Last Heritage, by Mark Sykes.
Great Britain and Palestine, by H. Sidebotham.
Philosophical and Literary Pieces, by Samuel Alexander.
The Life of Joseph Chamberlain, by J. Amery.

METHUEN & CO., LTD.:
Studies in Diplomatic History, by J. Headlam-Morley.

JOHN MURRAY, LTD.:
Life of Benjamin Disraeli, by Monnypenny and Buckle.
Zionism and the Jewish Future, ed. Harry Sacher.
Lady de Rothschild and Her Daughters, by Lucy Cohen.
At Close Quarters, by Arthur Murray.

IVOR NICOLSON & WATSON, LTD.:
Lord Riddell's *War Diary.*

OXFORD UNIVERSITY PRESS:
A Diary with Letters, by Thomas Jones.
A Study of History, by Arnold Toynbee. (Published by the O.U.P. on behalf of the Royal Institute of International Affairs.)

MARTIN SECKER & WARBURG, LTD.:
Alfred Mond, by Hector Bolitho.

UNION OF LIBERAL & PROGRESSIVE SYNAGOGUES:
Dangers of Zionism, by C. G. Montefiore.

SONCINO PRESS, LTD.:
Anglo-Jewish Letters, by Cecil Roth.

ACKNOWLEDGMENTS

GEORGE WEIDENFELD & NICOLSON, LTD.:
  Ben-Gurion of Israel, by Barnet Litvinoff.

YALE UNIVERSITY PRESS:
  The George Eliot Letters, ed. G. Haight.

ZIONIST ORGANISATION:
  The Case of the Anti-Zionists—A Reply, by Leon Simon.
  The Jewish State, by Theodor Herzl, translated by Sylvie d'Avigdor
  Zionism in England, by P. Goodman.

BEAVERBROOK NEWSPAPERS, LTD.:
  Men and Power, by Lord Beaverbrook. (Published by Hutchinson.)

DAILY EXPRESS:
  War Memoirs of David Lloyd George. (Published by Ivor Nicolson & Watson, Ltd.)

PRESIDENT DR. CHARLES SEYMOUR:
  The Intimate Papers of Colonel House. (Published by Ernest Benn, Ltd.)

CAPTAIN B. H. LIDDELL HART:
  T. E. Lawrence to His Biographer. (Published by Faber & Faber, Ltd.)

DR. S. LEVENBERG:
  British Labour Policy on Palestine. (Published by Poale Zion.)

MRS. SARAH GERTRUDE MILLIN:
  General Smuts. (Published by Faber & Faber, Ltd.)

In addition to those already mentioned, I have had valuable help and advice, which are gratefully acknowledged, from Mr. H. R. Aldridge (British Museum), Mr. Eliahu Elath, Sir Keith Hancock, Sir Lewis Namier, Dr. A. J. Toynbee and Dr. A. Wiener,

ACKNOWLEDGMENTS

and I desire also to record my indebtedness to the Alliance Israélite Universelle, Mr. Julian Amery, M.P., Professor Max Beloff, Mr. B. B. Benas, Professor Norman Bentwich, Professor Sir Isaiah Berlin, Bet Ahad Ha'am (Tel-Aviv), Mr. T. Blackburn, Mr. A. G. Brotman, Mr. H. S. Deighton, Mr. Max Epstein, Mr. Josef Fraenkel, Mr. Vivian Gaster, Mr. A. Gordon (Zionist Information Office), the late Philip Graves, Dr. Gordon Haight, the late Dr. J. Heller, Dr. Z. Y. Hershlag, the late Albert Hyamson, the Italian Institute, Mrs. Sylvia Landress (Zionist Archives and Library, New York), Dr. S. Levenberg, Lord Melchett, Mrs. Sarah Gertrude Millin, the Hon. Lily Montagu, Mr. Dermot Morrah, Alderman A. Moss, the late Dr. D. Mowshowitch, Sir Lancelot Oliphant, M. Louis Oungre (Paris), Mr. J. M. Rich (Johannesburg), Mr. Bernard G. Richards (New York), Mr. P. H. Robb (Psywar Society), Lord Rothschild, Dr. Cecil Roth, Mr. G. Saron (Johannesburg), the late Mrs. A. O. Scott, Mrs. Irene Sholto, Mr. J. C. Smuts, M. André Spire (Paris), Mr. Barry Sullivan, the late H. Wickham Steed, Mr. A. J. P. Taylor, Mr. J. H. Taylor, the late A. P. Wadsworth, Dr. Robert Weltsch, Sir Arthur Willert, Sir William Wiseman, Dr. Curt Wormann (Jewish National and University Library, Jerusalem), and the Librarians of the Imperial War Museum, *The Jewish Chronicle,* The London Library, the *News Chronicle,* the Royal Institute of International Affairs, *The Times,* the War Office Library, and the Wiener Library. In excavating material I have had useful assistance from my son, Peter.

I desire to thank my publishers, Vallentine, Mitchell & Co., Ltd., represented by my friend, Mr. David Kessler, for their generous provision of facilities for the preparation of this book, as well as for their patience in waiting some eight years for its completion.

LEONARD STEIN

Leckhampstead
June 1959

Part I

The Background
1839-1914

CHAPTER 1

THE EUROPEAN POWERS, PALESTINE
AND THE JEWS

ZIONISM IS ROOTED in ideas as old as the Jewish Dispersion, but as an organised and articulate Movement with precise objectives its history begins in 1897, when, under the leadership of Theodor Herzl, the First Zionist Congress set up the Zionist Organisation and in the Basle Programme defined its purpose as 'the creation in Palestine of a home for the Jewish people secured by public law.'[1,2]

The British Government's first contact with the Zionist Movement was in 1902, but some sixty years before, when the Syrian question was in one of its critical phases, the idea of the restoration of the Jews to Palestine had, in that context, engaged the interest of Lord Palmerston. In Palmerston's instructions to British representatives in the East between 1839 and 1841 there is ample evidence of his desire that the Jews in Palestine, and, indeed, in the Turkish dominions generally, should be encouraged to look to Great Britain for protection, and of his unsuccessful efforts to persuade the Turks that the settlement of Jews in Palestine would be to their advantage.

Against an entirely different background, the Zionist cause was taken up in 1902 by Joseph Chamberlain. In Palestine itself the British Government could do nothing for the Zionists, but, at Chamberlain's instance, it examined sympathetically a scheme for the settlement of Jews on the threshold of Palestine in the Sinai Peninsula. This was found to be impracticable, but, again on Chamberlain's initiative, the Zionists were offered, as a second-

---

[1] 'Der Zionismus erstrebt für das jüdische Volk die Schaffung einer öffentlich-rechtlich gesicherten Heimstaette in Palästina.' Full text of Basle Programme (in Engl. transl.) in Sokolow, *History of Zionism* (London, Longmans, 1919), I, xxiv.

[2] For the history of the Movement to 1914 reference may be made to Sokolow's *History of Zionism* and Böhm's *Die Zionistische Bewegung* (Berlin, Jüdischer Verlag, 1935). There is a useful summary in I. Cohen's *The Zionist Movement* (London, Muller, 1945).

best, a tract of land in the then British East Africa Protectorate. Not only was the proposal unwelcome to the British settlers in East Africa, but the Zionists themselves were in two minds about entertaining it. Highly as they valued this mark of British good-will, the view which finally prevailed was that the Movement could not risk any deviation from its central purpose—the establishment of a home for the Jewish people in Palestine.

The East African episode ended in 1905. Once again before 1914 the British Government had occasion to interest itself in Zionism, but this time in a less friendly spirit. When, after the Turkish Revolution, the Young Turks began to veer towards Germany, it was believed in British circles in Constantinople that the Zionists were working with pro-German elements among the Jews and crypto-Jews prominently associated with the Committee of Union and Progress. Reports to this effect which reached London from Constantinople in 1910-1912 did the Zionists no good in British eyes. At the highest level they seem to have made little impression, but in some influential British circles the idea gained ground that the Zionists were somehow linked with the Jews behind the Turkish Revolution and with the forces interested in swinging Turkey into the German orbit.[3]

Up to 1914 Great Britain was alone among the leading Powers in having shown some serious interest in Zionism. In the 1860s, when French prestige in the Levant was at its height, it had looked for a year or two as though France might be disposed to do something for the Jews in Palestine. Nothing had come of this, just as nothing had come of Herzl's approach to the Kaiser in the late 1890s, when Germany, then doing her best to advertise and assert herself in Palestine, had played for a moment with the idea of a Zionist Movement under German patronage and protection. During the war of 1914-1918 it was to occur both to the French and to the Germans that the Zionists might be useful friends, but in the last years of peace they were in disfavour both in Paris and in Berlin. In Paris they were seen as tools of Germany. In Berlin the Foreign Office noted with irritation and resentment the Zionist campaign against the use of German as a language of

---

[3] As to Sir Mark Sykes' view, see below, page 273. Sir Cecil Spring-Rice's remarks on this subject in the context of the Balfour Declaration (see below, p. 582) are also relevant and instructive.

approach to the Sultan. He had no illusions about Turkish benevolence, but he dreamed of a bargain on a strict *do ut des* basis; he would dangle before the Turks the prospect of being extricated, with Jewish help, from the financial embarrassments which made them a prey to exploitation by the Powers. His advances were not rebuffed out of hand. In May 1901 he was received in audience by the Sultan, and in the following year he was twice in Constantinople for conversations with members of the Imperial entourage. But he commanded no such resources as might have made him interesting to the Turks, and they were not to be bluffed. They soon realised that he was in no position to help them, while he, on his part, came to understand that, though they might be disposed, for their own purposes, to encourage Jews to immigrate to other parts of the Turkish Empire, there was no question of their permitting any mass settlement in Palestine.[79]

If the front door to Palestine was barred, possibly a side-entrance could be found. Perhaps the Zionists could establish settlements somewhere in the neighbourhood of Palestine and there bide their time. As early as July 1898 Herzl had been thinking vaguely of Cyprus.[80] When it became clear to him in 1902 that there was little to be hoped for from the Turks, his thoughts again turned to Cyprus, but by this time it had occurred to him that a half-way house might also be found in what he sometimes described as 'Egyptian Palestine', or, in other words, on the Egyptian side of the Turco-Egyptian frontier in the Sinai Peninsula. What he had particularly in mind was the El Arish area. This, he thought, might be 'an assembly centre for the Jewish people in the neighbourhood of Palestine.'[81] In a letter to Lord Rothschild,[82] who was at this time showing some interest in his proposals, he suggested that the El Arish scheme might appeal to the British Government, since British influence in the Eastern Mediterranean would be strengthened by 'a large-scale settlement of our people at a point where Egyptian and Indo-Persian interests converge.'[83]

[79] For a description of Herzl's visits to Constantinople see Bein, op. cit., pp. 352-366; 377-380; 391-393.
[80] *Tagebücher*, II, 94 (1 July 1898).
[81] Ibid., III, 298 (23 October 1902).
[82] The first Lord Rothschild.
[83] Herzl to Rothschild, 21 July 1902: *Tagebücher*, III, 236-237.

One of the small group of British-born Jews who had in these early days identified themselves with Zionism was Leopold Greenberg.[84] Greenberg came from Birmingham, where, as an ardent young Radical, he had become well known to Joseph Chamberlain. In the autumn of 1902, when direct contact with the British Government had become essential to the Zionists if anything was to be achieved either in the El Arish area or in Cyprus, Greenberg induced Chamberlain, then Colonial Secretary, to give Herzl a hearing. At two interviews with Herzl in the autumn of 1902 Chamberlain made it clear that, for political reasons, nothing could be done in Cyprus but showed serious interest in the El Arish proposal.[85]

There is no reason to doubt that, quite apart from other considerations, Chamberlain was genuinely concerned about the position of the Jews in Eastern Europe and anxious that Great Britain should do something to help them. On this point his Limehouse speech in 1904 rings true.[86] So does his letter of 11 November 1905, in which, writing to a Jewish friend from South Africa, Max Langermann, he denounces the persecution of the Jews as ' a disgrace and a danger to European civilisation ' and declares his readiness ' to give all support to any scheme that offers a hope of practical relief from their sufferings.'[87] Chamberlain sincerely desired to see something done for the Jews, but Herzl seems to have convinced him that the El Arish scheme had also certain attractions from a British point of view. His biographer writes:

> ' Herzl's arguments had undoubtedly made a deep impression on Chamberlain. Hitherto his interest in Zionism had been chiefly humanitarian; he now saw in it some positive opportunities for British policy. By supporting Zionism, Britain could enlist the sympathies of world Jewry on her behalf. She could also secure Jewish capital and settlers for the

---

[84] 1861-1931. Editor of *The Jewish Chronicle,* 1907-1931, and of *The Jewish World,* 1913-1931.

[85] *Tagebücher,* III, 295-299 and 304-305, describing interviews with Chamberlain on 22 and 23 October 1902.

[86] See below, p. 33.

[87] Quoted by Julian Amery, *Life of Joseph Chamberlain* (London, Macmillan, 1951), IV, 268.

development of what was virtually British territory. Looking, moreover, to the future, a Jewish colony in Sinai might prove a useful instrument for extending British influence in Palestine proper when the time came for the inevitable dismemberment of the Ottoman Empire.'[88]

Herzl describes in his diaries an interview with Chamberlain in April 1903, when the El Arish scheme was again discussed. He told Chamberlain, he says, that ' we shall get [Palestine] not from the goodwill but from the jealousy of the Powers. And if we are in El Ārish under the Union Jack, then our Palestine will likewise be in the British sphere of influence.' This suggestion, Herzl writes, was not at all ill-received.[89]

Chamberlain's own Department, the Colonial Office, was not concerned with Egyptian affairs. The El Arish scheme was a matter for the Foreign Office, and the day after his first interview with Herzl Chamberlain arranged for him to be received by the Foreign Secretary, Lord Lansdowne.[90] Lansdowne showed some interest and, after receiving Herzl's proposals in writing, passed them on to the British Agent in Cairo, Lord Cromer.[91] Cromer's

[88] Ibid., IV, 261. Mr. Julian Amery writes (to the author, 1 July 1955): ' I have already returned the papers dealing with this period to the Chamberlain Trustees and would hate to be categorical from memory. Speaking from memory, however, my impression is that the disruption of the Turkish Empire was a matter of continuous speculation at this time, and that, as the dominant Power in Egypt, we were already concerned with what would then happen in the territories lying immediately north of the Canal. Chamberlain certainly encouraged the El Arish proposal from the start, and in view of his very close interest in Egyptian affairs, and his personal friendship with Cromer, he must surely have had the Imperial as well as the humanitarian aspects of the problem in mind. There is some confirmation of this in the extracts from Herzl quoted at the bottom of page 263 and page 264 of my book. I rather think, too—but here I am relying on memory—that I read a Foreign Office memorandum of that period . . . in which this aspect of the matter was also considered.'

[89] *Tagebücher*, III, 412-413 (24 April 1903). (This is the passage referred to by Mr. Amery.)

[90] For a full account of the El Arish episode, see Bein, op. cit., pp. 418ff. A detailed account of the discussion between the Zionists and the British authorities up to January 1903, based on an examination of the relevant Foreign Office files, is to be found in Dr. O. K. Rabinowicz's *Herzl and England* (New York, 1951).

[91] Lansdowne to Cromer, 21 November 1902, quoted by Rabinowicz, op. cit., p. 33.

comments, though critical, were not altogether discouraging.[92] But in the end the project had to be abandoned. The Egyptian Government objected. The Turkish Government, through its Commissioner in Cairo, also objected. Doubts were raised as to whether the Imperial Firman, which was supposed to be the ultimate source of the Khedive's authority, empowered him to grant a Charter for the setting up of a more or less autonomous Jewish colony. There was, moreover, the important question whether the amount of water which would be required to satisfy the minimum needs of the settlement was not more than Egypt could reasonably be expected to provide.[92a] Cromer had second thoughts about the scheme and in the summer of 1903 gave it its *coup de grâce*. Herzl was informed by the Foreign Office that Cromer had advised that the project should be dropped, giving three main reasons—first, that the Egyptian Government persisted in its opposition, secondly, that the experts believed the scheme to be unsound, and lastly (this may well have been the decisive consideration), that the administration of Egypt already presented problems enough and it would be unwise to add to them. ' It can hardly be doubted,' Herzl was told, ' that, whatever might be the conditions of the settlement, the establishment of a large cosmopolitan society in the Sinai Peninsula would entail a material increase of the difficulties which the Egyptian Administration has already to encounter.'[93]

Soon after his meetings with Herzl in the autumn of 1902 Chamberlain left England on an official visit to Africa. The Jewish problem was still in his mind, and it occurred to him during his travels that there would not be much difficulty in finding room in British East Africa for a Jewish settlement under Zionist

---

[92] Cromer to Lansdowne, 29 November 1902, Rabinowicz, loc. cit.

[92a] A Committee of technical experts, headed by Leopold Kessler, had reported to Herzl, after investigations on the spot, that the crucial question was that of irrigation. For a summary of the report see Bein, *Herzl*, pp. 433–434.

[93] Foreign Office to Herzl, 19 June 1903: *Zionist Archives* (Jerusalem). This was followed a month later by another letter making it clear to Herzl that it had been finally decided to abandon the El Arish project; F.O. to Herzl, 16 July 1903: Z.A. Though unable, in the end, to support the El Arish scheme, Cromer later showed himself sympathetically interested in Zionism—see below, pp. 173, 300.

auspices.[94] In his diary there is a note, dated 21 December 1902, to the effect that if Herzl was inclined to consider East Africa, suitable land could be found there; 'but I assume this country is too far removed from Palestine to have any attraction for him.' This is quoted by his biographer as the first reference in the Chamberlain papers to the idea of a Jewish settlement in East Africa.[95]

On returning home in the spring of 1903 Chamberlain put this suggestion to Herzl, who was in London in the interests of the El Arish scheme. According to Herzl's diary, Chamberlain spoke of Uganda,[96] but, if he did, it was a slip of the tongue; it is clear that he was not, in fact, thinking of Uganda but of the East Africa Protectorate, soon to become the Colony of Kenya.[97] Still dreaming of El Arish, Herzl refused to entertain any alternative, but he changed his mind when he heard, a few weeks later, that in conversation with Greenberg Chamberlain had again raised the question of a Jewish settlement under the British flag in East Africa.[98] There was in Herzl's mind no question of the Zionist Movement being diverted from its central purpose—the creation of a home for the Jewish people in Palestine.[99] Palestine was the goal and East Africa could be no substitute. It was, however, strongly represented to Herzl by Greenberg that an offer from the British Government was not lightly to be rejected and that by

---

94 For a detailed account of the East African episode see Bein, op. cit., pp. 435ff., and Böhm, I, 254ff. See also the Foreign Office material drawn upon by Dr. O. K. Rabinowicz in *Fifty Years of Zionism* and in *New Light on the East Africa Scheme*, reprinted from *The Rebirth of Israel* (London, 1952).

95 Amery, op. cit., IV, 262.

96 *Tagebücher*, II, 412 (24 April 1903), describing an interview with Chamberlain on the 23rd: 'On my travels I have seen a land for you—Uganda. It is hot on the coast, but in the interior the climate is excellent for Europeans.' In Zionist circles the project was almost always referred to as the 'Uganda' scheme.

97 Amery suggests (op. cit., IV, 263) that Herzl may have misunderstood something said by Chamberlain about land he had seen from the Uganda Railway.

98 *Tagebücher*, III, 437 (23 May 1903), recording a message from Greenberg about an interview with Chamberlain on May 20th: 'He [Chamberlain] offers us an area for colonisation large enough for a million souls, with local self-government. Not in Uganda, but in that region.'

99 See, on this point, Dr. O. K. Rabinowicz, *Herzl* (New York, Herzl Press, 1958), pp. 11ff.

enlisting its active interest the Movement might be brought a step nearer to its final destination.[100] Realising that the El Arish scheme was a forlorn hope, Herzl had already authorised Greenberg to investigate the East African project and to find out more precisely what Chamberlain had in mind.[101] He now agreed that the Zionists should frame their own proposals and submit them to the Government for comment. Greenberg acted promptly and early in July 1903 sent Herzl a draft scheme prepared, on his instructions, by a firm of solicitors, Lloyd George, Roberts and Company. These, he explained, ' in addition to being excellent people, have a great advantage—Lloyd George, as you know, is a Member of Parliament ; he, therefore, knows the ropes of these things and can be helpful to us.'[102] Having been approved by Herzl, the scheme was sent to Chamberlain on July 13th.

Though the initiative had come from Chamberlain, the Foreign Office, and not the Colonial Office, was the competent Department.[103] The scheme was passed on by Chamberlain to the Foreign Secretary, and Lansdowne, already knowing something about Zionism from his handling of the El Arish project, gave the matter some personal attention.[104] As in the case of El Arish, he was cautious but by no means unsympathetic. Without committing himself to the proposals set out in the Lloyd George, Roberts draft, he agreed in August to provide Greenberg with a letter suitable for communication to the Sixth Zionist Congress, then about to meet at Basle. The letter, dated 14 August 1903,

[100] Greenberg to Herzl, 1 June 1903 : Rabinowicz, *New Light on the East Africa Scheme*, p. 78.

[101] *Tagebücher*, III, 437 (23 May 1903).

[102] Greenberg to Herzl, 4 July 1903 : an extract from this otherwise unpublished letter is printed by Rabinowicz, op. cit., p. 79. For permission to use the letter the author is indebted to Greenberg's daughter, Mrs. Sholto. So far as is known, this was Lloyd George's first contact with the Zionist Movement.

[103] For the reason that the territory in question was in a Protectorate and not a Colony.

[104] Though the initiative came from Chamberlain and the matter was handled by Lansdowne, the project would clearly have required the approval of the Prime Minister, Arthur Balfour, and was, in fact, actively supported by him : see Sokolow, I. xxix. No correspondence on the East African offer between Balfour and Chamberlain has, however, been found in the Balfour papers : Mrs. Dugdale in Goodman's *Jewish National Home*, p. 3.

was in guarded language but made it clear that the East African project was being taken seriously.[105] It began with a reference to 'the form of an agreement which Dr. Herzl proposes should be entered into between His Majesty's Government and the Jewish Colonial Trust, Ltd.,[106] for the establishment of a Jewish settlement in East Africa,' and continued:

> 'I am now directed by His Lordship to say that he has studied the question with the interest which His Majesty's Government must always take in any well-considered scheme for the amelioration of the position of the Jewish Race. The time at his disposal has been too short to enable him to go fully into the details of the plan or to discuss it with His Majesty's Commissioner for the East Africa Protectorate and he regrets that he is unable to pronounce any definite opinion on the matter.'

This was, however, followed by an assurance that, subject to certain provisos,

> 'Lord Lansdowne will be prepared to entertain favourably proposals for the establishment of a Jewish colony or settlement on conditions which will enable the members to observe their National customs. For this purpose he would be prepared to discuss (if a suitable site had been found and subject to the views of the advisers of the Secretary of State in East Africa) the details of a scheme comprising as its main features: the grant of a considerable area of land, the appointment of a Jewish official as chief of the local administration, and permission to the Colony to have a free hand in regard to municipal legislation and as to the management of religious and purely domestic matters, such local autonomy being conditional upon the right of His Majesty's Government to exercise a general control.'

The letter was read by Greenberg to the Zionist Congress on 26 August 1903, and the project thus became public property.

At this point things began to go wrong. When the British settlers in the Protectorate learned of what was on foot, they lost

[105] VI Z.C. Prot., pp. 215-216; see also The Times, 27 August 1903.
[106] The J.C.T. was the main financial instrument of the Movement.

no time in expressing their indignation.[107] A protest against 'the introduction of alien Jews' was cabled to the Foreign Office by their spokesman, Lord Delamere, and published in *The Times*,[108] where it appeared together with a letter in opposition to the proposal (though on different grounds) from a well-known Jewish publicist, Lucien Wolf. The British Commissioner for the Protectorate, Sir Charles Eliot, was from the first half-hearted about the scheme and in the end advised against it.[109] The Zionists themselves were confused and disunited. At the Zionist Congress the delegates were deeply moved by the British offer and unanimous in welcoming it as evidence that their Movement had engaged the serious attention of a great World Power. But there agreement ended. With gratitude to the British Government and pride in the enhanced status of the Zionist Organisation were mingled the doubts and misgivings of those who saw in the proposal the beginning of the end of Zionism as a Movement dedicated to the creation of a home for the Jewish people in Palestine. The connection between the Jews and Palestine was of the essence of the Zionist creed. Once let the Organisation deviate even momentarily from its real purpose and it might never find its way back. These views were held with passionate conviction by a large part of the Congress, including most of the delegates from Russia. In the end it was decided to temporise. The Congress agreed by a majority, a large number of delegates abstaining, that a Committee should be set up to consider whether a commission of enquiry should be sent to East Africa. After an interval of some sixteen months, a Zionist Commission did go out to the Protectorate, but in the meantime the protests of the Zionists in rebellion against the scheme had become louder and more insistent, while the British settlers had shown no sign of having changed their minds and the British Commissioner had passed from doubt

---

[107] See Elspeth Huxley, *White Man's Country* (London, Chatto and Windus, 1953), pp. 118ff.

[108] Ibid.; *The Times*, 28 August 1903.

[109] Elspeth Huxley, op. cit., p. 123. In the House of Commons, on 20 June 1904, it was officially stated that 'Sir Charles Eliot's last opinion was unfavourable to the scheme': O.R., Col. 578. In the same debate a Member said that in 1903 'he had found the country seething with indignation at the proposition to make these settlements of Russian and Rumanian Jews': Col. 562.

to disapproval.[110] By the end of 1903 the Foreign Office seems already to have become weary of a project so beset with difficulties: a note by Lord Lansdowne on a Foreign Office memorandum on the subject, dated 14 December 1903, reads as follows: 'We shall probably be well out of it! But it was right to treat the application considerately.'[111]

The scheme had become burdensome to the Government, but it was by no means extinct and was assumed to be still in being when the whole question of the settlement of Jews in East Africa was debated in the House of Commons on 20 June 1904. The Government spokesman was the Under-Secretary of State for Foreign Affairs, Earl Percy. After giving particulars of 'the lease of land which they had provisionally offered to the Jews,' he went on to explain the Government's attitude in language not unlike that of the Foreign Office letter of 14 August 1903:

'The motives which had actuated the Government had not been of a purely financial character; they had been inspired by those feelings of sympathy which ought to be felt by every Christian nation, and which had always been felt by the British race, for that persecuted and oppressed people.'[112]

Earl Percy was followed by Sir Edward Grey, who, while asking for fuller information about the scheme, expressed his sympathy with its purpose:

'Something had turned on the point that it was a Jewish settlement that was contemplated. They all knew what anti-Semitic feeling was and what it gave rise to. But there was another view of the Jewish race, that of millions of persecuted people who had been through generation after generation scattered without homes and without hope; and he said frankly that if it were the intention to attempt to provide a refuge and a home for people of that description in the British dominions, it would have his entire sympathy.'[113]

[110] See preceding note.
[111] Quoted from F.O. files by Rabinowicz, *Fifty Years of Zionism*, p. 56.
[112] H.C., 20 June 1904: O.R., Col. 571ff.
[113] Col. 575.

A Zionist Commission of Enquiry was at length appointed and left for East Africa at the end of 1904. Its unenthusiastic report helped to extricate both the Zionists and the British Government from what had now become, for both, a somewhat embarrassing position. On 30 July 1905 the Seventh Zionist Congress adopted by an overwhelming majority a statement in which it affirmed its rejection of all Zionist activity outside Palestine and its immediate neighbourhood, and, while thanking the British Government for its offer to make land available for a Jewish settlement in East Africa, resolved not to engage itself further with the proposal. The statement went on to declare that ' the Congress recalls with satisfaction the recognition accorded by the British Government to the Zionist Organisation in its desire to bring about a solution of the Jewish problem, and expresses a sincere hope that it may be accorded the further good offices of the British Government, where available, in any matter it may undertake in accordance with the Basle Programme.'[114]

Thus ended the second of Joseph Chamberlain's attempts to help the Zionists. They were made at a time when the arrival in England of considerable numbers of Jewish refugees from Eastern Europe had given rise to an agitation against alien immigrants and a demand that the influx be checked. After an enquiry by a Royal Commission on Alien Immigration,[115] certain restrictions on the entry of aliens were proposed in a Bill introduced by the Balfour Government in the spring of 1904.[116] By that time Chamberlain had resigned from the Government, but when he interested himself in the El Arish scheme and, later, in the East African project, it was already common knowledge that some such legislation was to be expected. Though Chamberlain was satisfied of its necessity, he seems also to have felt that the Jews who were thus to be denied asylum in England ought, if possible, to be offered some compensation, and it looks as though this accounts, at least in part, for the East African offer. Speaking at a public meeting at Limehouse on 15 December 1904, he said: [117]

[114] Transl. from the original German text, *VII Z.C. Prot.*, p. 132. Printed also in Böhm, I, 315.
[115] Report in Cmd. 1741 (1903).
[116] As to this legislation, see below, pp. 79, 150.
[117] *The Times*, 16 December 1904.

'You are suffering from the unrestricted import of cheaper goods. You are suffering also from the unrestricted immigration of the people who make these goods. . . . Now a word as to the people themselves. I, for one, am not going to press hardly upon these poor people. . . . I think they are subjects for pity and for practical sympathy. There is a problem, how are they to be saved from the fate which is befalling them, how is their salvation to be accomplished without the ruin of our own people at home? While I was in office, I did what I could. I had many conferences with the late Dr. Herzl,[118] a man who made upon me the greatest impression, whose sincerity, patriotism and ability were such as must have provoked the regard of anyone who became aware of him. And in principle, at any rate, I can say that we were agreed that the best solution of this question was to find some country in this world of ours, if possible under the ægis of the British flag, or under the protection, if you please, of a Concert of nations—some place in which these poor exiles from their native land, who do not leave it out of caprice or with any desire to injure us, could dwell in safety, following their own religion and their own aspirations, and where they could find subsistence without in any way interfering with the subsistence of others. . . . I think that within the present week a Commission is leaving for East Africa . . . to see whether there cannot be found an asylum for these persecuted people. That is the solution of the question. . . .'

The East African episode left deep scars on the Zionist Movement. It came near to splitting the Organisation and, even though this was averted, it gave rise to bitter personal feuds which for years poisoned the relations between some of the principal Zionist leaders. But it also left another legacy. From the 1840s onwards, well-remembered instances of British concern for the welfare of the Jews,[119] coupled with Great Britain's liberal treatment of her

---

[118] Herzl died, at the age of 44, on 3 July 1904.

[119] In connection with the Rumanian question, the British Government declared in 1867 : ' The peculiar position of the Jews places them under the protection of the civilised world ': L. Wolf, *Diplomatic History of the Jewish Question*, p. 24, citing *British and Foreign State Papers*, LXII, 705.

own Jewish population, had caused her name to be held in honour by Jews everywhere in the world, and especially by the Jewish masses in Eastern Europe. Whatever view might be taken of its merits, the Zionists, and not only the Zionists, saw in the East African offer a striking re-affirmation of British goodwill. Writing privately to a colleague in 1911, Wolffsohn, Herzl's successor as President of the Zionist Organisation, said in a sentence what most Jews felt: 'The Jews generally, and especially the Zionists, have more to thank England for than all the other Powers put together.'[120]

After the Turkish Revolution of 1908-1909 there was some revival of British interest in Zionism, but it was now a less friendly interest. In British circles in Constantinople it became an *idée fixe* that powerful Jewish forces closely linked with Germany were working to undermine the British position in the East, and that among these must be counted the Zionists. The British Ambassador reported unfavourably on Jewish activities in Turkey. The Chief Dragoman at the Embassy, G. H. Fitzmaurice,[121] busied himself with a close study of Jewish financial, commercial and political contacts in the Balkan Peninsula.[122] The Constantinople correspondent of *The Times* sent home reports warning British public opinion against Zionist and other Jewish manœuvres for the benefit of Germany. How firmly the idea took root that Zionism was a movement directed by German Jews in German interests is shown by a passage in the volume on *Syria and Palestine* in the series of Foreign Office Handbooks published

[120] Wolffsohn to Victor Jacobson, 15 February 1911: Z.A.

[121] According to T. E. Lawrence, Fitzmaurice 'was a rabid Roman Catholic and hated Freemasons and Jewry with a religious hatred. The Young Turk Movement was 50 per cent. crypto-Jew and 95 per cent Freemason': *T. E. Lawrence to his Biographers, Liddell Hart and Robert Graves* (London, Faber and Faber, 1938), p. 88. Fitzmaurice seems later to have modified his views about Jews to the extent of showing some friendly interest in Zionism in the Balfour Declaration period, as evidenced by his contacts with Weizmann and Aaron Aaronsohn: Weizmann to Sokolow, 18 February, 1917, *Ch.W.P.* (Papers of Dr. Chaim Weizmann in the Weizmann Archives, Rehovoth, Israel); *Aaronsohn Diaries* (Diaries of Aaron Aaronsohn, in the possession of the Aaronsohn Memorial Foundation, Zikhron Ya'akov, Israel), 24 November 1916.

[122] Philip Graves, *Briton and Turk* (London, Hutchinson, 1941) p. 158. Graves was Constantinople correspondent of *The Times,* 1908-1914.

in 1920 substantially in the form in which they had been originally prepared for the use of the British Delegation at the Paris Peace Conference. After a reference to Abdul Hamid's objection to 'a German Palestine,' it is explained that 'only after the Revolution of 1908 could the German-Jew institutions, which had come into existence to take control of the Hebrew movement in Palestine, begin to make headway, and the German era of Jew colonisation increased materially the number and holdings of alien settlers,'[123]

British opinion in Constantinople began to turn against the Jews about the time when Turkey, after a brief change of heart in the earlier phases of the Revolution, was seen to be swinging back into the Geman orbit.[124] The Revolution had been organised from Salonica, where the Jews, together with the crypto-Jews known as Dönmeh, formed a majority of the population. Salonica Jews and Dönmeh had taken an important part in the events associated with the Revolution and had provided the Committee of Union and Progress with several of its ablest members. The Turks needed no prompting to be suspicious of Russia, but for all Jews everywhere Russia was the enemy, and it was a natural assumption that the Jewish elements in the C.U.P. would not be backward in pushing Turkey in an anti-Russian and, as a corollary, in a pro-German direction.

On the other hand, it was an error to suppose that they were somehow associated with the Zionists. Zionism had never gained a hold on the Oriental Jews. In Turkey, in particular, the Alliance Israélite, which, because of its educational work, had acquired considerable influence and prestige, had done and continued to do all it could to obstruct and discredit the Zionist Movement.[125] Nor would it, in any case, have been possible for the Jews

---

[123] F.O. Handbook, *Syria and Palestine*, p. 45.

[124] British resentment against the Jews is illustrated by a passage in R. W. Seton-Watson's contribution to *The War and Democracy* (London, Macmillan, 1915), at p. 284: 'Since 1908 the fate of Turkey has passed from the control of the Turk and is being decided by an alien clique of infidels, renegades, political freemasons and Jews.' Seton-Watson, however, distinguishes between 'pseudo-national' and 'national' Judaism and speaks favourably of the Zionist Movement.

[125] See Böhm, I, 396 ; R. Gottheil, *Zionism* (Philadelphia, 1914), pp. 157, 227.

associated with the C.U.P. to interest themselves in Zionism without imperilling their precarious position as members of a non-Turkish and non-Moslem minority. As a matter of self-preservation, they had to be more Turkish than the Turks. Nothing could have been worse for their standing with their ultra-nationalist colleagues than any sign of friendliness for Zionist aspirations in Palestine. Far from being influenced by their Jewish associates in favour of Zionism, the Young Turks showed themselves immovably opposed to it.

All the same, it is possible to understand why responsible British observers in Turkey gained the impression that the Zionists were playing the German game. There was, first, the behaviour of the Zionist Agency in Constantinople, and there were, secondly, the peculiar activities of a Jewish adventurer, Alfred Nossig, who, soon after the Revolution, appeared on the scene from Berlin.

A Zionist Agency had been established in Constantinople in 1908. Its Director, Victor Jacobson,[126] was a Russian-born Jew who had spent his student-years in Germany and, as was to be more clearly shown during the Balfour Declaration period, had become firmly convinced that German goodwill was more important to the Zionists than that of any other Power. The Constantinople Agency's subsidised organ, Le Jeune Turc, lent itself to German propaganda and more than once published articles unfriendly to Great Britain. The business manager of the paper was a German, Samy Hochberg, and among those invited to contribute was Alexander Helphand who, under his pseudonym 'Parvus,' was later to become an important link between the Germans and the Bolsheviks.[127] It is impossible to say with certainty that Jacobson actively encouraged Le Jeune Turc in its pro-German bias, but at least he gave a free hand to German or pro-German writers. Far from approving of his handling of the paper, the headquarters of the Zionist Executive in Cologne were embarrassed by what were regarded as serious indiscretions. It was in protesting to Jacobson against an anti-British article in Le Jeune Turc that Wolffsohn, in a letter already quoted,

[126] 1869-1934. Elected a member of the Zionist Executive, August 1911. Appointed Director of the Copenhagen Zionist Bureau, 1916.
[127] Lichtheim, Memoirs (see Note on sources), Chapt. XII.

reminded him that Great Britain had done more for the Jews, and especially for the Zionists, than all the other Powers put together. Nevertheless, it was common knowledge that *Le Jeune Turc* was subsidised from Zionist funds, and it is not surprising that its pro-German tone was assumed in British circles to be a reflection of Zionist policy.[128]

The Zionists were still further prejudiced in British eyes by the activities of Dr. Alfred Nossig. Soon after the Revolution Nossig presented himself in Constantinople with ambitious plans for the settlement of Jews both in Palestine and elsewhere in Asiatic Turkey, notably in Mesopotamia, under the auspices of a German-Jewish organisation founded by himself and having its seat in Berlin.[129] Coming from Berlin, the suggestion that Jews should be encouraged to establish themselves in Mesopotamia served only to aggravate British suspicions, since in no part of the Turkish Empire were British and German interests so near to colliding.

Nossig had at one time been an active Zionist, but at the Ninth Zionist Congress in 1909 he had been publicly disowned by the President of the Organisation, and Zionists had been warned to have nothing to do with his unauthorised activities.[130] All the same, he had a Zionist past, and the proposals which he brought to the Turks from his Organisation in Berlin, coupled with his bombastic hints that, if Turkey would do as he suggested, she would be helped to secure 'influential alliances,' went to strengthen the impression prevailing in British circles in Constantinople that the Zionists were somehow linked with Germany and working in German interests. 'As Dr. Nossig comes from Berlin, it may be assumed,' said the *Times* correspondent, 'that these alliances would be with the Central European Powers.'[131]

All this did not pass unnoticed at the British Embassy. In

[128] This brief account of the *Jeune Turc* episode is based on material from the following sources: Böhm, I, 393-394 ; Philip Graves, op. cit., p. 154 ; Lichtheim, *Geschichte,* pp. 104, 204 ; Lichtheim, *Memoirs,* Chapters X and XII.

[129] *Allgemeine Jüdische Kolonisations-Organisation :* see Lichtheim, *Geschichte,* pp. 205, 211 ; Böhm, I, 496 ; *The Times,* 14 April 1911.

[130] Böhm, loc. cit.

[131] *The Times,* 14 April 1911.

August 1910 the Ambassador, Sir Gerard Lowther, reported to London as follows: [132]

'In its internal form the Committee [of Union and Progress] appears to be a Judeao-Turkish dual alliance, the Turks supplying a splendid military material and the Jews the brain, enterprise, money . . . and a strong press influence in Europe, while, as shown by Sionist [sic] literature since the Revolution, the Jewish world seems to have now turned its eyes towards Mesopotamia as the land best suited for Jewish colonisation and the ultimate formation of a Jewish autonomous State. The Jews who now seem to inspire and control the inside machinery of the State and are bent on the economic and industrial capture of Young Turkey appear determined that no important enterprise shall be started in Mesopotamia, without their participation, if not control. . . . The Jews, in order to maintain their position of influence in Young Turkey [sic] circles, have to play up to, if not encourage, Turkish "nationalistic" tendencies, and the two elements make a distinctive strong combination which has to be reckoned with, especially by those interested in Mesopotamia. . . .'

After speaking of the chauvinism of the Young Turks and the probability of conflict between British and Ottoman interests in several parts of the Arab world, especially in Mesopotamia and the Persian Gulf, the Ambassador continued:

'In this connexion, I have the honour to enclose copies of three articles which have recently appeared in the *Jeune Turc*, a Committee-inspired paper, which, like the *Neue Freie Presse* of Vienna, is financed and directed by Jews. The latter's detestation of Russia, which is one of the features of Young Turkey, is frequently reflected in its columns. . . . The articles inveigh against what they erroneously call the Triple Entente and try to make Young Turkey incline towards the Triple Alliance.'

In 1911-1912 Zionism was receiving some unfavourable publi-

[132] 22 August 1910: G. P. Gooch and H. W. V. Temperley (Ed.), *British Documents on the Origins of the War*, 1898-1914 (London, H.M.S.O.), Vol. X, Pt. II, No. 1.

city in *The Times,* whose Constantinople correspondent shared the Embassy's view of Jewish activities in Turkey. In a message published in *The Times* of 14 April 1911 he drew attention to the *Jeune Turc's* ' violent hostility to England ' and ' its Germanophile enthusiasm,' and to the propaganda carried on among Turkish Jews by ' German Zionist agents.' Commenting on ' the unconcealed activities of the advocates of Jewish immigration ' in favour of ' the introduction of great numbers of Jews into the thinly populated lowlands of Mesopotamia,' he asked:

> ' What would be the political bearing of such an event as the colonisation of parts of Mesopotamia and Syria by Jews from Central and Eastern Europe, whose language would be Judæo-German, whose leaders would be German and Austria Jews . . . ?'

Three months later *The Times* published at length, in a message from Constantinople, the remarks of ' a well-known Arab divine ' to the effect that the policy of the Committee of Union and Progress was affected by ' the presence in the [Masonic] Lodges of strong Jewish influences, working in favour of Zionism and also for the exploitation by Jewish capitalists of the Ottoman provinces of Syria and Palestine.'[133] In September 1912 *The Times* Constantinople correspondent again sounded a note of warning about the Zionists. ' Judging from the attitude of the principal Zionist organ in Constantinople, there is,' he reported, ' a strong Anglophobe current among many of the Eastern Jews.' He went on to suggest that

> ' given the predominantly German-Jewish character of Zionism, the British public and those who guide its political opinion will be well advised to take more than a platonic interest in the Movement,'

adding that, apart from other considerations,

> ' there is the question of the maintenance of British prestige in the Arab world. . . . Indiscreet manifestations of sympathy with Zionism on the part of any important section of the British public might conceivably cost us the confidence of the

[133] *The Times,* 12 July 1911.

best elements in the Arab world from Mohammerah to Mombasa.'[134]

Read together with the extract already quoted from the British Ambassador's dispatch, these reports suggest that in British circles in Constantinople it was believed that the Jewish politicians in Turkey were somehow linked with the Zionists and that both were working for Germany; that it was also believed that an attempt should be made to discredit the Jewish members of the C.U.P., and to drive a wedge between them and their Turkish colleagues, by suggesting that they were pursuing hidden ends of their own; and, lastly, that it was thought expedient to hint to the Arabs that, whatever the Zionists might be planning to their disadvantage, Great Britain was their friend.

The charge that the Zionists were working for Germany was answered in *The Times* by Wolffsohn, Herzl's successor as President of the Zionist Organisation, in May 1911,[135] and at the Tenth Jewish Congress, a few months later, was brushed disdainfully aside by Max Nordau: 'In England it is proclaimed that the Zionists are enemies of the British and are the advance-posts of Germany, whose power in Turkey they seek to establish in strength at England's expense. Whoever knows Zionism and the Zionists ever so little laughs at all that asinine talk.'[136] At the Eleventh Congress, in the summer of 1913, Dr. Moses Gaster[137] dealt with the matter more fully[138]:

'[Zionism] is not a German Movement. I wish you to understand this, because it has been described as such in the English press, from *The Times* downwards. It has been said that the centre is in Germany, and the Zionists serve German

---

[134] *The Times*, 28 September 1912.
[135] *The Times*, 11 May 1911. Further letters on the subject from a prominent English Zionist, Herbert Bentwich, and from Max Nordau were published in *The Times* of 7 October and 30 December 1912.
[136] Quoted from the report in *J.C.*, 18 August 1911. A leading English Zionist said, at a meeting of the English delegates, that the transfer of the headquarters of the Movement from Cologne to Berlin would be unfortunate, 'since the Zionists were accused already of being the cat's paw of German politics, and if the Central Office was at Berlin it would make matters worse.' *J.C.*, 11 August 1911.
[137] See below, pp. 286–287.
[138] Translated from German text in *XI Z.C. Prot.*, pp. 111-112.

political interests. . . . We are fighting everywhere to make it clear that we feel neither German nor English nor French nor Russian, but that our feelings and our thoughts are solely and exclusively Jewish.'

Here was the germ of the principle of neutrality, which, though generally accepted by Zionists at the time, was soon, as we shall see, to give rise to unforeseen difficulties. In 1913 Gaster seemed to most Zionists to be propounding a simple and self-evident truth: the *raison d'être* of the Zionist Organisation was to serve the Jewish people, and not to promote the interests, or put itself at the service, of this or that Great Power. Within little more than a year it began to be seen that it was easier to affirm the principle of neutrality than to be sure how it was in practice to be interpreted and applied to the advantage of the Zionist cause in the circumstances of a war which split Europe in two. Had 'neutrality' been strictly observed, there could have been no Balfour Declaration.

After the liquidation of the East African project in 1905 it was some years before the Zionist leaders attempted to re-establish contact with the British Government. In the summer of 1912, Nahum Sokolow,[139] a Russian-Polish member of the Zionist Executive, the directorate of the Movement, was sent from Berlin[140] to take some soundings in London. He does not appear to have visited the Foreign Office or to have seen any member of the Government, and he returned to Berlin with nothing much to report beyond his impression that in English public life, and especially in religious circles, Zionism had some influential friends.[141]

A few months later war broke out in the Balkans. The Powers were once more confronted with the Eastern Question in an acute and urgent form, and there was in some Zionist circles a strong feeling that now was the time for a fresh approach to the British

[139] See below, pp. 167–170.
[140] The seat of the Executive had been moved from Cologne to Berlin in 1911.
[141] For Sokolow's visits to England in 1912 and 1913 see S. Rawidowicz, ' Nahum Sokolow in Great Britain' in *The New Judæa*, May 1941 ; J. Hodess, ' Dr. Chaim Weizmann,' in *Zion*, January 1953.

Goverment. From England this view was pressed upon the Executive by Weizmann, who, though not yet in a position of leadership, was one of the British members of the Zionist General Council and already an important figure in the Zionist world. In November 1912 he wrote to Berlin urging that Sokolow should come to England without delay. He asked that in the meantime he himself should be authorised to approach certain important personages to whom, he said, he could get access—among them Balfour and Haldane.[142] The Executive declined to sanction such conversations but early in 1913 arranged for Sokolow to spend some time in London on his way to the United States.

Sokolow had the advantage of a letter of recommendation from the British Ambassador in St. Petersburg, and this time he established direct contact with the Foreign Office. Soon after his arrival he was seen by a high official, Sir Louis Mallet,[143] and on 3 March 1913 he had a lengthy interview with some other senior members of the Department. There is no record of his having been received by the Foreign Secretary or any other Minister, but he felt that he had at least broken the ice and left London satisfied, as he reported to his colleagues, that 'in case the question of Palestine is put before any future Conference, this will prove to have been our preparatory step.'[144] He had started on his mission with no excessive optimism. 'Zionism,' he wrote in one of his reports, 'has no longer the attraction of novelty which it had before. One has also to pay attention to the general increase of anti-Semitism. This has now become epidemic in France and also in England.'[145] Nor was he under any illusions as to what he had achieved. Though the Foreign Office had seemed to be genuinely interested in what he had to say, he realised that at a moment when the Balkan crisis was at its height the British Government was not likely to busy itself with the Jews and their aspirations in Palestine.

Whatever impression Sokolow may have made at the Foreign

---

[142] Weizmann to Zionist Executive, 20 November 1912: Z.A. As to his conversation with Balfour in 1906, see below, p. 151.

[143] Then an Assistant Under-Secretary of State; later, Ambassador in Constantinople.

[144] Quoted by Rawidowicz, loc. cit.

[145] Ibid.

Office, it seems clear that in the early stages of the War of 1914-18 the view held in the Department was that the Zionists and their claims were of little practical importance. When Sokolow came to London at the end of 1914, the Foreign Office politely excused itself from receiving him, explaining that it already possessed ample information about Zionism and could see no need for an interview.[146] In some higher quarters, as we shall see, the Zionists enjoyed from the start more sympathy than they themselves realised, but at the official level the Foreign Office was not disposed to give them any encouragement.

[146] See below, p. 170.

CHAPTER 2

GREAT BRITAIN AND FRANCE IN THE LEVANT

'The political problem in Palestine is at once intensely interesting and immensely critical by reason of its complexity. . . . England alone stands outside the arena of strife and intrigue ; her interests in the land are few, and her policy continues to be one of restraint. . . . England may find herself forced to interfere, suddenly, silently, but very definitely. Palestine and Syria have been ere now the battleground of European politics. The future defies our speculation ; but the last few years should have prepared us for any change, however startling.'

The Near East,
21 November 1913

IN THE LAST years of peace before 1914 France was insisting energetically on the recognition of her moral and material interests in Syria. Well entrenched there at the outbreak of war, she was not slow to make it clear to her Allies that in any partition of the Turkish Empire her claims would extend to a Greater Syria, including Palestine. The events which were, step by step, to drive her back from that position and to end in a British Mandate for Palestine form an indispensable part of the background to the Balfour Declaration.

When France had begun, after 1815, to re-establish her Great Power status and, in doing so, to rebuild her position in the Levant, her Eastern policy had at first pivoted on Egypt. This chapter had been closed by the events of 1882. The French had had to recognise that effective control of Egypt, and all that went with it, had passed irrevocably to Great Britain, but they had been slow to reconcile themselves to the new situation. They had brought themselves in the end to assent, at a price, to British predominance in the Nile Valley, but the Anglo-French Agreement of 1904, though it had put an end to French obstruction, had not wholly extinguished French resentment.[1] All the more

---

[1] As late as the summer of 1917, Sir Mark Sykes, describing his difficulties in working for Anglo-French co-operation in the East, mentioned among them 'the Fashoda memories of the British and French functionaries in Cairo': *Sledm.* (papers of Sir Mark Sykes in the possession of Sir Richard Sykes, Bart., at Sledmere, Yorks), No. 63—Sykes to Eric Drummond, 20 July 1917.

tenaciously did France cling to the position she had built up for herself in Syria. From this she had no intention of being dislodged, and on the eve of the War she was doing her best to consolidate it by a vigorous assertion of her rights and interests.

Her rights, as she conceived them, included the recognition of her claim to a privileged status as the leading Christian Power, with the responsibility which went with it for the protection of Christian shrines and religious and educational establishments. Prestige and sentiment apart, French interests included investments of capital greatly exceeding those of any other foreign country and, if all went well, soon to be increased to a point at which the whole economic life of the region would be under French control. On the eve of the War plans were in hand for an ambitious programme of public works to be carried out by a French consortium which already had within its grasp valuable concessions for railways and harbours both in Syria proper and in Palestine.[2]

It was of Syria that Frenchmen were accustomed to speak, but the distinction between Syria and Palestine was blurred.[3] On the delicate questions connected with the custody of the Holy Places and the protection of Christian establishments France was well aware that she must reckon with other Powers, and more particularly with Russia. Neither on these points nor on some others did she specify the exact nature and limits of her claims, but, while refraining from too precise a definition of her rights and interests, she was on the eve of the War doing her best to stake out for herself a sphere of influence, if not something more, in a Greater Syria in which Palestine, or most of it, would be included.

[2] See below, p. 50.

[3] 'In the south the boundary between Egypt and Syria . . . follows an arbitrary line drawn from slightly west of Rafa on the Mediterranean to slightly east of Taba . . . on the Red Sea. . . . In modern usage the expression " Palestine " has no precise meaning but is taken as being equivalent to Southern Syria': F.O. Handbook, *Syria and Palestine*, p. 2. 'At present the great mass of Frenchmen interested in Syria mean Palestine when they say Syria': Sir Mark Sykes to F.O., 8 April 1917: *Sledm.*, No. 49. Palestine is included in 'Southern Syria' as defined in the Acte Séparé annexed to the London Convention of 15 July 1840: *Brit. & For. St. Pap.*, XXIX: 345ff.

By her severance of official relations with the Holy See in 1905 France had seriously weakened her position in the Levant. Her denunciation of the Concordat had embarrassed her in the rôle she had been accustomed to play and had encouraged her Austrian and Italian rivals to challenge her pretensions as the leading Catholic Power. When the Poincaré Government came into office in 1912, it felt strongly that the time had arrived for a determined effort to restore the situation and to make it clear that, whatever her domestic policies, France had no intention of renouncing her 'traditional mission' in the East.

A fresh impetus was given to this campaign when, towards the end of 1912, French public opinion began to be disturbed by persistent rumours, prominently reported in a section of the press, of British activities in Syria, where British agents were said to be courting the Arab Nationalists and encouraging them to work for the union of Syria with Egypt—all this, it was alleged, as part of a plan conceived by Lord Kitchener for bringing the entire Middle East under British control.[4] Warnings to much the same effect were being conveyed to the French Foreign Office from sources connected with the francophile elements among the Syrian Arabs.[5]

Whatever effect they may have had on the public, it seems clear from Poincaré's comments that the French Government was prepared to believe that these reports should be discounted. What Poincaré says on the subject in his Memoirs[6] is that some excess of zeal on the part of British agents in Egypt had helped to give currency to rumours about a British move in Syria. These fears, he writes, were entirely baseless and he goes on to mention,

---

[4] See Gooch and Temperley, X, Pt. II, App. III.

[5] Jung, *La Révolte Arabe* (Paris, 1924), pp. 47-57. This was not the first time such reports had been in circulation. On 6 June 1913 the German Ambassador in London (Lichnowsky) reported to Berlin: 'That the French have designs on Syria is just as well known as that these designs are being opposed by England. Kitchener's attempts to carry on from Egypt a campaign of English propaganda in Syria . . . were doubtless by no means welcome in Paris. But from here [London], too, he was given to understand that the British Government was opposed to such plans. . . .': Lichnowsky, *Heading for the Abyss* (London, Constable, 1928), pp. 318-319.

[6] Poincaré, II. 400.

accepting it at its face-value, Grey's assurance[7] that Great Britain had no aspirations in Syria and could be relied upon to leave it alone.

The reports of British activities in Syria which were circulating in Paris in the winter of 1912 coincided with the re-opening of the Eastern Question as a result of the First Balkan War. The shattering defeats inflicted on the Turks by the Balkan Alliance had shown how precarious was their foothold in Europe. They had already been forced to capitulate to Italian aggression in North Africa. In Asia their Empire was still held together by its Moslem cement, but cracks were beginning to appear, and the already restive non-Turkish elements, notably the Arabs, had been encouraged in their aspirations by the exposure of their masters' military weakness. At a moment when the Eastern Question seemed to be entering upon a new and critical phase French public opinion was bound to be particularly sensitive to any suggestion of British designs on Syria. That such suspicions should be promptly dispelled was all the more imperative because about this time the French saw, or thought they saw, signs of an Anglo-German rapprochement and scented danger, fearing some deal behind their backs and at their expense.[8]

It was in these circumstances that the British Foreign Secretary felt it necessary to clear the air by an explicit denial of the disquieting rumours which were gaining currency in France. On 5 December 1912 Sir Edward Grey informed the British Ambassador in Paris of an interview he had had that day with the French Ambassador, Paul Cambon:

' I recurred in conversation with M. Cambon to-day to what he had said about the uneasiness caused by Herr von Kiderlen's reference to Germany's good relations with England. I said that I had observed that the French press still continued to talk of British intrigues in Syria, and I thought that this report, combined with what Herr von Kiderlen had said, might put it into people's heads that we

---

[7] See below, p. 48.

[8] See Siebert, *Entente Diplomacy in the World War* (New York and London, 1921), Nos. 766, 767 ; Harold Nicolson, *Lord Carnock* (London, Constable, 1930), pp. 384-386 ; *Grosse Politik*, XXXIII, No. 12284.

had been making some arrangement with Germany. . . . During the whole of this Balkan crisis, nothing in Asia Minor, not even the Bagdad Railway, had been discussed between Germany and ourselves. We were carrying on no intrigues in Syria and we had no intentions or aspirations respecting it.

'M. Cambon readily accepted what I said.'[9]

Grey's assurance was promptly communicated by Poincaré to Parliament. In a speech on the Turkish Question on 21 December 1912 he assured the Senate that France intended to ensure respect for her traditional interests in the Lebanon and in Syria, and that it was quite untrue that on this point the French and British Governments held divergent views. 'The British Government', he said, 'has in a very friendly manner declared to us that in these regions it has no intention of taking any action nor has it any designs or political aspirations of any kind.'[10] A year later the British declaration was again invoked by the French Government. In December 1913 the then Prime Minister, Doumergue, speaking of French activities in Syria, observed that 'our task in developing this part of the Ottoman Empire is remarkably facilitated by the assurance given by the British Government in December 1912 to our Ambassador in London.'[11]

On three points Grey's assurance was open to more than one interpretation. First, had Great Britain simply disinterested herself in Syria without recognising it as a French sphere of influence[12] or had she, as the French preferred to think,[13] conceded a shadow protectorate to France? Secondly, having regard

---

[9] Gooch and Temperley, IX, Pt. II, No. 336.

[10] This account of what Poincaré said is taken from his own extracts from his speech as set out in *Au Service de la France*, VI, 411-412. An editorial in *The Times* of 23 December 1912 notes with satisfaction that Poincaré had been able to say that there were no differences between France and Great Britain concerning Syria. The passage in question is not, however, to be found in the official report of the Senate debate on 21 December 1912, and it may be that, though Poincaré describes his statement as having been made to the Senate, it was made to the Foreign Affairs Commission of that body.

[11] 24 December 1913: reported in *The Times, 26* December 1913.

[12] This was the British interpretation: Gooch and Temperley, IX, Pt. II, No. 555—Grey to Goschen (Berlin), 24 January 1913.

[13] Ibid.; see also Poincaré, VII, 244.

to the sense in which the loose expression ' Syria ' was commonly used in France, to the special position so persistently claimed by France in relation to the Holy Places, and to the concessions held or sought by French financial interests in Palestine as well as in Syria proper, was it clear that the British ' désinteréssement ' did not apply to Palestine? Lastly, if it did, did it apply only *rebus sic stantibus,* so as to make second thoughts admissible should the situation be radically changed by a war which might end with the break-up of the Turkish Empire?

One at least of Grey's parliamentary supporters felt misgivings about the British assurance and spoke his mind on the subject in a debate in the House of Commons on 18 March 1914.[14] Doumergue's allusion to Grey's conversation with Cambon served as a text for a vigorous protest by the Conservative Member for Central Hull against British acquiescence in the exploitation of Syria by ' a cosmopolitan group of financiers' protected by France. At the age of thirty-five Sir Mark Sykes had already gained an established reputation as a student of Turkish affairs and an independent critic of British policy in the East. In his speech on March 18th he insisted that French activities in Syria, when their implications were fully understood, represented a veiled threat to vital British interests, because ' the policy of the French financiers would eventually destroy the Ottoman Empire,' and because Great Britain would then be faced with ' a European frontier in the Sinai Peninsula.'

The French claim to a special position in Syria, including Palestine, was strengthened by the arrangements provisionally agreed upon on the eve of the War for the settlement of the disputes associated with the Baghdad Railway and its ramifications.

During the last two years of peace Great Britain, France and Germany were moving towards an adjustment of these long-drawn-out controversies, and by the summer of 1914 a number of interlocking agreements had been initialled.[15] War broke out

---

[14] O.R., col. 2162ff.

[15] Including Anglo-Turkish Agreement, 29 July 1913 (Gooch and Temperley, X, Pt. II, No. 124) ; Franco-German Agreement, 15 February 1914 (ibid., X, Pt. II, No. 201) ; Franco-Turkish Agreement, 10 April 1914 (ibid., X, Pt. II, p. 367) ; Anglo-German Agreement, 15 June 1914 (ibid., X, Pt. II, No. 249). A German-Turkish Agreement was under negotiation in the summer of 1914—ibid., X, Pt. II, No. 260.

before any of them could be ratified, but they are of interest as indicating the lines on which a shadow partition of the Turkish Empire had been conceived. In the course of these transactions the French fought hard and successfully for a privileged position in Syria. In the autumn of 1913 it became known in Paris that German interests were pressing for a lease of the Damascus-Haifa branch of the Hedjaz Railway. It was foreseen that this would be followed by a German demand for the Haifa port concession.[16] The French group interested in the Syrian ports and railways stood to lose heavily by such intrusion and was prepared to pay a price to get rid of it. The bargaining which followed ended in an Agreement initialled in February 1914.[17] What this amounted to was that, in return for an undertaking not to get in the way of German enterprise further north, the French group gained a free hand in Central and Southern Syria, including Palestine.

This cleared the way for a Franco-Turkish Agreement initialled some two months later.[18] French interests identical, or closely associated, with those controlling the existing French railways in Syria were promised (among other favours) concessions for harbour-works at Haifa and Jaffa, as well as at Tripoli, and for the fuller development of the Syrian railway-system, including its southward extension to a point on the French-owned railway running from Jaffa to Jerusalem.

These were matters between France and Turkey, but the British Government had been kept informed. Tacitly acquiescing in arrangements which would put French interests in control of the principal Syrian ports and railways, it had, but for one reservation, found nothing to object to in the French programme. The reservation, however, was significant. The French official communiqué summarising the Franco-Turkish Agreement announced that ' it was hoped that the British Government would eventually agree to an extension connecting the Rayak-Ramleh

---

[16] These matters were discussed at length in an article in the *Revue de Paris,* summarised in *The Times,* 16 September 1913.

[17] Gooch and Temperley, X, Pt. II, No. 201 (15 February 1914).

[18] Gooch and Temperley, X, Pt. II, p. 367 (10 April 1914): see also *The Times,* 27 April 1914. In *Grosse Politik,* XXXVII (2), a note at p. 610 gives the date as 9 April 1914.

line[19] with the Egyptian railway-system.'[20] The British Government had from the start looked coldly on such proposals and had no intention of facilitating them. On the contrary, it had been doing everything in its power to obstruct any arrangement for bringing the Syrian railways up to the Egyptian frontier and had plainly made up its mind that any such project must be resisted as a threat to the security of the Canal Zone. In the summer of 1913 the French Government had told Sir Edward Grey that a French group was applying for certain railway concessions in Syria, ' with the right of eventual extension to El Arish.'[21] Grey had objected and had been assured that the idea would be dropped.[22] When, nearly a year later, it became apparent that both the French and the Turks were still thinking on these lines,[23] Grey intervened to make it clear that the British attitude was unchanged. He reminded the Turkish Ambassador that Great Britain, as was well known, was opposed to any railway connection with Egypt from the east, and he went on to press for an assurance that, should this view be modified at any future time, a concession would be granted only to a British group acceptable to the British Government.[24]

Grey's firm attitude reflected the British Government's fixed determination that nothing should be done to open up the overland approaches to Egypt across the desert. In 1840 Palmerston had been prepared to risk a head-on collision with France rather than allow her Egyptian protégé, Mehemet Ali, to make good his claim to the possession of Syria.[25] British interests, as then con-

---

[19] I.e., the line which was to link up the Syrian system with the Jaffa-Jerusalem railway.

[20] Gooch and Temperley, X, Pt. II, p. 367. About the same time, the Turkish Finance Minister, Djavid Bey, told the Constantinople press that the Rayak-Ramleh line would later be linked up with the Egyptian railways: *The Times,* 27 April 1914.

[21] On the Mediterranean.

[22] See Grey to Lowther (Constantinople), 6 June 1913—Gooch and Temperley, X, Pt. II, No. 88. Grey returned to the subject in a Note to the French Ambassador dated 7 July 1913—ibid., No. 115.

[23] See foot note 20.

[24] 4 May 1914—Gooch and Temperley, X, Pt. II, No. 239.

[25] See Webster, *The Foreign Policy of Palmerston,* 1830-1841, II, 628 ; Temperley, *England and the Near East,* p. 106.

ceived by Palmerston, required that, for the protection of Turkey, there must be firm resistance to the incorporation of Syria in an Egyptian principality backed by France. Palmerston had made his stand because ' the permitting Mehemet to retain Syria is to all intents and purposes sanctioning the dismemberment of the Turkish Empire.'[26] What was then at stake was the integrity of Turkey. But since 1882 the situation had been reversed. It was Egypt and not Turkey which now required British protection against any threat from the direction of Syria. In the earlier days of the British occupation of Egypt the desert barrier had been assumed to be a sufficient guarantee of the landward security of the Canal Zone. British sensitiveness to any Turkish encroachment on the Sinai Peninsula to the disadvantage of Egypt[27] was demonstrated by Cromer's determined stand in 1892, and again in 1906, when Turkish probings in the neighbourhood of the boundary-line provoked energetic British protests, backed by an ultimatum. The Turks were forced to give way, but it was now seen to be uncertain whether the desert barrier was as impassable as had been supposed. The defences of Egypt were re-examined by the British General Staff, which came to the conclusion that the desert could be crossed by an enemy force of about 5,000, though not more.[28] This was on the assumption that no railway transport was available.[29] If there were railway connections, not under British control, between Palestine and a point on the Sinai Peninsula, a very different situation would arise. Even if Palestine remained Turkish, the existence of such railways would from a British point of view be highly unwelcome. In 1913-14 those responsible for the defence of the Suez Canal had to consider what the position would be if, as a result of the collapse and

---

[26] Palmerston to Beauvale (Vienna), 25 August 1839, quoted by Temperley, loc. cit.

[27] The Sinai Peninsula was also of importance to Great Britain in relation to the naval position in the Red Sea. See Cromer's observations in 1906, quoted by Grey, *Twenty-Five Years* (London, Hodder and Stoughton, 1925), I, 124.

[28] Wavell, *The Palestine Campaigns* (London, Constable, 1928), p. 5.

[29] By 1914 it had become possible for a force destined for the invasion of Egypt to be moved by the Hedjaz Railway as far as Ma'an, but no further.

partition of Turkey, Egypt came to have as her eastern neighbour a Power with the ambitions and resources of France.

Nor was a potential threat to the security of Egypt the only danger which could be foreseen from a French occupation of Syria. In 1840 one of Palmerston's reasons for resisting Mehemet Ali's pretensions had been that, if France, through her Egyptian satellite, became mistress of the Syrian coast, she might be capable of challenging British sea-power in the Mediterranean.[30] Between 1840 and 1914 the French, though they had lost their hold on Egypt, had greatly improved their position in Algeria and had made further important gains on the North African seaboard in Tunis and Morocco. If in the Eastern Mediterranean they were to acquire potential naval bases at Alexandretta and Haifa, they would have materially strengthened their already considerable sea-power in Mediterranean waters. This was precisely one of the reasons why, in pressing for a strong foreign policy, French politicians of the type of Georges Lèygues attached so much importance to Syria. Within a few months of the entry of Turkey into the War in October 1914 Lèygues[31] was asserting the French claim to Syria in language which showed that by Syria he meant, as did most Frenchmen of his way of thinking, a Greater Syria including Palestine:

> ' The Mediterranean will not be free for us . . . unless Syria remains in our sphere of influence. By Syria must be understood, not a Syria mutilated and discrowned, but Syria in its entirety, that which extends from El Arish to the Taurus.'[32]

Nor was this merely the rhetoric of an extremist. How sweeping were the French demands appears from a memorandum by the

---

[30] Palmerston to Granville (Paris), 15 November 1840—text in H. Lytton Bulwer, *Life of Lord Palmerston*, (London, 1871), p. 351 ; Guizot, *An Embassy to the Court of St. James's in 1840* (London, 1862), p. 40, recording conversation with Palmerston, 4 March 1840. See also H. F. Frischwasser-Ra'anan, *The Frontiers of a Nation* (London, Batchworth, 1955), p. 29.

[31] Then Chairman of the Foreign Affairs Committee of the Chamber ; later (1920), Prime Minister.

[32] Quoted by Gontaut-Biron, pp. 28-29; Lèygues was addressing the French Geographical Society.

then Lord Chancellor, Lord Maugham, the principal British representative on the Anglo-Arab Committee which in 1939 examined the letters exchanged in 1915-16 between Sir Henry McMahon and the Sharif Hussein.[33] Describing the situation at the time of the British assurances to the Sharif in the autumn of 1915, Lord Maugham says: ' It can be stated as a fact that at the time of the correspondence [with Hussein] France claimed the Mediterranean littoral as far south as the Egyptian border and as far east as Damascus.'[34]

Besides the latent threat to the security of Egypt and to the British naval position in the Mediterranean, French designs on Syria could in yet another respect be embarrassing to Great Britain. Plans for the building of a British-controlled railway from the Mediterranean to the Persian Gulf had many times during the nineteenth century been discussed and set aside, but the idea was still alive.[35] Apart from its naval importance, the Bay of Acre would be highly suitable as the starting-point of such a railway. Exclusive French control of the Syrian coast would mean that if the project was to be proceeded with, it would be necessary to rely on the much less satisfactory alternative of a trans-Arabian railway, with its western terminus in the neighbourhood of Aqabah.

The position at the outbreak of the Great War was that the British Government had, at least by implication, agreed that France was entitled to the leading rôle in the economic development of Syria, Palestine being plainly included. It had not positively conceded any larger French pretensions, but it had expressly disavowed any political aspirations of its own in a region vaguely described as Syria—a name which had no precise geographical connotation but might well be taken to cover Palestine. Yet in any partition of Asiatic Turkey, should this become unavoidable, could Great Britain stand aside and let the French have their way in Syria to the full extent of ' la Syrie intégrale '? Could France safely be permitted to dominate both

[33] See below, p. 267.

[34] Cmd. 5974 (1939), p. 27.

[35] See Gooch and Temperley, X, Pt. II, No. 259, Grey to Mallet (Constantinople), 14 July 1914.

the overland approaches to Egypt and the whole Mediterranean seaboard from Alexandretta southwards?

These were questions to which Lord Kitchener would have been bound to give thought while in Egypt as British Agent in the years immediately before the War. His ideas had behind them all the weight of his military prestige, and on taking over the War Office in August 1914 he was in a strong position for pressing them upon his Cabinet colleagues. That he held and expressed decided views about the conflict between French and British interests in the Levant can be inferred from a passage in the memorandum, already quoted in another context, in which the British construction of the McMahon correspondence was expounded by Lord Maugham for the benefit of the Anglo-Arab Committee set up to examine it in 1939. Lord Maugham was inviting the Arab delegation to agree that Palestine was excluded from the British undertaking to recognise the independence of the Arabs, since this was limited to areas 'in which Great Britain is free to act without detriment to the interests of her ally, France.' It was certain, he declared, that Great Britain was not free, in October 1915, to act in Palestine without detriment to French interests.

> 'It may be perfectly true,' he went on, 'that under the influence of Lord Kitchener and others His Majesty's Government before and after the outbreak of war were anxious to restrict the French claims on the Levant coast if they could find a legitimate means of doing so. But there is a great difference between desiring an object and attaining it. . . .'[36]

It is implied, as could, indeed, be assumed, that Kitchener took a leading part in pressing for a policy designed to keep as much of the Levant coast as possible out of French control.

The exact nature of Kitchener's proposals is not disclosed. From Sir Philip Magnus' study of the Kitchener papers it appears that in the early part of the War he was particularly pre-occupied with the question of a British claim to Alexandretta, and that it was only with some difficulty that he was eventually persuaded to

[36] Cmd. 5974 (1939), p. 27. Then follows the passage already quoted concerning French claims to the Mediterranean littoral down to the Egyptian frontier.

accept Haifa as a substitute.[37] There is, however, good reason to believe that he had, while in Egypt, formed strong views as to the strategic importance of Palestine,[38] and these may well have been reflected in the handling of the Anglo-French negotiations leading up to the Sykes-Picot Agreement of May 1916. Kitchener actively concerned himself with these discussions, and since, as his biographer tells us,[39] he ' personally supervised . . . every detail,' it may be inferred that he had something to do with the firm refusal on the British side to concede the French claim to Palestine.

Material is lacking for an exact assessment of Kitchener's influence on British thinking about the future of Palestine. What is clear is that at a very early stage of the War the idea was gaining ground that this was a matter in which important British interests were at stake, it being assumed that the war-time alliance with France was no guarantee of lasting good relations or of an end to Anglo-French rivalry in the Levant. In January 1915 Lloyd George was already playing with the idea of a Jewish buffer-state in Palestine.[40] About the same time the British Agent in Cairo, evidently assuming that the information would be of interest in London, was reporting that a large part of the population of Palestine would welcome a British occupation.[41] In March, in a memorandum on Palestine of which more will be said later, Herbert Samuel—on this point possibly reflecting Kitchener's views—suggested to his Cabinet colleagues that ' the establish-

[37] Sir Philip Magnus, *Kitchener* (London, John Murray, 1958), pp. 313, 314.

[38] At the end of 1913 Kitchener gave orders for the surveys of Palestine carried out in the 1870s by Colonel Conder and himself to be completed by their extension southwards down to Aqabah, camouflage for the work of the Royal Engineers being provided by an archæological expedition sponsored by the Palestine Exploration Fund: see *T. E. Lawrence, by his Friends* (London, Cape, 1937), pp. 105ff. ; *T. E. Lawrence to his Biographers, Liddell Hart and Robert Graves* (Faber and Faber), p. 86; *The Letters of T. E. Lawrence*, ed. David Garnett (London, Cape, 1938), p. 181. These operations were mentioned at the time, with suspicious comments, by *L'Egypte* (Cairo), and *Le Marché* (Paris): Jung, op. cit., I, 82. The archæologists employed were Lawrence and Leonard (later Sir Leonard) Woolley. Soon after Turkey entered the War both were taken into the British Intelligence Service in Cairo.

[39] Magnus, op. cit., p. 314.

[40] C. P. Scott to Weizmann, 14 January 1915: *Ch.W.P.*—quoted below p. 141.

[41] Mentioned in Samuel memorandum, March 1915—see below, p. 109.

ment of a great European Power so close to the Suez Canal would be a continual and formidable menace to the essential lines of communication of the British Empire. . . . We cannot proceed on the supposition that our present happy relations with France will continue always.' After a conversation, at the end of March, with C. P. Scott, the Editor of the *Manchester Guardian*, Dr. Weizmann told Samuel that Scott's view was that 'events are shaping in favour of a British Palestine.'[42] About the same time, T. E. Lawrence, then a member of the British Intelligence organisation in Egypt, was privately expressing his much more advanced opinions. 'One cannot,' he wrote to D. G. Hogarth, 'go on betting that France will always be our friend,' and he went on to suggest means by which 'we can . . . biff the French out of all hope of Syria.'[43] These were merely the personal opinions of a very uninhibited junior officer, but it may reasonably be surmised that Lawrence was reflecting ideas current at the time in some military circles in Cairo, where Kitchener had recently been the leading figure.

By the end of 1915 French hopes of British acquiescence in the incorporation of Palestine, or most of it, in French Syria had begun to flicker out, and in 1916 they were to be extinguished by British insistence on an international régime in which France would be only one of two or more partners. From this point the French were to be again pressed back until, almost immediately after the Armistice, an unencumbered claim to Palestine was conceded by Clémenceau to Lloyd George.[44] France was in the end to come out of the War with nothing in Palestine and even in Syria proper with a good deal less than she had foreseen.

Looked at through British eyes, all this represented, as to Palestine, Great Britain's just reward for the exertions which had brought the Turks to their knees and, as to Syria, a settlement doing less than justice to the legitimate expectations of the Arabs. Seen through French eyes, the picture was different. Because of his association with Georges-Picot,[45] Gontaut-Biron may well have

---

[42] Weizmann to Samuel, 21 March 1915: *Ch.W.P.*

[43] Lawrence to Hogarth, 22 March 1915—*The Letters of T. E. Lawrence,* ed. David Garnett, pp. 195-196.

[44] Below, p. 614.

[45] Gontaut-Biron had served in the East on Picot's staff.

had a keener sense of frustration than the average Frenchman, but he was only expressing, in rather intemperate language, what many of his compatriots felt, when, looking back in 1922, he recalled that as soon as France found it necessary to assert her long-standing interests in the East, she at once found herself in collision with her Allies of the moment, ' whose old rivalries had not been disarmed.'[46] We shall see later how the conflicting interests of Great Britain and France were related to the origins of the Balfour Declaration.

[46] Gontaut-Biron, p. 3.

CHAPTER 3

THE ZIONIST MOVEMENT IN 1914

THE PURPOSE OF these introductory chapters is to sketch the salient features of the remoter background to the Balfour Declaration. Something has already been said about the relations, up to 1914, between the Zionists and those Governments—foremost among them the British Government—which had taken notice of the Movement. To complete the picture, we must now look a little more closely at the Zionist Organisation itself. What was its standing in the Jewish world? How did it expect to attain its objects, and how had its policies been affected by the Turkish Revolution of 1908? What had it actually achieved in Palestine, and what were the relations between the Jewish settlers and the Arabs?

In answering these questions, we may take as a starting-point Weizmann's presidential address at the Twelfth Zionist Congress, the first to meet after the War, in the summer of 1921.[1] He began by recalling the circumstances in which the last pre-War Congress had met eight years earlier:

' What was the situation then? After many years of striving the conviction was forced upon us that we stood before a blank wall, which it was impossible for us to surmount by ordinary political means. But the strength of the national will forged for itself two main roads towards its goal—the gradual extension and strengthening of our Yishuv[2] in Palestine and the spreading of the Zionist idea throughout the length and breadth of Jewry. Our colonisation work . . . could look forward to a period of steady growth. . . . In the Diaspora we saw our national idea gaining ground and were justified in hoping that by steady work we should succeed in winning for it its rightful place in the life of the Jewish people.'

[1] *Report of the Twelfth Zionist Congress* (Central Office of the Zionist Organisation, London, 1922), pp. 13ff.
[2] Yishuv (Heb.: literally, ' settlement '), a collective name for the Jewish settlers in Palestine.

This was broadly the situation on the eve of the War, as seen through Zionist eyes. Two potential sources of trouble not mentioned by Weizmann and not fully present to the mind of the 1913 Congress were, first, the unabated hostility of many influential Jews and Jewish organisations and, secondly, the effect of the Turkish Revolution in accelerating the growth of Arab nationalism.

1

The weak diplomatic position of the Zionist Movement on the eve of the War has already been described. In England it had, for reasons connected with events in Turkey, come under a cloud, and there had been no renewal of the close and friendly relations with the British Government which it had enjoyed in the days of the Balfour Administration between 1902 and 1905. The French remained convinced that it was working for Germany, while the Germans had begun to accuse it of working for their enemies. The Turks, for their part, were adamant in their hostility to the Movement and deaf to Zionist protestations of loyalty and goodwill.

This was the 'blank wall' which 'it was impossible for us to surmount by ordinary political means.' Recognising that, as a political movement, Zionism did stand before a blank wall, the Tenth Zionist Congress, meeting in 1911, had announced a change of direction, or more accurately, perhaps, a change of emphasis, by electing a re-constituted Executive pledged to concentrate its efforts on practical work in Palestine—a policy re-affirmed by the Eleventh Congress in 1913.[3] At both Congresses it was made clear that 'practical work' was intended to include, not only colonising activities, but also an effective contribution to the revival of the Hebrew language and of Jewish culture—all this to be combined with a more determined effort to give effect to that part of the Basle Programme which called for 'the strengthening of Jewish sentiment and national consciousness.' Staunch upholders of the Herzlian tradition objected to the Movement's becoming either an emigration agency or—as Wolffsohn put it—something like a German Students' Corporation.[4] Addressing the 1913 Congress as

[3] See Böhm, I, 502, 608 ; I. Cohen, *The Zionist Movement*, pp. 91ff.
[4] *J.C.*, 5 September 1913.

Chairman of the Executive,[5] Otto Warburg, himself a leading exponent of 'practical' Zionism, took occasion to repudiate the idea that political work had become obsolete. 'Our Palestine work,' he said, 'is not merely a factor of equal rank with our political work but is the necessary forerunner of our political efforts.'[6] In other words, piecemeal colonisation was not an end in itself; the central purpose of the Movement remained what it had always been—the creation in Palestine of a home for the Jewish people. What happened during the War showed that the 'practical' Zionists—Weizmann was one of them—had not lost sight of the larger aspirations of Zionism, but their coming into power in 1911 meant that the Movement had made up its mind that it must adjust itself to changed conditions.

The establishment of a home for the Jewish people in Palestine, 'secured by public law,' had originally been conceived by the Zionists as a planned operation to be carried out systematically by agreement with the Sultan and with the approval of the Powers. For the first few years of its existence the Zionist Organisation adhered to the principle that it must conserve its resources until the grant of what came to be vaguely described as 'the Charter' gave the signal for mass immigration. Not until 1908 did the Organisation start some preparatory work in Palestine, and then only on a small scale and without much enthusiasm on the part of the Old Guard. The 'political' Zionists were still in the saddle and in their hearts unshaken in the belief that no good could come of what they disdainfully called petty colonisation. Between 1908 and 1911 there were some modest concessions to the 'practical' Party,[7] but all the time the 'political' Zionists were fighting a rearguard action against the encroachment of the heresy that practical work could and must be undertaken in Palestine, even though no such political guarantees as Herzl had thought indispensable had been secured or were in sight.

In the minds of its founders, the distinctive feature of the Zionist Organisation had been that it set out to raise the Jewish

[5] When Wolffsohn's Presidency ended in 1911, no new President was elected, but Warburg was appointed Chairman of the Executive.

[6] XI Z.C. Prot., p. 10.

[7] See Bein, Return to the Soil (Jerusalem, Z.O., 1952), pp. 57, 65, 76, 104.

Question to the plane of international politics. Herzl's original conception, baldly stated, was simply that, with the help and under the ægis of the European Powers, most of whom would—he assumed—not be sorry to see part of their Jewish population drained away, there should be organised an orderly exodus of Jews to some territory, still to be selected, in which they could build up an autonomous society. Herzl laid it down as a cardinal feature of his plan that the Jews should not get on the move until they were assured of a home which they were entitled to enter *en masse* as of right. There was to be no creeping in by the back-door.[8]

Through contact with Jews bred in a different and more authentic Jewish tradition, Herzl soon became convinced that his Movement would make no appeal to the Jewish imagination, and would, therefore, be still-born, unless it took as its starting-point the historic connection between the Jews and Palestine.[9] It was on this basis that the Zionist Organisation was founded in 1897. But in adopting as its central purpose the creation of a home for the Jewish people in Palestine the Organisation retained as an essential part of its doctrine the principle that this was to be achieved by political means. Not until the Charter had been secured and underwritten by the Powers[10] was mass settlement to begin. The 'Back to Palestine' Movement did not start with the Zionist Organisation. In the early 1880s Societies known as *Choveve Zion* ('Lovers of Zion') had sprung up in Eastern Europe, and under their auspices Jews had been trickling into Palestine for some fifteen years before the Zionist Organisation came into existence. What distinguished the Zionists from the *Choveve Zion* was not only that their plans were more ambitious and their aims more clearly defined, but that their Movement, as they conceived it, was essentially a political Movement having as its first objectives the Charter and the international guarantee. Of

[8] *The Jewish State*, pp. 20, 29, 30, 56, 73.

[9] Even in his *Jewish State*, Herzl, though asking only for 'a portion of the globe sufficiently large to satisfy our just requirements' (p. 67), had recognised the special significance of Palestine for the Jews: 'Palestine is our ever-memorable historic home. The very name of Palestine would attract our people with a force of marvellous potency' (p. 30).

[10] This was the real meaning of the words in the Basle Programme, 'secured by public law.'

the efforts of the early settlers—the founders of the first agricultural colonies—Max Nordau wrote in 1900: 'The colonies are
wholly without significance for the redemption of the Jewish
people.'[11] When a second wave of immigration from Eastern
Europe started in 1904, the Zionist Organisation tried—but in
vain—to discourage it, in the belief that the time was not ripe.[12]

It is easy to understand why the 'political' Zionists, clinging
stubbornly to the ideas with which Herzl had started, were not
prepared to yield without resistance to the forces which finally
prevailed in 1911. But, though they were well entrenched in their
orthodoxy, they had for some years been fighting a losing battle.
Long before the issue was at length decided against them at the
Tenth Congress there had been Zionists who suspected that the
political activities of the Movement were leading nowhere and
believed that, if it was not to stagnate and in the end die of
frustration, it must begin to think less of diplomacy and more of
practical work in Palestine. It was as an advocate of this view that
Weizmann, not then a leader but only a young man of promise,[13]
established his reputation at the Eighth Zionist Congress in 1907.
Diplomatic Zionism, he said, had failed.

> 'The Charter is to be aimed at, but only as a result of our
> endeavours in Palestine. If the Governments give us a
> Charter to-day it will be a scrap of paper. Not so if we work
> in Palestine; then it will be written and indissolubly
> cemented with our blood.'[14]

This was not an unqualified rejection of the Charter idea. Weizmann seems still to have been thinking of a Charter to be given to
the Zionists by 'the Governments,' meaning, presumably, Turkey
and the European Powers. His point was simply that a Charter
would be meaningless unless the Jews had already established
themselves in Palestine by the work of their hands.

The idea of a Charter to be underwritten by the Powers dis-

---

[11] Quoted by Böhm, I, 231, from Nordau's *Gesammelte Schriften*
(Berlin, 1923), p. 78.

[12] Bein, op. cit., p. 40.

[13] He was then 32.

[14] *VIII Z.C. Prot.*, pp. 299ff. English translation in *Chaim Weizmann*,
ed. P. Goodman (London, Gollancz, 1945), pp. 147-148.

appeared altogether after the Turkish Revolution of 1908. It now began to be clear even to the most politically-minded Zionists that the old conceptions must be discarded or at least temporarily set aside. If even in the days of Abdul Hamid the Movement had never come within sight of the Charter, it was plain that, with their fanatical nationalism and their fierce determination to resist any encroachment on Ottoman sovereignty, the Young Turks would be still more unaccommodating. If their distrust of Zionism was to be dispelled, there must be no more talk of a Charter or, even worse, of an international guarantee; still less must there be any room for the suspicion that the real purpose of the Zionist Movement was to detach Palestine from Turkey and turn it into a Jewish State. However reluctant they might be to acknowledge that Herzl's ideas were outmoded, even the 'political' Zionists were forced to recognise that, without abandoning the essence of its aspirations, the Movement must change its tactics.

Within a few months of the beginning of the Revolution in the summer of 1908, the official organ of the Movement, *Die Welt*, published an article by Nahum Sokolow, then the General Secretary of the Zionist Organisation, in which he protested that there was no truth whatever in the allegation that Zionism aimed at the establishment of an independent Jewish State.[15] *The Jewish Chronicle*, which, under the editorship of Leopold Greenberg, had become an ardent supporter of the Zionist cause, was quick to point out that in the Basle programme there was 'not a word of any autonomous Jewish State.'[16] At the Ninth Zionist Congress in 1909 Max Nordau—the Public Orator of the Movement—declared that 'we respectfully deposit the Charter idea in the archives of modern political Zionism and speak of it no more.'[17] At the same Congress, Wolffsohn, the President of the Organisation, made an elaborate statement to the effect that the Zionists unreservedly accepted the obligations of loyalty to the Ottoman State and its institutions and implicit obedience to its laws.[18] At the Tenth Congress in 1911 Wolffsohn said, in his presidential

[15] *Die Welt*, 22 January 1909.
[16] *J.C.*, 16 October 1908.
[17] *IX Z.C. Prot.*, p. 22.
[18] *IX Z.C. Prot.*, pp. 6-8.

address, that what the Zionists wanted was not a Jewish State but a homeland,[19] while Nordau denounced the 'infamous traducers,' who alleged that ' the Zionists . . . wanted to worm their way into Turkey in order to seize Palestine. . . . It is our duty to convince [the Turks] that . . . they possess in the whole world no more generous and self-sacrificing friends than the Zionists.'[20] At the Eleventh Congress in 1913 Otto Warburg, speaking as Chairman of the Zionist Executive, gave similar assurances of loyalty to Turkey, adding that in colonising Palestine and developing its resources the Zionists would be making a valuable contribution to the progress of the Turkish Empire.[21]

These protestations fell upon deaf ears. The Turks were unimpressed and did all they could to keep Jews out of Palestine. If means were found of surmounting the barrier, this was due partly to the venality of Turkish officials[22] and partly to the diligence of the Russian Consuls in Palestine in protecting their Jewish nationals and saving them from expulsion.[23] Nevertheless, the idea of 'loyalty' to Turkey, so often and so emphatically asserted in the years immediately before the War, became in the minds of many Zionists something like an article of faith, and, coupled with the principle of 'neutrality,' helped—as we shall see—to account for the cool response of the Russian Zionist leaders when they were pressed in 1917 to join in demanding openly a British trusteeship for Palestine.

Thus, the position on the eve of the War was as Weizmann described it in his retrospect in 1921. As a political movement Zionism stood, or appeared to stand, before a blank wall. Neither from the Turkish nor from any other Government could it expect any encouragement. At the 1913 Congress it was Weizmann himself who, little more than a year before he was to start on the road leading to the Balfour Declaration, declared that there was little or nothing to be hoped for from the Great Powers:

---

[19] *X Z.C. Prot.*, p. 11.

[20] Ibid., p. 26.

[21] *XI Z.C. Prot.*, p. 6.

[22] See Bein, op. cit., p. 27.

[23] *The Near East*, 31 October 1913 ; A. M. Hyamson, *Palestine* (London, 1917), p. 68.

'The greatest of the Great Powers we have to deal with is the Jewish people. From this Power we expect everything; from the other Powers very little.'[24]

2

In his presidential address in 1921 Weizmann remarked that, though in 1913 the political outlook was bleak, an encouraging feature of the situation was 'the spreading of the Zionist idea throughout the length and breadth of Jewry.'

Of this, however, there was no clear indication in the enrolled membership of the Movement. At the time of the last pre-War Congress—September 1913—the figure was of the order of 130,000.[25] This was the highest total reached before the War, but it represented no marked improvement on a membership of 114,000 in 1899.[26] In the interval the numbers had fallen a little,[27] but the most that could be said was that by 1913 the Organisation had regained the lost ground and made a slight advance.

As was before long to become evident, the underlying strength of the Movement was vastly greater than the membership figures would have suggested. Its slow growth is attributable partly to the inhibitions imposed upon the Russian Jews by the disabilities under which they laboured until 1917, but partly also to a widespread feeling in the Jewish world that the Zionists were beating the air. Before the War they were looked upon by most of their fellow-Jews as unworldly dreamers out of touch with realities. Once satisfied that Zionist aspirations were not mere fantasies, many Jews who had stood aloof were quick to show where their sympathies lay. This was true even in Great Britain and the United States, where before the War Zionism had made little headway. Great Britain, with a Jewish population of about

---

[24] *XI Z.C. Prot.*, p. 168.

[25] The right to vote for delegates to the Zionist Congress depended on the payment of the 'Shekel'—a nominal registration-fee fixed by the First Congress at one French franc or its equivalent. In what follows, membership figures represent 'shekel-payers.' At the 1913 Congress the number was given as 'over 130,000': *XI Z.C. Prot.*, p. 43.

[26] J. Frankel, *The History of the Shekel* (London, 1952), p. 10.

[27] Figures in *XI Z.C. Prot.*, p. 113.

300,000, had in 1913 some 8,000 enrolled Zionists.[28] in 1919 a petition urging the Peace Conference to give effect to the Balfour Declaration was stated to have been signed by 77,039 ' adult Jews and Jewesses of the United Kingdom.'[29] A pro-Zionist petition submitted about the same time to President Wilson is said to have been signed by more than 500,000 American Jews,[30] though in 1913, out of the three million Jews in the United States, only some 12,000 had enrolled themselves as Zionists.[31] By 1921 the total membership of the Organisation had risen from the 1913 figure of 130,000 to 778,000[32] and would have shown a still more striking increase if events in Russia had not interposed a barrier between Russian Jewry and the rest of the Jewish world.[33]

The Zionists had always believed that there were many Jews outside their Movement who were only waiting for a sign. In this they turned out to be right, but on the eve of the War their visible strength was not impressive. Zionism was, in fact, and had been from the start, the faith of a comparatively small minority of Jews. Nowhere in the Jewish world—not even in Eastern Europe—was there before the War any evidence of active mass-support for the Movement, while from two opposite quarters it was under persistent and determined attack—in Russia by the Jewish Socialists of the Bund and in the West by the leaders of the assimilated Jewish bourgeoisie.

The Bund—' Der Algemeiner Yidiche Arbeterbund in Rusland und Poiln ' (The General Jewish Workers' Organisation in Russia and Poland)—was founded at Vilna in 1897, which was also the year of the first Zionist Congress.[34] It was a proletarian organi-

---

[28] The author is indebted for this information to Dr. S. Levenberg.

[29] *The Peace Conference, Paris, 1919* (London, Joint Foreign Committee, 1920), p. 115.

[30] J. de Haas, *Louis Dembitz Brandeis* (New York, Bloch, 1929), p. 70.

[31] *Die Welt*, 1913, No. 35, p. 1146.

[32] *Report of the Twelfth Zionist Congress* (London, 1922), p. 9.

[33] Sixty-four Russian Zionists were admitted to the 1921 Congress in a consultative capacity, but, except for ten from the Ukraine, there were no elected Russian delegates: ibid.

[34] What follows is based mainly on material from the following sources : E. H. Carr, *The Bolshevik Revolution* (London, Macmillan, 1950), I, 1, 2, 6, 30 ; R. R. Abramovitch, *Jewish Socialist Movements in Russia*, and Ben-Adir, *Modern Currents in Jewish Social and National Life* (Jewish Encyclopædic Handbooks, New York, 1948, Vol. II) ; L. Greenberg, *The Jews in Russia* (New Haven, 1951), Vol. II.

sation with strong Marxist leanings, its purpose being to represent the Jewish contribution to the Russian revolutionary movement and, within the movement, to safeguard what it conceived to be the interests of the Jewish working-class. The Bund helped to organise the Minsk Congress, which in 1898 founded the Russian Social Democratic Party, and it was represented at the Second Party Congress in 1903. But by this time its separatism and its interest in the rights of national minorities, meaning especially the Jewish minority, had begun to bring it into disfavour. These features of the Bundist ideology were particularly obnoxious to Lenin and his 'Iskra' group, who denounced the Bundists as reactionaries, deviationists and a hindrance to the class-war. At the 1903 Party Congress the Bund's claim to be the representative, and the sole representative, of the Jewish proletariat was overwhelmingly rejected, and its delegates withdrew in protest. But before long the breach had been repaired. In 1906 the Bund was re-admitted to the Party as a Jewish Social Democratic Organisation, and in 1912 the Party approved its programme of 'national-cultural autonomy' (the culture in question being Yiddish and not Hebrew culture) for the Russian Jews.

Thus the position on the eve of the War was that in Russia the Zionists had to compete for the allegiance of the more ardent spirits with a Jewish proletarian movement which invited Jews not to waste their time dreaming about Palestine, but to do their duty nearer home by playing their part, side by side with the rest of the Russian proletariat, in the Social Revolution. From a Bundist point of view, Zionism was much worse than an idle dream ; it distracted Jews, if, indeed, it was not designed to distract them, from the revolutionary struggle and the class-war, by which alone the Jewish question could be solved, encouraging the Jewish workers to forget the fight against their class-enemies and staking its hopes on the goodwill of bourgeois Governments. What made it all the more imperative for the Bundists to be relentless in their war on Zionism was that in the light of their demand for a measure of Jewish autonomy, they themselves could be suspected of a species of deviation. The Bund by no means lived up to its magniloquent title—the General Jewish Workers' Organisation of Russia and Poland. In 1907, when the Jewish population of the Russian Empire was about six millions, the Bund had only some 25,000 members.[35] It must, however, be borne in mind that the Bund was an illegal organisation and that its influence certainly extended well beyond its active membership. In 1913 the Zionist Organisation, whose activities were likewise illegal in Russia, had only about 36,000 Russian members.[36] Bundist ideas commanded enough support to compete seriously with Zionism in Russia, and not only in Russia but in other parts of the Jewish world to which they were brought by Russo-Jewish immigrants. Both Zionism and anti-Zionist Socialism of the Bundist type were represented among the two million Jews, nearly all from Eastern Europe, who flooded into the United States from 1881 onwards, but at the beginning the Socialist element may well have been the larger.[37] In England, Jewish immigration from Eastern Europe provided the Zionist Movement with most of its rank-and-file, but Bundist ideas had a considerable hold on the Jewish proletariat, and before the War the leaders of the Jewish Labour Movement in England were, on the whole, anti-Zionist.[38]

The Bund persisted to the end in its hostility to Zionism and helped in 1917 to make it impossible to represent the Russian Jews as substantially united in demanding the establishment of a Jewish National Home in Palestine. The Bundist representative on a Russian delegation which visited London in August 1917 made a statement deliberately designed to undermine support for Zionism in British Labour circles.[39] But though the Bund's activities somewhat weakened the Zionist position, they never seriously endangered it. In the Balfour Declaration period a much more formidable threat was to come from a very different quarter —the lay leaders of Anglo-Jewry.

---

[35] Abramovitch, op. cit., p. 390.

[36] *Die Welt,* 1913, No. 35, p. 1146.

[37] See Maurice Samuel, *Level Sunlight* (New York, 1953), p. 214 ; see also A. Goldberg, *Zionism in America* ('Theodor Herzl, A Memorial,' New York, 1929), p. 211.

[38] P. Goodman, *Zionism in England,* p. 46. This was not true of all of them. The General Secretary of the (predominantly Jewish) United Garment Workers spoke in friendly terms of Zionism in his evidence before the Royal Commission on Alien Immigration: Cmd. 1742 (1903), p. 502.

[39] Below, p. 475.

As it turned out, it was the Anglo-Jewish opposition which counted most, but it was not only in England that the Zionists found themselves before the War in conflict with the established order in Jewish communal life. In France the influential Alliance Israélite was vehemently opposed to Zionism, seeing in Zionist propaganda a weapon which might be used by the anti-semites against the Jews in France, and fearing, also, that the position of the Jews in Turkey, and its own educational work in the East, might be gravely compromised if the Young Turks were given cause to suspect the Jews of designs on Palestine. In the United States the proceedings of the first Zionist Congress (1897) were condemned by the Central Conference of American Rabbis on the ground that Zionist activities

> ' do not benefit but infinitely harm our Jewish brethren, where they are still persecuted, by confirming the assertion of their enemies that the Jews are foreigners in the countries in which they are at home and of which they are everywhere the most loyal and patriotic citizens.'[40]

The Conference was not as fully representative as its name might suggest, but it reflected the views of an important section of the Americanised Jewish bourgeoisie.[41] In 1907 Jacob Schiff, then generally recognised as the lay leader of the American Jewish community, publicly dissociated himself from Zionism.

> ' Speaking as an American, I cannot for a moment consider that one can be at the same time a true American and an honest adherent of the Zionist Movement.'[42]

In Germany a protest against ' the attempts of the so-called Zionists to found a Jewish national State in Palestine ' was published in July 1897, on the eve of the first Zionist Congress, in the name

---

[40] *Year Book of Central Conference of American Rabbis, 1897-98*, p. xli ; see also O. Handlin, *Adventure in Freedom* (New York, 1945), p. 168.

[41] The Conference spoke only for ' Reform ' Judaism. But at this time ' Reform stood dominant in the religious topography of American Jewry ': R. Learsi, *The Jews in America* (Cleveland, 1954), p. 123.

[42] Schiff to Professor Schechter, 8 August 1907: quoted, Cyrus Adler, *Jacob Schiff* (London, Heinemann, 1929), II, 165. ' Schiff exchanged views fully with him [Schechter] and agreed to have the letters published ': ibid., 164.

of the Association of German Rabbis.[43] In 1913 the Central Union of German Citizens of the Jewish Faith adopted and published a resolution sympathising with the Zionists in their efforts ' to find homes for the Jews of Eastern Europe and to increase the pride of the Jews in their history and religion,' but declaring that the Union could have nothing to do with Zionism ' in so far as it was a Jewish Nationalist Movement which disclaimed the sense of German nationality.'[44] In February 1914 a statement published in the German press on behalf of three hundred well-known German Jews declared that ' it is essential in the interests of Judaism that a line be drawn between the German Jews and the Zionists.'[45]

It would be a mistake to suppose that the anti-Zionists were simply Jews who turned their backs on Palestine because to them it meant nothing. The first important Jewish organisation to encourage the settlement of Jews in Palestine on the land was the Alliance Israélite. In the years immediately before the War Jacob Schiff and other American Jews of the same type and the same way of thinking were taking an active personal interest in various Jewish undertakings in Palestine, such as the Atlit Agricultural Experiment Station and the projected Technical Institute at Haifa. In rejecting the nationalist element in Zionism, the Central Union of German Citizens of the Jewish Faith took care, as has been seen, to disclaim any lack of sympathy with the practical part of the Zionist programme. As for the English Jews, Sir Moses Montefiore's seven visits to Palestine were among his principal claims to the pre-eminence assigned to him in the Anglo-Jewish hagiology. The Anglo-Jewish Association, though never identified with Zionism, is mentioned by Sokolow as one of two bodies—the other being the Alliance Israélite—to which ' no inconsiderable share of the interest in the Western world in the foundation of the Jewish colonies in Palestine may justly be credited.'[46] In the early 1890s the *Chibbath Zion* Movement[47] had a considerable following in England and counted among its adherents men like Colonel Albert Goldsmid, Sir Joseph Sebag-

---

[43] Lichtheim, *Geschichte*, p. 134.
[44] *The Times*, 1 April 1913.
[45] *J.C.*, 20 February 1914.
[46] Sokolow, II, 324.
[47] Above, p. 62.

Montefiore, Elim d'Avigdor, Sir Samuel Montagu (later, the first Lord Swaythling) and other members of the Anglo-Jewish élite.[48]

If, then, the leaders of the Jewish communities in the West were, generally speaking, unfriendly or even, in some cases, violently hostile to Zionism, it was not because for them the historic ties between the Jews and Palestine had no significance; it was because they were alarmed by what they conceived to be the implications of the Zionist philosophy. A mystical or sentimental or philanthropic interest in Palestine was a very different matter from assent to the Zionist doctrine that only by creating a home for the Jewish people in Palestine could the Jews purge themselves of their inhibitions, obsessions and split personalities— that only thus could they put themselves right with the world and ensure their own survival. Cherishing the equality of status to which they had, in most countries, been admitted only a generation or two earlier, the Western Jews or the vast majority of them—for there were some who at once rallied to Herzl's side—saw in the conception of a Jewish State an invitation to their enemies to raise the question of divided loyalties, and that at a time when anti-semitism was rampant in France and Central Europe, and when xenophobia with unmistakably anti-semitic overtones was gaining ground in the United States[49] and even in England.[50]

Herzl had at first spoken in terms of a Jewish State.[51] The Basle

---

[48] Norman Bentwich, *Early English Zionists* (Tel Aviv, n.d.), pp. 10-11.

[49] Handlin, op cit., pp. 184ff. ; Learsi, op cit., pp. 224-225.

[50] ' In the first ten years of this century, which, unfortunately, I am old enough to remember, there was a very strong xenophobia in this country about the tremendous number of people who had come into the country from Eastern Europe '—The Right Hon. J. Chuter Ede, House of Commons, 26 November 1953: O.R., col. 556. Besides the East European influx, the climate was somewhat unfavourable to the Jews for other reasons, such as the alleged connection of Jewish financiers with the origins of the South African War and the rapid social advance of certain members of the Jewish plutocracy as part of the entourage of King Edward VII. Full advantage was taken of their opportunities by anti-semites like G. K. Chesterton and Hilaire Belloc.

[51] He is said to have explained later that he was not thinking of a full-blown Jewish State. ' Had I wanted a State like all other States of the world, I would have labelled it as " ein jüdischer Staat " . . . I was thinking of a Jewish territory . . . run by a modern Company on the lines of rational and progressive colonisation. Such territory I would

Programme did not, it was true, go so far, but it could be seen to point in that direction. Moreover, with 'the creation in Palestine of a home for the Jewish people' the Programme coupled 'the strengthening of Jewish national consciousness,' thus proclaiming that the Jews were a people or a nation, and not a sect or religious brotherhood. If so, where—it could be asked—did the British (or French or American) Jews stand? Were they being invited to regard themselves, not as part of the British (or French or American) people, but simply as fragments of a scattered Jewish nation, faithfully discharging their civic obligations in the country in which they lived but not identifying themselves with its national life? The overwhelming majority of Jews in Europe, and some two-thirds of World Jewry, were in Russia or Austria-Hungary. In these multi-national Empires there might well be a case for what was known in the controversies of the time as Diaspora Nationalism—the conception of a Jewish 'nationality' sharing a common citizenship with other 'nationalities' but living its separate national life. But were ideas springing from a wholly different environment and experience to be translated to the West? Was there to be a kind of Pan-Judaism, with Jerusalem signifying for Jews everywhere what Berlin signified for the Pan-Germans and Moscow for the Pan-Slavs?

In their approach to Zionism assimilated Jews were genuinely troubled by such questions. The answers were not self-evident, nor were misgivings about the ambiguity of words like 'nation' and 'nationality' peculiar to anti-Zionists. In a slightly different but relevant context, the point was put by Herbert Samuel, not long before the Balfour Declaration, at a Conference of which we shall hear again later: [52]

> 'If it was intended to create in Palestine a Jewish nation
> *eo nomine,* care must be taken to explain the sense in which
> the term was used, because there was much misunderstand-
> ing, among Jews of the West, and some fear, owing, to that

[52] 7 February 1917—see below, p. 370. The record of the Conference, from which this quotation comes, is not a verbatim report.

> call "Judenstaat." . . . We want a Jewish Gemeinwesen [Common-
> wealth] with all securities for freedom. . . .' (From Sokolow's ' Reminis-
> cences of the First Zionist Congress,' *Zionist Review,* October 1917,
> pp. 86-89.)

misunderstanding, that a Jewish State in Palestine might be incompatible with their loyalty. So long as it was claimed that by nation is meant an organised community, well and good, but it might be misunderstood as meaning that the Jews in Great Britain, for instance, would constitute, as a result of a Jewish Palestine, a separate nation in the same sense as the British are a nation.'

This was early in 1917. Eight years later Samuel returned to the subject in his final report to the Colonial Office at the end of his term of office as High Commissioner for Palestine.[53] Speaking of the background to the Palestine White Paper of 1922,[54] he wrote:

'. . . It was asked what was the meaning of the word "national" in the Balfour Declaration. . . . If the Jews were declared to be a "people" and entitled to a "national home," a member of that people, it would seem, must possess that nationality. But if he were already a national of England, for example, or of France or of the United States, was the citizenship that he cherished unaffected by this or was it not? . . .

'As a result of these doubts, many Jews, patriotic citizens of the countries in which their families had lived, often for generations, regarded the Declaration, and indeed the whole Zionist Movement, with embarrassment, and sometimes with hostility. Others, equally patriotic, held the contrary view. . . . They refused to engage in fine-drawn discussions as to the meaning of "national" and "people." They were deeply interested in the return of a body of their co-religionists to Palestine . . . and at the same time they saw no reason why they should not remain, in spirit and in action, as loyal citizens of the States to which they belonged as if Palestine had not entered the field of political discussion and as if the Balfour Declaration had never been made. . . .'

The debate continued long after these words were written. But the anti-Zionists were fighting a losing battle. The Zionists

[53] Report on the Administration of Palestine, 1920-25, Colonial No. 15 (1925), pp. 26-27.
[54] Cmd. 1700 (1922).

might be unable to provide a tidy answer to every question, but
they had two irresistible advantages—a constructive programme
and a positive faith. The anti-Zionists had nothing to offer but
negations. The problems concerning the relations between
Palestine and the Diaspora which tormented many thoughtful
and sensitive Jews never were—perhaps never could be—satis-
factorily resolved, but in the end it was tacitly agreed that ' fine-
drawn discussions as to the meaning of " national " and " people " '
were sterile and unprofitable. When it came to the point, most
Jews—even those who had at no time identified themselves with
Zionism—found no insuperable difficulty in accommodating themselves to the emergence of the State of Israel. What had at first
been frowned upon as a dangerous heresy or laughed away as
a whimsical aberration became gradually respectable, and, in
the end, positively fashionable in the most select Jewish circles.[55]

But this was the close of a chapter which had opened more
than fifty years earlier with the appearance of Herzl's ' Jewish
State.' In the 1890s the first impact of the Zionist challenge
shocked the leaders of the Jewish communities in the West into
indignant protest. Believing that implicit in Zionism was a denial
of the principles on which the emancipation of the Jews had been
based, they denounced it as an invitation to go back to the ghetto.
In 1914 this view was still widely held in influential Jewish circles,
and nowhere more strongly than in England.

Writing in a leading English Review in 1878, the then Chief
Rabbi, Hermann Adler, took up a question which seemed to him
to call for an answer. What, it had been asked, was ' the political
bearing of Judaism?' The Chief Rabbi's reply was very simple:
' Judaism has no political bearing whatever.'

> ' Ever since the conquest of Palestine by the Romans we
> have ceased to be a body politic. We are citizens of the
> country in which we dwell. We are simply Englishmen or
> Frenchmen or Germans, as the case may be, certainly holding

[55] Among the contributory causes were the response to the Nazi challenge,
and also, perhaps, a half-conscious feeling that the establishment of a
Jewish State actually eased the situation by drawing a clear dividing-
line between those Jews who did and those who did not desire to be
citizens of such a State.

particular theological tenets and practising special religious ordinances; but we stand in the same relation to our country-men as any other religious sect, having the same stake in the national welfare and the same claim on the privileges and duties of citizens.'[56]

This was the classic Anglo-Jewish doctrine. In England, where there were no minority problems and where the Jews had since 1858[57] enjoyed full equality of status, there was no room for any we-and-they relationship between the Jews and their fellow-citizens. The English Jew was, or ought to be, simply an English-man of the Jewish persuasion. This—'the liberal compromise'[58] —was how the Jews of Victorian England sought to harmonise their genuine desire to preserve their Jewish heritage with their equally genuine desire to identify themselves with the national life. It could be objected that their picture of themselves did not correspond to realities, since, whatever Dr. Adler might say, it was plainly not the case that they were just a sect like any other sect or that they had nothing in common with one another or with Jews elsewhere but certain purely religious beliefs and prac-tices. It would be absurd to pretend that other people saw the Jews as the Jews saw, or wished to see, themselves.[59] Nor were the Jews, for their part, wholly at ease. There is an illuminating passage in a sermon preached by Israel Abrahams[60] in 1894:

' If we will but use our eyes and see the finger of God bring-ing us again to this land to fulfil Israel's mission of spreading God's truth over the world; if we will but see Him guiding

---

[56] *The Nineteenth Century*, July 1878.

[57] In 1858 a modification of the Parliamentary oath made it possible for a Jew to sit in Parliament. Jews had before that date been returned to Parliament but had been precluded by the nature of the oath from taking their seats.

[58] The phrase is Mr. Richard Crossman's: *Palestine Mission* (London, Hamish Hamilton, 1946), p. 75.

[59] The relations between the Jews and their neighbours in an English provincial city in the early 1900s are described by a talented and sensitive British-born Jew in Humbert Wolfe's reminiscences of his boyhood years in Bradford: *Now a Stranger* (London, Cassell, 1933), pp. 124ff. (Wolfe was born in 1886.)

[60] 1858-1925: Reader in Talmudic Literature and Rabbinics at Cam-bridge University, 1902-1925.

our destinies here and to-day as he guided our destinies elsewhere and in Israel's past; then, my friends, the coming generation of English Jews will not be torn by that bitterest of internal conflicts, by that most hopeless of dilemmas: Are we Jews or Englishmen first? . . . Ah, but you will respond to God's mercies now, even as your fathers did in their day. Your life and your religion will both perfect themselves when your life and your religion as Englishmen and as Jews form one harmonious whole . . .'[61]

The vehemence of the Anglo-Jewish protest against the Zionist intrusion may be partly accounted for by a sub-conscious awareness of an 'internal conflict' still to be resolved. But even if some of the more sensitive spirits would have felt compelled to admit the existence of such a conflict, their inference would have been merely that the process of adjustment was not yet complete. Firmly rooted in the established tradition, most English-born Jews looked to the future without anxiety, confident that the next generation, if not their own, would find a sure anchorage in the liberal compromise.

Zionism came on the scene at a time when in England, as in the United States, the structure of the Jewish community was being drastically changed by immigration from Eastern Europe.

Almost immediately after the accession of the Czar Alexander III. in 1881, fresh turns of the screw brought the repression of the Jews in Russia to a point at which many of them found their miseries unendurable. In Rumania, where the Jews had been intended by the Powers to benefit by the guarantees of religious liberty contained in Article XLIV of the Treaty of Berlin, they had in practice no relief from their disabilities. A westward exodus of Jews from Russia began in 1881 and from Rumania in 1899, and to this was added a steady stream of emigration from Austrian Poland (Galicia), though there the spur was not so much persecution as sheer poverty.[62]

Of the two-and-a-quarter million Jews who streamed out of Eastern Europe between 1881 and 1914, some two million found

---

[61] *J.C.*, 13 January 1894.
[62] See A. Ruppin, *The Jews of Today* (London, Bell, 1913), pp. 85ff.

their way to the United States, where the Jewish population rose in these thirty-three years from less than 250,000 to something like three million.[63] But for the influx of Jews steeped in a tradition which made them sensitive to anything concerning Palestine, it is unlikely that Zionist or pro-Zionist sentiment in the United States would have been strong enough in 1915-1917 to command the attention of the British Government in its political warfare. In so far as the Balfour Declaration, in its propagandist aspect, was aimed at American Jewry, its main target was the mass of unassimilated or half-assimilated Jews from Eastern Europe who, impressed by left-wing pacifist propaganda and remembering resentfully the British alliance with Czarist Russia, were noticeably apathetic about the War.

In England Jewish immigration from Eastern Europe was not on the same spectacular scale as in the United States, but it was large enough to bring about a radical change in the make-up of the Jewish community. In 1880 there were about 60,000 Jews in England,[64] many of them British-born and nearly all of them more or less anglicised.[65] When the impact of Zionism first began to be felt in the late 1890s, Anglo-Jewry had already ceased to be the compact and cosy little group that it had been some twenty years earlier. Between 1881 and 1905 Jewish immigrants, mainly from Eastern Europe, settled in England in numbers not precisely known but usually estimated at about 100,000.[66] Though cut down by the restrictive legislation introduced in 1905, immigration continued up to 1914, when about one-half of a total Jewish population of some 300,000[67] would appear to have consisted of fairly recent arrivals from Eastern Europe and their dependents.[68]

[63] Ruppin, loc. cit.; H. S. Lindfield in *American Jewish Year Book* (Philadelphia, 1927), pp. 241, 250ff.

[64] V. D. Lipman, *Social History of the Jews in England, 1850-1950* (London, Watts, 1954), p. 61.

[65] Ibid., p. 84.

[66] Ibid., p. 89.

[67] Ibid., p. 160 ; M. Freedman (ed.), *A Minority in Britain* (London, Vallentine, Mitchell, 1955), p. 73.

[68] Freedman, op. cit., p. 63. In connection with the British Census of 1911, it was thought necessary to issue 30,000 forms printed in Yiddish. The forms were for heads of households, so that, accepting Dr. Redcliffe Salaman's estimate (*J.C. Supplement*, 1921, Nos. 4-8) of five as the average size of the Jewish family, the inference would

To the leaders of the Anglo-Jewish community it seemed self-evident that, if immigration on this scale was to be digested, everything possible must be done to anglicise the newcomers. With its insistence on the distinctiveness of the Jews, not merely as a religious group but as a people or a nation, Zionist propaganda appeared to them to point in the opposite direction and was feared and resented accordingly. From this point of view it was all the more embarrassing at a time when England was showing distinct symptoms of xenophobia. The Protectionist agitation was gaining ground, and the 'keep out foreign goods' campaign slid easily into 'keep out the foreigner,' which, on the facts of the case, came near to meaning 'keep out foreign Jews.' It was the influx of Jews from Eastern Europe which led to the setting up in 1902 of a Royal Commission on Alien Immigration, and the introduction by the Balfour Government of the Aliens Bill which became law in the summer of 1905. There was here a warning that there was a limit to the number of Jews whom the country was prepared to absorb, and that even in England the Jewish Question might arise, as it was already beginning, just about this time, to arise in the United States.[69] It was not only the Act itself that was disturbing, but the line of argument adopted by some of its leading supporters in its passage through Parliament. *The Jewish Chronicle,* which had strongly objected to the measure, did not question Balfour's sincerity in his emphatic disclaimer and denunciation of anti-semitism. The fact remained that even Balfour, in asserting the right of every country to choose its immigrants, had declared that no one could seriously say that the question of race could be ignored,[70] and that in another speech on the Bill he had spoken still more pointedly of 'the undoubted evils that had fallen upon the country from an immigration which was largely Jewish.'[71] A widespread uneasiness

---

[69] See Handlin, op. cit., pp. 184, 192.

[70] H.C., 2 May 1905: O.R., col. 795.

[71] H.C., 10 July 1905: O.R., col. 155.

---

be that about 150,000 Jews belonged to Yiddish-speaking households: Freedman, loc. cit. In 1916 the number of male Russian nationals of military age resident in the United Kingdom (most of them certainly Jews) was estimated at 25,000: *J.C.,* 4 August 1916.

among English Jews was reflected in an article in *The Jewish Year Book* for 1905:[72]

> '. . . Everywhere abroad the [Aliens] Act is interpreted as meaning that England recognises itself as face to face with a growing Jewish Question, and the Jew in England has by universal foreign opinion been brought into line with his brethren elsewhere as one against whom special legislation is directed. . . .'

The writer was Leopold Greenberg. Greenberg was an ardent and prominent Zionist. Far from drawing the inference that to be a Zionist was to harbour dangerous thoughts, he remained unshaken in his Zionist faith. Anti-semitism could work in either of two opposite directions. According to their backgrounds and temperaments, it made Zionists of some Jews and anti-Zionists of others. In the decade before the War the effect of the anti-alien agitation on the lay leaders of the Anglo-Jewish community was to fortify them in their uncompromising opposition to Zionism. The anti-Zionist case is summed up in a statement issued in 1909 in protest against the establishment of Zionist Societies by Jewish undergraduates at certain English Universities. Nearly all the best-known Anglo-Jewish families were represented among the twenty-five signatories.[73]

> 'We regard it,' they wrote, 'as dangerous that the rising generation of educated Jews should be encouraged in opinions which (a) must tend to alienate them from other Englishmen, (b) demolish the structure of the argument advanced, for example, by Lord Macaulay, on which the Act for the removal of Jewish disabilities was supported, and (c) are likely to arouse some suspicion in all classes of society, and particularly in the working-classes, among whom Jewish immigrants have to make their way, as to the measure of patriotism among English Jews. . . .'[74]

[72] p. 465.

[73] They included Leopold de Rothschild, Claude Montefiore, Sir Philip Magnus, Robert (later, Sir Robert) Waley Cohen and Osmond (later, Sir Osmond) d'Avigdor Goldsmid.

[74] *J.C.*, 9 April 1909. This statement was reprinted in 1917 and circulated by the anti-Zionists in support of their propaganda.

The Chief Rabbi, Hermann Adler, endorsed the statement, declaring that 'since the destruction of the Temple and our dispersion, we no longer constitute a nation ; we are a religious community.'[75]

Here were the seeds of the bitter controversy which in 1917 rent Anglo-Jewry, startled and embarrassed the War Cabinet and looked for a moment as though it might result in the Balfour Declaration being strangled at birth.

3

There were in 1914 about 85,000 Jews in Palestine[76] and about 600,000 Arabs,[77] some of them belonging to one or other of the Christian Churches, but with Moslems in an overwhelming majority. The Jewish population had more than doubled since the beginning of the Back to Palestine Movement in the early 1880s, when it is believed to have numbered about 35,000.[78] Allowing for natural increase, the difference of 50,000 represents a net immigration of the order of 30,000-35,000 in the thirty-two years from 1882 to 1913.[79] [80]

The new settlers included Yemenites from Southern Arabia and, at the other end of the scale, a sprinkling of German intellec-

---

[75] *J.C.*, 23 April 1909.

[76] A. Ruppin, *The Jews in the Modern World* (London, Macmillan, 1934), pp. 55, 389 ; Bein, *Return to the Soil*, p. 138 ; Luke and Keith-Roach, *Handbook of Palestine* (London, Macmillan, 1930), p. 58.

[77] No reliable statistics are available but the generally accepted figure for the total pre-War population is in the neighbourhood of 700,000: see Bein, loc. cit. ; Luke and Keith-Roach, op. cit., p. 38. A Census taken in 1922 showed a total population of 757,000, of whom 590,000 were Moslems, 83,000 Jews and 73,000 Christians: Colonial No. 15 (1925), p. 48. (Druzes made up most of the remaining 11,000.)

[78] Ruppin, *The Jews of Today*, p. 284 ; Luke and Keith-Roach, op. cit., p. 58.

[79] Ruppin, op. cit., p. 284, estimates the aggregate increase by immigration from 1881 to 1910 at 32,500. According to Ruppin (*The Jews in the Modern World*, p. 389), 'in 1914 about two-thirds of the 85,000 Jewish inhabitants of Palestine still belonged to the old Orthodox type and only one-third to the new national, progressive section.'

[80] Except for the 1922 Census returns, all the figures mentioned above are only estimates, no reliable statistical data being available.

tuals, but the bulk of them came from Russia, Rumania, Austrian Poland and Hungary, with the Russians leading both in numbers and in influence and bringing with them ideas derived from the Russian intellectuals by whose teachings many of them were inspired. Among these immigrants from Eastern Europe were the founders of the agricultural settlements which, though still in their infancy, had by 1914 become a distinctive feature of the revival of Jewish life in Palestine and symbolised the cleansing of the stains of the ghetto by a return to the soil.[81]

The Turkish Government wanted no more Jews in Palestine, and immigration was possible only to the extent to which it was unable to enforce its will. If Jews managed to filter in, this was in part thanks to the good offices of the foreign—notably the Russian—Consuls, and in part—as it was delicately put in a Zionist report—because ' it was always possible to get round the individual official with a little artifice.'[82] In these respects nothing was changed by the Turkish Revolution. Turkish policy remained at least as obstructive as in the days of Abdul Hamid, the local officials as inefficient and venal, and the foreign Consuls as ready to invoke the Capitulations for the benefit of their nationals and in the interests of their own prestige.

The Jews who elected to take their chance in Palestine were only an insignificant fraction of the more than two million who between 1882 and 1914 poured forth from Eastern Europe in the mass migration which changed the face of the Jewish world. Those who settled in Palestine did not go there because they had no choice. They were free to emigrate to America or, at least until 1905, to England. If they decided for Palestine, it was not from necessity but because of an inner compulsion to satisfy needs which, for them, could be fully satisfied nowhere else. Not all of them were strong-minded and purposeful enough to stay the course, but the best of them formed an élite under whose

[81] Estimates of the aggregate population of these settlements in 1914 vary from 15,000 (*Zionism and the Jewish Future*, London, 1916, p. 155) to 10,500 (*The Jewish Colonies in Palestine, 1882-1914*, Admiralty Naval Staff Intelligence Department, January 1919—I.D. 1203). This N.I.D. paper may be consulted for a detached view of the position in 1914. A good description of the history of the settlements up to that date can be found in Bein's *Return to the Soil*.
[82] Z.C. 1921 *Reports*: " Palestine Report," p. 7.

leadership a new type of Jewish society began gradually to take shape in Palestine—a society seeking to build up by its own efforts a home which would be truly its own, and inspired by *Da'at Haavodah* (' the religion of work '), whose gospel was the redemption of the individual Jew, and of the Jewish people, through productive labour.[83]

By 1914 only a small beginning had been made, but enough had been achieved not only to inspire the Zionists with confidence in the future but to enlist the sympathy of many Jews who did not call themselves Zionists, and to attract some attention in the outside world. The Jewish agricultural colonies, though not yet self-supporting, had profited by their mistakes and were beginning to develop on sounder lines. In the towns there was now a nucleus of Jewish skilled labour. The Jewish settlers were no longer isolated groups of individuals but were developing on a miniature scale some of the institutions of an organised society. The Hebrew language was coming back to life and was permeating the schools. In the twelve months ended August 1914 there was a larger immigration than had ever before been recorded in a single year.[84] On the eve of the War preparations were well advanced for the early opening of a Jewish Institute of Technology, and there was already talk of a Hebrew University. The exertions of the early Lovers of Zion, the lavish benefactions of Edmond de Rothschild, the stolid perseverance of the Jewish Colonisation Association, and the expanding activities, from 1908 onwards, of the Zionist Organisation and its Palestinian offshoots were now seen not to have been wasted or misdirected. Thanks to the quality of the human material, they were beginning to bear fruit.

It was all on a very small scale. Even in 1914 a large proportion of the Jewish population of about 85,000 consisted of Orthodox Jews carrying on in the Holy Cities the traditional study of the

---

[83] See Böhm's chapter on Aaron David Gordon, I, 549ff. ; J. L. Teller, ' The Making of the Ideals That Rule Israel ' in *Commentary* (New York), January 1954 ; Joseph Baratz, *A Village by the Jordan* (London, Harvill, 1954).

[84] The Report cited in Note 82 gives a figure of 6,000, adding, however: ' Many of them drifted away again, but a portion remained and took root.'

Law and living on gifts provided by pious supporters abroad.[85] These remained stagnant in their seclusion. The dynamic element —the immigrants who had come in after 1882—was, after all, only some 35,000 strong. What had been achieved was not spectacular, but it was just enough to make a difference—it may well have been a decisive difference—to the standing of the Zionists and their claim to a hearing when, with the entry of Turkey into the War, the future of Palestine became an open question. It needs no great effort of the imagination to realise how much weaker the Zionist case would have been if it had had to be presented solely in terms of a paper programme and a set of abstract ideas. It was fortunate for the Zionist leaders that, in approaching the British Government, they could point to what had already been accomplished in Palestine under highly adverse conditions as evidence that the Zionists were not mere talkers or dreamers but deserved to be taken seriously.

4

When Jewish immigrants began trickling into Palestine in the early 1880s, the Arab population did not at first show any sign of alarm or resentment. The Jewish colonies were sometimes raided by Arabs out for loot, but these were isolated incidents without serious significance. Though there may even then have been some latent fear or suspicion of the newcomers, they aroused no strong feeling. There were not enough of them to attract much attention ; apart from Jews coming to Palestine to pray and study in the Holy Cities, the total number of immigrants up to 1900 cannot have amounted to much more than about 12,000.[86] Jewish immigration brought money into the country, and part of it went to provide wages for Arab workers in the Jewish colonies. The Arab national movement was still in its infancy and negligible as a political force.

By 1914 the Arabs had begun to be somewhat more sensitive to the impact of Jewish immigration. There was still an Arab majority of about six to one, but the Jewish population had grown

[85] See Note 79.
[86] Ruppin, *The Jews of Today*, p. 284.

and was slowly but steadily increasing. It was not only a question of numbers. The Jews were finding their feet and were working energetically and with mounting confidence to consolidate their position in Palestine. As their expanding activities became more noticeable, there were Arabs who began to be conscious of a potential threat to the established order and to Arab predominance. This was more particularly the case in the towns, where the Arab commercial classes were becoming anxious about Jewish competition in trade and industry.[87] In the rural areas there was some feeling against the acquisition of land by infidel foreigners, but Arab interests were not directly threatened, as they were in the towns, by Jewish competition. Arab-Jewish relations had, however, deteriorated for another reason. The older Jewish colonies in the coastal plain gave employment to some thousands of Arab workers,[88] but there was no employment for Arabs in the settlements which had in the decade before the War sprung up further north in Galilee.[89] These had been founded by men who believed with religious fervour that the Jews must redeem themselves by the work of their own hands and insisted that they must rely upon themselves alone.[90] These ideas spread to the towns, and, as the Jewish Labour Movement gained strength, it pressed for the acceptance of the principle that employment provided by Jews or Jewish institutions must be reserved for Jewish workers. There was here a genuine dilemma. Not only was there some force in the contention that it would be morally degrading for the Jews to become mere overseers of Arab labour, but the building up of a Jewish working-class population with varied skills was clearly indispensable to the development of a healthy economy. On the other hand, what amounted to a boycott of Arab labour was not calculated to improve Arab-Jewish relations.

[87] Ibid., p. 292.

[88] 'Five thousand Arab labourers are today working in the colonies of Judea alone': S. Tolkowsky, in *Zionism and the Jewish Future* (London, 1916), p. 156.

[89] See B. Litvinoff, *Ben-Gurion of Israel* (London, Nicolson and Watson, 1954), p. 59. Speaking of agricultural colonisation generally, Ruppin said, at the 1913 Zionist Congress: 'The objective we have in view [is] the creation of a Jewish milieu and of a closed Jewish economy, in which producers, consumers and middlemen shall all be Jewish': *Three Decades of Palestine* (Jerusalem, Schocken, 1936), p. 62.

[90] Litvinoff, loc. cit.

On a different level, the situation had changed since the early days of immigration, first because of the emergence of Zionism as a political movement and, secondly, because of the growing strength of Arab nationalism in response to the Turkish Revolution and its aftermath.

The main features of Zionist history from 1882 to 1914 have already been outlined. The *Choveve Zion,* under whose auspices the Back-to-Palestine movement had begun, had operated on a modest scale and with no clearly defined objective. The Zionist Organisation had come into existence in 1897 with much larger ideas and a much more precise programme, proclaiming as its purpose the creation in Palestine of a home for the Jewish people and making it clear that what was contemplated was a massive Jewish immigration with the backing of some kind of international guarantee. After the Turkish Revolution the 'practical' Zionists had come gradually into the ascendant and the political aspect of the Movement had receded into the background. To this extent the original conception had been modified, but the Basle Programme still held the field and the main purpose of the Movement remained in essence unaltered.

Among the Palestine Arabs there was as yet no well-developed national consciousness, but since the Turkish Revolution Arab nationalism had been gaining ground, and, though its main centres were in other parts of the Arab world, Palestine had begun to feel its backwash.[91]

The Arab national movement came to birth about the middle of the nineteenth century with the efforts of a small group of Syrians and Lebanese—mainly Christians—to promote an Arab literary revival and to remind the Arab people of their rich cultural heritage. The Syrian Protestant College founded at Beirut, under American auspices, in 1866[92] played an important part in fostering this Arab renaissance and, as time went on, became a seed-bed of Arab nationalism. The close ties between this in-

---

[91] For the origins and growth of the movement, see George Antonius, *The Arab Awakening* (London, Hamish Hamilton, 1938); E. Atiyah, *The Arabs* (London, Penguin, 1955); G. Haddad, *Fifty Years of Modern Syria and Lebanon* (Beirut, 1950); Philip Graves, *The Land of Three Faiths* (London, Cape, 1923); Gooch and Temperley, X., Pt. II, App. III; F.O. Handbook, *Syria and Palestine,* pp. 46-48.

[92] In 1920 re-named The American University of Beirut.

THE ZIONIST MOVEMENT IN 1914

fluential American institution and the Arab national movement help (among other reasons) to explain why in 1917 Zionism found little favour in the eyes of the State Department in Washington.[93]

Little by little the Arab intelligentsia began to develop vague national aspirations, but up to the time of the Turkish Revolution there was no strong emotional impulse behind them, nor did they command any widespread support. It was not until the Committee of Union and Progress had begun, after 1909, to show its hand that Arab nationalism acquired a sharper edge. In the false dawn which followed the collapse of the old régime politically-minded Arabs, like other non-Turkish elements in the Ottoman Empire, were encouraged to hope for equality of status with the former master-race and for some measure of home rule. On both points they were quickly disillusioned. In the recoil from the frustration of the hopes aroused by the fall of the Sultan Abdul Hamid, Arab nationalism, especially in Syria, gained momentum. In a predominantly Moslem society the position of a Christian minority was bound to be precarious, but Islam was a powerful unifying force, and Moslem Arabs, accustomed, as Moslems, to regard themselves as members of the ruling caste, had not had the same incentive as the Christians to press separatist demands. But it was now becoming clear to them that, in the eyes of the Young Turks, Moslem Arabs were none the less Arabs and, as such to be kept in their place.[94] They, too, had their grievances, and what had been, in its origins, largely a Christian movement commanded a growing measure of Moslem support. But the Turks were not prepared to make any far-reaching concessions. The Arab nationalist societies never came within sight of their objectives, and by 1914 they had reached a dead end of frustration.

Though up to 1914 the movement had achieved nothing, there was potency in the ideas behind it. On the other hand, its real strength and dimensions should not be over-rated. While George Antonius commands respect, there is no compulsion to accept uncritically his romantic picture of Moslems and Christians

[93] See below, p. 597.
[94] 'The undisguised contempt testified by the Turks towards Arab Moslems warned these to expect no superior offices or emoluments': F.O. Handbook, *Syria and Palestine*, p. 47.

welded into a *union sacrée* in support of the national aspirations of the Arab people. How feeble the movement really was can be inferred from the failure of the Arabs, after 1914, to take advantage of Turkey's war-time embarrassments by a revolt *en masse*. According to Antonius,[95] the Arabs formed nearly half the population of the 1914 Turkish Empire—about 10½ out of 22 million, yet nowhere outside the Arabian Peninsula was there any armed rebellion. The overwhelming majority of the Arabs remained completely passive. In Syria there was some conspiring and plotting against the Turks, but nothing came of it. Some Arabs from other parts of Turkey joined the forces of the Sharif of Mecca, but in no great numbers,[96] and in no other part of the Arab area—neither in Mesopotamia nor in Syria nor in Palestine—did the Arabs rise against the Turks. It would be wrong to say that the Arabs contributed nothing to their own liberation, but in terms of active co-operation with their real liberators, the British Armies which forced the Turks out of the War, their contribution was unimpressive. The seeds of what was, in the end, to become a genuine national movement had already been sown in 1914, but it was a plant of slow growth. At the time of which we are speaking—the eve of the War—it was supported by a considerable part of the Arab intelligentsia and by a number of notables, but it had no mass following. A well-informed and by no means unsympathetic student of Arab affairs has described the position as follows:

> '... After the Balkan war, little more survived of the movement than a secret understanding among Arab officers in the Ottoman army and a freemasonry of discontent among Arab intellectuals, landed notables, tribal and family chiefs, and ambitious men of substance. ... Through lack of single aims,

[95] p. 104. (The figures are estimates.)

[96] At the Peace Conference, on 20 March 1919, President Wilson said that ' Feisal had said that he could not say how many men he had had in the field at one time, as it had been a fluctuating figure, but from first to last he had probably had 100,000 men.' The *procès-verbal* continues: ' General Allenby said that he had never had so many at one time ': *Foreign Relations of the United States* (Washington, Government Printing Office), *Paris Peace Conference*, V, 1-14 ; Lloyd George, *The Truth about the Peace Treaties* (London, Gollancz, 1938), II, 1067. (100,000 would be rather less than one per cent. of the Arab population of the then Turkish Empire.)

of effective organisation, and of strong leading, nothing practical came of it before the outbreak of war in 1914.'[97]

If even in Syria proper the movement had at this time no strong hold on the mass of the Arab population, Palestine, a backwater of the Arab world, felt its impact still less. Nevertheless, it did not leave Palestine entirely untouched. Of the seven Arab nationalists who in 1911 founded the secret society known as al-Fatat two were from Palestine, and so were three of the fourteen Arabs indicted by the Turks at the Aley treason trial in 1915.[98] After the Turkish Revolution there were distinct signs of stiffening Arab opposition to Jewish activities in Palestine, and especially to Jewish purchases of land.[99] There was no acute tension—still less was there any violent collision—between Jews and Arabs, but there was some hardening of Arab hostility to Zionism both in Palestine and in the Arab world generally.

It was not that there was no Arab recognition of the obvious fact that Palestine stood to gain by the immigration of Jews with a European standard of living and by the investment of Jewish capital. In a debate in the Turkish Chamber in May 1911, the Arab deputy for Jerusalem, while objecting to ' political ' Zionism, is reported to have said that Jewish activities had been of advantage to Palestine and that Jewish settlers would be welcome, provided that they identified themselves with the rest of the population by adopting Ottoman nationality.[100] In April 1914 one of the Arab nationalist leaders wrote in the Cairo newspaper

[97] D. G. Hogarth in H. W. V. Temperley (ed.), A *History of the Peace Conference* (published under the auspices of the British [later Royal] Institute of International Affairs, London, 1924), VI, 119. For T. E. Lawrence's equally candid appraisal, see his *Secret Dispatches from Arabia* (London, Golden Cockerel Press, 1939), p. 158.

[98] Antonius, pp. 111, 187.

[99] In 1910 the inhabitants of Nazareth agitated strongly against the sale of certain lands in the district to Jews: Bein, *Return to the Soil*, p. 75. In March 1911 the Director of the Zionist Office in Palestine reported that Arab protests against Jewish land purchases had been telegraphed to Constantinople: Lichtheim, *Memoirs*, Chapter 10. In 1912 Arab Deputies protested in the Turkish Chamber against Jewish land purchases in Palestine: Antonius, p. 259. In May 1914 the Beirut correspondent of *The Near East* reported: ' The Arab press continues to be deeply perturbed by the rapid growth of Jewish influence and colonial expansion.'—*The Near East*, 22 May 1914.

[100] Böhm, I, 403 ; *Juedische Rundschau* (Berlin), 24 December 1929.

al-Muqattam that the reason why Arab public opinion had turned against the Jews was that they kept strictly apart from the Arabs and aimed at establishing a Jewish State.[101] Even among the Arab nationalists there seem to have been some who were prepared to admit that Jewish immigration might in itself be of advantage to Palestine. What they were not prepared to admit was that there could be room in Palestine both for Arab nationalists and Zionist Jews. When the War came, British policy required that both the Jews and the Arabs should be encouraged in their respective national aspirations. We shall see later how it was sought to resolve the contradiction by suggesting to the Arab nationalists that, in the wider interests of their own cause, it might be to their advantage to let the Jews have their way in Palestine.

On returning from a visit to Palestine in 1912, Ahad Ha'am[102] reported, with his usual candour, that 'many natives of Palestine, whose national consciousness has begun to develop since the Turkish Revolution, look askance, quite naturally, at the selling of land to "strangers" and do their best to put a stop to this evil.'[103] About the same time the Constantinople correspondent of *The Times* was warning the British public against forfeiting the good-will of the Arab world by indiscreet manifestations of sympathy with Zionism.[104] Writing just after the outbreak of war, a British friend of Zionism, R. W. Seton-Watson, drew attention to the growing strength of Arab nationalism and continued: 'Nor can we afford to ignore the possible effect of such an Arab movement upon the state of Palestine and the future of the healthy Jewish nationalism which is at length striking root in its original home.'[105] It seems clear that these three observers, diverse as were their standpoints, were at one in seeing in the impetus given to Arab

---

[101] Nafik Bey Hakim in *al-Muqattam*, 14 April 1914, quoted in *Juedische Rundschau*, loc. cit.
[102] Pen-name of Asher Zvi Ginzberg, b. near Kiev, 1856; d. Tel-Aviv, 1927. Foremost Hebrew writer of his day; originator and leading advocate of 'Spiritual Zionism.'
[103] *Ten Essays on Zionism and Judaism*, transl. by Leon Simon (London, Routledge, 1922), p. 140.
[104] *The Times*, 28 September 1912; see above, p. 39.
[105] *The Round Table*, December 1914.

nationalism by the Turkish Revolution a danger-signal for the Zionists.

The warning sounded by Ahad Ha'am in 1912 was in keeping with views which he had expressed more than twenty years before. In an article published in a Hebrew periodical in 1891 he wrote, on his return from his first visit to Palestine:

> 'We are in the habit of thinking that all the Arabs are wild men of the desert and do not see or understand what goes on around them. But that is a great mistake. The Arabs, especially the town-dwellers, see and understand what we are doing and what we want in Palestine, but they do not react and pretend not to notice, because at present they do not see in what we are doing any threat to their own future. ... But if ever we develop in Palestine to such a degree as to encroach on the living space of the native population to any appreciable extent, they will not easily give up their place.'[106]

Ahad Ha'am by no means drew the inference that there was no future for the Jews in Palestine; he was simply trying, as a realist, to dispel the illusion that the Arabs could be relied upon to remain as apathetic as they then appeared and could safely be left out of account. But Ahad Ha'am's warning made little impression at the time. A good many years were to pass before the Zionist leaders began seriously to concern themselves with the problem of Arab-Jewish relations. The subject was not discussed by Herzl in any of his six presidential addresses to successive Zionist Congresses between 1897 and his death in 1904, nor is there any evidence in his other speeches and writings of his having considered it important.[107] This can more easily be understood when it is remembered that Herzl was thinking all along of a mass immigration of Jews under the authority of a formal Charter and had insisted from the start that there must be no attempt at piecemeal infiltration. It was not that he was under the illusion that Palestine was empty. In *The Jewish State* (1896) he expressed the view that, wherever his State might be founded, whether in Palestine or in

---

[106] *Hashiloah* (Odessa), April 1891; reprinted in *Collected Works* (Berlin, 1895), I, 26ff. For the English translation from the original Hebrew the author is indebted to Sir Leon Simon.

[107] See, as to this, Böhm, I, 271; Bein, *Return to the Soil*, pp. 423ff.

Argentina (for at this stage he was still thinking of Argentina as a possible alternative), 'infiltration is bound to end badly. It continues until the inevitable moment when the native population feels itself threatened and forces the Government to stop a further influx of Jews.'[108] It was precisely for this reason that Herzl staked his hopes on the Charter and the international guarantee. As appears from his *Altneuland* (1902), he assumed that the Arabs would share in the prosperity to be brought to Palestine by the Jews and would have no reason to find a Jewish régime unacceptable.

It was not until several years after Herzl's death that the Zionist leaders began to think more seriously about Arab-Jewish relations. In 1908 the Zionist Organisation, which, in accordance with Herzl's principles, had till then abstained from any practical activity in Palestine, began for the first time to supplement the work of other Jewish bodies already in the field by promoting colonisation on its own account. This of itself brought the Organisation into closer contact with the realities of the situation in Palestine. In the same year, 1908, when signs were beginning to appear of the growing strength of Arab nationalism, a Zionist Agency was established in Constantinople under the direction of Victor Jacobson, with the result that the Zionist Executive now had its own sources of information as to political developments in Turkey. Thus, in the circumstances of the years immediately before the War, the Zionist leadership became alive to the need for some accommodation, if such were possible, with the Arabs. In 1908 there was an exchange of views on the subject between Victor Jacobson and the then President of the Zionist Organisation, David Wolffsohn.[109] In a work published three years before the War, the relations between Jews and Arabs in Palestine were discussed at length by Arthur Ruppin, the Director of the Palestine Office of the Zionist Organisation. While recognising that certain difficulties might arise from Jewish competition with the Arabs in trade and agriculture, Ruppin expressed the optimistic view that, if these could be overcome, 'there is not much to fear from the national jealousy of the Arabs.'[110] But he struck

[108] English translation (see above, p. 18, note 58), p. 29.
[109] Bein, *Return to the Soil*, p. 424.
[110] *The Jews of Today*, pp. 291-292.

a rather more cautious note in addressing the Eleventh Zionist Congress in 1913. 'We have before us,' he told the Congress, 'the task, which can in no wise be evaded, of creating peaceful and friendly relations between the Jews and the Arabs. In this respect we have to catch up a great deal that we have neglected, and to rectify the errors that we have committed. It is, of course, quite useless to content ourselves with merely assuring the Arabs that we are coming into the country as their friends. We must prove this by our deeds. . . .'[111]

About this time the Arab problem was engaging the serious attention of the Zionist General Council. It was felt that some contact ought to be established with the main centres of Arab nationalism, and in the spring of 1914 it was decided that Sokolow[112] should visit Egypt and Syria. There he did his best to conciliate Arab opinion, pleading for a joint effort by Jews and Arabs to develop the resources of Palestine for the benefit of both, and advocating the teaching of the Arabic language and literature in Jewish schools.[113]

When Sokolow left on this mission, Jacobson was already in contact in Constantinople with a group of Arab politicians and journalists. He did his best to persuade them that if the Arabs would relax their opposition to Jewish activities in Palestine, the Jews could and would help them to realise their own national aspirations. The discussions went on from January to July 1914 but in the end came to nothing.[114] Jacobson had, in fact, nothing of substance to offer the Arabs, and the whole proceedings were all the more unreal because by this time Arab and Turkish interests were clearly in conflict, and in no circumstances could the Zionists afford to antagonise the Turks. At the Aley trial in 1915, when a number of Syrian nationalists were indicted for treason, the documents produced by the Turkish prosecutors included records of Jacobson's discussions with representative Arabs. It was fortunate for the Jews in Palestine—already suspect in Turkish eyes—that the papers included a memorandum which

111 Reprinted, in English translation, in *Three Decades of Palestine*, pp. 35ff.
112 Now a member of the Zionist Executive—see below, p. 168.
113 Böhm, I, 403 ; *Juedische Rundschau*, 24 December 1929.
114 Lichtheim, *Memoirs*, Chapter 12.

made it clear that the Arabs had been unimpressed by Jacobson's advances, being satisfied that the Zionists would and could do nothing to support the Arab cause at the cost of loyalty to Turkey.[115]

Though at least from 1908 onwards the Zionist leaders were alive to the importance of the Arab problem, it was not until after the War that the Zionist rank-and-file in Eastern Europe began to realise that Palestine was already the home of a considerable Arab population, which could not be brushed aside. In his first report on the administration of Palestine, Herbert Samuel, writing in the summer of 1921, remarked that among the Zionists

> 'there are those . . . who sometimes forget or ignore the present inhabitants of Palestine. Inspired by the greatness of their ideals, feeling behind them the pressure of two thousand years of Jewish history, intent upon the practical measures that are requisite to carry their purpose into effect, they learn with surprise and often with incredulity that there are half-a-million people in Palestine, many of whom hold, and hold strongly, very different views.'[116]

It is no wonder that when the time came to give effect to the Balfour Declaration, there was a strong sense of disillusionment among the more unsophisticated Zionists, who had seen in the Declaration a promise of a free hand for the Jews in Palestine and found it hard to reconcile themselves to the more realistic view presented to them by Weizmann.[117]

---

[115] Ibid., Chapter 18.

[116] Cmd. 1499 (1921), p. 7.

[117] ' . . . It would be idle to blame the extremists. They were taking the Balfour Declaration at its face-value, putting upon it the most reasonable and natural interpretation. . . . Only after five years' experience of Arab opposition has Dr. Weizmann, like a statesman, accepted the depreciated currency which we have found the best we can offer today': D. G. Hogarth, Introduction to Philip Graves' *The Land of Three Faiths* (London, Cape, 1923), pp. 5-6.

Part II

The Preliminaries
1914-16

CHAPTER 4

ZIONIST POLICY ON THE OUTBREAK OF WAR

THE ZIONIST ORGANISATION had no ready-made plans for dealing with the difficult position in which it found itself when war broke out in the summer of 1914.

The Central Office of the Organisation and the seat of its directorate, the Zionist Executive, were in Berlin, but it had adherents in all parts of the Jewish world, including all the countries at war. Its main strength was in Russia and Austria-Hungary. Some of its most important institutions—the Jewish Colonial Trust, the Anglo-Palestine Company, the Jewish National Fund—were incorporated in England. Of the six members of the Executive, two—Otto Warburg and Arthur Hantke—were Germans, and three—Yechiel Tschlenow, Nahum Sokolow and Victor Jacobson—were Russians. The sixth member, Shmarya Levin, was of Russian origin but had recently acquired Austro-Hungarian nationality.[1] The twenty-five[2] members of the General Council included twelve from Germany or Austria-Hungary, together with seven from Russia, two (Weizmann and Leopold Kessler) from England, and one each from Belgium, France, Holland and Rumania.[3]

With Europe split asunder by war, how would it be possible for such an Organisation to continue to function and retain its unity? How was effect to be given to the principle of neutrality so emphatically proclaimed and so warmly approved only a year before at the Eleventh Zionist Congress?[4] Did neutrality require that the Organisation should abstain from any political activity during the War, making no attempt to stake out in advance a claim to a hearing at a future Peace Conference? If, on the other hand, it did attempt to stake out such a claim, might it not find

[1] Böhm, I, 626. Levin had gone to the United States on Zionist business in the summer of 1914 and remained there throughout the War.
[2] Exclusive of the former President of the Organisation, Wolffsohn, who died in September 1914.
[3] For details see *1921 Z.C. Reports*, ' Organisation Report,' pp. 15-16.
[4] See above, p. 41.

itself on a slippery slope leading to its taking sides in the War ?

The practical question which at once arose for decision was whether the headquarters of the Organisation should be left in Berlin or moved to some neutral country. On this point there were sharp differences of opinion.[5] In favour of removal it could be argued that, if the seat of the Executive remained in Germany, the Organisation would be bound, in the end, to compromise itself by drifting into the German orbit. How easily this could happen was shown, it was contended, by the action of some prominent German Zionists, including several who held office in the Movement,[6] in identifying themselves with a newly founded organisation known as the 'Komitee für den Osten.' The K.f.d.O. represented its rôle as being that of an intermediary between the Jewish population and the German authorities in those parts of Eastern Europe which had been or might be over-run by the German armies.[7] This might, in itself, be a laudable object, but the K.f.d.O. had other and larger purposes. The point was put very plainly in a letter from one of its founders, Max Bodenheimer, one of the German members of the Zionist General Council, to the Chairman of the Zionist Executive, Otto Warburg: 'As I see it, the Russian Jews have precisely the same interest as the German Reich in a decisive German victory.'[8] It was evident that, whatever its ostensible aims, the K.f.d.O. was, and was meant to be, at the disposal of the German Government

---

5 See *Organisation Report*, pp. 27-28 ; *procès-verbal* of General Council Meeting, 3-6 December 1914 (Z.A.) ; Weizmann to Shm. Levin, 18 October 1914 (*Ch.W.P.*) ; letter of 14 December 1914 from the Belgian member of the General Council, Jean Fischer, to his colleagues (*N.S.P.*). (The accuracy of Fischer's account of the General Council meeting was disputed by the Executive—Hantke to members of the Council, 8 January 1915 [*N.S.P.*].)

6 Among them, two members of the Zionist General Council, Max Bodenheimer and Adolf Friedemann: Lichtheim, *Geschichte*, p. 212.

7 Ibid.

8 Bodenheimer to Warburg, 22 November 1914 (Z.A.). Böhm, I, 631, quotes Friedemann as having stated the aims of the K.f.d.O. as follows: 'To place at the disposal of the German Government the special knowledge of the founders and their relations with the Jews in Eastern Europe and in America, so as to contribute to the overthrow of Czarist Russia and to secure the national autonomy of the Jews.' (The date of this statement is not given by Böhm.) In 1915 the K.f.d.O. started pro-German propaganda work in the United States— see below, p. 215.

for the purposes of its political warfare and the furtherance of its ulterior designs in Eastern Europe.

Disturbed by the activities of the K.f.d.O. and anxious that they should not be allowed to compromise the Zionist Movement, influential Zionists outside Germany pressed all the more strongly for the removal of the Zionist headquarters from German soil. Among them was Weizmann, who took the view that not only should the Central Office be moved from Berlin, but the existing Zionist Executive should cease to function. Almost immediately after the outbreak of war, an *ad hoc* body known as the Provisional Executive Committee for General Zionist Affairs had been set up in the United States under the chairmanship of Louis D. Brandeis.[9] Weizmann's advice was that the conduct of Zionist affairs during the War should be entrusted to Brandeis' Provisional Committee. ' I do not doubt,' he wrote to Shmarya Levin, ' that by this way only the Organisation could be saved from falling to pieces.'

> 'In view of the tension now prevailing, I consider the activities of the old Actions Committee[10] impossible and even dangerous for the future of our cause. . . . The American Provisional Committee should be given full power to deal with all Zionist matters until better times come. As soon as the situation is somewhat cleared up, we could talk plainly to England and France with regard to the abnormal situation of the Jews. . . . It is in the interest of peoples now fighting for the small nationalities to secure for the Jewish nation the right of existence. Now is the time when the peoples of Great Britain, France and America will understand us. . . . The moral force of our claims will prove irresistible; the political conditions will be favourable to the realisation of our ideal. . . . We must unite the great body of conscious Jews in Great Britain, America, Italy and France. The German and Austrian Jews will also understand us better later . . .'[11]

[9] Later, Justice Brandeis of the United States Supreme Court. As to the Provisional Committee, see below, p. 189.

[10] The official (German) style of the Executive was 'Engeres Aktionskomitee.'

[11] To Shm. Levin, 18 October 1914: *Ch.W.P.*

Weizmann's instinct was already telling him in what direction the Zionists must look for their friends.

His proposal for the handing over of control to the New York Committee was put forward at a time when he himself had barely begun to make the contacts by which he paved the way for the Balfour Declaration. Had his view prevailed, his activities would have been subject to remote control from New York and would, in all probability, have been severely circumscribed. He was able to ignore a rump Executive sitting in enemy territory in Berlin. He would not have had the same free hand if authority had been formally transferred to a predominantly American body sitting in New York and, at least so long as the United States was outside the War, conceiving itself to be bound by the principle of neutrality.

Weizmann's view did not gain acceptance, nor did the less drastic proposal, favoured by some other prominent Zionists, that the seat of the Executive should be moved to some neutral part of Europe—preferably to The Hague. If the headquarters of the Movement were removed from Germany, might not this, it was argued, be noted and resented by the German Government and so antagonise a Power which, for all anyone could tell, might have a large voice in the post-War settlement? Would it not be more prudent to leave the seat of the Executive where it was, and to set up somewhere in neutral Europe a separate Bureau which could serve as a clearing-house for Zionist affairs? What finally decided the issue in favour of this view was the situation which arose when Turkey, in November 1914, entered the war on the side of the Central Powers. The position of the Jews in Palestine at once became highly precarious. About half of them were Russian nationals.[12] Some of the leading Zionist institutions had been incorporated as English companies. Both Russia and Great Britain were at war with Turkey. The Turks had all along been antagonistic to Zionism; now was their opportunity to work their will on the Jews and all they had created in Palestine. Was not the best—perhaps the only—hope of averting that disaster to prevail upon the Germans to intervene in favour of the Jews with their Turkish allies?[13] Was it not, therefore, of paramount

[12] Lichtheim, *Geschichte*, p. 208.
[13] Lichtheim, *Memoirs*, Chapter 14.

importance that the Zionist Executive should be left in as strong a position as possible for invoking the friendly interest and good offices of the German Government?

Early in December 1914 the whole situation was reviewed by the General Council at a meeting (its first since the outbreak of war) held at Copenhagen and attended by nine of its twenty-five members—five Germans, three Russians and one Belgian. Neither of the two English members was present.[14] The outcome of the proceedings, together with certain supplementary decisions taken by the Executive, was, briefly, as follows: The Central Office was left in Berlin in charge of the two German members of the Executive, Warburg and Hantke. It was not expressly laid down that the Berlin members of the Executive should have authority to act for that body as a whole, but this appears to have been the intention.[15] Jacobson, who had been temporarily in Berlin, returned to his post as Director of the Zionist Agency in Constantinople. A Zionist Bureau, which was to work in close conjunction with the Berlin Executive,[16] was opened in Copenhagen under the direction of a Russian member of the General Council, Leo Motzkin. It was further decided that two Russian members of the Executive, Tschlenow and Sokolow, should go on a special mission to the United States, with a view to a programme of political action being worked out with the New York Provisional Committee. The general idea seems at this stage to have been that responsibility for the conduct of the Movement, and for the protection of Zionist interests in Palestine, should be divided between Berlin (with its Constantinople and Copenhagen subsidiaries) and the American Provisional Committee. As for England, it was arranged that Tschlenow and Sokolow should visit London en route for New York, but the main emphasis was on the exchange of views with the American Committee.[17] In the

---

[14] 3-6 December 1914: *procès-verbal* in Z.A.; decisions summarised in *1921 Z.C. Reports*, 'Organisation Report,' pp. 28-29.

[15] Lichtheim, *Memoirs*, Chapter 14.

[16] 'Organisation Report,' p. 28: 'An Office was to be opened in Copenhagen to work in conjunction with the Berlin Executive.' It was opened in February 1915—ibid., p. 30.

[17] The 'Organisation Report' does not mention the proposed mission to the United States but says simply: '[The Conference decided that] Mr. Sokolow and Dr. Tschlenow should go to London.' The decisions

event, the mission to the United States was dropped. Sokolow arrived in England on 31 December 1914 and, finding himself fully occupied, stayed there throughout the War. Tschlenow came with him but decided, after a few months in London, that he was needed at home. He remained in Russia until, in the autumn of 1917, he returned to England, where he died a few months later.

At a meeting of the General Council in March 1916 it was explained that Sokolow and Tschlenow had been sent to England soon after the outbreak of war because in England itself the right people for political work were hard to find. It was also stated at the same meeting that Sokolow and Tschlenow had set out for London bound by a resolution declaring that the Zionist Executive (of which both were members) could not be a party to negotiations with the Government of any country at war with Turkey.[18]

On the first point the Berlin Executive turned out to have been misinformed. On the second point its views were—fortunately for the Movement—disregarded. By the time Sokolow and Tschlenow reached London at the end of December 1914 the course of events had already begun to be shaped by other hands.

---

[18] *Procès-verbal* of General Council meeting, The Hague, 23-24 March 1916—Z.A. Hantke said (p. 18): 'When Yechiel [Tschlenow] and Nahum [Sokolow] went to England, it was expressly resolved that no negotiations (" Verhandlungen ") could be allowed to be conducted by the Executive [" Engeres Aktionskomitee "] with any Government which was in a state of war with Turkey. In England itself there was a lack of suitable persons who could give effective help in political work' ('die die politische Arbeit wirksam hätten unterstützen können').

recorded in the *procès-verbal* provide in general terms for 'special missions to various countries,' but the only country specifically mentioned in this connection is the United States. A summary (Z.A.) of the results of an Executive meeting held concurrently with the General Council meeting (3-7 December 1914) refers to a mission to New York to be undertaken by Sokolow and Tschlenow, and also speaks of a specific piece of work to be done by Tschlenow in London in connection with the purchase of a site in Jerusalem for the projected University. In February 1915 the Executive still assumed that Tschlenow and Sokolow would be going to the United States: circular letter to members of General Council, 26 February 1915—Z.A. In June 1915 Tschlenow told the General Council that he intended going there with Sokolow in September: Berlin office to Shm. Levin, 21 June 1915—Z.A.

CHAPTER 5

HERBERT SAMUEL

GREAT BRITAIN DECLARED war on Turkey on 5 November 1914.
In his speech at the Lord Mayor's Banquet on November 9th,
the Prime Minister, Mr. Asquith, made it clear that, in the light
of the new situation, Great Britain had finally abandoned her
traditional Eastern policy and now included among her war aims
the dismemberment of the Turkish Empire. 'It is the Ottoman
Government,' he declared, 'and not we who have rung the death-
knell of Ottoman dominion not only in Europe but in Asia.'[1] On
the same day the Turkish question seems to have been discussed
by the Cabinet, probably in connection with Asquith's Guildhall
speech; at all events, we know from Lord Samuel's memoirs[2]
that at a meeting of the Cabinet on that day Lloyd George
'referred to the ultimate destiny of Palestine.'

Samuel (then Mr. Herbert Samuel) had a seat in the Cabinet
as President of the Local Government Board. After the meeting
he broached the subject of Zionism in a talk with Lloyd George,
who assured him (this is all we are told) that 'he was very keen
to see a Jewish State established'[3] in Palestine. On the same day
Samuel developed his views more fully in a conversation with the
Foreign Secretary, Sir Edward Grey.[4] Pointing out that 'the
jealousies of the great European Powers would make it difficult
to allot [Palestine] to any one of them,' he suggested that 'perhaps the opportunity might arise for the fulfilment of the ancient
aspiration of the Jewish people, and the restoration there of a
Jewish State.' He suggested, further, that 'British influence
ought to play a considerable part in the formation of such a
State,' since 'the geographical situation of Palestine, and
especially its proximity to Egypt, would render its goodwill a
matter of importance to the British Empire.' Such a State, he

---

[1] *The Times*, 10 November 1914.
[2] Viscount Samuel, *Memoirs* (London, Cresset Press, 1945), pp. 139ff.
[3] Ibid.
[4] Ibid.

said, 'could not be large enough to defend itself,' and it would, therefore, be essential that it should be neutralised.

Grey showed marked sympathy with these ideas. He told Samuel that Zionism had always had a strong sentimental attraction for him. According to Samuel's note of the conversation, 'he was quite favourable to the proposal and would be prepared to work for it if the opportunity arose.' He went so far as to say that 'if any proposals were put forward by France or any other Power with regard to Syria, it would be important not to acquiesce in any plan which would be inconsistent with the creation of a Jewish State in Palestine.' Thinking, perhaps, of what the French were accustomed to describe as the 'accord' of 1912,[5] he enquired whether Syria must necessarily go with Palestine. Samuel's reply was that this was not only unnecessary but inadvisable, since it would bring in a large and unassimilable Arab population; 'it would,' he said, 'be a great advantage if the remainder of Syria were annexed by France, as it would be far better for the State to have a European Power as neighbour than the Turk.'

To Samuel's account of this interview may be added Weizmann's note of what he was told about Grey's views on Zionism when, accompanied by Dr. Moses Gaster, he saw Samuel a few weeks later:

> 'He [Mr. Samuel] further communicated to us that Sir Edward Grey is interested in the project, especially from the point of view of creating a Jewish cultural centre, a "nidus," as Sir Edward called it, which would reflect glory not only on the Jews, but on the whole world; a sort of generating-station which would set in motion all that is best in Israel.'[6]

To Asquith, as we shall see, it seemed incredible that Zionist fantasies should have found their way into Herbert Samuel's 'well-ordered and methodical brain.' Even Lloyd George,

---

[5] Above, p. 48.

[6] 'Report submitted to the Members of the Executive of the International Zionist Organisation [i.e., Sokolow and Tschlenow] by Dr. Ch. Weizmann, London and Manchester, 7 January 1915'—*Ch.W.P.* (hereafter referred to as 'Weizmann's January 1915 Report'). For a further reference to this interview (25 December 1914) see below, p. 139.

though himself attracted by Zionism, had not expected it to appeal to Samuel. One of his intimates, Sir George Riddell,[7] wrote in his diary (17 January 1915): ' L.G. said there was a scheme on foot to take the Jews back to Palestine . . . and that, much to his surprise, Herbert Samuel is very keen on it.' Samuel's outstanding abilities were universally recognised, but he was generally imagined to be lacking in emotional warmth and to combine with the intellectual efficiency of the typical product of Balliol something of its alleged *atrofia del cuore*.[8]

But Samuel's colleagues in the Government were not more surprised by his espousal of the Zionist cause than were the Zionists themselves. If his public personality did not suggest that he was likely to interest himself in Zionism, neither did his background and environment. His family had for several generations been firmly rooted in England, and he was connected by birth or marriage with many prominent members of the old-established Anglo-Jewish community. In the family circle to which he belonged Jewish loyalties and traditions were cherished, but there was little sympathy with Zionism. He himself had taken no public part in Jewish life. From the time he left Oxford in 1893 he had been actively engaged in politics. He had entered the House of Commons in 1902, had been given junior office when the Liberals returned to power some four years later, and in 1914, at the age of forty-four, had for five years had a seat in the Cabinet. He had remained in the fullest sense a member of the Anglo-Jewish community, but, immersed as he had been in politics, he had never taken an active interest in its affairs.

In the years immediately before the War, an influential group of British Jews had, as we have seen, set on foot a vigorous anti-Zionist campaign. Samuel had kept his opinions to himself. Except for Dr. Moses Gaster, who was in the secret, it would never have occurred to the Zionist leaders that a man of Samuel's type and standing was not against them. We now know that without going deeply into the question, he had given it some

[7] Later, Lord Riddell. *War Diary* (London, Nicholson & Watson, 1933), p. 52.

[8] ' He conveys no impression of enthusiasm and is as free from passion as an oyster. . . . For him one can conceive . . . no time when he cherished a sentiment or coquetted with an illusion ': A. G. Gardiner, *Prophets, Priests and Kings* (London, Alston Rivers, 1908), pp. 247-248.

thought, and, to use his own words, had, even in those days, had
'a benevolent goodwill towards the Zionist idea.'[9]

In his early enquiries into Zionism he had turned for enlightenment to Dr. Gaster.[10] There was a personal connection between
the two men, in that their wives were lifelong and intimate
friends.[11] Gaster certainly helped to bring Samuel closer to
Zionism, but this was not the beginning.[12] It seems clear that even
before he had started his talks with Gaster, something he had
heard or read about Zionism must have excited his sympathy and
fired his imagination. What it was that attracted him may be
conjectured from the way in which he put the case for Zionism
in his conversation with Grey in November 1914: 'If a Jewish
State were established in Palestine, it might become the centre
of a new culture. The Jewish brain is rather a remarkable thing,
and under national auspices the State might become a fountain
of enlightenment and a source of a great literature and art and
development of science.'[13]

At the outbreak of war these ideas must already have been
latent in his mind. So long as Palestine was in Turkish hands
the whole question had seemed to him to be of no more than
academic interest, but the moment Turkey entered the War on
the side of the Central Powers he was moved to action. In his
Lucien Wolf Memorial Lecture (1935) he explained his position
as follows: [14]

> 'With the Zionist Movement I had had no connection ; the
> prospects of any practical outcome had seemed remote ; I
> had much to do in other directions. Now, suddenly, the con-
> ditions had been entirely altered. As the first member of the
> Jewish community to sit in a British Cabinet (Disraeli had
> left the community in boyhood and never re-joined) I felt

[9] Address to the West London Zionist Association, *J.C.*, 28 November 1919.
[10] Lord Samuel to the author, 6 December 1951.
[11] Ibid.
[12] Ibid. What follows is the author's interpretation of the facts and is not based on the letter cited above.
[13] Samuel, *Memoirs*, p. 140.
[14] *Great Britain and Palestine* (London, Jewish Historical Society of England, 1935), pp. 11-12.

that in the conditions that had arisen there lay upon me a special obligation. . . . I made, therefore, a study of the aims of the Zionist Movement and of its achievements till then, and I learned all that I could about Palestine itself. . . .'

In December 1914, a few weeks after his conversation with Grey, Samuel came for the first time into personal contact with Weizmann[15] and, though he never became a member of the Zionist Organisation, he was from that time forth in constant touch with its leaders.

On further reflection, Samuel modified in certain respects the views he had expressed in his first talk with Grey. He had started with rather vague ideas about Palestine and its population. In this he was not alone ; in February 1915 he himself had to remind Grey that the Arabs were in an overwhelming majority.[16] Talks with (among others) former British Consuls in Jerusalem and the United States Consul[17] opened his eyes to the facts of the situation. A memorandum which he circulated to some of his Ministerial colleagues in January 1915[18] shows that by that time he had already recognised that, on a realistic view of the conditions prevailing in Palestine, the immediate or early establishment of a Jewish State was impracticable. 'To attempt to realise the aspiration of a Jewish State one century too soon might,' he wrote, 'throw back its `actual realisation for many centuries more.' A few weeks later, he told Lucien Wolf[19] that 'on the question of Palestine . . . he had convinced himself that something would have to be done . . . the Jews would seem to be insensible to their great traditions if they did nothing. Still, he agreed that immediate political privileges would be impossible, partly because the Jews were in a minority in Palestine . . . and partly because any attempt at a Jewish State would at this moment fail with very great scandal to the whole of Jewry.' According to Wolf's note of the conversation, '[Mr. Samuel] thought the cultural plan, with free opportunity for political development,

---

[15] 10 December 1914: see below, p. 137.

[16] Samuel, *Memoirs*, p. 144.

[17] Ibid.

[18] See below, p. 109.

[19] As to Lucien Wolf, see below, p. 173.

would suffice. It would be safe from the political point of view, and as an effort to create a great spiritual and cultural centre for Judaism in the Holy Land would probably satisfy the imagination even of Christian well-wishers.'[20]

If, however, the setting up of a Jewish State was, under existing conditions, impracticable, what was to be done with Palestine in the post-War settlement, and how were British interests to be safeguarded? Very early in the War Samuel formed the view that the only effective safeguard would be the annexation of Palestine or some other form of direct British control. In the memorandum already mentioned we find him, in January 1915, speaking of the 'annexation of the country to the British Empire,' and of 'British suzerainty in Palestine.' In February 1915 he pressed upon Grey 'the danger of any other Power than England possessing Palestine.'[21] In a revised version of his memorandum, circulated in March 1915,[22] he advocated a British protectorate. In November 1915 he suggested, in conversation with Lloyd George, that Great Britain should work for 'a mediatised' Palestine under British protection.[23] The course of events in the war with Turkey—the Turco-German threat to the Suez Canal and, at a later stage, the strong French pressure for a predominant position in Palestine—made Samuel all the more zealous an advocate of the view that on no account could Great Britain afford to let Palestine fall into the sphere of any other Great Power ; that a Franco-British condominium was unacceptable ; and that Great Britain should agree to no arrangement which did not leave her in exclusive *de facto* control.

Though on these points Samuel departed in some degree from his original conception, his main thesis remained unchanged. His talks with Lloyd George and Grey in November 1914 were the first steps in a sustained effort to interest the British Government in Zionism and to convince it, as he was profoundly convinced himself, that Zionist aspirations were not only worthy of respect on their merits, but ought on grounds of policy to command

[20] 28 February 1915: *C.F.C.* 1915, 26ff. A note by Wolf states: 'The above report has been seen by Mr. Samuel and approved by him.'

[21] Samuel, *Memoirs*, p. 144.

[22] See below, p. 109.

[23] *C. P. Scott's Jnls.*, 26 November 1915.

British support. By filling the dangerous vacuum which would be left in Palestine by the collapse of Turkey, the Zionists could to this extent, he believed, help Great Britain to consolidate her position in an area of high strategic importance.

During 1915 Samuel developed his argument in further talks with Lloyd George[24] and Grey,[25] and, more formally, in the memorandum already mentioned. There were two versions of this document. Copies of the memorandum in its original form were sent by Samuel to Asquith and some others of his colleagues towards the end of January 1915.[26] A revised text was circulated to the Cabinet in the middle of March, at a time when the whole Eastern Question was being forced into the foreground by the Russian demand for Constantinople and the Straits.[27]

The January version opens with the Zionist question and is mainly concerned with the arguments, including the strategic argument, in favour of combining a British annexation of Palestine with British support for Zionist aspirations. Only towards the end does the memorandum discuss alternative solutions of the Palestine problem and the objections to each of them. In the March version the order is reversed. The memorandum now starts by asking what should be the policy of the British Government in considering the future of Palestine. Annexation by France would be highly undesirable ; ' the establishment of a great European Power so close to the Suez Canal would be a continual and a formidable menace to the essential lines of communication of the British Empire.' To leave Palestine to the Turks would be unthinkable. Internationalisation would not work and might prove to be a stepping-stone to a German protectorate. The establishment of an autonomous Jewish State had been suggested, but ' it is certain that the time is not ripe for it.' The conclusion reached is that the only satisfactory arrangement would be a

---

[24] Samuel to Weizmann, 11 January 1915: ' Mr. Lloyd George, whom I have seen today, would be very glad if you would breakfast with him next Friday . . .'; *Ch.W.P.*, ' In January and February 1915 . . . there were . . . two more conversations with Lloyd George, at one of which Dr. Weizmann was present': Samuel, *Memoirs*, p. 144.

[25] 5 February 1915: ibid., p. 143.

[26] Ibid., p. 142.

[27] The full text of the final (March) version is printed by Mr. John Bowle in his *Viscount Samuel* (London, Gollancz, 1957).

British protectorate (the word 'annexation' is dropped), since Great Britain cannot safely accept a common frontier with a European neighbour at El Arish. It is at this point that, nothing having so far been said about Zionism except that the establishment of a Jewish State is impracticable, the memorandum goes on to express the hope that

> 'under British rule facilities would be given to Jewish organisations to purchase land, to found colonies, to establish educational and religious institutions, and to co-operate in the economic development of the country, and that Jewish immigration, carefully regulated, would be given preference, so that in course of time the Jewish inhabitants, grown into a majority and settled in the land, may be conceded such degree of self-government as the conditions of that day might justify.'

Then follows an elaboration of the case for British sponsorship of Zionism on much the same lines as in the earlier version, but omitting what Lord Samuel himself has described as 'a somewhat rhetorical peroration'.[28]

Though there is some difference between the two documents in the distribution of emphasis, the conclusions reached are substantially identical. In starting, in the later version, with a carefully worked-out argument in favour of a British protectorate, Samuel may, perhaps, have been influenced by a talk he had had with Grey on 5 February 1915.[29] While again expressing sympathy with Zionist aspirations, Grey had suggested that the French might have views of their own as to the future of Palestine and had made it clear that in any case he would be indisposed to saddle Great Britain with the fresh responsibilities which would be involved in a British protectorate. What he was inclined to favour was the neutralisation of Palestine under an international guarantee, coupling this with the rather surprising suggestion that the government of the country should be vested in 'some kind of Council to be established by the Jews.' Samuel having remarked that it was doubtful 'whether the Arab population, who number five-sixths of the inhabitants, would accept such a

[28] Samuel, *Memoirs,* p. 142.
[29] Ibid., p. 143.

government,' Grey had proposed as a possible alternative some arrangement by which Palestine, while remaining under Turkish suzerainty, should have a Governor appointed by the Powers. To this also Samuel had demurred on the ground that an international régime would be dangerous to Great Britain, since it might well end in some other Power becoming predominant in Palestine.

It is impossible to say with certainty whether the Samuel memorandum was formally considered by the Cabinet. In Asquith's diary there is an entry, dated 13 March 1915,[30] in which he speaks rather disrespectfully of Samuel's ' dithyrambic memorandum,' adding that ' the only other partisan of this proposal is Lloyd George, who I need not say does not care a damn for the Jews or their past or their future, but thinks it will be an outrage to let the Holy Places pass into the possession or under the protectorate of " agnostic, atheistic France." ' The March version of Samuel's memorandum had been circulated a few days earlier, and Asquith may well have been referring to some discussion which had taken place in the Cabinet. The words in quotation-marks—" agnostic, atheistic France "—suggest that he may be alluding to something actually said by Lloyd George.

However that may be, Samuel's memorandum does not seem to have made any marked impression on his colleagues. He points out in his Memoirs that Lloyd George was not, in fact, his only ' partisan.' On receiving a copy of the January version of the memorandum, Haldane had written to him expressing a friendly interest in his proposals.[31] It is a little surprising that he does not mention the Marquess of Crewe,[32] for Crewe had expressed privately some sympathy with Zionism,[33] and an entry in Lord Bertie's diary shows that in January 1915 he was already claimed

[30] Earl of Oxford and Asquith, *Memories and Reflections* (London, Cassell, 1928), II, 65.
[31] Samuel, *Memoirs*, p. 143. In his letter of 20 November 1912 to the Zionist Executive Weizmann mentioned Haldane as one of the important persons to whom he thought he could get access: see above, p. 42.
[32] Secretary of State for India.
[33] In his January 1915 Report Weizmann said that he had had a letter from Mrs. James de Rothschild ' in which she informed me of a very favourable opinion expressed by Lord Crewe.' (The letter, dated 19 November 1914, is in *Ch.W.P.*)

by the Zionists as a supporter.[34] From Samuel's silence it may be inferred that Crewe did not express in the Cabinet any decided views on the memorandum. Since Samuel himself mentions no allies other than Lloyd George and Haldane, it is clear that his colleagues did not give him much encouragement.

From the Prime Minister he received none at all. Asquith's view can be inferred from the passage already quoted from his diary.[35] An earlier comment, dated 28 January 1915, is equally bleak. Speaking of the January version of Samuel's memorandum, a copy of which had just reached him, Asquith wrote:

> '. . . I confess I am not attracted by the proposed addition to our responsibilities, but it is a curious illustration of Dizzy's favourite maxim that "race is everything" to find this almost lyrical outburst proceeding from the well-ordered and methodical brain of H.S.'[36]

From first to last Asquith found it impossible to take Zionism seriously. When he visited Palestine in the winter of 1924, he was quite unimpressed. 'The talk of making Palestine a "Jewish National Home" seems to me', he wrote, 'as fantastic as it has always done.'[37] If he was not disposed to excite himself about the Jewish Question, it was, perhaps, because he hardly recognised its existence. He was the last man to harbour prejudices against Jews; in his matter-of-fact way, he took men as he found

---

[34] Lord Bertie (then Sir Francis Bertie), British Ambassador in Paris, wrote in his diary (25 January 1915): 'Edmond de Rothschild sent a co-religionist established in Manchester to "talk" about what *I* think an absurd scheme, though they say it has the approval of Grey, Lloyd George, Samuel and Crewe': *The Diary of Lord Bertie of Thame*, ed. Lady Algernon Gordon Lennox (London, Hodder and Stoughton, 1924), I, 105. In a message to the London Opera House meeting, on 2 December 1917, to celebrate the Balfour Declaration, Crewe wrote: 'I have long hoped that it would be possible to make such a Declaration': *Sokolow*, II, 114. On 12 July 1920 he was one of the principal speakers at a Zionist Demonstration in London: the speeches are reported in *Great Britain and Zionism* (London, Zionist Organisation, 1920). As to Lady Crewe (whose mother, the Countess of Rosebery, was the daughter of Baron Mayer de Rothschild), see below, p. 184.

[35] Above, p. 111.

[36] *Memories and Reflections*, II, 59.

[37] Spender and Asquith, *Life of Lord Oxford and Asquith* (London, Hutchinson, 1932), II, 352-353 (26 November 1924).

them. Samuel was the first professing Jew to enter a British
Cabinet, and it was Asquith who selected him. His 'dithyrambic
memorandum' did him no harm in Asquith's eyes. He temporarily
lost his seat in the Cabinet because of the re-shuffling of offices
when some leading Conservatives joined the Government in May
1915, but Asquith brought him back to Cabinet office a few
months later. One of Asquith's closest political and personal
friends among the younger Liberals was another Jew—Samuel's
cousin, Edwin Montagu,[38] whose views on Zionism (Montagu was
vehemently opposed to it) may conceivably have helped to colour
his own. Weizmann never met Asquith, but, if he had, it is
unlikely that it would have made much difference. Cautious and
level-headed, warily feeling his way by the light of common-sense,
Asquith was not the man to be moved by the considerations
which made Zionism interesting and attractive to more adventurous minds and more romantic temperaments. He could see in
Zionist aspirations nothing but a rather fantastic dream, and in
proposals for British control of Palestine merely an invitation
to Great Britain to accept an unnecessary and unwanted addition
to her Imperial responsibilities.[39] Samuel, though he talked to
others of his colleagues about Zionism, nowhere records any conversation on the subject with the Prime Minister. Perhaps he
knew that it would be useless.

Grey's attitude was different. Zionism did not interest Asquith.
It did interest Grey. When he told Samuel, in November 1914,[40]
that the Zionist idea had always had a strong sentimental attraction for him, this was not a mere form of words. In his speech

---

[38] See below, pp. 496ff. As to Asquith's friendship with Montagu, see
Spender and Asquith, op. cit., I, 202, II, 13, 254.

[39] Asquith was Prime Minister when, presumably, with his approval,
Grey, in March 1916, proposed to the French and Russian Governments that the three Entente Powers should join in a pro-Zionist
declaration concerning the future of Palestine: below, pp. 219ff. The
explanation may be that Asquith regarded this purely as a propagandist
move and that there was no implication of any special *British* responsibility. Colonel Meinertzhagen describes in his diary (7 February
1918) a private luncheon-party shortly after the Balfour Declaration
at which the guests included Lord Rothschild, Balfour and Asquith.
The Declaration was the main topic of conversation, but 'Asquith
kept out of it': Meinertzhagen, *Middle East Diary* (London, Cresset
Press, 1960), pp. 8-9.

[40] Samuel, *Memoirs*, p. 141—see above, p. 104.

in Parliament on the East African project in 1904 he had shown his sympathetic concern about the position of the Jews. In his talk with Samuel in February 1915 he spoke with obvious sincerity of his desire to do something for the Zionists and of his readiness to support any scheme which would help them to realise their aims without making Great Britain responsible for the administration of Palestine. When the Balfour Declaration was published, he expressed his warm approval,[41] from which it may be inferred that, had he then been in office, he would have supported the Declaration in the Cabinet. The reservations that he made in his talks with Samuel can easily be understood in the light of the situation at the time. As shown by their vehement opposition, early in 1915, to proposals for a British landing at Alexandretta,[42] the French were in a touchy frame of mind and highly suspicious of British intentions in Syria. No Palestine campaign was in prospect, and it could not be foreseen that the War would end with Palestine in British military occupation. Lastly, it had to be borne in mind, as was recognised by Lloyd George,[43] that there was a considerable body of British opinion, and especially Liberal opinion, which was strongly averse to anything savouring of an extension of British responsibilities.

Though the Prime Minister was against him and the Foreign Secretary's undoubted sympathy was tinged with caution, Samuel remained unshaken in his views and continued to urge them in

[41] 'I am entirely in sympathy with the declaration made by Mr. Balfour, and am very glad that this has been announced publicly as the view of the British Government': *Zionist Review*, December 1917, p. 133. After the War, however, Grey felt doubts about the Declaration and expressed them in a speech in the House of Lords on 27 March 1923. '. . . A Zionist home undoubtedly means or implies a Zionist Government over the district in which the home is planned, and if 93 per cent. of the population of Palestine are Arabs, I do not see how you can establish other than an Arab Government, without prejudice to their civil rights': O.R., col. 655. (One of the main topics in the debate was the question of the consistency of the Declaration with the promises to the Arabs in the McMahon correspondence, as to which see below, p. 267.)

[42] See, for example, Poincaré, VI, 33, VII, 254.

[43] Samuel having suggested, in conversation with Lloyd George, 'a mediatised Palestine under British protection,' 'George remarked that France . . . wanted Palestine for herself . . . that, moreover, there would be an objection in this country to such an extension of our responsibilities': *C.P.S. Jnls.*, 26 November 1915.

every likely quarter. He pressed them particularly on Lloyd George, to whom he talked Zionism in April 1915[44] and again in November.[45] By this time he had returned to the Cabinet and was once more at the centre of affairs. The negotiations which were to lead up to the Sykes-Picot Agreement were now under way and soon afterwards reached a point at which it became necessary for the British Government to give serious thought to the future of Palestine. In March 1916 Samuel sent copies of his memorandum to those members of the Cabinet who had not seen it when it was originally circulated. He had already shown it to Sir Mark Sykes.[46] Sykes had till then known little about Zionism and disliked what he knew, but he was impressed by Samuel's proposals and responded immediately to the ideas underlying them, with results which, as we shall see, became apparent when the Zionist question entered the sphere of practical politics in 1917.

In the Sykes-Picot Agreement of May 1916 the Zionists were ignored. The British Government and its advisers, notably Mark Sykes, were alive to the strategic importance of Palestine both from a military and a naval point of view and had done their best to keep it out of exclusive French control, but so far as Zionism was concerned, the Government was still uncommitted. Samuel refused to be discouraged, and in November 1916 he seems to have been preparing the ground for a fresh approach to Grey.[47] Before anything could come of this, both he and Grey had followed Asquith out of office, and the issue was left to be finally decided by a Cabinet of which he was not a member. He could, had he wished, have had an important place in the Lloyd George Administration,[48] but, though on the Zionist question Lloyd George had been, of all his former colleagues, the closest to his views, there were other and weightier considerations which made him unwilling to serve under the new Prime Minister.

[44] Weizmann to Sokolow and Tschlenow, 15 April 1915 (*Ch.W.P.*): 'I saw Scott today, and he told me he lunched with Samuel and Lloyd George the day before yesterday and they talked Zionism. Samuel talked very warmly and called Zionism "a splendid ideal" . . .' (trans. from the Russian).

[45] See note 41 above.

[46] See below, p. 233.

[47] See below, p. 298.

[48] Samuel, *Memoirs*, p. 123.

Out of office he continued to exert his still considerable influence in the same direction as before. He brought his proposals to the notice of Lord Milner and was almost certainly the first to awaken the active interest of one of the most influential members of Lloyd George's War Cabinet.[49] Though not himself a member of the Zionist Organisation, he was present, and played a leading part, at the important conference at which, in February 1917, Mark Sykes for the first time exchanged views with a group of representative Zionists.[50] In the following October, when the fate of the Balfour Declaration was in the balance, he was consulted by the War Cabinet[51] and in his reply set out with all the weight of his authority the case for the policy which, in and out of office, he had consistently advocated for nearly three years.

When Turkey entered the War, Samuel had seen at once that the Zionists might now have a chance of achieving their purpose and had satisfied himself that it would be to Great Britain's advantage to encourage them. So had Weizmann, but the two had never met, and neither knew what the other was doing or had in mind. We shall see later how, as a sequel to a chance encounter with C. P. Scott of the *Manchester Guardian*, Weizmann was put in touch with Samuel and, meeting him for the first time early in December 1914, made the astonishing discovery that he was fully committed to the Zionist cause. A letter from Weizmann, dated 21 March 1915, shows how much the Zionists had already come to rely on Samuel. After telling him of some recent developments, Weizmann continues: ' I know you must be very busy now, but I hope you won't mind my informing you of the state of our affairs. Perhaps it is not the worst thing which may follow from this war. You were good enough to guide us up to now, and I am sure you will continue to help us. We look to you and to your historical rôle which you are playing and will play in the redemption of Israel.'[52]

---

49 See below, p. 315.
50 See below, p. 370.
51 See below, p. 527.
52 Orig. in *H.S.P.*; copy in *Ch.W.P.*

CHAPTER 6

WEIZMANN

In 1914 Chaim Weizmann, then a man of forty,[1] had lived in England for ten years. He had left his native Russia in 1893 to complete his education in the more hospitable atmosphere of the West and had spent most of the next eleven years in Germany and Switzerland, first as a student and then as a teacher of chemistry.[2] He had settled in England in 1904, had become a naturalised British subject and, after holding some less important appointments, had in 1913 become Reader in Bio-Chemistry at the University of Manchester. He had hoped for a Professorship, but when a vacancy arose shortly before the War, he had been passed over. Hurt by what he felt to be an injustice, he had been half-inclined to accept a pressing invitation to join the Zionist Central Office in Berlin. It was not without some hesitation that he had in the end rejected the proposal and remained in Manchester.[3]

When Weizmann came to England in 1904, he had already begun to interest himself in applied chemistry and had several discoveries of some importance to his credit. During his years in Manchester he made further progress in this field, applying himself particularly to the study of fermentation. By 1914 he had published a considerable number of scientific papers and had acquired an established reputation in certain branches of industrial chemistry.[4]

When war came, Weizmann's scientific attainments enabled him to render valuable services to the British Government. His impressive performance in solving some difficult and urgent

[1] Born at Motol, White Russia, 1874.
[2] At Darmstadt, Berlin, Freiburg and Geneva.
[3] *Trial and Error*, p. 173.
[4] For a popular description of Weizmann's chemical work up to 1914 see article by S. S. Israelstam in *The Jewish Observer*, 14 November 1952. His first application (jointly with others) for an English patent was accepted in December 1905: Patent Office Library to the author, 27 February 1953.

problems relating to the production of explosives enhanced his personal standing and made him well known to important Ministers and their entourage. The Admiralty began to interest itself in one of his fermentation processes in April 1915.[5] A few weeks later, his expert knowledge in this field was brought to the notice of Lloyd George, then struggling to organise the newly formed Ministry of Munitions, by C. P. Scott,[6] in whom by this time he already had a staunch friend and admirer. In September 1915 he entered the service of the Ministry as Chemical Adviser on acetone supplies, accepting at the same time a similar post under the Admiralty,[7] which was engaging on its own account in experiments in the production of acetone.

One result of these appointments was that from the spring of 1915 until somewhere near the end of 1916 Weizmann was absorbed in his scientific work, and his Zionist interests, though he still contrived somehow to find time for them, had to be fitted in with his prior obligations to the Government. From a Zionist point of view, his enlistment in the Government service had one important advantage ; it brought about his removal, towards the end of 1915, from Manchester to the centre of affairs in London. But his official duties weighed heavily upon him. They not only used up his energies but frayed his nerves. Because of the urgency of his work and its confidential nature, his freedom of movement was restricted.[8] While his processes were on trial, he was in a state of constant anxiety. He was disturbed by what he considered to be the mishandling of some of the experiments[9] and complained, apparently not without cause, of obstruction by a certain high

5 Weizmann to Sir F. Nathan, 27 February 1916. (Nathan was head of the propulsive explosives branch of the Ministry of Munitions.)

6 Scott to Lloyd George, 6 June 1915 ; *C.P.S. Jnls.*, 16 June 1915 ; Lloyd George, *War Memoirs* (London, Nicholson and Watson, 1933-1936), II, 584.

7 See note 5.

8 *C.P.S. Jnls.*, 26 November and 11-15 December 1915. As late as 8 April 1917 Weizmann wrote to Brandeis: ' I was asked yesterday to go to Egypt so as to be on the spot when a possibility arises to proceed further into Palestine. . . . As you are aware, I am in the service of the Admiralty, and unless I can satisfy my chiefs that the work here will not suffer in my absence, I could not even think of applying for leave. . . .': *Ch.W.P.*

9 Weizmann to Scott, 1 December 1915: *Ch.W.P.*

official of the the Ministry of Munitions.[10] On 1 December 1915 he wrote to Scott: '[11] . . . My position is becoming untenable . . . I may find myself *vis-à-vis de rien*.' Three months later he unburdened himself in a letter to Sir Frederick Nathan, pointing out that his status was unsatisfactory and had still to be regularised. 'Somehow,' he wrote, 'I remain a temporary and anonymous worker.'[12]

With the help of Scott, who on at least four occasions intervened on his behalf,[13] Weizmann was able to bring his difficulties and frustrations to the personal notice of Lloyd George. His complaints received serious attention, and by the time Lloyd George left the Ministry of Munitions for the War Office in July 1916 they had been in large measure redressed. Weizmann was now in smoother waters, but it was not until later in the year that, the experimental period having ended successfully and production begun, his official duties began to press on him rather less heavily. He was still in Government service and not entirely his own master. Even in 1917 there were times when problems connected with his chemical work caused him acute anxiety,[14] but, fortunately for the Zionist cause, it so happened that the extreme pressure relaxed about the time when the change of Government at the end of 1916 opened the final phase of the events leading up to the Balfour Declaration.

A misreading of some loose language used by Lloyd George, in his picturesque way, in his *War Memoirs*[15] is the source of the

---

[10] C.P.S. *Jnls.*, 26 November and 11-15 December 1915; 24-29 January 1916. The obstruction appears to have been due partly to mistrust of Weizmann as a 'foreigner,' but Scott seems to have thought that there might also be an element of jealousy.

[11] Copy in *Ch.W.P.*

[12] 27 February 1916.

[13] C.P.S. *Jnls.*, 14 October, 26 November, 15 December, 1915; 27 February-3 March 1916.

[14] Scott to Weizmann, 9 March, 12 September, 24 September, 1917: *Ch.W.P.*

[15] II, 584. Lloyd George writes: 'When our difficulties [about acetone] were solved through Dr. Weizmann's genius, I said to him: "You have rendered great service to the State, and I should like to ask the Prime Minister to recommend you to His Majesty for some honour."' Lloyd George goes on to say that Weizmann replied that he wanted nothing for himself but that he would like something to be done for his people. 'He then explained his aspirations as to the repatriation of the Jews to the sacred land they had made famous. That was the fount and origin

myth that the Balfour Declaration was Weizmann's reward for his personal services in the War. It is, on the face of it, nonsensical to imagine that the Declaration was handed to him as a kind of good conduct prize. We shall see later how closely the case for the Declaration was considered before being finally approved by the War Cabinet as a deliberate act of policy. It does not, however, follow that Weizmann's war-time services to the State were wholly irrelevant to the history of the Declaration. His war work brought him into close personal contact with Lloyd George and, because of the confidence and respect he inspired, placed him in a strong position for talking Zionism to a Minister who was before long to become the head of the Government. This is what Lloyd George seems really to have meant when, speaking at a Jewish meeting in 1925, he declared that 'acetone converted me to Zionism.'[16] After the change of Government at the end of 1916, the fact that Weizmann was already well and favourably known to the Prime Minister gave him readier access than he might otherwise have had to the real seat of power. His war work has a bearing on the origins of the Declaration to the extent, though only to the extent, that, by raising his stature and adding to his prestige, it made him so much the more effective an advocate of the Zionist cause.[17]

[16] Afterword to *Napoleon and Palestine*: see note 15.
[17] At the Weizmann Forest Dinner in London (1949), Field-Marshal Smuts said: ' [Weizmann's] outstanding war service as a scientist had made him known and famous in high Allied circles, and his voice carried so much the greater weight in pleading for the Jewish National Home': *J.C.*, 25 November 1949.

of the famous declaration about the national home for Jews in Palestine.' Lloyd George had previously referred to this incident in his Afterword to Philip Guedalla's *Napoleon and Palestine* (London, Allen & Unwin, 1925), p. 50, and in a speech reported in the *North Wales Chronicle* of 27 August 1927. He told Tom Jones, in 1936, that this was the origin of the Balfour Declaration: Thomas Jones, *A Diary With Letters* (O.U.P., 1945), diary entry 14 June 1936 ; see also Lloyd George's *The Truth About the Peace Treaties* (1938), II, 117, and his Foreword to *Chaim Weizmann*, ed. P. Goodman (London, 1945).

Mrs. Weizmann has informed the author, from her personal recollection, that Lloyd George's account of his offer to Weizmann and Weizmann's reply is correct. In describing this as the 'fount and origin' of the Declaration he is obviously not to be taken as making a serious contribution to history ; this is simply his rhetorical way of saying that he was impressed and moved by the incident.

Weizmann had from his early youth been an active Zionist and by 1914 had risen to a prominent, though not a commanding, place in the Zionist Movement. At the Zionist Congress of 1913 he had occupied the important position of Chairman of the Standing Committee and as *rapporteur* on the proposed Jewish University had added to the reputation he had already won as the foremost advocate of that project. He was one of the two English Zionists (the other was Leopold Kessler) with seats on the Zionist General Council and one of the two Vice-Presidents of the English Zionist Federation. He did not, however, belong to the inner circle consisting of the members of the Zionist Executive. The offices he held gave him a recognised standing in the Movement but no authority to speak even for its English branch—still less for the Organisation as a whole.

Nor had he at this time any large popular following; indeed, it was not in his nature to court popularity. Jealously guarding his own inner integrity, he despised the arts of the demagogue. Even at the height of his fame, when his ascendancy was established and unchallengeable, he remained somewhat aloof. He declined to seek cheap applause by feeding the masses on illusions, and in his relations with his colleagues and associates he did not exert himself to flatter their self-esteem. His contempt for the shoddy, the spurious, the second-rate was at times reflected in a certain hauteur which could be mistaken for arrogance. He could rise to the majesty of a prophet, but he had none of the meekness of a saint. If he was not interested, he showed it. If he had personal dislikes, he made no great effort to conceal them. He was apt to be impatient or even resentful of criticism or dissent and preferred —rightly, as a rule—to rely on his own judgment or intuition. In his management of a difficult team he could not afford too tender a regard for the feelings or *amour propre* of collaborators who had ceased to be useful or to fit in with his plans. For anyone who commanded his confidence and esteem there was no man with or under whom it was easier or more exhilarating to work, but he did not suffer fools gladly, and he had a mordant wit which could wound.

An American Zionist who became one of his most devoted disciples has provided a vivid picture of Weizmann as he

appeared to an eye-witness at the last pre-War Zionist
Congress: [18]

> 'When I first met Weizmann at the Vienna Congress in 1913,
> he seemed indifferent to its proceedings. . . . He was pointed
> to as the promising young man who had crossed swords in
> debates with Theodor Herzl in the early Congresses. . . .
> He was not yet a westerner and was losing his credentials as
> a Russian Zionist. He hovered between the two worlds, his
> destinies not yet determined. I remember that as the Chair-
> man of the Standing Committee . . . he was meticulous, but
> often frivolous. . . . He was counted as a member of the
> Russian delegation, but was not excited by their disputes.
> At their caucuses Weizmann stood in the rear of the hall,
> his eyes half-closed, seemingly bored. . . . The last scene
> I remember was the languid appearance of Dr. Weizmann
> in the plenum reporting the nominations for his Committee.'

This may be taken to represent with a fair degree of accuracy
the average Zionist's impression of Weizmann on the eve of the
War. He was an important but not a dominating figure. He had a
status in the Movement which ensured respect for his views, but
he was just one prominent personality among others.[19] Outside a
limited circle of intimate friends and admirers the Zionist world
had no conception of his real quality and stature. Thus, when war
broke out, he had no such pre-eminence as to make it seem
natural to turn to him for leadership in the emergency. In some
quarters there was a demand for Max Nordau.[20] In England, some
of the leading Zionists—notably Cowen, the President of the
English Zionist Federation, and Leopold Greenberg—thought of
Israel Zangwill.[21] They had not forgotten that in 1905 he had

[18] Louis Lipsky in *The American Zionist* (New York), 15 December 1952.
[19] When the nominations for the General Council were read out at the
1913 Congress, the loudest applause was reserved for the former President of the Organisation, David Wolffsohn; next came the Russian
leader, Ussishkin; after these a mildly applauded group of five, of
whom Weizmann was one: *Protocol*, pp. 358-359.
[20] An appeal to Nordau was resolved upon by the General Council at a
meeting in Copenhagen in June 1915, but nothing came of this: see
Protocol of meeting 10-11 June 1915 in Z.A.
[21] In deference to their views, Weizmann made the gesture of approaching
Zangwill and appears to have met him in October 1914 and again in

broken away from the Organisation on the East African issue, but, because he had a name and was in the public eye, they were desperately anxious to bring him back. One of the main reasons for Sokolow's journey to London at the end of 1914 was, as we have seen, that there appeared to his colleagues in Berlin to be no one in England capable of carrying on political work in that country. As for the English Zionists, how far they were from perceiving in Weizmann a successor to Herzl can be inferred from an editorial in *The Jewish Chronicle* of 2 July 1915: 'Today, in this gathering of favourable omens, we miss the inspiring leadership of a Herzl—of a man who can seize with imagination and vigour the Jewish interests at stake and present them to the world when the welter of the conflict has subsided.'

It was not in response to any popular demand or to any prompting by his colleagues, but because of his own belief in himself and his mission, that almost immediately after the outbreak of war Weizmann took command of such forces as he could muster and started on the road which was to lead in the end to the Balfour Declaration. He travelled as light as he could, not wanting to be encumbered by uncongenial company. He was not on cordial terms with other leading Zionists in England. Greenberg had never forgiven him for his opposition to Herzl nor forgotten that he was, after all, an Ostjude.[22] Gaster's view of

22 In 'A Letter to Dr. Weizmann,' 'Mentor' (Greenberg's pseudonym) writes (*J.C.*, 25 May 1917): 'A Russian by birth and a chemist by profession, you arrived in this country with not more, perhaps less, than the average material wealth possessed by thousands of your compatriots who . . . have come to these shores. But you possessed not less, certainly more, than the average of intellectuality. . . . Your self-confidence, based upon what you have in yourself managed to overcome, tends to minimise difficulties for you and to exaggerate points of encouragement. That is a real danger in a man like you. . . .'

November: see 1914 correspondence between Weizmann and Zangwill in *Ch.W.P.* and Weizmann's January 1915 report to the Zionist Executive. It seems clear that Weizmann had little real belief in Zangwill's usefulness and no liking for these pourparlers, which in the end led nowhere—see Weizmann to Harry Sacher and Leon Simon, 3 December 1914 (Z.A.): 'I had to be amenable to concessions, as my intention was to build a golden bridge for him and also to satisfy all our "Zangwillians," who may do mischief. So far I succeeded in keeping them quiet and it was morally very obnoxious to me to enter into negotiations at all with the I.T.O. [Zangwill's ' Jewish Territorial Organisation '], but it is a military necessity and I ask to be forgiven. . . .'

Weizmann is unmistakably reflected in his unpublished diaries, and Weizmann's view of Gaster is known to readers of his autobiography.[23] He had no personal quarrel with Joseph Cowen but held no high opinion of his abilities or judgment.[24] After the first few weeks of the War, Weizmann was not in the habit of taking any of these men into his confidence, nor did he normally use the machinery of the English Zionist Federation.[25] In the report which he submitted to Sokolow and Tschlenow shortly after their arrival in England at the end of 1914,[26] he singles out as his closest associates Ahad Ha'am,[27] 'who at all times gave us the advantage of his valuable advice and his full moral support,' and two of his own younger disciples, Leon Simon[28] and Harry Sacher.[29] Among other members of his inner circle were Simon Marks[30] and Israel Sieff,[31] and, on the fringe of it, Albert Hyamson [32] and Samuel Landman.[33] He and the little group he gathered round him were, in his own words, 'a small band of workers, not official, not recognised, out of contact with Jewry at large.'[34] When echoes of his activities penetrated to Zionist circles outside England, they were criticised in some

[23] *Trial and Error*, pp. 117, 229, 230.
[24] Weizmann to Sacher and Simon, 15 December 1914: *Ch.W.P.*; to Mrs. Weizmann, 24 December 1914: *V.W.P.*
[25] Weizmann did, however, take part in the setting up, under the auspices of the E.Z.F., of a Political Committee, which functioned from January 1916 to January 1917: P. Goodman, *Zionism in England*, pp. 38-40; Goodman's *Jewish National Home*, pp. 16-17. This Committee played a certain rôle as a consultative body, but Weizmann's real coadjutors were (apart from Sokolow) his own inner circle.
[26] See above, p. 104, note 6.
[27] See above, p. 90, note 102.
[28] B. 1881. Later, Sir Leon Simon, C.B. A member of the Civil Service, in which he later rose to high rank; a distinguished Hebraist and translator of Ahad Ha'am.
[29] B. 1881. On editorial staff of the *Manchester Guardian* 1905-1909 and 1915-1919, and of the *Daily News* 1909-1915.
[30] B. 1888. Later, Sir Simon Marks.
[31] B. 1889. Associated with Simon Marks in the business which later became Marks & Spencer, Ltd.
[32] 1875-1954. Civil servant and Anglo-Jewish historian. Director of Jewish Section, Ministry of Information, 1917-1918—see below, p. 568.
[33] B. 1884. Later, Secretary of the World Zionist Organisation.
[34] Address delivered at London Zionist Conference, 21 September 1919 (text in *Zionist Policy*, British Zionist Federation, 1919).

quarters as a breach of discipline, since he had no authority to speak for the Organisation; as a breach of the principle of neutrality; as a danger to the Jews in Palestine, since the Yishuv was at the mercy of the Turks, with whom England was at war.[35] One advantage of Sokolow's arrival in London at the end of 1914 was that it provided Weizmann with a colleague who, unlike himself, had the status and authority of a member of the Zionist Executive.

It has been said by Sir Charles Webster[36] that in diplomatic transactions success is most often obtained by 'the method, always preferable, if it is possible, of a direct and candid approach to the objective because of the conviction that it is such that, in the long run, the interests of all concerned are best served by it.' 'One of the best examples,' Sir Charles continues, 'of such successful diplomacy is that by which Dr. Weizmann brought into existence the Jewish National Home.' In the two thousand interviews by which, as he has told us,[37] he paved the way to the Balfour Declaration, the bio-chemist from Manchester showed diplomatic address of the highest order. He was much more than a skilful negotiator. Before the discussion could be got on its feet, the British statesmen and public servants with whom he had to deal had first to be satisfied that there was something to discuss; they had to be convinced that Zionism was to be taken seriously— that the Zionists, weak and scattered though they were, possessed, nevertheless, certain intangible assets—that the Zionist Movement was not merely interesting but important. Weizmann told Ahad Ha'am that, when he saw Balfour in December 1914, Balfour had mentioned a talk he had had with a distinguished British Jew who had appealed for his intervention on behalf of the Jews in Rumania. 'What a profound difference,' Balfour had remarked,

---

[35] See Weizmann to J. L. Magnes, 9 January 1915: Z.A.; Julius Simon to V. Jacobson, 4 April 1916: Z.A.; Jacobson to S. Pewsner, 25 October 1916. Z.A. At a meeting of the Berlin Zionist Executive, 29-31 July, 1917, it was reported that the Zionist Committee at The Hague considered that 'the whole work of Weizmann and his friends was in too one-sided an English direction.': Z.A.

[36] *The Listener*, 28 February 1952.

[37] In his speech of 21 September 1919—see above, p. 124, note 34.

' there is between you and him! For you do not beg for anything—
you demand; and people must listen to you because you are a
statesman speaking for [literally, " a statesman of "] a powerful
moral Government.'[38]

Weizmann was not only a dexterous and resourceful advocate—
flexible, sure-footed, highly sensitive to atmosphere, and with an
unerring instinct for timing; he possessed in a high degree the
power to kindle the imagination and to impart to others some of
his own mystical faith in the destiny of his people and the significance of its survival. Among the principal architects of the
Declaration two at least—Balfour and Mark Sykes—were highly
sensitive to the Jewish mystique. The Declaration itself pre-
supposed that the Jewish people counted for something in the
world and that the ideas bound up with the connection between
the Jews and Palestine had not lost their potency. But the war
years were not a time for sentimental gestures. The British
Government's business was to win the War and to safeguard
British interests in the post-war settlement. Fully realising that
these must in the end be the decisive tests, Weizmann was never
under the illusion that the Zionists could rely on an appeal
ad misericordiam. Zionist aspirations must be shown to accord
with British strategic and political interests. This was not merely
part of an advocate's brief; that Great Britain needed Palestine,
and needed the Jews if the best use was to be made of it, was for
Weizmann as axiomatic as that that, from a Zionist standpoint,
British sponsorship of a home for the Jews in Palestine was
beyond all comparison more to be desired than that of any other
Power.[39]

Even before Turkey had entered the War Weizmann had
already started thinking on these lines. Writing to Zangwill on
10 October 1914, he said:

' My plans are based naturally on one cardinal assumption—
viz. that the Allies will win and, as I sincerely wish and
hope, win well. . . . I have no doubt in my mind that Palestine

[38] Weizmann to Ahad Ha'am, 14 December 1914, describing an interview
with Balfour on December 12. Original in possession of Ahad Ha'am's
executors: see further, as to this letter, below, p. 153. For the translation
from the original Russian the author is indebted to Mr. J. M. Japp.

[39] For his reasons, see below, pp. 375, 392.

will fall within the sphere of England. Palestine is a natural continuation of Egypt and the barrier separating the Suez Canal from . . . the Black Sea and any hostility which may come from that side . . . it will be the Asiatic Belgium,[40] especially if it is developed by the Jews. We—given more or less good conditions—could easily move a million Jews into Palestine within the next fifty to sixty years, and England would have an effective barrier and we would have a country. . . .'[41]

This was before Weizmann's first meeting, on 10 December 1914, with Herbert Samuel, whose views turned out, to his amazement, to be closely parallel to his own. If there was any difference, it was that, according to Weizmann's contemporary record[42] of the interview, Samuel's plans were rather more ambitious:

' He believed that my demands were too modest, that big things would have to be done in Palestine.[43] Mr. Samuel preferred not to enter in[to] discussions of his plans as he would like to keep them liquid, but he suggested that the Jews would have to build railways, harbours, a University, a network of schools, etc. . . .'

Weizmann had already heard somewhat similar comments on his proposals at an interview with James de Rothschild on 25 November 1914:

' He [de Rothschild] thought that the demands, which only amount to asking for an encouragement of colonisation of Jews in Palestine, are too modest and would not appeal sufficiently to statesmen. One should ask for something which is more than that and which tends towards the formation of a Jewish State.'[44]

Weizmann was thus encouraged to go forward with a rather

---

40 ' The Asiatic Belgium '—an echo, perhaps unconscious, of a passage in *Daniel Deronda*, Chapter XLII, where this phrase occurs.

41 Copy in *Ch.W.P.*

42 Weizmann's January 1915 Report.

43 In his conversation with Grey about a month earlier Samuel had spoken of a Jewish State: above, p. 103.

44 Note of the conversation in *Ch.W.P.*

bolder programme than he had originally had in mind. His aims eventually crystallised in 1917 in the conception of a Jewish Commonwealth in Palestine under British protection, but in essentials his views had already taken shape before the end of 1914, and especially the pivotal idea of an identity of British and Zionist interests.

In his dealings with the British Government and its representatives Weizmann had the twofold advantage that he was a British subject of undoubted loyalty and was not, on the other hand, an assimilated English Jew.

It has been said of him by one of his admirers that 'he was made of one piece.'[45] This is not quite apt, and certainly not as applied to the Weizmann of 1914. Lipsky was nearer the mark when, describing Weizmann as he appeared at the 1913 Zionist Congress, he said that ' he was not yet a Westerner and was losing his credentials as a Russian Zionist. He hovered between these two worlds. . . .'[46] Another of Weizmann's associates in Zionism, Kurt Blumenfeld, put the same point with a different emphasis when he observed that ' Weizmann invariably lived on different levels . . . it was Chaim Weizmann's luck that West and East did not blend in him. Thus, as with a Janus-like mind, he saw the one and the other world.'[47]

In 1914 Weizmann had, with brief interruptions, been away from Russia for the best part of twenty years and had lived for ten years in England. He had not forgotten, nor did he ever forget, the rock whence he was hewn, but he had outgrown his original environment. He could no longer look at the outside world with quite the same eyes as the Jewish masses in Eastern Europe, while they, on their part, wondered at times whether he had not somehow grown away from them. On the other hand, in his relations with British statesmen and public men it was part of his strength that, when he took the field in 1914, he was not only a British subject, but was already attuned to English ways and habits of thought. More than that, he was, and was known to be, not merely a loyal citizen but a true friend and admirer of his

45 *The Times,* 17 November 1952.
46 Above, p. 122.
47 *Zion* (Jerusalem), November 1952.

adopted country. The genuine respect he had felt for England even before he settled there was already beginning to grow into an emotional attachment destined, in the end, to cost him much anguish in the years of frustration and estrangement which lay in the still distant future. If he retained, in English eyes, a certain exotic quality, this, far from prejudicing him, served only to make him more interesting and impressive, and to heighten the impact of his personality on men who found themselves—many of them for the first time—in the presence of an authentic Jew. It may as well be frankly recognised that among the most ardent Gentile pro-Zionists were some who, until they came into contact with Zionism, had had no particular liking for Jews. There were anti-semites with a conscience who found Zionism attractive because, by supporting it, they could purge themselves of a certain sense of guilt. For these especially it was a refreshing experience to find themselves in the presence of an unhyphenated and uninhibited Jew, who could talk and be talked to about the Jewish Question with no embarrassing reticences or evasions.

How was it that Weizmann, starting with such slender resources in terms of visible power and prestige, was able to make so profound an impression upon men accustomed to great affairs, coming to them with none of the conventional credentials and from a quite different world? Harold Nicolson, who, as a young Foreign Office official, assisted Mark Sykes in his handling of the Zionist question in 1917, has spoken of Weizmann's personal dignity—' I do not think that I ever met a man quite as dignified as Dr. Weizmann '—and of a certain awe which he inspired: ' I sometimes wonder whether his fellow-Jews realise how deeply he impressed us Gentiles by his heroic, his Maccabean quality.'[48] If Weizmann was seen a little larger than life, it was not because he struck heroic poses. He was far from being austere or other-worldly. In his good moods—for he had a mercurial temperament —he could be higly companionable, witty and entertaining. He enjoyed the pleasures of life and was well endowed with worldly wisdom. In appearance (he was slightly above middle height, with a powerfully built frame and a physiognomy which people

[48] *The Jerusalem Post*, 2 November 1954.

not used to Russian Jews might well have thought more Russian than Jewish) he was striking rather than handsome, but a certain elegance which distinguished his work both in science and in politics was reflected also in his bearing, his manners and even in his dress. If, as Harold Nicolson has said, he inspired a certain awe, it was not because he exerted himself to be impressive, but because it was impossible, in his presence, not to be conscious of his reserves of strength or to resist the enchantment of his magnetic eyes. Man of the world though he was or became, he preserved inviolate an inner sanctuary. It was the mystical element mingled with his realism which gave him his charismatic quality and was the hidden source of his power.

Weizmann was not spectacularly effective as a public speaker. Though he could dominate an audience by the weight of his authority and could sometimes move it with a telling phrase or dazzle it with a shaft of wit, his gifts were most effectively exercised in intimate conversation. They were tested to the full in the innumerable interviews by which, little by little, he edged his way towards his goal. Of these, in the nature of the case, only scattered traces have survived. His writings and speeches, impressive as some of them are—even his own revealing autobiography—will give future generations but a faint impression of the impact of his personal presence at the height of his powers.

CHAPTER 7

C. P. SCOTT

On 16 September 1914 Weizmann wrote to Greenberg:

'. . . I had a long talk with C. P. Scott (the editor of the
" Guardian ") to-day, and he will be quite prepared to help us
in any endeavour in favour of the Jews. He expressed his will-
ingness to see Grey, when we have a practical proposal to
submit. He carries great weight and may be useful . . .'[1]

The celebrated editor of the *Manchester Guardian* had long
been an influential and highly respected figure in public life. A per-
sonage in his own right as well as by virtue of his office, he had
widespread connections, enjoyed access everywhere, and was a
close political and personal friend of Lloyd George.[2] The talk
reported by Weizmann to Greenberg had taken place at a private
party at which he had been introduced to Scott, and, availing himself of a chance opening, had brought the conversation round to
Zionism. The meeting had not been pre-arranged, and the introduction was a pure accident; indeed, Weizmann did not at first
realise that the guest he was talking to was Scott.[3]

Zionism, as Weizmann expounded it, was new to Scott. Though
now approaching seventy,[4] he was open, as he had always been,
to fresh ideas. What Weizmann told him aroused his interest, and
he expressed a wish to hear more. The two met again, and by the
end of November Scott's first favourable impression had been fully
confirmed. ' I was immensely interested,' he wrote to Weizmann,
' in what you told me of your hopes and plans. There are so few
people who have the courage of an ideal and at the same time the
insight and energy which make it possible.'[5]

[1] Copy in *Ch.W.P.*
[2] Tom Jones describes him as ' probably Lloyd George's closest political
confidant': *Lloyd George* (O.U.P., 1951), p. 48.
[3] The incident has been described to the author by Mrs. Weizmann, who
was also at the party, from her personal recollection. See also *Trial and
Error*, p. 190.
[4] Born 1846. He died in 1932.
[5] Scott to Weizmann, 22 November 1914: *Ch.W.P.*

Scott's approach to Zionism and the admiration he felt for Weizmann personally are more fully brought out in a letter to Harry
Sacher, dated 16 January 1915:[6]

> 'I have had several conversations with Dr. Weizmann on the
> Jewish Question, and he has, I think, opened his whole mind
> to me. I found him extraordinarily interesting—a rare com-
> bination of idealism and the severely practical which are the
> two essentials of statesmanship. . . . What struck me in his
> view was, first, his perfectly clear conception of Jewish
> nationalism—an intense and burning sense of the Jew as
> Jew . . . and, secondly, arising out of that and necessary for
> its satisfaction and development, his demand for a country,
> a homeland, which for him, and for anyone sharing his views of
> Jewish nationality, could be no other than the ancient home
> of his race. To you no doubt these ideas are familiar . . . but
> they are not to most people and were not to me. . . . It seems to
> me a big idea and is, I fancy, already producing a revolution
> in Jewish thought—a painful one, no doubt, to many. But the
> fundamental conception—to make the Jew a whole Jew . . .
> to clear him up in his own eyes and the eyes of the world—
> that seems to me sound, at least as an ideal. And there may be
> a chance now of moving a long way towards it.'

In this letter there are three points which call for notice. First,
Scott by implication accepted the view that the position of the
Jews generally was anomalous and unsatisfactory and would
remain so until something was done—as he put it—'to make the
Jew a whole Jew, to clear him up in his own eyes and the eyes
of the world.' Secondly, he foretold—and he was right—that 'the
revolution in Jewish thought' of which he spoke would encounter
some strong Jewish resistance. Lastly, he was dealing exclusively
with the Jewish aspect of the matter. He said nothing about any
special British interest in the future of Palestine.

When Scott and Weizmann first met in the middle of September
1914, Turkey had not yet entered the War, and there was no reason
to assume that an Allied victory would involve the break-up of the
Turkish Empire; the Entente Powers, had, in fact, offered to
guarantee its integrity if Turkey would undertake to remain

[6] *L.S.P.*

neutral.[7] Scott's interest was aroused, to begin with, because, without having found it necessary to give any close thought to the subject, he was vaguely uncomfortable about the position of the Jews and so predisposed to be in sympathy with a Movement which recognised that there was something wrong and proposed a radical solution.

Scott's offer to talk to Grey suggests that, even in September 1914 he thought that it might be possible for something to be done for the Zionists in the peace settlement, but, as matters then stood, it was not obvious that Zionism had any special significance from a British point of view. Once Turkey had entered the War, Scott began to think on different lines and to link the Zionist Question with that of the future of Palestine in relation to the defence of Egypt and the Suez Canal. It was not long before he was firmly convinced that in any partition of Turkey it was essential that Palestine should fall to Great Britain. In March and again in April 1915 Weizmann reported to his colleagues that Scott had talked to him on these lines.[8] Scott himself records in his Journal the views he expressed in a luncheon-table conversation with Lloyd George, Samuel, and Weizmann in November 1915. Samuel had argued in favour of ' a mediatised Palestine under British protection.' Scott's note continues:

' George remarked that France would probably object and wanted Palestine for herself . . . that, moreover, there would be an objection in this country to such an extension of our responsibilities. I suggested that if France got Syria, that should satisfy her, and that Russia would certainly object to a Catholic Power holding the Holy Places and would much prefer a Protestant one as being quasi-neutral in the religious question. Also that in regard to responsibility we had already the responsibility of defending Egypt and that it was only a question of how that could best be done in face of new danger. George thought a condominium of the three Powers might be proposed, but Samuel and Weizmann agreed that from their point of view this would be the worst solution and it seemed to me not good from ours.'[9]

[7] See Grey, *Twenty-Five Years*, II, 173 ; Pingaud, I, 98ff.
[8] To Sokolow and Tschlenow, 20 March and 15 April 1915: *Ch.W.P.*
[9] (See opposite page for footnote.)

It is interesting to note the distinction drawn by Scott between Samuel as well as Weizmann on the one hand and himself on the other. Samuel and Weizmann agreed that a condominium would be bad from 'their' point of view; Scott thought that it would also be bad from 'ours.'

It may at first sight seem somewhat curious that Scott, who would have been ranked as the opposite of an Imperialist, should have taken so strong a line about Palestine. Like Lloyd George, he had been identified with the Radical wing of the Liberal Party and, like him, had, in opposition to the Liberal Imperialists, been on the unpopular side in the South African War.[10] In the years before 1914 the *Guardian* had been highly critical of Grey's diplomacy and up to the last moment, and certainly until the invasion of Belgium, had taken the view that, if war broke out in Europe, Great Britain could and should keep out of it.[11] Nevertheless, Scott was a realist. Once the War had started, all doubts were cast aside ; it might or might not have been possible to avert the catastrophe, but all that mattered now was that the War should be won.[12] So also, once Turkey had chosen to enter the War and thus made it inevitable that an Allied victory would mean the dissolution of the Turkish Empire, Scott took a realistic view of the new situation. He could see no reason for being content with a settlement which would place Great Britain at a disadvantage in the Middle East for the benefit of France, and both personally and through his paper he fought hard in defence of what he conceived to be a vital British interest in that part of the world.

We have seen already how clearly Scott defined his views in

[10] See J. L. Hammond's *Life of C. P. Scott* (London, Bell, 1934), p. 185.

[11] Hammond, op. cit., p. 181 ; Ivor Brown, *The Way of My World* (London, Collins, 1954), pp. 190-191.

[12] See *Manchester Guardian* leader, 5 August 1914.

[9] *C.P.S. Jnls.*, 26 November 1915. Lloyd George's reserve can be better understood when it is remembered that at the time of this discussion the Anglo-French tug-of-war, which ended, in May 1916, in the Sykes-Picot Agreement, had just started. Lloyd George himself seems always to have hankered after some arrangement which would keep the French out of Palestine and put Great Britain in effective control, and from 1917, as Prime Minister, he pursued this object with the greatest determination.

C. P. SCOTT

private conversation with Lloyd George and others on 26 November 1915. A few days earlier, the *Manchester Guardian* had for the first time devoted a leading article to a discussion of the Palestine question on the lines on which Scott had been thinking, though avoiding any explicit reference to a possible conflict of interests betwen Great Britain and France. The main burden of the article was that a friendly Palestine was essential to the defence of Egypt and the Suez Canal. 'Moreover,' it continued, 'we are in Mesopotamia engaged in operations which seem likely to give us a new province, which ought not to be separated from Egypt by hostile territory.' The whole situation, it was argued, would be different ' if Palestine were now a buffer-State between Egypt and the North, inhabited, as it used to be, by an intensely patriotic race, friendly, as it was in the past, to Egypt. . . . It is to this condition that we ought to work. . . . On the realisation of that condition depends the whole future of the British Empire as a Sea Empire.'[13] The writer was the *Guardian's* Military Critic, Herbert Sidebotham,[14] who needed no prompting to express views in the fullest accord with his own,[15] but the article, whether or not it was inspired by Scott, could not have appeared without his approval.

How strongly Scott felt on the Palestine question and how unreservedly he identified himself with the Zionist cause is attested, not only by the policy of his paper, but also by his personal exertions behind the scenes from 1914, when he was the first to bring Weizmann to the notice of Lloyd George, to 1917, when his long-standing association with the new Prime Minister placed him in a particularly advantageous position for advocating the Zionist cause in the highest quarters. His private Journals, and the correspondence preserved in the Weizmann archives, show, as we shall see later, how hard he worked to create a favourable atmosphere

[13] The *Manchester Guardian*, 22 November 1915.
[14] Sidebotham, *Great Britain and Palestine* (London, Macmillan, 1937), p. 32. Sidebotham adds in a footnote: ' As the article was an editorial leader, the credit (or discredit) of the opinion is, of course, with the Editor.' (At p. 29, Sidebotham makes the surprising statement that ' if Scott believed in Zionism, he never sought to communicate his faith to any member of his staff.' This is difficult to reconcile with Scott's letter [16 January 1915] to Sacher, quoted above, Note 6.)
[15] See below, p. 302.

135

for the Zionists in their plea for British support. They also provide ample evidence of the warm admiration he came to feel for Weizmann personally. He saw in Weizmann, not only the embodiment of all that appealed to him in Zionism, but also of the qualities which his long experience of public life had taught him to value most—' a rare combination,' as he said in a letter already quoted, ' of idealism and the severely practical, which are the two essentials of statesmanship.' When, in September 1917, Weizmann found himself at variance with his colleagues and was thinking of resignation, Scott appealed to him not to leave his people leaderless. ' You,' he wrote, ' are the only statesman among them.'[16] At every awkward turn in the long road leading to the Balfour Declaration Scott is to be found at Weizmann's side as a steadfast friend and sagacious adviser. The close relations which existed between the two are reflected also in Scott's solicitude for Weizmann's interests in the difficulties—and they were many—which he encountered in connection with his scientific work for Government Departments.[17] In these matters likewise Scott was able to intervene the more effectively because of the personal connections which made him a powerful ally. The background to the Declaration cannot be fully understood without reference to the triangular relationship between Scott, Weizmann, and Lloyd George.

[16] 14 September 1917: *Ch.W.P.* See below, p. 496.
[17] See above, p. 119, and also *C.P.S. Jnls.*, 29 February, 3 March, 22-26 May, 26-28 July 1916; 27 February, 19 April, 30 April-4 May, 8 June 1917.

CHAPTER 8

WEIZMANN, SAMUEL AND LLOYD GEORGE

It was Scott who first brought Weizmann to the notice of Lloyd George and paved the way for his introduction to Herbert Samuel. On 29 November 1914 he wrote to Weizmann: ' I saw Lloyd George on Friday[1] and spoke about the Palestine question. It was not new to him, as he had been reading the *New Statesman* article[2] and talking to Herbert Samuel. He was interested and would like to see you and would ask Herbert Samuel to meet you too.'[3] As it turned out, Lloyd George found it impossible to give Weizmann an early appointment and suggested that he should see Samuel.[4] An interview was arranged by Scott, and on 10 December 1914 Weizmann called on Samuel at his office at the Local Government Board.

In a report prepared a few weeks later,[5] Weizmann describes

---

[1] November 27.

[2] ' The Future of Palestine,' *The New Statesman,* 21 November 1914. The article, signed ' A.M.H.,' was written by Albert Hyamson. ' Mr. Asquith,' it begins, ' has announced that the end of the Turkish Empire is at hand.' After setting out the Zionist case, the article concludes: ' Let Britain remember her past and think of her future and secure to the Jews, under her protection, the possibility of building up a new Palestine on the ruins of their ancient home.'

[3] Scott to Weizmann, 29 November 1914: *Ch.W.P.*

[4] Weizmann's January 1915 Report: ' Mr. Scott . . . intimated to me that he had spoken to Mr. Lloyd George, that he had found him interested and that also Mr. Herbert Samuel was particularly interested in the question, and that Mr. Lloyd George would receive me some day in London. As it happened, Mr. Lloyd George, having several engagements for the week, suggested that I should see Mr. Herbert Samuel, and an interview took place at his office.' The date is fixed by Weizmann's letter of 10 December 1914 to Mrs. Weizmann (*V.W.P.*), and his letter of 13 December 1914 to Scott (*Ch.W.P.*). To Mrs. Weizmann he wrote: ' I wired you today after my conversation with S. Really messianic times are upon us. . . .' To Scott he wrote (13 December): ' As you kindly arranged, I saw Mr. Samuel at his office on Thursday . . . and his views, I must say, were quite a revelation to me. . . .' [Thursday = 10 December.]

[5] The January 1915 Report (dated 7 January 1915).

the conversation in considerable detail. The salient passages are as follows:

> 'I suggested that [the] abnormal position of our people in East and West is due to one fundamental cause, that we are a nation inasmuch as we resist all influences making for the destruction of our race, and not a nation because we assimilate ourselves superficially, and are always ready to attach ourselves quickly to surroundings. . . . We are a people without a status, and if in normal times such a position is tolerated, in times of crisis it becomes dangerous. If the Jews had at present a place where they formed the important part of the population and led a life of their own, however small this place might be, for example, something like Monaco, with a University instead of a gambling-hall, nobody would doubt the existence of the Jewish nation. . . . We should have a definite passport and we should, therefore, not be suspected. . . .
>
> 'Mr. Samuel . . . remarked that he was not a stranger to Zionist ideas; he had been following them up a little of late years, and although he had never publicly mentioned it, he took a considerable interest in the question. Since Turkey had entered the war he had given the problem much thought and consideration, and he thought that a realisation of the Zionist dream was possible. He believed that my demands were too modest, that big things would have to be done in Palestine; he himself would move, and would expect Jewry to move, immediately the military situation was cleared up. He was convinced that it would be cleared up favourably. The Jews would have to bring sacrifices, and he was prepared to do so.
>
> 'At this point I ventured to ask in which way the plans of Mr. Samuel were more ambitious than mine. Mr. Samuel preferred not to enter in[to] a discussion of his plans, as he would like to keep them "liquid," but he suggested that the Jews would have to build railways, harbours, a University, a network of schools, etc. The University seems to make a special appeal to him. . . .
>
> 'He also thinks that perhaps the Temple may be rebuilt,

as a symbol of Jewish unity—of course in a modernised form.
'After listening to him, I remarked that I was pleasantly
surprised to hear such words from him; that if I were a
religious Jew I should have thought the Messianic times
were near. . . . He added that these ideas are in the mind of
his colleagues in the Cabinet. He advised me to work quietly
. . . and prepare for the hour to come. . . . [I said that] what
I asked for was simply encouragement from the British
Government, which we hoped would be the master of
Palestine, in our work there and, further, a wide measure of
local government and freedom for the development of our
own culture.'

Weizmann goes on to say that 'on taking leave from Mr.
Samuel he asked me whether I knew his friend Dr. Gaster, to
which I replied in the affirmative.' On December 25th, Weizmann, this time accompanied by Gaster, saw Samuel at his private
house. It was explained to Samuel that 'in view of the atomised
state of Jewry, there is a grave danger that all sorts of local and
self-appointed bodies may flood him or the Foreign Office with
projects and memoranda,' to which Samuel replied that 'the
British Government would not look at any project which did not
emanate from and was not backed by international Jewry. . . .
He urged that we should try to create a representative instrument
which would be sufficiently strong to negotiate when the time
came.'[6] Samuel's insistence on this point helps to account for the
efforts made on the Zionist side—in the end, as we shall see, with
little success—to win the support, or at least to blunt the opposition, of those sections of Jewry which had stood aloof from
Zionism, and, in particular, to bring into line the influential body
of Anglo-Jewish opinion represented by the Conjoint Foreign
Committee of the Board of Deputies of British Jews and the
Anglo-Jewish Association.

Samuel's next step was to arrange for Weizmann to see Lloyd
George. He wrote to Weizmann (11 January 1915): 'Mr. Lloyd
George, whom I have seen to-day, would be very glad if you
could breakfast with him next Friday. I should be there also, and
we should have a good opportunity of discussing the matter in

[6] Weizmann's January 1915 Report.

which we are both interested.'[7] Two days later he told Lloyd
George that Weizmann had accepted the invitation. Scott knew
of it and on January 14th wrote to Weizmann, who had evidently
asked for guidance, forewarning him of the questions he might
expect. They are obviously questions raised by Lloyd George
with Scott and show that he was sufficiently interested in Zionism
to be realistic about the difficulties.

> '... You will probably find that he [Lloyd George] will take
> the lead in the conversation and put questions to you which
> will give you plenty of openings. . . . He will, I am sure, be
> much interested in your view of the Jews of Judæa as a
> possible link between East and West . . . and as a channel of
> ideas and of enterprise in the Arabian Peninsula. But no
> doubt he will want to discuss with you much more concrete
> matters than those—the present strength of the Jewish
> element in Palestine and the possibility of its rapid expan-
> sion; its relation to the local Arab population which so
> greatly outnumbers it; the potential value of Palestine as a
> " buffer-State " and the means of evading for ourselves an
> undesirable extension of military responsibility ; the best way
> of allaying Catholic and Orthodox jealousy in regard to the
> custody of the Holy Places—and the like.'[8]

Lord Samuel records in his Memoirs[9] that in January and February 1915 he had ' two more conversations with Lloyd George,
at one of which Dr. Weizmann was present.' In a letter dated
15 April 1915 Weizmann tells his colleagues, Tschlenow and
Sokolow, that ' Scott will write to-day to Herbert Samuel and will
suggest to him that he should see me together with Lloyd George
again' (author's italics). It is quite clear that arrangements had
been made for Weizmann to breakfast with Lloyd George, in
company with Samuel, on 15 January 1915, and as good as certain
that the breakfast took place, but it is a puzzling fact that no
record of the conversation has come to light.

A few months later, Lloyd George became Chairman of the
Munitions Committee (soon to develop into the Ministry of Muni-

[7] *Ch.W.P.*, ' Friday '=January 15.
[8] *Ch.W.P.*
[9] Samuel, *Memoirs*, p. 144.

tions)[10] and almost at once found himself in trouble about the production of acetone. He happened to mention his difficulties to Scott, who suggested that Weizmann might be able to help.[11] After an interview early in June 1915, Lloyd George was satisfied that Weizmann knew his business and should be given a trial. His signal success in evolving a new and relatively economical method of producing acetone established him firmly in Lloyd George's favour and was the beginning of a personal association which continued after Lloyd George had left the Ministry of Munitions to become, first, Secretary of State for War, and, later, Prime Minister.

In Lloyd George's allusions to the Balfour Declaration in later years there is ample evidence of the impression made upon him by Weizmann. 'I am his proselyte,' he told a Jewish audience in 1925; 'acetone converted me to Zionism. . . . There is no man with a greater part in the conversion of the Gentiles running the war than my friend Dr. Weizmann.'[12] Addressing another Jewish audience in 1927, he said : ' I was glad to take part in the Zionist Declaration. It was a very remarkable member of your race who directed and guided me in that—Dr. Weizmann, whom I regard it as a great privilege to have met, one of the noblest and most unselfish men I have ever met.'[13] In his *Truth About the Peace Treaties* (1938)[14] he associates the Balfour Declaration with ' the initiative, the assiduity and the fervour of one of the greatest Hebrews of all time, Dr. Chaim Weizmann.' Though Lloyd George's rhetorical exuberance has usually to be discounted,

[10] The Committee was set up in April 1915. Lloyd George's appointment as Minister of Munitions was announced at the end of May.

[11] Lloyd George, *War Memoirs*, II, 584ff. Scott wrote to Lloyd George, 6 June 1915: ' If you are seeing Dr. Weizmann tomorrow (he is calling, as directed, on your Secretary, Mr. Wolf), you may like to ask him about the War Office contract with a certain Company for the manufacture of acetone. They are paying a considerable sum . . . for a process originally devised by Weizmann himself and which is now worthless, as Weizmann's new process (which he offered to the War Office for nothing) . . . will work out, he says, very much cheaper.'

[12] Afterword to Philip Guedalla's *Napoleon and Palestine* (London, Allen & Unwin, 1925), pp. 49-51.

[13] The *North Wales Chronicle*, 27 August 1927. The author is indebted to Mr. I. Wartski, of Bangor, for drawing his attention to this speech, which was delivered at a Jewish Summer School in Wales.

[14] II, 1117.

these are not empty words. It is clear that any allusion to the Balfour Declaration evoked in Lloyd George's mind the image of Weizmann and, linked with this, genuinely grateful recollections of his war-time services. This is of itself sufficient proof that Weizmann's advocacy of the Zionist cause made a powerful impression upon Lloyd George and carried added weight because of his esteem for Weizmann personally.

But this was not quite the beginning. Lloyd George had first come into contact with the Zionist Movement in 1903, when Greenberg, on Herzl's behalf, consulted him, in his professional capacity, on the British Government's tentative offer of land for Jewish colonisation in East Africa.[15] It may be surmised—though there is no positive proof of it—that this was the real starting-point of his interest in Zionism. When, at the end of 1905, he was given Cabinet office in the newly-formed Liberal Administration, *The Jewish Chronicle*[16] remarked that ' as becomes the doughty Welsh Nationalist, Mr. George is an ardent believer in the Zionist Movement.' His ardour was kept well under control. He made a rather tepid speech in support of the East African project in the debate in Parliament in 1904,[17] and in 1906 he sent, through Greenberg, a friendly message to a Zionist meeting at Cardiff.[18] Beyond this there appears to be no record, up to 1914, of his having expressed himself publicly on the subject. But neither had Herbert Samuel. It does not follow that he was not interested; on the contrary, it seems clear that at the outbreak of war vague ideas about the restoration of the Jews to Palestine were already floating in his mind. Within a few days of the declaration of war on Turkey in November 1914, he was, as we have seen, telling Herbert Samuel that he ' was very keen to see a Jewish State established' in Palestine, and when, later in the month, Scott sounded him on the Palestine question, he found him already prepared to interest himself in Zionism.[19] If Weizmann gained and held his attention, it was in part at least because he was predisposed to be receptive.

[15] See above, p. 28.
[16] 15 December 1905.
[17] H.C., 20 June 1904: O.R. col. 577.
[18] *J.C.*, 9 March 1906.
[19] Above, p. 137.

Like some other eminent pro-Zionists, Lloyd George had mixed feelings about Jews. In some of his speeches on the South African War and its aftermath there can be discerned a streak of ordinary vulgar anti-Semitism.[20] There is a trace of it also in his parting shot at Sir Alfred Mond, when his former friend and colleague went over to the Conservatives in 1926.[21] Even in the debate in Parliament in 1904 on the East African offer to the Zionists he had not been able to resist a gibe at the Jews : ' There were a good many Jews they could well spare. . . .'[22] Yet another side of his nature was sensitive to the Jewish mystique. Though he had lost the unquestioning faith which had once sustained him, he still bore the impress of the Welsh Chapel where, he said, ' I was taught far more about the history of the Jews than about the history of my own people. . . . We were thoroughly versed in the history of the Hebrews. We used to recite great passages from the Prophets and the Psalms . . . that great literature which will echo to the very last days of this old world. . . .'[23] It was not for nothing that bound up with the memories of his childhood were the prophecies which foretold the restoration of the Jews to the Holy Land.

He was drawn to Zionism for another reason. In the address just quoted he reminded his Jewish audience that he, like them, belonged to a small nation. ' It is an ancient race, not as old as yours, and, although I am very proud of it, I am not going to compare it with yours . . . but all I know is that up to the present it is the small races that have been chosen for great things. . . .'[24] Unlike Balfour, he had not thought deeply about the relations

---

[20] The following is an extract from a speech by Lloyd George at the Finsbury by-election in 1905 ; quoted by Frank Owen, *Tempestuous Journey* (London, Hutchinson, 1954), p. 141 : ' Would you like to know how to make a fortune ? First, get up a war like Mr. Chamberlain's. . . . Having got your war, go down there and start business. If you have a British name, like Jones, or Smith, or Baker, change it at once: make it Beit, or Dunkelsbuhler, or, say, Cohen.' (The Conservative candidate's name was Cohen.) For other examples, see extracts quoted by Mr. Owen from speeches in 1899 (p. 95) and 1904 (pp. 138-139).

[21] ' Like another notorious member of his race, Alfred Mond has gone to his own place ': see Hector Bolitho, *Alfred Mond* (London, Secker, 1932), p. 274.

[22] H.C., 20 June 1904: O.R., col. 579.

[23] Afterword to P. Guedalla's *Napoleon and Palestine*, p. 48.

[24] Ibid., p. 49.

between Jew and Gentile, nor was he above playing on anti-Semitic prejudices when it suited him, but the Jews in the abstract—the Jews as a small nation struggling for its place in the world—evoked in him the same kind of instinctive sympathy as did the Boers and, in later years, the Greeks in 1919 and the Abyssinians in 1935.

In expressing gratitude for the Balfour Declaration, the semi-official *Zionist Review*,[25] assigned to Lloyd George ' the foremost place inside the Cabinet among the architects of this great decision. Next to him comes Mr. Balfour. . . .' There could obviously have been no Declaration without the Prime Minister's express approval, but there are, in fact, clear indications of Lloyd George's active personal interest. In April 1917 he personally impressed upon Mark Sykes, then about to leave for the East as the head of the Political Mission to be attached to the British Army in Palestine, the importance of doing nothing to prejudice the Zionist Movement and the possibility of its development under British auspices.[26] In the following August he took the initiative in informing the Foreign Office, through Philip Kerr, that an official statement concerning Palestine was under consideration. At the end of September 1917, when, after an abortive discussion in the War Cabinet earlier in the month, the question of a declaration in favour of Zionism had been shelved, Lloyd George personally gave instructions for it to be restored to the agenda for early consideration. Thanks to the efforts of Edwin Montagu, no decision was reached when the War Cabinet re-examined the proposal early in October, but a few days later Montagu himself told Scott that he recognised that the game was up ; Lloyd George, like Balfour, was, he said, ' immovable.'[27]

Lloyd George has been described by one who knew him intimately as 'basically a hard realist with no illusions about men or movements.'[28] No one would be so naïve as to suppose that his active interest in Zionism was accounted for by mere emotion

[25] December 1917, p. 214.
[26] Below, p. 384.
[27] Below, p. 473.
[28] Thomas Jones, *A Diary with Letters* (O.U.P., 1954), p. 30.

or sentiment, or that he would have exerted himself in favour of the Balfour Declaration if he had not been fully satisfied that a pro-Zionist policy accorded with British interests as he conceived them. In an address already quoted, he himself, after explaining why Zionism had appealed to him, gave a perfectly realistic account of some of the motives for the Balfour Declaration: 'There we were, confronted with your people in every country of the world, very powerful. You may say you have been oppressed and persecuted—that has been your power ! You have been hammered into fine steel. . . . And therefore we wanted your help. We thought it would be very useful.'[29]

Lloyd George's personal interest in the Balfour Declaration can without difficulty be related to his views on wider issues covering the conduct of the War and the post-War settlement. In the controversy between the Western and Eastern schools of strategy he had long been among the most persistent of the Easterners. For him the operations in Palestine were, as he confided to Scott, ' the one really interesting part of the War.'[30] It was he who was primarily responsible, after the setback at Gaza early in 1917, for the decision to take the risk of a large-scale campaign for the conquest of Palestine—an enterprise which he pressed insistently upon a reluctant Chief of the General Staff. He was inflexible in his determination that Great Britain should gain control of Palestine to the total exclusion of France. ' The French,' he declared to Lord Bertie in the spring of 1917, 'will have to accept our protectorate ; we shall be there by conquest and shall remain.'[31] Of all the military experts in the press much the best, he told Scott,[32] was the *Manchester Guardian's* ' Student of War'—the *nom de plume* of Herbert Sidebotham, who had persistently urged the vital importance of ensuring that Palestine should in some way be incorporated in the system of Imperial defence.

Weizmann and his friends being strongly pro-British, a pro-

---

[29] Afterword to P. Guedalla's *Napoleon and Palestine*, p. 49.

[30] *C.P.S. Jnls.*, 3 April 1917.

[31] *The Diary of Lord Bertie of Thame* (London, Hodder & Stoughton, 1924), II, 122 (20 April 1917).

[32] *C.P.S. Jnls.*, 10 August 1917: ' G. suddenly put it to me: " Do you know who is the best military critic in the press ? " I said I could guess. " The military critic of the *Manchester Guardian*—much the best . . . and I have told Hankey to cut out his articles." '

Zionist policy fitted comfortably into this order of ideas. But this does not fully account for the personal satisfaction which Lloyd George seems to have felt in identifying himself with the Zionist cause. After talking to Lloyd George about the Samuel memorandum, Lord Reading, who knew him intimately, told Samuel, early in 1915, that 'he was certainly inclined to be on the sympathetic side. Your proposal appealed to the poetic and imaginative as well as to the romantic and religious qualities of his mind.'[33] Lloyd George may not have cared greatly about the Jews for their own sake, but, just as in the Palestine campaign the very names of the battlefields stirred his imagination, so he was still capable of being moved by his memories of the sacred writings, familiar to him from childhood, which foretold the restoration of the Jewish people to the Holy Land. The question of policy which arose in 1917 was decided by the War Cabinet in favour of the Zionists on strictly rational grounds, but it does not follow that in Lloyd George's personal approach to it sentiment played no part.[34]

[33] Samuel, *Memoirs*, p. 143.

[34] ' Balfour went on to say that he himself was not in favour of a British Mandate over Palestine, but that he would not oppose it. The Prime Minister was very anxious to secure a British Mandate for purely sentimental reasons': Colonel Minertzhagen, *Middle East Diary* (diary entry 30 July 1919), pp. 24-27.

CHAPTER 9

BALFOUR

IT WAS TO his chance meeting with Scott in September 1914 that Weizmann owed his introduction, first to Herbert Samuel and then, through Samuel, to Lloyd George. At the outbreak of war he had hardly any direct contacts of his own in the higher reaches of public life. There was one British statesman of the first rank who might, perhaps, give him a hearing, but this depended on whether Mr. Balfour remembered a young University lecturer who had talked to him about Zionism in 1906. Balfour did remember. By the end of 1914 Weizmann had seen him again, and from this sprang an association which had already begun to acquire a certain intimate quality when Balfour joined the Lloyd George Government as Foreign Secretary at the end of 1916.

Weizmann met Balfour for the first time in January 1905, when he had been in England less than a year. During a visit to his Manchester constituency, Balfour, then Prime Minister, addressed a Conservative meeting on January 27th.[1] Weizmann went to hear him and was introduced to him at the meeting, almost certainly by Dr. Charles Dreyfus, who, besides being an active Zionist, was personally known to Balfour as a prominent Manchester Conservative and one of his most energetic supporters. 'We couldn't talk much,' Weizmann told Ussishkin,[2] 'but he [Balfour] invited me to see him in London.' At this time the handling of the British Government's East African offer was still causing violent dissension within the Zionist Movement. Ussishkin was campaigning strongly against the East African project. Dreyfus, like Weiz-

---

[1] *The Times,* 28 January 1905.

[2] Weizmann to Ussishkin, 29 January 1905 (*Ch.W.P.*): 'The day before yesterday I saw Balfour, the Prime Minister. This was at a mass meeting. We couldn't talk much, but he invited me to see him in London. The local leader of the Zionists, Dr. Dreyfus, is a very close friend of Balfour. . . .' (Transl. from the orig. Russian.) M. M. Ussishkin was a leading Russian Zionist. Dreyfus controlled the Clayton Aniline Works, which were in Balfour's constituency. Weizmann was employed there as a part-time research chemist. At the 1906 Election Dreyfus was Chairman of Balfour's Election Committee.

mann,[3] was also opposed to it. Weizmann clearly hoped that, with Dreyfus' help, Balfour might be brought to see that true Zionism did not admit of any deviation from Palestine. 'Dreyfus,' he told Ussichkin in the letter just quoted, 'is pro-Palestine, and we could submit to Balfour and the others a memorandum on our true purposes . . . so we could *eo ipso* paralyse Greenberg and Co.,' Greenberg and his friends sharing Herzl's view that the East African offer ought not to be rejected out of hand.

All this came to nothing. No memorandum was submitted to Balfour, nor did Weizmann succeed in seeing him in London.[4] Weizmann's first opportunity of talking to him about Zionism came twelve months later during the General Election which followed the resignation of the Balfour Government in December 1905. Balfour, now Leader of the Opposition, was fighting—as it turned out, unsuccessfully—to retain the seat he had held since 1885 in the East Division of Manchester. In the near-by constituency of North-West Manchester the Liberal candidate was Winston Churchill, who had in the spring of 1904 broken with the Conservatives on the Free Trade issue and, soon after changing sides, had accepted an invitation from the North-West Manchester Liberals to oppose the sitting Conservative Member at the next Election. Having been given junior office in the newly formed Liberal Administration as Under-Secretary of State for the Colonies, he was now exerting himself with every weapon at his command to make sure of a seat in the new Parliament.

There was no candidate whom on personal as well as political grounds the Conservatives were more anxious to see defeated. Neither was there any candidate who could make so effective an appeal for the support of Jewish voters. North-West Manchester happened to be one of the few constituencies with enough Jewish electors to make a difference, and this happened to be one of the rare occasions when there was something resembling a Jewish

---

[3] After some wavering at the start (see Shm. Levin, *The Arena* [London, Routledge, 1932], p. 256), Weizmann had become an out-and-out 'anti-Ugandist.'

[4] 'When I'll be in London (in ten days from now), I'll see Gordon [Sir W. Evans-Gordon] and Balfour. . . .': To Ussishkin, 11 April 1905. (*Ch.W.P.*) 'I haven't seen Gordon and the others; they are not in London': to Ussishkin, 15 June 1905. (*Ch.W.P.*) (Transl. from the orig. Russian.)

issue. Twice during its last two years of office the Conservative Government had come forward with proposals for restricting alien immigration. In 1904 a Government Bill which had reached the Committee stage had at that point been held up by Liberal obstruction and had in the end been withdrawn.[5] A somewhat milder version of the same proposals had formed part of the Balfour Government's legislative programme for what turned out to be its last year of office. This measure had found its way to the statute-book and had become law in the summer of 1905, a few months before the General Election.[6]

Aimed as it obviously was—indeed, Balfour himself had said as much[7]—at Jewish immigration from Eastern Europe, the Aliens Act, 1905 was seen by many English Jews (though there were some who took a different view[8]) both as a harsh restriction of the right of asylum and as a slur upon themselves. It was resented all the more because in the years 1903-1904 a fresh wave of pogroms had increased the pressure upon the Russian Jews to find a way of escape. From the British Government's point of view this may well have seemed to underline the need for some measure of control, but to many Jews, especially to those who were themselves of East European origin or descent, the moment seemed particularly ill chosen for a partial closing of the doors. Their fears turned out, in the event, to have been exaggerated. The Act did not, in practice, operate as harshly as they had foreseen,[9] but in 1906 there was strong feeling against the Conservatives among those Jews, and they were many, who were sensitive on the subject.

Balfour had not only been the head of the Government responsible for the Aliens Act but had personally taken an active part in piloting it through the House of Commons. In doing so he had taken occasion to denounce in the strongest language the persecution of the Jews in various parts of the Christian world. 'The treatment of the race,' he said in his Second Reading speech, 'has been a disgrace to Christendom.'[10] All the same, he had found it

[5] H.C., 11 July 1904: O.R., cols. 1220-1221.
[6] The Aliens Act, 1905 (Royal Assent, 11 August 1905).
[7] H.C., 10 July 1905: O.R., col. 155.
[8] See *The Jewish Chronicle, 1841-1941* (London, 1949), p. 120; C. C. Aronsfeld, 'Britain and Aliens,' *J.C.*, 19 August 1955.
[9] V. D. Lipman, *Social History of the Jews in England* (London, Watts, 1954), p. 143.
[10] H.C., 2 May 1905: O.R., col. 795.

necessary to defend his Party against imputations of anti-semitism.[11] *The Jewish Chronicle*[12] had voiced a widespread feeling among Jews when, in May 1905, it invited Balfour to explain how his sympathy with persecuted Jews could be reconciled with a policy which led him 'to refuse asylum to Jewish religious refugees.' Churchill, on the other hand, had exerted himself vigorously on the opposite side. Shortly after being approached by the North-West Manchester Liberals in the spring of 1904, he had assured a leading member of the Manchester Jewish community, Nathan Laski, of his opposition to the Aliens Bill then before Parliament.[13] He had been as good as his word. He had taken a prominent part in the strangling of the 1904 Bill by obstruction in Committee, and only a few weeks before the dissolution of Parliament at the end of 1905 he had been publicly thanked by the Board of Deputies of British Jews for his efforts to improve the measure which had just become law.[14] He had thus established a strong claim upon the Jewish voters in his constituency, and in his election campaign he made the most of it.[15]

On 27 December 1905 Weizmann had a letter from Churchill's election agent. Would he use his influence among the Jews in Churchill's favour? Weizmann replied that he must consult the President of the Zionist Organisation—at that time David Wolff-sohn.[16] [17] He wrote to the Zionist headquarters at Cologne asking

[11] See his letter to a correspondent, *The Times*, 11 May 1904 ; also his letter to Sir F. Milner, 19 July 1905, quoted below, p. 165.

[12] 5 May 1905.

[13] *The Times*, 31 May 1904.

[14] *J.C.*, 24 November 1905.

[15] On 7 January 1906 he addressed a Jewish meeting in his constituency and, according to the *J.C.* report (January 12), 'appealed for the support of the Jewish community on account of the work he had done for them in connection with the Aliens Bill.' On January 19 the *J.C.* wrote that his victory at the Election 'was in considerable measure due to the support of the Jews.'

[16] Weizmann states these facts in a letter to Wolffsohn dated 28 December 1905: Z.A.

[17] Earlier in the month (10 December 1905) Weizmann had been among the guests invited to meet Churchill at a dinner-party given by Nathan Laski, one of his most active Jewish supporters, after a public meeting, at which Churchill had spoken, to protest against the recent pogroms in Russia: see O. K. Rabinowicz, *Winston Churchill on Jewish Problems* (London, Lincolns-Prager, 1956), p. 36.

for guidance, but, instead of answering him direct, Wolffsohn left it to Greenberg to advise him.[18] What advice, if any, he received from Greenberg is unknown, but in writing to Wolffsohn he had pointed out that he was a foreigner and had questioned the advisability of his intervening in the Election. It seems clear that he did not, in fact, take any part in it.

Dr. Dreyfus, who had taken Weizmann to Balfour's Manchester meeting in January 1905, was now the Chairman of Balfour's Election Committee. In the course of the campaign he arranged for Weizmann to call on Balfour at a Manchester hotel. Mrs. Dugdale explains, in her biography,[19] that Balfour, who had been Prime Minister at the time of the East African offer to the Zionists, had been puzzled by its cool reception and had mentioned this to Dreyfus. Dreyfus, she writes, had suggested that Weizmann might be able to throw some light on the matter, whereupon Balfour had asked to see him. Dreyfus, who had, like Weizmann, disapproved of the East African project, may possibly have hoped that Weizmann would convince Balfour that he and those who shared his views had been right. It would not have been altogether out of keeping with Balfour's character and temperament to welcome a change from a candidate's routine bill-of-fare. On the other hand, the middle of a hotly contested Election was hardly the time which an astute electioneerer might have been expected to select for a deviation from the matter in hand. Dreyfus must have been aware that in a near-by Manchester constituency Churchill was bidding strongly for Jewish support, and it may possibly have occurred to him—especially if he knew that Weizmann had been approached in Churchill's interests—that a meeting between Weizmann and Balfour could do no harm.

The exact date of the interview is not known,[20] nor has any contemporary record of it come to light.* But, whatever may have been the real background to the conversation, and whether or not it has been accurately remembered in later attempts to reconstruct it, on three points there is no room for doubt. First, what

[18] Wolffsohn to Greenberg, 4/1/06: Z.A.   [19] Dugdale, *Balfour*, I, 433.
[20] Since this was written, there has been discovered in Dr. Weizmann's papers a letter to Mrs. Weizmann, dated 9 January 1906, in which he writes: 'I saw Balfour to-day, and had quite a long conversation with him about Zionism.'
* See note at foot of p. 667.

Balfour and Weizmann talked about was Zionism. Secondly, the interview convinced Balfour that Zionist aspirations could be satisfied nowhere but in Palestine. Lastly, Balfour was greatly impressed, not only by what he heard from Weizmann, but by the man himself. Writing a few weeks after the Election to a Jewish friend—an anti-Zionist, he said: 'I enclose a letter from Dr. Dreyfus, to whom I wrote to find out the name of the Russo-Jewish gentleman of whom I spoke to you. I did not, as you will see by Dr. Dreyfus's account of him, in any way overstate his intellectual qualifications.'[21] In his Introduction to Sokolow's *History of Zionism*[22] Balfour says of the East African project that, well-intentioned as it was, 'it had one serious defect. It was not Zionism. . . . Conversations [*sic*] I held with Dr. Weizmann in January 1906 convinced me that . . . if a home was to be found for the Jewish people, homeless now for nearly nineteen hundred years, it was in vain to seek it anywhere but in Palestine.' In 1929, having been reminded by Mrs. Dugdale of his meeting with Weizmann more than twenty years before, he said: 'It was from that talk with Weizmann that I saw that the Jewish form of patriotism was unique. Their love of their country refused to be satisfied by the Uganda scheme. It was Weizmann's absolute refusal even to look at it that impressed me.'[23]

Looking back in 1930 on his association with Balfour, Weizmann recalled, in an obituary tribute in *The New Judæa*,[24] an incident which had happened not long before the War. 'I think,' he wrote, 'it was in 1911 that Lord Balfour visited Manchester again to receive an honorary degree from the University. . . . The Vice-Chancellor came . . . to tell me that Lord Balfour remembered a conversation he had had with a young lecturer five years before and would like to resume it. I was to meet him at a garden-party. Unfortunately, he was called away to London, and the

21 Letter dated 13 April 1906 (copy in *Dugdale papers*). In reply to Balfour's enquiry, Dreyfus had told him something about the background and attainments of 'the Russian gentleman who had the honour of an interview with you in Manchester': Dreyfus to Balfour, 24 March, 1906 (ibid.).

22 I, xxix-xxx.

23 Conversation with Balfour, 7 August 1929, recorded by Mrs. Dugdale (*Dugdale papers*).

24 March-April 1930.

meeting did not take place.' Though in 1914 eight years had
passed since his meeting with Balfour, Weizmann had reason to
believe that it had not been forgotten. On 12 November 1914 he
wrote to Ahad Ha'am: 'You have probably noticed Asquith's
speech. . . .[25] It is time we came out of our stupor and did something. I have written to Balfour and am now awaiting his reply.'[26]
A few days later, he told Ahad Ha'am that he had invoked the
good offices of his friend and senior colleague, Samuel
Alexander[27]: 'After I had written to Balfour . . . I decided that
it would be better if Professor Alexander, who knows B. well,
would approach him. He did so, and to-day has come the answer,
which I enclose herewith.'[28] This was a letter from Balfour to
Alexander, dated November 17th:

> ' I have the liveliest and also the most pleasant recollections
> of my conversation with Dr. Weizmann in 1906, and should
> be very pleased to hear from him. If I am in London later in
> the year, and he happens to be up in Town, I shall be happy
> to see him; but my plans are uncertain, and it is safer for
> him to write. This would not prevent our talking matters over
> if opportunity served.'[29]

Thus encouraged, Weizmann secured an appointment, and on
12 December 1914—two days after his first meeting with Herbert
Samuel—he called on Balfour at his house in Carlton Gardens.
Writing to Scott the next day, Weizmann begins by describing his
talk with Samuel and then goes on to speak of his meeting with
Balfour: 'Our conversation was more of an academic nature, as
I did not outline fully the practical problem. He was much more

---

[25] I.e., Asquith's Guildhall speech, 9 November 1914: above, p. 103.

[26] Copy in *Ch.W.P.* (transl. from the Russian).

[27] The eminent philosopher, Samuel Alexander (1859-1938) was at this
time Professor of Philosophy at Manchester University. In a letter to
Alexander's literary executor, John Laird, Weizmann wrote: 'He said
of himself that he was a total assimilationist who had ceased to believe
in the possibility of assimilation': *Philosophical and Literary Pieces by
Samuel Alexander,* ed. by his Literary Executor (London, Macmillan,
1939), p. 93.

[28] *Ch.W.P.* (transl. from the Russian).

[29] *Ch.W.P.*

than sympathetic. . . .'[30] With the interview fresh in his mind, Weizmann wrote to Ahad Ha'am on December 14th[31]:

' I saw Balfour on Saturday. . . . Our talk lasted an hour and a half. Balfour remembered everything we had discussed eight years ago, and this made it superfluous for me to repeat my exposition of the Jewish problem in its national aspect. . . . When I expressed my regret that our work [in Palestine] had been interrupted, he said: " You may get your things done much more quickly after the war. . . ." [Words in quotation-marks are in English] . . . He said that, in his opinion, the [Jewish] problem would not be solved until either the Jews became completely assimilated here or a normal Jewish society came into existence in Palestine, and, moreover, he was thinking more of the West European Jews than of those of Eastern Europe. He told me how he had once had a long talk with Cosima Wagner at Bayreuth and that he shared many of her anti-semitic postulates. I pointed out that we, too . . . had drawn attention to the fact that Germans of the Mosaic persuasion were an undesirable and demoralising phenomenon, but said that we wholly disagreed with Wagner and Chamberlain[32] both as to diagnosis and prognosis. . . . These Jews had built up Germany, had contributed much to her power . . . at the cost of the Jewish people as a whole, whose sufferings increased in proportion to its desertion by its most active elements and their absorption by their milieu, while the same milieu later criticises us on account of this very absorption and reacts in the form of anti-semitism. He listened for a long time and was, I assure you, most deeply moved—to the point of tears. . . . He asked me if I wanted anything practical now. I replied that I did not; I only wanted to explain to him how vast and

---

[30] Copy in *Ch.W.P.*

[31] Orig. (in Russian) in Ahad Ha'am archives, Tel Aviv ; Hebrew transl. in *Ch.W.P.* The author is indebted to the executors of Ahad Ha'am for kindly making this document available ; to Mr. B. Schochetmann, of the Hebrew University, for a copy of the full Russian text ; to Sir Leon Simon for his good offices in the matter ; and to Mr. J. M. Japp for the English translation.

[32] Houston Stewart Chamberlain, author of *Grundlagen des Neunzehnten Jahrhunderts.*

deep was the Jewish tragedy, and that I would like to see
him again, if he agreed, when the thunder of the guns had
ceased. . . . In bidding me good-bye, he said with warmth:
" Mind you come again to see me. I am deeply moved and
interested. It is not a dream. It is a great cause, and I understand it." ' [Words from ' Mind you come again ' to ' I understand it ' are in English.]

Weizmann saw Balfour again in March 1915, but no record
of the conversation has come to light, except for a brief allusion
to it in a letter dated 21 March 1915 from Weizmann to Herbert
Samuel: ' I had an opportunity of talking to Mr. Balfour, who
would help us if the situation with regard to France would be
clearer.'[33] Two months later the Asquith Government was reconstructed on a broader basis by the inclusion of a number of leading
Conservatives—among them Balfour, who replaced Winston
Churchill as First Lord of the Admiralty. The Admiralty had
already begun to interest itself in Weizmann's chemical processes,
and in September 1915 he became its Technical Adviser on
acetone supplies,[34] with the result that he now had Lord Balfour
as his official chief. There is no evidence of frequent contact
between them, but, just as Weizmann's work for the Ministry of
Munitions brought him prominently to the notice of Lloyd
George, so his Admiralty appointment helped to keep alive his
relations with Balfour. In March 1916 Mrs. Waldorf Astor[35] gave
a luncheon-party at which Weizmann was to talk about Zionism
to a select company of important persons, among them Balfour.
Mrs. Weizmann records in her diary[36] that he was prevented
at the last moment from being present, ' but he rang up and
expressed the wish to meet Chaim next Sunday evening.' Later
in March, Mrs. Astor brought Weizmann and Balfour together as
her guests at dinner and invited them to talk about Zionism.[37]
    When they next met is uncertain, but at some time in 1916—
probably in the autumn—Weizmann once again found himself at
Carlton Gardens talking to Balfour about Palestine. There appears

[33] Copy in *Ch.W.P.*
[34] Above, p. 118.
[35] Later, Viscountess Astor.
[36] 15 March 1916: *V.W.P.*
[37] Mrs. Weizmann's diary, 25 March 1916: ibid.

to be no contemporary record of the interview, and the fullest
description of it is that given by Weizmann, drawing, presumably,
on his memory, in an article published in *The New Judæa* in
1930.[38] He began, he says, by speaking of the tragic position of
the Jews in Eastern Europe. ' I pointed out to Lord Balfour that
this could not have happened but for the peculiar homelessness
of the Jews. He said: " Christian civilisation owes to the Jews a
debt which it cannot repay. . . . Our religion—our science—our
philosophy—dispersed and scattered as you have been, you have
made a contribution to them all—and what a contribution it is!"'
The conversation, Weizmann writes, then passed to Palestine.
' We talked of English co-operation. He agreed but said that, were
England to assume the responsibility for Palestine, she would be
suspected of seeking territorial aggrandisement . . . ,' to which
Weizmann replied that ' it was a combination of both material
and idealistic motives which would induce England to sponsor
the upbuilding of a national home in Palestine.' Weizmann goes
on to say that Balfour insisted that the United States should be
asked to undertake this task, ' and if she [the United States]
refused to do so alone, possibly England and America might
combine to do it together. . . . He strongly objected to strategic
or other opportunist considerations being brought forward as an
argument for assuming the responsibility for Palestine. . . .'

Balfour long persisted in the view that, if the Americans could
be induced to agree, the sponsorship of a Jewish national home in
Palestine should be undertaken by the United States rather than
by Great Britain. His dismissal of ' strategic or other opportunist
considerations' accords with what Weizmann is reported to have
said on the subject in conversation with Mrs. Dugdale in 1926.[39]
' Whenever during that time I gave him other arguments, or
spoke of things like the effect on American opinion or the value
of Jewish settlement of Palestine to the Empire, he never seemed
to be interested. He made me often ashamed of my niggling
mind.'

Weizmann does not seem to have seen Balfour again until the
end of March 1917. ' For the first time,' he told one of his Zionist

[38] *The New Judæa*, March-April 1930, p. 110.
[39] Conversation recorded by Mrs. Dugdale, 5 October 1926 (*Dugdale
papers*).

colleagues, 'we had a serious talk on practical suggestions connected with Palestine. He gave me a good opening to put before him the importance of Palestine from a British point of view, an aspect which was apparently new to him.'[40] By this time Lloyd George had become Prime Minister, Balfour had moved from the Admiralty to the Foreign Office, and the events which were to lead to the Balfour Declaration were already in train.

Balfour's inquisitive and speculative mind ranged widely over matters remote from politics. In his interest in Zionism there may well have been an element of sheer intellectual curiosity, but there was also a tinge of emotion out of keeping with the generally accepted view of his character and temperament. 'Behind all this glitter lay a hardness,' says one historian, quoting Neville Chamberlain's verdict: 'He always seemed to me to have a heart like a stone.'[41] Another writer has spoken of him as 'never allowing enthusiasm to colour his innate and detached cynicism.'[42] This is not the Balfour who was moved to the point of tears by Weizmann's exposition of the Zionist case at their interview in 1914, nor the Balfour who, in 1917, in conversation with Harold Nicolson, explained his approach to the Jewish question in words like these[43]: 'The Jews are the most gifted race that mankind has seen since the Greeks of the fifth century. They have been exiled, scattered and oppressed. . . . If we can find them an asylum, a safe home, in their native land, then the full flowering of their genius will burst forth and propagate. . . . The submerged Jews of the ghettoes of Eastern Europe will in Palestine find a new life and develop a new and powerful identity. And the educated Jew from all over the world will render the University of Jerusalem a centre of intellectual life and a radiant nurse of science and the arts.' 'Such, more or less,' Nicolson recalls, 'were the exact words he used.' 'I never knew A.J.B.,' Lord Vansittart

---

[40] To Joseph Cowen, 26 March 1917: *Ch.W.P.*

[41] Robert Blake, *The Unknown Prime Minister* (London, Eyre & Spottiswoode, 1955), p. 41.

[42] A. P. Ryan, *History Today*, June 1952, p. 421.

[43] Sir Harold Nicolson in *The Jerusalem Post*, Weizmann Memorial Issue, 2 November 1952.

writes, ' care for anything but Zionism.'[44] The cynic with ' a heart like a stone' was capable of a sensitive understanding of the Jewish predicament and threw himself into the Zionist cause with an ardour in which there was plainly an element of emotion.

Balfour was not moved by any mystical ideas about the return of the Chosen People to the Holy Land, but his niece and biographer, Mrs. Dugdale, testifies to his lifelong interest in the Jews and their history, ascribing this to the early Scottish training which had woven the Old Testament story into the texture of his mind.[45] This at least, widely different as were their origins and backgrounds, he had in common with two others of the architects of the Balfour Declaration—Lloyd George and Smuts. Mrs. Dugdale speaks also of the concern he felt, long before he ever heard of Zionism, about the treatment of the Jews at the hands of the Christian world.[46] ' I remember in childhood,' she writes,[47] ' imbibing from him the idea that Christian religion and civilisation owed to Judaism an immeasurable debt, shamefully ill repaid.' The deep and lasting impression made upon him by his first serious conversation with Weizmann in 1906 is more easily understood when it is remembered that to this extent the ground was already prepared.

There is a legend—but it is only a legend—that at a meeting with George Eliot in 1876 Balfour, then a young man of twenty-nine, applauded the Zionist theme of *Daniel Deronda*. This story is apocryphal,[48] but long before his first contact with Zionism

---

[44] *The Mist Procession* (London, Hutchinson, 1958), p. 232.

[45] Dugdale, *Balfour,* I, 433.

[46] Ibid., II, 216-217.

[47] Ibid., I, 433.

[48] Dr. Gordon S. Haight, of Yale University, to whom the author is greatly indebted for kindly providing him with authoritative information on the subject, has told him that neither in George Eliot's 1876 Journal nor anywhere else in the George Eliot papers is there a reference to anything said by Arthur Balfour about *Daniel Deronda.* How the story originated is not quite clear, but it looks as though it may have been set afloat by an article in the *J.C.* Supplement, June 1931 (reprinted in *The Jewish Annual,* 1947-48, pp. 144ff.). The article was, of course, accepted for publication in all good faith, but the author is informed by Dr. Haight that the writer was drawing on his imagination. The reader will hardly need to be told that this is a subject on which Dr. Haight speaks with unrivalled authority.

Balfour was interesting himself in the Jews. When Lady Battersea, one of the daughters of Sir Anthony de Rothschild, was staying with him at Whittingehame in 1895, they 'talked about J. Morley's and Chamberlain's religious views, also about Claude [Montefiore] and the Jews. . . . [After luncheon] talked again about Claude, whom he wishes to know. After dinner talked a great deal about the Jews, alien immigration, synagogues. . . .'[49]

Balfour's patriotic devotion to his native Scotland and his belief in the virtues of pride of race and country helped to make Zionism intelligible and attractive to him as a movement designed to satisfy aspirations which he was predisposed to regard with respect. Asked at a private gathering a few months after the Declaration about the real motives behind it, he replied: ' Both the Prime Minister and myself have been influenced by a desire to give the Jews their rightful place in the world; a great nation without a home is not right.'[50] In his Introduction to Sokolow's *History of Zionism* (1918),[51] he argues against the anti-Zionists that ' everything which assimilates the national and international status of the Jews to that of other races ought to mitigate what remains of ancient antipathies; and evidently this assimilation would be promoted by giving them what all other nations possess: a local habitation and a national home.' In a conversation recorded by Mrs. Dugdale in 1926[52] he said: ' As you know, I have always been a Zionist, long before the War. Therefore, when the problems of nationalism . . . began to occupy my mind when I was at the Foreign Office during the War, it isn't likely that I would be less keen to satisfy Jewish nationalism than any of the others.' In a memorandum written during the Peace Conference in 1919 he brushed aside the argument that this was not the normal case of a nation seeking the right to live its own life on soil which it already occupied. ' The four Great Powers are committed to Zionism. And Zionism, be it right or wrong, good or bad, is rooted in age-long traditions, in present needs, in future hopes of far profounder import than the desires and prejudices of

---

[49] Diaries of Lady Battersea (8 September 1895). Quoted by Lucy Cohen, *Lady de Rothschild and her Daughters* (London, John Murray, 1935), p. 250.
[50] Meinertzhagen, op. cit. (diary entry 7 February 1918), pp. 8-9.
[51] Sokolow, I, xxxiii.
[52] 16 July 1926, *Dugdale Papers.*

the 700,000 Arabs who now inhabit that ancient land.'[53] ' I was very sympathetic to Arab nationalism, too,' he told Mrs. Dugdale in 1926, ' though I always felt that, as far as Palestine went, Arab claims were infinitely weaker than those of the Jews.'[54]

Zionism appealed to Balfour, not only because he saw in it a national movement at least as worthy of respect as any other, but also because the unhappy history of the Jews seemed to him to give them a special claim to some measure of reparation. When he thought of the wrongs they had suffered at the hands of their persecutors, he was oppressed by a certain sense of guilt, and his passionate advocacy of Zionism is accounted for, at least in part, by the promptings of a troubled conscience. The idea of atonement is brought out strongly in the concluding passages of his speech in the Palestine debate in the House of Lords on 21 June 1922[55]:

> ' Consider whether the whole culture of Europe, the whole religious organisation of Europe, has not from time to time proved itself guilty of great crimes against this race. Surely it is in order that we may send a message to every land where the Jewish race has been scattered, a message which will tell them that Christendom is not oblivious of their faith, is not unmindful of the service they have rendered to the great religions of the world . . . and that we desire, to the best of our ability, to give them the opportunity of developing in peace and quietness, under British rule, those great gifts which hitherto they have been compelled . . . only to bring to fruition in countries which know not their language and belong not to their race. . . . That is the aim which lay at the root of the policy I am trying to defend; and though it is defensible on every ground, that is the ground that chiefly moves me.'

[53] *Documents on British Foreign Policy 1919-1939, First Series* (London, H.M.S.O.), IV, No. 242, p. 345 (11 August 1919). The memorandum continues: ' In my opinion, this is right. What I have never been able to understand is how it can be harmonised with the declaration [i.e., the Anglo-French declaration of November 1918], the Covenant [of the League of Nations], or the instructions to the [American] Commission of Enquiry.' For a discussion of this memorandum see below, pp. 649-650.
[54] See note 52.
[55] O.R., col. 1008-1009.

In an interview, in June 1919, with the American Zionist leader, Justice Brandeis, Balfour approached the subject from a different angle. According to a memorandum by Justice Felix Frankfurter (then Professor Frankfurter), who was present at the conversation,[56]

'Mr. Balfour . . . said the Jewish problem (of which the Palestinian question is only a fragment but an essential part) is to his mind as perplexing a question as any that confronts the statesmanship of Europe. He is exceedingly distressed by it and harassed by its difficulties. Mr. Balfour rehearsed summarily the pressure on Jews in Eastern Europe, and said that the problem was, of course, complicated by the extraordinary phenomenon that Jews are now not only participating in revolutionary movements but are actually, to a large degree, leaders in such movements. He stated that a well-informed person told him only the other day that Lenin also on his mother's side was a Jew.'

After denying the story about Lenin, Brandeis said that he believed 'that every Jew is potentially an intellectual and an idealist and the problem is one of the direction of those qualities. . . . As an American, he was confronted with the disposition of the vast number of Jews, particularly Russian Jews, that were pouring into the United States year by year.' This, he said, had led him to a study of the Jewish question 'and to the conviction that Zionism was the answer.' 'The very same men with the same qualities that are now enlisted in revolutionary movements would find (and in the United States *do* find) constructive channels for expression and make positive contributions to civilisation.' Balfour interrupted to express his agreement, adding: 'Of course, these are the reasons which make you and me such ardent Zionists.'

The Balfour Declaration took shape in the interval between the Russian Revolution of March 1917 and the events immediately preceding the Bolshevik *coup d'état* in the following November.[57] Considering how Czarist Russia had treated its Jews, it is a little surprising that it should have struck Balfour as an 'extraordinary

---

[56] B.F.P., *First Series*, Vol. IV, Appendix (ii), p. 1276 (24 June 1919).

[57] These and all other dates referring to Russian events or documents are those of the Western calendar (*N.S.*).

phenomenon' that many Jews were active, and some were conspicuous, in the revolutionary movements. But Balfour's remark that 'these are the reasons which make you and me such ardent Zionists,' is significant. The events of 1917 made it natural to turn to Zionism as a stabilising force in the Jewish world, and to value it for its power, if given its chance, to provide an antidote to the destructive mania of Jews in rebellion against their lot by offering them a healthy outlet for their frustrated energies. This was part of the case for Zionism as presented at the Peace Conference by Weizmann, who in February 1919 told the Council of Ten that 'the solution proposed by the Zionist Organisation was the only one which would in the long run bring peace and at the same time transform Jewish energy into a constructive force instead of its being dissipated in destructive tendencies or bitterness.'[58] At the time of the Balfour Declaration these ideas were already coming to the fore, but, strongly as they appealed to Balfour in the light of the Russian Revolution, they served only to fortify him in beliefs which on other grounds he had come to hold with firm and, indeed, passionate conviction.

The general nature of these beliefs has already been indicated. It is not altogether surprising that to some Jews they appeared to have disturbing implications. From the conception of a nation without a home might it not be a short step to that of a man without a country? If Zionism was 'the Jewish form of patriotism'—if it was, as Balfour seems to have felt, an expression of Jewish nationalism not essentially different from other national movements—what inferences were to be drawn as to the real, as distinct from the legal, status of Jews who lived, and would continue to live, outside Palestine? Was the true position that, though they might be excellent citizens of their respective countries, patriotism was not to be expected of them, since their real emotional attachment was, or ought to be, elsewhere?

On these matters the views of some other Gentile pro-Zionists come out much more plainly than Balfour's ever did. Josiah Wedgwood declared that 'when a Jew was asked whether he was a Jew, he must be able to reply proudly: "Yes, I am a Jew.

---

[58] *For. Rns. U.S.*, Paris Peace Conference 1919, IV, 164 (27 February 1919).

Palestine is my country . . . and the Lion of Judah is my flag." '[59] Wyndham Deedes wrote disdainfully about Jews who were anti-Zionists from fear of losing their 'acquired nationality' in countries 'where they may happen to reside.'[60] Mark Sykes, Sokolow tells us, 'had no liking for the hybrid type of the assimilating Jew.'[61] Even C. P. Scott, in a letter already quoted,[62] speaks approvingly of the conception of 'the Jew as a whole Jew, with a country and a patriotism to which any other country and any other patriotism will be secondary or adoptive.' There was, in fact, a kind of pro-semitism which to some Jews looked like the opposite—the pro-semitism which put all the emphasis on the distinctiveness of the Jews and seemed almost to imply that emancipation had done them a wrong by blurring their identity as a nation.

Balfour, for his part, seems to have told Weizmann in 1914 that he agreed with some of Cosima Wagner's 'anti-semitic postulates.'[63] All the same, he was not indifferent to the anxieties of the assimilated Jews. 'Doubtless,' he writes in his Introduction to Sokolow's *History*,[64] 'there are difficulties, doubtless there are objections—great difficulties, very real objections. And it is, I suspect, among the Jews themselves that they are most acutely felt.' He goes on to suggest that the fears of the anti-Zionists are baseless, since 'everything which assimilates the national and international status of the Jews to that of other races ought to mitigate what remains of ancient antipathies.' Nevertheless, there is a certain ambiguity in the words with which he ends his Introduction. Zionism, he says, 'will do a great spiritual and material work for the Jews, but not for them alone. For, as I read its meaning, it is, among other things, a serious endeavour to mitigate the age-long miseries created for Western civilisation by the presence in its midst of a Body which it too long regarded as alien and even hostile, but which it was equally unable to expel or to absorb.'

If Balfour became an ardent pro-Zionist it was not simply out

---

[59] *J.C.*, 26 October 1917.
[60] Quoted in *Deedes Bey*, by John Presland (pseud.) (London, 1942), p. 290.
[61] Sokolow, II, xxi-xxii.
[62] Above, p. 132.
[63] Above, p. 154.
[64] I, xxixff.

CHAPTER 10

THE ZIONISTS AND THE ANTI-ZIONISTS

WHAT WEIZMANN CALLED his reconnaissance was already well under way when, at the end of 1914,[1] he was joined by two Russian members of the Zionist Executive, Tschlenow and Sokolow. As a result of the Copenhagen meeting of the Zionist General Council, the Central Office of the Movement had remained in Berlin, but, as we have seen, arrangements had been made for Tschlenow and Sokolow to visit London and then go on to New York. In the end, their American mission was abandoned. Tschlenow, after a few rather unfruitful months in England, went home to Russia. Sokolow remained in England for the rest of the War, and, working closely with Weizmann, played an active and important part in the preliminaries to the Balfour Declaration.

Yechiel Tschlenow,[2] a Russo-Jewish physician of high professional standing, belonged to the small class of Jews privileged to reside in Moscow. After serving for some years on the Zionist General Council, he had been elected a member of the Zionist Executive at the last pre-War Congress in 1913 and had thereupon sacrificed his professional career in order to give whole-time service to the Zionist cause. Though he was highly esteemed in the Movement, he was not a forceful personality. One of his Russian colleagues has described him as a man who ' did not command, but requested, even implored, like a doctor who begs a recalcitrant patient to be reasonable and take his medicine.'[3] In London he was ineffectual, and his six months' work there in 1915 left no visible mark. On returning home, he threw himself into the uphill struggle to keep Zionism alive in Russia under highly adverse conditions. His hour came in 1917, when, as a result of the March Revolution, the Russian Jews were relieved of their

[1] ' The Russians arrive at Newcastle today ': Weizmann to Mrs. Weizmann, 31 December 1914: V.W.P.
[2] 1863-1918. For biographical sketch see Sokolow, II, 281, and obituary in *Zionist Review*, March 1918.
[3] Shm. Levin, *The Arena*, p. 185.

disabilities and Zionism, in common with other Jewish movements, could come freely into the open. The Zionists were now in
a position to assert themselves as a force to be reckoned with in
Russo-Jewish life, and Tschlenow came into the foreground as
their most authoritative spokesman. On a wider stage he became
important soon after the Revolution, when the Zionist leaders in
England were doing their utmost to unite the British, American
and Russian Zionists in a clear demand for British sponsorship of
Jewish aspirations in Palestine. It was largely because of
Tschlenow's doubts as to the outcome of the War, his scepticism
as to British intentions and his nervousness about a breach of
Zionist 'neutrality' that Sokolow was frustrated in his efforts to
bring the Russian Zionists into line. When Tschlenow died before
his time early in 1918, he left an honoured name in the annals of
the Zionist Movement, but, in contrast to Sokolow, who was cast
for one of the leading rôles, he has no notable place in the history
of the Balfour Declaration.

Nahum Sokolow[4] was born in 1860 in a small town in Russian
Poland. At the age of about twenty he moved to Warsaw, where
he started his literary career on the editorial staff of a Hebrew
periodical and gradually built up a reputation not confined to
Eastern Europe but extending to most parts of the Jewish world.
When Herzl appeared on the scene in 1896 with his brochure,
The Jewish State, Sokolow was at first unimpressed by proposals
which he described as 'a fanciful dream.'[5] After attending the
First Zionist Congress in 1897 he changed his mind[6] and from that
time forth identified himself unreservedly with the Zionist Movement. In 1905 he agreed to become General Secretary of the
Zionist Organisation and left Warsaw for Cologne, then the
seat of the Central Office. Discouraged by the defeat of the
'practical' Zionists at the Ninth Congress in 1909, and convinced
that this was a disaster, he resigned his appointment, but when

---

[4] 1860-1936. Biographical details in *J.C.* obituary, 22 May 1936 ; Böhm,
I, 92, 99, 380, 499. There is a penetrating character-sketch by Harry
Sacher in *The New Judæa,* February 1944, reprinted in *Zionist Portraits*
(London, Blond, 1959). A biography by Mr. Florian Sokolow is under-
stood to be in preparation.

[5] *Hazefirah* (Warsaw), 1896, No. 218, quoted by Greenberg, *The Jews in
Russia* (New Haven, 1951), II, 177.

[6] *Hazefirah,* 1897, No. 191 : ibid.

at the Tenth Congress, two years later, the 'practical' Zionists came decisively into the ascendant, he re-entered the whole-time service of the Organisation as a member of the Executive. He was re-elected at the Eleventh Congress in 1913 and was now firmly established as one of the leading figures in the Movement. Until his departure for London at the end of 1914 he was in charge of a department at the Central Office in Berlin, where, notwithstanding that, as a Russian national, he had become an enemy alien in Germany, he was allowed to remain unmolested after the outbreak of war.

Sokolow had had a thorough grounding in the limited range of studies prescribed by tradition for Jews in Eastern Europe. For the rest, he was self-taught, but his native talents, which might have withered in the townlet from which he came, began to flower when transplanted to Warsaw, in those days one of the main centres of Jewish intellectual life. Well before reaching middle age he had built up an established reputation as a man of letters. Though much of his best work was in Hebrew, he was at home in half-a-dozen languages and wrote fluently in all of them—a little too fluently, perhaps, for he had a well-stocked but not a tidy mind, and in the vast mass of his literary output can be found much rambling discourse and many loose ends. Neither as a thinker nor as a stylist was he in the same class as Ahad Ha'am, but he commanded a large popular audience, and among contemporary Jewish writers in Eastern Europe there was none more widely read and admired. By the time he came to London in 1914 he had become an eminent figure in Jewish life, not only as a Zionist leader, but also as one of the best known Jewish littérateurs of his day.

Not only had he raised himself by his own exertions to a prominent position in the Jewish world, but, springing though he did from the Polish ghetto, he had somehow acquired a poise and *savoir faire,* an air of breeding and distinction, which helped him to hold his own in much more sophisticated circles than those into which he had been born. Some may have found him a little tedious; one of them seems to have been Harold Nicolson, who, looking back on many meetings with him at the Foreign Office in 1917, sees him as 'slow, solemn, patriarchal, intense.'[7] Sokolow

[7] *The Spectator*, 3 January 1947.

had none of Weizmann's dynamic quality, but he had certain gifts of a different order which enabled him, on the diplomatic plane, to render valuable service to the Zionist cause, as shown— to take a notable example—by the skill with which, in the spring of 1917, he skated over thin ice on somewhat embarrassing missions to Paris and Rome.

When Sokolow arrived in England at the end of 1914, he was fifty-four and Weizmann was forty. Not only was he much the older of the two, but as a member of the Executive, he was Weizmann's senior in the Zionist hierarchy. He found Weizmann already taking the lead and gaining access to influential circles to which he himself did not penetrate until 1916 or later, and then only because Weizmann had paved the way. In these circumstances, and considering also how widely the two men differed in temperament and training, it was creditable to both, but especially, perhaps, to Sokolow, that they managed during the Balfour Declaration period to work together, not without occasional clashes, but on the whole without serious friction.

Nor should Sokolow's contribution to the partnership be underrated. In 1917 he played a leading part in the framing and submission of proposals for the consideration of the War Cabinet. He represented the Zionists in important discussions with Mark Sykes and Georges-Picot and was charged, among other responsibilities, with the delicate task of sounding the French and Italian Governments and the Holy See. At an earlier stage, when Weizmann had had to give first place to his scientific work for Government Departments, it had often devolved upon Sokolow to hold the fort. He was important also for another reason. He was, and Weizmann was not, a member of the Zionist Executive. As such, he had a measure of formal authority which Weizmann did not possess and did not claim. In May 1917, when a memorandum was being drafted for submission to the British Government, Weizmann agreed with Gaster that Sokolow's signature was essential, observing that 'it is obvious that he [Sokolow] is the only responsible person who is entitled to carry out negotiations on behalf of the whole Movement.'[8] Sokolow was in a position to legitimise Weizmann's free-lance activities, though in endorsing

[8] Weizmann to Gaster, 9 May 1917: copy in *Ch.W.P.* In the end, the memorandum in question was not submitted to the Government.

them he himself had to throw overboard the resolution adopted earlier in the War by the Executive in Berlin purporting to forbid 'negotiations,' as distinct from non-committal contacts, with the Government of any State at war with Turkey. Had Sokolow not been in England and prepared to co-operate, it is at least uncertain how far Weizmann would have felt entitled to go on his sole responsibility.

When Tschlenow and Sokolow came to England at the end of 1914, they had two main objects in view—first, to bring Zionist aspirations to the notice of the British Government and important persons in British public life, and, secondly, to secure as much backing as possible among British Jews.

One of the leading Russian Zionists, Israel Rosoff, happened to be on friendly terms with James Whishaw, an influential member of the British community in Petrograd. Knowing that Whishaw would be in England when Tschlenow and Sokolow arrived there, Rosoff had asked him to do what he could for them.[9] Their modest estimate of their own standing is shown by the fact that, instead of approaching the Foreign Office direct, they thought it better to rely on Whishaw's good offices. He did his best to get them a hearing but was rather coldly informed that 'as the Foreign Office has already in its possession a good deal of information with regard to the Zionist Movement,' Sir William Tyrrell 'does not feel that a personal interview with Mr. Sokoloff and Dr. Tschlenoff would be of advantage at the present time.'[10]

This was only a few days before Herbert Samuel's conversation with Grey on 5 February 1915,[11] when Grey said that 'he [was] still anxious to promote a settlement of the [Palestine] question in a way favourable to Zionist ideas.' This being so, it is at first sight somewhat surprising that the Department showed as little interest as it did in the two Zionist leaders. It seems clear that, although Zionism had engaged Grey's personal sympathy, at a lower level it was not considered to be of much practical importance. A few weeks earlier Tyrrell had been approached by

[9] Rosoff to Whishaw, 22 December 1914 (copy): *N.S.P.*
[10] F.O. to Whishaw, 28 January 1915 (copy): *N.S.P.* Tyrrell was Grey's Principal Private Secretary.
[11] Above, p. 110.

Lucien Wolf, representing the anti-Zionist Conjoint Foreign Committee,[12] and it is at least conceivable—though there is no proof of it—that Wolf had influenced him in an anti-Zionist direction. It is also possible that Sokolow's standing in the eyes of the Foreign Office may have been prejudiced by the fact that he had come straight from the Zionist Central Office in Berlin, where he had stayed on, though a Russian national, after the outbreak of war. Lastly, there may have been lingering memories at the Foreign Office of the supposed association between the Zionists and the Young Turks, and of the dubious behaviour of the Zionist Agency in Constantinople. All this is only conjecture. Whatever the explanation, Sokolow and his colleague were cold-shouldered by the Foreign Office and got no further in their attempts to put their case before the British Government.

In January or February 1915 Sokolow, almost certainly accompanied by Tschlenow, had an interview with Herbert Samuel,[13] but no record of the conversation has come to light. Whishaw seems to have arranged for the two to be received—probably in April 1915—by Lord Cromer, who had come into contact with Zionism when, as British Agent in Cairo, he had had to deal with the El Arish scheme in 1902-1903.[14] There is no contemporary record of the conversation, but, writing some years later, and

---

[12] 'I had a long talk with Mr. Wolf this afternoon. . . . He has been in communication with Sir Wm. Tyrrell, and he understands that the Foreign Office are going to appoint a man specially to deal with Jewish matters. . . . He expressed the view that the British Government would do nothing for the Jews which would irritate the Arabs. . . .': Sacher to Tschlenow and Sokolow, 5 January 1915 (copy): N.S.P.

[13] See Samuel, Memoirs, p. 144. Dr. O. K. Rabinowicz, Fifty Years of Zionism, says (p. 68, note 3) that he understands from Lord Samuel that 'at the end of 1914 all three [Weizmann, Tschlenow, and Sokolow] visited Herbert Samuel, and that conversation, so far as he recollects, was the latter's first serious conversation with Dr. Weizmann about Palestine.' This cannot be correct, since (1) Tschlenow and Sokolow did not arrive in England until 31 December 1914, and (2) by that time Lord Samuel had already had the two conversations with Weizmann (December 10th and 25th) described at pp. 138-139.

[14] On 8 March 1915 James Whishaw wrote to Sokolow: 'I will write to Lord Cromer's son, whom I know very well, and ask him if he can arrange an interview': N.S.P. There is in N.S.P. a copy of a letter (undated) from Cromer to his son, in which Cromer writes that he would be happy to see 'the gentleman mentioned in Mr. Whishaw's letter' after his return to London 'early next month.'

erroneously attributing the interview to December 1914, Sokolow says: ' [Lord Cromer] told us: " It is not necessary to appeal to England—England is favourable to your ideas ; address yourselves to France." '[15]

This, so far as can be ascertained, was the sum-total of what Tschlenow and Sokolow were able to achieve on the political plane. It was not impressive. Had the Foreign Office been less frigid, they might have been better placed for achieving their other main purpose—to strengthen the Zionist position by bringing the Anglo-Jewish community into line in support of an agreed programme.

This meant, first and foremost, coming to terms with the Conjoint Foreign Committee, the recognised spokesman of the British Jews in matters affecting Jewish communities abroad. It was through the Conjoint Committee that the two principal lay organs of Anglo-Jewry—the Board of Deputies of British Jews[16] and the Anglo-Jewish Association[17]—had since 1878 worked together in a sustained effort to secure a more tolerable existence for those Jews, numbering at least seven millions, who in various parts of the world, and more especially in Eastern Europe, were still subject to crippling disabilities. In 1914 the fourteen members of the Committee were drawn without exception from the assimilated Jewish bourgeoisie. They were men who, while they felt themselves firmly rooted in England, were loyal to a well-established tradition which made it incumbent upon British Jews to take up the cause of oppressed or under-privileged Jews in other parts of the world. Not one of them was a Zionist, and most of them—though, as it turned out, not all—were not only outside the Zionist Movement but, for reasons which will appear later, strongly opposed to it.

The British Government had interested itself from time to time in the grievances of Jewish minorities, and as a responsible body backed by Jewish names commanding respect the Conjoint Com-

---

[15] *N.S.P.* The document is a typescript consisting, apparently, of a German translation of a Hebrew essay by Sokolow on Baron Edmond de Rothschild—from internal evidence clearly written not earlier than 1919. For a further reference to Cromer see below, p. 300.

[16] A body of elected representatives of synagogues and other Jewish institutions, founded 1760.

[17] A membership organisation, founded 1871.

mittee had acquired a certain *locus standi* at the Foreign Office. Thus, in 1914-15 the Committee, secure in the belief that it had the ear of the Government, was inclined to deal with the Zionists *de haut en bas*. It was not until considerably later that the Zionists came into the ascendant, while the Conjoint Committee lost ground both because it was opposing a pro-Zionist policy which the Cabinet was inclined to favour, and also because it was embarrassing and irritating the Foreign Office by its insistent pressure for British intervention with the Russian Government in favour of the Russian Jews.

For many years before the War the Conjoint Committee had been mainly concerned with the position of the Jews in Russia and Rumania and had sought by every means at its disposal, but with no perceptible success, to secure the acceptance by the Governments concerned of the principle of equal rights. Soon after the outbreak of war the Committee set up a new department, known as the Special Branch, 'for dealing with the Jewish questions in connection with the eventual reconstruction of Eastern Europe,' and also 'for watching subsidiary Jewish questions arising out of the War.'[18]

The direction of the Special Branch was entrusted to Lucien Wolf,[19] who was to play a leading part on the anti-Zionist side in the feud between the Conjoint Committee and the Zionists which began to develop half-way through 1915 and ended two years later with the discomfiture of the Committee, quickly followed by its dissolution. Wolf was well qualified for his appointment. Born in London in 1857 and educated in Paris and Brussels, he had gained a position for himself in English journalism as a specialist in foreign affairs, and as 'Diplomaticus' of *The Fortnightly* was well known to readers of the serious Reviews. He had also specialised in the Jewish field and had, in fact, begun his newspaper career on the London *Jewish World,* of which he later became Editor.[20] He was not only a distinguished journalist but a scholar whose painstaking study of sources never before fully

---

[18] *The Peace Conference, Paris, 1919 :* 'Report of the Delegation of the Jews of the British Empire' (London, 1920), para. 13. The setting up of the Special Branch was announced in *J.C.* of 22 January 1915.

[19] 1857-1930. Biographical sketch by Dr. Cecil Roth in Introduction to Wolf's *Essays in Jewish History* (London, 1934).

[20] 1906-1908.

excavated had enabled him to throw new light on obscure places in Jewish, and especially Anglo-Jewish, history.[21] He was a skilful —some would have said an astute—negotiator, and his immense store of well-ordered knowledge made him a formidable controversialist. He was fifty-seven when, soon after the outbreak of war, he gave up journalism in favour of whole-time service to the Jewish cause as he saw it and became the mainspring of the Conjoint Committee.

The essence of the Jewish problem, as conceived by the Committee, was simply that some six million Russian Jews— nearly half the Jews in the world—were still denied the equality of status and opportunity which, once conceded, would produce the same beneficent results as had followed from the emancipation of the Jews in the more enlightened parts of Europe. If Russia could only be moved to relieve her Jewish subjects of their disabilities, there might still be some black spots here and there, but the end of the Jewish problem would be in sight.

These were, in substance, the ideas underlying the activities of the Conjoint Committee. To Lucien Wolf their validity seemed self-evident. For him it was axiomatic that the key to the solution of the Jewish problem lay in the emancipation and assimilation of the Jews of Eastern Europe, and equally axiomatic that, bleak though the outlook might appear, this would, in the end, assuredly come to pass. ' The whole tendency of the national life in Eastern Europe,' he wrote in 1915, 'is necessarily towards a more enlightened and liberal policy. . . . It may well take more than one generation to make [the Russian and Polish Jews] as indistinguishably Russian or Polish as their co-religionists in this country or in France are British or French. Of the final result, however, we need have no doubt.'[22] ' Our sole aim and purpose,' he declared, ' is to serve the welfare of our co-religionists by obtaining for them full rights of citizenship in the lands in which they are still oppressed and by protecting them in the enjoyment of such rights where they are already in possession of them.'[23] With this aim and purpose Zionism seemed to him to be in conflict, because its ' national postulate ' implied ' the perpetual

[21] He was the first President of the Jewish Historical Society of England.
[22] C.F.C., 1915/145-146 (April 1915).
[23] Ibid., 143

174

alienage of the Jews everywhere outside Palestine.',[24] and because the Zionists seemed to him to concede and, indeed, to affirm an essential unassimilability of Jews in other countries.'[25] On the view he took, it was clear to Wolf that in looking for ' the eventual establishment of a Jewish nation and State in Palestine, not as a mere spiritual community, but as a political Common-wealth,' the Zionists were not only undermining the case for the emancipation of the Jews in Eastern Europe, but, by playing into the hands of the anti-semites, were imperilling the status of the Jews in countries where their emancipation was already complete[25a]

Hard as they were fought by Wolf, the Zionists had an equally determined and in some respects a still more formidable antagonist in Claude Montefiore. As President of the Anglo-Jewish Association, Montefiore was one of the two Joint Presidents of the Conjoint Committee.[26] By reason of his lofty character, his learning and his philanthropy, and of his high standing and reputation outside as well as inside the Jewish community, he was an important and impressive figure in Anglo-Jewish life and was recognised by the Zionists themselves as an opponent worthy of respect.[27] Like Wolf, he saw in Zionism a capitulation to the anti-semites. Recalling many years later a conversation with Herzl in the early days of the Zionist Movement, ' I rejected the defeatist theory ', he said, ' and I reject it still.'[28] ' I must combat this doctrine of despair,' he declared in 1912. '. . . I still believe that what has happened in England can be even translated into Russian.'[29] ' We know ', he wrote in 1918, ' that the Zionists keep insisting that the Jews . . . even outside Palestine . . . possess a nationality of their own. And we have seen how fully

[24] Ibid., 150.

[25] C.F.C., 1917/169-170 (20 November 1916).

[25a] Ibid.

[26] The other Joint President was D. L. Alexander, K.C., the President of the Board of Deputies.

[27] See, for example, Leon Simon's *The Case of the Anti-Zionists* (London, 1917), p. 9.

[28] Quoted from an address delivered in 1935 in *Some Recollections of C. G. Montefiore*, by Lucy Cohen (London, Faber and Faber, 1940), p. 227.

[29] *Outlines of Liberal Judaism* (London, Macmillan, 1912), p. 296.

the anti-semites agree with the Zionists.'[30] But Montefiore raised
the argument to a higher plane. For him the fundamental objection to Zionism was and had always been that 'the stress . . .
is being laid upon nationality and not upon religion.'[31] 'It is ',
he wrote in 1899, 'the religious factor which must either be the
rock against which Jewish nationalism will suffer shipwreck or
which must itself be ruined in the fray.'[32] Believing as he did in
'the essential universalism of the Jewish religion,'[33] he insisted
that 'we have come forth from the Ghetto to be worldwide and
free ; we cannot again be cribbed and confined by geographical
limitations. . . . If there is still work for the Servant to do, it
can only be if the word " Jew " denotes not a member of a given
nation but a member of a a given religion.'[34]

It is not surprising that an open conflict between the Zionists
and the Conjoint Committee turned out in the end to be unavoidable, but it looked for a time as though a collision might be
averted. When Weizmann and Gaster saw Herbert Samuel in
December 1914, he warned them that the British Government
would not interest itself in any project which was not backed by
Jewry as a whole. Even before this it had been clear to Weizmann
and his friends that it would be essential for the Zionists to
command, and to demonstrate that they commanded, the support
of an imposing body of Jewish opinion not only in England but
elsewhere. It was also clear to them that in any dealings with
the British Government they would be at a serious disadvantage
if they had the leading British Jews against them. This did not
necessarily mean that they must at all costs come to terms with
the Conjoint Committee. Weizmann was not prepared to con-

[30] *The Dangers of Zionism* (London, 1918), p. 9.
[31] Ibid.
[32] *Nation or Religious Community* (London, Jewish Historical Society, reprint, 1917), p. 4.
[33] Ibid., p. 14.
[34] *The Dangers of Zionism*, p. 12. Montefiore was speaking as a Liberal Jew. Though many Orthodox Jews disliked Zionism as much as he did, the view that it was a threat to the Jewish religion was shared neither by the Chief Rabbi, Dr. Hertz, nor by the Haham (the ecclesiastical head of the Sephardic section of the community), Dr. Gaster, both of whom were avowed Zionists.

cede that the Committee was truly representative of Anglo-Jewry, but as a realist he recognised that it could exert some influence and was in a position, if so minded, to be an obstacle to his plans.

He decided, therefore, to sound the Committee, but on the footing that there was no need to go to it cap in hand. Writing on 28 November 1914 to Harry Sacher and Leon Simon,[35] he stated his position with uncompromising frankness: 'The gentlemen of the type of L.W. [Lucien Wolf] have to be told that we and not they are the masters of the situation; that if we come to them, it is only and solely because we desire to show the world a *united* Jewry, and we don't want to expose them as self-appointed leaders. . . . I am going to fight openly *sans trêve*, but before opening the fight we will attempt everything to rope these Jews in and work with them harmoniously. If they don't come they will be removed from their pedestal '—as in the end, in fact, they were.

The soundings had begun, shortly before this letter was written, with an interview on 17 November 1914 between Sacher and Lucien Wolf.[36] The atmosphere was friendly. Wolf's attitude was not discouraging, while Sacher, on his part, assured Wolf that ' we were most anxious, if it were possible, to find some tolerable common ground on which the " leading " Jews and Zionists could unite.' Wolf had his own reasons for being conciliatory. From his point of view, an understanding with the Zionists was clearly to be desired, if it would help, as it might, to head them off from demands which the Conjoint Committee would regard as unwarrantable and dangerous. He told Sacher that on November 12th there had been a meeting of leading British and French Jews; they had talked, he said, among other matters, about Palestine, and ' they are apprehensive that the Powers might give them the terrible gift of Palestine to rule for the Jews.'[37] ' I said,' Sacher writes, ' that I was not a political Zionist, and what I was concerned about was that we should have full liberty to colonise in Palestine and to develop Jewish culture; that we should have the active sympathy of the rulers of Palestine

[35] *Ch.W.P.*
[36] The interview is described in a letter of the same date from Sacher to Weizmann: *Ch.W.P.* The words in quotation-marks are Sacher's.
[37] It is not clear whether these are Wolf's words or Sacher's paraphrase.

in doing so ; and the financial assistance of Western Jewry. Political demands or [*sic*] a Jewish State I should not press for or raise if we could get Jewish unanimity on such a basis as this.' Wolf replied, Sacher reports, that ' he thought that such a programme would be welcomed by the leaders as, among other things, a mode of countering any embarrassing offer of a Jewish State,' adding that ' for such work in Palestine there was more sympathy than we imagined.'

Two points will at once strike the reader—first, that so much was Zionism even then in the air that, when Turkey entered the war, it immediately occurred to the Jewish leaders in London and Paris that the peace settlement might quite possibly include proposals for making Palestine into a Jewish State; secondly, that Sacher made it clear that he, for his part, did not regard a demand for a Jewish State as an indispensable feature of the Zionist programme.

Sacher having broken the ice at his interview with Wolf on November 17th, Weizmann, accompanied by Sacher, saw Wolf a few weeks later and was rather favourably impressed. ' I am very glad,' he wrote to Sacher (17 December 1914[38]), ' that Wolf takes such a reasonable view.' Weizmann's comment on these talks, in a memorandum written early in January 1915, makes it clear that they had left him with the impression that they might lead to an understanding. ' These preliminary conversations,' he remarks, ' yielded one result, namely, that it might be possible under certain conditions to establish an *entente* between the nationalist sections of Jewry and their former opponents, so as to appear before the Powers as a united body.'[39]

This was the stage which had been reached when Tschlenow and Sokolow appeared on the scene at the end of December 1914. They at once asked for a meeting with the Conjoint Committee. They were told that this could be arranged, but it was apparent that, before going further, Wolf wished to pin them down to the programme outlined to him by Sacher in conversation on 17 November 1914, and to extract from them an assurance that it had their imprimatur as members of the governing body of the Zionist Organisation. Sacher told Wolf on their behalf that ' they

[38] *L.S.P.*
[39] Weizmann's January 1915 Report (7 January 1915):*Ch.W.P.*

178

do not think it altogether opportune to put in writing any definite proposals,' but that they would welcome a preliminary exchange of views.[40] Then followed some rather inconclusive bickering between Wolf and Sacher as to what precisely Sacher had said on November 17th, and on whose authority. After a little more preliminary sparring, the Conjoint Committee waived its demand for a written statement of the Zionist proposals, and on 14 April 1915 the two sides met for an unfettered exchange of views.

In the meantime the Conjoint Committee had begun to formulate its own policy on the Palestine question. It looks as though Wolf was anxious to secure the support of Herbert Samuel for the kind of programme which the Conjoint Committee would be prepared to entertain, thus materially strengthening its position in any future dealings with the Zionists. Something has already been said about Wolf's interview with Samuel on 28 February 1915.[41] Wolf propounded the view that ' the " cultural " policy, including perhaps a Hebrew University, free immigration and facilities for colonisation, together with, of course, equal political rights with the rest of the population, should be the limit of our aims at the present time.' Asked whether he agreed, Samuel, according to Wolf, ' answered unhesitatingly " yes." ' A similar programme was proposed by Wolf in a letter dated 2 March 1915 to the Secretary of the Alliance Israélite.[42] Here was the germ of the Conjoint Committee's ' formula,' round which a furious battle was to rage when the controversy between the Committee and Zionists came to a head in the spring of 1917.

The Conference of 14 April 1915 between the Conjoint Committee and the Zionists was unfruitful.[43] The Zionist position was explained at length by Tschlenow, Sokolow and Gaster.[44] Weiz-

[40] Sacher to Wolf, 6 January 1915 (copy): *L.S.P.*
[41] *C.F.C.*, 1915/26ff. See above, p. 108. The words in quotation-marks are from Wolf's note of the interview, which ends: ' The above report has been seen by Mr. Samuel and approved by him.'
[42] *C.F.C.*, 1915/22.
[43] What follows is based on Wolf's report of the proceedings: *C.F.C.*, 1915/156ff. It should be borne in mind that this is not an agreed report, but no other is available. No report from the Zionist side has been found in the *Zionist Archives*. The words in quotation-marks are from Wolf's note and are not necessarily the words actually used by the speaker.
[44] The Zionist representatives included also Joseph Cowen and Herbert Bentwich.

mann was not present; it was just about this time that the Admiralty began to interest itself in his fermentation processes, and his scientific work had now to come first. According to Wolf's record of the proceedings, Tschlenow said that ' there is a good chance that Palestine may fall to England and that England may give the Jews the chance of creating and developing a big [*sic*] Jewish Commonwealth.' Sokolow explained that ' what was anticipated and desired was that England should assume the control and protectorate of Palestine on behalf of the Jews and in order to solve the Jewish problem.' On the question whether any ' special rights ' would be needed for the Jews, Dr. Gaster ' said most frankly that . . . it would be necesary to have those special rights and privileges till the Jews were so numerous . . . that they would predominate by weight of numbers.' After the Zionist representatives had spoken, the Conference adjourned until April 29th, when the Conjoint Committee handed in a written statement of its views.

Why the parties failed to find enough common ground for co-operation can be clearly seen from the Committee's memorandum, read together with the Zionist rejoinder.[45] The Committee insisted that ' the most hopeful solution of the Jewish problem still lies in the direction of civil and political emancipation in lands in which the Jews are persecuted or oppressed.' It denied that Zionism offered any solution ' either by way of appreciably diminishing the number of Jews in Eastern Europe or by abating the rigours of their oppression.' Lastly, the Committee considered that ' the nationalist postulate of the Zionists, and their scheme of special rights for Jews in Palestine[46] [are] calculated to stimulate anti-semitism and to imperil the rights enjoyed by Jews in countries where their political emancipation has already been won.' In their rejoinder, the Zionist representatives expressed the view that ' while . . . civil and political emancipation is a demand of elementary justice in all civilised countries, it cannot be regarded as a solution of Jewish difficulties. . . . Only when the Jewish people is itself emancipated will Jews attain to

45 C.F.C., 1915/166ff. (27 April 1915) ; 170ff. (11 May 1915).
46 The nature of the ' special rights ' in question is not specified either in Wolf's note of the April conference or in the subsequent exchange of memoranda between the two sides.

that status which is necessary to secure for them immunity from persecution. . . .' This required 'the creation of a Jewish centre—a Home for Jews as well as for Judaism—in the old Jewish land.' There was nothing to support the suggestion that 'the "nationalist postulate" of the Zionists, or their scheme of special rights for the Jews in Palestine, is calculated to stimulate anti-semitism. . . . There is abundant evidence that Jewish attempts at assimilation have often been a strong stimulus for anti-semitic agitations.' Finally, the Zionist representatives pointed out that the Conjoint Committee 'ignores the question of its own attitude towards an English Protectorate or other scheme of control of Palestine by the British Government.'

On this last point the Conjoint Committee, in a letter dated 11 June 1915,[47] observed with some hauteur that 'it would be highly inopportune, and even tactless, from the point of view of the harmonious co-operation of the Allies, to raise this question in any formal shape. Moreover, the Committee, as an exclusively British body, cannot well discuss, and still less concert, measures in regard to a question of British Imperial policy with other bodies largely composed of foreign, and to some extent even of enemy alien, elements.' In spite of this rather bellicose paragraph, the letter ends by assuring the Zionists that the Committee 'join in the hope that the progress of events may lead to such an approximation of the views of the two parties as to render some useful scheme of co-operation yet possible.' On this note the exchange of views came to an end, not to be resumed until Weizmann and Wolf met, and failed to agree, in August 1916.[48]

[47] *C.F.C.*, 1915/177-178.
[48] Below, p. 443.

CHAPTER 11

THE ROTHSCHILDS

BY THE MIDDLE of 1915 it had become evident that there was little prospect of an accommodation between the Zionists and the governing circles in Anglo-Jewry. The Chief Rabbi, Dr. Hertz, was a Zionist, and so was Dr. Gaster, the ecclesiastical head of the Sephardic congregations, but from the exchanges between the Zionists and the Conjoint Foreign Committee it was evident that the lay leaders of the community were still unreconciled to Zionism and viewed it with much the same dislike and suspicion as before the War. In this they had with them nearly all the old-established families from which most of them were drawn. But there was one important exception. At the summit of the Anglo-Jewish aristoplutocracy the Zionists found, not merely friends, but active allies among the members of the house of Rothschild.

Not that the Rothschilds were all of one mind. Leopold de Rothschild,[1] who was until his death in May 1917 one of the mainstays of the Conjoint Committee, was vehemently opposed to Zionism. So was his son, Lionel, who, soon after the Balfour Declaration, joined with Claude Montefiore and other leading anti-Zionists in forming the League of British Jews.[2] On the other hand, the senior branch of the family was identified with Zionism through the first Lord Rothschild's elder son and successor, Walter,[3] and his younger son, Charles. Charles Rothschild and his wife had been captured by Weizmann, with the help of Mrs. James de Rothschild, by the middle of 1915.[4] Walter, the

[1] The younger brother of the first Lord Rothschild.
[2] Below, 565-566.
[3] Walter Rothschild (1868-1937) succeeded to the peerage in 1915. It was through him that the Balfour Declaration was formally communicated by the British Government to the Zionists in November 1917. He took no part in the Rothschild banking business and, apart from his public services as a Member of Parliament and the holder of various offices in the Anglo-Jewish community, was best known for his work in zoology, which was recognised by his election as a Fellow of the Royal Society.
[4] Mrs. James de Rothschild to Weizmann, 19 November 1914 ; 7 June 1915 : Ch.W.P.

182

second Lord Rothschild, appears on the scene rather later. Exactly when and how he was moved to take an active interest in Zionism is uncertain.[5] Neither in the Weizmann papers nor, so far as can be ascertained, in the Sokolow papers does his name appear until 14 November 1916, when Weizmann writes to Sokolow[6]: ' Jimmy[7] to-day informed me that on Thursday there will be a lunch at Lady R.'s . . . at which will be present Charles, Lord Walter and [Herbert] Samuel. It will be a Zionist lunch. . . .' That the holder of the Rothschild peerage had identified himself with Zionism did not become generally known until, in *The Times* of 28 May 1917, British Jews, some to their dismay and others to their astonished delight, found Lord Rothschild explaining exactly what it was that ' we Zionists ' desired.

Both Walter and Charles were influenced by their knowledge of the views expressed by their father, the first Lord Rothschild, during the last months of his life. He had had some friendly contacts with Herzl in 1902-1903,[8] but after the collapse of the El Arish project he had shown no further interest in Zionism, dismissing it as an idle dream so long as Palestine was in the hands of the Turks. The idea of a resettlement of the Jews in Palestine seems, nevertheless, to have touched his imagination, and shortly before his death in the spring of 1915 it had become clear that he was prepared to revise his views on Zionism in the light of the changed situation brought about by the War.[9] In this he appears to have been influenced mainly by Herbert Samuel,[10] but he had also been approached in the same sense by his kins-

---

[5] His papers were, in accordance with his directions, destroyed after his death. No relevant papers have been found in the New Court archives.

[6] *N.S.P.*

[7] James de Rothschild.

[8] Herzl, *Tagebücher,* III, 215, 221, 232, 306, 325, 333, 358, 408, 410, 415.

[9] Speaking at the Jewish Board of Deputies on 17 June 1917, his son, the second Lord Rothschild, said: ' I know, as I have read his letters on the subject and heard his statements, that when it was a question of a national home for the Jews under one of the Allied Powers, he was prepared to throw himself wholeheartedly into the question ': *J.C.,* 22 June 1917.

[10] ' As you know, my late father was strongly in favour of Mr. H. Samuel's scheme ': Charles Rothschild to Weizmann, 9 June 1915: *Ch.W.P.* Samuel had seen Lord Rothschild early in 1915: Samuel, *Memoirs,* p. 144.

man, Baron Edmond de Rothschild,[11] the head of the French branch of the family, who, though he did not call himself a Zionist, had supported the Jewish agricultural settlements in Palestine with a lavish munificence to which many of them owed their survival.

Shortly before the War, Weizmann had enlisted Baron Edmond's interest in his plans for a Jewish University in Palestine and had thus become personally known both to the Baron and, through him, to his elder son, James,[12] who had settled in England and had in 1913 married an English-born wife. When Weizmann began to put out feelers in the winter of 1914, one of his first steps was to sound Mr. and Mrs. James de Rothschild. Both of them instantly became his allies[13] and from that time forth placed their contacts and social prestige at the disposal of the Zionist cause. It was thanks largely to them that Weizmann gained the entrée to a world which he might otherwise have found it difficult to penetrate. Charles Rothschild and his wife have already been mentioned. In June 1915 Weizmann heard from Mrs. Charles Rothschild that she had begun to interest Lady Crewe. The Marquess of Crewe had married as his second wife Lady Margaret Primrose. She was the daughter of the fifth Earl of Rosebery by his marriage with Hannah, daughter of Meyer Nathan Rothschild,[14] so that on her mother's side Lady Crewe had family connections which linked her with the Rothschild circle. Weizmann saw her, on Mrs. Charles Rothschild's introduction, in the summer of 1915. She hesitated to commit herself[15] and it was not until after a talk with Baron Edmond some six months later that she was finally won over to the Zionist side.[16] On 20 March 1916, Mrs. Weizmann wrote in her diary[17]: ' Mrs. James [de Rothschild] . . . has been to dinner at Lady Crewe's and over-

---

[11] Mrs. James de Rothschild to Weizmann, 21 March 1915: *Ch.W.P.*

[12] 1878-1957. Born in Paris ; acquired British nationality 1920. M.P. for Isle of Ely, 1929-1945.

[13] Weizmann's January 1915 Report.

[14] An uncle of the first Lord Rothschild.

[15] Mrs. Charles Rothschild to Weizmann, 9 and 29 June 1915: *Ch.W.P.*

[16] Mrs. Charles Rothschild to Weizmann, 13 December 1915: *Ch.W.P.* Her hesitation is rather curious, since Lord Crewe seems already to have expressed some interest in Zionism: see above, p. 111.

[17] *V.W.P.*

heard the conversation between Lord Robert Cecil and Lady Crewe. She asked Cecil what he thought of Zionism and declared that "we all in this house are Weizmannites," and asked whether the time was right to start a Zionist campaign.'

Lady Crewe was not the only one of Lord Rosebery's children to be attracted by Zionism. When Neil Primrose,[18] the younger of her two brothers, was killed in action in Palestine in November 1917, *The Zionist Review* wrote[19]: ' It is no secret that Captain Neil Primrose was much interested in the Jewish National Movement of late years, and that since the War he had, in conjunction with his cousin, Mr. James de Rothschild, followed the progress of Zionist efforts to identify the British Government with the Jewish restoration to Palestine.'

Neil Primrose's first known contact with Zionism was a meeting with Gaster in March 1915.[20] In January 1917, when, because of the energy with which the French were pressing their claims, the Palestine question was coming to a head, Primrose went with James de Rothschild to see C. P. Scott and listened (though apparently without taking part in it) to their discussion of British policy in Palestine.[21] He was at this time a member of the Lloyd George Administration as Joint Chief Whip. Early in April 1917, while still in the Government, he was present, together with (among others) Weizmann, Herbert Samuel and James de Rothschild, at a meeting called to consider, in consultation with an influential American, Norman Hapgood, what could be done in the United States to strengthen the case for a Jewish national home in Palestine under British protection.[22] In the summer of 1917 arrangements were being made for the recruitment of a Jewish infantry unit for service on the Palestine Front. Primrose, who had by this time left the Government to rejoin the Army, on his own initiative associated himself with the project; indeed, there is some evidence that at one stage he himself offered to

---

[18] 1882-1917. Under-Secretary of State for Foreign Affairs, 1915 ; Parliamentary Secretary to Ministry of Munitions, 1916 ; Joint Chief Government Whip, December 1916-May 1917.

[19] December 1917, p. 153.

[20] Weizmann to Tschlenow and Sokolow, 11 March 1915: *Ch.W.P.*

[21] Below, p. 365.

[22] Below, p. 423.

serve as an officer in a Jewish battalion.[23] In the event, he went to Palestine with his own Yeomanry regiment and, at the age of thirty-five, was killed in action during the advance to Jerusalem in November 1917.

Outside their own family circle the Rothschilds began at a very early stage to win friends for Zionism in influential quarters. Two of these call for special mention because of the positions they occupied at the Foreign Office in the year of decision, 1917. In May 1915 Mrs. Charles Rothschild wrote to Weizmann: ' I have had several long conversations with Mr. Theo. Russell, who is staying with us, about the great question. I found him very sympathetic, and he quite agreed that something will have to be done for the Jews and that this is the moment for it.'[24] Russell had just been appointed Diplomatic Secretary to Sir Edward Grey, a post which he retained when Balfour succeeded Grey as Foreign Secretary on the change of Government at the end of 1916.

In August 1915 Mrs. Rothschild arranged for Weizmann to meet Robert Cecil.[25] ' With Lord Robert Cecil,' he wrote to Sacher (21 August 1915), ' I had a very interesting conversation. . . . We spoke chiefly about Palestine, and I tried to make it clear to him that it would be good not only for us but for England and gave him the reasons, which he found " very weighty and serious." '[26] Cecil was at this time Under-Secretary of State for Foreign Affairs. He served in the Lloyd George Administration as Assistant Foreign Secretary and, as Balfour's deputy, was closely concerned with the handling of the Palestine question in the critical months of 1917.

Speaking in 1920 at a Zionist Demonstration in London, Cecil said that he could not recall the details of his first conversation with Weizmann, but ' I know this, that I was a convinced Zionist in opinion before he came, and that, when he left, I was a Zionist by passionate conviction.'[27] Weizmann came away from the inter-

[23] J. H. Patterson, *With the Judæans in the Palestine Campaign* (London, Hutchinson, 1922), pp. 19-21.

[24] *Ch.W.P.*

[25] Mrs. Charles Rothschild to Weizmann, 8 August 1915: *Ch.W.P.*

[26] *Ch.W.P.*

[27] Albert Hall, 12 July 1920. Speeches in full in *Great Britain and Zionism* (London, Zionist Organisation, 1920).

view fully satisfied that Cecil was not only in sympathy with Zionism but was disposed to agree that the building up of a Jewish Palestine under British protection 'would be good not only for us but for England.' When it came to the point, Cecil seems not to have been quite so sure. At the end of the War the British Government had to make up its mind whether to press its claim to the Palestine Mandate. Cecil did not actually oppose that policy, but he acquiesced without enthusiasm, gloomily predicting that because of the tension between Jews and Arabs, 'whoever goes there will have a poor time,' and that the Jews 'are likely to quarrel with the Protecting Power.'[28] However fervently he believed in the justice of the Zionist cause, it seems clear that by the end of the War Cecil had come round to the view that, from a purely British standpoint, the Palestine Mandate must be regarded rather as an inescapable burden than as a coveted prize.

[28] Lloyd George, *Treaties*, II, 1150: see below, pp. 610, 612.

CHAPTER 12

AMERICAN JEWRY

In 1914 there were about three million Jews in the United States
but not more than about 12,000 enrolled members of the Zionist
Organisation.[1] The relatively insignificant number of Zionists is
at first sight surprising, when it is remembered that since the early
1880s some two million Jews had flooded into the country, and that
of these the overwhelming majority were from Eastern Europe. To
Jews of this type Zionism might have been expected to make a
strong appeal. If, up to 1914, only a negligible proportion of them
had actively identified themselves with the Movement, this was
partly because most of them, flung into a highly competitive
society, were absorbed in the day-to-day struggle for existence,
but partly also because many of those who did find time for
dreams were wedded to a Socialist ideology with which Zionism
was, or was thought to be, in conflict. But the membership figures
were even further than they were in England from reflecting the
real strength of Zionist sentiment. The immigrant masses were
not as indifferent as they seemed. When Herzl died in July 1904,
there was general mourning in the Jewish sections of New York.
' I was amazed,' an eye-witness recalls, ' at the almost unanimous
display of sentiment and enquired of the man I was visiting
whether all these people belonged to the Zionist Movement. He
replied that few, if any, of them would so much as buy a
shekel . . . let alone join a Zionist society; nevertheless, the news
of Herzl's death . . . had touched at the hearts of Zionist and non-
Zionist alike.'[2] There was a vast fund of inarticulate sympathy
waiting to be drawn upon when the time came for the Zionists to
appeal to American Jewry for support in the light of the new
situation arising from the War.

The outbreak of war not only threatened the Zionist Movement with disintegration by drying up its resources and dislocating

[1] See above, p. 67. See also Z.C. 1921 Rpts., ' Organisation Report,' p. 113,
where a still smaller figure is mentioned.
[2] Julius Haber in The American Zionist, June 1954.

188

the machinery; the shock to the precariously poised economy of the Yishuv, coupled with the undisguised ill-will of the Turkish Government and its local representatives, could have calamitous consequences for the Jewish settlements and institutions so laboriously built up in Palestine over the past thirty years. When this was brought home to them, a good many American Jews who had, before the War, shown little interest in the abstractions of the Zionist ideology found themselves moving in a Zionist direction. Among the Jews more firmly rooted in American life there were many who still held aloof, but even in these circles the ice began to melt.

Within a few months of the outbreak of war, a newly formed emergency organisation, headed by Louis D. Brandeis, inspired by his personal exertions and fortified by the prestige of his name, had already begun to transform the struggling movement of the pre-War years into a powerful force in American Jewish life.[3] Not that the Zionists had it all their own way. At no time during the War did they command anything like the unanimous support of American Jewry. In January 1918 Brandeis was reported by the British Ambassador, Sir Cecil Spring-Rice, to have told him that the Zionists were ' violently opposed by the great capitalists and by the Socialists, for different reasons.'[4] It could have been added that there were a good number of American Jews of the type broadly represented by the American Jewish Committee— members of the comfortably placed bourgeoisie, but by no means all of them ' great capitalists '—whose attitude towards Zionism, if not positively hostile, showed signs of nervousness and embarrassment.[5] Nevertheless, from the outbreak of war the Zionists were moving into the ascendant, steadily increasing their numbers and attracting allies among Jews who, even though they might not elect to wear the Zionist label, recognised that something of importance to themselves was at stake in Palestine. By the end of 1915 the tide was already flowing so strongly that Lucien Wolf, himself an anti-Zionist, felt obliged to advise the

[3] By the summer of 1919 enrolments had risen to 173,000: de Haas, *Louis Dembitz Brandeis*, p. 70.

[4] Spring-Rice to Balfour, 4 January 1918: *Spring-Rice*, II, 421.

[5] See N. Schachner, *The Price of Liberty* (New York, American Jewish Committee, 1948), pp. 65-66, 68, 70.

British Government, in the light of an objective study of the situation, that 'in America, the Zionist organisations have lately captured Jewish opinion,' and that 'in any bid for Jewish sympathies to-day very serious account must be taken of the Zionist Movement.'[6]

Almost immediately after the outbreak of war, the Federation of American Zionists called an Extraordinary Conference to consider what could be done in the United States to tide the Movement over the emergency. The Conference met in New York on 30 August 1914 and resulted in the setting up of an *ad hoc* body under the name of 'The Provisional Executive Committee for General Zionist Affairs,' with Brandeis as Chairman. The words 'General Zionist Affairs' were significant. The functions of the Provisional Committee, as originally conceived, are explained in a statement issued by Brandeis after his acceptance of the Chairmanship:

> 'The members of our Actions Comité are scattered. Our Central Bureau in Berlin is crippled. The Federations of England, Germany and Austria are partially or wholly disabled. The Zionists of those countries and of Russia are bound to take thought for themselves alone. At an Extraordinary Conference . . . held in New York . . . a Provisional Executive Committee for General Zionist Affairs was formed to act until such time when the Actions Comité shall re-assemble . . . .'[7]

On the assumption that the normal machinery of the Zionist Organisation had come to a standstill, the Provisional Committee was prepared to take control and to become responsible, for the time being, for the central direction of the Movement. Towards the end of 1914 it suggested to the Zionist Executive in Berlin that the headquarters of the Organisation should be transferred to the neutral United States.[8] Weizmann, as we have seen, was disposed at the time to favour this idea, believing it to be essential

6 *C.F.C.*, 1916/119 (16 December 1915).
7 *Brandeis on Zionism* (Washington, Zionist Organisation of America, 1948), pp. 46-47.
8 *Z.C. 1921 Reports*, 'Organisation Report,' p. 28.

that the Movement should neither be nor appear to be directed from Berlin, and that the best alternative was New York. But nothing came of the American proposal. The Copenhagen meeting of the Zionist General Council in December 1914, though it was agreed that there must be some decentralisation, ended with a decision to leave the headquarters in Berlin. The New York Committee did not press its point. It had advocated the transfer on the assumption that the European organs of the Movement would be paralysed, but it became apparent that it had taken too alarmist a view, and in a report issued in March 1915 it noted with relief that ' in spite of the War, the Inner Actions Comité and the general organisations in the several countries [have] been able to continue, or to resume, to a far greater extent than we had deemed possible their activities in Zionist affairs.'[9]

The rôle which the Provisional Committee was called upon to play was not precisely that originally conceived for it, but it was fortunate for the Zionist cause that it was brought into existence. It was due largely to its exertions, and to its success in enlisting the benevolent interest of the United States Government, that the Jewish population of Palestine was preserved from the disasters which would almost certainly have overwhelmed it had it been left without generous benefactors and powerful friends in the critical period which followed the entry of Turkey into the War. ' From the day when war broke out,' said a report submitted to the 1921 Zionist Congress,[10] ' Palestine had appealed to America for help. America was at that time the one country which, through its political and financial position, was able to save Palestine from permanently going under.' Though there was generous assistance from outside the Zionist ranks, the mainspring of the American effort was the Provisional Executive Committee. But the Committee was much more than a relief agency. It was under its guidance, and as a result of its energetic and intelligent propaganda, that the Zionist Movement in the United States began to build up the mass support which it had hitherto lacked. Nor was it only a question of numbers. The Committee succeeded in kindling the imagination of the Jewish masses, but it also attracted from a very different milieu supporters of the quality

9 Copy in *N.S.P.*
10 ' *Palestine Report,*' p. 16.

and standing of men like Felix Frankfurter[11] and Julian W. Mack.[12]

This hastily improvised body could never have accomplished what it did without outstanding leadership. It was to its immeasurable advantage that it had for its first Chairman so commanding a personality as Brandeis.

When he agreed to head the Committee, Brandeis, then in his fifty-eighth year, was committing himself for the first time to an active part in Jewish affairs. Until he became interested in Zionism, his whole life, he told Balfour at their interview in 1919,[13] 'had been free from Jewish contacts or traditions.' In a passage already quoted, in another context, from Felix Frankfurter's note of the conversation, Brandeis explains that he had first become interested in Zionism when, 'as an American, he was confronted with the disposition of the vast numbers of Jews, particularly Russian Jews, that were pouring into the United States.'[14] A Zionist pamphlet which happened to come his way led him, he says, to a study of the Jewish problem and to the conviction that Zionism was the answer.

He had come to Zionism, he told Balfour, 'wholly as an American.' This note is struck again and again in his war-time speeches as Chairman of the Provisional Committee. Some of them are in curious contrast to the views he had held earlier in his career. In an address delivered in 1905 he said:

> 'There is room here for men of any race, of any creed, of any condition in life, but not for Protestant-Americans or Catholic-Americans or Jewish-Americans, nor for German-Americans, Irish-Americans or Russian-Americans. . . . Habits of living or thought which tend to keep alive differences of origin, or to classify men according to their religious beliefs, are inconsistent with American ideals of brotherhood and are disloyal.'[15]

[11] Later, Justice Frankfurter of the U.S. Supreme Court.
[12] Judge of the U.S. Circuit Court of Appeals.
[13] *B.F.P., First Series,* Vol. IV, Appendix (ii), pp. 1276ff.
[14] Brandeis seems to have been alluding to his experiences as a mediator in the Garment Workers' strike of 1910: see A. T. Mason, *Brandeis* (New York, Viking Press, 1946), p. 442 ; R. Learsi, *The Jews in America* (Cleveland and New York, World Publishing Company, 1954), p. 158.
[15] Quoted by Mason, op. cit., p. 442.

Ten years later he was saying almost the opposite:

> 'Every Irish-American who contributed to advancing Home Rule was a better man and a better American for the sacrifice involved. Every American Jew who aids in advancing the Jewish settlement of Palestine . . . will likewise be a better man and a better American for doing so.'[16]

Brandeis developed this theme in many others of his war-time speeches. 'My approach to Zionism was through Americanism. . . . Gradually it became clear to me that to be good Americans we must be better Jews, and to be better Jews we must become Zionists.' 'Loyalty to America demands . . . that each American Jew become a Zionist. For only through the ennobling effects of its stirrings can we develop the best that is in us and give to this country the full benefit of our great inheritance.' 'The Jewish renaissance in Palestine will help us to make toward the attainment of the American ideals of democracy and social justice that large contribution for which religion and life have peculiarly fitted the Jew.' 'Let no one of you, if he be a true American, shirk his duty.'[17]

What Brandeis was saying was that, far from its being the duty of American Jews to be unhyphenated Americans, they owed it to America as well as to themselves to preserve their distinctive identity. 'Assimilation,' he declared in 1915, 'is national suicide.' And 'assimilation cannot be averted unless there be re-established in the fatherland a centre from which the Jewish spirit may radiate and give to the Jews scattered throughout the world that inspiration which springs from the memories of a great past and the hope of a great future.'[18]

The heavy emphasis on Americanism does not, at first sight, cohere comfortably with the equally emphatic rejection of assimilation and seems to point to some sub-conscious tension. Perhaps Brandeis' real reasons for becoming a Zionist were not exactly what he thought they were. It almost looks as though, having felt the impact of Zionism as an emotional experience, he may have been trying to rationalise his feelings and to state the

16 From extracts from speeches 1914-15, quoted by de Haas, op. cit., p. 169.
17 *Brandeis on Zionism*, pp. 29, 49–50, 54, 88.
18 *The Menorah Journal* (New York), Vol. I, No. 1, January 1915.

Zionist case in a form adapted to the conditions of American life at a time when there seemed to be a place and, indeed, a need for the 'cultural pluralism' of which his close friend, Norman Hapgood, was a leading advocate.

For Brandeis, an American rooted in and deeply attached to his native country,[19] it was clearly impossible to see the Jewish question with the same eyes as a Russian or Rumanian Jew who had no such roots and knew no such loyalties. Fervently as he identified himself with Zionism, his approach to it was not and could not be the same as that of Jews of the type which predominated in the Movement and provided most of its leaders. In the end, the latent conflict came to the surface and worked up to a climax in 1921, when, after a fierce struggle between opposing groups of Zionists, Brandeis, together with most of his closest and most distinguished American associates, was swept aside. By this time growing differences between Brandeis and other Zionist leaders on various questions of policy had widened into an open breach. But this was after the War. In the war-years, Weizmann and Sokolow in London and Brandeis in Washington together represented *de facto* the main directing force of the Movement, except so much of it as recognised the jurisdiction of the rump Executive in Berlin.

Brandeis first began to interest himself in Zionism in 1910. He joined the Federation of American Zionists towards the end of 1912 and made his first appearance on a Zionist platform early in 1913.[20] But at the outbreak of War he was not generally regarded as a Zionist leader—still less as one of the leaders of American Jewry. When, in August 1914, he became Chairman of the Provisional Committee, his spectacular identification with Zionism impressed the Jewish community all the more because he had not involved himself in its domestic affairs but had made his name on the larger stage of American public life. He had already risen to a position of the highest eminence at the Bar and was before

[19] He was born at Louisville, Kentucky in 1856 of foreign-born parents.
[20] de Haas, op. cit., p. 57 ; Mason, pp. 443-444 ; *Brandeis on Zionism*, p. 37.

long to become a Justice of the Supreme Court.[21] But he was much more than a successful lawyer. He had a highly developed social conscience and had fought the trusts and monopolies with a zeal which had brought him into disfavour with some sections of the élite but had made him a national figure as 'the people's attorney.' By 1914 he had become known throughout the country as a great Liberal, humanitarian and social reformer.

In politics Brandeis had started as a Republican, but he had broken away from his Party and, after veering towards La Follette's Progressive Republicanism, had eventually come down on the Democratic side as a supporter of Woodrow Wilson in the presidential campaign of 1912.[22] He was recognised as an important recruit and was considered for office when the time came for President Wilson to select his first Cabinet.[23] Faced with strong opposition from various quarters—some of it from the moneyed interests and some of it of an anti-semitic hue[24]—Wilson decided at the last moment to drop Brandeis from his list. Brandeis never held political office, but his association with Wilson developed into a relationship which gave him an influential position as one of the President's most highly esteemed unofficial advisers.[25] In 1916, when Wilson, having nominated Brandeis to fill a vacancy in the Supreme Court, was encountering some opposition in the Senate, he wrote in support of the appointment:

> 'I have known him. I have tested him by seeking his advice upon some of the most difficult and perplexing public questions about which it was necessary for me to form a judgment. I have received from him counsel, singularly enlightened,

---

[21] After his elevation to the Supreme Court in the summer of 1916, Brandeis resigned the Chairmanship of the Provisional Committee and was succeeded by Rabbi Stephen Wise. He accepted the title of Honorary President and continued to take an active interest in the work of the Committee.

[22] Mason, op. cit., p. 376.

[23] Ibid.; A. S. Link, *Wilson, the New Freedom* (Princeton University Press, 1956), pp. 10ff., 13ff.

[24] Mason, op. cit., p. 387.

[25] '[Brandeis] wielded a large influence on the formulation of domestic policies because he was one of the few persons in the country whose judgment on economic questions the President respected': Link, op. cit., p. 95.

singularly clear-sighted and judicial and, above all, full of moral stimulation . . . .'[26]

When the nomination had at length been approved by the Senate and Wilson was free to proceed with the appointment, he wrote to Henry Morgenthau: 'I never signed any commission with such satisfaction.'[27]

That Brandeis stood high in Wilson's confidence and esteem was common knowledge, and in the eyes both of the Zionists and of other interested observers this gave an added significance to his assumption of the Zionist leadership in the United States. The prestige of his name, enhanced by his close relations with the President, was an asset of which full use was made by the Zionist leaders in London in their dealings with the British Government. His reputation as one of Wilson's most trusted advisers materially influenced the course of events in so far as it improved the standing of the Zionists and gave them an added claim to attention.[28] But, surprising as it may appear, it seems clear that when, early in September 1917, Wilson was first sounded by the British War Cabinet as to his views on a pro-Zionist pronouncement, he looked for advice, not to Brandeis, but to his still more intimate confidant, Colonel House. After consultation with House, he sent a discouraging reply to which Brandeis cannot possibly have been a party. On the other hand, there is reason to believe that Brandeis had something to do with Wilson's second thoughts when a further enquiry on the same subject reached Washington from London a few weeks later. This time Wilson let it be known, through House, that he would favour the proposed British

[26] President Wilson to Senator Culbertson, 5 May 1916. Quoted by Mason, op. cit., p. 499.

[27] R. S. Baker, *Woodrow Wilson, Life and Letters* (London, Heinemann, 1937), VI, 116.

[28] There is an absurd myth to the effect that in the autumn of 1916 the British Government caused it to be intimated to Brandeis that it would undertake to do something for the Jews in Palestine in consideration of Brandeis' using his influence with the President to bring the United States into the War. This 'silly nonsense' (Justice Frankfurter to the author, 8 December 1952) appears to have been hatched in the inventive mind of James Malcolm, as to whom see below, pp. 363-364.

declaration. It seems to have been House who finally persuaded him to assent, but in the interval between the two British enquiries Brandeis had intervened to some purpose, though it looks as though his influence had been exerted through House rather than by a personal approach to the President.[29]

Weizmann and his London colleagues had hoped that Brandeis would be able to induce Wilson actively to press their case on the British Government. This did not happen, but in so far as Brandeis helped to swing Wilson from discouragement to approval of a British assurance to the Zionists, he rendered a signal service to the Zionist cause. Wilson's September message had come near to killing the Balfour Declaration.[30] Had his reply to the second British enquiry been equally chilling, it is quite possible that the Declaration would never have seen the light.

Brandeis had in his youth studied for a short time at Dresden, and his contact with the Germany of the 1870s, exulting in the recent triumphs of her war-machine, had left him with a deep-seated fear of Prussian militarism.[31] When war broke out in 1914, his personal sympathies were from the start unreservedly with the Allies. The same was true of most of his principal lieutenants— notably the British-born Dr. Richard Gottheil, Jacob de Haas (likewise British-born), Rabbi Stephen Wise and Felix Frankfurter.

Among the leading American Zionists there were only two who are known to have felt differently. One of these was Dr. Judah Magnes, of whom his biographer writes that 'he had, from his American background, a deep distrust of British Imperialism and, from his Jewish background, a hatred of Russian tyranny. The alliance of England and France with Russia . . . seemed to him unholy.'[32] Having quarrelled with Brandeis, though on a different issue, Magnes resigned from the Provisional Executive Committee in September 1915 and thereafter went his own way, to become

[29] The facts on which this paragraph is founded are set out and discussed below, pp. 506-508, 529-530.

[30] Below, pp. 505, 510.

[31] Justice Frankfurter to the author, 8 December 1952.

[32] N. Bentwich, *Judah L. Magnes* (London, East & West Library, ?1955), p. 97.

an embarrassment to the American Jewish community, and more particularly to the Zionists, by persisting in pacifist propaganda even after the United States had entered the War.

Magnes' coldness towards the Allied cause was shared by Dr. Shmarya Levin, the only member of the Zionist Executive who was in the United States during the War. For Levin, as for Magnes, Russia was the enemy, but he may well have been influenced also by his recently acquired Austro-Hungarian nationality and, still more, by his German education and his long residence in Berlin. It was not long before it became apparent to his colleagues that his sympathies were not with the Allies, and by the middle of the War he was showing openly where they lay by contributing to *The American Jewish Chronicle*, which was known by all well-informed persons to be a subsidised organ of German propaganda. Though Levin was not, strictly speaking, a member of Brandeis' Provisional Committee, he had helped to organise it and was, indeed, treated at the beginning as sharing responsibility with Brandeis. But he soon ceased to have any real influence on policy. Writing privately to Weizmann in December 1915, Kallen,[33] one of the associate members of the Provisional Committee, told him that '[Levin's] chief value has been that of an agitator rather than that of a responsible executive leader.' In view of 'the general attitude of Dr. Levin on the issues of the war,' Kallen agreed that Weizmann had done wisely in ceasing to correspond with him and went on to point out that 'if you will examine the personnel of the Committee, both the regular members and associate members, you will notice that there is not a single one whose personal sympathies are not definitely with the forces of democracy.'[34]

It was not only in Zionist circles that the Allied cause commanded the sympathy of leading American Jews. Writing to the Conjoint Foreign Committee in May 1916, Louis Marshall, the President of the American Jewish Committee, took occasion to assure his friends in London that he and many of his colleagues were whole-heartedly on the side of the Entente: 'While there is doubtless a division of sentiment among the members of our Committee, acting in their private capacities, the majority of its

[33] Dr. H. M. Kallen, of the New School for Social Research, New York.
[34] Kallen to Weizmann, 16 December 1915: *Ch.W.P.*

most influential members are strongly pro-Ally in sentiment. I may say that, personally, there is no member of the Committee who more strongly adheres to the cause of the Allies than I do.'[35] At the same time, Marshall made it clear that there could be no question of any open demonstration of sympathy with the Allies. In the interests of the Jews directly affected by the War (and also, it may be suggested, because of the neutral position of the United States and the neutral behaviour officially enjoined upon responsible citizens), ' the Committee has deemed it to be a sacred duty to refrain from doing aught that would indicate partisanship, in so far as the American Jews are concerned, with respect to the conflict which is now in progress.'[36]

For similar reasons, the Zionist leaders in the United States, irrespective of their personal views, felt obliged to adhere to the principle of neutrality. They were, indeed, under a still more compelling inhibition. If the American Zionists openly identified themselves with one group of belligerents, this would not only tend to undermine still further the already precarious unity of the Zionist Movement, but might seriously compromise the position of the Jews in Palestine. Hence it was that, at the end of 1915, when preparations were begun, under Zionist leadership, for the organisation of a representative American Jewish Congress, Brandeis declared that the Preparatory Committee ' maintains a strict neutrality towards the nations now at war.'[37] As late as January 1917 Gottheil was severely criticised at a meeting of the Provisional Executive Committee for having attacked the Turkish Government in *The New York Times,* thus violating the rule of neutrality, which was still, it was insisted, as binding as it had always been.[38]

While both Brandeis and Marshall felt that open partisanship would be inconsistent with their public duty, both were at heart unreservedly on the side of the Allies. But it must not be supposed that they, and those who shared their views, represented the prevailing mood in American Jewry. On the contrary, they were swimming against the stream. For the vast majority of the

[35] *C.F.C.* 1916/252 (15 May 1916).
[36] Ibid.
[37] *J.C.*, 26 November 1915.
[38] P.E.C. Minutes, 10 January 1917: *Brandeis Papers.*

American Jews one simple fact was decisive: one of the partners in the Entente was Russia. Of the three million Jews in the United States, by far the greater part were immigrants, or the children of immigrants, who had escaped during the past thirty years from the Russian ghetto. Many of them had their own resentful memories of what it meant to live as a Jew in the Pale of Settlement. Most of them still had near relatives in Russia, where a large part of the Jewish population was now in the war zone and exposed to the uncouth brutality of the Russian High Command. With this they were invited by pro-German propagandists to contrast the German General Staff's studiously correct treatment of the Jews in the occupied territories in Russian Poland.[39] All of them to a man saw Czarist Russia as the enemy and prayed for the War to end with the downfall of their oppressors. Nor were they interested only in seeing their enemies brought low. For the sake of their kinsmen still living in the Pale they had solid practical reasons for praying that Russia might be defeated. If she were, this would almost certainly mean that Russia would lose to Germany precisely those Russian or Russo-Polish territories in which the bulk of the Jewish population was concentrated. Germany might have no particular love for her Jews, but if a Jew were asked whether he would rather live under the Kaiser or the Czar there could be but one answer. A French Jew, Professor Victor Basch, who, towards the end of 1915, went to the United States in the interests of French propaganda, reported that on this point Jewish opinion, as reflected in the Yiddish press, was unanimous and emphatic.[40]

Thus, for the overwhelming majority of the American Jews the Front which mattered was the Eastern Front. What really interested them and engaged their emotions was the struggle between Germany and Russia. It would not be quite accurate to say that the Jewish masses in the United States were pro-German. Had the War been a duel between Germany and Great Britain, or between Germany and France, there is no reason to suppose that their sympathies would have been on the German side. They well

[39] As to the behaviour of the Germans, see interview with B. Goldberg in *J.C.*, 22 October 1915.

[40] *C.F.C.* 1916/193 (undated extract from letter from Basch to the French parliamentarian, Marius Moutet).

knew that the Western Allies, and especially Great Britain, had much stronger claims on their goodwill than the Kaiser's Germany. A Jewish writer of the day was at pains to point out that ' the headlines of [the Yiddish] newspapers do not celebrate German victories—they celebrate Russian defeats.'[41] But the distinction was a fine one. Those who desired Russian defeats desired German victories, and to them it made little difference that Germany was also at war with Great Britain and France, which, compromised by the Russian alliance, were held to have a measure of guilt by association.

Of the American Jews who had no personal ties with Eastern Europe a large proportion were of German origin or descent. Swamped by the immigrant masses, the German Jews had by 1914 shrunk to a small minority, but they had had time to become integrated in American life and, retaining the prestige attaching to their superior social status, still provided American Jewry with a large part of its recognised leaders. Their feelings about Russia were what those of any Jew were bound to be, but besides this there was the pull of the ties which many of them still had with Germany because of the memories of their early years or because of still existing family connections and the business interests often interwoven with them. Some of them were not merely anti-Russian but frankly pro-German. Others, in spite of their antipathy to Russia and their own German associations, sided with the Allies. Others, again, started as out-and-out pro-Germans but had second thoughts and began to waver.

Of these last an outstanding example was Jacob Schiff, the senior partner in the eminent banking firm of Kuhn, Loeb and the most influential figure of his day in American Jewish life. In April 1915 Schiff wrote in *The Menorah Journal*: ' It is well known that I am a German sympathiser. . . . England has been contaminated by her alliance with Russia. . . . I am quite convinced that in Germany anti-semitism is a thing of the past.' By the second year of the War he was already modifying his views. In December 1915 he declined to support the German-American Literary Defence Committee, explaining that, although ' my sympathies for the land of my birth are as warm as anyone's. . . . I cannot sanction some of the things to which officers of your

[41] H. M. Kallen in *The Menorah Journal*, April 1915.

Committee have given public expression.'[42] How completely he came to reverse his position is shown by a letter in which, in March 1917, he opened his mind to his friend, Charles W. Eliot, the President of Harvard: 'Ever since the sinking of the Lusitania and the subsequent ruthless and inhuman acts of the German Government my attitude has undergone a thorough change, and I now only hope that before very long Great Britain and France will be able to force a peace which shall prevent the return of conditions that have brought upon the world the present ghastly situation.'[43]

In some British circles the idea seems still to have persisted that Schiff was incurably pro-German. In a memorandum written in July 1917 Mark Sykes, discussing the forces working, as he believed, for a soft peace with Turkey, refers disdainfully to ' the Lucien Wolf and Jaky Schiff anti-Zionists,' describing them as ' Russophobe pro-Turks who have become pro-German and now are definitely fixed in that camp.'[44] Incensed by the opposition to Zionism in certain Jewish circles, Sykes was evidently carried away by his indignation. At the time they were made, his remarks had as little application to Schiff as they would have had at any time to Lucien Wolf. From the moment the United States entered the War, Schiff had, as in duty bound, backed his country's war effort to the full extent of his influence and resources and had done so all the more whole-heartedly because by this time the Czarist régime, and all that it had meant for the Russian Jews, had been swept away by the March Revolution. But, as we have seen, Schiff's change of heart had, in fact, begun a good deal earlier. Far from being in the pro-German camp in July 1917, he had begun moving out of it while the United States was still neutral and while the Czar was still on the throne.

The fact remained that Germany had ready-made friends among the German Jews in the United States, and that any attempt to win the sympathies of American Jewry for the Allied cause had to contend, not only with the emotional hatred of Russia which all American Jews had in common, but also with the pro-German sentiments of a relatively small but influential

[42] Cyrus Adler, *Jacob H. Schiff* (London, Heinemann, 1929), II, 192.
[43] Ibid., II, 201.
[44] *Sledm.*, No. 44 (29 July 1917).

minority. The picture changed with the American declaration of war on Germany, which happened to coincide almost exactly with the March Revolution in Russia, but in the earlier stages of the War it would have been broadly true to say that the American Jews—not, indeed, without some important exceptions—looked coldly on the Allied cause.

The British Ambassador in Washington, Sir Cecil Spring-Rice, was convinced that American Jewry was on the side of Germany and said so plainly and resentfully both in reports to Grey and Balfour and in private correspondence. ' Dernburg[45] and his crew,' he told Sir Valentine Chirol[46] (13 November 1914), ' are continually at work, and the Germans and the German Jew bankers are toiling in a solid phalanx to compass our destruction.' On the same date he wrote in a similar strain to Sir Edward Grey: ' The Jews show a strong preference for the Emperor, and there must be some bargain.' A year later he was telling a private correspondent that the German element in the United States had for thirty years been consolidating its position, and ' the active co-operation of the Jews has very much assisted in the process.' In January 1916 he wrote despondently to Grey: 'All the enemies of England have been marshalled against us, and the Irish have lent their unequalled power of political organisation to Jews, Catholics and Germans.' Reporting to Balfour a few weeks after the Balfour Declaration, he remarked ironically: ' It was not the general impression here that Jews and Catholics were to be counted as our best friends. The result of the capture of Jerusalem has been to reveal the fact that throughout the War they have been panting for our success and are now eagerly and confidently expecting their reward.'[47]

Spring-Rice's rather crudely coloured picture was in some respects misleading. The impression he gave was that, from a British point of view, the whole American Jewish community must be written off as irreconcilably hostile, and that its leaders

---

[45] Dernburg, a former Colonial Minister, was in charge of German propaganda in the United States. He was a half-Jew by birth but had never considered himself a Jew.

[46] Director of the Foreign Department of *The Times* from 1899 to 1912.

[47] *Spring-Rice*, II, 242, 245, 285, 309, 373.

must be assumed to be playing deliberately into Germany's hands. He made no allowance for the intensity of anti-Russian feeling among the American Jews or for the effect which this might have had in determining their view of the War. On these points the balance was to some extent redressed by various references to the Jews in a series of reports on the state of American opinion prepared in London, for the information of the British publicity services, in the light of material received from British or pro-British sources in the United States. There were warnings against the mistaken idea that the coolness of the Jews towards the Allied cause could be accounted for simply by a tenderness for Germany skilfully exploited by German propaganda. Speaking of the treatment of the Jews in the Russian war zone, a report compiled in April 1915 commented that ' the cumulative effect of these revelations has been extensive not only upon Jewish opinion in America but on American opinion as a whole.' In February 1916 a well-informed observer in the United States was quoted as saying on the same point that he 'knew many Americans both Jew and Gentile who felt very strongly on this matter although . . . wholly uninfluenced by German propaganda.' The same report, dealing generally with the strength of anti-Russian sentiment in the United States, observed that 'German agents have sedulously fostered it, but . . . its importance must be attributed not solely, perhaps not even principally, to this cause.' It would almost certainly be true to say that, had there been no German propaganda at all, the presence of Russia among the Allies would have been enough of itself to deter the great majority of the American Jews from supporting the Allied cause and to drive some of them in the opposite direction. But German agents were, in fact, energetically at work and making the most of their advantages. Russia's black record in the past, her treatment of the Jews in the War zone, the contrast between Russian inhumanity and the well-publicised good behaviour of the Germans in occupied Poland—all this was nourishing diet for the German propagandists. But even this was not the whole of their case. The American Zionists and those in sympathy with them could be invited to reflect upon what the Germans could do and, in fact, were doing to restrain their Turkish allies from working their will on the Jews in Palestine. More than that, there were vague suggestions that a victorious Germany, with the Turks securely in tow, would be relied upon not to overlook Zionist aspirations. It was largely, though not exclusively, in the interests of their propaganda in the United States that at a very early stage of their political warfare the German authorities began to concern themselves with Zionism, in response to approaches made to them by the Zionist Central Office in Berlin and its annexe, the Zionist Agency in Constantinople.

ZIONIST MOVES IN BERLIN AND CONSTANTINOPLE

THE CENTRAL OFFICE of the Zionist Organisation remained throughout the War in Berlin and, after the departure of Sokolow and Tschlenow at the end of 1914, was directed by the two German members of the Executive, Professor Otto Warburg and Dr. Arthur Hantke. They worked in close association with Victor Jacobson—the third member of a triumvirate which, because Berlin was still the official seat of the Zionist Executive, claimed to represent the lawfully constituted governing body of the Movement.[2]

Jacobson, who was of Russian origin but seems somehow to

---

[1] The author desires to acknowledge his indebtedness to Mr. Richard Lichtheim for much valuable information concerning the war-time relations between the Zionist Movement and the Central Powers. Mr. Lichtheim, a German Zionist, who was for many years an important figure in the Zionist Organisation, was in Constantinople as a representative of the Berlin Executive from the outbreak of war in 1914 until the spring of 1917. He was then transferred to the Berlin Office, where he occupied a responsible position until the end of the War. He was thus, throughout the War, intimately acquainted with what was going on behind the scenes, and his Memoirs, published in 1953 in a Hebrew translation (*She'ar Yashoov*, Tel Aviv, M. Newman), contain a large amount of new and interesting material. Mr. Lichtheim has generously permitted the author to draw freely on this work, and has placed him under a further obligation by dealing fully with certain specific points on which he has allowed himself to be consulted. Information derived from Mr. Lichtheim's book is denoted in the footnotes by the word 'Memoirs.' The source used by the author is the German typescript of the *Memoirs*. The chapter references will enable the passages in question to be identified in the published Hebrew version. The citation 'Lichtheim, *Geschichte*' refers to another of Mr. Lichtheim's works— *Geschichte des Deutschen Zionismus* (Jerusalem, Rubin Mass, 1954). As regards references in this and later chapters to documents from the captured archives of the German Foreign Office, it should be made clear that these represent only a superficial skimming of a mass of material of Jewish interest which has not yet been fully investigated—a task on which the Yad Va'shem (Jerusalem) and the American Jewish Historical Society are understood to be engaged.

[2] See Lichtheim, *Geschichte*, p. 209.

have acquired Ottoman nationality,[3] was at the outbreak of war at the head of the Zionist Agency in Constantinople. When, in the spring of 1915, he joined the Central Office in Berlin, his place was taken by Richard Lichtheim, who remained in charge of the Agency until recalled to Berlin some two years later. Jacobson was subsequently transferred to Copenhagen as Director of the Zionist Bureau which had been installed there soon after the out-break of war. Its *raison d'être* was, as has been seen, to provide Zionist leaders in all parts of the world with a clearing-house on neutral soil, but it was impossible for it to exist in a vacuum. Its face was turned to Berlin, and it was, for all practical purposes, an emanation of the Berlin Executive.

On taking charge at Copenhagen at the end of 1916, Jacobson began an assiduous courtship of the German Legation. Till then the political activities of the Copenhagen Bureau had been unim-portant, but very early in the War the Constantinople Agency was in contact with the German Embassy, and it was not long before the Zionist leaders in Berlin had established relations with the German Foreign Office.

The immediate purpose of the Zionist approaches to the German Government was to invoke its help in averting the danger overhanging the Jews and Jewish institutions in Palestine from the moment Turkey entered the War. That in this they had a measure of success is, at first sight, surprising. Ever since the Kaiser's interest had flickered out after his momentary flirtation with the Zionists in 1898, Germany, having nothing to gain by irritating the Turks for the sake of the Jews, had consistently refrained from showing any interest in Zionist aspirations. Not long before the War the Zionists had incurred the positive dis-pleasure of German Foreign Office circles by their emotional protest against the use of German, in competition with Hebrew, as a language of instruction in the Jewish educational system in Palestine. Certain influential elements among the German Jews had been incensed by the incident and in the early years of the War were still trying to discredit the Zionists in the eyes of the German Government.[4]

[3] At a meeting of the Zionist General Council in March 1916 Jacobson explained his reasons for acquiring Ottoman nationality—Minutes, pp. 24-25: Z.A.

[4] Lichtheim, *Memoirs*, Chapter XVII ; *Geschichte*, pp. 174, 211.

Quite apart from this, the Germans might have been expected, on broad grounds of policy, to keep the Zionists at arm's length. If even before the War one of their main reasons for steering clear of Zionism was that it was obnoxious to the Turks, the case against intervening in their affairs for the benefit of the Jews was all the stronger at a time when they were Germany's allies, and allies so touchy and so sensitive to German interference that they required the most tactful handling. But the question was not so simple. Germany needed all the friends she could get among the neutrals and needed them above all in the United States, whose three million Jews formed too important a group to be left out of account and might well be influenced in either direction by what happened in Palestine. If the Turks committed outrages against the Jews, Entente propaganda would make the most of them, and Germany, as Turkey's ally, would share the blame. In its effect on public opinion, and especially Jewish opinion, in the United States the Turkish alliance was capable of damaging Germany in much the same way as the Russian alliance damaged Great Britain and France. Messages reaching Berlin and Constantinople from the German Ambassador in Washington, Count Bernstorff, showed how seriously he was embarrassed by reports of harsh treatment of the Jews by the Turks.[5] But, whereas Great Britain and France were impotent to do anything for the Jews in Russia, the Germans, especially in the earlier stages of the War, when their star was in the ascendant and their prestige stood high, could risk going a certain distance in restraining the Turks. If there was evidence of successful intervention by the Germans in favour of the Jews in

---

[5] Lichtheim, *Memoirs*, Chapter XVI. Lichtheim's information on this point seems to have been derived from the German Embassy in Constantinople and also, perhaps, from his correspondence with Isaac Straus, Bernstorff's adviser on Jewish Affairs, as to whom see below, p. 215. Its accuracy is confirmed by documents which have since become available from the files of the German Foreign Office (hereinafter referred to as *D.G.F.O.*); the reference numbers are those identifying the relative microfilm at the Record Office (London): Washington to Berlin, 30 October 1914 (K692/K176709-10)—' Jewish circles here, who, as is known, are favourably disposed towards Germany, are concerned lest massacres of Jews might take place in Turkey, for which we might be held indirectly responsible. . . .'—Berlin to Washington, 1 November 1914 (K692/K176711-12)—' Some time ago we already strongly advised Turkey, on account of international Jewry, to protect Jews of every nationality, and we are now reverting to the matter once more.'

Palestine, this would be so much to their credit, and their stock would rise. There might be some difficulty with the Turks, but it could be put to them that they had a common interest with their allies in conciliating neutral opinion.

These considerations told strongly in Lichtheim's favour when, in the winter of 1914,[6] he appealed to the German Embassy in Constantinople to do what it could to relieve the pressure on the Jews in Palestine.[7] The Germans not only listened sympathetically but showed that they were able and willing to be helpful. In November 1914 the German Embassy, on instructions from Berlin, recommended the Turks to sanction the re-opening of the Anglo-Palestine Company's Bank—a Zionist institution which rendered important services to the Yishuv. In December the Embassy prevailed upon the Turks to refrain from a projected mass deportation of Jews of Russian nationality.[8] In February 1915 German influence helped to save a number of Jews occupying prominent positions in Palestine from imprisonment or expulsion. These are only a few instances—according to Lichtheim,[9] there were many more—of German intercession with the Turks

6 Jacobson did not finally leave Constantinople until April 1915, but in the winter of 1914 he spent some time in Berlin, and Lichtheim acted as his deputy.

7 A memorandum by Lichtheim, undated, but initialled by a Foreign Office official on 2 November 1914 (*D.G.F.O.*, K692/176701-02), expresses anxiety about the treatment of the Jews in Palestine and urges the German Government to interest itself in Zionism, pointing out that the headquarters of the Movement are in Germany. On November 3rd the Foreign Office informed the Constantinople Embassy that Lichtheim had been told that the Ambassador would do what he could, but that his ability to intervene was limited ' in view of the international character of Zionism and of the well-known mistrust of the Turks.' The dispatch continues: ' It cannot be denied that, especially at the present moment, it would be a wise act on the part of the Porte to win the sympathies of international Jewry, especially in America, through a conciliatory treatment of Zionism ' (*D.G.F.O.*, K692/K176716-17).

8 Lichtheim, *Memoirs*, Chapters XV, XVI: corroborated by *D.G.F.O.*, Berlin to Constantinople, 8 November and 28 December 1914 K692/K176723 and 176745). A little later, however, the Ambassador reported (24 March 1915) that he must move cautiously, since the Turks would regard it as an unfriendly act if Germany claimed to occupy the rôle of protector of the Jews in Turkey (*D.G.F.O.*, K692/K176968-69).

9 ' A dozen or twenty times [the Germans] intervened with the Turks at our request, thus saving and protecting the Yishuv.' Mr. Lichtheim to the author, 12 February 1952.

at the instance of the Constantinople Zionist Agency or of the Zionist Executive in Berlin. Reporting in March 1915 on the situation in Palestine, the New York Provisional Executive Committee mentioned a perceptible improvement in the attitude of the Turkish authorities and explained that this ' is, we believe, largely due to the efforts of the Governments of both the United States and Germany and their Ambassadors in our behalf.'[10] A report laid before the 1921 Zionist Congress, after speaking of the helpful conduct of the German Consulates in Palestine during the War, goes on to say that ' the Jewish population benefited by the presence of the head of the German Military Mission in Palestine, who on several occasions exerted his influence on behalf of the Jews.'[11]

The Germans showed their goodwill in other ways. The Constantinople Zionist Agency was from December 1914 allowed the use of the German diplomatic courier service and telegraphic code for communicating with Berlin and with Palestine.[12] Tschlenow and Sokolow, both Russian nationals, were allowed to remain unmolested in Berlin until their departure for London at the end of 1914. Jacobson, though not a German national, was provided with German diplomatic travel documents for moving between Constantinople and Berlin.[13] On 5 June 1915 Jacobson, having finally left Constantinople and settled for the time being in Berlin, was received at the German Foreign Office by the Under-Secretary of State, von Zimmermann,[14] and, parallel with the conversations started earlier in the War between Lichtheim and the German Embassy in Constantinople, regular contact now began to be established between the Berlin Zionist Executive— Warburg, Hantke and Jacobson—and the German Foreign Office.

It was fortunate for the Zionists that the Germans had their own good reasons for interesting themselves in the fate of the Jews in Palestine. It was, as we have seen, due largely to the energy and generosity of the American Jews, and their success in securing the benevolent co-operation of their Government, that the Jewish population of Palestine was kept alive during the early

[10] Report dated 8 March 1915: *N.S.P.*
[11] ' Palestine Report,' p. 34.
[12] Lichtheim, *Memoirs,* Chapter XV.
[13] Ibid., Chapter XIV.
[14] Ibid., Chapter XVIII.

part of the War. But, though in terms of relief work the American effort was decisive, the Jews had still to contend with the malevolence of a régime implacably hostile to Zionism and bent on mischief. It is doubtful whether they could have been saved from disaster by anything short of sustained diplomatic pressure on the Turks by Powers in a position to exert it. One such Power was the United States. The American Ambassador to Turkey, Henry Morgenthau, did, in fact, do all he could to protect the Jews.[15] But, though the representations of the most powerful neutral had to be listened to with respect, it is reasonable to suppose that it was still more difficult for the Turks to be deaf to the remonstrances of their principal ally at a time when the Germans were in the full tide of their early victories and at the height of their prestige. Lichtheim, who was in Constantinople and behind the scenes throughout the critical period, is almost certainly right in thinking that, while the Jews owed much to Morgenthau, it was German protection which turned the scale.[16]

The starting-point of the Zionist approaches to the Germans was the emergency in Palestine, but the conversations soon began to broaden out to larger issues. The Germans might be induced to come to the rescue of the Jews in Palestine in the interests of their war-time propaganda, but, from a Zionist point of view, would it not be still better if they could be persuaded to see long-term advantages for Germany in favouring Zionist aspirations? On the German side there were signs of interest as early as November 1914, when the Counsellor at the German Embassy in Constantinople, von Kühlmann,[17] told Lichtheim that he would like to see the Zionists concentrating all their activities in Germany, plainly hinting, says Lichtheim, that he looked forward to a time when the Zionist Movement would be within the German sphere of influence.[18] To Germans who foresaw the War ending with

[15] Ibid., Chapter XIII.
[16] Lichtheim, *Geschichte,* p. 210 ; letter to the author, 5 February 1952.
[17] Later, Foreign Minister (1917-18).
[18] Lichtheim, *Memoirs,* Chapter XV. More than a year later (F.O. to Recruiting Centre, Wilmersdorff, 10 February 1916—*D.G.F.O.,* K692/K177584) the Foreign Office is to be found explaining to the military authorities that the activities of the [Berlin] Zionist Executive are of political advantage to Germany in so far as they serve to bring Zionist bodies and the Zionist press in all countries under the direction of the Berlin Central Office.

Turkey a German satellite and Turkey in Asia thrown wide open to German enterprise it might well appear that in such a situation the Jews could be useful and that it would do Germany no harm to have them on her side.

These ideas were elaborated and publicised by Zionist propagandists in Germany. In *Die Juden der Türkei*[19] Davis Trietsch argued that 'in a certain sense the Jews are a Near Eastern element in Germany and a German element in Turkey,' and suggested that 'there are possibilities in a German protectorate over the Jews as well as over Islam.' Because of his official status in the Zionist Movement, a more important contributor to the discussion was Kurt Blumenfeld, one of the principal members of the Secretariat of the Berlin Central Office. In an article published in *Preussicher Jährbucher* (August-September 1915), under the heading 'Zionism as a question of German policy in the East,' Blumenfeld expounded at length the thesis that Germany would be well-advised, in her own interests, to co-operate with the Zionists. Zionism, he declared, had no political aims of a separatist nature; in other words, there was no question of any attempt to detach Palestine from the Turkish Empire. On the contrary, the Turks would have in the Jews a completely reliable element and one which could do much to raise the level of their economic and cultural life. The English press, said Blumenfeld, might be professing a friendly interest in Jewish nationalism, but British control of Palestine would from a Zionist point of view be unattractive, since Great Britain's policy in the Middle East hinged on Egypt. The Jews could not, therefore, rely on her to put her weight behind their aspirations in Palestine, the implication being—though this is not said in so many words—that Great Britain would lean towards the Arabs. Blumenfeld went on to argue that a revival of Jewish life in Palestine would not only benefit Germany by strengthening her friend and ally, Turkey, but would be of direct advantage to Germany herself. The Jews, nearly all of whom, it was pointed out, spoke as their mother-tongue a language closely akin to German, were the natural intermediaries between Germany and the East, and the Jews who settled in Palestine would thus form

[19] Leipzig, 1915. The quotations are from an extract printed in *The Times History of the War*, Vol. XIV, pp. 320-321.

a bastion of German influence in that part of the world. Given their chance, they could be relied upon to spread German culture, and promote German economic penetration, throughout the Turkish Empire.

An advance copy of this article was sent by Lichtheim in July 1915 to von Neurath,[20] who had replaced von Kühlmann as Counsellor at the German Embassy. After an interview with von Neurath in the same month, Lichtheim, who had found him ready to be helpful, suggested to the Berlin Zionist Executive that the Foreign Office should be asked formally to notify the German Consuls in Palestine of the German Government's friendly interest in Zionism. In October 1915 von Neurath, then acting as Chargé d'Affaires, was asked by Berlin for his views and replied in favour of the proposal. In November the text of a document approved for circulation to German Consulates in Turkey was communicated to the Berlin Zionist Executive by the German Foreign Office and to Lichtheim by the Embassy in Constantinople. The Consuls were instructed that the German Government looked favourably on ' Jewish activities designed to promote the economic and cultural progress of the Jews in Turkey, and also on the immigration and settlement of Jews from other countries.' The Consuls were 'authorised to adopt a friendly attitude towards such Jewish activities' and were asked to report on the action taken by them in the light of these instructions.[21]

The document was cautiously worded. It spoke vaguely of 'Turkey,' with no express mention of Palestine. The Consuls were told to act with discretion and to be careful to respect Turkish susceptibilities. All the same, the German Government would not have troubled to issue such instructions at all if it had not made up its mind that good relations with the Zionists would be to its advantage. According to Lichtheim, the matter was taken so

[20] Later, Foreign Minister (1932-38) and 'Protector' of Bohemia (1939-43). It appears from *D.G.F.O.* that an advance copy was also sent by the Berlin Zionist Executive to the German Foreign Office.

[21] This paragraph is based on Lichtheim, *Memoirs*, Chaper XVIII, where the instructions are set out in full. Lichtheim's version corresponds to the text of the instructions as set out in *D.G.F.O.*, K177405-06 (22 November 1915). In a further communication of the same date (K177407) the Ambassador in Constantinople informs the Consuls confidentially that the instructions are dictated by considerations of policy, but that care should be taken not to offend non-Zionist elements [i.e., anti-Zionist Jews].

seriously that the final text of the document was submitted for approval to the German Chancellor, Bethmann-Hollweg.[22]

On the Zionist side it was felt that an important advance had been made towards a firm assurance of German support. But as it turned out, the Germans were not, at this stage, prepared to go any further. Elated by the progress already made, the Berlin Zionist Executive pressed for a public assurance of German sympathy and support. Well aware that any such public commitment would be furiously resented by the Turks, the Germans politely excused themselves, telling the Zionists to wait until the end of the War, when a victorious Germany could be relied upon to demonstrate her goodwill.[23]

With this the Berlin Zionist Executive had, for the time being, to rest content. For them the instructions to the German Consuls in Palestine were only a first step in the right direction, but something had been gained, and they did their best to turn it to account. On 29 December 1915 Warburg and Jacobson called at the Foreign Office to express their thanks to the Under-Secretary of State, von Zimmermann, and to ask leave to bring the German Government's friendly gesture to the notice of leading Zionists in various parts of the world. Von Zimmermann agreed in principle, provided that this was done with great discretion. On no account must there be any publicity, since the Turks, he said, were touchy and suspicious. Warburg explained that he was thinking especially of the United States, where the news would undoubtedly make a most favourable impression, and that the moment was particularly opportune in view of plans which were being made for the organisation, on an imposing scale, of an American Jewish Congress.[24]

Warburg and Jacobson would have known that the German move would be particularly helpful to Isaac Straus, who very early in the War had gone from Germany to the United States to assist the German Ambassador as his adviser on Jewish affairs.

---

[22] Ibid. From *D.G.F.O.*, however, it looks as though the actual drafting was left to the discretion of the Ambassador in Constantinople: K692/ K177404 ; 177420.

[23] Mr. Lichtheim to the author, 12 February 1952.

[24] A note of this interview is in Z.A.

Straus had been sent out under the auspices of the Komitee für den Osten,[25] which, though at the start concerned mainly with Eastern Europe, was interesting itself in pro-German propaganda among Jews in other parts of the world, and especially in the United States. An apparently well-informed article in *The Jewish Chronicle* of 2 March 1917 quotes a confidential memorandum, dated November 1915, in which the K.f.d.O. claims credit for having sent to America 'one of our gentlemen [obviously Isaac Straus], who has been in close connection with the German Ambassador, Count Bernstorff, and the State Secretary, Dr. Dernburg,[26] to win over the ghetto masses, who come mainly from Russia, and to win over their press.' Straus' position was all the stronger because it was generally accepted in American Jewish circles that he was not simply a paid agent, but a man of wealth and position who had, as a patriotic German citizen, placed his services at the disposal of his country.[27] Though his mission to the United States had been sponsored by the Komitee für den Osten and not by the German Zionists, he himself was a member of the Zionist Organisation and made it his business to keep in close touch both with the Zionist leaders in Berlin and with Lichtheim in Constantinople. The more evidence they could provide of German sympathy with Zionism and of German solicitude for the Jews in Palestine, the better for Straus' propaganda in the United States. He, on his side, could reciprocate by impressing upon Bernstorff the importance of the Zionist Movement and its claim to German support.[28]

Straus, as in duty bound, did his best to get himself accepted in Zionist circles in the United States. Writing to Otto Warburg on 12 April 1915, he reported that he had been present at 'a Zionist dinner' attended by (among others) Brandeis and Shmarya Levin.[29] He persisted in his courtship of the American Zionists, but without much success. Brandeis was the last man to be influenced in a pro-German direction, and nearly all his leading associates were as unshakable as he was in their sympathy with

---

[25] See above, p. 98.
[26] As to Dr. Dernburg, see above, p. 203.
[27] Mr. Bernard G. Richards to the author, 11 December 1951.
[28] See Lichtheim, *Memoirs*, Chapter XVI ; *Geschichte*, p. 209.
[29] Z.A.

the Allies. The only notable exception was Shmarya Levin. Something has already been said about Levin's pro-German proclivities and his contributions to a periodical—*The American Jewish Chronicle*—founded in 1916 by Isaac Straus in the interests of his pro-German propaganda.[30] But Levin, though important because of his membership of the Zionist Executive, was not an American, nor does he appear to have had much influence on his American colleagues. Straus moved about as much as he could among the Zionists, but he was never admitted to their inner circle. Stephen Wise[31] has spoken of ' the hints from the Bernstorff-Dernburg-Isaac Straus group that the victories of the Central Powers, including Turkey, would result in handing over Palestine to the Jews. This promise, reinforced by the wishful thinking or the real confidence of the Jewish pro-German group of those days, was rejected out of hand by Brandeis and his closest followers.'

But this is not to say that it had no effect on the Jewish masses. For Jews already inclined in a pro-German direction out of hatred for Russia such an assurance might well have some attraction, and that more particularly at a time when the Germans were gaining victories and a German promise was not to be disdained. Though German propagandists already had a winning card in Czarist Russia, there was no reason why they should not strengthen their hand by an appeal to the Jewish feeling for Palestine.

It was, as it turned out, greatly to the advantage of the Zionists that the Berlin Zionist Executive succeeded in interesting the German Foreign Office, and that Zionism was taken up by German and pro-German propagandists. When, in the autumn of 1917, the British War Cabinet was being pressed by the Foreign Office for prompt approval of the Balfour Declaration, one of the main short-term arguments was that the Germans were courting the Zionists and might at any moment come out with a pro-Zionist declaration of their own.[32] So, also, it was fortunate for the

---

[30] Levin's contributions to this paper were mentioned with disapproval by Dr. Gottheil at a meeting of the New York Provisional Executive Committee, 10 January 1917: *Brandeis papers*. As to the *provenance* of the *A.J. Chronicle*, see *J.C.*, 3 May 1918.

[31] In a paper contributed to Goodman's *Jewish National Home*. Wise succeeded Brandeis as Chairman of the New York Provisional Committee.

[32] See below, pp. 516, 528, 544.

Zionists that the American Jews as a whole (though not without notable exceptions) showed no enthusiasm for the Allied cause. If they had all along been reliable friends, there would have been no need to pay them any special attention. How greatly it was desired to win them over, and how strongly it was believed, long before the Balfour Declaration, that an appeal to Zionist sentiment might be effective, can be seen from the events which have now to be described.

CHAPTER 14

SIR EDWARD GREY'S PROPOSAL, MARCH 1916

BOTH IN LONDON and in Paris serious notice was taken of the state of feeling among the American Jews. The tenor of the reports sent to London by the Washington Embassy can be inferred from the extracts already quoted from the correspondence of Sir Cecil Spring-Rice.[1] Lucien Wolf was told at the Foreign Office, early in 1916, that anything which could discreetly be done by the Conjoint Foreign Committee to influence Jewish opinion in the United States would be a helpful contribution to Allied propaganda. It was suggested to him that the most useful point to make might be that the attitude of American Jews was creating a most unfortunate impression in England and France and was bound to prejudice the British and French approach to any questions relating to Jews which might come up for discussion. Some three months later, Wolf reported to his Committee[2] that he had had an interview at the Foreign Office with the head of the Publicity Section, Hubert Montgomery, who 'read me extracts from a long dispatch which had been received from Sir Cecil Spring-Rice. . . . He [Spring-Rice] seems to be disposed, like Lord Robert Cecil, to hold all the Jews responsible for this attitude of their American co-religionists, and I was surprised to find Mr. Montgomery hinting at the same thing.'

By this time some counter-propaganda had already been attempted, with no marked success, by the French Government, which had received disturbing reports about the sympathies of the American Jews from its own Embassy in Washington.[3] It had chosen as its instrument Victor Basch, a French Jew of Hungarian origin, who was a Professor of some distinction at the Sorbonne. In November 1915[4] Basch was sent to the United

[1] Above, p. 203.

[2] *C.F.C.*, 1916/210 (5 April 1916).

[3] The Conjoint Foreign Committee was so informed by Wolf, who was in contact with well-informed circles in Paris: *C.F.C.*, 1915/340.

[4] The date is given by Basch in an article in *Hatikvah* (Antwerp), Dec. 1927.

States, ostensibly as an official representative of the Ministry of Public Instruction, but in reality in the hope that he would be able to exert some influence on the American Jews through personal contact with their leaders.[5] He was armed with a message to American Jewry from the Prime Minister, Briand,[6] and on his return to France in the spring of 1916 he was asked to report in person to President Poincaré.[7] His mission was clearly regarded as important, but it produced no perceptible results and had in the end to be written off as a failure.[8]

Through his connections in French parliamentary circles, Lucien Wolf was provided with a summary of Basch's reports to the French Government.[9] Basch had encountered one insurmountable obstacle—the Russian alliance. 'For Russia there is universal hatred and distrust. . . . We are reproached with one thing only, the persecution of the Russian Jews, which we tolerate—a toleration which makes us accomplices. . . . It is certain that measures in favour of Jewish emancipation would be equivalent to a great battle lost by Germany.'[10] This, Basch insisted, was the crux of the problem, but he suggested that the American Jews might be favourably impressed by an Anglo-French assurance that, when the time came for a Peace Conference, the two Governments would press for the redress of Jewish grievances and would interest themselves in the future of the Jews in Palestine. Basch returned to this point in a memorandum prepared by him in the summer of 1916 for the information of the Conjoint Foreign Committee.[11] While again insisting on the paramount importance of the Russian Question, he drew attention to the growing strength of the Zionist Movement in the United States and urged that this should not be overlooked by the French and British Governments in their political warfare.

Soon after Basch's departure for the United States, the French

---

[5] *C.F.C.*, 1915/340.

[6] See note 4.

[7] Poincaré, VIII, 220 (15 May 1916).

[8] Its failure was referred to by Picot at his interview with Sokolow on 9 February 1917: below, p. 375.

[9] *C.F.C.*, 1916/183ff.

[10] Transl. from the French.

[11] *C.F.C.*, 1916/275ff. (Undated, but evidently written in the summer of 1916.)

Government approved the setting up of a ' Comité de Propagande français auprès des Juifs neutres,' to be presided over by Georges Lèygues, the Chairman of the Foreign Affairs Commission of the Chamber of Deputies. The members of the Committee included, in addition to Basch, several other well-known Jewish names. One of the secretaries was Jacques Bigart, the secretary of the Alliance Israélite.[12]

Bigart suggested to Lucien Wolf that a similar Committee should be formed in London. Wolf consulted the Foreign Office and was invited by Lord Robert Cecil to provide the Department with a full statement of his views.[13] In December 1915 he submitted a memorandum[14] in which he analysed the make-up of the Jewish population in the United States and reached the conclusion that ' the situation, though unsatisfactory, is far from unpromising.' He made various suggestions for surmounting or evading the difficulties of the Russian Question and then went on to speak of Zionism.

> ' I am not,' he said, ' a Zionist, and I deplore the Jewish National Movement. . . . Still, the facts cannot be ignored, and in any bid for Jewish sympathies to-day very serious account must be taken of the Zionist Movement. In America the Zionist organisations have lately captured Jewish opinion. . . . This is the moment for the Allies to declare their policy in regard to Palestine. . . . If, for example, they would say they thoroughly understand and sympathise with Jewish aspirations in regard to Palestine, and that when the destiny of the country comes to be considered, these aspirations will be taken into account, and that, in addition, they would be guaranteed reasonable facilities for immigration and colonisation, for a liberal scheme of local self-government for the existing colonists, for the establishment of a Jewish University, and for the recognition of Hebrew as one of the vernaculars of the land, I am confident they would sweep the whole of American Jewry into enthusiastic allegiance to

[12] C.F.C., 1915/339ff.; 1916/124ff.
[13] C.F.C., 1916/110, 124.
[14] The full text of the memorandum, dated 16 December 1915, is set out in C.F.C., 1916/111ff.

their cause. What the Zionists would especially like to know is that Great Britain will become mistress of Palestine. This may be difficult to say in view of French claims and of the assurances which have already been given to France in regard to the whole of Syria, which is held in Paris to include Palestine. But if, without dealing with this question, the guarantees I have indicated could be given, I am sure they would suffice . . . .'

Early in 1916 a further memorandum was submitted to the Foreign Office—this time as a formal communication from the Conjoint Foreign Committee.[15] The gist of it was that 'the London and Paris Committees[16] formed to influence Jewish opinion in neutral countries in a sense favourable to the Allies' had agreed to make certain representations to their respective Governments. First, the Russian Government should be urged to ease the position of their Jews by some immediate concessions. Secondly, in view of 'the great organised strength of the Zionists in the United States,' the Allied Powers should authorise a public statement on the Palestine question, giving certain assurances to the Jews. The assurances proposed were substantially identical with those which had been suggested by Wolf in his memorandum of 16 December 1915.

On 24 February 1916 Wolf was informed by Cecil that 'as to the formation of the American Committees that you have spoken to me about more than once,' there was no objection to this proposal, but that 'any attempt at the present moment to influence the British and French Governments to intervene directly or indirectly in Russian internal questions would be a great mistake'[17] Noting that Cecil, while holding out no hope of any British or French intervention in favour of the Jews in Russia, had said nothing about Palestine, Lucien Wolf, on 3 March 1916, submitted to the Foreign Office 'the text of the formula I would suggest on the Palestine question.' 'I do not think,' he wrote, 'that anything less would impress the Zionists, but there is noth-

[15] C.F.C., 1916/130ff. (18 February 1916).
[16] No separate London Committee seems, in fact, to have been set up for this purpose, but the Conjoint Foreign Committee was working in close contact with the Lèygues Committee, as to which see above, p. 220.
[17] C.F.C., 1916/182.

ing in it that need involve His Majesty's Government in any difficulty, or to which my Committee would raise any objection.'[18] [19]

Wolf's formula was as follows:

> 'In the event of Palestine coming within the spheres of influence of Great Britain or France at the close of the War, the Governments of those Powers will not fail to take account of the historic interest that country possesses for the Jewish community. The Jewish population will be secured in the enjoyment of civil and religious liberty, equal political rights with the rest of the population, reasonable facilities for immigration and colonisation, and such municipal privileges in the towns and colonies inhabited by them as may be shown to be necessary.'

Since the whole point of his proposal was that the best hope of winning over the American Jews lay in an appeal to their emotional feeling for Palestine, Wolf, himself an anti-Zionist, was in the awkward position of having to find a form of words which would go far enough to achieve its purpose and yet not so far as to be intolerably heretical in his own eyes and in those of like-minded members of his Committee. As he explained later, his formula had been framed as a concession to the Zionists.[20] He would appear to have had some excuse, at the time, for believing that they would be content with it. According to his note of an interview with Herbert Samuel early in April 1916, 'he [Samuel] seemed to think that, when it comes to the point, the Zionists will be quite satisfied if we obtain the adoption of our formula.'[21] During a visit to Paris some three months later Wolf saw Baron

[18] Ibid., 203.

[19] Though the formula was, in the first instance, communicated to the F.O. under cover of a personal letter from Wolf to Lancelot (later, Sir Lancelot) Oliphant, it was not long afterwards adopted officially by the Conjoint Foreign Committee. In a memorandum submitted to the F.O. on 10 October 1916, the C.F.C. said, with reference to the Palestine question, that it was proposed to amplify in due course the views which 'have already been set forth in broad outline in the formula submitted to His Majesty's Government on March 3 last': *The Jews and the War, No. 1* (London, Conjoint Foreign Committee ; 1917), p. 9.

[20] See below, p. 231.

[21] C.F.C., 1916/267 (7 April 1916).

Edmond de Rothschild and showed him the formula. According to his account of the conversation, ' he [the Baron] thought the Zionists should be satisfied with it.'[22] But Wolf had not consulted the Zionist leaders, and by the time the text became public property the scales were tilting so heavily in their favour that such insipid and inhibited language seemed to them to savour of sabotage. The formula which in March 1916 represented, as Wolf saw it, a concession to the Zionists was to become the focus of a furious controversy when, in the spring of 1917, it was incorporated by the Conjoint Foreign Committee in a public statement in which the Zionists indignantly perceived a declaration of war.

On 9 March 1916 Wolf was informed by the Foreign Office that ' your suggested formula is receiving [Sir Edward Grey's] careful and sympathetic consideration, but it is necessary for His Majesty's Government to consult their Allies on the subject.'[23] The British Government did consult their Allies, and without delay. On March 11 identical instructions were telegraphed to the British Ambassadors in Paris and Petrograd.[24] The Ambassadors were told that ' it has been suggested to us that if we could offer to the Jews an arrangement in regard to Palestine completely satisfactory to Jewish aspirations, such an offer might appeal strongly to a large and powerful section of the Jewish community throughout the world.' If so, it would follow ' that the Zionist idea has in it the most far-reaching political possibilities, for we might hope to use it in such a way as to bring over to our side the Jewish forces in America, the East, and elsewhere which are now largely, if not preponderantly, hostile to us '. Then followed the text of Lucien Wolf's proposal, with the comment that ' this formula seems to us unobjectionable,' but that

[22] *C.F.C.*, 1916/489 (10 July 1916).

[23] *C.F.C.*, 1916/206.

[24] The substance of Grey's telegram, as communicated by the British Ambassador to the Russian Foreign Minister, is included (No. 78) in ' Die Europäische Mächte und die Türkei während des Weltkrieges—Die Aufteilung der Asiatischen Türkei' (Dresden, 1932), a German translation of Vol. VI (Moscow, 1924) of the series of documents from the archives of the Russian Foreign Office, ed. E. Adamov (hereinafter cited as ' Adamov ').

'we consider that the scheme might be made far more attractive to the majority of Jews if it held out to them the prospect that when in course of time the Jewish colonists in Palestine [have] grown strong enough to cope with the Arab population, they may be allowed to take the management of the internal affairs of Palestine (with the exception of Jerusalem and the Holy Places) into their own hands.'

'We have,' it was added, 'been given to understand that some influential Jewish opinion would be opposed to an international protectorate, but we do not desire to state a preference for any particular solution. Our sole object is to find an arrangement which would be so attractive to the majority of Jews as to enable us to strike a bargain for Jewish support'. The telegram ends: 'We should be glad if you would submit the matter to the serious consideration of the Government to which you are accredited and ask them to favour us with their views as soon as possible'.

It will be noticed that Grey is uncomfortable about the state of Jewish opinion, not only in America, but also in 'the East and elsewhere'. Apart from the East European Jews, he may have been thinking particularly of Salonica, which, with its large and influential Jewish population, had, as a result of the Balkan Wars, passed from Turkey to Greece. Greece occupied a key-position in Anglo-French strategy in the Eastern Mediterranean, and it was a matter of some concern to the Allies that the Salonica Jews seemed to have retained their pro-Turkish sympathies. One of the first decisions of the Franco-Jewish propaganda committee formed in Paris at the end of 1915 was to send an eminent French Rabbi, Israel Lévi, on a mission to Salonica.[25] When Lucien Wolf was received by Briand in July 1916, one of the subjects discussed is stated by Wolf to have been 'the importance of the Russian question in relation to the Jewish electorate of Salonica.'[26] After the Russian Revolution Mark Sykes thought that the appeal of Zionism might help 'to draw the Salonica Jews out of the Ottoman rut.'[27]

[25] *C.F.C.*, 1915/341.

[26] C.F.C., 1916/483 (10 July 1916): 'The Russian question'—i.e., the effect on Jewish opinion of the Russian persecution of the Jews.

[27] Shane Leslie, *Mark Sykes—His Life and Letters* (London, Cassell, 1923), p. 270.

It is interesting—and, seeing that Asquith was still Prime Minister, somewhat surprising—to find Grey coming forward, as early as March 1916, with a proposal that the Jews should be offered by the Allies, if not a Jewish State in Palestine, at least something in the nature af an autonomous Jewish Commonwealth. Who it was that prompted or inspired this suggestion is uncertain. In thinking, as they evidently did, that the Wolf formula was inadequate and that something more impressive was required, it is possible that Grey and his advisers may have been influenced by a study of Herbert Samuel's Palestine memorandum.[28] Just about this time Samuel had sent copies of the memorandum to those of his colleagues who were not in the Cabinet when it was originally circulated early in 1915, and this may have helped to bring it back to life. But these are mere conjectures. Precisely what lay behind Grey's instructions still remains to be discovered. Whatever their paternity, they speak for themselves as evidence of the growing strength of the Zionist Movement and of the British estimate both of its aims and of its importance. Though the Foreign Office was evidently quite alive to the fact that the Jews were heavily outnumbered in Palestine by the Arabs, Grey's proposals imply that the conception of something like a Jewish State was not regarded as too fantastic to be taken seriously; indeed, in the spring of 1916 the British Government seems to have been prepared to join with its allies in giving assurances to the Zionists going well beyond those which it felt able, eighteen months later, to offer them, on its own responsibility, in the Balfour Declaration.

Since in the end nothing came of them, Grey's proposals need not be closely analysed, but on certain points they call for comment.

First, they throw some indirect light on the disputed question whether Palestine fell within the area in which Sir Henry McMahon, in his letter of 24 October 1915 to the Sharif Hussein, pledged the British Government to 'recognise and support the independence of the Arabs'.[29] Grey seems clearly to have assumed

---

[28] Lord Samuel has told the author that he has no recollection of having been consulted about Grey's proposals. There is no evidence of Grey's ever having been seen by Weizmann or any other Zionist leader.

[29] Printed in Cmd. 5957 (1939), pp. 7ff.

that Palestine was excluded, for, if not, it is inconceivable that, within a few months of authorising the British promise to the Sharif, he would have suggested, as a preferable alternative to the Lucien Wolf formula, a scheme holding out to the Jews the prospect of their being eventually 'allowed to take the management of the internal affairs of Palestine (with the exception of Jerusalem and the Holy Places) into their own hands.'[30]

Secondly, what was the real point of Grey's remark that ' some influential Jewish opinion would be opposed to an international protectorate '? The alternative to an international protectorate would be either complete independence, which Grey can hardly have contemplated, or the protectorate of a single Power. The British Government could not possibly have desired that that Power should be France. Grey would have known that a British protectorate was strongly favoured in Zionist circles both in England and in the United States, but the introduction of the topic is rather puzzling, since it must also have been obvious that there could be no question of the French being persuaded to join in sponsoring a scheme which ruled out an international protectorate without substituting their own.

Lastly, why was so much importance attached to the Jews ? Why did Grey go so far as to say that, if it was true, as had been suggested, that the Jews could be won over by a gesture of sympathy with Zionist aspirations, then ' the Zionist idea has in it the most far-reaching political possibilities '? This is strong language. How is it to be explained? It cannot be accounted for merely by an exaggerated belief in the money-power of the Jews. The Jewish banking houses in the United States, though two or three of them were important, were far from dominating the American money-market. Moreover, Grey was speaking in terms of ' political '—not financial—advantages, and, in any case, the most superficial enquiry would have shown that Jews of the type associated with high finance were much more likely to be alarmed than elated by an Allied declaration in favour of Zionism. Is it, then, to be supposed that the Foreign Office was thinking of the intellectuals and the unassimilated or half-assimilated masses,

---

[30] After the War, Grey expressed doubts as to the compatibility of the promise of a Jewish National Home in Palestine with the McMahon pledge ; see above, p. 114, note 41.

from whom the Zionists drew most of their strength? These were a political factor to the extent that even in those days the Jewish vote in the United States counted for something in certain important electoral districts, especially in New York. There is some reason to believe that in 1916 Woodrow Wilson gave a prominent New York Zionist an assurance of his benevolent interest in Zionism in return for a promise of support in the presidential campaign of that year.[31] There was also the widespread impression that both as proprietors and as writers the Jews were strongly represented in the newspaper world and were thus influential out of all proportion to their numbers in shaping public opinion. We may recall what Thomas Masaryk said about the American Jews in acknowledging their help in popularising the Czech cause in the United States: 'In America, as in Europe, the Jews have great influence in the field of journalism; it was highly advantageous to us not to have this Great Power against us.'[32]

The Foreign Office may have had such considerations in mind, but there is no evidence to show, nor is there any need to assume, that Grey's views of what the Allies stood to gain by winning over the Jews was based on any closely reasoned calculation. The influence of the Jews may have been over-estimated, but, in England in particular, there was a traditional belief that, for reasons not precisely definable, world Jewry was important and its friendship worth acquiring.[33] In 1840 Palmerston, in recommending the Turks to encourage Jewish colonisation in Palestine, pointed out that 'the Jews . . . are . . . a sort of Freemason

[31] Speaking of discussions with Wilson in 1916, de Haas (*Brandeis*, p. 88) writes: 'The assurances, reduced to a six-line memorandum with the initials "W.W.," were wholly satisfactory.' De Haas' daughter, Mrs. de Haas Dembitz, wrote to the author (27 October 1954): 'I presume you know that President Wilson, before he was elected, promised my father active support in return for my father's support in getting him elected.'— 'President Wilson . . . was the first occupant of the White House to feel the full force of Zionist pressure. It may be assumed that domestic political repercussions were not ignored, either': *Early History of Zionism in America*, ed. I. S. Meyer (New York, 1958), p. 292.

[32] Quoted from Masaryk's *Die Welt Revolution*, pp. 249-250, by Josef Cohn, *England und Palästina* (Berlin, 1931), p. 221.

[33] In his *A Piece of My Mind* (London, W. H. Allen, 1957), Edmund Wilson analyses (pp. 78-80) the once widely read novels of George du Maurier as reflections of the popular conception of the Jew 'as a spirit from an alien world, who carries with it an uncanny prestige.'

fraternity whose good word would be useful to the Sultan.'[34] In 1904, when Herzl came forward with his El Arish scheme, Joseph Chamberlain was impressed, his biographer tells us, because (among other reasons) 'by supporting Zionism Britain would enlist the sympathies of World Jewry on her behalf.'[35] Balfour told Weizmann in 1914 that he saw in him the representative of 'a powerful moral Government.'[36] The same order of ideas was reflected in the Balfour Declaration, of which Mark Sykes said, in 1918, that, combined with the British victories in Palestine, it gave England, and the Entente as a whole, 'a hold over the vital vocal and sentimental forces of Jewry.'[37]

On the assumption that the War in the East would end with the collapse of Turkey and the partition of the Turkish Empire, the Entente Powers had been moving forward towards an agreed delimitation of their claims. Grey's telegram of March 11th, raising the question of 'a bargain for Jewish support,' reached Paris and Petrograd just after the opening of the final stage of these involved discussions. Russia's main interests in Turkey in Asia were in the north. As to Mesopotamia, Syria and Palestine, and the rest of the region south of the zone already conceded to Russia, negotiations conducted on the British side by Sir Mark Sykes and on the French side by François Georges-Picot had resulted, at the beginning of 1916, in the approval by both Powers of the arrangements soon afterwards to be embodied in the Sykes-Picot Agreement. Having reached an understanding between themselves, the two Governments had proceeded to bring their intentions to the notice of their Russian ally. Sykes and Picot had been sent to Petrograd, and on March 9th the outcome of the Anglo-French discussions had been made known to the Russian Foreign Minister, Sazonov.[37a] Without, at this stage, going closely into the Sykes-Picot scheme, it will be enough to say that, in dealing with Palestine, it ignored the Jews and, far

[34] Above, p. 7.
[35] Above, p. 24.
[36] Above, p. 126.
[37] *Milner papers* 'Palestine' file (1 January 1918).
[37a] Adamov, No. 74.

from being designed to encourage Zionist hopes, was, on the face of it, much more likely to work the other way. The offer to the Jews now favoured by Grey—an offer which would invite them to expect eventual predominance in Palestine—would, therefore, involve a reconsideration of the proposals on which Great Britain and France had agreed, and in which Russia was being invited to concur.

On March 13th the substance of Grey's message of the 11th was communicated to the Russian Government by the British Ambassador, Sir George Buchanan.[38] No direct reply was received, but an oblique allusion to Grey's *démarche* was inserted by Sazonov in a Note addressed four days later to Buchanan and his French colleague.[39] The Ambassadors were informed that, subject to its being satisfied on certain specified points not relating to Palestine, the Russian Government would concur in any proposals agreed upon between Great Britain and France as to the future of those parts of Asiatic Turkey lying south of the Russian zone in Armenia. Having given this general assurance, Sazonov went on to say that, with regard to Palestine, Russia would agree to any arrangement providing adequate guarantees for the Orthodox Church and its establishments and would be prepared, in principle, to raise no objection to the settlement of Jewish colonists.

In the interval between the end of his negotiations with Picot and his departure for Petrograd late in February 1916 Mark Sykes had had a talk with Herbert Samuel and had read his Palestine memorandum. Zionism had till then made no appeal to Sykes, but he had been impressed by the case which could be made out for it and had gone to Russia fully satisfied that the Zionists deserved to be taken seriously.[40] When, about a year later, he addressed a group of leading Zionists in London,[41] he told them that, while in Petrograd, he had sounded Sazonov on the Zionist question. Sazonov, he said, ' had objected that there was no room in Palestine for all the Jews of Russia.' He had then put ' the case for Palestine as a spiritual centre for the Jews,' and ' Sazonov had admitted its force.'[42]

[38] Adamov, No. 78.
[39] Ibid., No. 80.
[40] See below, p. 233.
[41] See below, p. 370.
[42] The quotations are from the procès-verbal of the meeting: *Ch.W.P.*

In assuring Grey that the settlement of Jews in Palestine would not, in principle, be objected to by the Russian Government, Sazonov may have reflected that, since most of the immigrants would come from Eastern Europe, this would, from his point of view, have the twofold advantage of reducing the number of Jews in Russia and increasing the number of Russian nationals in Palestine. But on the other and larger questions raised by Grey the Russian Note was silent. There was no comment on Grey's suggestion that, if the Jews were to be won over to the Allied cause, an offer of something like a Jewish Commonwealth in Palestine might have to be considered. Grey had also mentioned the objections from the Jewish side to an international protectorate. On this point likewise Sazonov said nothing. From the exchanges which took place a few weeks later between Sazonov and the French Ambassador[43] it can be inferred that the Russians proposed to insist on an international régime for all those parts of Palestine in which there were Orthodox institutions —a formula plainly embracing a much larger area than Jerusalem and its surroundings.

The Russian reply to Grey's enquiry, though reserved, was not wholly negative. If what Lucien Wolf was told by the Foreign Office was the whole story,[44] it was the French who finally killed his proposals by rejecting the Wolf formula as inadequate without responding to Grey's clear indication of his own preference for a more attractive offer to the Zionists.

On 4 July 1916 the Foreign Office informed the Conjoint Committee that Sir Edward Grey 'has given his careful consideration to the publication of some such formula as you suggest, but he is of opinion that the present moment is not opportune for making any official announcement on the subject.'[45] The next day Wolf reported to his Committee that it had been explained to him at the Foreign Office that what lay behind Grey's decision was the attitude of the French Government. The French, he had been told, 'had taken the view that it would be useless to make the announcement we propose at this moment, as they had ascer-

[43] Below, pp. 260-261.
[44] The author has not had access to the French documentary material which might throw light on the French side of the story.
[45] C.F.C., 1916/397.

tained that it would not satisfy a very large body of Jewish opinion.' Wolf's comment was that this meant that 'the Zionists have used their efforts to get our formula, which was intended as a concession to them, rejected.'[46]

During a visit to Paris a few days later Wolf did his best to find out what had really happened. On July 12th he was received by the Prime Minister, Briand, and, after some conversation on other matters, raised the question of his Palestine formula and its rejection by the French Government on the ground that it would be unsatisfactory to the Zionists. He had, he said, the authority of Baron Edmond de Rothschild for assuring Briand that the Zionists were not opposed to the formula. This opening led nowhere, Briand's reply being merely that no formula on the Palestine Question had ever come before him.[47] Two days earlier Wolf had seen Baron Edmond, who, according to Wolf's note of the conversation, thought that the Zionists should be satisfied with the Palestine formula and could not imagine who had misled the French Government.[48] After his interview with Briand on July 12th Wolf had a further talk with Baron Edmond, who, he says, 'was inclined to think that the Foreign Office had misunderstood the French Government, or that, if the French Government had made the excuse attributed to them, it was really because they did not want to make a public declaration on the Palestine question, which would either tie their hands in any future negotiations with Turkey or would have the effect of admitting that the destiny of Palestine was not exclusively a French concern.'[49]

[46] Ibid., 396.
[47] Ibid., 489.
[48] Ibid., 478.
[49] Ibid., 493. It is not to be inferred that Edmond de Rothschild was fully identified with the standpoint of the Conjoint Committee or enthusiastic about the 'formula.' At the end of his visit to Paris, Wolf himself expressed the view that 'the most important concrete result of my conversations with the Baron is that for the moment at least he is in agreement with us on our formula, although we start from different premises and perhaps with different aims' (*C.F.C.*, 1916/488). Baron Edmond seems to have thought that the 'formula' was as much as could be hoped for at the moment, and that, without necessarily renouncing their larger aspirations, the Zionists, not being (as it seemed to him) in a particularly strong position, would be well advised to take what they could get.

The French may well have been advised—possibly by Victor Basch—that, if the Zionists, the Jews who really mattered in this connection, were to be impressed, the Lucien Wolf formula would not serve and something much less milk-and-watery would be needed. But if the French Government was, indeed, convinced that the Wolf formula would not appeal to the Zionists, it could not have failed to observe that Grey himself had, in effect, said much the same and had gone on to outline proposals to which the Jews would, he suggested, be much more likely to respond. On this point the French were as silent as the Russians had been. The inference seems to be that, for the reasons suggested by Baron Edmond, the French were disinclined to join with the British in any far-reaching declaration concerning the future of Palestine and preferred to ride off on the rather lame pretext that the Wolf formula was inadequate. Whatever its real motives, the French Government's refusal to co-operate, added to the significant reticence of the Russians, gave Grey's proposals their *coup de grâce*, and by the middle of 1916 they were dead.

CHAPTER 15

SIR MARK SYKES' INTRODUCTION TO ZIONISM

GREY HAD PUT the case for a concerted effort by the Allies to get the Jews on their side by identifying themselves with Jewish aspirations in Palestine. This proposal had been made with a view to 'a bargain for Jewish support' in the interests of the Entente as a whole. But Great Britain had interests of her own to safeguard in Palestine, and just about the time of Grey's abortive move, Mark Sykes' introduction to Zionism by Herbert Samuel was opening the way to some fresh thinking on the British side about the possible advantages of an understanding with the Zionists.

On the eve of his departure for Petrograd, Sykes wrote to Samuel (26 February 1916)[1]:

> 'I read the memorandum and have committed it to memory and destroyed it, as no print or other papers can pass the R[ussian] frontier except in the F.O. bag. There is one suggestion which I forgot to mention to you, at least I did not put it properly, that is that Belgium should assume the administration as the trustee of the Entente Powers. I have no personal opinion on the merits of this, but I believe that it might be more acceptable to France as an alternative to an international administration. I think on the whole that the boundaries as marked[2] are more favourable than if they were wider. By excluding Hebron and the East of the Jordan there is less to discuss with the Moslems, as the Mosque of Omar then becomes the only matter of vital importance to discuss with them and further does away with any contact with the Bedouin, who never cross the river except on business.
>
> 'I imagine that the principal object of Zionism is the realisation of the ideal of an existing centre of nationality rather

---

1 *H.S.P.*

2 This refers, presumably, to the map annexed to the Sykes-Picot Agreement, then in draft.

than boundaries or extent of territory. The moment I return I will let you know how things stand at Pd.'

There is nothing here that points, in itself, to the building up of a special relationship between Great Britain and the Zionists, but this was the central theme of the Samuel memorandum, and it was not long before Sykes' mind began to move in that direction. Because of his reputation as an expert on Eastern affairs and his access to the men in power, his views were important. His ideas about British war-aims in the East already carried weight and were to become still more influential when, after the change of Government at the end of 1916, he was given a key-position in the War Cabinet Secretariat.

For Sykes—it may not be irrelevant that he was a Kitchener man—it was axiomatic that, for reasons, mainly strategic, of high Imperial policy, the future of Palestine was of vital concern to Great Britain. Above all, on no account must Palestine either be conceded to France or allowed to pass under *de facto* French control.

When, in February 1916, Sykes began to interest himself in Zionism, he had recently emerged from the tough negotiations with the French delegate, Georges-Picot, which had resulted in an Anglo-French accord as to the respective claims of the two Powers in the partition of Asiatic Turkey. Among the most hotly disputed questions had been that of the future of Palestine. In the end, the French had reluctantly agreed that Palestine, or the greater part of it, should be internationalised. But, though they were well aware that there was a Russian as well as a British barrier to the full achievement of their ambitions in Palestine, it was with an ill grace that they had conceded, under British pressure, the principle of internationisation. From the standpoint of anyone who saw the situation as Sykes saw it, their presence in Palestine, even as equal partners in a condominium, might well turn out to be embarrassing. Nor could they be relied upon to be content with such a partnership. It was tolerably certain that, given the opportunity, they would try to make good the claim to predominance which at heart they had never renounced.[3]

In his anxiety about the future of Palestine Sykes was moved

[3] 'Ne pouvant souscrire, malgré l'accord signé, à l'abandon de ses révendications sur la Palestine. . . .': Pingaud, III, 230.

to consider how the British position could be strengthened. As shown by his letter to Samuel, he had played with the idea of proposing a Belgian trusteeship. This would have the advantage of keeping out the French, but what Sykes really wanted was a firm British foothold in Palestine. Was it not possible that here the Zionists could be of some assistance? Having regard to the strong pro-British bias of the Zionist leaders, not only in England but also in the United States, to say nothing of the long tradition of friendship and admiration for Great Britain among the Jews of Eastern Europe, might there not be room for an understanding which would tend to bring the Zionist Movement into the British orbit? Might not this lead to an alliance which could be as useful to Great Britain in dealing with the Palestine Question as it would assuredly be welcome to the Zionists themselves?

These ideas, at first only floating vaguely in Sykes' mind, began to crystallise as his contact with Zionism grew closer. He found them still more attractive in the light of his conversations with Weizmann and Sokolow after meeting them for the first time at the beginning of 1917. By the spring of that year competition between Great Britain and France for eventual predominance in Palestine had been sharpened by clear indications that Russia—an important third party—was drifting out of the War and might before long cease to count. The French could hope that this would tell in their favour. On the other hand, a start had now been made with the British invasion of Palestine, which would mean, if all went well, that the War would end with Jerusalem, if not the whole country, in British occupation. It was in these circumstances that, having found favour at a higher level, Sykes' ideas began to be translated into a plan of action designed to help the British Government to extricate itself, so far as Palestine was concerned, from the Sykes-Picot Agreement by demonstrating to the French that the Jews were solidly opposed to a condominium in Palestine and overwhelmingly in favour of a British trusteeship.

It will be seen, when we reach this point, that Sykes was identified with almost every move. But all this was in the context of a new turn of events—the Russian Revolution and the British invasion of Palestine. When he went to Petrograd at the end of February 1916 Sykes was only just beginning to think about the Jewish aspect of the Palestine Question and to consider whether the Jews could somehow be fitted into the arrangements he had agreed upon with Picot a few weeks earlier.

The situation at the start of the War has already been described. The French had placed themselves in a strong position for claiming that, should the War end with the collapse of Turkey and the partition of the Turkish Empire, they should be recognised as the natural heirs to Syria, which, in their eyes, included Palestine. In some influential British circles the prospect of French control of Palestine was viewed with anxiety, but the British Government had not shown its hand, nor, indeed, had it made up its mind as to how far the French could safely be allowed to have their way. In the end it came round to the view that the French claim must be cut down, and Palestine, or the greater part of it, reserved for an international régime in which Great Britain would be represented. In the Sykes-Picot discussions it declined to recede from this position, and by the end of January 1916 the French had unwillingly acquiesced.

For Great Britain it was an advantage that it was not solely a question between herself and France. British pressure for an international régime would in any case have been hard to withstand. What made it irresistible was the presence in the background of another interested party—Russia.

Rapacious as was Russia's programme of territorial expansion, it did not extend to Palestine. She was, however, well entrenched there. For some years before the War Russian influence in Palestine had been growing steadily stronger. The subsidies lavished by Russia on the Orthodox Church and its institutions, the impressive building programme which had provided not only Jerusalem but most of the other religious centres with visible symbols of her presence, the annual influx of Russian pilgrims shepherded and watched over by the Imperial Orthodox Society —all this had redounded to Russia's credit in the eyes of the Palestine population and noticeably enhanced her prestige. In 1913 a well-informed English periodical published a series of articles on 'The Powers in Palestine.' The conclusion reached was that 'Russia stands first of the European Powers . . . Germany has come up very close. France's . . . old proud pre-eminence has been lost. . . .'[4] The tension still prevailing between the Greek and Russian elements in the Orthodox Church was enough, of itself, to make it important for Russia to sustain her pretensions as the Orthodox Power *par excellence* by showing no weakness or lack of zeal in her defence of Orthodox interests in Palestine.

Hence, quite apart from such resistance as there might be from the British side, the French could not hope to get all they wanted in Palestine without a deal with Russia. On the other hand, if subject only—should this be unavoidable—to some special provision for the Holy Places, Russia could be induced to acquiesce in French predominance in Palestine, the British position would be seriously weakened. Before the opening of the Sykes-Picot negotiations at the end of 1915 the French had already made at least two attempts to get their Russian ally on their side in the matter of Palestine,[5] but, though the Russians had made some soothing noises, their attitude had been equivocal and their claims had been neither relinquished nor clearly defined.

As was later to appear, the French went on hoping against hope that the Russian barrier to their aspirations in Palestine might somehow be charmed away.[6] But all they could do was to bide their time. When the results of the Sykes-Picot discussions were reported to Paris in January 1916, the French Government had to face the distasteful fact that the British demand for internationalisation would be pressed and could not be resisted. On this, as on various other points, it was compelled reluctantly to give way, and in May, the Russians having been duly consulted, the Sykes-Picot scheme, with some variations not here material, was formally ratified by the two Governments in an exchange of letters between the British Foreign Secretary, Sir Edward Grey, and the French Ambassador, Paul Cambon.

The effect of the Agreement was briefly as follows[7]:

[4] *The Near East,* 21 November 1913.
[5] See below, p. 244.
[6] See below, p. 260.
[7] The full text, as set out in Sir Edward Grey's letter of 16 May 1916 to M. Cambon, is printed in *B.F.P., First Series,* Vol. IV, pp. 245ff. The map annexed to the Agreement is not reproduced in *B.F.P.,* but the reader is referred (p. 245, note 1, and p. 642) to the map printed in Lloyd George's *The Truth about the Peace Treaties,* II, 1024, and to the more instructive map printed at the end of Aldrovandi Marescotti's *Guerra Diplomatica* (Milan, 1936).

First, Great Britain was to exercise authority in Southern Mesopotamia (referred to in the Agreement as ' the red area ') and, on
the Palestine coast, was to acquire the ports of Haifa and Acre.
Secondly, parallel to the British Zone in Southern Mesopotamia,
there was to be a French Zone (' the blue area ') including the
coastal strip of Syria and the Lebanon, together with so much of
Palestine west of the Jordan as lay north of a line running,
roughly, from just north of Acre to a point near the head of Lake
Tiberias. The ' blue area ' assigned to the French extended north-
wards from Syria so as to take in Cilicia and, still further north,
a triangular block of territory with its apex deep in Asia Minor.
Thirdly, south of the ' blue area ' there was reserved for separate
treatment as an international zone a ' brown area ' bounded on
the south by a line starting just north of Gaza, then running north
of Hebron, and ending at a point near the northern end of the
Dead Sea. The ' brown area ' thus consisted of what was left of
Palestine west of the Jordan, after allowing for the French claim
to the strip to be merged with Syria in the north and for the
British claim to Haifa and Acre.

It was agreed, lastly, that, as to the future of the predominantly
Arab territories outside the red, blue and brown areas, or, in other
words, the interior of Syria and Mesopotamia, Great Britain and
France would be prepared to recognise and uphold[8] an independent Arab State, or a Confederation of Arab States, ' under
the suzerainty of an Arab chief.' The whole area of the Arab State
or Confederation was to be divided into French and British
spheres of influence (' area A ' and ' area B '), to be separated by
a line running roughly north-eastwards from Lake Tiberias to the
Turco-Persian frontier and plotted so as to award Mosul to the
French sphere.

More will need to be said about the Agreement as a whole, but
it will be convenient at this point to set out the provisions
specially relating to Palestine, it being borne in mind that a strip
of northern Palestine was included in the ' blue area ' assigned
to France.

' 3. That in the brown area[9] there shall be established an

[8] The word ' uphold ' was substituted for ' protect ' by an amendment
agreed to in August 1916: *B.F.P., First Series*, Vol. IV, p. 249.
[9] As to the limits of the 'brown area' see above.

international administration, the form of which is to be decided upon after consultation with Russia, and subsequently in consultation with the other Allies, and the representatives of the Shereef of Mecca.

' 4. That Great Britain be accorded the ports of Haifa and Acre. . . .

' 5. . . . That Haifa shall be a free port as regards the trade of France, her dominions and protectorates. . . . There shall be freedom of transit for French goods through Haifa and by the British railway through the brown area. . . .

' 7. That Great Britain has the right to build, administer and be sole owner of a railway connecting Haifa with area B.[10] . . . It is to be understood by both Governments that this railway is to facilitate the connexion of Bagdad with Haifa by rail, and it is further understood that, if the engineering difficulties and expense entailed by keeping the connecting line in the brown area only make the project unfeasible, that the French Government shall be prepared to consider that the line in question may also traverse the polygon Banias-Keis Marib-Salkhad Tell Otsda-Mesmie before reaching area B.'

This was the situation in the spring of 1916. How that position had been reached must now be more fully explained, if the events which followed are to be understood.

[10] I.e., the British sphere of influence in Mesopotamia.

CHAPTER 16

THE SYKES-PICOT AGREEMENT

THE ANGLO-FRENCH naval attack on the Dardanelles forts opened on 19 February 1915. It was in the interval between the commencement of the attempt to force the Dardanelles and the landing of British troops on Gallipoli on April 25th that the Russians succeeded in extorting from their allies the recognition of their claim to Constantinople and the Straits.

The Anglo-French operations had been undertaken partly with a view to relieving Turkish pressure on the Russians in the Caucasus. On the other hand, if they succeeded, the Russians would be left in the, for them, embarrassing position of finding the Straits controlled, and Constantinople occupied, by Allied naval and military forces to which they had made no contribution.[1] Obsessed by what they conceived to be a threat to their vital interests, they resolved to insure against it by a prompt and determined assertion of their demands at a moment when their partners in the Entente could ill afford to quarrel with them. On 4 March 1915 Sazonov startled London and Paris with what amounted to a peremptory announcement by the Russians to their British and French allies of their fixed resolve to ensure, not merely the neutralisation or internationalisation of the Straits, but the incorporation in the Russian Empire of the Straits, Constantinople and an extensive hinterland.[2] The War was going none too favourably for the Entente ; Russia was an unreliable ally ; and, though the extent of the claims so abruptly advanced was unexpected and alarming, Great Britain and France were in no position to resist them. The British reluctantly acquiesced, followed, after an interval, and still more reluctantly, by the French.

Once the Russian demands had been accepted, it was clear that the partition of Turkey, if she lost the War, had become unavoid-

---

[1] Adamov, Vol. II ('Constantinople and the Straits'), No. 46 ; Pingaud, I, 247 ; Grey, *Twenty-Five Years,* II, 187.

[2] *B.F.P.,* pp. 635-636. All *B.F.P.* citations in this chapter refer to First Series, Vol. IV.

able. With the Russians installed in Constantinople and in control of the Straits, Turkey would simply become a Russian satellite unless Great Britain and France had taken steps to reserve appropriate slices of the Turkish Empire for themselves or their protégés. Sazonov himself, in his telegram of March 4th, had assured the British and French Governments that Russia could be relied upon not to stand in their way in making good any claims of their own in other parts of Turkey or elsewhere. This assurance was taken up by Grey, who, on March 12th, while agreeing to the Russian demands, made it clear that this was subject to the War being carried on to victory, and 'to the desiderata of Great Britain and France in the Ottoman Empire and elsewhere being realised.'[3]

Grey was, however, in no hurry to specify the British desiderata. In conversation with the Russian Ambassador, Benckendorff, on March 3rd,[4] just before the arrival of Sazonov's bombshell, he had said, according to Benckendorff, that, while Great Britain had certain interests in the region of the Persian Gulf, she had no aspirations in any part of Syria or Asia Minor. Nine days later, in a memorandum amplifying his acceptance of the Russian demands, Grey said plainly that both Great Britain and France would now have to see to the protection of their own interests in the East, but in regard to British claims he was vague, the only question explicitly raised being that of a revision in favour of Great Britain of the Anglo-Russian agreement concerning spheres of influence in Persia. As to Turkey, Grey's only express stipulation at this stage was that 'the Mussulman Holy Places and Arabia shall under all circumstances remain under independent Mussulman dominion.'[5]

Grey's insistence on this last point reflects his anxiety to place himself in as strong a position possible for cultivating the goodwill of the Arabs, in pursuance of the policy, now already beginning to take shape, of widening the breach between the Arabs and the Turks, and creating in Arabia a rallying-point for Moslem loyalties, as an answer to the Holy War proclaimed by the Ottoman Khalif. What was in Grey's mind is clearly brought out by a memorandum dated 20 March 1915,[6] in which Sazonov is

[3] *B.F.P.*, p. 636.
[4] Adamov, No. 13.
[5] *B.F.P.*, pp. 636-638.
[6] Adamov, No. 32.

informed that His Majesty's Government attach great importance
to the creation of an independent Mussulman State as the political
centre of Islam. It is not yet possible, it is pointed out, to say
whether such a State should include, in addition to Arabia, any
other part of Asiatic Turkey, and it would, therefore, be premature for the Powers, pending a settlement of that question, to
discuss a possible partition of Mesopotamia, Syria, Palestine and
the adjacent territories.

It will be noticed that Grey seems to contemplate as at least
a possibility the inclusion of Palestine in the Moslem Arab State,
though only a few weeks earlier he had told Herbert Samuel that
he was still anxious to promote a settlement of the Palestine question in a sense favourable to Zionist ideas.[7] Quite apart from this,
it might have been expected that the British Government would,
on other grounds, regard an Arab claim to Palestine as inad-
missible. There is, however, some reason to believe that Kitchener
favoured the award of Palestine to the Arabs,[8] assuming, presumably, that the result would be to bring it indirectly under
British control.

Uncertainty as to what it might be necessary or expedient to
offer the Arabs helps to account for Grey's delaying tactics, but
he had other reasons for being vague about the British claims.
Even apart from the Arab question, Great Britain's Eastern policy
had not yet been fully thought out in the light of the new situation
created by the entry of Turkey into the War, followed by the
Russian demand for Constantinople and the Straits. In the
intricate negotiations which had resulted, immediately before the
War, in interlocking agreements between the Powers mainly
concerned as to their respective spheres of interest in Asiatic
Turkey the British Government's principal concern had been to
safeguard the British position in the region of the Persian Gulf.
On this point there was no room for any deviation from a well-
established policy, but for the rest there was no consensus of

[7] Above, p. 110.
[8] See Sir Vivian Gabriel's letter to *The Times* (12 July 1922): 'In 1915,
when Lord Kitchener laid the proposition [concerning negotiations with
the Sharif of Mecca] before the Cabinet, of which he was a member, I
was acting as his personal assistant in regard to Arab matters, and know
that his scheme, on which the letter to the Sharif was based, would
certainly not have admitted the exclusion of Palestine.'

opinion in the British Cabinet. In March 1915, when the Cabinet must have been considering the Turkish question in the light of Sazonov's demands, Samuel was inviting his colleagues to interest themselves in the future of Palestine. In a passage already quoted from his diary (13 March 1915), Asquith refers to Samuel's memorandum, but only to brush it aside with the comment that Samuel's sole supporter is Lloyd George.[9] There were other proposals for British participation in the carving-up of Turkey. From an entry in Asquith's diary twelve days later[10] it appears that Winston Churchill (who, as First Lord of the Admiralty, would have been interested in oil supplies) was urging that, if other Powers were to be awarded their shares of the spoils of war, Great Britain should insist on hers and should claim (*inter alia*) 'Mesopotamia, with or without Alexandretta.' Only two members of the Cabinet seem to have been against an expansionist policy on principle, but these two were the Prime Minister and the Foreign Secretary. 'Grey and I,' Asquith writes, 'are the only men who doubt and distrust any such settlement.'

Grey, therefore, was not in a hurry to discuss the partition of Turkey. The French were. On 7 March 1915 Benckendorff reported to Petrograd that it appeared to him that, while Grey was anxious to steer clear of the subject, the French Foreign Minister, Delcassé, wanted to deal with it as a matter of urgency.[11] Benckendorff's impression was correct. The French were alarmed by the extent of the Russian demands and unwilling to concede them, but, should this become unavoidable, they were determined to do everything in their power to make sure that their own claims were not overlooked. They knew that Russia was greedy and unreliable, and as for Great Britain, the resentful memories still lingering in their minds of what had happened in Egypt and at Fashoda nourished their distrust of British intentions in other parts of the East. From the start they had borne the brunt of the fighting in the Western theatre of war, and, as the War went on, the strain on their resources was bound to be reflected in a deterioration of their bargaining-power in relation to their Allies.

[9] The passage is quoted above, p. 111.
[10] *Memories and Reflections*, II, 69 (25 March 1915).
[11] Adamov, No. 19. See also Grey, *Twenty-Five Years*, II, p. 230.

Time was not on their side. If the British could afford to wait, the French could not.

Quite early in the War the French had tried to arm themselves with an assurance that, so far as Russia was concerned, their claim to a Greater Syria, including Palestine, as well as to certain areas further north, was conceded.

On 21 November 1914 the French Ambassador in Petrograd, Paléologue, was received in audience by the Czar. Having listened deferentially to the Czar's exposition of Russian war-aims in Europe and Asia, Paléologue took occasion to remind him that ' in Syria and Palestine France has a precious heritage of historical memories and moral and material interests.' Would His Majesty acquiesce in any measures which France might think fit to take to safeguard that heritage? Without making any reservations in regard to Palestine, the Czar, according to Paléologue, gave the assurance he had been asked for.[12]

This was only a few weeks after Turkey had entered the War. Some four months later, after the Russians had announced their intentions concerning Constantinople and the Straits, they were again invited to recognise the French claim to Syria and again reminded that it extended to Palestine. Paléologue saw the Czar on 16 March 1915 and explained to him ' the full programme of civilising work France intends to undertake in Syria, Cilicia, and Palestine.' After examining the area in question on the map, the Czar declared: ' I agree to all you ask.' This is Paléologue's account of the conversation.[13] Pingaud, however, says that the Czar made some reservations concerning Palestine and the Holy Places.[14]

Such reservations were certainly made by Sazonov when Paléologue saw him later on the same day. According to Pingaud,[15] Paléologue pointed out that from the time of the Crusades Palestine had, in French eyes, always been indissolubly linked with Syria, but Sazonov was not impressed. This is borne out by his telegram of March 16th to the Russian Ambassador in Paris,

[12] M. Paléologue, *An Ambassador's Memoirs* (London, Hutchinson, 1923), I, 193.

[13] Ibid., I, 303.

[14] Pingaud, I, 253.

[15] I, 254.

Iswolsky.[16] Paléologue, he said, had given it to be understood that in their claim to Syria the French included Palestine. This point, Iswolsky was told, would have to be clarified, since it raised the question of the Holy Places, which would call for special consideration. Nor was Russia interested only in the Holy Places as commonly understood. In a reference in his diary (March 18th) to Paléologue's interviews with the Czar and Sazonov, President Poincaré recorded his strong impression that Russia would never agree to a Roman Catholic protectorate over ' Jerusalem, Galilee, the Jordan, and Lake Tiberias.'[17]

The French, on their side, began to retreat a little. On March 17th Delcassé told the Russian Ambassador that, while France might claim possession of certain parts of Palestine, he agreed that the question of the Holy Places must be reserved for separate discussion.[18] It looks as though Delcassé was still hoping to strike some bargain about Palestine with the Russians. When he told the Foreign Affairs Commission of the Chamber of Deputies, in the middle of March, that France would have to give way to Russia on the matter of Constantinople and the Straits, the Commission was much perturbed but was left under the impression that the Russians had at least conceded the French claim to Palestine. ' Delcassé,' the British Ambassador wrote in his diary (28 March, 1915), ' had spoken to the Deputies in the autumn of Palestine but lately had not mentioned it ; they, therefore, concluded that Russia had been squared.'[19] The Russians had not been squared, but Delcassé may still have thought they might be, in which case the Palestine question would be so much the easier to handle when it came to discussions with the British.

But any hopes that he may have had of a firm Franco-Russian understanding about Palestine had in the end to be set aside. Much as they disliked the Russian claim to Constantinople and the Straits, and hard as they had tried to get full consideration for assenting to it, the French had to be content with a vague assurance that Russia was prepared to let them have what they wanted in Syria and Cilicia.[20] On 12 April 1915, a month after the British,

[16] Adamov, No. 29.
[17] Poincaré, VI, 118.
[18] Adamov, No. 31.
[19] Bertie, I, 134-135.
[20] Adamov, Nos. 29, 31.

and, apparently, under British pressure,[21] they informed the Russian Government that they agreed to its demands on condition that the War was carried on to victory and that France and Great Britain realised their aims in the East and elsewhere.[22]

But France and Great Britain had still to define their aims and to agree upon them between themselves, and many months were to pass before that point was reached. If Delcassé had had his way, there would have been a prompt exchange of views.[23] But however desirable it might be to clear up the position as between the two Powers, the British Government was not yet ready to enter into any binding commitments. Before doing so, it would have to make up its mind as to its own objectives, and these, in turn, would depend in some measure on the nature and extent of the promises to be made to the Arabs as the price of the Arab rising which it was intended to encourage.

As a first step towards a definition of British war aims in the East, Asquith decided early in April 1915 to set up an Inter-Departmental Committee under the chairmanship of Sir Maurice de Bunsen.[24] The de Bunsen Committee's terms of reference were to consider the nature of British desiderata in Turkey in Asia in the event of the successful conclusion of the War. The Committee submitted its report on June 30th. With the exception of one short extract, the report has not been published, but the exception is important, since it is a passage relating to Palestine[25]:

'Still less do the Committee desire to offer suggestions about the future destiny of Palestine, but since that territory has been included within the geographical limits assigned to the British sphere in the two schemes, of partition, and of zones of interest, they desire to repeat that they see no

[21] Poincaré, I, 336 ; Ribot fils, *Journal d'Alexandre Ribot* (Paris, 1936), p. 130.
[22] *B.F.P.*, p. 638.
[23] Grey, op. cit., II, 230 ; Pingaud, III, 224.
[24] The date and terms of reference are given in a memorandum by Sykes: *Sledm.*, No. 15 (1 July 1916). Sir M. de Bunsen had been British Ambassador in Vienna.
[25] Cmd. 5974 (1939), Annex J, p. 51.

reason why the sacred places of Palestine should not be dealt with as a separate question. They have felt free to deliberate on the assumption that the French claim will be rejected, since they are convinced that the forces opposed are too great for France ever to make that claim good, but for the same reason they consider that it will be idle for His Majesty's Government to claim the retention of Palestine in their sphere. Palestine must be recognised as a country whose destiny must be the subject of special negotiations, in which both belligerents and neutrals are alike interested.'

From this it may be inferred that by the middle of 1915 it had come to be generally accepted that there could be no question of acquiescing in the French claim to Palestine. It also appears that beyond that point opinions were sharply divided. One school of thought, represented, it may be guessed, by the War Office, was evidently pressing for a policy designed to bring Palestine directly or indirectly under British control. The de Bunsen report discouraged any such ambitions and advised the Government to take its stand on the principle that the future of Palestine was a matter of international concern. The Committee expressed no view as to the kind of régime which would be suitable for Palestine. It did not, in terms, advocate an international administration, or, still less, an international administration representing the Allied Powers to the exclusion of others ; on the contrary, it proposed that neutrals as well as belligerents —meaning, apparently, belligerents on both sides—should be consulted.

The de Bunsen report, or at least the published extract,[26] does not enter into any close examination of the nature and extent of British interests in Palestine. The whole tone is rather detached. The Government is simply advised to abandon any idea of a British claim to Palestine and to rest content with the certainty that the French claim must fail. Nevertheless, it looks as though British thinking began soon afterwards to move towards a more active interest in the Palestine question. As soon as the de Bunsen Committee had reached its conclusions and

[26] The words 'they desire to repeat . . .' seem to suggest that the published extract may not represent the only reference in the report to Palestine.

247

THE BALFOUR DECLARATION

was ready to draft its report, Sykes, who had been in touch with the discussions, was sent (according to his biographer, by Kitchener) on an extended tour of the East.[27] From Cairo, where Picot had been before him, he wrote:[28] ' From what I have heard of M. Picot's mission I believe that the French will give up the coast to the south of Akka. This, indeed, is essential to our position in Mesopotamia.'[29] Considering how close Sykes was to the inner circle, there is here an indication that by the summer of 1915 it was beginning to be taken for granted that Great Britain must make sure of a permanent foothold in Mesopotamia, with the corollary that she would also need Haifa, which the French must be invited to renounce in her favour. As to the Palestine question generally, it has been authoritatively stated that ' in the autumn of 1915 His Majesty's Government wished to restrict the claims of their Ally to Palestine ',[30] the implication being that this was a matter in which the British Government was now actively interested.

In March 1915 the British Cabinet had been divided on the question whether Great Britain should demand anything for herself in the partition of Turkey in Asia. Quite apart from anything that may have been contained in the de Bunsen report, a decision to take a firm line in the assertion of British interests in that part of the world may have been in some degree influenced by the reconstitution of the Cabinet, and the introduction of a number of Conservative Ministers, two months later. Whatever the explanation, substantial British claims in the

---

[27] Shane Leslie, *Mark Sykes—His Life and Letters*, pp. 20, 238. Lawrence, however, referring, apparently, to Sykes's mission to the East in 1915, said: ' The mission was on Sykes's own initiative, not Kitchener's. He fixed it up with Sir A. Nicolson ': *T. E. Lawrence to his Biographers, Liddell Hart and Robert Graves*, p. 60. Sykes left England on 1 June 1915 ; Shane Leslie, p. 227.

[28] Shane Leslie, p. 241.

[29] Basra had been occupied by British forces early in the War, and a further advance was in preparation.

[30] ' He [the Lord Chancellor] does not deny that in the autumn of 1915 His Majesty's Government wished to restrict the claims of their ally to Palestine if they could do so in the only way open to them, i.e., by an understanding with that ally ': Statement by the Lord Chancellor (Lord Maugham) printed in ' Report of a Committee set up to consider certain correspondence between Sir Henry McMahon and the Sharif of Mecca ' —Cmd. 5974 (1939), p. 46.

partition of Turkey were advanced in the Anglo-French negotiations which began towards the end of the year, while, as to Palestine, Great Britain insisted on internationalisation with a firmness which showed that what was considered to be at stake was not just an abstract principle but an important British interest.

The time proposed by the British Government for the opening of the Anglo-French discussions was obviously related to the progress of its negotiations with the Sharif of Mecca. In his letter of 24 October 1915[31] the British High Commissioner in Cairo, Sir Henry McMahon, defined, not with absolute precision but as clearly as seemed possible in the circumstances, the area in which Great Britain would be prepared to recognise and support the independence of the Arabs. Four days earlier, and, presumably, after the terms of the McMahon letter had been finally settled, Grey had, in conversation with the French Ambassador, proposed that the British and French Governments should appoint representatives to discuss the frontiers of Syria, and, by inference, of the projected Arab State.[32] It would, from a British point of view, have been premature to embark on such discussions before the British offer to the Arabs had been formulated. On the other hand, once the ground had thus been cleared, it was highly desirable that any possible misunderstandings between Great Britain and France should be disposed of before the expected Arab rising took place.[33] Such misunderstandings could well arise from British assurances to the Sharif which might be considered by the French to derogate from the position they claimed for themselves in Syria, and to conflict with what they had become accustomed to describe as the Anglo-French accord of 1912. Interpreting this as entitling them, as between themselves and the British, to a free hand in Syria, they scented danger in the relations between the British Government and the Sharif. It was important that they should be persuaded, not only that Great Britain was not seeking by devious

[31] Text in Cmd. 5957 (1939), pp. 7ff.
[32] B.F.P., No. 334, p. 481.
[33] As to the real dimensions of the events, sometimes rather bombastically described as the Arab Revolt, which began with the rising in the Hedjaz in June 1916, see above, p. 88.

means to undermine the French position in the Levant, but that the two Powers had a common interest in fomenting an Arab rising and, as a corollary, in encouraging Arab national aspirations. The British had from the start been convinced that substantial advantages to the Allied cause could be expected from a successful courtship of the Arabs. The French were much less enthusiastic. Not only might the mere existence of an Arab State carved out of the former Turkish Empire turn out to be a standing threat to their interests in the Levant, but they had also to consider what effect it might have on the situation in North Africa,[34] where they had, only two years before the War, considerably increased their stake in the Moslem Arab world by the veiled annexation of Morocco.

It was in the light of this situation that, at an interview with the French Ambassador on 21 October 1915, Grey suggested that representatives of the two Powers should meet to discuss the frontiers of Syria.[35] Grey's primary purpose was to reconcile French claims with Arab aspirations, and both with British commitments, in the matter of Syria, but what was eventually to emerge was an Anglo-French understanding covering a wider range of questions relating to the post-War settlement in the East, including that of the future of Palestine.

Grey's proposal was promptly agreed to by the French Government, which looked forward hopefully to an acceptable definition of its sphere of interest in Syria. This, Poincaré wrote in his diary (27 October 1915),[36] would be a happy complement to the accord of 1912. Within a few days of the receipt of Grey's invitation the French Government had selected its representative and sent him to London.[37]

---

[34] Poincaré, VII, 362 (Diary, 28 December 1915). A memorandum stating Sykes's views on the Syrian question (*Sledm.*, No. 4, 16 December 1915) draws attention to French anxiety about North Africa.

[35] See Note 32.

[36] Poincaré, VII, 206.

[37] Delcassé had just resigned, and at the moment of Grey's *démarche* the French Foreign Office was temporarily in charge of the Prime Minister, Viviani. Viviani himself resigned almost immediately afterwards and was succeeded, on October 30th, by Briand, who, as Prime Minister and Minister of Foreign Affairs, was in control of French policy throughout the negotiations leading to the Sykes-Picot Agreement.

François Georges-Picot[38] had at the outbreak of war been French Consul-General in Beirut. After leaving Syria when Turkey entered the War, he had been sent on a special mission to Egypt, with results reflected in Mark Sykes's discovery, on his arrival in Cairo in the summer of 1915, that Anglo-French rivalry was being vigorously exploited.[39] Besides some personal knowledge of the Levant, Picot's qualifications included twenty years in the French diplomatic service, a fervent belief in France's mission in the East, and a keen awareness of the weak position in which she might find herself if she failed, while there was still time, to insist firmly on her fair share of the spoils in the Levant and elsewhere. In negotiation Picot was tough and tenacious ; his friend, and (later) his junior colleague, Gontaut-Biron describes enthusiastically his conduct of the rearguard action he was compelled to fight in the Anglo-French talks, ' disputing foot by foot every scrap of territory, countering every manoeuvre aimed at our rights.'[40]

The Anglo-French discussions opened on 23 November 1915 with a meeting between Picot and Sir Arthur Nicolson.[41] Marked divergencies emerged on the Syrian question, and no agreement was reached.[42] At a further meeting on December 21st Picot was somewhat less unaccommodating in regard to Syria,[43] but the British and French positions were still far apart. According to Poincaré,[44] Briand reported to his colleagues that it appeared from what Nicolson had said that the British Government was prepared to agree that the French Zone should extend to Cilicia and that it should take in Alexandretta but was asking for large concessions in return. First, Syria and the Lebanon were to be under the suzerainty of the Sharif, the French having only the

[38] 1870-1951.
[39] Shane Leslie, p. 241.
[40] Gontaut-Biron, pp. 33-34.
[41] Permanent Under-Secretary of State for Foreign Affairs ; later, Lord Carnock.
[42] B.F.P., No. 334, p. 481 ; Pingaud, II, 225.
[43] B.F.P., loc. cit.
[44] VII, 362ff. (Diary, 28 December 1915).

right to appoint the Governor.[45] Secondly, the French were to agree to the building of a British trans-Asiatic railway with a Mediterranean terminus at Haifa.

As to Palestine, it seems clear that, apart from any question that may have been raised on the British side as to the future of Haifa, it was by this time common ground that some special provision would have to be made for the Holy Places. It seems also to have been conceded by the French, at least in principle, that for this purpose, a reserved area would have to be carved out of Palestine and placed under some kind of international régime.[46] The position at this stage appears to have been that to this limited extent the French had receded from their extreme demands, but that no agreed decision had been reached as to the delimitation of the reserved area, nor had the French relinquished the hope that even there they might secure a special status giving them *de facto* control.

In the interval between Picot's interview with Nicolson on 23 November 1915 and their further meeting a month later Mark Sykes had returned from his mission to the East. His travels had brought home to him the dangers inherent in the strained relations between British and French functionaries on the spot and in the smouldering suspicions and resentments which kept them apart. He had come back convinced that the Arab rising which he confidently foresaw might well result in serious tension between the two Powers, if, when it began, they were still at cross-purposes in the East. On arriving in England early in December he pressed this view strongly upon Kitchener, Grey and Nicolson.[47] Recognising that the Anglo-French discussions could not safely be left where they were and that the deadlock must somehow be resolved, the British Government decided to make a fresh start, with Sykes as its representative.

[45] It must be borne in mind that this is only Poincaré's impression of the British proposals as reported, or as he understood them to have been reported, by Briand.

[46] This seems to be implied in the reference to 'the Jerusalem enclave' in the statement of Sykes' views in a memorandum dated 16 December 1915 (*Sledm.*, No. 4).

[47] In a memorandum written in September 1917 Sykes recalls that, as a result of his representations in this sense to Kitchener, Grey and Nicolson, he was invited to carry on the negotiations with Picot: *Sledm.*, No. 68 (25 September 1917).

Though Sykes was not, like Picot, a professional diplomat, he was well equipped to deal with that tough and experienced negotiator. At the age of thirty-six, he had by his writings and his speeches in Parliament built up an established reputation as an expert on Eastern affairs. He had travelled widely before the War in nearly all parts of the Turkish Empire and had studied at close quarters the forces making for its disintegration, believing that the break-up of Turkey would, from a British point of view, be a misfortune, but giving thought to the situation which would arise if it could not be averted. To his discussions with Picot he brought, not only the fruits of his intimate acquaintance with pre-War Turkey, but the fresh knowledge and enhanced authority derived from his association with the de Bunsen Committee, followed by nearly six months' travel, with all doors open to him, in the East. As an ardent Roman Catholic he was immune from any suspicion of anti-Catholic bias in dealing with the delicate issues involved in certain aspects of the French claim to a predominant position in the Levant, and more particularly in Palestine. If there were some who thought him too impressionable and impulsive to be always reliable in his judgments, there could be no doubt as to the gifts which gave him his distinctive quality and flavour— his well-stored, active and agile mind, his lively imagination, his accessibility to new ideas and the exuberant vitality which sustained him in his invincible optimism.[48]

Sykes' general view of the Middle Eastern situation—a view which he consistently expressed throughout the War—was that the corner-stone of a stable settlement in harmony with British interests must be close and permanent co-operation between Great Britain and France. It was because he was convinced that Anglo-French rivalry, if left unchecked, could only play into the hands of the Turco-German combination that he pressed for a determined effort to put an end to it in time to clear the ground for the Arab rising on which he counted. But he was far from suggesting that the price to be paid for an Anglo-French under-

---

[48] In addition to Sir Shane Leslie's excellent biography of Sykes (*Mark Sykes—His Life and Letters*), there is a brilliant character-sketch by his son, Christopher Sykes, in *Two Studies in Virtue* (London, Collins, 1953), pp. 173ff.

standing must be a capitulation to French demands, and least of all in the matter of Palestine. Among his papers is a memorandum, dated 16 December 1915,[49] which shows how his mind was working on the eve of his conversations with Picot. He took the view which a Kitchener man might be expected to take of the strategic importance of Palestine. Assuming that there would have to be a ' Jerusalem enclave,' he thought that, the enclave excepted, Great Britain should claim for herself, or for her sphere of influence, the whole area south of a line reaching the Mediterranean at Acre down to the Egyptian frontier. Sykes' purpose is self-evident. His scheme would secure British control of the Palestine coast, save for any part of it which might be reserved as an outlet for the enclave. It would give Egypt the full benefit of the desert barrier, and it would interpose a substantial belt of British-controlled territory between the Sharif's Arabian homeland and the French. On the assumption that even the enclave would not be left to France but would be internationalised, Sykes' proposals would mean that, far from securing their ' Syrie intégrale,' the French would find the southern limit of their sphere pushed back from the borders of Egypt to the northernmost part of Palestine. It was not until some two months later that, as a result of his talk with Herbert Samuel and his study of Samuel's Palestine memorandum, Sykes began to interest himself in the Jewish aspect of the Palestine question. In the scheme he outlined in December 1915 it was ignored.

In his approach to the French claims generally Sykes was influenced by his dislike and suspicion of the French financial interests which had before the War involved themselves heavily in Turkey. In the paper just mentioned we find him dwelling upon two themes which continued to pre-occupy him throughout the War. First, he was convinced that French co-operation in a pro-Arab policy was being, and would continue to be, obstructed by ' Franco-Levantine finance,' meaning the holders of profitable Syrian concessions which, having been granted by the Turks, might be threatened by a change of régime. Secondly, Sykes was impressed, almost to the point of obsession, by the dangers which he believed to be implicit in the pre-War links between the French and German groups jointly concerned with the Baghdad

[49] *Sledm.*, No. 4.

railway and its ramifications. He was satisfied that these connections had not been completely severed and that the two groups were still in touch with each other through a Swiss intermediary. Resistance to the French demands for ' la Syrie intégrale ' was, in his view, all the more imperative because among its principal supporters he perceived financial interests tainted by association with the Germans.[50]

These were some of the ideas in Sykes' mind when, towards the end of December 1915, he began the conversations with Picot which paved the way for the Anglo-French accord popularly known as the Sykes-Picot Agreement. As Sykes himself more than once pointed out,[51] ' the Sykes-Picot Agreement ' is a misnomer. Because he was recognised as an expert on the matters in question, Sykes, though not a member of the Foreign Office nor a professional diplomat, had been brought in from outside in the hope that he would succeed in breaking the deadlock which had been reached in the talks between Picot and Nicolson. His advice would naturally carry weight and would play its part in moulding British policy, but, like Picot, he was not a plenipotentiary but a delegate acting under instructions and with no power to make binding commitments. For reasons to be given later, it may be doubted whether, from a British standpoint, the Sykes-Picot Agreement was as unsatisfactory as has sometimes been suggested, but, whatever view may be taken of its merits or shortcomings, final responsibility rests with the Department which, to quote Sykes' biographer, ' employed him, supervised him, and, in fact, amended his draft agreement.'[52]

By the time the Anglo-French negotiations had begun to get under way, the Russians had provided their British and French allies with a strong incentive to compose their differences. Early in December 1915 information had reached Petrograd from Armenian sources to the effect that Djemal Pasha, the Turkish Commander-in-Chief in Syria and Palestine and a member of the

[50] *Sledm.*, No. 4 (16 December 1915); No. 14 (20 June 1916); No. 68 (25 September 1917).
[51] *Sledm.*, No. 62 (19 July 1917); F.O. memorandum quoted by Shane Leslie, p. 252.
[52] Shane Leslie, p. 21.

inner circle which ruled Turkey, might be prepared, given certain assurances, to march on Constantinople, overthrow the régime, put an end to the Turco-German alliance and take Turkey out of the War. His terms, as reported to Petrograd, were that the *Entente* Powers should recognise him as Sultan of an independent State comprising the greater part of Turkey in Asia, it being understood that Turkey would submit to the loss of Constantinople and the Straits.[53] This information was passed on by the Russians on December 25th to their British, French and Italian allies.[54]

The effect of any such deal with Djemal would be to leave Russia in possession of Constantinople and the Straits, while the incorporation in Djemal's Empire of Syria, Palestine, Mesopotamia and the Arabian Peninsula, all of which were expressly mentioned in the Russian Note of December 25th, would mean that Great Britain and France would be dismissed empty-handed, to say nothing of the Arabs. There would likewise have been an end to Jewish aspirations in Palestine, but the Jews were not then in the picture. The obvious objections were promptly pointed out to the Russians by Briand on December 29th[55] and by Grey on the 30th.[56] Since it was evident that the Russians were, for comprehensible reasons, inclined to favour a flirtation with Djemal, it was all the more essential that Great Britain and France should lose no time in staking out their own claims in Asiatic Turkey after reaching agreement between themselves.

In the end, the Djemal plan faded out. After some further inconclusive exchanges with the other Governments concerned, the Russians learned in June 1916 that the whole question had become unreal, Djemal having abandoned any intention he might have had of treating with the Allies.[57] By this time, the exchange

[53] Adamov, Nos. 50, 52.

[54] Adamov, No. 52.

[55] Adamov, No. 58.

[56] In explaining why the French urged, and the British agreed, that it had become imperative for the two Powers to delimit their respective spheres in Asiatic Turkey, Grey (*Twenty-Five Years*, II, 230-231) does not mention the Djemal episode but says that an impetus was given to the Anglo-French discussions by the Russians' successes in Asia Minor and their announcement that they must not be expected, at the end of the War, to withdraw from the conquered territories.

[57] Adamov, No. 135.

of views between Great Britain and France had been concluded and its results endorsed, in substance, by Russia. The whole episode had no longer any significance, but at the end of 1915 the Russians were clearly interested in the idea of a bargain with Djemal, and the disturbing inferences which could be drawn from their attitude must be borne in mind as part of the background to the Anglo-French conversations.

Sykes came to his discussions with Picot armed with a memorandum in which the British Government, now plainly showing its hand, set out its proposals in some detail. They included the main features of the scheme eventually assented to by the French and, in May 1916, embodied in the Sykes-Picot Agreement, the general purport of which has already been described.[58]
As to Palestine, the British Government did not advance the sweeping demands which had been favoured by Sykes. On the eve of his negotiations with Picot, Sykes, as we have seen, had taken the view that Great Britain should aim at control of the whole country south of Acre, with the exception of a Jerusalem enclave to be reserved for special treatment. Had this proposal been adopted, the British Government would have been interested in keeping the enclave as small as possible, since it would, in effect, be carved out of a British zone. But the idea advocated by Sykes, perhaps influenced by Kitchener, of a small enclave embedded in a British zone was set aside in favour of a less ambitious policy, closer to the recommendations of the de Bunsen report. Haifa, with the Bay of Acre, was to become British, but, subject to this, it was proposed that Palestine should be internationalised. Once it had been decided to work for a condominium in Palestine, it followed that British interests required that the area to be internationally administered should not be confined to Jerusalem and its immediate surroundings but should be considerably more extensive, the line dividing the international zone from the French zone in Syria being pushed well to the north. This was essential if the French in Syria were to be kept at a safe distance from the approaches to Egypt, and if Haifa was to have a hinterland not under purely French control. As to the desert barrier, the British scheme would leave within the British sphere of influence the

[58] As to the British proposals see Pingaud, III, 225.

257

Negev and the rest of southern Palestine down to the Egyptian frontier, as well as the area later to become known as Trans-Jordan.

Far from being offered anything resembling their 'Syrie intégrale,' the French were being invited to submit to a drastic cutting down of their claims. Stubborn resistance was to be expected, and Gontaut-Biron is to be believed when he says that Picot disputed every inch of the ground.[59] Sykes made one concession: he agreed that, instead of being assigned to that part of the projected Arab State which was to be within the French sphere of influence, Beirut should go to France as part of her own Syrian coastal zone.[60] On other points Picot had to give way, and the discussions closed on 3 January 1916 with an agreement on the lines of the British memorandum.[61]

The proposed arrangements were not yet binding on the French, since Picot was not a plenipotentiary. He promptly passed them on to Paris, where Briand—speaking as Poincaré records, 'avec une spirituelle imprécision'—reported on the matter to his colleagues on January 4th.[62] Poincaré records in his diary[63] his pained surprise at British proposals which would, he complains, violate the 1912 accord by leaving the French in Syria under the suzerainty of the Sharif. He recognises with satisfaction that Great Britain has acceded to the French claim to Alexandretta, but a later entry in his diary (January 13th)[64] suggests that, because of the doubtful attitude of the British Admiralty, even this point had not been finally cleared up. As to Palestine, the French had by this time been forced to recognise that eleventh-hour attempts to secure some concessions from the British had failed and that the British Government was not to be deflected either from its demand for Haifa or from its insistence, subject to that demand, on the internationalisation of Palestine.[65] Alexan-

---

[59] Gontaut-Biron, pp. 33-34.
[60] Pingaud, III, 227.
[61] Ibid., 228.
[62] Poincaré, VIII, 8.
[63] Ibid.
[64] Ibid., 26.
[65] Ibid., 23-24, 26.

dretta was in the end left to the French. For the rest, they felt that they had no choice but to give way.[66]

Why did the French think it impossible to hold out against proposals which administered so severe a check to their ambitions both in Syria and in Palestine? The answer, it may be suggested, is that they were acutely conscious of the twofold weakness of their position. First, in the then military situation they could ill afford to quarrel with their partner in the Western theatre of war. Secondly, in the war with Turkey they were not taking, and were not likely ever to be in a position to take, any significant part. It was the British and not the French who were fighting the Turks, and, although at this stage they had not gone beyond defensive operations in Egypt, it was at least conceivable that they might eventually launch an offensive which would result in their emerging from the War in effective control of large slices of Turkish territory, including precisely those areas which were of special interest to France. Would it not, then, be better for France to strike the best bargain she could with Great Britain while the situation was still fluid, rather than run the risk of delaying until the scales had been still further weighted against her? It was precisely because Picot foresaw a weakening of France's bargaining position if her claims were left in the air until the War had been won that, when summoned to Paris for consultation in the spring of 1915, he had urged Delcassé to press for an early and precise agreement between the three leading members of the *Entente* as to their shares in the partition both of Asiatic Turkey and the German colonial Empire.[67]

It is not difficult to understand why, in the situation in which they found themselves at the time of the Sykes-Picot negotiations, the French felt obliged to yield to British pressure rather than risk

[66] Though on the evidence at present (1959) available it is not possible to say precisely when the settlement provisionally reached in London on 3 January 1916 was assented to in Paris, it seems clear that before the end of the month the two Powers had committed themselves, subject to the concurrence of Russia, to the scheme to be embodied, in May, in the Sykes-Picot Agreement.

[67] Picot on *The Origins of the Balfour Declaration*: address delivered in Paris, 1 March 1939 ; verbatim report in *Questions d'Israel* (Paris), 1939, pp. 676-687.

a deadlock by insisting on what they conceived to be their rights. As to Palestine, though they agreed in the end to what was asked of them, they did so with mental reservations, still hoping that, if they could strike a bargain with the Russians, they might be able to press successfully for the question to be re-opened.

When the outcome of the Sykes-Picot discussions was communicated to the Russians early in March 1916, Sazonov noticed that the proposed French sphere of influence ('Area A') extended well into the heart of Armenia, thus impinging on the zone which Russia proposed to claim for herself.[68] In the full tide of their recent successes against the Turks—they had just launched a vigorous offensive on the Armenian Front—the Russians were not disposed to forego any of the fruits of their victories. They insisted on the Sykes-Picot map being revised in their favour at the expense of the French, and in the negotiations which followed the French tried to compensate themselves for the concessions which were being asked of them by some strengthening of their claim to Palestine.   '

It looks as though at one stage Sazonov had been inclined to give them some encouragement. In a memorandum circulated to his Ministerial colleagues in the middle of March he summarised the Anglo-French proposals, pointing out that, if Russian interests were to be safeguarded, it was essential that the northern boundary of the proposed French sphere of influence should be substantially modified. After outlining certain territorial concessions which could safely be offered to the French in return, he suggested that they might also be told that, in regard to Palestine, Russia would be prepared to concern herself solely with the Holy Places and to agree, accordingly, to the cutting down of the area to be internationalised.[69] On March 26th Sazonov was sounded on the Palestine question by the French Ambassador, Paléologue, who wrote on the same day to thank him for having intimated in conversation that, if Great Britain were agreeable to Palestine being included in French Syria, no objection would be raised from the Russian side.[70] But Sazonov seems already to have had second thoughts. In replying to Paléologue[71] he was careful not

[68] Adamov, No. 77 ; Pingaud, III, 230.
[69] Adamov, No. 77.
[70] Adamov, No. 91.
[71] Ibid.

to commit himself unambiguously as to the extent of the Russian interest in Palestine. He agreed that he had told the Ambassador that Russia would probably assent to Palestine going to the French as part of Syria. He went on, however, to qualify this by making it clear that Russia would have to insist, nevertheless, that not only the Holy Places, but all towns and localities in which there were religious establishments belonging to the Orthodox Church, should be placed under an international administration, with a guarantee of free access to the Mediterranean coast. What this equivocal formula really meant was that Sazonov was taking away with one hand a large part of what he gave with the other.

A firm assurance of Russian support for the French claim to Palestine would have knocked away one of the main props of the case for internationalisation. No such assurance was forthcoming, and the Franco-Russian negotiations ended with an arrangement from which the French could derive no great satisfaction. Russia successfully insisted on a re-shuffling, on balance substantially in her favour, of the proposed French and Russian zones in Armenia and adjacent areas. In return, she was prepared to assent, as between herself and France, to the Anglo-French proposals with regard to the establishment of an Arab State or Confederation and 'the disposal of the territories of Syria, Cilicia and Mesopotamia,' Palestine not being expressly mentioned. A Franco-Russian agreement on these lines was embodied in an exchange of Notes dated 26 April 1916,[72] to be followed, a few weeks later, by the formal adoption of the Sykes-Picot scheme by Great Britain and France. The French had had, for the time being at least, to accept defeat in their claim to Palestine, but they were still not prepared to abandon it. In consenting to the sacrifices imposed upon them by the Franco-Russian agreement of April 26th, they had given way, says Pingaud,[73] in the hope that they might yet be in a position to press, with Russian support, for the Palestine question to be re-considered.

In his letter of 16 May 1916 to the French Ambassador,[74] Grey prefaced his ratification of the Sykes-Picot Agreement by observ-

---

[72] *B.F.P.*, pp. 241-243 ; Adamov, Nos. 103, 104. The tripartite agreement was rounded off, in the autumn of 1916, by an exchange of Notes between Sir E. Grey and the Russian Ambassador: *B.F.P.*, pp. 249-251.
[73] III, 232.
[74] *B.F.P.*, pp. 245ff.

ing that 'the acceptance of the whole project will involve the abdication of considerable British interests.' By 'the whole project' Grey evidently meant, not simply the accord between Great Britain and France, but the entire tripartite arrangement in the form in which it had emerged after the discussions in Petrograd. On the footing that this included the acceptance by the other two Powers of the Russian claim to Constantinople and the Straits, with its far-reaching strategic and political implications, Grey's comment can be well understood. As between Great Britain and Russia, the agreed partition might also involve certain other disadvantages from a British point of view. There was good reason to fear that, no matter what safeguards it might be possible to extract from the Russians,[75] the large areas destined to be incorporated in the Russian Empire would no longer be open to British trade and shipping as freely, or on such favourable terms, as in the days of the Turks.

On the other hand, as between Great Britain and France, the British sacrifices are less self-evident. No British markets were being given away, since it had been agreed that trade should be allowed to flow freely and without discrimination throughout the Sykes-Picot area.[76] Mosul with its oil-fields, in which a British group had a predominant interest, had been assigned to the French sphere of influence, but it had been agreed that existing concessions should not be interfered with,[77] and in any case the British Government had, for reasons of its own,[78] deliberately preferred to see Mosul left on the French side of the dividing-line between the two spheres. One point which Grey may have had in mind was the inclusion in the French zone of the Bay of Alexandretta. This was subject to a French undertaking to provide free port facilities for British trade, in return for a reciprocal British undertaking in respect of Haifa. Nevertheless, the recognition of the French claim to Alexandretta did involve some

---

[75] As to these, see Grey to the Russian Ambassador, 23 May 1916: *B.F.P.*, 247-248 ; see also Adamov, Nos. 83, 93, 138.

[76] Sykes-Picot Agreement, para. 8.

[77] Grey-Cambon letters, 15 May 1916: *B.F.P.*, pp. 244-245.

[78] Mosul was left on the French side of the line 'in consequence of a miscalculation by Lord Kitchener, who was unwilling to have territories in which Britain was interested coterminous with a military monarchy such as Russia then was. I remember agreeing with him ': Balfour's memorandum of 9 September 1919: *B.F.P.*, No. 265.

sacrifice of British interests. Both for strategic and for commercial reasons, the British Government had long been sensitive
about the future of this important natural harbour, which
not only had the makings of a valuable naval base but might one
day become one of the principal maritime outlets for trade routes
connecting the Mediterranean with Mesopotamia and the Persian
Gulf.

Whatever concessions the Sykes-Picot Agreement may have
called for on the British side, there is no difficulty in perceiving
its shortcomings from a French point of view. It represented,
says Gontaut-Biron,[79] a painful sacrifice forced by cruel necessity
on those who signed it on behalf of France at a time when,
fighting for her life, she was despoiled by her closest allies. This
almost hysterical outburst can be discounted as an echo, it may
be guessed, of Picot's personal resentment. The French had by
no means come away empty-handed. They were to have what
amounted to direct control of a zone comprising the coastal strip
of Syria, together with a substantial slice of south-eastern Anatolia. They were also to have what amounted to indirect control
of, roughly the north-eastern half of the large inland territories to
be assigned to the projected Arab State or Confederation. Lastly,
the Agreement clearly implied, as was well understood, that they
were to have an influential voice in the setting up of an international régime for Palestine. But all this fell far short of the hopes
cherished by Frenchmen who had dreamed of a veiled annexation
of a Greater Syria stretching from the Taurus to the Egyptian
frontier and standing in much the same relation to France as
Tunis or Morocco. These were not merely the fantasies of a few
extremists. As the representative of the French Government, Picot
had started by demanding the annexation by France of the whole
Mediterranean zone from the Taurus to the borders of Egypt.[80]
The Sykes-Picot Agreement deflated this grandiose conception
and, from a French point of view, signified a wholesale renuncia-
tion of legitimate claims for the sake of a settlement ostensibly
designed to reconcile the interests of the two Powers with the
national aspirations of the Arabs but in reality telling heavily in
favour of Great Britain.

[79] P. 34.
[80] Pingaud, III, 226.

How successfully British interests had been asserted becomes apparent when, leaving the Arabs, for the moment, out of account, the Agreement is looked at simply as a bargain between Great Britain and France. The British claim to a predominant position in Mesopotamia (the 'Red Area' of the Agreement, together with part of 'Area B') had not been in dispute, but in the Mediterranean zone and its hinterland the Agreement left the British much more strongly entrenched than they would have been had they not been in a position to put strong pressure on the French. First, Haifa, which, besides being a potential naval base, was on the eve of the War becoming one of the focal points of French economic penetration in the Levant, was to pass to Great Britain in full ownership. Secondly, Great Britain was to be entitled to build a railway from Haifa to Baghdad, with the right to carry it across the international zone in Palestine, or, if necessary, across the French sphere. This was agreed to by the French notwithstanding any adverse effect it might have on the prospects of the entrepôt trade which they could reasonably hope to attract to Alexandretta. Thirdly, the line dividing the projected Arab State or Confederation into British and French spheres of influence was drawn so as to leave on the British side most of the eastern part of the Jordan Valley, together with the rest of what was later to become the principality of Transjordan. Since the British sphere would also include the desert region south of Hebron down to the Egyptian frontier, the result would be to enclose the approaches to the Suez Canal in a solid block of British-controlled territory.

Lastly, the dispute concerning the future of Palestine was settled decisively in favour of the British demand for internationalisation. The French might well have been prepared to concede an international régime for a small area limited to Jerusalem and its surroundings, but the Sykes-Picot Agreement pushed them far beyond that point and, except for the merger with Syria of the area north of the Acre-Lake Tiberias line, left no part of Palestine under French control.

The delimitation of the 'Brown Area' of the Agreement was later to be severely criticised on the ground that it wantonly mutilated Palestine by leaving a slice of Galilee to be incorporated in Syria. But the Sykes-Picot line was not, perhaps, as arbitrary as it looked. The Russians had let it be known that they would insist upon an international régime, not only for the Holy Places, but for all localities in which there were religious establishments belonging to the Orthodox Church.[81] This would mean that the internationalised zone must at least take in Nazareth. The Russians, moreover, had made it clear to the French in 1915 that they would not accept Roman Catholic control of an area described by Poincaré at the time as including Galilee, the Jordan and Lake Tiberias.[82] If the boundaries of the ' Brown Area ' were drawn far enough, but only just far enough, to the north to satisfy these Russian requirements, this might help to explain the apparent eccentricities of the Sykes-Picot line, which happens also to bear some resemblance to the northern boundary of ' Southern Syria ' as defined by the Sultan of Turkey in the 'Acte Séparé' annexed to the London Convention of July 1840.[83] British interests would have been better served by a more rational line drawn somewhat further to the north and making the ' Brown Area ' to that extent a more effective barrier between Syria and Egypt. Nevertheless, there was no reason to complain of a settlement by which the French, having aspired to the possession or control of a Greater Syria extending to the borders of Egypt, were pushed back to the northern fringe of Palestine.

Not that the British position had been in all respects fully secured. In the ' Brown Area ' it would still be necessary to reckon with the presence of the French and with the claim which was sure to be advanced by them to a predominant place in the international régime. Haifa would be a valuable acquisition, but not as valuable as it would have been with a British or British-controlled hinterland. The building of a British-owned railway connecting Haifa with Baghdad was both from a military and a commercial point of view an attractive prospect, but with the disadvantage that, even if French Syria could be avoided, the line would in any event have to run through the internationalised area. All the same, a fair verdict on the Sykes-Picot Agreement would be that it was at least as favourable to Great Britain as could reasonably be expected in the circumstances of 1916. Those who negotiated it on the British side had no reason to be dissatis-

[81] Above, p. 261.
[82] Above, p. 245.
[83] *Brit & For. St. Pap.*, XXIX, 245ff.

fied with the results of their labours. Not until the following year did the time arrive for an attempt to improve upon it by a determined bid for British predominance in Palestine.

All this is on the footing that the Agreement represented, basically, a bargain between Great Britain and France. So, indeed, it did, but one of its main purposes was, or was supposed to be, the clearing of the ground for a joint effort by the two Powers to detach the Arabs from the Turks and, with that end in view, to lay the foundations of an Arab State or a Confederation of Arab States. This underlying motive is clearly brought out in the Grey-Cambon correspondence by which the Agreement was ratified in May 1916.[84] By the middle of 1917 Sykes himself was beginning to doubt whether, looked at in this light, the Agreement was well conceived. Its weakness, he wrote,[85] was that it left open the door to annexation. This could now be seen, he declared, to be contrary to the spirit of the times, and it had become imperative that Great Britain and France should shape their course accordingly. As to Palestine, he suggested that the French should be invited to agree to a British trusteeship. As to the rest of the area covered by the Agreement, the two Powers should abjure all annexationist designs and, without disturbing the French and British spheres of interest as shown on the Sykes-Picot map, should renounce direct control of any part of the area,[86] contenting themselves with the rôle of advisers.

This vague foreshadowing of the mandatory system is of interest as showing the direction in which Sykes' mind was now beginning to move. Looking back in 1929, Lawrence seems to have seen the position rather differently. ' The Sykes-Picot treaty,' he wrote,[87] ' was the Arabs' sheet-anchor. The French saw that and worked frantically for the alternative of the mandate. . . . By the mandate swindle England and France got the lot. The

[84] B.F.P., pp. 244, 245.

[85] Sledm., No. 61 (14 August 1917).

[86] I.e., the ' blue area ' and the ' red area ' (areas of direct French or British control) should be merged in ' area A ' and ' area B ' (areas of indirect French or British control).

[87] Letters of T. E. Lawrence, ed. David Garnett, No. 397 (22 October 1929).

Sykes-Picot treaty was absurd in its boundaries, but it did recognise the claims of Syrians to self-government and was ten thousand times better than the eventual settlement.'

With these questions in their broader aspects we are not here concerned, but it is relevant to enquire whether there is any reason to think that the Sykes-Picot Agreement, in its application to Palestine, involved a violation of British assurances already given to the Sharif of Mecca. Did Palestine form part of the area in which the British Government had, through Sir Henry McMahon, promised in the autumn of 1915 to recognise and support the independence of the Arabs?[88]

In his letter of 24 October 1915 McMahon explained to the Sharif the territorial limits of the British undertaking in language meant to indicate that Palestine was not included. No map, however, was attached to the letter, nor was the excluded area defined with the geographical precision which would have been appropriate in a treaty relating to the demarcation of a frontier. The wording of the letter was microscopically examined by a Joint Committee of British and Arab representatives set up by the British Government in the spring of 1939.[89] Disagreeing with their Arab colleagues, the British representatives came to the conclusion that ' on a proper construction of the correspondence, Palestine was, in fact, excluded,' adding, however, that ' they agree that the language in which its exclusion was expressed was not so specific and unmistakable as it was thought to be at the time.'[90] Thus, even the British representatives felt obliged to concede that, on a verbal analysis of the McMahon formula, it was at least arguable that it did not exclude Palestine.

But the question is not merely whether the choice of language was such as to close any possible loophole for the contention that the British undertaking, literally construed, could be made to extend to Palestine. It is material to enquire whether it was so intended by the British Government and so understood in good faith by the Sharif. On neither point is there room for any serious doubt as to the answer. As to the British intentions, McMahon's

---

[88] Cmd. 5957 (1939), pp. 7ff.
[89] The Committee's report is printed in Cmd. 5974 (1939).
[90] Loc. cit., p. 10.

own statement[91] that ' it was not intended by me in giving this pledge to [the Sharif] to include Palestine in the area in which Arab independence was promised ' is borne out by the testimony of Sir Gilbert Clayton,[92] who was in constant touch with McMahon throughout the negotiations with the Sharif and made the preliminary drafts of all the letters. It is clear that Grey, who was Foreign Secretary at the time of the British undertaking to the Sharif, took it for granted that it did not cover Palestine, for, if not, he could not possibly have advanced the proposals concerning Zionist aspirations in Palestine which he communicated to the French and Russian Governments in March 1916.[93] That there were no British commitments to the Arabs in the matter of Palestine was likewise taken for granted by the Lloyd George Government when giving Sykes his instructions on the eve of his departure for the East in April 1917. It was, as we shall see, impressed upon Sykes that he was to do nothing which might prejudice the Zionist cause and was to enter into no commitments to the Arabs with regard to Palestine, upon which he observed that the Arabs probably realised that there was no prospect of their being allowed any control over Palestine.[94] Strongly as Sykes favoured a pro-Arab policy, it had clearly never occurred to him, any more than it had occurred to those instructing him, that Arab control of Palestine had already been promised to the Sharif. Nor can it be suggested with any plausibility that, whatever may have been the British Government's intentions, the Sharif himself was, in fact, bona fide under the impression that the assurances given to him by McMahon extended to Palestine. No evidence to that effect is adduced by Antonius in his elaborate and well-argued statement of the Arab case,[95] while from the British side there is some evidence to the contrary. McMahon himself has stated that he ' had every reason to believe at the time that the fact that Palestine was not included in my pledge was well understood by [the Sharif].' According to Colonel Vickery, who in 1920 was sent on an official mission to the Sharif, the latter ' stated

[91] *The Times,* 23 July 1937.
[92] Sir G. Clayton to Lord Samuel, quoted by Lord Samuel, House of Lords, 20 July 1937: O.R., Col. 629.
[93] Above, pp. 223-224.
[94] *Sledm.,* No. 41 (3 April 1917).
[95] *The Arab Awakening,* pp. 176ff.

most emphatically that he did not concern himself at all with Palestine and had no desire to have sovereignty over it for himself or his successors.'[96]

The truth seems to be that while, on a minute examination of the language used by McMahon in describing the areas outside the scope of his assurances, a case can be made out for the view that Palestine was not unambiguously excluded, it is a purely verbal case, unrelated to the substance of the matter and devoid of merits. This is not to say that the position in Palestine was unaffected by British encouragement of Arab national aspirations; but if the question is whether the British Government had committed itself in 1915 to leaving Palestine under Arab control, the answer seems clearly to be that there was no such commitment.

[96] *The Times,* 23 July 1937 ; 21 February 1939.

CHAPTER 17

MARK SYKES

IT WAS, AS has been seen, during the pause between the provisional signature of the Sykes-Picot Agreement in January 1916 and
its ratification in May that Mark Sykes first began to interest himself in Zionism. He was all the more receptive because his mind
was full of the Palestine question, on which he had had to fight so
hard a battle with Picot. It was not long before he had become a
convinced pro-Zionist, and, because of the influence which he was
able continuously to exert behind the scenes, his adhesion to the
Zionist cause was, as time went on, to tell heavily in its favour.
Not only had he an established reputation as an expert on Eastern
affairs, but his position as a Member of Parliament, his social
standing and his personal connections in high quarters combined
to give him an exceptional freedom of access to the real seats of
power.

When his education in Zionism began with his study of the
Samuel memorandum in February 1916,[1] Sykes already had
the prestige attaching to his part in the discussions between the
three Entente Powers, then about to enter on their final phase.
Soon after his return from Petrograd a few weeks later he
was attached to the Secretariat of the Committee of Imperial
Defence and was thus brought into close contact with the
War Committee of the Cabinet.[2] He became responsible for
providing the Committee with periodical notes, known as 'the
Arabian Reports,' on the situation in the Middle East, acted
as liaison officer between the Government Departments concerned with Middle Eastern affairs,[3] and by the autumn of 1916
had been entrusted, in addition to his other duties, with the study
of the Zionist question. On the change of Government at the end
of the year, he stepped at once into a key-position as one of the
Assistant-Secretaries to Lloyd George's War Cabinet, with functions which, though rather vaguely defined, enabled him to play

[1] Above, p. 233.
[2] Shane Leslie, pp. 22-24, 259.
[3] Ibid.

a significant part in the shaping of British policy in the East.[4]
Decisions did not rest with him—his rôle was to provide the
Cabinet with information and advice—but he was not the man to
shrink from taking the initiative or from pressing his own ideas.
Entrenched at the centre of affairs and credited with an expert
knowledge of the East in which no member of the War Cabinet,
with the possible exception of Curzon, could compete with him,
he was an adviser whose views on the subjects he had made his
own, though not decisive, were highly influential.

In February 1917 he moved to the Foreign Office, where he
carried on the discussions already tentatively begun with the
Zionist leaders to a point at which, some five months later,
a draft declaration in favour of Zionism was ready for submission to the War Cabinet. Sykes was in the Foreign Office
but not of it. He was unfettered by the hierarchical discipline of
the Department, and there is reason to believe that permanent
officials noticed with no particular pleasure his free-lance status
and his direct access to the Secretary of State. On his missions
abroad his diplomatic activities were not invariably viewed with
complete approval by the professionals. Speaking of Sykes' visit
to Rome in April 1917, the then British Ambassador, Sir Rennell
Rodd, remarks in his memoirs[5] that ' in his case, as in that of
other Members of Parliament who visited Rome disguised as Staff
Officers, it was always rather difficult to grasp what they were
doing, or, rather, what they were authorised to do and say.' In the
same strain, Sir Reginald Wingate's biographer speaks of the
appearance in Palestine, early in 1918, of ' General Smuts, Sir
Percy Cox . . . and others of a more amateur status, such as Sir
Mark Sykes. . . .'[5a] But though Sykes' status was a little vague and,

---

[4] Sykes, like Leopold Amery, was graded, for administrative purposes, as
an Assistant to the Secretary to the War Cabinet, Sir Maurice (later,
Lord) Hankey: Amery, *My Political Life* (London, Hutchinson, 1953),
II, 92. Hankey was provided with ten Assistant-Secretaries (see Thomas
Jones, *A Diary with Letters* [O.U.P., 1954], p. xxiv). Sykes and Amery,
however, both Members of Parliament, were in a special position in
relation to the War Cabinet: '. . . we were to be kept at the disposal of
its members and at the same time free, as a kind of informal " brains
trust," to submit our ideas on all subjects to our chiefs ' (Amery, loc. cit.).
[5] *Social and Diplomatic Memories* (London, Arnold, 1925), p. 335.
[5a] R. Wingate, *Wingate of the Sudan* (London, John Murray, 1955),
pp. 225-226. Wingate was at the time British High Commissioner in
Egypt.

perhaps a little anomalous, there can be no doubt about the measure of his influence on British policy in the East, and especially in Syria and Palestine. As to his part in the making of the Balfour Declaration Leopold Amery, his closest colleague in the War Cabinet Secretariat, said of him, looking back ten years later, that ' no one who was concerned with the inside working of affairs during those years would fail to place his name in the very front as the man who by his restless vigour and profound faith brought that question to a definite conclusion.'[6] Another of Sykes' friends and war-time colleagues, Lord Harlech, has expressed himself to the same effect: '[Sykes] inspired both the Arab and Jewish policies and was chiefly responsible for securing their adoption by Ministers at home.'[7] Had Sykes taken a different view, his advice might well have been fatal to the policy embodied in the Declaration, and it is at least doubtful whether the obstacles in its way would have been surmounted if he had not worked actively and persistently in its favour.

Before his sympathetic interest in the Zionist approach to the Jewish Question was awakened by Herbert Samuel, Sykes had been no friend of Zionism and no admirer of the Jews. A fervent patriot and a firm believer in the virtues of nationalism, he had seen in the Jew the archetype of the cosmopolitan financier whose iniquities were among his favourite themes. He had been ready to accept the stereotyped picture of the Jews as rootless money-grubbers, all the more contemptible in his eyes when they tried to disguise themselves as something else. Among Sykes' youthful experiments in the art of caricature are three drawings—they reflect his mood (he was then in his twenties) at the time of the South African War—showing hideous Jewish types labelled respectively ' A boy of the bulldog breed,' ' A Welsh Nationalist,' and ' An earnest Christian.'[8] It is not surprising to learn from his biographer that ' he was interested in the ethos of the real

---

[6] Speech at Johannesburg, *The Zionist Record*, 16 September 1927. In his memoirs (*My Political Life*, II, 114-115), Amery writes: ' Sykes practically took charge of all negotiations which led up to the Balfour Declaration.'

[7] Shane Leslie, pp. 288-289.

[8] Shane Leslie, facing p. 85.

Hebrew, not the Anglicised Jew,[9] and from Sokolow[10] that 'he had no liking for the hybrid type of assimilating Jew.'

As a specialist in Eastern affairs, Sykes had no reason to think any the better of the Jews for the part generally considered to have been played by Salonica Jewry in the Turkish Revolution and its aftermath. In the years immediately before the War, the view taken in British circles in Constantinople was, as has been seen,[11] that the leading Turkish Jews were pro-German, that they were deliberately doing their best to steer the new Turkey into the German orbit, and that in all this the Zionists were implicated. Sykes at this time knew little of Zionism, but his dislike of what little he knew seems to have been connected with a vague idea that Zionism was somehow mixed up with the activities of Jews or crypto-Jews associated with the Committee of Union and Progress. Describing a visit to Turkey soon after the Revolution, 'the Jews, he wrote contemptuously,[12] 'were beginning to peer and peep and talk of Zionism.' Revisiting Turkey shortly before the War, he noticed, among the misdeeds of 'the new occult powers' which had supplanted the old régime, that 'Zionism was backed because it was bad cosmopolitanism and finance.'[13] The allusions are obscure, but cosmopolitan finance, symbolised by the Jews, duly appears as the enemy.

The Jews and the Zionists were not the only people about whom Sykes was known to change his mind. Important as was the place occupied by the Arabs in his plans for a new order in the Middle East, he had spoken of them in the past with anything but respect. 'The inhabitants of Mosul,' he wrote in 1904, 'are of the true proud, bigoted, conceited Arab tribe, such as inhabit Hama, Homs and Damascus. Eloquent, cunning, excitable and cowardly, they present, to my mind, one of the most deplorable pictures one can see in the East.'[14] In his last book, completed in 1913, there

9 Ibid., p. 269.
10 II, xxi.
11 Above, pp. 34ff.
12 *The Caliph's Last Heritage* (London, Macmillan, 1915), p. 465.
13 Ibid., p. 509.
14 *Dar-ul-Islam* (London, Bickers, 1904), p. 178.

is an entry in the Index reading: ' Arab Character: see also Treachery.'[15] So it was with the Armenians. His pre-war picture of them was unflattering to the point of contempt,[16] yet in 1917 he was thinking of them as partners, together with the Jews and the Arabs, in an alliance which, closely linked with Great Britain and France, would help to fill the void left by the collapse of the Turkish Empire.

Vehemently as he was wont to express himself, Sykes was not inflexible in his views nor immovable in his prejudices. Readily responsive to new ideas and impressions, especially when associated with something colourful, adventurous and a little exotic, he had on closer acquaintance with Zionism no difficulty in recognising that he had misjudged it. Without having given any serious thought to the Jewish Question, he had before the War had a distaste for Jews which was reflected in an instinctive mistrust of the Zionists. Once his eyes had begun to be opened by his contact with Herbert Samuel, he began to see the Movement in a different light.

Because he had no taste for the kind of Jew who seemed to him to sail under false colours, he was predisposed to look favourably on a Movement founded upon the conception of the Jews as a people with a distinctive heritage of its own. Far from being a sinister conspiracy organised in the interests of international finance, Zionism, he discovered, stood for the very opposite of a rootless cosmopolitanism and was sustained by idealists drawn mainly from the disinherited Jews of Eastern Europe. That, with the exception of certain members of the House of Rothschild, they had no backing among the Jewish financial magnates was, in his eyes, to their credit.

Zionism appealed to Sykes as a fervent believer in the virtues of nationalism, but it attracted him also for another reason. A member of the landed gentry, he had little respect for what he conceived to be the typical Jewish way of life, with its commercial bias and its strong urban flavour. All the more warmly did he applaud the Zionists for their pride in their agricultural settlements in Palestine and the faith which this proclaimed in the cleansing quality of contact with the soil. Sykes' approach to

15 *The Caliph's Last Heritage,* p. 596.
16 Ibid., pp. 417-418.

Zionism is well brought out in a letter in which he tells Sokolow how he put the case for Zionism to the Papal authorities during his visit to Rome in the spring of 1917[17]:

> '. . . The main object of Zionism [is] to evolve a self-supporting Jewish community which should raise not only the racial self-respect of the Jewish people, but should be a proof to the non-Jewish peoples of the world of the capacity of the Jews to produce a virtuous and simple agrarian population, and, by achieving these two results, to strike at the roots of those difficulties which have been productive of so much unhappiness in the past.'

There was yet another aspect of Zionism which made it interesting to Sykes. He saw in it, as Balfour did, a stabilising element in Jewish life. He perceived that among the enemies of Zionism were not only the international financiers whom he so strongly disliked, but also, at the opposite pole of the Jewish world, those subversive forces which he saw working in Russia to undermine the established order of society. In a memorandum written in September 1917 he contrasts the Zionists with 'the extreme Socialist Jews of the underworld, who regard Karl Marx as the only prophet of Israel and who work towards the destruction of the present nationalistic basis of the world and the setting up of a World State.'[18]

All this helps to explain why Zionism touched Sykes' imagination and engaged his personal sympathy, but it does not account, of itself, for the energy with which he worked for an understanding with the Zionists designed to draw them into the Allied orbit and, more particularly, to link them with Great Britain.

Sykes became seriously interested in Zionism just about the time when the British Government was suggesting to its allies that a statement on the Palestine question in language to which Zionists would respond would be an effective answer to German propaganda among the Jews in the United States and elsewhere.

[17] Sykes to Sokolow, 12 April 1917: Orig. in *N.S.P.*, copy in *Sledm.*, No. 49.

[18] *Sledm.*, No. 66 ; see below, p. 511.

It is natural to suppose that Sykes must have had something to do with this move, but on such evidence as there is this seems unlikely. However that may be, it was clearly the accepted view in Foreign Office circles at the time that in their political warfare the Allies could not afford to disregard the Jews, and that an appeal to Zionist sentiment might be well rewarded.

This was certainly a part, though by no means the whole, of what was in Sykes' mind. In what may well be a paraphrase of something said to him by Sykes when in Rome in 1917, the then British Ambassador, Sir Rennell Rodd, records in his memoirs[19] that 'Sykes had, I believe, been instrumental in convincing the Jewish idealists that their aims would best be served by associating themselves with the Allies in opposition to the international financiers, whose interests were for the most part pro-German.' This sounds like an authentic echo of Sykes, in whose demonology international finance had a prominent place. Sykes knew that the moneyed classes among the Jews were almost to a man anti-Zionist. Believing, as he did, that the Jewish international financiers, or nearly all of them, were somehow linked with Germany, he drew the inference that the Zionists were the natural enemies of the German or pro-German elements in Jewry. He would also have known that most of the leading Zionists in the United States were, in fact, friendly to the Allies. Moreover, apart from any question of sentiment, the Zionists must surely realise, or could be made to realise, that, whatever the German propagandists might promise, it would never pay the Germans to antagonise the Turks, and that only an Allied victory could give the Jews anything worth having in Palestine. It followed that it should be possible, and might well be profitable, to draw the Zionists into the orbit of the *Entente*.

There were times when Sykes went so far as to suggest that to be anti-Zionist was to be pro-German. The 'Semitic anti-Zionists,' he declared,[20] were 'undisguised pro-Turco-Germans'—they were 'Russophobe pro-Turks who have become pro-Germans and are now definitely fixed in that camp.' As this outburst shows, Sykes' indignant contempt for the Jewish opponents of Zionism was capable of impairing his judgment. He must have realised

[19] Rennell Rodd, op. cit., p. 335.
[20] *Sledm.*, No. 59 (29 July 1917).

himself that he was in danger of over-simplifying the position, for, though there is no evidence of his having ever been in direct contact with British Jews of the type represented by the Conjoint Foreign Committee, he came in the end to take a less uncharitable view of the Jewish assimilationists and their motives. His ' cosmo-politan Jew ' remained, in his eyes, an object of contempt, but, though he was not impressed by their anti-Zionist reasoning, he came to see that the assimilated Jews had a case.[21] The supposed identity between anti-Zionists and pro-Germans faded out of the foreground of his argument, but he remained unshaken in his belief that in the Zionists the Entente Powers had natural allies whose support could be won and was worth winning.

Looking further into the future, Sykes began to think of the Zionists as partners, together with other natural allies of the Entente—the Arabs and the Armenians (for such he conceived these to be), in a combination which would be of permanent value as a stabilising force in the Middle East. This became one of his favourite dreams. ' If,' he wrote (July 1917),[22] ' Great Britain and France would go in sincerely for Arab nationalism, the French suppressing their financial and the British their Imperialist leanings, then it would be possible to make an Arab-Jewish-Armenian barrier between Persia-Egypt-India and the Turco-German combine.' He put forward a proposal (but nothing came of it) for the setting up in London of a Joint Committee ' for the protection of Arab, Armenian and Jewish national rights,'[23] and urged the Arab Committee in Cairo ' to accept the policy of [an] Arab-Armenian-Zionist Entente.'[24] He wanted the foundations of such an Entente to be laid without delay, believing that it could be made to play a useful part at a future Peace Conference. ' I hold very strongly,' he wrote (August 1917), ' that we have certain big Entente war and [Peace] Conference assets in the Arabs, Zionists and Armenians, and that it is certainly our duty to get these people righted and that it will be in our interest to

[21] *Sledm.*, No. 66, memorandum of September 1917—see below, p. 511.

[22] *Sledm.*, No. 62 (19 July 1917). This looks like an amplified version of Kitchener's idea of ' an autonomous Arabia between Teutonised Turkey on the one hand and Egypt and India on the other '—Temperley, *H.P.C.*, VI, 120.

[23] Ibid., No. 71 (16 November 1917).

[24] Ibid., No. 61 (14 August 1917).

get them righted on lines compatible with our economic and
political interests.'[25] These ideas formed part of the background
to Lord Robert Cecil's declaration, on behalf of the British
Government, at the Zionist Demonstration at the London Opera
House on 2 December 1917: 'We welcome among us not only
the many thousands of Jews that I see, but also representatives
of the Arabian and Armenian races, who are also in this great
struggle struggling to be free. Our wish is that Arabian countries
shall be for the Arabs, Armenia for the Armenians and Judæa
for the Jews.'[26]

But these were not Sykes' only reasons for interesting himself
in Zionism. When his education in the subject began in February
1916 he had just emerged from his duel with Picot. On the
Palestine question the French had, under strong British pressure,
reluctantly accepted the principle of internationalisation, but
Sykes must have known or suspected that they had not at heart
renounced their claims. One point clearly brought out in Samuel's
Palestine memorandum, and, presumably, brought out also by
Samuel himself when he talked to Sykes, was that a British
protectorate was 'the solution of the question of Palestine which
would be by far the most welcome to the Jews throughout the
world.' It would have been surprising if it had not occurred to
Sykes that here might be something he could build upon in an
effort to strengthen the British position in Palestine in competition
with the French.

Immediately after returning from Petrograd in April 1916 he
produced some new ideas on the Palestine question and communicated them to Samuel, who passed them on, but without
specifying the source, to Gaster, Sokolow and Weizmann. His
plan provided for an Anglo-French condominium, but, according
to Gaster's summary of the scheme, it also contemplated 'as part
of the Constitution a Charter to Zionists for which England would
stand guarantee and which would stand by us in every case of
friction.'[27] The language is Gaster's, but there is no reason to

[25] *Sledm.*, No. 61 (14 August 1917). This sounds like an echo of Cromer's
quotation from Demosthenes at p. 256 of his *Modern Egypt* (London,
1911).

[26] Sokolow, II, 101—see below, p. 565.

[27] The following are extracts from Gaster's diaries: *11 April 1916*—
'H. Samuel rang up. Important changes foreshadowed for our Palestine

doubt that it correctly represents the substance of the proposal, the point of which was plainly that the Zionists were to be encouraged to regard the British as their patrons and protectors.

Nothing more was heard of this at the time, but it indicates the direction in which Sykes was beginning to move. His fertile mind later devised other proposals with the same underlying purpose. We find him, early in 1917, suggesting to the Zionists that they should operate in Palestine through a Chartered Company to be incorporated in England and enjoying British protection.[28] About the same time he was inviting them to consider whether they would not do well to make their headquarters at Haifa.[29] This would have the advantage of diverting the attention of the Jews from the sensitive Jerusalem-Jaffa area, but it would also mean that they would be expanding into the international zone from a British base and would help to provide Haifa with a friendly hinterland. The pro-British bias of the Movement, as represented by Weizmann and his associates, made it still more interesting to Sykes when, in the spring of 1917, the Lloyd George Government decided not to be content with a Franco-British condominium in Palestine, but to aim at a settlement leaving Great Britain in sole control. Sykes pointed out that, when the time arrived for Great

[28] Conference with Zionists, 7 February 1917—see below, p. 373.
[29] ' He [Sykes] mentioned the Haifa Zone, which seems to have been secured by England against French insatiable greed and this could be the new nucleus and centre of the Charter ': Gaster diaries, 30 January 1917. ' It seems that the Old City of Jerusalem will find itself inside the somewhat isolated " religious zone," and, as we must have a centre, Sir Mark suggested Haifa because of its situation near Galilee, its harbour and other natural advantages ': Sokolow to Weizmann, 1 May 1917 (transl. from the Russian); N.S.P.

work. Asks whether I could come with Weizmann Friday or Saturday. I suggested Sokolow to be added. Willingly agreed.' April 16th— ' Sokolow, Weizmann and Herbert Samuel. H.S.'s meeting of far-reaching and momentous importance. It practically comes to a complete realisa- tion of our Zionist programme. We are offered French-English condo- minium in Palest. Arab Prince to conciliate Arab sentiment and as part of the Constitution a Charter to Zionists for which England would stand guarantee and which would stand by us in every case of friction. We insisted on: national character of Charter, freedom of immigration and internal autonomy, and at the same time full rights of citizenship to [illegible—? Arabs] and Jews in Palestine.' May 2nd—' Lt.-Col. Sir Mark Sykes. Very long interview. He is the man who made the proposal to H. Samuel.'

Britain openly to press her claim to Palestine, 'the situation would be more favourable to British suzerainty with a recognised Jewish voice in favour of it.'[30]

Implicit in all this was the assumption that the Jews counted for something in the world and that Zionism was the most vital force in Jewry. In the Sledmere papers the earliest mention of Zionism is in a memorandum by Sykes, written in June 1916.[31] Dwelling on the disastrous consequences which would follow if the War were allowed to end with Turkey a German satellite, he remarks, among other considerations, that this would leave Germany with 'an international pawn in Palestine, which gives her a hold at once over the Zionists, the Papacy and the Orthodox.' It may seem surprising that Sykes should have ranked the Jews, or the Zionists, with the Roman Catholic and Orthodox Churches among the impalpable forces which counted in world affairs, but elsewhere in his papers there is ample evidence of the importance he attached to the Jews and of his belief in the potency of the Zionist idea. 'If the great force of Judaism feels that its aspirations are not only considered but in a fair way towards realisation, then,' he wrote to Picot (February 1917), 'there is hope of an ordered and developed Arabia and Middle East.'[32] A few weeks after the Balfour Declaration he told the Arab Committee in Cairo that 'the British Government have recognised Zionism as the greatest motive-force in Jewry. . . . If Zionism and Arab nationalism joined forces, I am convinced that the liberation of the Arabs is certain.'[33] In a memorandum already quoted he discusses the situation in the Middle East at the beginning of 1918 and, speaking of 'the assets we now have at our disposal,' points out that 'Palestine and our Zionist declaration combined gives us and the Entente as a whole a hold on the vital vocal and sentimental forces of Jewry.'[34]

It was Sykes' business to estimate as objectively as he could the value of Zionism as a political asset, but we find him, as time

[30] *Sledm.*, No. 49 (9 April 1917)—see below, p. 402.
[31] *Sledm.*, No. 14 (20 June 1916).
[32] *Sledm.*, No. 50 (28 February 1917).
[33] *Sledm.*, No. 71 (16 November 1917).
[34] *Milner Papers*, 'Palestine' file (1 January 1918).

goes on, beginning to speak of it in language which suggests that it had touched his emotions. In his speech at the London Opera House Demonstration in December 1917[35] he describes in words which ring true his vision of ' the return of Israel, with his majesty and tolerance, hushing mockery and dispelling doubt.' ' I foresee myself,' he writes a few months later to Sokolow,[36] ' handed down to posterity as one of those enduring obscurities who did nothing in any way remarkable, yet whose names last for all time because they scratched their fleeting impressions on the Memnon at Luxor. Your cause has about it an enduring quality which mocks at time. When all the temporal things the world now holds are as dead and forgotten as the curled and scented Kings of Babylon who dragged your forefathers into captivity, there will still be Jews, and so long as there are Jews there must be Zionism.'

At the time of the Balfour Declaration, Sykes had little more than a year to live. In the interval before his death, at the age of just under forty, in February 1919, it had been borne in upon him that the difficulties in the way of his pro-Zionist policy were more serious than he had realised. He was disturbed, and as a loyal Catholic, distressed, by the attitude of powerful elements in the Church, nor could he close his eyes to the signs of growing uneasiness in the Arab world.

When in Rome in the spring of 1917, Sykes had used all his influence as a distinguished Catholic layman, whose devotion to the Church was beyond doubt, to persuade the Papal authorities to look favourably on Zionism.[37] He seemed to have succeeded, but when he was again in Rome in November 1918, he realised that anti-Zionist forces were at work in the Vatican and was particularly disturbed by a marked lack of sympathy on the part of the Papal Secretary of State, Cardinal Gasparri. On the other hand, describing his impressions in a confidential letter to Ormsby-Gore[38] (' this is for you, Sokolow and Weizmann alone '), he went on to say that he had had a more friendly hearing from

[35] Sokolow, II. 106ff.
[36] 27 May 1918: Sokolow, I, xxxvii.
[37] See below, p. 405.
[38] The Hon. W. Ormsby-Gore ; later, Viscount Harlech.

the Under-Secretary, Monsignor Ceretti, who understood that 'the motives of Zionism were pure, natural, irresistible, inevitable and anti-materialist.'[39]

From Rome Sykes travelled to Palestine, where he hoped to create a better atmosphere by talks with the Franciscan Custos and the Latin Patriarch. In this he seems to have had little success. He arrived at the Paris Peace Conference, his biographer writes, 'with feelings shocked by the intense bitterness which had been provoked in the Holy Land.'[40] For him this would have been all the more distressing because, as he had told Ormsby-Gore, he was convinced that an estrangement between the Zionists and the Catholic Church would mean that 'two moral forces pivoted on the same centre, instead of radiating outwards, will consume their strength inwardly.'[41]

To add to Sykes' discomfort, it was becoming clear that he had under-rated the obstacles in the way of the Arab-Jewish under-standing which he had relied upon as one of the pillars of his policy. Immediately after the Balfour Declaration he had done his best to reassure the Arab nationalists, asking Sir Gilbert Clayton to tell the Arab Committee in Cairo that 'all the Zionists desire is to have the right of colonisation in Palestine and in their colonies to live their own national life.'[42] Clayton warned him that the news of the Declaration had been received by Moslems and Christians alike, 'with little short of dismay,'[43] and in 1918 he began to be seriously disturbed by evidence of mounting Arab hostility.

Powerful as was the influence which he had expected the

[39] This letter, signed by Sykes and dated Rome, 5 November 1918, was found among Sokolow's papers but was subsequently mislaid after being sent for copying and has not been recovered. Before parting with it, the author made a *précis*, with certain passages reproduced verbatim. The sentences in quotation-marks in the text appear as quotations in the *précis*

[40] Shane Leslie, p. 284. Sir Shane Leslie writes (loc. cit.): 'To Cardinal Gasquet he admitted the change of his views on Zionism, and that he was determined to qualify, guide and, if possible, save the dangerous situation which was rapidly arising.'

[41] See Note 39.

[42] *Sledm.*, No. 71 (16 November 1917).

[43] *Sledm.*, No. 75 (28 November 1917). Brigadier-General Sir Gilbert Clayton was on the Staff of the Egyptian Expeditionary Force as Chief Political Officer.

Zionists to exert in the Middle East, Sykes does not appear at any time to have thought of Zionism in terms of a Jewish State in Palestine or even of Jewish predominance. Grey's proposal, in March 1916, for an Allied declaration in favour of Zionism pointed plainly in that direction, but Sykes seems all along to have been thinking on rather different lines. He told Herbert Samuel at the very start that he imagined that Zionism was concerned with 'the realisation of the ideal of an existing centre of nationality, rather than boundaries or extent of territory.'[44] He came later to recognise that there could be no fulfilment of Zionism without the settlement of Jews in Palestine, and especially their settlement on the land, in substantial numbers, but the conception which he pressed upon the Zionists was that of a Jewish 'national unit,'[45] living side by side with other 'national units' with similar rights and status, on the footing that each enjoyed unfettered freedom to develop its distinctive way of life. In a note on 'Palestine and Zionism' prepared in September 1917[46] he declared explicitly that the objects of Zionism did not extend to the setting up of any form of State in Palestine or any part of it.

Desperately anxious as he was—for it was of cardinal importance for his plans—that the Arabs and the Jews should understand each other, he was disturbed by what seemed to him to be a failure on the part of the Zionists, or some of them, to appreciate the delicacy of the situation. Surveying the situation in Palestine early in 1918, he pointed out in a memorandum already quoted that the advantages flowing from the British successes in Palestine, coupled with the Balfour Declaration, were not being fully exploited: 'a whole crowd of weeds are growing around us'—among them, Arab unrest in regard to Zionism, and also 'Zionist anticipations undirected or [? un]controlled, running to suspicion and chauvinism.'[47] Again and again he told his Zionist audiences that co-operation with the Arabs was indispensable to the success of their cause, urging

44 Above, p. 233.
45 In his memorandum of September 1917 (see below, p. 511) he speaks of 'the recognition of the Jewish inhabitants of Palestine as a national unit, federated with [other] national units in Palestine': *Sledm.*, No. 66.
46 Ibid. Sykes' definition of the objects of Zionism is discussed at p. 523, below.
47 *Milner Papers*, 'Palestine' file (1 January 1918).

the Jews, in their own interests, ' to look through Arab glasses.'[48]
He returned to this theme in his last letter to Weizmann, written
less than three weeks before his death[49]: ' . . . I am convinced
that as regards the Palestine non-Jewish people and Zionists,
there is nothing that cannot be overcome by firmness and strict
adherence to a definite plan with which both sides are conversant.
What has to be made clear is that the Zionists do not desire that
the non-Jews should become in any sense a subject-people.'

This letter reflects Sykes' anxieties, but it also shows that,
seriously as he was troubled by difficulties not fully foreseen,
he had not lost faith in the fundamental soundness of a pro-
Zionist policy. That in this he stood firm seems clearly to be
demonstrated by the close and friendly relations which he maintained to the end with the Zionist leaders. From the time that
Sykes arrived in Paris for the Peace Conference, Sokolow saw
him almost daily on Zionist business and the very day before his
death received from him, through Lady Sykes, a message which
showed that the Zionists were constantly in his thoughts.[50]

[48] ' Therefore he warned the Jews to look through Arab glasses ': speech
at Zionist meeting in Manchester: *J.C.*, 9 December 1917.
[49] *Ch.W.P.* The letter is undated but was obviously written while Sykes
was at the Peace Conference in Paris. It begins: ' I am going over to
London to-night to return Saturday. I have 3 small things to do in
London and want to get them done before the Middle East turns up
here, which I expect will occur next week.' Sykes arrived in London
from the East on 30 January 1919 and left for Paris on February 1st.
He died in Paris on February 16th. (Dates given by Shane Leslie,
pp. 281, 292.)
[50] Sokolow, II, xxxvi: ' On the 15th [February] Lady Sykes sent for me.
. . . " My chief reason for troubling you," she added, " is because my
husband wants to know how Zionist matters went yesterday." I gave
full details to Lady Sykes. In the afternoon of the 16th Sir Mark died.'

CHAPTER 18

MOSES GASTER—AARON AARONSOHN

WE MUST NOW go back to April 1916, when Sykes, having returned from Petrograd with some ideas of his own for a fresh approach to the Palestine question, brought them to the notice of Herbert Samuel, who, without mentioning Sykes' name, communicated them to Weizmann, Sokolow and Gaster. The exact nature of the proposals is unknown. Gaster's description of them in his diary has already been quoted,[1] and from this it can be inferred that they pointed to a close association between Great Britain and the Zionists.

Soon afterwards Sykes began an exchange of views with Gaster, who, having been encouraged by Samuel to approach him, remained intermittently in contact with him until early in 1917, when the discussions were taken over on the Zionist side by Weizmann and Sokolow. By this time Sykes had been made still more receptive to Zionist ideas by what he had seen and heard of that enigmatic but impressive personality, Aaron Aaronsohn. Once brought into personal relations with Weizmann, Sykes was quick to recognise his commanding stature, but even Weizmann might have found it harder going had Sykes not already been indoctrinated, first by Samuel, and then by Gaster and Aaronsohn.

On 27 April 1916 Gaster, writing, as he explained, at Samuel's suggestion, asked Sykes for an interview 'concerning the question of recruiting Russian subjects.'[2] Sykes agreed and on May 2nd had a lengthy conversation with Gaster, not about the recruiting of Russian Jews, but about Palestine.[3]

[1] Above, p. 278.
[2] *Gaster papers.* Gaster was alluding to the controversy, then becoming acute, as to the enlistment in the British Army, under pressure amounting to compulsion, of Russian nationals resident in the United Kingdom (nearly all of them Jews) who, not having become British subjects, had escaped military service ; see below, p. 488.
[3] *Gaster Diary,* 2 May 1916. The opening words of this entry have already been quoted—above, p. 278, note 27. It continues: 'Had

This was the beginning of an association which Sykes made a point of recalling in his speech at the London Opera House meeting on 2 December 1917[4]: 'I should like to say, before I say one other word, that the reason I am interested in this Movement is that I met one some two years ago who is now upon this platform and who opened my eyes as to what the Movement meant. . . . I mean Dr. Gaster.' This is conclusive as to the impression made upon Sykes by Gaster. What is not altogether clear is why Samuel put Gaster in touch with him, but not Weizmann or Sokolow, though these were, in fact, the most authoritative representatives of the Movement in England at the time. Samuel knew Gaster not only as an old personal friend but as one who had played an important part in his own education in Zionism. In deciding who was the right person to introduce to Sykes, he may have felt that Sokolow was unsuitable as a foreigner, and Weizmann because he was in Government service and absorbed in his official duties. He may also have thought that Gaster would make an impression on Sykes as an ecclesiastical dignitary with a colourful Sephardic background.[5] These are merely conjectural explanations of an episode which is, on the face of it, a little puzzling.[6]

Not that there could be any doubt of Gaster's eminence both as an outstanding figure in the Zionist Movement and as a personality in his own right. In Rumania, where he was born in 1856, he had shown his strength of character by his vigorous part—too vigorous for the taste of the Rumanian Government, which expelled him—in the agitation for the removal of Jewish disabilities. He had shown it again when, after settling in England

4 Sokolow, II, 106ff.
5 He had since 1887 held the office of Haham—i.e., Chief Rabbi of the Sephardic (Spanish and Portuguese) congregations in England.
6 Lord Samuel has informed the author that he has no recollection of the incident. (To the author, 15 January 1954.)

seen Sazonov and whom he has won over to Zionist problem. . . . After long wrangle got his French colleague, George Picot, to see the point of Jewish help. He first dead against. Then agreed condominium. I put the case clearly. Warned him against France and even prefers [? preferred] to have German condominium, as latter's interests not in Egypt. Wants me to influence *Daily Telegraph* and then to work on America. I advise fait accompli. He answers to occupy Jerusalem—I, *not* by Jews, but by *English* soldiers. . . .'

in 1885, he had had the courage, eleven years later, openly to identify himself with Herzl—this at a time when Zionism was frowned upon by the leaders of Anglo-Jewry and not least by his own Sephardim. His prestige was enhanced by his international reputation in certain fields of scholarship[7] and by the dignity of his position as Haham. Long before the War his powerful personality, his imposing presence and his gifts of oratory, combined with an oracular manner suggesting that he had access to mysteries hidden from others, had made him an important figure at Zionist Congresses and on Zionist platforms in England and abroad. At the last pre-War Congress in 1913 he had served as one of the five Vice-Presidents, and he had been one of the principal Zionist spokesmen at the abortive conference with the Conjoint Foreign Committee in April 1915. All this attested his standing in the Movement, but he held no position which entitled him to speak for it with authority. He was not, like Sokolow, a member of the Zionist Executive, nor even, like Weizmann, a member of the General Council, nor had he held any office in the English Zionist Federation since retiring from the presidency of that body, after two troubled years, in 1909. Since then he had gone his own way, recognised on all hands as an imposing personality, but kept out of the main stream by an autocratic temperament which made him a difficult colleague. Convinced that he knew best and—as he never tired of explaining—preferring to work quietly behind the scenes, he accepted no leader and commanded no personal following. He kept his secrets to himself. Throughout his dealings with Sykes he appears to have confided only once in Sokolow,[8] and in Weizmann not at all. Not until the end of January 1917 did Weizmann learn for the first time, and then not from Gaster, of the conversations with Sykes which had started more than seven months earlier.

Gaster's first meeting with Sykes on 2 May 1916 was followed by another two days later.[9] At a third meeting not long afterwards

---

[7] See *Gaster Centenary Publication*, ed. B. Schindler (publ. for Royal Asiatic Society by Percy Lund, Humphries, 1958).

[8] He told Sokolow about his first meeting with Sykes on 2 May 1916 (*Diary*, under that date).

[9] *Gaster Diary*, 4 May 1916: ' . . . Warned him [Sykes] again about French manœuvres. . . . Will bring about meeting with Picot.'

Sykes was accompanied by Picot.[10] Early in July Gaster saw Picot again.[11] He wrote to Sykes during the summer,[12] but after May 10th there is no mention in his diaries of any further interview until the middle of November.

Gaster's rather cryptic notes are not always easy to interpret or even to decipher, but it is possible to extract from them some idea of the drift of the conversations. Sykes impressed upon Gaster that he had exerted himself to win support for the Zionist cause both in Petrograd and in Paris. He had talked to Sazonov and engaged his interest, and he had ' after [a] long wrangle got his French colleague, Georges Picot, to see the point of Jewish help.' He had, moreover, he told Gaster, persuaded Picot to agree to a Franco-British condominium in Palestine, the point being, appa-rently—though Gaster does not say so in terms—that, having gone so far as to concede that there was a British interest in Palestine, and having conceded also that ' Jewish help' would be useful, Picot could not disregard the strength of pro-British sentiment among the Zionists. Gaster, for his part, took a strong anti-French line in his talks with Sykes, begging him to beware of ' French manœuvres' and mentioning, in this connection, Victor Basch's mission to the American Jews.[13]

Gaster's dislike of French pretensions in the matter of Palestine did not prevent him from telling Picot, on being first introduced to him by Sykes on May 10th, that ' against positive assurances we would do our best for creating [a] public opinion favourable to France.' When, some two months later, he again saw Picot, this time alone, he told him, in effect, that, if the Jews were promised

[10] *Diary*, 10 May 1916: ' . . . I believe I made them [Sykes and Picot] [? see] the importance of Jewish Commonwealth in Palestine and the ideal for which the Republic is at war. . . . Told him of reverence foi memory of Napoleon among Jews. . . . His idea of a Jewish Kingdom in Palestine. . . . Against positive assurances *we* would do our best for creating public opinion favourable to France. . . .'

[11] *Diary*, 7 July 1916: ' . . . Fr. Govt. wishes a manifestation by Jews in favour of Entente. Asked also to define our wishes. I summed them up: Lebanon [word illegible], local autonomy, freedom of exercising civil rights, protection of property and recognition as Jewish enclave so that Jews may develop in peace. He fully understood and seemed satisfied. Told him of S.'s resignation and . . . elimination of German preponderat-ing influence in U.S. . . .' (' S.' has not been identified.)

[12] May 24th, July 3rd: *Gaster papers*.

[13] *Diary*, 2 and 4 May 1916: as to Basch, see above, p. 218.

what they wanted (which he defined as local autonomy in Palestine, the free exercise of civil rights, the protection of Jewish property and 'recognition as [? of] a Jewish enclave, so that Jews may develop in peace'), then Great Britain and France could count upon the overwhelming majority of Jews rallying to their side.[14] In Gaster's conversations with Sykes in May there had been some talk about propaganda in the United States,[15] but it is not clear whether what they were discussing was simply pro-Ally propaganda or, as the context seems rather to suggest, an attempt to influence American Jewry in favour of a British in preference to a French régime in Palestine.

But there would be little profit in trying to construct a coherent story out of rough notes which, though of value as contemporary documents and almost certainly reliable as far as they go, are plainly not to be regarded as an exact or exhaustive record of Gaster's dealings with Sykes and Picot. What can with some confidence be inferred from them is that both Sykes and Picot were now beginning to take the Zionists seriously, that they recognised a common interest in Zionism as a potential asset to the Allied cause, but that they had also opposing interests related to the Anglo-French competition which neither of them considered, in his own mind, to have been finally disposed of by the Agreement they had helped to negotiate.

On May 21st, three weeks after Gaster's first meeting with Sykes, Henry Morgenthau, who had just returned to the United States after relinquishing his appointment as Ambassador to Turkey, referred to the Palestine question in a widely publicised speech at Cincinnati. He announced that he had recently suggested to the Turkish Government that Turkey should sell Palestine to the Zionists after the War. This proposal, he said, had been well received, and figures had been discussed.[16] Sykes had always been inclined to suspect the Jews of a weakness for the Young Turks. That he had been disturbed by what he had heard about Morgenthau's speech can be inferred from Gaster's evident anxiety to satisfy him that it had misfired and that hints of a

[14] See note 11.
[15] See note 3.
[16] *J.C.*, 26 May 1916.

possible deal between the Turks and the American Jews were not to be taken seriously.[17]

Sykes may also have been unfavourably impressed by a certain ambiguity in Gaster's views about the ultimate control of Palestine. At their first meeting on May 2nd Gaster had made the rather surprising suggestion that even Germany might be preferable to France as a partner in a condominium in Palestine, since she was not specially interested in Egypt. 'You probably remember,' he wrote to Sykes a few weeks later,[18] 'that . . . I suggested eventually a different combination for a possible condominium. . . . Too many interests are involved to be decided only by one single set of Powers.' This, combined with the Morgenthau episode, may possibly have had a discouraging effect on Sykes and may help to explain why, after the beginning of July, when Gaster wrote to him about Morgenthau, it was some months before there was any further contact between them. On the other hand, Sykes may simply have felt that the exchange of views had gone as far as it could usefully be taken for the time being, and that until there was some change in the situation, further talks would be pointless. Whatever the explanation, Gaster had not been dropped. Sykes had not forgotten what he had learned from Gaster and, as we shall see, turned to him for guidance when, towards the end of the year, with the British Army in Egypt poised for an advance into Palestine, it looked as though quick decisions might have to be taken about British relations with the Zionists.

In the meantime, Sykes had been in contact with a Zionist of a different type. This was Aaron Aaronsohn,[19] who had managed by devious ways to travel from Palestine to England on a mission which he had reason to believe would be of interest to the British War Office.

Aaronsohn was a key-figure in a small group of Palestinian Jews who had, in the summer of 1915, got in touch with the British

[17] Gaster to Sykes, 3 July 1916: *Gaster papers.*
[18] 24 May 1916: ibid.
[19] 1876-1919. For biographical data the author is indebted to Dr. Hershlag, of the Hebrew University, who has made a close study of the Aaronsohn papers.

Intelligence centre at Port Said.[20] He had worked as a secret
agent under the direction of Leonard Woolley,[21] and it was with
Woolley's encouragement[22] that he had set out on his journey to
England with a view to placing his intimate knowledge of
Palestine at the disposal of the British military authorities and
interesting them in his plans for more systematic work behind the
Turkish lines.

Aaronsohn had been brought to Palestine as a child when his
parents—among the earliest Jewish immigrants from Rumania—
settled there in the early 1880s. He had studied agriculture in
France, Germany and the United States and, as one of the few
highly trained agricultural scientists in Palestine, had done
experimental work which had gained him more than a local reputation. In the spring of 1915, when there was a locust-plague in
Palestine, the Turkish authorities had put him in charge of the
anti-locust campaign,[23] an appointment which gave him an official
status and free access to all parts of the country, including areas
normally closed to civilians. He had thus been well placed for
accumulating information which could be put to good use in his
intelligence work for the British.

He had engaged in that work, not because of any special ties
with England, but because the behaviour of the Turks in the first
year of the War had convinced him and his friends that there was
no future for the Jews in a Turkish Palestine. At the start they
had believed that the Yishuv would best serve its own interests
by affirming and demonstrating its unqualified loyalty to its
Turkish rulers. Many others were of the same opinion. Early in
the War two leading members of the Jewish Labour Movement,
Ben-Zvi and Ben-Gurion, appealed to Djemal Pasha, the Turkish
Commander-in-Chief in Syria and Palestine, to recognise the

[20] See Basil Thomson, *The Scene Changes* (London, Collins, 1939),
pp. 308-309. (Sir Basil Thomson was engaged during the War in counter-
espionage work for the War Office and the Admiralty.) For an account
of the activities of Aaronsohn and his associates see *History of the
Hagana* (publ. in Hebrew), ed. by B. Dinur and Others (Israel Army
Publications), Pt. I ; Anita Engle, *The Nili Spies* (London, Hogarth
Press, 1959).

[21] Later, Sir Leonard Woolley.

[22] *A.A. Diaries*, 17 November 1916.

[23] Bein, *Return to the Soil*, p. 171.

strength of the ties binding the Jews to the Ottoman Empire, ' which has given our people shelter for hundreds of years.'[24] The Turks were unimpressed and showed by their harsh treatment of the Jews how little hope there was of any change of heart. Knowing that Djemal was in an ugly mood, most of the accredited Jewish leaders in Palestine felt strongly that on no account must anything be done to provoke the Turks or excite their suspicions. Aaronsohn and his friends, however, were not prepared to remain passive. Running counter to the main current of Jewish opinion, but convinced that they were justified in taking certain risks, they made up their minds that they could best serve the Jewish cause by working underground for the British.

In the summer of 1916 Aaronsohn set out for England, relying upon his own ingenuity and the benevolent interest of the British Intelligence network to see him through. He manœuvred his way, viâ Constantinople and Berlin, to Copenhagen, where, after making himself known to the British Legation, he boarded a liner bound for the United States. London had been informed of his movements, and the British North Sea Patrol had been instructed, when his ship was brought in to Kirkwall, to remove and detain him. Against his feigned resistance this was done, and by the end of October he was in London.[25]

The Zionist leaders were not in the secret, and throughout his four weeks' stay in London[26] Aaronsohn was careful to steer clear of them.[27] At the War Office the final result of a long series of interrogations was that the General Staff was satisfied of his reliability and decided that he should be put at the disposal of British Headquarters in Egypt. To this extent he was on the way to achieving his purpose. He was convinced—rightly, as it turned out—that he and his friends could give valuable assistance to the

[24] B. Litvinoff, *Ben-Gurion of Israel* (London, Weidenfeld & Nicholson, 1954), p. 72.

[25] Sources: *Arab Bulletin,* December 1916 ; *A.A. Diaries,* 22 October 1916 ; Basil Thomson, op. cit., pp. 308-309 ; Lichtheim, *Memoirs,* Chapt. 20 ; N. Bentwich, *Judah L. Magnes* (London, East and West Library, [1955]), p. 73.

[26] 26 October-24 November 1916.

[27] *A.A. Diaries,* 24 November 1916. Aaronsohn's presence in London was, however, disclosed by Sykes to Gaster, who warned him that Aaronsohn might be working for the Turks: *Gaster Diary,* 14 November 1916.

British Army in its operations against the Turks, and, in particular, in the planning of a campaign in Palestine. It looked as though they were now to be given their chance to show what they could do. But Aaronsohn had also hoped—and in this he was disappointed—that he might leave England fortified by some assurance of British sympathy with Zionist aspirations. It had been explained to him that on this point the General Staff could not commit the Foreign Office.[28] Three interviews with Mark Sykes,[29] together with other conversations he had in London, had left him with the impression that the Foreign Office was favourably disposed,[30] but no firm promise was obtainable. An entry in his diary on the eve of his departure from London records his sense of frustration: 'Au point de vue diplomatique, fiasco.'[31]

We shall hear of Aaronsohn again, but something may be said at this point about his place in the history of the Balfour Declaration. He had no significant part in the Zionist activities in London which led up to the Declaration, but he did more than has been generally recognised by Zionist historians in helping to create a favourable atmosphere. By the time he left England for Egypt in the winter of 1916, Aaronsohn had not only met and impressed Mark Sykes[32] but had gained a hearing for Zionism at the War Office. This was important because it meant that the subject was not entirely strange to the General Staff when it began, a few months later, to be more closely studied at the instance of the Director of Military Intelligence, General Macdonogh.[33] The relations later established by Weizmann with Macdonogh and his staff had much to do with their conversion into staunch supporters of the Zionist cause, but what made them all the more receptive was their admiration for the courageous work of Aaronsohn and his associates behind the Turkish Front.[34]

When Aaronsohn arrived in Egypt towards the end of 1916, he

[28] A.A. *Diaries*, 17 November 1916.
[29] Ibid., 27 October, 30 October, 6 November.
[30] Ibid., 17 November.
[31] Ibid., 24 November.
[32] As is shown by Sykes's confidential relations with him after his arrival in Egypt.
[33] See Sir Charles Webster's *The Founder of the Jewish National Home* (Rehovoth, [1955]), pp. 13, 21.
[34] Ibid., p. 21.

was somewhat coldly received by the British military authorities, who required to be convinced of his bona fides.[35] In the end he won their unqualified confidence, and by the spring of 1917 he had built up a strong position for himself at the Cairo head-quarters of the British Intelligence services. How highly his work was valued is shown by the tribute paid to him by Allenby after his untimely death in 1919: 'The death of Aaron Aaronsohn deprived me of a valued friend and of a staff officer impossible to replace. He was mainly responsible for the formation of my Field Intelligence organisation behind the Turkish lines. . . . His death is a loss to the British Empire and to Zionism, but the work he has done can never die.'[36] Among the soldiers who became convinced pro-Zionists was at least one officer in a key-position on the staff of the Egyptian Expeditionary Force, Colonel Richard Meinertz-hagen, whose contact with Aaron Aaronsohn in Egypt and Palestine was the starting-point of his active interest in Zionism.[37]

At the Arab Bureau, where political outweighed military considerations, Aaronsohn felt that his activities were viewed with some misgiving. His own impression was that in these circles it was feared that any services which he and his friends might succeed in rendering to the Army might be used as a justification for Zionist demands which would complicate British relations with the Arabs. After an interview with Lawrence, Aaronsohn's comment was that he thought that he was listening to ' a Prussian anti-semite talking English.'[38] Nevertheless, it was through his relations with the Arab Bureau that he acquired at least one valu-able friend for the Zionist cause. This was Major Ormsby-Gore, who, not long after being introduced to Zionism by Aaronsohn, was recalled to London and from the spring of 1917 was near the

---

[35] In January 1917 Norman Bentwich, then serving with the E.E.F., was sent to Cairo to interrogate Aaronsohn and test his story: Bentwich, *Wanderer Between Two Worlds* (London, Kegan Paul, 1941), pp. 75ff.

[36] Orig., dated 14 July 1919, in Allenby's own hand, in Aaronsohn Archives, Zichron-Ya'acov, Israel.

[37] ' It was Aaron Aaronsohn, by his dynamic personality, courage and enthusiasm, who developed an already natural sympathy for the National Home and the injustice inflicted on the Jews by Gentiles. It was he who first made me active.': Colonel Meinertzhagen to the author, 27 February 1955.

[38] For this information the author is indebted to Dr. Hershlag: see also Anita Engle, op. cit., p. 231.

centre of affairs as personal assistant to Lord Milner and Sykes' understudy in the War Cabinet Secretariat.[39]

Aaronsohn was not of a conciliatory disposition and was accustomed to speak his mind with more vigour than tact. He was a man who walked alone, and his relations with the official Zionist leadership were never particularly cordial. Except for a small minority, he was unpopular with the Palestinian Jews, who always feared that his activities would, in the end, bring reprisals from the Turks on their heads. They had, in fact, to pay dearly for the partial exposure of the Aaronsohn spy-ring when, in the autumn of 1917, one of its members fell into Turkish hands. Partly for these reasons, partly also because his influence on the course of events was indirect and not plainly visible, descriptions of the events connected with the Balfour Declaration have usually given Aaronsohn less than his due and under-rated his services to the Zionist cause.

[39] 'From early days [in the Arab Bureau in Cairo] I got into contact with Aaron Aaronsohn. I think he was my first " tutor " in Jewish Palestinian affairs ': Lord Harlech to the author, 16 November 1951.

CHAPTER 19

THE SITUATION AT THE END OF 1916

AARONSOHN LEFT ENGLAND in November 1916 disappointed by his failure to extract any firm assurance of British backing for the Zionists. But this does not mean that, after the failure of Grey's approach to the French and Russian Governments, British interest in Zionism had evaporated. Though the evidence is fragmentary and the picture is blurred, it looks as though about the time of Aaronsohn's visit to London some thought was again being given to this and other aspects of the Jewish question.

First, there was the renewal, late in 1916, of Sykes' contact with Gaster. Early in November we find Gaster sending him, ' according to promise,' a map of Europe marked to show ' all the places where there are Jewish settlements. I mean thereby established Jewish communities.' ' I am still owing you,' Gaster continued, ' a map of Western Asia, Palestine, and the northern coast of Africa. . . . I will be especially careful with the names and places of Jewish settlement in the Holy Land.'[1]

We know, further, that in the winter of 1916 the Alliance Israélite was asked by Briand to defer the submission of a memorandum on peace aims as affecting the Jews, for the reason, it was explained, that the French and British Foreign Offices were exchanging views on these matters.[2] It does not necessarily follow that the discussions touched on Palestine, but it would be surprising if that subject had been overlooked.[3]

---

[1] To Sykes, 3 November 1916: *Gaster papers.* A marked map of Palestine followed on 3 January 1917: ibid.

[2] *C.F.C.*, 1917/18: Wolf's report for period 16 September 1916 to 6 February 1917.

[3] In Vol. VI of his *Study of History* (O.U.P., 1939), at pp. 302-303, Professor Toynbee describes the Russian Imperial Government as having been ' intransigeant in vetoing any inclination on the part of its Western Allies to grant satisfaction to Zionist aspirations in Palestine.' The evidence is not specified and the point of time to which Professor Toynbee is referring is not quite clear, but it looks as though he may be speaking of the situation shortly before the collapse of the Czarist régime in March 1917. In March 1916 the Russian Government had not been

It seems clear that the Jewish question was in the air, but, whatever may have been the exact scope and purpose of the Anglo-French conversations, nothing positive came of them. The Conjoint Foreign Committee had for some time been pressing the British Foreign Office for an indication of its policy on various post-war questions of Jewish concern. These related mainly to Eastern Europe, but Palestine had also been mentioned. In January 1917 the Committee was informed that the Foreign Office could not usefully offer any comment on its proposals: ' In view of the general situation in Europe, [Mr. Secretary Balfour] is unable to hold out any hopes of an understanding being arrived at now or in the immediate future between the Allied Governments.'[4]

The Zionist leaders had gained the impression that a fresh wind was blowing, and towards the end of 1916 they decided that the time had come for them to make up their minds what to ask for and to be ready with a clear statement of their aims. This view seems to have been strongly held by the pro-Zionist members of the Rothschild family, with James de Rothschild taking the lead in pressing Weizmann and Sokolow to produce their programme.[5] On 15 November 1916 he, together with Lord Rothschild and his brother, Charles, discussed the position with Herbert Samuel at a luncheon-party given by the Dowager Lady Rothschild.[6] Weizmann reported to Sokolow that he had heard from Mrs. Charles Rothschild ' that the lunch was a success, that Samuel was very interesting and spoke with great enthusiasm about our cause, that

[4] C.F.C., 1917/54: F.O. to Wolf, 20 January 1917.
[5] Weizmann to Sokolow, 12 October 1916: Ch.W.P.
[6] Weizmann to Sokolow, 14 November 1916: ibid.

entirely intransigeant on the question of the settlement of Jews in Palestine: see above, p. 229. On the other hand, Gaster, recording in his diary an interview with Sykes on 30 January 1917, writes that, after discussing difficulties with the French on the Palestine question, ' I then referred him to Russia as the third partner, but he seemed to shake his head as if not sure of that help.' This fits in with the suggestion that Russia was unfriendly, but not with the idea that both her Western allies, France as well as Great Britain, were favouring a pro-Zionist move. It may be noted that towards the end of 1916 the Palestine question had been revived by the Italian demand for (inter alia) a share in the proposed international régime: see Sonnino's memorandum of 20 November 1916 (Adamov, No. 208).

he is going to see Grey to-morrow or the next day. Jimmy insists that the memo. should be submitted immediately. . . .'[7]

The preparation of the memorandum had already been taken in hand but had presented some difficulty, because, as Sokolow later explained to Brandeis, 'perhaps for the first time in the history of our Movement we felt the necessity of clothing Zionism in the garment of political reality.'[8] In the same letter Sokolow tells Brandeis that what had to be aimed at was a document which would be acceptable both to the English Zionists and also to 'the members of the family R,' adding that 'the greatest efforts were made, especially by our friend Chaim, to induce the members of the R family to accept and sign the programme. I need not dwell on the value of their support. . . .' A first draft was ready by the end of October[9]; but this was not considered satisfactory and was superseded by a second and drastically altered draft, which, in turn, was thought to need amendment. A revised version was ready by the end of November but does not appear to have been used until it was sent to Sykes by Gaster on 1 February 1917.

By that time Asquith had been succeeded as Prime Minister by Lloyd George, and both Grey and Samuel had followed him out of office. Whether in the closing days of the Asquith Government any fresh approach had been made to Grey[10] is uncertain, but, if it had, there had been no visible result. At the change of Government in December the situation was still as it had been described a few weeks earlier by Ahad Ha'am in a letter to Tschlenow in

7 Same to same, 15 November 1916: ibid. (Transl. from Russian).

8 Sokolow to Brandeis, 7 April 1917: Z.A. In what appears to be a draft of this letter (dated 2 April 1917), Sokolow states that he and certain of his colleagues started to consider the preparation of a programme in September 1916: N.S.P.

9 This is the document printed as Appendix I to the Political Report of the Executive to the Twelfth Zionist Congress (1921) and incorrectly stated in the Report (pp. 9-10) to have been submitted to the British Government in October 1916. The document in question was, in fact, never submitted to the Government, and Sokolow's letter to Brandeis of 7 April 1917 shows that it was superseded by a revised draft. This draft No. 2 is the document quoted in part in *Trial and Error* (pp. 235-236). This, in turn, was superseded by draft No. 3, which was almost certainly the document shown to Sykes early in 1917. Sokolow's draft letter of 2 April 1917 speaks explicitly of three successive drafts of the programme. A copy of the final draft, endorsed 'Settled 25/11/16,' is preserved among the papers of Herbert Bentwich.

10 See Weizmann's letter of 15 November 1916—above, note 7.

Moscow: ' It is impossible,' he writes, ' to speak yet either of an " agreement" or even of "negotiations" worthy of that name. The matter is in a state of simple conversations with some influential people who show interest in the issue. At the request of these people we did put down a formal draft of our claims. . . .' ' It is difficult,' he goes on, ' to expect any important step in the near future. As you know, the general position is such that there is no concrete basis for any important decision on our issue. One must wait and prepare the ground for the time being.'[11]

Preparing the ground meant, in the first place, the cultivation of personal contacts with the men in power and those close to them—the patient work behind the scenes in which Weizmann excelled and for which he was in the end to be well rewarded. But, realising that Zionism meant almost nothing to the general public, Weizmann had from the start been thinking also of straightforward propaganda designed to make the Movement comprehensible and interesting to a somewhat wider circle. A few pamphlets had appeared in 1915 and there had been a certain amount of favourable publicity in the press, but it was not until 1916 that a more ambitious effort was made with the publication of *Zionism and the Jewish Future*, followed, towards the end of the year, by the formation of the British Palestine Committee.

Zionism and the Jewish Future,[12] published in the summer of 1916, was a collection of essays designed to present the British public with a clear and realistic picture of the Zionist Movement, its background, aims and composition, and its practical achievements in Palestine. It was skilfully planned as a serious and authoritative statement of the Zionist case. It was meant primarily for the enlightenment of the general reader, but it was also a challenge to the anti-Zionist Jews. Both Weizmann and Gaster expressed themselves in language not calculated to narrow the gulf between the Zionists and their opponents in the Anglo-Jewish community. The anti-Zionists were deeply offended by Weizmann's assertion that ' the position of the emancipated Jew,

11 Ahad Ha'am to Tschlenow, 19 November 1916: *Igrot,* V, 284-285 (transl. from Hebrew).
12 London, John Murray: Edited by Harry Sacher.

though he does not realise it himself, is even more tragic than that of his oppressed brother,'[13] and by Gaster's remark that 'the claim to be Englishmen of the Jewish persuasion—that is, English by nationality and Jewish by faith—is an absolute self-delusion.'[14]

For a book of this type a sale of 3,000 copies was not unsatisfactory, but *Zionism and the Jewish Future* appeared at a time when it could hardly be expected to make any strong impression on the general public. In the summer of 1916 everything else was blotted out by the blazing up of the war in the West with the opening phase of the Battle of the Somme. In the East the war had not yet spread to Palestine, and the average Englishman had no reason to be particularly interested in Zionism as a mere abstraction. But, though there is nothing to suggest that *Zionism and the Jewish Future* had any marked effect on public opinion, it had some respectful notices in the press, and at least one of these was important because the reviewer was Lord Cromer.

Writing in *The Spectator*,[15] Cromer, who had known the Zionist Movement in its early days, put all the weight of his authority behind the view that it had now become a force to be reckoned with. In England, he said, ' there has never been any " Jewish question " properly so-called,' partly because England had learned to cherish the principle of religious toleration, but partly also because ' the relatively small number of Jews in the United Kingdom . . . has prevented them from exercising so commanding an influence over national life as has been the case in some other countries.' But, while ' toleration . . . has tended to break up the solidarity of the Western Jews,' in Eastern Europe, where toleration was unknown, the idea of a Jewish national revival had taken so firm a hold that ' the most passionately ardent Jews prefer persecution, which keeps alive the flame of nationalism, to emancipation, which tends to quench it.' Hence the growing strength of Zionism. ' Although possibly the Jewish question will

[13] Pp. 6-7.
[14] P. 93. It was later explained that ' the appearance of " irreconcilable differences " between the views of Zionists and those of Lucien Wolf and his friends arises in a large measure from the ambiguity of the word " nationality " . . . Zionists think of nationality mainly in its ethnographical and cultural aspects. . . .': Zionist memorandum dated 11 October 1916: *C.F.C.*, 1917/246ff.
[15] 12 August 1916.

not mature quite so quickly as some of the more enthusiastic Zionists consider probable, it is rapidly becoming a practical issue and before long politicians will be unable to brush it aside as the fantastic dream of a few idealists.'

The purpose of *Zionism and the Jewish Future*, as explained by its editor, Harry Sacher, was simply 'to set before English-speaking readers the meaning and achievement of Zionism.' It was concerned more with the Zionist approach to the Jewish question than with the political future of Palestine. One contributor vaguely hoped that the peace settlement would establish stable conditions in the Middle East and that 'under an efficient régime the Land of Promise will again become a land of fulfilment,'[16] but, though Weizmann and his friends had from the start staked their hopes on a British protectorate, the nature of the 'efficient régime' and the identity of the ruling Power were not discussed.

On the other hand, the *raison d'être* of the British Palestine Committee was to argue the case for British sponsorship of Zionist aspirations. The moving spirits were a group of Weizmann's Manchester friends—Sacher, Simon Marks and Israel Sieff, working in close alliance with Herbert Sidebotham.[17] The Committee started its campaign towards the end of 1916 with the circulation of a 'Memorandum of Policy'[18] announcing that it had been formed 'to interest English people, English men and women, in the idea of a Jewish Palestine under the British Crown.' This, it was declared, would be 'a noble ideal, worthy of the British nation.' Quite apart from any question of sentiment, it was argued that British strategic and political interests pointed in the same direction: 'British and Jewish interests coincide. . . . This harmony between the right of the oldest claimants to Palestine and the Imperial interests of Great Britain imposes upon both the duty of framing a scheme whereby both claims can be brought into unison.'

The ideas underlying the 'Memorandum of Policy' had some

16 Norman Bentwich, p. 197.
17 Two members of Weizmann's London circle, Leon Simon and Albert Hyamson, were in regular contact with the Manchester group.
18 For a copy of the Memorandum the author is indebted to Sir Leon Simon. There is also a copy in Z.A.

twelve months earlier been put forward by Herbert Sidebotham, though in a less elaborate form and in less colourful language, in a leading article in the *Manchester Guardian*.[19] The substance of the article must, presumably, have been approved by Scott, but Sidebotham, far from merely echoing his Editor, was advocating a policy in which he personally believed with a fervour all the more remarkable in one who had no Jewish connections and had never had any discussion with any of the Zionist leaders.[20] It so happened that among his colleagues on the staff of the *Guardian* was Harry Sacher, one of Weizmann's intimate advisers, but in his own account of his association with Zionism he emphasises that he had argued the case for the restoration of the Jews to Palestine without prompting of any kind. He had, he writes, advocated a pro-Zionist policy 'on grounds of British interest and with the single idea of helping the victory of the Allies in the War.'[21]

Sidebotham[22] was not only a brilliant journalist; he was the *Guardian's* military expert—the 'Student of War' whose daily commentaries were gaining him a solid reputation as one of the most knowledgable of the military critics. When the authorship of the *Guardian* leader became known in Zionist circles, it was realised that here was a valuable ally whose active co-operation must be secured. About the beginning of 1916 Sidebotham was brought by Sacher into contact with Marks and Sieff, and from this time forth the four worked closely together.

As a first step, it was suggested to Sidebotham that he should expand his leader into a memorandum for submission to the Foreign Office. This he did, and in the late spring of 1916 he handed in his memorandum at an interview with a senior official of the Department. It was in no way concerned with British or Allied propaganda in the United States or elsewhere, but solely with the long-term requirements of Imperial defence. It was the first closely reasoned exposition of views which were not, indeed, entirely novel, for not only Weizmann, but Samuel, Lloyd George

---

[19] Above, p. 135.
[20] In his *Great Britain and Palestine* (London, Macmillan, 1937) Sidebotham says (p. 29) that he did not meet Weizmann until 1916.
[21] Ibid., pp. 32-33.
[22] 1872-1941.

and Scott had already been thinking on similar lines, but had never before been so fully worked out. This was just about the time when Sykes was discussing Zionism with Gaster, but the Foreign Office was not to be drawn. Sidebotham was listened to politely but no more was heard of his memorandum and it was never discovered what impression, if any, it had made.[23]

The memorandum having elicited no response, Sidebotham and his Manchester friends had now to decide on their next move. This was to form themselves into a British Palestine Committee, which, modelling itself upon the Balkan Committee, would, they hoped, attract enough influential supporters to be in a position to press its views on the Government. Some might have thought the name a little misleading, since, with the exception of Sidebotham, all the members of the British Palestine Committee were Jews and Zionists, whereas the Committee purported to be a body which, approaching the question from a purely British point of view, was satisfied that Great Britain ought to back the Zionists in her own interests. The answer would have been that the Committee was intended to be merely the nucleus of a larger organisation, most of whose members would not be Jews.

This expectation, as we shall see, was disappointed, and the Committee had to look for other means of achieving its purpose. In January 1917 it began the publication of a weekly journal, *Palestine*,[24] which announced its policy in the heading to every issue: ' The British Palestine Committee seeks to reset the ancient glories of the Jewish nation in the freedom of a new British dominion in Palestine.'

Palestine was not under the direct control of the Zionist leaders, and there were times when the freedom which its writers allowed themselves caused Weizmann and Sokolow some embarrassment. More than once in the early part of 1917 Sykes pointed out that over-zealous advocacy of a British protectorate in Palestine might defeat its own purpose by hardening French opposition.[25] He objected also to what he regarded as indiscretions in an article discussing the future boundaries of Palestine.[26] *Palestine* may at

23 Op. cit., pp. 33ff., where the substance of the memorandum is set out.
24 The first number is dated 26 January 1917.
25 Note of Sykes' interview with Weizmann and Sokolow, 10 February 1917: *Ch.W.P.* Sidebotham to Weizmann, 9 March 1917: *Ch.W.P.*
26 Weizmann to Sokolow, 18 February 1917: *Ch.W.P.*

times have overshot the mark, but it stimulated fresh thinking by its sustained argument for British sponsorship of Zionism on the ground of enlightened self-interest. Though there were no signed articles, it was known to the initiated that among the regular contributors was Sidebotham, who often wove into his editorials a penetrating analysis of the military situation in the Turkish theatre of war. Partly for this reason, and partly also because it contained out-of-the-way information of interest to specialists and not easily to be found elsewhere, *Palestine* was taken seriously and regularly read at the War Office, in newspaper offices and in other influential quarters.

But *Palestine* did not make its appearance until the end of January 1917. By this time it was already assured of a more receptive audience than it would have had before General Murray, having occupied Rafa, stood on the threshold of Palestine, poised for the invasion now seen to be imminent. The British Palestine Committee's opening move a few weeks earlier had resulted in a fiasco. Towards the end of 1916 the Committee had sent a statement of its aims to some hundreds of eminent individuals in various walks of life. They had not been asked for any financial support but had been invited, if they agreed with the objects of the Committee, to identify themselves with it as patrons. A report circulated to the Committee in the middle of December 1916 describes the response as 'most discouraging.'[27] According to Sidebotham,[28] ' several hundred circulars were sent out to men famous in politics, letters and learning. I think we received about ten replies in all, of which half were purely formal acknowledgments. Of the remainder, two were opposed to us.'

The massive indifference of a group of representative Englishmen suggests that the impact of Zionism on British public opinion had so far been insignificant. In the select circle in which policy was made the Zionists could already count upon some important friends, but nothing had been decided, nor did they themselves believe that any firm commitment was in sight. This was the

[27] The author is indebted to Sir Leon Simon for a copy of this report. It is undated, but the covering letter is dated 13 December 1916.
[28] *Great Britain and Palestine*, pp. 41-42.

position towards the end of 1916. At that point the tide began to turn. As a result of the Cabinet crisis in December 1916, Lloyd George became Prime Minister and Balfour moved from the Admiralty to the Foreign Office. Soon afterwards the war with Turkey entered on a new phase, in which Palestine became of cardinal importance. In March the Russian Revolution set in train a succession of events which, though not in all respects advantageous to the Zionists, worked, on the whole, in their favour. It so happened that by the turn of the year Weizmann's scientific work for the Government had passed its most critical stage and left him freer than he had been in 1915-1916 to devote his energies to Zionism. Taking full command precisely at the moment when his leadership could be most effective, he used his opportunities with masterly skill. From the beginning of 1917 the Zionists were steadily gaining ground, and by the spring they were already well on the road to the Balfour Declaration.

One of Field-Marshal Smuts' last public speeches was at a London Dinner in honour of Weizmann in 1949. Recalling the circumstances in which the War Cabinet, of which he had been a member, had resolved to approve the Declaration, he spoke of the 'moral and religious motives' which had reinforced the political argument. 'We were persuaded. But remember that it was Weizmann who persuaded us.'[29]

---

[29] *J.C.*, 22 November 1949.

Part III

The Year of Decision—1917

w

CHAPTER 20

THE CHANGE OF GOVERNMENT

THE POLITICAL UPHEAVAL at the end of 1916 was in one important respect unfortunate for the Zionists. Herbert Samuel was invited by Lloyd George to retain his position as Home Secretary, but he declined the offer and followed Asquith out of office. So did Edwin Montagu, but, though the Zionists were thus relieved for the time being of their most determined opponent in the Government,[1] this was only partial compensation for the loss of their most active friend. Samuel's resignation was final; Montagu, on the other hand, was before long to change his mind about serving under Lloyd George and to reappear as a Minister in time to conduct from within the Government a relentless campaign against any pro-Zionist Declaration. Besides Herbert Samuel, the Liberal Ministers who resigned with Asquith included also another member of his Cabinet whom the Zionists could count as a friend, the Marquess of Crewe.

But though the change of Government was not all gain for the Zionists, it was on balance immeasurably to their advantage. Asquith had never given them the slightest encouragement. Both the new Prime Minister and the new Foreign Secretary were strongly predisposed in their favour, and, unlike Asquith and Grey, neither of whom Weizmann had ever met, were men whom he could approach with the knowledge that he had already won their confidence. Because of a long-standing personal friendship, Lloyd George was freely accessible to Weizmann's staunch friend and supporter, C. P. Scott, while Balfour had at his side, as Assistant Foreign Secretary, Lord Robert Cecil, who, after meeting Weizmann in 1915, had become, in his own words, 'a Zionist by passionate conviction.'[2]

---

[1] Montagu was already fighting Zionism in 1916: see his letter of 3 August 1916 to Sir Eric Drummond, quoted by Christopher Sykes, *Two Studies in Virtue* (London, Collins, 1953), pp. 212ff.

[2] Above, p. 186.

Under the new régime instituted by Lloyd George, final decisions on questions of high policy rested with a small War Cabinet presided over by the Prime Minister and composed, in principle, of Ministers free from departmental duties.[3] Balfour had all the authority attaching to his office as Foreign Secretary and to his standing as an elder statesman of the highest eminence, but he was not a member of the War Cabinet, though he was more often than not present at its meetings and in practice enjoyed a privileged position by reason of his close relations with the Prime Minister.[4]

One result of the change of Government was the introduction into the inner circle of Lord Milner, who, though he had till then evinced no particular interest in Zionism,[5] was to become a firm supporter of a pro-Zionist policy and, in the end, to share with Balfour and Lloyd George the main responsibility for the Balfour Declaration.

It was only at the last moment that Lloyd George, having reserved a seat in his War Cabinet for Sir Edward Carson, decided to offer it instead to Milner.[6] It did not take him long to discover how fully his choice had been justified and how reliable an adviser he had secured. Milner, he told the French Prime Minister, Ribot, was the only independent mind among his colleagues.[7] Leopold Amery has spoken of Milner as 'the hub of the machine' and

---

[3] The one exception was Bonar Law, who was Chancellor of the Exchequer but was included by virtue of his special position as Leader of the House of Commons and Leader of the Conservative Party.

[4] According to Mr. Robert Blake (*The Unknown Prime Minister*, London, 1955, p. 341), Balfour had the right to attend War Cabinet meetings on matters arising within his own Department. Mrs. Dugdale puts it rather higher: 'The Foreign Secretary was not a member of the War Cabinet, but alone among the Departmental Ministers was given the right to attend whenever he thought fit.' *Arthur James Balfour*, II, 241. Mrs. Dugdale goes on to say that out of more than five hundred meetings held under the Second Coalition Government, Balfour was present at more than three hundred. As to his access to the Prime Minister, 'Balfour had only to turn the handle of the door and saunter in': ibid.

[5] The contrary has been suggested, but on unconvincing evidence: see below, p. 312, note 15, and p. 314, note 21.

[6] Robert Blake, op. cit., p. 341; see also Sir Evelyn Wrench, *Alfred, Lord Milner* (London, Eyre & Spottiswoode, 1958), p. 315.

[7] Ribot's diary, 28 May 1917: '[Lloyd George] se plaint de son cabinet, où il n'y a qu'un homme ayant l'esprit libre, Lord Milner': Ribot fils, *Journal d'Alexandre Ribot* (Paris, 1936), p. 134.

' the acknowledged mainstay of the Cabinet,'[8] and, because of the weight he carried in that body, one historian has described him as occupying *de facto* ' the second position under the Crown.'[9] This may be an overstatement; Bonar Law's biographer brings out clearly the deference paid by the Prime Minister to the views of the Conservative leader,[10] and Milner's own biographer writes that ' Bonar Law, as Leader of the House of Commons, of course exercised the greatest influence on the political side after Lloyd George.'[11] What is certain is that Milner occupied a key-position in the War Cabinet and, once convinced that British interests would be served by an understanding with the Zionists, was able to exert a powerful influence in its favour. Looking back some ten years later, Smuts reminded a Zionist meeting in South Africa that ' the man who worked hardest for the formula of the national home was Lord Milner. He is dead to-day and his name is seldom or never mentioned in this connection, but a tribute to him is due for the work he did.'[12]

Though it was not until he had joined the War Cabinet that Milner first began actively to interest himself in Zionism, the Jewish Question was by no means new to him. In 1906 he had been one of the principal speakers at a Queen's Hall meeting called to protest against the persecution of the Jews in Russia. ' When British citizens,' he said, ' declared their conviction that the only final remedy for these fearful evils was complete equality of status, they were only preaching precisely what they had been the first to practise and had practised with magnificent results.'[13]

Milner had recently returned to England after seven years' service under the Crown in South Africa, where as High Commissioner, and especially in his capacity as Administrator of the Transvaal, he had shown marked consideration for the Jews in his handling of various problems affecting their interests. In 1902 it was rumoured in Jewish circles that foreign-born Jews in the Transvaal were to be considered ineligible for naturalisation. At

8 *My Political Life*, II, 98.
9 *History of The Times*, Vol. IV, Pt. II, p. 1068.
10 Blake, op. cit., pp. 343-344.
11 Wrench, op. cit., p. 333.
12 *The Zionist Record* (Johannesburg), 30 April 1926.
13 *The Times*, 9 January 1906.

a Zionist meeting in Johannesburg, the Chairman, Samuel Goldreich, read a letter from Milner in which he declared emphatically
that neither in this matter nor in regard to the franchise would
there be any question of discriminating against Jews. ' The principles which I have indicated are,' he wrote, ' part of a long
settled policy, universal throughout the Empire, from which no
British Government would think of departing. As far as I am
personally concerned, any such departure would be entirely
repugnant to my convictions and feelings. Equally repugnant to
me is anything like an ungenerous attitude towards Jews of
foreign origin who are either already resident in the Transvaal
or intending to enter it.'[14] In the autumn of 1902 Milner did his
best to ease the position of such Jews by authorising the South
African Zionist Federation, of which Goldreich was President, to
act, where Jews were concerned, as the channel for applications
for permits to enter or leave the Transvaal.[15]

In 1903 Milner again showed a friendly interest in the Jews by
attending the inaugural meeting of the South African Jewish
Board of Deputies. ' This great community,' he said, ' has its own
race traditions and its own race loyalty. There is absolutely
nothing incompatible in this with the most thoroughgoing British
patriotism.' The Board, he continued, could render a valuable

[14] 11 July 1902: printed in the report of the Johannesburg meeting in
J.C., 10 October 1902. Printed also in *The Milner Papers*, ed. Cecil
Headlam (London, Cassell, 1933), II, 378-379.

[15] Text of announcement by South African Zionist Federation printed in
the official Zionist organ, *Die Welt* (Vienna), 10 October 1902. Text of
official letter to Goldreich printed in *The Vision Amazing* by M. Gitlin
(Johannesburg, 1950), p. 74. Since a foreigner had normally to apply
through his Consul, the concession was of great benefit to Jews who
were Russian nationals or of doubtful national status. The Zionists
naturally made the most of this incident, which has sometimes been
construed as an indication that Milner was interested in Zionism long
before the War: see, for example, O. K. Rabinowicz, *Herzl* (New York,
1958), pp. 81ff.; cf., Wrench, op. cit., p. 364. It must, however, be
borne in mind (1) that the President of the Zionist Federation, Goldreich,
was personally known to Milner as a man who could be trusted, and
(2) that this was before the setting up of the South African Jewish Board
of Deputies, so that the Zionist Federation may well have been considered at the time to be the best available representative of the South
African Jews. That Milner had heard of Zionism before the War can be
taken for granted, but there are no grounds for thinking that he had
given it serious thought ; indeed, the evidence is all the other way—
see below, p. 314, note 21.

service to South Africa because of 'the bond which the Jews, whether born on British soil or not, who are British citizens, not merely in the legal sense but in the sense of deep-rooted loyalty and affection to our common country—the bond which they alone can create between [Jewish] newcomers and their non-Jewish fellow-citizens. . . . It is for you . . . to take them by the hand and draw them into fellowship with us in language, in sentiments and in ideas.'[16]

Milner's views, as reflected in his relations with the Jews in South Africa, were those of a liberal-minded Englishman for whom toleration was not a gratuitous condescension but a moral imperative, and anti-semitism an offence against civilised behaviour. He recognised that the Jews had their own traditions and loyalties, which they rightly cherished. All he asked of them was that, in return for the full equality of status to which they were justly entitled, they should respond by accepting not only its legal but its moral obligations, not holding themselves apart as a separate unit within the State but identifying themselves with the national life.

Milner's feelings about the Jews were coloured by his regard for Jews with whom he was on terms of personal friendship. 'Some of the best people I have ever known,' he wrote to Goldreich in 1902, 'are Jews, and Jews intensely devoted to their race and religion.'[17] With one of the most distinguished families in Anglo-Jewry, the Montefiores, Milner had long-standing ties associated with the memory of his Balliol contemporary, Claude Montefiore's brilliant elder brother, Leonard, by whose death, at the age of twenty-six, in 1879 he lost a much-loved companion of his youth.[18] The Montefiores were, indeed, intensely devoted to their religion, but this was not a circle in which Milner was likely to hear much good of Zionism. In South Africa he did meet many Zionists; most of the Jews he knew best—men like Goldreich, Max Langerman and Joseph Hertz (later to become the British

---

[16] *J.C.*, 28 August 1903.

[17] 11 July 1902: see above, note 14.

[18] Lucy Cohen, *Some Recollections of Claude Goldsmid Montefiore* (London, Faber, 1940), pp. 14, 146 ; Wrench, op. cit., pp. 50, 52, 232. Milner was the author of an unsigned biographical sketch included in *Essays and Letters by Leonard A. Montefiore* (privately printed, London, 1881)—see Wrench, op. cit., p. 52.

Chief Rabbi)—had strong Zionist sympathies. In 1903 Herzl, impressed by Milner's friendly attitude towards the Jews, appealed to Goldreich to interest him in the Movement,[19] and two years later Goldreich told Herzl's successor, David Wolffsohn, that he had tried: ' I did my best,' he wrote, ' to convince Lord Milner that what he called Imperialism is identical with Zionism, and that the highest and noblest ideals of Britain and the world demand the restoration of Israel to Zion.'[20] But Milner does not seem to have responded; neither in his South African days nor at any time up to 1917 is there any evidence of his having seriously interested himself in Zionism.[21] He had a sincere respect for Jews and was neither blind nor indifferent to the difficulties of their position, but he seems before the War to have had more in common with the views of Claude Montefiore and his colleagues in the Conjoint Foreign Committee than with those of the Zionists, for whom equality of status in the Diaspora, even if it were everywhere fully obtainable, would not of itself solve the Jewish problem as they conceived it.

Soon after joining the War Cabinet in December 1916, Milner received from Herbert Samuel a copy of his Palestine memorandum. ' It contains,' he wrote to Samuel, ' suggestions which are new to me. Among the possible alternatives which you review the one which you yourself favour certainly appears to me the most attractive.'[22] The alternative favoured by Samuel was some

19 Herzl to Goldreich, 16 June 1903: Z.A.
20 Goldreich to Herzl, 2 April 1905: Z.A. Quoted M. Gitlin, op. cit., p. 74.
21 ' I doubt whether he [Milner] had had any contacts with the Zionist Movement or any of its pre-war leaders, and I imagine Zionism only came within his consciousness when he contemplated the consequences of the defeat and break-up of the Turkish Empire': Lord Harlech to the author, 20 November 1951. 'Nor have I any recollection of Milner talking to me about Zionism before he joined the Lloyd George Government': Leopold Amery to the author, 1 July 1952. 'As to Milner, my recollection is pretty clear that he said that the Memorandum I had sent him was the first time his attention had been specially drawn to the subject': Lord Samuel to the author, 29 January 1952.
22 Samuel, Memoirs, p. 145. The date of Milner's letter is not given in the Memoirs but appears from Mr. John Bowle's Viscount Samuel (London, Gollancz, 1957), at pp. 178-179, to have been 17 January 1917. Samuel told Gaster, on 1 February 1917, that he had sent his memorandum to Milner, from whom he had had a very satisfactory answer: Gaster Diary.

form of British protectorate for Palestine, coupled with the encouragement of Jewish immigration, so that 'in course of time the Jewish inhabitants, grown into a majority, may be conceded such degree of self-government as conditions of that day might justify.'

There is good reason to believe that the Samuel memorandum was the starting-point of Milner's active interest in Zionism.[23] Samuel's contention that Great Britain could on no account afford to acquiesce in French predominance in Palestine—'the establishment of a great European Power so close to the Suez Canal would be a continual menace to the essential lines of communication of the British Empire'—would certainly have appealed to Milner, a strong Imperialist and all the more Egypt-minded because of his own experiences in Cairo, where from 1889 to 1892 he had served as Under-Secretary for Finance and had been a resentful observer of French manœuvres designed to shake the British position.[24] Since then there had been the Anglo-French Accord of 1904, but Milner would doubtless have agreed with Samuel that 'we cannot proceed on the supposition that our present happy relations with France will continue always.'

A policy designed to result in 'the gradual growth of a considerable Jewish community in Palestine under British suzerainty' was likewise calculated to appeal to Milner, not for sentimental reasons, but because, having had a good many contacts with Jews in Egypt and in South Africa, he had been impressed by their abilities and was ready to believe that, if the Jews were encouraged to establish themselves in Palestine, they might well make a success of it. He felt serious doubts as to the capacity of certain (as he thought) less advanced or less gifted peoples to govern themselves efficiently or at all, but he had much more confidence in the Jews.[25] Once presented with the idea of a British protectorate over Palestine, combined with a large-scale settlement of Jews under the British flag, he was disposed from the start to be sympathetic.

Lord Bertie mentions in his diary[26] a meeting with Milner in

23 See Lord Samuel's letter to the author, quoted above, note 21. There is no evidence of Milner's having ever met Weizmann.
24 See his *England in Egypt* (London, 1899), pp. 342-346.
25 The author is indebted for this point to Lord Harlech.
26 II, 168 (24 December 1917).

Paris a few weeks after the Balfour Declaration. 'Milner,' he writes, 'is not a Zionist engagé; he only hopes that the adoption of Zionism will benefit us. *I* think that Zionism is rot.' What Milner actually said was very likely less cynical than Lord Bertie makes it sound, but it seems true that his approach to Zionism was realistic. He was and had always been well disposed towards the Jews, but his feelings about them were not coloured by a sense of guilt calling for expiation, nor was he sensitive to the Jewish mystique nor excited by romantic dreams of the restoration of the Chosen People to the Holy Land. He began thinking about Zionism in the context of the impending break-up of the Turkish Empire, and it seems clear that the question which mainly interested him was whether co-operation with the Zionists would be of practical advantage to Great Britain in the new situation which was developing in the Middle East.[27]

Milner was not the man to be hurried into a decision, and he took his time in finally making up his mind about Zionism in its bearing on British policy. Lord Harlech, who, in March 1917, was brought back from Cairo to become Milner's Parliamentary Private Secretary, at the same time serving as Sykes' understudy in the War Cabinet Secretariat, recalls that early in their association Milner told him that he was a convinced supporter of Zionism.[28] On the other hand, C. P. Scott came away rather disappointed from an interview with Milner towards the end of April 1917. 'As a member of the War Cabinet,' he writes in his Journal,[29] 'I thought he [? might] have views about Palestine, but he was rather vague about it—seemed to think that it would have to be internationalised, evidently knew nothing of the Zionist view that this would be fatal for Zionism and therefore for our whole policy in Palestine. Spoke of the French assertiveness in regard to it, and of "unfortunate engagements" entered into a year ago. I said Palestine was a small thing compared with

[27] In the foregoing analysis of Milner's approach to the Zionist question the author has received valuable guidance, which he desires gratefully to acknowledge, from the recollections of Lord Harlech, who, as Major Ormsby-Gore, M.P., was in 1917 in close personal relations with Milner, and from the impressions, also based on personal contact with Milner, of Colonel Richard Meinerthagen.

[28] Lord Harlech to the author, 16 November 1951.

[29] 20 April 1917.

the vast territory we were overrunning in Mesopotamia, but it was the thing that mattered.'

Milner expressed himself more positively when he was seen about a month later by Claude Montefiore. Montefiore's report to his colleagues in the Conjoint Foreign Committee[30] was, from their point of view, somewhat discouraging. 'Milner,' he said, 'agreed that Mr. Lloyd George was impressed by, and sympathetic to, many of the ideas of the Zionists. His own views appeared to lie between our formula and the full Zionist scheme. He seemed to favour the establishment of a Jewish community in Palestine, or parts of Palestine, under a British protectorate. Within its own borders such a community would be autonomous, but it would not be an independent State.... He was very emphatic in his opinion that I exaggerated the dangers of Zionism. . . . He clearly thought that in our dislike of Zionism we greatly exaggerated its importance and its dangers. . . .' By this time the Government's pro-Zionist leanings had begun to crystallise into a settled policy. The Zionists were being encouraged to ask for a British protectorate over Palestine, and Milner was evidently no longer in the despondent mood in which he had talked to Scott about unavoidable concessions to the French.

At the end of Montefiore's note of the interview there is a significant reference to the situation in Russia: 'It has obviously been represented to H.M. Government that the Russian Jews are all enthusiastic Zionists. I said that I did not believe that this was by any means the case.' Part of the background to the Balfour Declaration was, as we shall see, the British Government's impression that, if the Russian Jews could be made to understand that the fulfilment of Jewish aspirations in Palestine was bound up with the victory of the Allies, this might help in some measure to counteract the subversive forces which were threatening to sweep Russia out of the War and into a separate peace with the Central Powers. About the time of his conversation with Montefiore in May 1917 Milner was inquiring into the strength of Zionist sentiment among the Russian Jews. He had headed a British Mission to Petrograd almost immediately before the March Revolution and was, within the War Cabinet, the Minister best qualified to advise on Russian affairs. He had begun moving

[30] *C.F.C.*, 1917/474ff. (16 May 1917).

towards an interest in Zionism before the Russian Revolution was foreseen, but the course of events in Russia strengthened the case for some such understanding with the Zionists as he was already disposed to advocate on broader grounds of long-term policy in the East.

It will be noticed that, while Milner favoured the establishment of an autonomous Jewish community in Palestine, he distinguished, in his talk with Montefiore, between this and an independent State. That the Jews should be promised a State in Palestine was at no time proposed by any member of the War Cabinet, but in his judgment of what the Zionists should be encouraged to expect Milner seems all along to have taken a rather more cautious line than some of his colleagues. It was he who was mainly responsible for the actual phraseology of the Balfour Declaration, and the formula which eventually emerged was based upon his amendment of a draft in somewhat less guarded language which Balfour had originally been prepared to recommend.[31] When the House of Lords debated the Palestine question in 1923, Milner stoutly defended the Declaration but made it clear that he was speaking of that document as interpreted in the Churchill memorandum of 1922,[32] and not of ' the policy which is advocated by the extreme Zionists, which is a totally different thing.' ' I think,' he concluded, ' that we have only to go on . . . with the policy of establishing, not a Jewish Government of Palestine but a Jewish home there . . . we have only to go on steadily in the policy which has already been laid down, and I think it will not be many years before Palestine . . . will become a source of strength and credit to us.'[33]

With Lloyd George and Milner dominating the War Cabinet and with Balfour and Cecil at the Foreign Office, the Zionists were in no danger of being overlooked in any fresh appraisal of British war aims or of long-term British policy in the Middle East. At a lower but still influential level they had friends in key-

[31] See below, pp. 521-522, and Appendix.
[32] Cmd. 1700 (1922), pp. 17ff.
[33] H.L., 27 June 1923: O.R., col. 664-671.

positions in the War Cabinet Secretariat, at the War Office and in the Prime Minister's personal entourage.

When Lloyd George became Prime Minister and set up his War Cabinet he introduced two other innovations in the machinery of government. He provided the War Cabinet with its own strongly staffed Secretariat under the direction of Sir Maurice Hankey, and at the same time he surrounded himself with a group of personal advisers, known to those who disliked his propensity for using them to short-circuit the dispatch of business as the Downing Street kindergarten. As his specialist in foreign and Imperial affairs he selected Philip Kerr,[34] the Editor of *The Round Table*, who was thus in a position to play an informal part in the shaping of policy, while at the same time making it his business to keep the Foreign Office informed when—as could happen under Lloyd George—it was in danger of being by-passed.[35] Weizmann had met Kerr at the Astors' early in 1916[36] and had got to know him well enough to be able to rely on his good offices in the critical months when, with the Balfour Declaration in the balance, it was useful to have a friend in the 'Garden Suburb.'

At the War Office, the Chief of the Imperial General Staff, Field-Marshal Sir William Robertson, was never interested in the Palestine campaign, which he regarded as a deviation from the real business in hand—the defeat of Germany in the West, nor was he, in any case, the man to concern himself with anything as exotic and as far outside the range of his experience as Zionism. On the other hand, the more imaginative and more politically-minded Director of Military Intelligence, General Sir George Macdonogh, did attach importance to the place of Palestine in the scheme of Imperial defence. He listened to and was impressed by Weizmann,[37] and by the time the Balfour Declaration was beginning to take shape he had become a strong supporter of a pro-Zionist policy, believing that this would help to open the

---

[34] Later, Marquess of Lothian.
[35] Joseph Davies, *The Prime Minister's Secretariat* (Newport, Mon., 1951), p. xix.
[36] Mrs. Weizmann's Diary, 25 March 1916: *V.W.P.*
[37] Sir Charles Webster, *The Founder of the Jewish National Home* (Rehovoth, n.d., ? 1955), p. 21. Sir Charles (then Lieutenant) Webster was in 1917 a junior member of General Macdonogh's staff.

door to a British trusteeship for Palestine or some other form of *de facto* British control, while at the same time giving the British and the Jews a common interest in pressing the case for the rectification of the unsatisfactory northern frontier.[38]

In another quarter, and one close to the seat of power, the Zionists had influential friends in a group of younger men— Sykes, Amery and Ormsby-Gore—belonging or attached to the War Cabinet Secretariat, but with a privileged status which gave them direct access to leading Ministers. On joining the Secretariat, Amery was told by Milner that, besides being at the disposal of members of the War Cabinet, he and Sykes, acting, as he puts it, as a kind of informal brains trust, were to be free to take the initiative in submitting ideas of their own.[39]

Middle Eastern affairs were the special province of Mark Sykes, who, as we have seen, had been interested in Zionism since early in 1916. Ormsby-Gore, the youngest of the three, assisted Sykes and deputised for him when he was away. He had come to London from Cairo impressed by what he had heard about Zionism from Aaron Aaronsohn and ready to learn more by direct contact with Weizmann, for whom he soon conceived a warm personal admiration. Amery, like Ormsby-Gore, owed his appointment to Milner, but, unlike him, had had no contact with Zionism and had, indeed, been barely aware of the existence of the Movement.[40] It was Sykes who introduced him to Zionism and convinced him that it was worth his attention. Looking back in 1945, 'Sykes,' he writes,[41] 'soon persuaded me that, from the purely British point of view, a prosperous Jewish population in Palestine, owing its inception and its opportunity of development to British policy, might be an invaluable asset as a defence of the Suez Canal against attack from the North and as a station on the future air-routes to the East. Both of us, too, as old travellers in the Middle East, believed that nothing could bring so regenerating an influence to those ancient centres of the world's civilisation . . . as a fresh contact with Western life through a people who yet regarded the East as their true home.'

[38] There is reason to believe that Macdonogh was thinking along these lines.
[39] Amery, *My Political Life,* II, 92.
[40] Ibid., II, 115.
[41] Preface to *Chaim Weizmann,* ed. P. Goodman (London, Gollancz, 1945), p. 11.

THE CHANGE OF GOVERNMENT

What is missing here is any reference to an aspect of the matter which Sykes and Amery can hardly have overlooked in their discussions. Sykes, says Amery, convinced him that Great Britain stood to gain by sponsoring the settlement in Palestine of a Jewish population closely linked to herself and providing her with a reliable barrier against an attack on the Suez Canal 'from the North,' meaning, presumably, from the direction of Syria. The whole conception pre-supposes a state of affairs in which the internationalised Brown Area of the Sykes-Picot Agreement has somehow been converted into a British sphere of influence. It is difficult to suppose that Sykes and Amery did not ask themselves how this condition was to be satisfied, or, in other words, how Great Britain was to extricate herself from the 'unfortunate engagements' to the French so despondently alluded to by Milner, in April 1917, in his conversation with Scott.

The idea of a special relationship between Great Britain and the Jews in Palestine, with the same underlying assumption that the French interest in Palestine was not an insuperable obstacle, was introduced in veiled language into a discussion of the future of Turkey in the June 1917 issue of *The Round Table*. The contents of this issue had been discussed at a *Round Table* committee meeting in March,[42] and the proofs of the article dealing with the Palestine question had been sent before publication to Weizmann.[43] After a sympathetic account of the progress already made by the Jews in Palestine, 'there are,' said the writer, 'Zionists who would like to see Palestine a British Protectorate, with a prospect of being able to grow into a British Dominion.' 'As for the British side of the question,' he went on, 'we may consult Dr. Trietsch,'[44] and he proceeded to set out at some length Trietsch's exposition of the potential advantages to Germany of

---

[42] For this and other information based on the records of *The Round Table* the author is indebted to Mr. Dermot Morrah.

[43] 'Please convey my compliments to Dr. Weizmann and thank him for having been so kind as to read the proofs of the article for *The Round Table* dealing with Palestine': Reginald (later, Professor Sir Reginald) Coupland, Acting Editor, to Vladimir Jabotinsky, 22 May 1917: *Ch.W.P.*

[44] As to Trietsch's pro-Zionist propaganda in Germany see above p. 212.

' a protectorate over the Jews.' ' Other Powers than Germany,' he remarked, 'may take these possibilities to heart.'

All this might have been of no particular significance if *The Round Table* had not been what it was—the organ of a group of liberal-minded Imperialists, having Milner as its presiding genius and Philip Kerr and Amery among its members. Though Milner had joined the War Cabinet and both Kerr and Amery were, at a lower level, associated with the Government, all three had continued to take an active interest in *The Round Table*. The *Round Table* article, therefore, with its strong hint in the direction of a pro-Zionist policy, was more than an abstract expression of opinion ; it meant that by March 1917, when its publication was approved, the case for British sponsorship of Zionism had made a serious impression on a group which had before the change of Government commanded more respect than influence but was now represented in key-positions in, or on the fringe of, the inner circle.

When, towards the end of May 1917, *The Times* showed its hand, it was seen that the Zionists had gained another important ally. The Editor, Geoffrey Dawson, was a member of the *Round Table* group and was in 1917 in close touch with Milner, but on the Zionist question the policy of *The Times*, though he must have acquiesced in it, was not shaped by him, but by the Foreign Editor, Wickham Steed.[45]

Before the War the general impression among Jews was that *The Times* was no friend of theirs, nor was Wickham Steed. In June 1914 *The Times* gave great offence in Jewish circles by a leading article in which, in effect, it condoned the Russian Government's refusal to relieve the Jews of their disabilities, observing that ' were the Jews free to move and trade amongst them at pleasure, they would soon eat up the tillers of the soil. Peddling, liquor-dealing and money-lending are pursuits to which the Oriental Jews naturally take, and no Russian statesman can desire to see them extended.'[46] In a letter to *The Times*, the Conjoint Foreign Committee, through its Presidents, Claude

[45] Wickham Steed to the author, 1 July 1952.
[46] *The Times*, 5 June 1914.

THE CHANGE OF GOVERNMENT

Montefiore and D. L. Alexander, K.C., protested strongly against these remarks.[47] In the light of what was to happen three years later, when *The Times,* under the guidance of Wickham Steed, backed the Zionists in their collision with the Conjoint Foreign Committee, there is a certain irony in a paragraph in *The Zionist* complimenting Montefiore and Alexander on their effective reply to ' a crude and violent anti-semitic outburst justifying the persecution of the Jews in Russia and exhorting the Russian Government to persist in it.'[48] As for Wickham Steed, who in 1917 was to become so stout a supporter of the Zionist cause, *The Zionist* observed that there was nothing very surprising in the behaviour of *The Times,* since ' the present Foreign Editor of *The Times* was until a short time ago that paper's correspondent in Vienna[49] and in that capacity specialised in transmitting anti-semitic news and views.'[50]

After the outbreak of war Jews still detected an undercurrent of illwill in *The Times.* We find *The Jewish Chronicle,* for example, protesting, in May 1915, against ' the frequency with which *The Times* has during the last few days permitted the name of Jew to be dragged into its columns, usually in an unfriendly connection.'[51] In 1917 the handling of the March Revolution in Russia by *The Times* Petrograd correspondent, Robert Wilton, was deeply resented by British Jews. A memorandum on the situation in Russia submitted by Lucien Wolf to the Conjoint Foreign Committee at the end of April 1917 dealt at length with ' the calumnies of *The Times.*'[52] A report from Petrograd which came before the Committee in June described the efforts of the Russian reactionaries to undermine the Provisional Government by inciting public opinion against the Jews, and their success in enlisting the co-operation of certain foreign correspondents. ' Thus, for instance,' the Committee was told, ' the correspondents of *The Times* and the *Morning Post* started their sinister work

---

[47] *The Times,* 9 June 1914.
[48] *The Zionist* (London), June 1914, pp. 3-4.
[49] Steed was Vienna correspondent of *The Times* from 1902 to 1913, in which year he became Foreign Editor.
[50] *The Zionist,* loc. cit.
[51] 14 May 1915.
[52] *C.F.C.,* 1917/328ff. (25 April 1917).

at the moment of the abdication of the Emperor.'[53] Early in May an article in Kerensky's organ stigmatising the *Times* correspondent as an anti-semite had embarrassed the Foreign Office and had been brought by its Propaganda Branch to Geoffrey Dawson's personal attention.[54]

But the marked lack of tenderness for the Jews shown by *The Times* in its handling of events in Russia did not prevent it from coming out in favour of the Zionists. Both matters were within the province of the Foreign Editor, but any apparent inconsistency is not difficult to explain when Wickham Steed's approach to the Jewish question is understood. It is worth analysis as illustrating the civilised type of anti-semitism—to be distinguished from paranoiac judæophobia—characteristic of some Gentile pro-Zionists.

In his ideas and feelings about Jews Steed had been greatly influenced by his experiences as *Times* correspondent in Vienna from 1902 to 1913. Like another close student of Austro-Hungarian affairs, Seton-Watson, who favoured Zionism for much the same reasons,[55] Steed had been struck by the strength of Jewish influence in the press and in high finance and had been offended by what seemed to him the unseemly zeal of the assimilated Jews in identifying themselves with one or other of the two master-races—the Germans in Austria and the Magyars in Hungary. In his *The Hapsburg Monarchy*,[56] published just before the War, Steed had used some highly unflattering language about the type of Jew he disliked. 'The Jews *quâ* Jews,' he wrote, 'are as entitled as any other people . . . in the world to full consideration of their rights and interests, but they cannot enjoy esteem so long as they attempt to out-German the Germans in Pan-Germanism or to out-Magyar the Magyars in oppression of the non-Magyar races of Hungary.'[57] From this distasteful spectacle he had turned with relief to the Zionists, whose creed was ' to be a Jew and to be proud of it, to glory in the power and pertinacity

[53] *C.F.C.*, 1917/589ff.
[54] *History of The Times*, Vol. IV, Pt. I, p. 248.
[55] See his contribution to *The War and Democracy*, by R. W. Seton-Watson and others (London, Macmillan, 1915), pp. 284ff.
[56] London, Constable, 1913. (The quotations are from the 1914 edition.)
[57] Pp. 174-175.

of the race, its traditions, its triumphs, its sufferings, its resistance to persecution. . . .'[58] Steed had known Herzl personally—they first met in 1896[59]—and had from the start been attracted by his ideas. In *The Hapsburg Monarchy* he is to be found describing the growth of Zionism as 'the most hopeful sign noticeable in Jewry for centuries,' and even going so far as to declare that 'Zionism in its territorial aspects is now an integral, if not indeed, the most significant, part of the Near Eastern Question, at least as regards the future of the Ottoman Empire.'[60]

One of Herzl's arguments in seeking support for Zionism in the early days had been that it would serve as a counterpoise to the revolutionary elements in Jewry.[61] On this point also Steed was receptive. 'When a young Russian Jew, who had been implicated in the abortive Revolution of 1905, confessed to me that the Zionist faith had transformed him from a sceptical desperado into a worker for Zionism, I understood,' he tells us, 'that Herzl's ideas might exert a regenerating influence upon the Jewish intellectuals no less than upon the masses of Jewry.'[62] Nor was it only the restless energies of the Jewish intellectuals that alarmed him. He suspected that astute Jews of quite a different type were exploiting leftist ideas for sinister ends of their own. 'Recognition of the fact that the capitalistic system tends to develop in the direction foreseen by Marx . . . has,' he declared, 'undoubtedly influenced the more wide-awake of the Jews and induced them to strive in time to control the masses through Socialist organisations in the hope of securing a potent influence upon legislation and upon the future construction of society.'[63]

It may now be easier to understand how it happened that, at the very time when, to the indignation of British Jews, the Petrograd correspondent of *The Times* was giving its readers a highly unfavourable impression of the behaviour of the Jews in Russia, the Foreign Editor was ardently backing the Zionists. What was

[58] Pp. 175-176.
[59] Steed in *Chaim Weizmann*, ed. P. Goodman, p. 69.
[60] Pp. 179, 175.
[61] Bein, *Herzl*, pp. 279, 295.
[62] Steed in *Chaim Weizmann*, ed. P. Goodman, pp. 71-72.
[63] *The Hapsburg Monarchy*, p. 156.

being alleged in quarters unfriendly to the Jews about their part in the leftward slide in Russia fitted in with his preconceived ideas, but it did not impair—on the contrary, it served only to strengthen—his Zionist sympathies. So it came to pass that by the spring of 1917 the Zionists had gained a firm supporter in *The Times*. At the end of May a leading article, written in the light of a discussion between Steed and Weizmann[64] and given the first position on the editorial page, pronounced an unequivocal verdict in favour of the Zionists in their conflict, then at the stage of open warfare, with the Conjoint Foreign Committee.[65] In the months which intervened before the Balfour Declaration, Steed was in frequent contact with Weizmann, Sokolow and Jabotinsky, and at several critical moments *The Times* threw all its weight into the scales on the Zionist side.[66]

[64] *Trial and Error*, p. 255.
[65] *The Times*, 29 May 1917.
[66] See *The Times*, 23 August, 3 and 13 September, 26 October 1917.

CHAPTER 21[*]

THE BRITISH INVASION OF PALESTINE

IF THE CHANGE of Government told strongly in favour of the Zionists, so also did the changes in the military situation which were to lead, in the end, to a firm decision by the War Cabinet in favour of a campaign on the grand scale in Palestine.

When Lloyd George became Prime Minister early in December 1916, the Egyptian Expeditionary Force under General Sir Archibald Murray had virtually completed its primary task—to clear Egypt of the Turks and to establish a reliable barrier against any further threat to the Suez Canal. It was still an open question whether, this once achieved, Murray's army should be relegated to an essentially defensive rôle or should pass to the offensive and carry the war across the Turco-Egyptian frontier. By the spring of 1917 the War Cabinet had committed itself to a forward policy designed to lead, first to the capture of Jerusalem, and then to the total expulsion of the Turks from Palestine.

That this would happen was by no means a foregone conclusion. There was no enthusiasm for the Palestine campaign on the part of the Chief of the Imperial General Staff, Sir William Robertson. Had his views prevailed, the Zionist question would have been a good deal less interesting to the British Government than it became in the light of the War Cabinet's strong desire, hardening into a fixed resolve, that the War should end with Palestine, or as much of it as possible, under British control.

[*] Apart from specific references in the footnotes, the authorities drawn upon in this Chapter, so far as it is concerned with military operations, are:
  (a) Official *History of the Great War: Military Operations in Egypt and Palestine from the outbreak of War to June 1917 ; Military operations in Egypt and Palestine from June 1917 to the end of the War.*
  (b) Colonel (later, F.-M.) A. P. Wavell, *The Palestine Campaigns* (London, Constable, 1928).
  (c) General Sir Archibald Murray, *Dispatches* (London, Dent, 1920).
  (d) Lloyd George, *War Memoirs*, Vol. IV.
  (e) Brig.-Gen. Sir James Edmonds, *A Short History of World War I* (O.U.P., 1951).

Weizmann was right when he told Brandeis, early in April 1917, that 'since the invasion of Palestine by the British Army, our problem has become much more tangible and " actual." '[1]

In his general approach to the strategy of the War Lloyd George's personal sympathies were and had long been with the Easterners. It would have been alien to his adventurous temperament to rest content with the austere doctrine, favoured by the Government's principal military advisers, that the War must be fought out in the West and that no good could come of attempts to dodge the issue by diversionary enterprises designed to break the deadlock in France and Flanders. So far as Palestine was concerned, it is clear that Lloyd George was influenced by other than purely military considerations. He writes in his *Memoirs*[2] that, when the question of going on with the Palestine campaign was discussed by the War Cabinet on 2 April 1917, ' we realised the moral and political advantages to be expected from an advance on this Front, and particularly from the occupation of Jerusalem.' He told Scott and Weizmann the next day that the campaign in Palestine was, for him, the one really interesting part of the War.[3] Some two months later, Smuts, in declining the offer of the Palestine Command, assured Lloyd George that ' the liberation of Palestine from the Turkish yoke appeals to me as strongly as it does to you on historical and human grounds.'[4]

But, although Lloyd George was personally predisposed in favour of a Palestine campaign, this question had to be considered in relation to Allied plans for a spring offensive on the Western Front, and to the limits thus imposed on the employment of British troops elsewhere. The War Cabinet wavered at first about an offensive in Palestine, and at the turn of the year Murray received a bewildering variety of instructions reflecting the Government's indecision and the restraining pressure exerted upon it by its military advisers in the interests of the forthcoming offensive in the West. Within a few days of the change of Government early in December 1916 Murray was asked to send his proposals for action beyond El Arish and directed to make the

[1] 8 April 1917: *Ch.W.P.*
[2] IV, 1829.
[3] *C.P.S. Jnls.*, 3 April 1917.
[4] Smuts to Lloyd George, 31 May 1917: quoted in Sarah Gertrude Millin's *General Smuts* (London, Faber, 1936), II, 39-40.

maximum effort possible during the winter. Almost immediately afterwards he was informed that, notwithstanding these orders, he was to consider his primary mission to be the defence of Egypt. In the end he was told, early in January 1917, that, while preparations were to be made for large-scale operations in Palestine, these would not be undertaken until the autumn.[5]

Mark Sykes, with his usual optimism, foresaw a rapid British advance and at the end of January was in a highly sanguine mood. Assuming that the British invasion of Palestine would before long have made substantial progress, he gave the Zionists a prominent place in his picture of the events which he believed to be imminent. He told Gaster on January 30th that at his first meeting with Weizmann two days earlier he had insisted, as a matter of urgency, that the Zionists 'should be prepared . . . to have men on the spot, when the English entered Jerusalem, so as to take effective part in the administration of at least the Jewish section of the population.'[6]

Two months later it looked for a moment as though Sykes had been right in counting upon an early British occupation of Jerusalem. To clear the way for the larger operations to be started later in the year, Murray decided, early in March, on an attempt to take Gaza by a *coup de main*. His assault, launched on 26 March 1917, ended in failure, but in the light of early reports was at first supposed in London to have been a success.[7] On March 30th he was instructed, 'in view of the altered situation, to make [his] object the defeat of the Turks south of Jerusalem and the occupation of Jerusalem,' and these orders were closely followed by an emphatic injunction to push forward with all possible energy.[8]

What was meant by 'the altered situation' was something more than the prospect of a rapid advance on the Palestine Front as a result of the supposed success at Gaza. In Mesopotamia the British campaign had taken a favourable turn under the leadership of General Maude, who had recaptured Kut in February and

---

[5] Murray's *Dispatches*, pp. 129-131 (Dispatch dated 28 June 1917).
[6] *Gaster Diary*, 30 January 1917. The words in quotation-marks are Gaster's version of what Sykes said to him.
[7] Wavell, p. 83 ; Edmonds, p. 372. See *The Times*, 31 March 1917, on 'a great victory in Palestine.'
[8] Murray, loc. cit.

in the middle of March had occupied Baghdad. At the same time the Turks were being pressed by the Russians in the Caucasus, and it looked for a moment as though the beginning of a pincer-movement against the Turks might be in sight when, at the beginning of April, Russian and British detachments made contact north-east of Baghdad.

Though the Russian Revolution had already taken place, the war-weariness of the Russian people had not been fully understood, and the demoralisation of the Russian armies, which were so soon to crumble, was not immediately foreseen. In some quarters it was at first naïvely believed that the disappearance of the corrupt and inefficient régime which the Revolution had brought to an end would galvanise Russia into the more vigorous prosecution of the War. If the Turkish army could be got on the run in Palestine, might not this, combined with the exploitation of the British successes in Mesopotamia and the Russian successes on the Caucasus Front, subject the Turks to irresistible pressure and force them to sue for peace?

A few days after the Battle of Gaza the military situation in Palestine was closely examined by the War Cabinet. By this time it was realised that something had gone wrong at Gaza, but the impression still prevailed that the Turks were weakening and, if resolutely attacked, would give way. The War Cabinet's considered view was that on this Front boldness was likely to be well rewarded, and that the campaign in Palestine should be vigorously prosecuted, with the occupation of Jerusalem as its objective.[9]

The War Cabinet's sanguine estimate of the prospects in Palestine had, among other consequences, the effect of bringing the Zionist question into the foreground. If all went well, it would not be long before the Turks had been swept out of Southern Palestine and a British army had entered Jerusalem. With this picture before it, the British Government had to think about its relations with the Zionists in the light of the new situation which would arise when a substantial part of Palestine was actually in British hands. If it seriously intended to identify itself with the Zionist cause, now was the time for it to begin moving in that direction. The impressive advance on the Palestine Front now

[9] Lloyd George, *Memoirs*, IV, 1828ff.

confidently foreseen would have, and was meant to have, political implications, and, in bidding for eventual control of Palestine, the British Government would, as Sykes pointed out,[10] stand to gain by a strongly expressed Jewish preference for a British rather than a French or Franco-British protectorate. Moreover, Jewish goodwill might have some value in the campaign itself. As Aaronsohn and his friends had shown, the inhabitants of the Jewish colonies scattered over the coastal plain and strung out along the line of the Jaffa-Jerusalem railway would be friends worth having for a British army advancing from the south.[11]

The War Cabinet took its decision in favour of a forward policy in Palestine on April 2nd.[12] On the 3rd, Lloyd George saw Weizmann, who came away from the interview in a highly optimistic frame of mind.[13] On the same day, Mark Sykes, then on the point of leaving London to take up his appointment as political adviser to General Murray, was told, as part of his instructions, that the door was to be left open to the development of the Zionist Movement under British auspices.[14] On the 4th, Sykes asked Weizmann to hold himself in readiness to leave for Egypt within the next ten days[15] and showed interest in his proposal that a statement of British policy in a pro-Zionist sense should be prepared for publication in Palestine at the first opportune moment.[16]

All this was clearly on the assumption that the setback at Gaza at the end of March would be quickly retrieved. Weizmann, said Sykes, when they met on April 4th, could be of great service in Palestine as soon as Gaza had been captured and the road thus

[10] *Sledm.*, No. 49 (9 April 1917).
[11] In conversation with Sykes on 4 April 1917 Weizmann pointed out that there was ' a considerable Jewish colony [at Jaffa] and other colonies all along the railway from Jaffa to Jerusalem ': quotation from Scott's note of the interview, at which he was present: *C.P.S. Jnls.* In conversation with Weizmann and Scott on 3 April 1917, Lloyd George said that the ex-members of the Zion Mule Corps then serving with a British unit in England (see below, p. 383) ought to be sent at once to Palestine, where ' they would be precious for " spying out the land " as in Joshua's day ': *C.P.S. Jnls.*
[12] See note 9.
[13] For a fuller reference to this interview see below, p. 383.
[14] *Sledm.*, No. 49 (3 April 1917).
[15] *C.P.S. Jnls.*, 4 April 1917, describing the conversation, at which he was present, mentioned in note 11.
[16] Weizmann to Sokolow, 4 April 1917: Z.A.

opened for an advance on Jerusalem.[17] But the Turkish resistance had been under-estimated. By the end of April a second attack on Gaza had miscarried and it had become clear that there was no prospect of a quick success on this Front. What made it worse was that, under the impact of the March Revolution, the Russian army in the Caucasus was now plainly disintegrating and there was no longer any question of the British and Russian forces in the Turkish theatre of war combining in a concerted effort to bring the Turks to their knees. Not only had that dream melted away, but the Turks might be in a position to turn the tables by putting pressure on the British. The Russian collapse would set free considerable numbers of Turkish troops which would now become available for strengthening the Turkish position in Palestine or— a still more serious danger—for threatening the British position in Mesopotamia. The Turks and their German advisers were fully alive to the situation, and by the end of April the German General von Falkenhayn had already been ordered to discuss with the Turkish High Command a campaign for the recovery of Baghdad.

The War Cabinet had now to make up its mind whether to cut its losses in Palestine or to double its stakes. Should it, for the time being at least, abandon the idea of pressing forward to Jerusalem or should it persist in the Palestine offensive, with the corollary that the British army in Palestine would have to be strengthened at the expense of some other Front, which would probably be Salonica? Had the first alternative been chosen the Zionist cause would have suffered a severe setback. This, at all events, was how the situation was seen by Mark Sykes. Telegraphing from Cairo on April 24th, he told the Foreign Office that, if the Egyptian Expeditionary Force, being too weak to hope for more than local successes, was not to be reinforced, then it would be necessary ' to drop all Zionist projects and all schemes involving negotiations with settled rural and urban elements in Syria. . . . [The] Zionists in London and U.S.A. should be warned of this through M. Sokolow, and the Jabotinsky scheme[18] should not be proceeded with.'[19]

[18] ' The Jabotinsky scheme '—i.e., the scheme for raising a Jewish Legion for service in Palestine—see below, p. 491.
[19] *Sledm.*, No. 42. The document in the Sledmere papers is a draft. It is here assumed that the telegram was sent as drafted.

Three weeks later, Sykes told Aaron Aaronsohn that reinforcements were coming to Palestine from Salonica and that, accordingly, Zionist propaganda could go on.[20] When he sent his despondent message to the Foreign Office on April 24th, he did not know that the day before, April 23rd, the War Cabinet had reviewed the situation in the light of the second reverse at Gaza and had decided that what was needed in Palestine was not a change of policy but more resolute leadership in the field.[21]

From a purely military point of view, a strong argument for that decision was that, by compelling the Turks to keep their eyes on the Palestine Front, vigorous preparations for a renewed British offensive would help to counter the Turco-German threat to the British position in Mesopotamia. On no account could the Turks afford to let Palestine look after itself, since a British breakthrough might end, if unchecked, in disrupting the communications of the Turco-German army destined for the recovery of Baghdad. Thus, fortunately for the Zionists, the same events—the Russian Revolution and its sequel, the crumbling of the Russian armies—which had shattered any hope of an early and spectacular British victory in Palestine told heavily in favour of the view that the British effort in that theatre of war, far from being abandoned or suspended, should be intensified.

Apart from purely strategical considerations, the War Cabinet had other reasons for persisting in an aggressive policy in Palestine. In reviewing the situation at the beginning of April, it had been impressed by the ' moral and political advantages '[22] to be expected from a successful campaign on that Front. Four weeks later those advantages stood out still more clearly in the light of what had happened since.

In the interval, the Allied spring offensive in the West had faded out with the disastrous collapse of General Nivelle's operations in Champagne almost at the moment of the second British failure at Gaza. Depressed by repeated disappointments, the British public badly needed the tonic of an impressive military success. There could be none more certain to fire its imagination and strengthen its morale than the entry of a British army into Jerusalem. This gave added weight to the military argument for

[20] *A.A. Diaries*, 15 May 1917.
[21] Lloyd George, *Memoirs*, IV, 1830.
[22] See above, note 2.

persisting in the Palestine campaign, but there was another and still more cogent consideration. If, as a result of her own exertions, Great Britain emerged from the War in actual occupation of Palestine, she would be in a strong position for insisting that, so far as the Brown Area was concerned, the Sykes-Picot Agreement should be set aside in favour of an arrangement more satisfactory to herself. That advantage was not lightly to be foregone.

This was a matter on which the Prime Minister held decided views. In his Journals for 1917 Scott records a breakfast with Lloyd George on March 16th. Lloyd George, he says, remarked that ' as to the future of Palestine, once we were in military possession, it would make a great difference. The French had an eye to it. . . . I [Scott] protested—he agreed that it was not to be thought of.' On April 3rd Lloyd George impressed upon Mark Sykes, just before his departure on his mission to the East, the importance of securing the addition of Palestine to the British area.[23] In conversation, earlier that day, with Weizmann and Scott, Lloyd George told them that ' he was altogether opposed to a condominium with France.' They heard the same from Sykes when they saw him the next day, April 4th. The Prime Minister, Sykes told them, was adamant against yielding anything to the French even in the matter of the Holy Places: ' George was against any concession and thought we could take care of the Holy Places better than anybody else.'[24]

It seems a safe guess that these ideas had their part in the Cabinet's decision on April 23rd not to be deterred by what had happened for the second time at Gaza from going forward in Palestine at the price of the still greater and more costly effort which this must be expected to entail. From that decision Lloyd George was not to be deflected even after Smuts, writing at the end of May in explanation of his unwillingness to accept the Palestine Command, had expressed his ' strong conviction that our present military situation on all Fronts does not really justify an offensive campaign for the capture of Jerusalem and the occupation of Palestine.'[25]

[23] *Sledm.*, No. 41.
[24] Both quotations are from Scott's *Journals*.
[25] The quotation is from Smuts' letter (dated 31 May 1917) as set out in Sarah Gertrude Millin's *General Smuts*, II, 39-40. An extract, but without the passage quoted in the text, is to be found in Lloyd George's *Memoirs*, IV, 1833.

As Lloyd George conceived the Palestine campaign, its object was not merely to inflict a military defeat on the Turks but to bring Palestine permanently under British control. If all went well, the War would end with Great Britain in possession, and Palestine, liberated from the Turks by her exertions, would, on a realistic view, be at her disposal.[26] But there were obstacles which, though doubtless not insurmountable, could be embarrassing. There was still the spectre of the Sykes-Picot Agreement and the encumbrance of engagements to the French which would certainly be invoked and could not peremptorily be repudiated. At his interview with Weizmann and Scott on April 4th Sykes told them, Scott notes in his Journal, that 'the French needed much careful handling.' Discussing the Palestine question with Scott on April 20th, Milner spoke wearily of 'the French assertiveness in regard to [Palestine]' and 'seemed to think that it would have to be internationalised.'[27] Their anxiety aroused by the prospect of a British occupation of Jerusalem, and their appetite, perhaps, already whetted by signs that Russia was weakening, the French were clearly going to be difficult. They might, in the end, be compelled to recognise a British title to Palestine by right of conquest and actual possession, but might not some moral weight be added to the British claim—was it not even possible that the French themselves might be impressed —if it could be shown that Jewish opinion throughout the world strongly favoured a British trusteeship for Palestine or some other form of British control?

Weizmann and his colleagues did not need to be convinced that British rule in Palestine was infinitely to be preferred to that of any other Power or to any type of condominium. For this, so far as their influence extended, they could be relied upon to work, once satisfied that they would not be working in vain. The incentive they needed was the twofold assurance that Great Britain was, in fact, seriously interested in bringing Palestine into the British orbit, and that she was also interested in the building up in Palestine, under her protection, of a home for the

[26] Speaking of Palestine, 'Lloyd George . . . said that the French will have to accept our protectorate; we shall be there by conquest and shall remain. . . .': *Diaries of Lord Bertie,* II, 122 (20 April 1917).
[27] *C.P.S. Jnls.,* 20 April 1917.

Jewish people. At an interview with Weizmann at the Foreign Office on 25 April 1917 Lord Robert Cecil, without giving him any precise undertaking as to British policy in Palestine, hinted plainly that the British Government would welcome a clear manifestation by world Jewry of its desire that Great Britain should be the protecting Power. With this went an implied assurance that the Zionists could count upon British goodwill.[28]

Encouraged by similar hints from other quarters, Weizmann and his associates had, earlier in April, already been representing to Brandeis that the time had come for the Zionists to anchor themselves firmly to Great Britain and to make it plain that they had done so. Almost immediately after Weizmann's interview with Cecil on April 25th suggestions to the same effect began to be pressed upon Tschlenow in Moscow. These moves were made with the Government's knowledge and approval, as is shown by the facilities given to the Zionist leaders in London for communicating with their American and Russian colleagues through the machinery of Government Departments.[29]

We shall see later, in greater detail, how energetic were their efforts, inspired and guided by Weizmann, to elicit from the American and Russian Jews, and through them, as was hoped, from their Governments, a clear expression of sympathy with the idea of a Jewish Commonwealth in Palestine under British protection. We shall see also what pains were taken to impress upon the sceptics in Russia and elsewhere that Great Britain's readiness to encourage Zionist aspirations showed that her intentions in Palestine were free from any annexationist taint.[30] What is here to be noted is that the turning-point for the Zionists was the spring of 1917, when the combined effect of the British invasion of Palestine and the March Revolution in Russia was beginning to be reflected in sharpened competition between Great Britain and France for eventual predominance in Palestine. It is at this point that the British Government can be perceived moving forward from a friendly interest in Zionism and semi-official encouragement to something not yet amounting to a commitment but not far removed from it.

[28] This is based on Weizmann's note of the interview in *Ch.W.P.* For a further reference to this conversation see below, pp. 391-392.
[29] See below, p. 377.
[30] See Chapters 28 and 29.

Neither at this nor, indeed, at any later stage was there a bargain in the sense in which that word suggests an arm's-length negotiation on a *do ut des* basis. Weizmann and his friends had from the start pinned their faith on Great Britain. Leading members of the Lloyd George Administration had long ago recognised that the Zionists deserved to be taken seriously and that their aims were worthy of sympathy and respect. It was not a case of concessions by one side as the price of equivalent concessions by the other. Both parties were moving in the direction in which it had all along been their inclination to move. What had happened was that events were now shaping in such a way as to provide a realistic basis for a closer understanding between the British Government and the Zionists—an understanding seen to correspond to the desires and interests of both.

It would have been disastrous for the Zionists if, in April 1917, the War Cabinet, weighing the lessons of the failure at Gaza, had shrunk from a further effort in Palestine instead of deciding, as it did, that a fresh start should be made on a larger scale and under different and more determined leadership. But this would call for much planning and preparation, and in the meantime there must be a pause in the campaign. After the War Cabinet's choice for the command in Palestine had fallen, in default of Smuts, on Allenby, he spent several months in laying the foundations of a renewed offensive and struck his first blow with the capture of Beersheba on October 31st—the day, as it happened, on which the War Cabinet finally approved the Balfour Declaration. Though in April Weizmann and his colleagues were being encouraged to popularise the idea of British sponsorship of Zionist aspirations, it was not until the late summer that the War Cabinet began to discuss the advisability of a public pronouncement in favour of a Jewish national home in Palestine. It was the Zionists' good fortune that, while the Palestine campaign was hanging fire, events in Russia were providing the British Government with a fresh and compelling incentive for interesting itself in Zionism.

Montefiore's interview with Milner on 16 May 1917[31] was far from dispelling his anxieties about the Government's intentions,

[31] *C.F.C.*, 1917/464ff. This is the interview already mentioned at p. 317.

but in one respect he found it reassuring. Milner, he reported to his colleagues,

> ' said that there had been many conversations about Palestine, but nothing more.
>
> ' Before the Russian Revolution it looked very likely that the Turks would soon be driven out of Jerusalem and Palestine, but now such an event was much less likely and was probably considerably distant.
>
> ' The Palestine question was, therefore, much less immediate and urgent than it seemed to be a couple of months ago.'

Montefiore concludes :

> ' The delay in the Palestinian campaign has clearly made the question much less immediately interesting to the Government, except in so far as it may affect Russian-Jewish opinion in Russia. It has obviously been represented to H.M. Government that the Russian Jews are all enthusiastic Zionists. I said that I did not believe that this was by any means the case.'

Only three weeks before, Robert Cecil had told Weizmann, with express reference to the question of bringing Palestine within the British sphere, that it would be helpful if the Jews were to express themselves in favour of a British trusteeship.[32] It can certainly not be the case that by the middle of May the British Government had begun to lose interest in Zionism except in so far as it could be turned to propagandist uses in Russia. All the same, Montefiore was right up to a point. In considering the impact of the Russian Revolution as it affected the Jews, we shall see how important a part of the background to the Balfour Declaration was the belief, based upon an exaggerated estimate of Jewish power and influence, that by rallying Russian Jewry in support of the Allied cause an appeal to Zionist sentiment might somehow help to check the drift to the Left and to keep Russia in the War.

[32] Above, p. 336.

CHAPTER 22

THE RUSSIAN REVOLUTION

WITHIN A MONTH of the March Revolution the Russian Jews had been relieved of their disabilities. One of the first acts of the Provisional Government was to issue a decree which, without expressly mentioning the Jews, annulled all restrictions imposed on any class of Russian citizens on account of their religion or nationality.[1] For the Russian Zionists, who under the old régime had had to walk warily, the Revolution meant that they could now come fearlessly into the open. Emancipation might have been expected to blunt the edge of Zionist propaganda in Russia, but this did not happen ; the number of enrolled Zionists, which had before the War been about 36,000, rose almost immediately after the Revolution to some 140,000,[2] and that out of a Jewish population reduced by at least one-third as a result of large slices of Russian territory, thickly inhabited by Jews, having passed under German or Austrian control.

On the other hand, anti-Zionists could and did contend that the new turn of events in Russia had knocked the bottom out of the Zionist case in so far as it had rested on the intolerable conditions of Jewish life in Eastern Europe.[3] Though the Zionist philosophy went deeper, it was true that, in seeking the sympathy of the outside world, the Zionists had, as was natural, buttressed their appeal by dwelling upon the miseries of the Jews cooped up in the Pale of Settlement. Given the opportunity, many of them, the argument had run, would be able to rebuild their lives in Palestine without forcing upon the United States and Great Britain a dis-

---

[1] 3 April 1917. Text, in English translation, in *Zionist Review*, August 1917. p. 51.

[2] Sokolow, II, 28. Sokolow gives the pre-war figure as 26,000, but this may be a slip for 36,000. According to the official figures submitted to the 1913 Zionist Congress, the number of ' shekel-payers ' in Russia was just under 36,000.

[3] This was one of the points made by Claude Montefiore in his reply to the War Cabinet's request for his views in October 1917 (see below, p. 525): 'A national home for the Jews on the score of the oppressed condition of the Jews is no longer necessary. . . .'

tasteful choice between turning back fugitives from persecution and admitting an influx of unwelcome immigrants.[4] All this, it could plausibly be represented, had now become unreal. The Russian Jews had been relieved of the disabilities which had made them rootless. Why, it could be asked, should they not settle down to enjoy the fruits of liberty in their native country? Never doubting that the new régime in Russia, with its liberal attitude towards the Jews, would endure, the assimilationists could declare that their optimistic predictions were coming true.

In another respect the Russian Revolution was not pure gain for the Zionists. They had cause for anxiety in the growing pressure on the part of the revolutionary forces in Russia, with some backing in the United States, for a peace without annexations. So far as Turkey was concerned, it could be made to appear that, once Russia had renounced her claim to Constantinople and the Straits, the Imperialist designs of the Western Allies were the only serious obstacle to a negotiated peace. A peace with Turkey on the basis of no annexations would blight the hopes of the Zionists, and even if the future of Syria and Palestine were left to be settled on the principle of self-determination, the outlook for Zionism would be no better. From a Zionist point of view, it was fortunate that the British Government had good reasons of its own for discouraging a soft peace with Turkey and a common interest with the Zionists in heading off any move in that direction.[5]

For yet another reason the Russian Revolution was of some disadvantage to the Zionists. The collapse of the Czarist régime had made Russia respectable in Jewish eyes and, so far as the Jews were concerned, had deprived pro-German propagandists of their trump card—the partnership between the Western Allies and the Russian anti-semites. The idea of counter-propaganda by way of an appeal to Zionist sentiment among the Jews was, there-

---

[4] There is an echo of this line of argument in the British Palestine Committee's *Memorandum of Policy*, circulated towards the end of 1916, para. 6 (b). As to this Memorandum, see above, p. 301. In Herzl's letter of 12 November 1902 to Lord Lansdowne concerning the Sinai project (see above, p. 24) a point is made of the emergence, both in England and in America, of 'an expression of public opinion distinctly averse to further immigration of Jews from Eastern Europe': Text in Dr. O. K. Rabinowicz's *Herzl and England* (New York, 1951), p. 29

[5] See below, p. 356.

fore, no longer as interesting as it had been before the pro-German elements in Jewry had been in large measure disarmed by the fall of the Czarist despotism.

But all this was of little significance in comparison with what the Zionists gained directly or indirectly by the change of régime in Russia and the events which flowed from it. First, it is, to say the least, very doubtful whether the Czarist Government could ever have been persuaded to countenance such an undertaking to the Zionists as was contained in the Balfour Declaration, and as good as certain that, had it remained in power, no such move would have been made against its wishes. Secondly, the fading out of Russia as an active partner in the War told in favour of the Zionists by opening the way to a direct conflict between British and French ambitions in Palestine. Lastly, the March Revolution enhanced their importance by leading to a situation in which it looked as though in Russia itself they might be able to render important services to the Allied cause by helping to stem the tide of pacifist propaganda.

On the question of the Czarist Government's attitude to Zionism the evidence is not all one way. The Zionists themselves seem to have been under the impression that it was not unfriendly. Early in 1915 Weizmann told Scott that he had heard from Russia that a memorandum stating the Zionist case had been submitted to Sazonov and had been well received.[6] According to Tschlenow,[7] the Director of the Near East Section of the Russian Foreign Office said, at an interview in 1915, that, having taken Sazonov's instructions, he could state that, except for the Holy Places, Russia was not interested in Palestine ; he had even, Tschlenow told his colleagues, gone so far as to say that, though she would not take the initiative in the matter, Russia would welcome any action in the interests of Zionism by other Allied Governments. At his meeting in London with some of the Zionist leaders in February 1917[8] Sykes spoke reassuringly about the Russian approach to the

---

[6] Weizmann to Scott, 16 February 1915: *Ch.W.P.*

[7] What follows was reported by Tschlenow at a meeting of the Zionist Executive in Copenhagen in July 1917: Z.A.

[8] See below, p. 370.

Palestine question: ' Sir Mark had gathered the impression that Russia wants to keep out of Palestine and that her interests there are only religious. She wants a definite say in the Holy Places and in the Jordan pilgrimage and, in general, guarantees for the Russian pilgrim-traffic.'[9]

This would not necessarily involve more than some special provision for the custody of the Holy Places and the setting aside of a reserved area comprising Jerusalem and its environs, with a corridor to the sea at Jaffa; indeed, Sykes seems to have thought that some arrangement on these lines might be expected to satisfy the Russians.[10] But they would almost certainly have been satisfied with nothing less, and even this would have meant the cutting off from the rest of the Yishuv not only of the large Jewish populations of Jerusalem and Jaffa but of a number of well-established Jewish settlements in the coastal plain. Nor would it be at all a safe assumption that, subject to this, Russia would have been content to let the Zionists have their way. The Czarist Government was, indeed, primarily concerned with safeguarding the interests of the Orthodox Church, but it is at least highly questionable whether its conception of Orthodox interests would have been found, when it came to the point, to be compatible with the establishment in Palestine of a national home for the Jews.

On the Zionist question, as on the Palestine question generally, the enigmatic behaviour of the Czarist Government makes it rash to dogmatise as to its real views and intentions. In the event, these were never to be tested, but it is difficult to believe that Czarist Russia could have swallowed any far-reaching commitment to the Zionists. However ready it may have been to tolerate, or even to favour, the settlement of Russian Jews in Palestine, it seems unlikely that it would ever have agreed to the Zionists being encouraged in their larger aspirations.

The changed situation in Russia not only made it easier than it might otherwise have been for the British Government to identify itself with the Zionists but helped indirectly to give it fresh incentives for doing so.

[9] The quotation is from the record of the Conference of 7 February 1917 (copies in *Ch.W.P.* and *Z.A.* and also in *H.S.P.*).
[10] Ibid.

So long as the Czarist Government was in power and Russia was an effective—albeit unreliable—member of the *Entente,* there could be no settlement of the Palestine question without her concurrence. This was clearly implied in the Sykes-Picot Agreement, which, in dealing with the Brown Area, provided that the form of the international administration should be decided 'after consultation with Russia.' Only after Great Britain, France and Russia had worked out an agreed plan was there to be discussion with other allies.[11] Russia had an acknowledged interest in Palestine and was in a position to insist upon its being safeguarded to her satisfaction. Exactly what this would involve was uncertain. The cat-and-mouse game played by the Russians with the French in 1915 and again in 1916 has already been described. The Czarist Government never clearly showed its hand in the matter of Palestine, but, whatever scheme it might agree to, one thing was certain ; it would not assent to any arrangement which would, in effect, hand over Palestine to the exclusive control of the French. Having good reasons of her own for not wanting to see France in control of Palestine, Great Britain had on this point a common interest with the Russians and could rely upon Russian resistance to the French in their more ambitious claims.

With the Russian Revolution, the picture changed. If, under the new régime, Russia were to weaken on the Palestine question or lose interest in it, or if she were to fade out of the War and cease to count, a barrier to the French claims would have fallen and Great Britain would have to find means of withstanding them without the help of a Russian veto. On the other hand, the disappearance of the Russian barrier to French aspirations for predominance in Palestine could also mean, for Great Britain, the removal of an obstacle to her own plans for turning the invasion of Palestine to account.

At the time of the Sykes-Picot Agreement the case for an international régime, which France had reluctantly accepted, would have been a good deal less cogent than it was had there been no need to reckon with Russia. If Russia were now to fall out, it

[11] ' In the Brown Area there shall be established an international administration, the form of which is to be decided upon after consultation with Russia, and subsequently in consultation with the other Allies, and the representatives of the Shereef of Mecca '—S.-P. Agreement, para. 3 : *B.F.P.,* p. 241.

could be argued that Palestine went naturally with Syria and, on the religious plane, that Great Britain, in contrast to France, had no traditional concern with the protection of Christian interests in Palestine and the custody of the Holy Places. To all this, however, a British military conquest and occupation of Palestine would, on a realistic view, be an effective answer, and, if Russia were out of the way, the weakening of the case for an international régime might, from a British point of view, be a positive gain. Discussing the prospects in Palestine with Weizmann and Scott early in April 1917, Sykes said that 'he thought that the new Government in Russia would be a good deal easier to deal with than the old,'[12] meaning, as would appear from the context, that a British claim to Palestine was less likely than it would otherwise have been to run up against Russian opposition. The Russian Revolution was of indirect advantage to the Zionists in so far as it tended to narrow down the Palestine question to a direct issue between Great Britain and France. Neither in resisting French pretensions nor in acquiring control of Palestine for herself were the Zionists indispensable to Great Britain, but their strong desire to see her installed as the protecting Power could be a useful makeweight both as an obstacle to a French claim and as a fortification of her own.

For another reason the Russian Revolution told indirectly in favour of the Zionists. In the spring of 1917 the British Government, and, it would seem, Milner in particular, began to be attracted by the idea that, in the steadily deteriorating situation in Russia, the Allied cause might benefit by an appeal to Zionist sentiment among the Russian Jews. At the end of April the British Ambassador in Petrograd, Sir George Buchanan, was asked for his views on the subject.[13] Sykes' comment was that this was the wrong approach. Telegraphing from Cairo on 27 April 1917,[14] he impressed upon the Foreign Office that enquiries as to the feelings of the Russian Jews could safely be made only through prominent Zionists 'such as Sokolow, Weizmann or Jabotinsky.'

[12] *C.P.S. Jnls.*, 4 April 1917.
[13] Memorandum by W. J. Childs, of the Foreign Office: *Dugdale Papers*.
[14] *Sledm.*, No. 42.

'It is also,' he added, 'to be noted that the result of satisfying
the Zionists would not be direct action and open propaganda on
the side of the *Entente* in Russia or elsewhere, but powerful, if
impalpable, benevolence, deflecting hostile forces, calming excitement and transmuting the various pacifist tendencies of thought
into friendly political elements. . . .'

The Ambassador seems to have advised against any appeal to
the Zionists, but his discouraging report did not close the matter.
Prince Lwow's first Foreign Minister, Miliukoff, had pledged
Russia to the vigorous prosecution of the War in concert with her
allies, but by the middle of May the left-wing agitation against
him was coming to a head and the situation in Russia was, from a
British point of view, taking a sharp turn for the worse. When
Montefiore saw Milner on May 16th, he came away, as we have
seen,[15] with the impression that the Zionist question had become
'less immediately interesting to the Government except in so far
as it may affect Jewish opinion in Russia.' 'It has,' he told his
colleagues, 'obviously been represented to H.M. Government that
the Russian Jews are all enthusiastic Zionists.' A few days later,
Lucien Wolf reported to the Conjoint Foreign Committee a
conversation he had had with a member of the Political Intelligence Department of the Foreign Office, R. A. Leeper. Speaking
of the situation in Russia, 'he [Leeper] said: "Suppose the
British Government were to authorise an official statement
expressing their readiness to establish a Jewish State in Palestine,
do you think this would make the Jews more friendly to
England?"' Wolf had replied that he thought not, giving as his
main reason that any such declaration would be resented by the
Jewish Socialists [in Russia], who, he told Leeper, had at the
moment much more political influence than the Zionists.[16]

Soon afterwards Milner received from Ormsby-Gore a note

---

[15] Above, p. 338.

[16] *C.F.C.*, 1917/615 (21 May 1917). In his telegram of 27 April 1917 (see
above, note 14) Sykes warned the F.O. that, in the matter of an appeal
on Zionist lines to the Russian Jews, 'H.M.G. should beware of the
activities of Mr. Lucien Wolf and those who think with him or are
inspired by him. He is an anti-Zionist who desires to focus Jewish power
at some point outside Palestine ; though he has on more than one occasion masqueraded as a Zionist, he has done this in order to thwart
Zionist aims.'

of an interview with a Russian Jew of some standing,[17] who had told him that 'with the poorer Jews [in Russia] Palestine is the one vital factor. He thought Palestine the best weapon to use against the " no annexation " cry both among Christians and Jews in Russia.' According to Ormsby-Gore's informant, ' the Jews were immensely influential in Russia owing to the fact that practically all could read and write, which the Russian workman and peasant cannot do.' Milner was impressed by the report, on which he noted: ' The source of the information is good.' An echo of what was in the Government's mind can be detected in a lengthy passage devoted by Weizmann to the Russian situation in addressing a Zionist Conference in London on May 20th. ' The fate of Jewry,' he said, ' the fate of the Zionist Movement, largely depends on stable conditions in that part of the world, and it will be, I am sure, an honourable task for the Zionist Organisation, and especially for our friends in Russia, to contribute as much as is in their power to the stabilisation of conditions in Russia.'[18]

Though some of the leading Bolsheviks were Jews or of Jewish birth, they had no ties with the Jewish masses and did not speak for them.[19] The Bolsheviks, from Lenin downwards, had been violently hostile to Zionism, and Jews with Zionist sympathies were, therefore, their natural enemies. Even the Bundists, the Jewish Socialist Party, were in the Menshevik camp and were to be found, when the crisis came in November 1917, in open opposition to Lenin's seizure of power.[20] The Bund, however, was and had always been anti-Zionist, and when, soon after the March Revolution, preparations began to be made for the organisation of an All-Russian Jewish Congress, the Bundists stoutly resisted the Zionist proposal that Palestine should be given a prominent place on the agenda.[21] Outside both the Zionist and the Bundist groups were assimilationists of the type of Baron Gunzburg, who took the view that, after the Revolution, ' we have become simply

[17] N. Alchevsky. Ormsby-Gore's note is dated 29 May 1917.
[18] Sokolow, II, 55: *Zionist Review*, June 1917, p. 35.
[19] See S. M. Schwarz, *The Jews in Soviet Russia* (Syracuse University Press, 1951), p. 93.
[20] L. Shapiro, *The Origins of the Russian Revolution* (London, 1955), p. 67.
[21] For a fuller account of the episode see below, p. 431.

Russians who go to Synagogue.'[22] The Bundists gradually lost
ground, and when delegates to the Russo-Jewish Congress were
at length elected early in 1918, the Bund obtained only nine per
cent. of the mandates.[23] The Zionists, with fifty-seven per cent.,
were much the largest group,[24] but the figures suggest that, even
after the Balfour Declaration had become known in Russia, the
Russian Jews were about equally divided between supporters of
Zionism and opponents or neutrals.

But in the spring of 1917 the British Government was not much
interested in the internal strains in Russian Jewry.[25] It was satisfied that Zionism was a potent force in Jewish life, and, over-
estimating the influence which the Jews were capable of exerting
in Russian affairs, it thought that the Allied cause might benefit
if an Allied victory were associated in their minds with the
fulfilment of Zionist aspirations. As the outlook in Russia grew
darker, it clung to the hope that, given a strong enough incentive,
the Russian Jews would throw their full weight against the left-
wing extremists and so help to keep Russia in the war, or at least
to restrain her from drifting into a separate peace or, should even
that become unavoidable, to obstruct the exploitation of Russian
resources by the Central Powers. When, in October 1917, the
Balfour Declaration was hanging in the balance, one of the points
most strongly emphasised by the Foreign Office in pressing for
an immediate British assurance to the Zionists was that the Jews
were playing an important rôle in Russia and that it could safely
be assumed that almost every Jew in Russia was a Zionist.[26]

A paper circulated to the British Delegation at the Paris Peace
Conference, but originally prepared early in 1918, discussed,
among other matters, the effect of the Balfour Declaration on the
state of feeling among the Russian Jews. The author, who, as a

[22] Gunzburg to Leopold de Rothschild, 12 May 1917: copy in *C.F.C.*, 1917/601.
[23] *J.C.*, 22 March 1918.
[24] Ibid. The Bolshevik Government refused to allow the Congress to meet.
[25] After an interview with Milner on 15 March 1917, just after Milner's return from his mission to Petrograd, Montefiore reported to the Conjoint Foreign Committee: 'I gathered that he had not been instructed to look into the Jewish question on his visit to Petrograd, and that he had not discussed it with anybody while he was there': *C.F.C.*, 1917/300.
[26] See below, p. 544.

member of the Intelligence Directorate at the War Office, had been personally concerned with the Zionist question,[27] went so far as to suggest that 'it is even possible that, had the Declaration come sooner, the course of the [Russian] Revolution might have been affected.' It is difficult to believe that he was right, but his comment provides a measure of the importance attached to Zionism as a weapon of political warfare in the period between the March Revolution in Russia and the November *coup d'état*.

Behind the short-term view of the propagandist value of Zionism in Russia lay the broader conception of a struggle between healthy and unhealthy elements in Jewish life—a point stressed by Weizmann in addressing the 12th Zionist Congress in 1921. 'Britain,' he said, 'with her political farsightedness, understood sooner and better than any other nation . . . that the Jewish question, which hangs like a shadow over the world, may become a gigantic force of construction or a mighty instrument of destruction.'[28]

The seizure of power by the Bolsheviks meant that the Russian Jews were to be sealed off from the rest of the Jewish world and the Russian Zionists made impotent to take their part—it would, in other circumstances, have been a leading part—in the building up of the Jewish national home. The effect of the November *coup d'état* was, therefore, to weaken the Movement internally, but, as against this, the Bolshevik threat to the established order of society, and exaggerated ideas as to the extent to which Jewish brains were behind it, served to strengthen the position of the Zionists in presenting their case to the Western world. When, at the Peace Conference, Weizmann appeared before the Council of Ten in February 1919, one of his main contentions was that 'the solution proposed by the Zionist Organisation was the only one which would in the long run . . . transform Jewish energy into a constructive force instead of its being dissipated in destructive tendencies.'[29] A few weeks later, Felix Frankfurter

---

[27] See Sir Charles Webster: Chaim Weizmann Memorial Lecture, *The Founder of the National Home* (Rehovoth, ? 1955), pp. 13-14.

[28] *Report of the Twelfth Zionist Congress* (London, 1922), p. 67.

[29] *For.Rns.U.S.: The Paris Peace Conference* (Washington, 1943), IV, 164 ; 27 February 1919.

struck the same note in appealing to President Wilson, at a time when the Americans were groping for a Middle Eastern policy, not to leave out of mind ' the conditions that now confront Jewry, above all Eastern Jewry.' ' As a passionate American,' Frankfurter wrote,[30] ' I am, of course, most eager that the Jew should be a reconstructive and not a disruptive force in the new world order.' In June 1919, on an occasion already mentioned, Brandeis put much the same point to Balfour, whose comment was: ' Of course, these are the considerations which make you and me such ardent Zionists.'[31] The ideas prevalent about this time are well brought out in a newspaper article written early in 1920 by Winston Churchill. After describing the Jews as ' beyond all question the most formidable and the most remarkable race which has ever appeared in the world,' he goes on to speak of ' the part played in the creation of Bolshevism . . . by . . . international and for the most part atheistical Jews,' and of Zionism as the Jewish answer to international Communism. ' The struggle which is now beginning between the Zionist and Bolshevik Jews is little less than a struggle for the soul of the Jewish people.'[3]

[30] 8 May 1919: *B.F.P., First Series*, Vol. IV, No. 180, Encl. No. 1, pp. 260-261.
[31] 24 June 1919: *B.F.P., First Series*, Vol. IV, p. 1276–see above, p. 161.
[32] *Illustrated Sunday Herald*, 8 February 1920.

CHAPTER 23

THE ENTRY OF THE UNITED STATES INTO
THE WAR

To COMPLETE THE background to the Balfour Declaration, it remains to consider how the course of events was affected by the entry of the United States into the War.

The American declaration of war on Germany in April 1917 made it certain that the United States Government, and the public opinion to which it was sensitive, would be in a position to play an influential and, it might well be, a decisive part in the shaping of the post-war settlement. The United States was, and was to remain to the end, outside the war with Turkey, but it was not to be expected that it would stand aside while the Powers more directly concerned agreed, or failed to agree, between themselves as to the future of the Turkish Empire. If the United States could be induced to favour Great Britain as the protecting Power in Palestine, or, as a possible alternative, to agree to an Anglo-American trusteeship, in either case the French claim would be blocked and what had now become one of Great Britain's principal war aims in the East would be within her grasp.

But this pre-supposed that British ideas about the future of Palestine could be reconciled with the American approach to the whole question of war aims, coloured as it was by the belief that, by keeping clear of any arrangements between the Allies, ' we [the Americans] could exert an influence against greed and the improper distribution of territory.' This was how President Wilson's most intimate confidential adviser, Colonel House, put it to Balfour at one of their first meetings after the arrival of the British Mission in Washington towards the end of April 1917.[1] House had been asked by Wilson ' to discuss with the [British] Foreign Secretary the general problems of war aims and ask him about the secret treaties.' House records in his diary (28 April

[1] *The Intimate Papers of Colonel House*, ed. Charles Seymour (London, Ernest Benn, 1928), III, 47.

1917)[2] that Balfour explained to him that by these treaties Russia was awarded a sphere of influence in ' Armenia and the northern part' and France and Italy in ' the balance of Anatolia up to the Straits,' while ' the British take in Mesopotamia [and the region] which is contiguous to Egypt,' on which House comments: ' It is all bad and I told Balfour so.' Wilson felt as strongly as House that these arrangements were ' all bad,' and he and his advisers made up their minds that, in dealing with the Eastern Question, the United States must insist on the secret treaties being set aside.

If the Americans were going to throw their weight into the scales against the partition of Turkey, it was all the more to be desired that Palestine, at least, should be shown to be a case apart. Nor was it only a question of the final peace settlement. Russia having renounced her territorial claims on Turkey, the United States might be attracted by the idea that, under American pressure, Great Britain and France could be made to follow suit and thus pave the way for an attempt to detach the Turks from their German allies by an offer of a soft peace. In the end, the Americans came to the conclusion that the idea of a negotiated peace with Turkey was a chimera,[3] but in the summer of 1917 it looked at times as though the United States might be veering in that direction.

In August, Kerensky's Foreign Minister, Terestschenko, instructed the Russian Ambassador in Washington to sound the United States Government as to its views on the future of Turkey. The Russian view, Terestschenko told the Ambassador, was that there was no longer any sense or meaning in the secret treaties concerning the partition of the Turkish Empire. He had reason to think that the American Government was of the same opinion, and he wished the Ambassador to ascertain whether there was any possibility of joint action by the United States and Russia with a view to bringing the war with Turkey to an end.[4] To this

---

[2] Ibid., III, 44. The words ' and the region ' are an insertion by the Editor.

[3] *For.Rns.U.S.*, 1917, Suppl. 2, I, 326: Lansing to Page, 30 November 1917. Lansing goes on to say that a separate peace with Turkey would, in any case, be of questionable advantage. ' It appears . . . to this Government that the only advantage to be gained by a separate peace with Turkey now would be to prevent the bargains of the Allies with regard to Asia Minor from being carried out at the end of the War.'

[4] Adamov, No. 325: Terestschenko to Bachmetyew, 18 August 1917.

the Ambassador replied[5] that, because of the rather strained relations which had recently developed between the two Governments, the matter needed cautious handling. He had, therefore, made no formal *démarche*, but he had broached the subject unofficially with President Wilson's son-in-law, McAdoo,[6] who—he said—was well-informed on what was going on in the inner circle. From him he had learned that there was influential support for the view that the United States, being now in a position to put effective pressure on the Allies, should insist on their facilitating the exit of Turkey from the War by renouncing all territorial claims at her expense.

What had looked like a tentative move by the United States in the direction of a peace offer to Turkey had already been checked by the British, with the help of a skilful diplomatic performance by Weizmann.

In the middle of May, Henry Morgenthau, the former United States Ambassador in Constantinople, told the Secretary of State, Robert Lansing, that he believed that the time was ripe for secret overtures to Turkey. He thought that he could be helpful and offered to arrange a meeting in Switzerland between himself and certain Turkish acquaintances of his who would be suitable intermediaries.[7] After two interviews with Wilson,[8] Morgenthau sailed on June 21st for Cadiz. Soon after he had left, Lansing instructed the United States Ambassador in London, Walter Page, to enquire whether the British Government could arrange for Weizmann to meet Morgenthau at Gibraltar. Page was told that he should 'leave nothing undone to secure Mr. Balfour's consent, as it is considered most important that Mr. Morgenthau see Mr. Weizmann.'[9]

Why was this considered important ? The answer is not quite clear, but it looks as though Morgenthau may have wanted a meeting with Weizmann because he believed that the Zionists

---

[5] Ibid., No. 326 (31 August 1917).

[6] McAdoo was Secretary of the Treasury.

[7] *For.Rns.U.S.*, 'Lansing Papers,' II, 17-19. Lansing to Wilson, 17 May 1917, reporting interview with Morgenthau on the previous day.

[8] May 28th and June 7th: W. A. Yale, 'Ambassador Henry Morgenthau's Special Mission of 1917,' *World Politics* (New Haven), April 1949.

[9] *For.Rns.U.S.*, 1917, Suppl. 2, I, 109 (25 June 1917).

could somehow be harnessed to his peace efforts. Such a meeting may have been thought all the more desirable because it would fit in with the ostensible purpose of Morgenthau's activities. According to a communiqué issued by the State Department, the Morgenthau mission had been authorised by the President 'in an effort to ameliorate the condition of the Jewish communities in Palestine.'[10] Putting it rather more colourfully, *The New York Times* had announced that Morgenthau was going to the East on a mission to prevent massacres of Jews in Palestine and elsewhere.[11] Though the whole affair had started with Morgenthau's offer of his services in connection with peace overtures to the Turks, it seems clear that by the time he left the United States his original purpose had come to be mixed up with relief work in Palestine. But even if this was not mere camouflage, the underlying intention remained what it had been from the start. Reporting to London on a conversation with President Wilson on July 13th, Sir William Wiseman said that the President had told him that ' Morgenthau was sent to the East for relief work and instructed that if opportunity arose to get in touch discreetly with some of the Turkish leaders, he might do so and sound them on the subject of peace. . . . The President asked me to assure Mr. Balfour that Mr. Morgenthau was not authorised to express his views to anyone or to approach any Turkish leaders officially.'

Balfour had been in the United States at the time when the Morgenthau mission was taking shape and had given the Americans some reason to suppose that the British Government would not be averse to an attempt to test the state of feeling in Turkey. On May 13th, a few days before Morgenthau made his offer to Lansing, House had reported to Wilson that Balfour had agreed with his (House's) suggestion that ' if Turkey and Austria were willing to break away from Germany . . . certain concessions should be made to them.'[12] In communicating Morgenthau's offer to the President on May 17th, Lansing remarked that he had recently asked Balfour for his views on the chances of a separate peace with Turkey and that Balfour had replied that, according

10 Ibid., I, 120.

11 Yale, loc. cit., quoting *New York Times*, 17 June 1917.

12 House, *Intimate Papers*, III, 58.

extinction of its hopes in Palestine.[21] It may be that, though interested in testing Turkish reactions to the idea of a separate peace, the Government had never been particularly enthusiastic about leaving this delicate matter to be handled by Morgenthau and was glad of the excuse provided by the Zionist and Armenian protests, coupled with a leakage of information in the press, for suggesting that the Morgenthau mission should be called off. Having proposed this to the Americans, but without success, on the eve of Sykes's return to London, it would have been all the readier to be impressed by his vigorous presentation of the case against any plan for letting the Turks out of the War on easy terms. In the end, it made up its mind that the time was inopportune for any approach to the Turks and that means must somehow be found of torpedoing the Morgenthau mission without antagonising Wilson.

The chosen instrument was Weizmann, who, at the request of the Foreign Office, was temporarily released from his work for the Admiralty[22] and sent to Gibraltar, where, together with a French representative, Colonel Weyl, he had conferences with Morgenthau and Frankfurter on July 4th and 5th.[23] Surprising as it may at first sight appear, Weizmann's selection for this rôle is easily explained when it is remembered that, while Morgenthau was on his way, Lansing had particularly asked that arrangements should be made for Weizmann to meet him at Gibraltar.

Weizmann handled the situation so adroitly that Morgenthau

[21] Writing to Sacher on 11 June 1917, Weizmann, referring apparently to his interview with Ormsby-Gore on the 10th, said that he had been told at the Foreign Office that ' it was axiomatic that no arrangements with Turkey can be arrived at unless Armenia, Syria and Arabia are detached ': *Ch.W.P.* This is not, however, mentioned in Ormsby-Gore's note of the interview.

[22] Sir W. Graham Greene (Admiralty) to Weizmann, 28 June 1917— *Ch.W.P.*: ' I am informing Sir Ronald Graham at the Foreign Office that the Admiralty have given permission for you to be absent for the period suggested in order to enable you to join the mission at Gibraltar.'

[23] A full report of the proceedings was sent by the ' special agents ' (Morgenthau and Frankfurter) to the Secretary of State in Washington in a telegram dated Madrid, 8 July 1917. This states (inter alia) that ' at the conference Weizmann announced that condition precedent in any negotiation with Turkey, so far as Great Britain was concerned, was the separation from Turkey of territory containing subject-races—in effect, Armenia and territory south of Taurus ': *For.Rns.U.S.*, 1917, Suppl. 2, 1, 120ff.

was forced to recognise the futility of his mission, abandoned his plans for meeting his Turkish friends in Switzerland,[24] and, soon after leaving Gibraltar, was peremptorily instructed by the State Department in no circumstances to enter upon any discussions bearing on a separate peace with Turkey.[25] In a letter already quoted,[26] Sykes, after describing his own efforts to deal with the situation he had found on his return to London, gave much of the credit to the Zionists: ' Luckily, Zionism held good and the plot to bring Morgenthau over and negotiate a separate peace with Turkey in Switzerland was foiled. Morgenthau was met at Gibraltar by Weizmann on behalf of British Zionism and was compelled to admit that no useful negotiations could be undertaken with the Turks until another victory had been gained.'

A curious feature of this episode is Morgenthau's evident belief that he could somehow interest the Zionists in his peace efforts. It is relevant to recall that in his speech at Cincinnati, which caused such a stir in the summer of 1916, he had hinted that he might be able, by his personal influence, to negotiate a sale of Palestine by the Turks to the Zionists.[27] In his report to the Foreign Office, Weizmann wrote (6 July 1917): ' I have asked Mr. Morgenthau several times why he had tried to enlist the support of the Zionists in his mission. Here again no clear answer was forthcoming and it was, therefore, found necessary to state clearly to Mr. Morgenthau that on no account should the Zionist Organisation be compromised by his negotiations . . . that on no account must the Zionist Organisation be identified or mixed up even with the faintest attempt to secure a separate peace . . . and we would like assurances from Mr. Morgenthau that he agrees and understands this position. This assurance was given.'[28]

Morgenthau had been duly headed off. The Zionists had gained by Weizmann's enhanced prestige, but they seem to have had a price to pay in Morgenthau's resentment at his discomfiture, for

---

[24] Weizmann to Sir Ronald Graham (telegram), 6 July 1917: copy in Ch.W.P.

[25] Acting Secretary of State (Polk) to Morgenthau, 14 July 1917: For.Rns.U.S., 1917, Suppl. 2, I, 129.

[26] To Sir G. Clayton, 22 July 1917: Sledm., No. 52.

[27] Above, p. 289.

[28] To Sir Ronald Graham (letter), 6 July 1917: copy in Ch.W.P.

it is not easy to find any other satisfactory explanation of the marked change in his feelings about the Zionist Movement. As American Ambassador to Turkey in 1913-16 he had shown himself sympathetically interested in Zionism and had done his best to be helpful to the Jews in Palestine. Early in 1918 he was being quoted by Walter Page as an anti-Zionist,[29] and in 1919 he was one of the prominent American Jews who signed an anti-Zionist petition submitted to President Wilson in the early days of the Peace Conference.[30] As an active and valuable member of the Democratic Party,[31] Morgenthau had some influence with Wilson and, though there is no proof of it, it is conceivable that his views may have had something to do with Wilson's rather cautious approach to the Zionist question.

Once the United States had entered the War, the views of Wilson and his advisers, with their anti-annexationist and anti-Imperialist bias, had to be reckoned with as a powerful influence in the shaping of the post-War settlement. The Zionist leadership in London and the British Government had, therefore, a common interest in inviting the American Jews to endorse the idea of a Jewish Commonwealth in Palestine under British protection. The support of the largest aggregation of Jews outside Russia would be valuable for its own sake, but still more valuable if it helped, as it was hoped that it might, to secure the backing of their Government.

For another reason the changed situation brought about by the American declaration of War encouraged the British Government

---

[29] Walter Page to A. W. Page, 19 January 1918: 'Morgenthau is dead right. I agree with him *in toto*. I do not think that anybody in the United States need be the least concerned about the Zionist Movement, and there isn't a single Jew in our country such a fool as to go to Palestine when he can stay in the United. The whole thing is a sentimental, religious more or less fantastic idea. . . ': *Life and Letters of Walter H. Page*, ed. B. J. Hendrick (London, Heinemann, 1922), II, 349-350.

[30] Manuel, op. cit., p. 237. For text of the petition (submitted 4 March 1919) see M. Jastrow, *Zionism and the Future of Palestine* (New York, 1919), pp. 151ff.

[31] Wilson 'rewarded two of his heaviest financial supporters, Frederick C. Penfield and Henry Morgenthau, with the ambassadorships to Austria-Hungary and the Ottoman Empire respectively': A. S. Link, *Wilson, The New Freedom* (Princeton, 1956), p. 102.

to interest itself in Zionist propaganda in the United States. An appeal to Zionist sentiment might stir the emotions of that not inconsiderable section of American Jewry which was apathetic about the War or even actively opposed to it. Among the Jewish immigrant masses there were many who, not yet firmly rooted in American life, felt that the War was no concern of theirs and whose left-wing sympathies made them all the easier a target for pacifist propaganda. It was not, as has sometimes been supposed, a question of melting the hearts of the Jewish money-barons. Despite the German connections of many of them, the Jewish moneyed classes could, generally speaking, be relied upon, without any special coaxing, to identify themselves with what had now become the American cause, and to do so all the more whole-heartedly because it was a cause not tainted by an association with Czarist Russia. Even had it been otherwise, nothing could have been better calculated to frighten them than the offer of a Jewish Commonwealth in Palestine. It was precisely in these circles that such ideas were indignantly rejected as dangerous heresies. With the immigrant masses it was different. For them Europe meant the Europe from which they had fled with bitterness in their hearts, and there were many among them who resented being dragged into its quarrels. It was this section of American Jewry that had to be made to feel that Jews, as Jews, had a direct concern in the outcome of the War, since an Allied victory would mean the realisation of Jewish hopes in Palestine.

Within the Zionist Movement itself the entry of the United States into the War had the effect of absolving the American Zionists from the obligation of neutrality. As Americans, they had been inhibited by President Wilson's warning to his fellow-citizens against openly taking sides in the War. As Zionists, they had not forgotten that neutrality as between rival groups of Powers had been accepted at the last pre-war Congress as a basic principle of Zionist policy. They had, moreover, been impressed by the argument that, in the interests of the Jewish population in Palestine, they must be careful to do nothing calculated to give offence to the Turks or to antagonise Turkey's German ally, who was alone in a position to restrain her from excesses against the Jews. As late as January 1917 a member of the New York Provisional Committee had been severely criticised by some of his colleagues for unneutral conduct in speaking his mind in the press about Turkish outrages in Armenia.[32] Up to the moment of the American declaration of war on Germany the Provisional Committee was still in contact with the Berlin-controlled Zionist Bureau at Copenhagen.[33] In the spring of 1917 the American Zionists finally cut loose from the rump Executive in Berlin and, abandoning even the semblance of neutrality, became free to associate themselves with Weizmann and Sokolow in their attempt to form, with Brandeis and Tschlenow, a London-Washington-Moscow combination unfettered by any inhibitions about an understanding with the British Government.

[32] See above, p. 199.

[33] Minutes, 2 April 1917: Brandeis said: 'We have had definite communication from Copenhagen notifying us that the changes which have come from the Russian Revolution have, in their opinion, greatly improved the Zionist situation. . . .'

CHAPTER 24

SYKES' CONTACTS WITH THE
ZIONIST LEADERS

AGAINST THE BACKGROUND which has now been sketched we can go on to look more closely at the events which, in the year of decision, 1917, were to lead to the Declaration communicated by Mr. Balfour to Lord Rothschild on November 2nd.

The year opened with Sykes still in contact with Gaster, who on January 3rd sent him a map of Palestine marked to show the exact position of the Jewish colonies[1] and two days later wrote to him again, evidently in reply to a request for an appointment.[2] But now that General Murray's Army had advanced to the threshold of Palestine and might at any moment begin to move forward, it had become essential for Sykes to know exactly where he stood with the Zionists and to be in touch with the responsible leaders who could really speak for them. Was it wise for him to rely exclusively on Gaster? He was beginning to have his doubts. Moreover, Picot seems to have told him that his talks with Gaster had been sterile and he would prefer to deal with someone else.[3] When, some three months later, Sykes met Aaron Aaronsohn in Cairo, he explained to him in confidence what had happened. Gaster, he said, had given him the impression that he could answer for the whole Zionist Movement. He had eventually realised that he had overestimated Gaster's authority and had

---

[1] 'I hope that the long delay in keeping my promise has not shaken your confidence in me. . . . At last I found the accompanying maps. . . . In order to make it as clear as possible, especially as regards the Palestine Jewish colonies, I have marked their spots with figures and I am enclosing the list of the names of the places to which these figures correspond': *Gaster papers.*

[2] Gaster to Sykes, 5 January 1917: 'I shall be glad to see you, of course, any time that you can spare. . . . If 9.30 is not too early for you . . . I shall be most happy to wait for you. . . .': *Gaster Papers.*

[3] In a lecture to a Jewish audience in Paris in 1939, Picot said that he had told Sykes that, though he had found Gaster's ideas interesting, he wished to meet someone on the Zionist side with a more realistic grasp of the situation: *La Terre Retrouvée* (Paris), 1 April 1939.

then, through an Armenian intermediary, Malcolm, got in contact with Weizmann and Sokolow, with whom he had established satisfactory relations.[4]

James Malcolm[5] belonged to a well-known Armenian family long settled in Persia. He had been educated in England, had become a British subject, and after leaving Oxford had gone into business in the City of London. He had been selected as one of the members of an Armenian National Delegation constituted early in 1916 under the auspices of the Armenian Catholicos, and, the seat of the Delegation being in Paris, he had become its London representative. In that capacity he had been brought into contact with Sykes, who, as shown by his proposals on the subject during the tripartite discussions in Petrograd in the spring of 1916,[6] took an active interest in the Armenian Question. One of Sykes' favourite dreams was, as we have seen, that in which he pictured the Armenians linked with the Jews and the Arabs in a permanent *entente* which would be a stabilising force in the Middle East and a barrier to German penetration. He had, therefore, good reason to cultivate friendly relations with the London representative of the Armenian cause.

Malcolm had many irons in the fire and an extensive range of personal contacts. C. P. Scott once described him, rather unkindly, as ' a self-important busybody.'[7] What Sokolow saw in him was a ' brasseur des affaires.'[8] However that may be, he had a wide circle of acquaintances, and it so happened that among

---

[4] A.A. *Diaries*, 4 April 1917: Chez Sykes. Enfin! Immédiatement abordons sujets intimes. Il m'assure que, parlant à un patriote juif, il me confiéra des choses très sécrètes, dont certaines sont même inconnues au Foreign Office. Lui, Sykes, depuis mon départ, s'est addressé à Dr. Gaster. Celui-ce . . . lui a assuré que lui est capable de faire marcher tout le Sionisme. Sykes s'est laissé gagner et a fini par reconnaître que Gaster a baissé. . . . Il s'est addressé alors à Weizmann et Sokolow par intermédiaire de l'Arménien Malcolm. Ces deux lui ont plu. Mais il s'agissait de ne pas froisser Gaster ; alors Sykes a suggéré une réunion chez Gaster à laquelle lui, Sykes, assistera en homme privé et on choisirait deux réprésentants qui traiteraient directement avec lui.' (As to the reliability of the Aaronsohn diaries, see List of Sources.)

[5] (1868-1952.) O.B.E., 1947. ' Malcolm ' appears to be an anglicisation of ' Malkom.' See, as to this Perso-Armenian family, Christopher Sykes, op. cit., p. 180.

[6] See Adamov, No. 76 (12 March 1916).

[7] Scott to Weizmann, 20 April 1917: *Ch.W.P.*   [8] See below, p. 395.

them was Leopold Greenberg, the editor of *The Jewish Chronicle*. When Malcolm helped to found the Russia Society in 1915, he had been anxious to induce one or two influential British Jews to give their names, and one of those approached had been Greenberg.[9]

At some date not precisely ascertainable but almost certainly towards the end of January 1917, Malcolm called at the *Jewish Chronicle* office and asked Greenberg to tell him who were the real leaders of the Zionist Movement in England. Greenberg named Weizmann and Sokolow[10]—a generous gesture on his part, since his relations with Weizmann were not notably cordial.[11]

The known facts fit in comfortably with Aaronsohn's account of what he was told by Sykes. Piecing them together, the episode can with reasonable confidence be reconstructed as follows: Having made up his mind that he could not afford to go on relying exclusively on Gaster, Sykes was anxious to meet the effective leaders of the Zionist Movement but was uncertain who they were. For obvious reasons, he could not ask Gaster, nor could he very well ask Herbert Samuel, who had put Gaster in touch with him. Malcolm, who seems to have been a kind of contact man, was invited, or offered, to help. Being as much in the dark as Sykes, he thought of Greenberg as a likely source of information, and it was as a result of Greenberg's reply to his enquiries that on 28 January 1917, a date which can be precisely

9 'The Russia Society, Inaugural Meeting, 10 March 1915': Greenberg's name is in the list of those invited (p. 50).

10 This is based on the personal recollection of Greenberg's daughter, Mrs. Sholto, who at the time was working with her father at the *Jewish Chronicle* office. Independently of her evidence, the author has been informed by Mr. J. Hodess (later, Editor of *The New Judæa*), who was during the 1914-1918 War in close contact with *The Jewish Chronicle*, that he remembers being told by Greenberg that Malcolm had called on him to enquire who were the Zionist leaders.

On the publication in 1921 of the Report of the Zionist Executive to the 12th Zionist Congress, Greenberg complained (24 August 1921) to the General Secretary of the Organisation that there was no reference to his part in bringing the Zionist leaders into contact with Sykes, though the author of the Report 'must have known that I had the honour of bringing Dr. Weizmann and Sir Mark Sykes into touch with one another.' (The author is indebted to Mr. S. Landman for kindly showing him this letter.)

11 Above, p. 123.

fixed,[12] there was a meeting—probably at Sykes' house—at which Weizmann, accompanied by Greenberg, was introduced to Sykes by Malcolm.[13]

Why did Sykes deal with the situation in this roundabout way instead of using the official machinery at his disposal? It is difficult to suppose that the Foreign Office could not have told him, or found out for him, who the Zionist leaders were and helped him to get in touch with them. It may be that, as he hinted to Aaronsohn, he preferred to keep what he was doing to himself: he told Aaronsohn that he was trusting him with secrets some of which were unknown even to the Foreign Office.[14] Whatever the explanation, it is clear that Malcolm was the intermediary and that it was he who, thanks to Greenberg, was instrumental in bringing Sykes and Weizmann together.

Entries in Scott's Journals for 27 and 28 January 1917 throw some light on the preliminaries to Weizmann's meeting with

---

[12] See below, p. 366.

[13] In an article published in *The New Judæa* (October-November 1944, pp. 9-10) Malcolm writes: 'In October 1916 the late Mr. L. J. Greenberg took me to his house in Kensington, where I found a small group of remarkable Jews assembled. . . . They were the leaders of the Zionist Movement, the men whom the British Government had asked me to find after the War Cabinet had adopted my suggestion to win the support of Jewry by a promise of Palestine. . . . The next day I introduced them to Sir Mark Sykes, and the vital messages were flashed by cipher to Washington and other parts of the allied and neutral world, thus beginning the close co-operation which resulted, in November 1917, in the issue of the historic Balfour Declaration. . . . The " gentlemen's agreement " between the Zionist leaders and the War Cabinet, which I was entrusted to bring about, was the basis of co-operation, and within a few months . . . solid progress was achieved. The support of President Wilson was, of course, the main achievement, because United States help was vitally needed by the Allies. It was only in the following April that the United States came into the war. . . .' All this is part of a fairy-tale invented by Malcolm to flatter his own megalomania and elaborated, with still greater fertility of imagination, in a memorandum privately circulated by him in July 1944. The one grain, or half-grain, of truth contained in it is that at the end of January 1917 Malcolm introduced Weizmann to Sykes in the circumstances described in the text. His story is not worth serious discussion and is mentioned here only to show that it has not been overlooked. Professor Trevor-Roper has remarked (*The Last Days of Hitler*, p. 24) that 'mythopœia is a far more common characteristic of the human race than veracity.' The Malcolm myth is a good example.

[14] See above, note 4.

6444

Sykes. The entry for January 27th includes the following: 'Saw Weizmann in morning about Palestine question. Sir Mark Sykes deputed by F.O. to deal with it. He and Lord Rothschild and James Rothschild and others to see him. Memorial was being prepared on whole question. Very important to obtain American Jews' support.[15] It would be unanimous if they could be assured that in event of a British occupation of Palestine the Zionist scheme would be considered favourably. Now was the moment for pressing the matter when British troops were actually on Palestinian soil.'

In the afternoon of the same day Scott met James de Rothschild; Neil Primrose accompanied de Rothschild but is not mentioned by Scott as having taken any part in the conversation. Scott writes in his Journal (January 27th): 'Met James Rothschild and Primrose at the Reform Club by appointment. Rothschild . . . said . . . that Sir Mark Sykes was being consulted as the expert on the whole question of the Near East. He was at present engaged in examining, What is Armenia? When I suggested that, in addition to Syria, France might have Damascus as a sop for resigning any pretensions in Palestine, Rothschild said that Sykes designed to include it in the new Arab State as its commercial capital—a strange idea.'

We know from Gaster's diary[16] that on the morning of that same day, January 27th, de Rothschild had asked Sykes for an appointment and had had some conversation with him about Palestine. It seems clear that both Weizmann and de Rothschild, having known nothing of the conversations which had been going on since the spring of 1916 between Sykes and Gaster, had just discovered that Sykes was handling the Palestine question and was, in fact, the Government's principal adviser on the subject.

On the morning of the next day, January 28th, Weizmann told Scott about an interview he had had with Malcolm. Weizmann, Scott writes, 'told me a curious story about an Armenian enjoying the name of "Malcolm," who appeared to be on intimate terms with Sykes and had approached W. with a view to gaining Zionist support for "stable"—i.e. bureaucratic and reactionary—government in Russia, alleging parallel between Russian pro-

15 I.e., presumably, for British control of Palestine.
16 30 January 1917, quoted below, p. 367.

tectorate in Armenia and British in Palestine. Apparently the idea was that if Zionists gave this support to the Russian protectorate, Russia would not make difficulties about a British protectorate. Weizmann replied that Armenia was completely outside the sphere of Zionist interests.' This is the only contemporaneous record which has come to light of what passed between Weizmann and Malcolm before the meeting at which Weizmann and Greenberg were introduced by Malcolm to Sykes.

It will be noticed that the Armenian question figured prominently in Malcolm's conversation with Weizmann. It may be more than a coincidence that almost at the same moment James de Rothschild, having just seen Mark Sykes, was telling Scott that Sykes was engaged in defining the boundaries of Armenia.[17] Any ideas that Sykes may have had as to the future of Armenia would naturally have been discussed by him with the London representative of the Armenian National Delegation. Malcolm may quite possibly have been echoing something he had heard from Sykes—he may even have been acting on a hint from Sykes—in sounding Weizmann as to his views on a kind of tripartite arrangement between Great Britain, Russia and the Zionists, by which, in return for Russian acquiescence in a British claim to Palestine, Great Britain would back a Russian claim to Armenia, and the Zionists, for their part, would use their influence against the revolutionary forces in Russia. Malcolm had not only taken a leading part in the foundation of the Russia Society in 1915 but had in other ways been active during the War in pro-Russian propaganda.[18] Whether prompted by Sykes or not, it would have been natural for him to grasp at the chance of a deal with the Zionists in the interests both of Russia and of the pro-Russian elements among the Armenians.

Except for the extract already quoted from Scott's Journals, nothing is known of what passed at Malcolm's interview with Weizmann, nor is there any first-hand record of the conversation at the meeting between Weizmann and Sykes, attended by Greenberg and Malcolm, on January 28th.

The date is fixed by entries in Gaster's diary for January 28th

[17] *C.P.S., Jnls.,* 27 January, 1917, quoted above, p. 365.
[18] This can be seen from the references to Malcolm in *The Times* Index for the War years.

and 30th. There is no reference to the meeting either in the Sledmere or in the Weizmann papers, and for an account of what happened we have to rely on Gaster's note of what Sykes told him two days later.

On January 28th Gaster wrote in his diary:

> ' Message from Weizmann, wants to speak to me. He rings up. . . . He had met Sir Mark Sykes and found out that he was an old friend of mine and that he referred W. and Baron James to me. . . . He realised that the whole problem rested now in Sir M.'s hands and that he was the man on whom our Zionist hopes hang.'

The entry for January 30th is more informative:

> ' Went to Sykes. Long conversation. Told me the whole history. On Saturday[19] wire from Baron James to meet him. . . . To his surprise it was about Zionism. . . . I asked him about W.'s visit and I learned that it was not Baron James at all who had introduced him. Sykes had told Baron James to come to me and did not hear another name. W. had rung up on Sunday[20] and came together with Greenberg. . . . Dr. Weizmann had made a more favourable impression [than Greenberg]. He was earnest in his plea for Zion. They then learned from S. that I had been in constant communication, etc. (sic). S. had not entered upon many details, but, as I learned from him, he had represented the situation as urgent and that steps should be taken to formulate proposals, to prepare for some machinery. As I understood him when he now spoke to me! that we should be prepared in men and [?] to put into immediate practice some of the principles of local Government and administration, to define our activity, to have men on the spot when the English entered Jerusalem so as to take effective part in the administration of at least the Jewish section of the population.'

After mentioning various matters discussed between Sykes and himself, Gaster writes: ' I then learned that W. had another

[19] Saturday = 27 January 1917.
[20] January 28th.

appointment with him that evening.' An entry in Gaster's diary, dated January 31st, reads:

> 'Weizmann came and told me . . . [about] the first and second interviews.[21] Had been introduced, as he alleged, by the Armenian Galman [sic] of [word illegible]. (I believe a doubtful customer) . . . He said that Sykes wanted a meeting with Herbert Samuel and other representatives. . . .'

As we know from Aaronsohn's diary,[22] Sykes wanted such a meeting, not only because it would be useful in itself, but also because he hoped that it would lead to the nomination of one or two genuinely representative Zionists with authority to carry on the discussions. In the end Gaster was to drop out altogether, but whether this was intended by Sykes is not quite clear. In the entry in Gaster's diary recording his meeting with Sykes on 30 January 1917 there is a passage which suggests that Sykes spoke to him as though taking it for granted that the two would remain in close contact. It may be that, knowing that Gaster would be difficult to work with, the other Zionist leaders now brought into the picture preferred to go on without him. What eventually happened was, as we shall see, that Gaster, though from time to time consulted by Sokolow and Weizmann, took no further part in the conversations with Sykes.

It was agreed that before meeting the Zionists, Sykes should be provided with an outline of their proposals. The memorandum laid before him was the latest version of a document—its antecedents have already been mentioned[23]—on which the Zionist leaders, in consultation with Herbert Samuel and the pro-Zionist members of the Rothschild family, had been working for some considerable time. The first draft had been abandoned in favour of a much less elaborate programme, and it was almost certainly an amended version of this second draft that was submitted to Sykes.[24] It

---

[21] 'I hope to see Dr. W. this afternoon and I shall probably hear from him the result of his visit to you last night' (i.e., January 30th): Gaster to Sykes, 31 January 1917: *Gaster papers*.

[22] 27 April 1917, quoted above, note 4.

[23] Above, pp. 297-298.

[24] What document was submitted to Sykes cannot, so far as the author has been able to ascertain, be established by direct evidence, but (1) we know from the Sokolow papers that there were three successive drafts;

ended by summing up the scheme as follows:

> 'Palestine to be recognised as the Jewish National Home, with liberty of immigration to Jews of all countries, who are to enjoy full national political and civic rights; a Charter to be granted to a Jewish Company; local government to be accorded to the Jewish population; and the Hebrew language to be officially recognised.'

The expression 'Jewish National Home,' devised by Sokolow[25] and later expanded, in the Balfour Declaration, into a 'National Home for the Jewish People,' here appears for the first time. In earlier versions of the Zionist programme the central idea had been what was described in the October 1916 draft as 'the recognition of a separate Jewish nationality or national unit in Palestine.'[26] It looks as though this would have alarmed the anti-Zionists less than did the conception of a Jewish National Home, which seemed to them to imply that the Jews throughout the world formed part of a single nation with its seat in Palestine. At an interview with Balfour on January 30th, almost at the moment when the Zionist memorandum was being submitted to Sykes, Lucien Wolf explained that the Conjoint Foreign Committee insisted that nothing should be done 'which might be calculated to compromise the position and aims of Jews else-

---

[25] Sokolow to his drafting Committee, 3 November 1916: *N.S.P.* The drafting Committee included, in addition to Sokolow, Herbert Bentwich, Cowen, Gaster and Weizmann and, at one stage, Ahad Ha'am.

[26] *Political Report of Zionist Executive to 12th Zionist Congress, App. I,* 'Summary,' para. (1).

---

(2) we know from the Sokolow papers, and also from the Herbert Bentwich papers, that the third draft was completed by 25 November 1916—the Bentwich papers contain the text of draft No. 3 endorsed 'Settled, 25/11/16'); (3) the first draft (that printed as an Appendix to the Report of the Zionist Executive to the 12th Zionist Congress and dated October 1916) had certainly been scrapped and is not in question, and, as between Nos. 2 and 3, it is a reasonable presumption that the final, and not the penultimate, version would have been submitted to Sykes; (4) references to the document in the procès-verbal of the conference on 7 February 1917 (see below) fit in better with No. 3 than with No. 2. The text of No. 3 (undated) is in *Ch.W.P.* and corresponds to the text, also in *Ch.W.P.*, of a French version of the Zionist proposals. It has, therefore, been assumed that what was submitted to Sykes was, in fact, No. 3.

where,' but that, subject to this, 'we should have no objection if [the Jews in Palestine] developed into a local Jewish nation and a Jewish State.'[27]

Not without some friction between Gaster on the one hand and Weizmann and Sokolow on the other,[28] a list of persons to be invited was agreed upon, and the meeting with Sykes took place at Gaster's house, and under his chairmanship, on February 7th.[29] Sykes explained that he was attending the conference in his private capacity. He was bound to make this clear, since he had no authority to bind the Government by any promises to the Zionists. Moreover, while he himself was strongly opposed to an Anglo-French condominium in Palestine, there are indications that at the Foreign Office the view then taken at the official level was that it would be better to be content with a condominium than to start a quarrel with the French. Reports to that effect had reached the Zionists, and Weizmann was anxious to bring them to the notice of Lloyd George. Scott wrote to him on February 3rd: 'I hope George will see you before the meeting with Sykes next Wednesday. The suggestion (which Sacher reports) of a condominium with France—a repetition of the ill-omened Egyptian "dual control"—would be fatal both for you and for all of us. I hope Sykes doesn't seriously entertain such a project, but the French are very astute and pressing diplomatists.'[30] Two days later, Scott wrote to Lloyd George, evidently at the instance of Weizmann: 'I hope you will be able to see Weizmann about the Palestine question. . . . I dread the matter being handled in the spirit of compromise by the F.O. I gather that the whole drift of F.O. policy is towards some sort of dual control—name of

[27] C.F.C., 1917/59.   [28] Gaster Diary, 1 and 6 February 1917.

[29] The account which follows of the conference of 7 February 1917 is taken from a record of the proceedings of which copies are in Ch.W.P. and Z.A. and also among the papers kindly placed at the author's disposal by Lord Samuel. From a letter preserved in the Gaster papers it looks as though the compiler must have been Sokolow. It has not been found possible to verify this, but the document gives the impression of having been prepared from a note taken at the time by one of those present at the meeting. It does not purport to be a verbatim report, and the quotations in the text must be understood accordingly. Those present, in addition to Sykes and Gaster, were Herbert Samuel, Weizmann, Sokolow, Lord Rothschild, James de Rothschild, J. Cowen, Sacher and Herbert Bentwich.

[30] Ch.W.P.

ill-omen—with France. . . . I don't believe it is your view and, personally, I believe it would be fatal to our interests.' As appears from Scott's letter to Weizmann of February 11th, Lloyd George was at the moment inaccessible: 'It is serious . . . that the F.O. is so weak in the matter. George, of course, could overrule it, but it is difficult to get him to give enough attention and study to anything not immediately urgent. . . . Still, if you can gain his whole attention even for a short time, no one is quicker to see and to decide.'[31] Scott need not have had any anxiety about Sykes's views on the question of a condominium, but it seems clear that they were not, at this time, the views of the Foreign Office.[32]

For another reason Sykes must have been conscious that in his dealings with the Zionists he was skating on thin ice. He knew, but the Zionists did not, that Great Britain's hands were tied by her engagements to the French under paragraph 3 of the Sykes-Picot Agreement. Having been a member of the Cabinet when the Agreement was negotiated, Herbert Samuel was fully informed, but he was not free to disclose Cabinet secrets. James de Rothschild, with his French connections, had heard some disturbing rumours, but, though the Zionists were aware that the French claims were being pressed, they did not realise that there were British commitments which made it difficult to resist a condominium, nor that Great Britain had agreed that a slice of northern Palestine should be added to the French zone in Syria. It was not until the middle of April that, as a result of a disclosure—very likely a calculated indiscretion—by a French journalist to C. P. Scott, it came to Weizmann's knowledge that a settlement on these lines had already been agreed upon between Great Britain and France.[33] At the conference on February 7th the Sykes-Picot Agreement was plainly an embarrassment to Sykes,

[31] *Ch.W.P.*

[32] As late as 19 April 1917 a high Foreign Office official, Sir Ronald Graham, wrote to Sykes: 'I had a letter from Bertie [Sir F. Bertie, British Ambassador in Paris], who is very pessimistic as to the chance of the French renouncing claims to Palestine. . . . I confess that I do not feel sanguine on the matter, and it is somewhat disquieting to see how entirely the Zionist plans and ideas are based on a British Palestine': *Sledm.*, No. 48.

[33] See below, p. 391.

who, in encouraging the Zionists to press for a British protectorate, had to give the impression that the future of Palestine
was still unsettled as between the two Powers. Sykes having said
that 'no pledges had been given to the French concerning
Palestine,' 'Mr. de Rothschild pressed for assurances on this
point, as he had been informed differently.' Towards the end of
the proceedings, 'Mr. de Rothschild again desired to know
whether any pledge had been given about Palestine. Sir Mark
Sykes suggested that Mr. Samuel might say what had taken place.
Mr. Samuel replied that he could not reveal what had been done
by the Cabinet. Sir Mark thereupon repeated that with great
difficulty the British Government had managed to keep the
question of Palestine open.'

It was no part of the purpose of the Conference to debate the
merits of Zionism or the advantages, from a Zionist point of view,
of British suzerainty in Palestine. On these points Sykes and the
Zionists came to the Conference fully agreed. Sykes told the
Zionists that 'he had long had the question of Palestine and
the Jews in mind and the idea of a Jewish Palestine had his full
sympathy.' Gaster declared, in his opening statement from the
Chair, that 'what Zionists in England and everywhere desired
was a British protectorate with full rights to the Jews to develop
a national life.' As to what the Zionists wanted, Gaster said that
'the Jews in Palestine must be recognised as a nation, a "millet."'
For Weizmann the essential point was that 'the Jews who went
to Palestine would go to constitute a Jewish nation and be one
hundred per cent Jews.' Sokolow spoke vaguely of the establishment in Palestine of 'a Jewish society.' On the other hand,
Lord Rothschild, going rather further, 'sympathised fully with
the development of a Jewish State in Palestine under the British
Crown.' Sacher, likewise, spoke, in terms, of a Jewish State, pointing out that 'Jews in Palestine would be members of the Jewish
State and owe it political obligation. Jews outside Palestine would
be members of the Jewish nation and owe Palestine such respect
as they thought fit, but would owe it no political obligation.'

Sacher was here dealing with the question of dual loyalties, on
which Herbert Samuel also had something to say: 'If it was
intended to create in Palestine a Jewish nation *eo nomine,* care
must be taken to explain the sense in which the term was used.

. . . So long as it was plain that by "nation" is meant an organised community, well and good, but it might be understood as meaning that the Jews in Great Britain, for instance, would constitute a separate nation in the same sense as the British are a nation.'[34]

Three points stand out in Sykes' speech. First, repeating what he had said to Weizmann on January 28th, he told the Zionists that the Palestine question was now becoming urgent. 'The soldiers, he thought, would soon find themselves in Palestine even though they might not think so. Time was pressing.' Secondly, he made no attempt to evade the Arab problem. 'One would have to go carefully,' he said, 'with the Arabs. The Syrians, in the organ of the King of the Hedjaz, had commenced attacking the Zionists. He had stopped that. The Arabs professed that language must be the measure and [they] could claim all Syria and Palestine. Still, the Arabs could be managed, particularly if they received Jewish support in other matters.'

Last and most important, Sykes declared that 'the French have no particular position in Palestine and are not entitled to anything there' and ended by proposing that the Zionists should see what they could do to induce the French to give way. 'He suggested that the Zionists should approach Monsieur Picot and convince [the] French,' on which Samuel's comment was that 'it is the business of the British Government to deal with the French and dispose of their pretensions. The French had no claims whatsoever in Palestine. . . . The Foreign Office should point out that Palestine was practically the only thing England was claiming[35] and should insist upon it.'

Sykes made no direct reply but gave the discussion a fresh turn by suggesting that 'all that the Jews desired could be embodied in the constitution of the Chartered Company, which would be British. As the Chartered Company bought land, it would come under British protection.' He went on to propose that 'a defined area should be put under the authority of the Company, with certain "islands" which should be under international control,' these to include Jerusalem and a belt of land from Jerusalem to

---

[34] Referring in his diary (27 April 1917) to what Sykes told him about the Conference, Aaronsohn writes: 'A cette réunion . . . Samuel, au sentiment de Sykes, était trop "English" et pas assez "Jewish."'

[35] He seems to have forgotten Mesopotamia.

the sea at Jaffa. Sykes' description of his ' defined area ' was clearly related to the Brown Area of the Sykes-Picot Agreement.

This ingenious device for circumventing the French made no marked appeal to the Zionists, and the discussion ended inconclusively. But the conference had helped to clear the ground for further conversations, and Sykes proceeded to ask that someone should be appointed ' to put the Jewish views before M. Picot and to continue negotiations with himself.' On the motion of James de Rothschild, the choice fell on Sokolow, and ' it was thereupon arranged that Mr. Sokolow should be introduced by Sir Mark Sykes to M. Picot.'

Sokolow's nomination had, before the conference, been suggested informally by Weizmann in conversation with Gaster.[36] Though Gaster might feel that his long association with Sykes gave him a prior claim, there could be no difficulty in justifying the selection of Sokolow. It was natural that the choice should fall on the only leading Zionist then in England who could speak with the authority of a member of the Zionist Executive. As de Rothschild pointed out, Sokolow had also the advantage of being in close contact with Russian Jewry and its leaders. Weizmann was fully agreeable to this arrangement and had, indeed, proposed it himself. He needed no formal credentials to give him the commanding position he occupied *de facto* in the transactions which followed.

Sykes had suggested at the conference that, if it was desired that Great Britain should be the protecting Power in Palestine, then ' the Zionists should approach M. Picot and convince the French.' This task now devolved upon Sokolow and was promptly taken in hand. On February 8th, the day after the conference, Sokolow was introduced to Picot by Sykes, who was present at the conversation which followed but took only a minor part in it.[37]

Picot manifested a strong desire to discuss the Jewish question

[36] Gaster to de Rothschild, 9 February 1917: copy in *Gaster papers*.

[37] The accounts which follow of Sokolow's discussions with Picot on February 8th and 9th, and of the meeting on the 10th between Sykes, Sokolow and Weizmann, are taken from notes of these conversations in *Ch.W.P.*—copies also in Z.A. The quotations in the text are from these notes. Picot was at this time temporarily attached to the French Embassy in London.

in Poland. Sokolow refused to be headed off and brought the conversation round to Zionism, dwelling on what the Jews had already achieved in Palestine under adverse conditions and on what they could hope to achieve 'if Palestine came under the control of a great civilised Power.' Asked point-blank to say what Power he was thinking of, Sokolow told Picot quite frankly that 'the Jews had long had in mind the suzerainty of the British Government.' The Jews, he said, remembered that 'for many years Great Britain had championed their cause and distinguished herself by benevolence towards them.' She had been the most successful of the colonial Powers and was believed by Jews to be 'the most fitted for developing a new colony.' They had observed that the British Government did not make a practice of imposing any stereotyped way of life upon the peoples it ruled. 'It did not try to suppress their individuality, but allowed them to live according to their own aspirations and ideas.' The Jews, Picot was assured, had profound respect for France and the French contribution to civilisation ; 'nevertheless, the feeling among Jews was very strongly in favour of British suzerainty in Palestine.'

Picot reminded Sokolow that the future of Palestine was, after all, a matter for the Entente. He could not say what Russia would do, but, personally, he anticipated serious difficulties from that quarter. There were also Italian claims to be considered. Picot went on to say bluntly that 'in his opinion there was no possibility of France renouncing completely its aspirations in Palestine in favour of Great Britain. Ninety-five per cent. of the French people were strongly in favour of the annexation of Palestine by France.' Sykes intervened to put forward the idea he had mentioned at the conference the day before of an English Chartered Company for the colonisation and development of Palestine on Zionist lines, but Picot was unimpressed. The end of it was that Picot conceded nothing except that 'so far as he was concerned, he promised to do his best to make known the Zionist aims.'

After Picot had left, Sykes suggested that Sokolow should ask to see him again. The next day, February 9th, Sokolow called on Picot at the French Embassy. Picot did not favour any immediate attempt to influence French public opinion in favour of Zionism. This, he said, might provoke a violent counter-agitation, but he

promised that 'he personally . . . would do his best to win for the Movement whatever sympathies were necessary to be won, so far as compatible with the French standpoint on the question.' As to the Zionist preference for Great Britain, he invited Sokolow to remember that France had shown the greatest ardour in championing the cause of small nations and so was naturally disposed to take a special interest in Zionism, adding, however, a warning that if the Zionists represented themselves as one of the small peoples struggling for liberation, they must expect strong opposition from the French Jews. Picot again expressed his objection to the Chartered Company scheme, strongly advising the Zionists, as a friend of the Jews, not to ask for the setting up of a Company enjoying special privileges. Sokolow having again inquired what the Zionists could do to interest France in their aspirations, 'Monsieur Picot assured Mr. Sokolow of the great and sympathetic interest which France took in their work,' but suggested that 'the more the Jews, as Jews, especially in the neutral countries, brought their support of the Entente into prominence, the better their chances of success.' There followed an inconclusive discussion about propaganda in the United States and Italy, and with this Picot and Sokolow ended their two-day fencing-match.

The next day, February 10th, Sykes, Weizmann and Sokolow met to review the situation in the light of Sokolow's exchanges with Picot. Sykes expressed satisfaction with what had been achieved. There might still, he said, be great difficulties with the French, but Picot would now be clearer in his mind as to what the Zionists wanted, and this was a useful first step. On the question of propaganda in England, Sykes could see no objection to a pro-Zionist campaign, 'but it was necessary to keep the idea of British suzerainty in the background for the time being, as it was likely to intensify the French opposition.' He thought that *Palestine,* the organ of the British Palestine Committee, was doing harm by over-emphasising the British interest in Palestine. After some further discussion , 'Mr. Sokolow and Dr. Weizmann said they were confident in the power and influence of Great Britain to remove whatever difficulties might arise in connection with the realisation of the Zionist demands.'

These 'demands' had been outlined in the memorandum

which Sykes had had before him at the conference on February 7th, but the only member of the Zionist Executive who was a party to the document was Sokolow. In order to give it greater authority, it was thought that steps should be taken to secure the assent of Sokolow's Russian colleague, Tschlenow, and also of Brandeis, who, though not a member of the Executive, could speak, with all the prestige of his name, for the powerful body of Zionist opinion in the United States. Recognising that it was desirable that on this and other matters the Zionist leaders in England should be in a position to communicate freely with Tschlenow and Brandeis, Sykes undertook to see that this was made possible.[38] Thus, from about this time Weizmann and Sokolow were able to send confidential information to Brandeis in Washington and to Tschlenow in Moscow with a minimum of interference by the war-time censorship and, in some cases, through official channels. A little later, the machinery at the disposal of the British military authorities began to be used for this purpose, and by the end of 1917 some two hundred letters and telegrams on their way from or to the Zionist leaders in London had been transmitted by the Military Intelligence Directorate of the War Office.

[38] Note of conversation on 10 February 1917—*Ch.W.P.* and *Z.A.*

CHAPTER 25

WEIZMANN'S MEETINGS WITH BALFOUR AND LLOYD GEORGE

ON 20 MARCH 1917 Weizmann wrote to Scott[1]: 'The Zionist negotiations with Sir Mark Sykes are entering upon their final stages. . . . I feel that our negotiations must be placed soon on a more definite practical basis. . . .'

In speaking of 'the Zionist negotiations with Sir Mark Sykes,' Weizmann was almost certainly not referring merely to what had passed between Sykes, Sokolow and himself early in February. There must in the interval have been further discussions, but of these no record has survived, except for a description by Sykes, in a letter to Picot,[2] of a conversation with Sokolow on February 22nd. Sokolow, he told Picot, had dwelt upon the Zionist objections to the internationalisation of Palestine and to any form of dual control or condominium. Sokolow had also pointed out that the Jews would be loth to disinterest themselves in parts of Palestine made precious in Jewish eyes by forty years of Zionist activity. This referred to a suggestion which had been put to Sokolow by Sykes that the Jews might be satisfied with facilities for colonising and developing an area rather vaguely described as comprising 'the country round Haifa and the arable lands east of the Jordan and south of Jerusalem.'

By the middle of March Weizmann was becoming impatient, and in his letter of March 20th he explained to Scott why he felt that the Government should now be pressed to show its hand more clearly. He believed, as Sykes did, that the British invasion of Palestine would soon be well under way ; 'after the occupation of Gaza,' he wrote, 'the military events may develop much more rapidly.' He had noted that, in drafting the proclamation published by General Maude on his entry into Baghdad on

[1] Orig. with *C.P.S. Jnls.*; copy in *Ch.W.P.*
[2] 28 February 1917: *Sledm.*, No. 50.

March 11th, Sykes had inserted an emphatic assurance of British support for Arab aspirations but had missed 'a splendid opportunity of saying a good word to the Jews. . . . I think Baghdad possesses the largest Jewish community in Asia; not a word has been said about them in this manifesto.' He feared that a situation might develop in which the Zionist question would be pushed into the background. 'Although Sir Mark is very keen on the Zionist scheme, I cannot help feeling that he considers it somewhat as an appendix to the bigger scheme with which he is dealing—the Arab scheme.' As to the competition for Palestine between Great Britain and France, Weizmann was still in ignorance of the Sykes-Picot Agreement and under the impression that nothing had been settled: 'I understand that the French people have not fully formulated their claims; they have not yet said whether they would limit their claims to Syria only or whether they would press some claims for the north of Palestine. Sir Mark is of the opinion that this may easily adjust itself, and I am perfectly convinced that it would be easily arranged if the British assert their claims, which I think they will do, with some force, when the country is occupied by British troops.'

'I feel, therefore,' he told Scott, 'that our negotiations must be placed very soon on a more definite basis,' and he went on to explain what he wanted:

> 'I should accompany Sir Mark to the East, enter there into negotiations with the leading Arabs from Palestine and see what can be done almost immediately in the way of acquisition of land in the Palestinian territory already occupied by the British. It is of the utmost importance . . . that the Palestinian people and the Jews at large should realise that we mean business. . . . In order that we should be able to begin our work in Russia and America, it is essential that our negotiations with the Government, which hitherto have been semi-official, should have a more definite character. . . . I could attempt to see Lloyd George in view of what he said last week but I do not want to do so before I have heard from you. . . .'

A few days before writing this letter, Weizmann had told Scott about a conversation he had had with Lloyd George at a dinner-

party at the Astors'[3] on March 13th. Scott wrote in his Journal
(March 15th): 'Breakfasted with Weizmann. Keen to see Lloyd
George. Had met him at dinner and had interesting conversation
but not yet got to grips about that (*sic*). When he asked for
appointment, George replied could make none, but "you must
take me by storm, and if Davies[4] says I'm engaged, don't be put
off but insist on seeing me. . . ."' Describing the same incident,
Mrs. Weizmann writes in her diary (March 13th): 'No sooner
Lloyd George came in than he asked Chaim if he liked the
situation in the campaign in the East. . . . Lloyd George said that
he must see Chaim to discuss the Eastern affairs, and when Chaim
remarked that he is afraid to take off his time, Lloyd George
simply said that Chaim ought to come and inflict himself upon
him.'

What advice Scott gave Weizmann in reply to his letter of
March 20th is unknown, but he arranged, as we shall see, for
Weizmann to breakfast with Lloyd George on April 3rd. In the
meantime, Weizmann had had an important interview with
Balfour—their first serious conversation about British policy in
Palestine since Balfour had gone to the Foreign Office. Balfour
as well as Lloyd George had been among the Astors' guests on
March 13th, and we know from Mrs. Weizmann's diary that after
Lloyd George had left, 'Balfour discussed Zionism with Chaim,
[but] merely academically.' They met again on March 22nd, and
this time the conversation was not so academic. Writing to Joseph
Cowen on the 26th,[5] Weizmann told him that at this interview
'for the first time, we had a serious talk on practical questions
connected with Palestine. He gave me a good opening to put
before him the importance of P[alestine] from [a] British point
of view, an aspect which was, apparently, new to him.' Another
matter touched upon at this interview is mentioned in a letter of
March 23rd from Weizmann to Scott[6]: 'Mr. Balfour dwelt upon

---

[3] The Astors are not mentioned by Scott in his reference to the matter in
his Journal, but are mentioned by Mrs. Weizmann in describing the
dinner-party in her diary: *V.W.P.*
[4] Later, Sir J. T. Davies, one of Lloyd George's Private Secretaries.
[5] *Ch.W.P.*
[6] *Ch.W.P.*

the difficulties arising from French (and Italian)[7] claims. He suggested that in case no agreement could be reached between England and France, it would be advisable to bring in the Americans and have an Anglo-American protectorate over Palestine,' on which Weizmann comments that 'attractive as such a project would appear, it is always fraught with the danger that there are two masters and we do not know yet how far the Americans would agree with the British on general principles of administration.'

Nothing more is on record as to what passed at this interview, but Weizmann was well satisfied with the outcome. 'I had,' he wrote to Brandeis (April 8th),[8] 'an opportunity of seeing Mr. Balfour on the 22 March and of discussing with him the Zionist position, and I have no hesitation in saying that the Secretary of State for Foreign Affairs is in full sympathy with our aspirations and I am sure that we may reckon on his support.'

We are now nearing a critical point in the history of the Declaration. From the beginning of 1917 the hopes of the Zionists had been rising, but it was not until the spring that they could begin to rely confidently on British support. The Zionist leaders had been encouraged by their talks with Sykes, but, as they themselves realised, these had been only at a semi-official level, leaving the British Government uncommitted. By the end of April the Zionists had moved forward from this position to one on which they could rely upon firm assurances of goodwill in the highest quarters. There were still no precise promises—still less any public undertakings, but the Zionist leaders were being encouraged to believe that, should Palestine come under the control of Great Britain, they could rely upon British support in laying the foundations of a Jewish Commonwealth. They were also being given to understand that the British Government would look favourably on Zionist propaganda designed to impress upon

---

7 Since the winter of 1916 the Italians had been pressing their claim to a share in the partition of Asiatic Turkey and demanding (inter alia) representation in the international régime to be set up for the Holy Places and, generally, guarantees for their interests in Palestine. For a full discussion of the subject from the Italian point of view see M. Toscano, *Gli Accordi di San Giovanni di Moriana* (Milan, 1936).

8 Copy in *Ch.W.P.*

world Jewry, or as much of it as could be reached, that a British trusteeship, or some other form of British control, would be the best guarantee for the fulfilment of Jewish aspirations in Palestine.

By popularising this idea the Zionists would be advancing British interests as well as their own. Moreover, a situation was developing in which an understanding with the Zionists might be in the interests of the Entente as a whole. In the United States a considerable section of the Jewish population was inclined to hold aloof from the American war effort or even to obstruct it. Above all, the Zionists might—it seemed—be helpful in checking the rising tide of pacifist propaganda in Russia. By the time that the Balfour Declaration was finally approved by the War Cabinet in October, these considerations had come, as we shall see, to be rated as the most cogent short-term arguments in its favour.

Statements by Zionist leaders in the spring of 1917 show that they were conscious that the situation was changing to their advantage. In a letter already quoted, Weizmann told Brandeis on April 8th that 'since the invasion of Palestine by the British Army our problem has become much more tangible and actual. I think that everybody here realises the importance of the Palestinian campaign, and the press on the whole is extremely favourable to a Jewish Palestine under a British Protectorate.' A few days earlier, Brandeis, addressing the Zionist Provisional Committee in New York, had spoken of a marked improvement in the outlook for Zionism. After mentioning a report from the Copenhagen Zionist Bureau to the effect that the Zionists stood to benefit by the Russian Revolution, he went on: 'We also have our advices from England—in fact, all the advices that have come recently have been full of hope and encouragement. . . . I think that we can feel to a degree as we have certainly never felt before that Zionism is taking its place in public consideration and it is one of the problems that the war is likely to settle for us.'[9]

By this time Weizmann could already count upon the assurances he had had from Balfour at their meeting on March 22nd. He had been encouraged by his talk with Lloyd George at the Astors' on March 13th, but this had been only an informal con-

[9] Minutes of Zionist Provisional Committee, 2 April 1917: *Brandeis papers.*

versation, and, as he had told Scott a few days later, he was anxious to see the Prime Minister again. His opportunity came on April 3rd, when he breakfasted with Lloyd George together with Scott, who had arranged for him to be invited. This was the day after the War Cabinet, having reviewed the situation on the Palestine Front in the light of the first attack on Gaza, decided that General Murray should be ordered to press forward as rapidly as possible, with the capture of Jerusalem as his objective. At breakfast the next morning, with Scott and Weizmann as his guests, Lloyd George had a good deal to say about Palestine. Scott writes in his Journal (April 3rd): ' He (Lloyd George) said that it was to him the one really interesting part of the War. Of the various possible solutions he said that he was altogether opposed to a condominium with France, to which Weizmann was no less hostile. " What about international control ?" he asked. Weizmann said that it would be a shade worse, as it would mean no control but mere confusion and intrigue. " What about joint control with the Americans ?" Weizmann said he could accept that. The two countries would pull together. " Yes," said Lloyd George, " we are both thoroughly materialistic peoples "—a remark, as I suggested, obviously dictated by the conscious superiority of the Kelt. . . .' The conversation passed to the question of the use to be made of a group of ex-members of the Zion Mule Corps[10]—mainly Jewish refugees from Palestine—who, after serving at Gallipoli, had enlisted in a Territorial Battalion in England and were still in training at Winchester, despite their entreaties to be sent to the Palestine Front. When told of this, ' George was furious and said they [were] the very men wanted where local knowledge was invaluable. . . . They would be precious, too, for " spying out the land," as in Joshua's day.'

On April 4th Weizmann wrote to Sokolow[11]: ' . . . I had the opportunity of seeing Lloyd George yesterday and he was very emphatic on the point of British Palestine. . . .' Writing to Brandeis a few days later, Weizmann, having spoken about his interview with Balfour on March 22nd, went on: ' We may also reckon on the full sympathies of the Prime Minister, with whom

[10] See below, p. 488.
[11] Z.A.

I had the honour of discussing the question on April 3rd.'[12] The whole tenour of the conversation, as recorded by Scott, implied that Lloyd George's support could be taken for granted, but in this informal table-talk there was nothing amounting to a positive commitment on his part as head of the Government. Weizmann was not, however, exaggerating when he said that 'we may reckon on the full sympathies of the Prime Minister.' On the afternoon of the same day, April 3rd, Lloyd George and Curzon saw Mark Sykes on the eve of his departure for the East to join the Egyptian Expeditionary Force as political adviser to the Commander-in-Chief. Three points were impressed upon him. First, every effort was to be made to secure the addition of Palestine to the British area. Secondly, no pledges should be given to the Arabs concerning Palestine. Thirdly, it was considered important that nothing should be done to prejudice the Zionist Movement and the possibility of its development under British auspices.[13]

The next day, April 4th, Weizmann and Scott called on Sykes and found him anxious that Weizmann should follow him out to the East. Scott writes in his Journal: 'Sykes . . . was very pressing for Weizmann to follow in a week or ten days. George had practically consented and Balfour was to be at once consulted. Thought Weizmann could be of great service as soon as Gaza was captured and the road thus opened for an advance to Jerusalem.' The same interview (or, possibly, another interview with Sykes on the same day) is mentioned by Weizmann in a letter of April 4th to Sokolow, then in Paris on a mission of which more will be said later: 'I have had a talk with Sir Mark with regard to a declaration to be issued in Palestine when the time arrives. He is fully agreeable, of course. . . . Please don't forget to talk the question of [the] declaration over with Sir Mark and try to come to some definite conclusion.'[14]

In the same letter Weizmann tells Sokolow that 'here last week practically every paper wrote about Jewish Palestine under British protectorate. . . . There can be no doubt that the feeling here is very strong and of course much more concrete than it was a

[12] 8 April 1917: *Ch.W.P.*
[13] *Sledm.*, No. 41.
[14] Z.A.

fortnight ago.' On April 7th a writer in *Palestine* observed that
'just as the British press sees that Palestine must be British, it
sees that to be British it must be Jewish.' In this connection,
Palestine, after quoting various other newspapers, drew attention
to two articles in the *Daily Chronicle* (an organ closely associated with Lloyd George)[15]—one of them a leader declaring that
'the project for constituting a Zionist State under British protection has much to commend it,'[16] and the other an article by the
paper's Military Correspondent, who asked 'What should we
do with Palestine?" and answered: 'There can be little doubt
that we should revive the Jewish Palestine of old and allow the
Jews to realise their dream of Zion in their homeland. . . .'[17]

15 This point is not mentioned in *Palestine*.
16 The *Daily Chronicle*, 30 March 1917.
17 Ibid. The author is indebted to the Librarian of the *News Chronicle* for
his help in tracing this article. Through the misguided zeal of the Publicity Department of the Zionist Provisional Committee in New York, a
passage, including the sentence quoted above, from an article by the
Military Correspondent of the *Daily Chronicle* was circulated to the
American press as 'an extract from a proclamation issued by General Sir
Archibald Murray': see 'Zionism Conquers Public Opinion' (New York,
1917), p. 7. There was, it need hardly be said, no such proclamation. This
is confirmed, if confirmation is needed, in a letter to the author from the
War Office (21 September 1954). Equally fictitious is 'a plan for the
establishment of a Jewish national home in Palestine,' said by J. de Haas
(*Louis Dembitz Brandeis*, p. 89) to be contained in 'a statement by the
British War Department in April 1917.' The 'plan' is, in fact, merely a
set of proposals formulated by the Zionists themselves. The War Office
letter mentioned above confirms that there was no such 'statement by
the British War Department.'

CHAPTER 26

THE PLAN OF CAMPAIGN

THE PLAN OF campaign now began to take shape. Weizmann was to join Sykes in Egypt and go on with him to Palestine when the time was ripe. Sokolow was to see what he could do to create a more favourable atmosphere in Paris, where the Government had been disinclined to take the Zionists seriously and the leading Jews were for the most part openly hostile. Sokolow's mission was in the end to take him to Rome as well as Paris, but this was not originally planned or foreseen. An organised effort was to be made to secure the support of the American and Russian Zionists, and, if possible, of their Governments, for what was now to be put forward openly as the Zionist programme—the building up of a Jewish Commonwealth in Palestine under the ægis of Great Britain. Sykes, for his part, was getting ready to break it to Picot that Great Britain meant to insist on some form of British suzerainty in Palestine and that the French would have to reconcile themselves to the relinquishment of their claims.

Sykes had begun to pave the way at the end of February, when he wrote to Picot about a conversation he had had with Sokolow on February 22nd.[1] In making their plans for the future, Great Britain and France were bound, he argued, to take the Zionists into account: 'If the great force of Judaism feels that its aspirations are . . . in a fair way towards realisation, then there is hope of an ordered and developed Arabia and Middle East. On the other hand, if that force feels that its aspirations will be thwarted by circumstance[s] and are doomed to remain only a painful longing, then I see little or no prospect for our own future hopes.'

[1] Sykes to Picot, 28 February 1917: *Sledm.*, No. 50. For a reference to Sykes's description, in this letter, of his conversation with Sokolow on February 22nd see above, p. 378.

He dwelt on the strong objections from the Zionist side to any
form of dual control or condominium and begged Picot to consider whether some means could not be found of satisfying the
Zionists, while at the same time making suitable provision for
Jerusalem and the Holy Places. An international régime might be
acceptable and workable in a small Jerusalem enclave, but, as to
the rest of Palestine, some one Power must be put in charge. To
propose either British or French control would only be asking
for trouble. Belgium or Switzerland might be considered, but in
Switzerland the German element was too large, while Roman
Catholic Belgium might be unacceptable to Russia. There
remained the United States, which, said Sykes, had no strong
bias in favour either of Great Britain or of France and would be
neutral on religious and racial questions, so that United States
rule in Palestine 'would have no political or strategic *sequelæ*
that we need anticipate with apprehension.'

Sykes was, in effect, telling Picot that there could be no question of an Anglo-French condominium, or, still less, of French
control, but without, at this stage, drawing the inference that
Palestine (except for Jerusalem and the Holy Places) must fall to
Great Britain. What he was really leading up to is fairly plain. The
day after he had put to Picot the case for an American protectorate, he had a talk with Scott, who wrote in his Journal (March
1st): 'Met Sir Mark Sykes by appointment, an interesting person
and one of the best of the progressive Tories. . . . An immense
believer in the future of the Arab race. . . . Syria, on the break-up
of Turkey, might go in full possession to France and she might
exercise a protectorate over the hinterland—i.e. the upper region
of the Tigris and Euphrates, while we should exercise a protectorate over Palestine and Mesopotamia and give support to the
new Arab Kingdom, which would include the Arabian Peninsula
and extend as far north as and include Damascus. . . . As to Palestine, he was rather inclined to compromise, since France was very
insistent in pressing her claims to something like condominium.
. . . This would not do, as we must have military control over the
country, except as regards the Holy Places and, perhaps, the railway from Jaffa, which might be internationalised and policed by
the French, but he thought we might secure all we wanted if we
acted as the "mandatories" of the Powers—i.e. exercised a dele-

gated authority.[2] But he said it would make a great difference, when we came to the Peace Conference, if we were already in military possession of the country, the invasion of which we had already begun.'

It can hardly have been either a surprise or a disappointment to Sykes to find that his tentative suggestion, in his letter to Picot, of a United States protectorate had a bleak reception in Paris. On April 8th he reported to the Foreign Secretary that 'the French are most hostile to the idea of the U.S.A. being the patrons of Palestine,' explaining (among other reasons) that both the French clericals and the French concessionaires 'naturally tremble at the prospect of dollars and " go " being brought into line against their sentiment and chicane.'[3] That either Sykes or the War Cabinet was seriously contemplating the handing over of Palestine to the United States it is difficult to believe. Balfour had all along hankered after bringing the United States into the picture, and the idea of an Anglo-American combination in Palestine had been thrown out by Lloyd George in his talk with Weizmann on April 3rd. But whatever advantages might be foreseen from an Anglo-American partnership, an undivided American trusteeship would clearly be inconsistent with the military control of Palestine which, as Sykes had told Scott on March 1st, he considered to be indispensable to Great Britain ; indeed, Lloyd George himself, in giving Sykes his instructions on April 3rd, had told him that every effort was to be made to bring Palestine within the British area.[4]

Sykes left London on April 5th and, while in Paris on his way to the East, followed up his letter of February 28th by suggesting to Picot that he should break it to his Government that it would have to agree to British suzerainty in Palestine. 'I have seen Monsieur Picot,' he telegraphed to London on April 6th,[5] 'and have impressed on him importance of meeting Jewish demands

[2] A memorandum supplied to the War Cabinet by the Foreign Office just after the end of the War suggested that, while 'under the agreement with France an international administration is to be established [in Palestine],' yet 'the provisions of the agreement will be sufficiently satisfied if a tutelary Power be appointed by the Treaty of Peace': Lloyd George, *Treaties*, II, 1151.
[3] *Sledm.*, No. 49.
[4] See above, p. 384.
[5] *Sledm.*, No. 42.

and expressed my opinion strongly that it would be advantageous to prepare French mind for idea of British suzerainty in Palestine by international consent. I pointed out to him that our pre-ponderant military effort, rights of trans-Palestine railway con-struction,[6] rights of annexation at Haifa, coupled with the general bias of Zionism in favour of British suzerainty, tended to make such a solution the only stable one.' He added that Picot had shown himself personally less hostile to this idea than might have been expected but had pointed out that it would be impossible to prepare the ground for its acceptance unless and until the French public, which imagined Palestine to be the greater part of Syria, could see evidence of favourable developments in Syria proper.

Picot seems to have been more severely shaken than Sykes had realised. He had been designated as French High Commissioner for Occupied Territories in Palestine and Syria and was on the point of leaving for the East, where he and Sykes were to double the rôles of colleagues and competitors, as they had done during the tripartite discussions in Petrograd in the spring of 1916. In the elaborate instructions given to Picot on April 2nd by the French Prime Minister, Ribot,[7] he was exhorted, while co-operat-ing with the British, to be constantly mindful of French interests and French prestige, remembering the special position tradition-ally occupied by France throughout the East, and especially in Palestine. Five days later, having by then had his interview with Sykes, Picot saw President Poincaré and gloomily reported his misgivings about British intentions. 'He [Picot] is convinced,' Poincaré wrote in his diary (April 7th), 'that in London our agreements are now considered null and void. British troops will enter Syria from the south and disperse our supporters.'[8]

When Sykes left London for the East at the beginning of April 1917, he expected Weizmann to join him shortly in Egypt and, in due course, to go on with him to Palestine. It was not

6 Sykes-Picot Agreement, paragraph 7.

7 Adamov, No. 282.

8 'Il [Picot] a la conviction que dès maintenant à Londres on considère nos accords comme caduces. Les troupes anglaises entreront en Syrie par le Sud et disperseront nos partisans': Poincaré, IX, 109.

until the middle of May that Weizmann finally decided that the time was not ripe and that he would do better to stay in London.

The suggestion that he should accompany Sykes to Palestine was first put forward by Weizmann himself in his letter of March 20th to Scott. He was then under the impression that the fall of Gaza was imminent and would be followed by a rapid advance on Jerusalem. Sykes had welcomed the proposal and on the eve of his departure was, as Scott noted in a passage already quoted from his Journal (April 4th), 'very pressing for Weizmann to follow him in a week or ten days.' On April 9th Weizmann received a telegram from Sokolow, who had seen Sykes in Paris, asking him to be ready to go to Egypt when Sykes gave the word.[9] Sykes arrived in Egypt on April 23rd and on the 28th telegraphed to the Foreign Office that Weizmann's presence was indispensable.[10] On May 5th he sent a further telegram to the effect that, unless all idea of a further advance in Palestine had been abandoned (in which case Weizmann should be advised to drop his propaganda), he should come out as soon as possible. 'I propose,' he continued, 'to use Weizmann to organise Zionist situation in Egypt, easing the Judæa-Arab [sic] situation by promoting good feeling and co-operation, assisting in the organisation of local Zionists, and improving such of our intelligence service as depends on Jewish information and making plans for political action against our advance.'[11]

But by this time Weizmann was beginning to have second thoughts. In the first place, Murray's second attack on Gaza had failed and there was no longer any likelihood of a rapid British advance. Writing to Weizmann on April 25th, Scott strongly advised him not to be in a hurry: 'You can do nothing till the army gets to Jaffa and very little then—how many months will that take? If it reaches Jerusalem (which it never may) by the end of [the] summer it will be lucky.'[12]

But the check to the Palestine campaign was not Weizmann's

---

[9] Text in letter of 9 April 1917 from Weizmann to Lord Rothschild: Ch.W.P.

[10] Sledm., No. 42. On May 1st Sir R. Graham wrote to Weizmann: '[Aaronsohn] advises and Sir M. Sykes agrees that your presence in Egypt is now essential': Ch.W.P.

[11] Sledm., No. 42.

[12] Ch.W.P.

only reason for hesitating. Since Sykes' departure he had for the first time become aware of the extent to which the British Government had tied its hands in the matter of Palestine by its engagements to the French. His letter of March 20th to Scott shows that he was then under the impression that there were as yet no binding British commitments and that the whole matter 'may easily adjust itself . . . if the British assert their claims.' A month later his eyes were opened by a letter from Scott, who wrote (April 16th)[13] : 'I ought to tell you that I met the Vicomte de Caix, the Foreign Editor and leader-writer of the *Débats* (who is obviously in close touch with the French Government), the other night and he assured me that it had been "settled" that France was to have not only northern Syria but Palestine down to a line from St. Jean d'Acre to Lake Tiberias and including the Hauran, and that the rest of Palestine was to be "internationalised."' Weizmann went to the Foreign Office and, in the light of what he now had good reason to suspect, told Sir Ronald Graham that there could be no question of his joining Sykes in Egypt without a clear mandate to rally Jewish opinion in support of British suzerainty in an undivided Palestine.[14] This was on April 24th. The next day Weizmann saw Robert Cecil, then in charge of the Foreign Office during Balfour's absence in the United States.[15] He began by explaining why Jews all over the world strongly desired that Great Britain and no other Power should have control of Palestine, giving much the same reasons as those given by Sokolow in his conversation with Picot early in February. Having stated the Jewish case against any type of condominium or internationalisation, he was asked by Cecil what would be the objection to purely French control. To this he replied that the French would not leave the Jews to develop their

13 *Ch.W.P.*

14 Mrs. Weizmann's diary, 24 April 1917: *V.W.P.*

15 The account of this interview which follows is taken from Weizmann's full note of the conversation, copies of which are in *Ch.W.P.* and *Z.A.* The day after the interview, Weizmann wrote to Scott: 'After this conversation [with Lord Robert Cecil] I saw Sir Ronald Graham and told him all that had passed and suggested that this interview should be written out and placed on record at the Foreign Office. He agreed with that course and I am at present writing out the interview practically on the lines of this letter ; I will send you a copy when it has been lodged at the Foreign Office': *Ch.W.P.*

own way of life but would try to impose ' l'esprit français '; that a French administration would lean on elements (obviously meaning the Catholic clergy and the Christian Arabs) which were unfriendly to the Jews; and, lastly, that the Jewish world as a whole had not the same confidence in France as it had in Great Britain.

Weizmann then turned to the proposed mutilation of Palestine by arrangements which would incorporate the northern Jewish colonies in the French zone in Syria and would condemn the rest of the country to all the disadvantages of an international régime. All this led up to what he had to say about his journey to the East. His note of the interview ends as follows: ' He would go on the clear understanding that he is to work for a Jewish Palestine under a British protectorate. Lord Robert agreed to this view; he mentioned that, of course, there are considerable difficulties in the way, but it would strengthen the position very considerably if the Jews of the world would express themselves in favour of a British protectorate. Dr. Weizmann replied that this is exactly the task which he would like to undertake, to bring about such an expression of opinion, and it is for that purpose that he would go to Palestine.'[16]

Weizmann was soon to have fresh cause for misgivings. Almost immediately after his interview with Cecil on April 25th the Italian press began to comment on the results, as it interpreted them, of the Inter-Allied Conference at St. Jean de Maurienne.[17] On April 27th the *Corriere della Sera,* in an article on ' The Inter-Allied Agreement concerning the Ottoman Empire,' welcomed the decision that French and Italian troops should take part in the Palestine campaign, describing this as an appropriate prelude to the setting up of an international régime for the Holy Places and northern [*sic*] Palestine.[18] It looked as though the Sykes-Picot arrangements concerning the Brown Area, far from being called in question, were being reaffirmed. *Palestine* made the article in

16 So far as Cecil's remarks are concerned, the last paragraph of Weizmann's note, as quoted above, is confirmed by a note, dated 8 May 1917, from Ormsby-Gore to Sykes: *Sledm.,* No. 47.

17 An Anglo-Franco-Italian conference, held at St. Jean de Maurienne (Savoy) on 19 April 1917, considered (among other matters) Italian claims on Turkey: see *B.F.P.,* pp. 638-639: Lloyd George, *Treaties,* II, 773ff.; Toscano, *Gli Accordi di San Giovanni di Moriana,* pp. 264ff.

18 Quoted, Toscano, op. cit., p. 291.

the *Corriere* the text for what amounted to a frontal attack on the Sykes-Picot Agreement.[19] There was no express reference to an Anglo-French understanding, but under the headings 'No Partition'—'No Condominium' *Palestine* expressed its views in language clearly suggesting some inside knowledge of the substance of the arrangements between the two Powers. This outburst was neither inspired nor approved by Weizmann ; on the contrary, he expressed his displeasure at what he regarded as a serious indiscretion.[20] The fact remained that, on top of what he had learnt from Scott about de Caix's disclosures, there was now a further indication that the Sykes-Picot plan still held the field.

Cecil had suggested, in effect, that if the Jews were strongly to express their preference for Great Britain as the protecting Power in Palestine, this might help in some measure to get the Sykes-Picot Agreement out of the way. The hint, as we shall see later, was followed up, but in spite of Cecil's encouragement Weizmann decided, in the end, not to go to Egypt. Though on April 28th, the Foreign Office telegraphed to Sykes that Weizmann would be leaving on May 11th, he changed his plans and stayed in London. He had been told by Cecil that he could work for a Jewish Palestine under British protection, but he now knew that Great Britain's hands were not free and that there was no certainty that the Sykes-Picot plan would or could be set aside. On April 24th Scott had warned him against going on a fool's errand.[21] A few days later Scott wrote in his Journal (April 30th): ' Saw Weizmann, who, in view of check to our advance in Palestine and the complete uncertainty as to British policy in relation to it, had finally decided to postpone his departure, as I strongly advised him.' The postponement was indefinite and nothing more was heard of the project. On May 19th Sykes suggested to the Foreign Office that Weizmann should be asked to appoint Aaronsohn to act in his place.[22] Aaronsohn did not stand high in Weizmann's favour and no such appointment was made, but until he left for London in the autumn of 1917 Aaronsohn was, in practice, treated by the British authorities in Cairo as their principal Jewish adviser.

[19] *Palestine*, 5 May 1917.
[20] Sacher to L. Simon, 9 May 1917: *Sacher letters.*
[21] *Ch.W.P.*
[22] *Sledm.*, No. 42.

CHAPTER 27

SOKOLOW IN PARIS AND ROME

AT THE CONFERENCE of 7 February 1917 Sykes had proposed that the Zionists should see what they could do to induce the French to give way on the question of British suzerainty in Palestine. At his interviews with Picot immediately after the conference Sokolow had done his best, but with no marked success. On 30 March 1917 he wrote to Herbert Samuel: 'I have the honour to inform you that the negotiations with Sir Mark, being very favourable as far as British views and interests are concerned, made it again clear that further pourparlers with M. Picot on behalf of the French Government are necessary. In accordance with an understanding between Sir Mark and M. Picot, I am leaving to-morrow evening for Paris, where I am to meet M. Picot[1] and others.'[2] Sykes had arranged to leave for Paris, on his way to the East, a few days later, so that Sokolow could count upon being able to consult him, should his further guidance be needed.

Sokolow had been provided with an unwanted escort in the person of James Malcolm. This may possibly have had something to do with Sykes's favourite idea of an Arab-Jewish-Armenian *entente*. He may have wanted to create the impression that the Zionist and Armenian causes were somehow linked together.[3] He may also have thought that, as a member of the Armenian National Delegation, which had its headquarters in Paris, Malcolm might have some useful contacts. Malcolm's company

---

[1] Picot had returned to Paris, where he was preparing for his departure for the East. He left Paris for Egypt and Palestine on April 11th.

[2] Copy in *N.S.P.*

[3] In his letter to Weizmann (20 April 1917), an extract from which is quoted below, Sokolow writes: 'You are, of course, acquainted with Mr. M.'s idea of an *entente* between Armenians, Arabs and Jews. I regard the idea as quite fantastic. It is difficult to reach an understanding with the Arabs, but we will have to try. There are no conflicts between Jews and Armenians because there are no common interests whatever.'

had not been sought by Sokolow, who wrote to Weizmann (April 20th)[4]:

'I wish to let you know what I think of [Malcolm]. . . . I must say I did not like to have a stranger in the centre of our work. But, as you know, he was thrown upon us. The chief[5] thought that he had connections here and demanded his participation. . . . There is no reason to expect any trouble from him ; he may even be useful in some way. He is a business man of the "brasseur des affaires" type, with a vivid imagination, an ardent Armenian patriot. He has great sympathy for Zionism (not for the Jews in general), is endowed with an esprit of a goyish kind, is very adroit and somewhat conceited. Our chief had an exaggerated idea of his connection with Government circles here. I am sure I would have achieved what I did without him, but I must say he worked well and behaved tactfully. I did not take him to the chiefs here nor to the Old Man. . . .[6] It is possible that he hoped to do some big business in the future or believes that the Jewish *haute finance* will help the Armenians. In any case, he is now sincerely devoted to our cause, and as both chiefs[7] sponsor him, I had to inform him about all " official " matters and keep him *au courant* of my strictly official work, but I would not initiate him into any confidential things in London. . . . We had to accept his co-operation, but I would not like to have him *à la longue* in the centre of our activities.'

Malcolm parted company with Sokolow towards the end of April,[8] when he returned to London and advised Weizmann that there was no possibility of excluding the French from a share in the control of Palestine. Writing to Sokolow on May 1st, Weiz-

4 Transl. from Russian: copy in *N.S.P.*

5 Presumably, Sykes.

6 Baron Edmond de Rothschild.

7 Presumably, Sykes and Picot.

8 A letter of 20 April 1917 from Malcolm to Weizmann (*Ch.W.P.*) shows that he was then back in London. He handed Weizmann a written report, but the author has not succeeded in finding a copy. After looking at the report, Scott wrote to Weizmann (April 28—*Ch.W.P.*): ' All that you have done seems to be done wisely and with a purpose. A precisely opposite description would, I fear, apply to the proceedings of Mr. Malcolm.'

mann told him that ' Malcolm frequently mentioned to me that we should have to make up our minds that a condominium will be the final result.'[9]

Had this defeatist view been accepted by the Zionists, Picot's main purpose in arranging Sokolow's visit to Paris would have been achieved. He had taken longer than Sykes to make up his mind on the Zionist question, but he was now satisfied that the Zionists were worth cultivating. If so, there was all the more reason why the British should not be left to make all the running.

Before the War, the French Government, so far as it thought about the Zionists at all, had thought of them as catspaws of Germany. This impression was not easily to be dispelled, nor did the French Jews exert themselves to correct it. Though the Zionists had a powerful friend in Edmond de Rothschild, the representative leaders of the Jewish community, and especially those associated with the influential Alliance Israélite, were, with hardly an exception, implacably opposed to Zionism and not sorry to see it discredited by its supposed links with Germany.[10] When the Syrian question came to life with the entry of Turkey into the War, the French Government had all the more reason for keeping the Zionists at a distance. Why should it interest itself in a movement so odious to the clerical elements which were working for France in the East and to her most reliable clients, the Syrian Christians ?

Not that the Zionists had no friends in France. In the early days of the War they had had some encouragement from the Socialist leader, Jules Guesde, who had joined Viviani's National Government as a Minister of State.[11] About the same time, another influential Socialist, Gustave Hervé, came out in his paper, *La Guerre Sociale*, with an emotional appeal for the restoration of the Jews to Palestine under the ægis of France.[12] Among the French intellectuals the Zionists had sympathisers of the standing of the historian, Charles Seignobos, Maurice Vernes of the Sorbonne, and the publicist and future Minister, de Monzie.

But the Ministry of Foreign Affairs was in no hurry to entangle

[9] Copy in *Ch.W.P.*
[10] See André Spire, ' Herzl's Influence in France,' in *Theodor Herzl : A Memorial*, ed. M. W. Weisgal (New York, 1929), p. 248.
[11] Weizmann to Sacher and L. Simon, 4 and 6 December 1914: *L.S.P.*
[12] *La Guerre Sociale*, 12 February 1915.

itself with the Zionists, and at the beginning its attitude was one of stony indifference. When Weizmann was in Paris at the end of 1914, he asked Jabotinsky[13] to see what he could do unofficially to sound the French Government on the Zionist question. Gustave Hervé took Jabotinsky to Delcassé, but the interview was a failure. The Foreign Minister showed no desire to discuss the subject and left Jabotinsky with the clear impression that the French Government was not interested in Zionism.[14] The ice had begun to melt a little by the end of 1915, when Briand thought it expedient to offer the Jews some vague assurances concerning Palestine in connection with Victor Basch's visit to the United States in the interests of French propaganda. A little later, the Lucien Wolf formula, mentioned by Grey in his proposals early in 1916 for a joint declaration by the Allies in favour of Jewish aspirations in Palestine, seems to have been objected to by the French on the ground that it would not satisfy a large body of Jewish opinion, or, in other words, the Zionists. This may have been merely a pretext for rejecting a suggestion which the French disliked on other grounds, but about this time the Zionist question was beginning to interest them more seriously as a result of Picot's education in the subject by Sykes, followed by his talks with Gaster. According to his own account, Picot was particularly impressed by his subsequent conversations with Sokolow and by the spring of 1917 he was fully convinced that the Zionists must be taken into account in the shaping of French policy in the East.[15] A reflection of his views can be seen in the instructions issued to him on April 2nd for his guidance as French High Commissioner-designate for Occupied Territories in Palestine and Syria. In the passage dealing with Palestine he was enjoined (among other duties) to be particularly careful to show a benevolent interest in the Jewish colonies and their future, remembering always how closely his attitude would be watched throughout the Jewish world.[16] In the course of his talks with Sokolow in February Picot had pointedly reminded him that, however strong might be the Zionist preference for Great Britain, the future of Palestine was, after all, a matter for the Entente. For Picot and his Government

[13] See below, p. 486.
[14] V. Jabotinsky, *Die Jüdische Legion im Weltkrieg* (Berlin, 1930), p. 37.
[15] Lecture in Paris, reported in *La Terre Retrouvée*, 1 April 1939.
[16] Adamov, No. 282.

the real significance of Sokolow's visit to Paris was that it could be used to drive this home.

Earlier in the War both the Russian and the American Zionists had pressed Sokolow to visit France, but he had firmly declined. Realising how delicately he would have to walk in Paris, he had had no taste for so embarrassing a mission and had excused himself from undertaking it.[17] But Sykes's plans required that he should accept the French invitation, and there was no holding back. 'There is no need,' he reminded Weizmann,[18] 'to tell you why I had to go to Paris. You know it as well as I do.' Weizmann had made it clear that he was uncomfortable about Sokolow's activities in Paris. He suspected that the French wanted to entice the Zionists into direct negotiations with themselves over the heads of the British, thus diverting them from their pro-British orientation and strengthening the case for an Anglo-French condominium.[19] This was not the first time that he had expressed such misgivings, nor was he alone in entertaining them; they were shared by Scott, Sidebotham and Sacher.[20]

But when Sykes joined with Picot in encouraging Sokolow to go to Paris, he knew what he was doing. He genuinely believed that the Entente as a whole stood to gain by convincing the Zionists that the Allied cause was their own. Up to this point he and Picot had a common purpose, but each had an ulterior motive. Just as Picot hoped to detach the Zionists from their exclusive reliance on Great Britain, so Sykes, for his part, thought that any expression of sympathy with Zionist aspirations which might be extracted by Sokolow from the French would, in the long run, serve to strengthen the British claim to Palestine. France would then have recognised that the future of Palestine was a matter on which the Zionists were entitled to be heard, and the Zionists could be relied upon to be immovable in their preference for Great Britain as the protecting Power. Telegraphing to the Foreign Office, almost immediately after his arrival in Paris, early in April 1917, on Sokolow's negotiations with the French, he said that 'Sokolow is of the opinion [that] [the] admission by France of [the] principle of [the] recognition of Jewish nationality in

17 Sokolow to Weizmann, 12 May 1917: *Ch.W.P.*
18 Ibid.
19 Weizmann to Sokolow, 1 May 1917: copy in *Ch.W.P.*
20 Sacher to L. Simon, 13 April 1917: Sacher letters.

Palestine will be a step in advance, and I agree.'[21] Writing privately the next day to a colleague in London, Sykes remarked that ' if the French accept the Zionist desiderata, a great step has been gained. . . . The element of Zionism is recognised and consequently a say in the matter is automatically accorded the Zionists.' He goes on to enumerate the favourable factors in the situation, beginning with ' British occupation of Palestine as a *fait accompli* ' and ending with ' French recognition of Jewish national aspirations '.[22]

In his opening conversations with Sokolow Picot's tactics were to put the French claims at their highest, while at the same time assuring Sokolow that France could be relied upon to take a favourable view of the Zionist proposals. Three days after his arrival in Paris, Sokolow reported to Weizmann that Picot had told him that, except for the idea of a Chartered Company, he regarded the Zionist programme as acceptable and would advise his Government to approve it. He had insisted, however, that France claimed Palestine for herself and would not hear of a combination with Great Britain or, still worse, with the United States.[23]

A day or two later, Sykes made it clear to Picot that the British claim to Palestine would be pressed,[24] and when Sokolow was received at the Quai d'Orsay on April 9th, the question of suzerainty was glided over.[25] The importance attached to the occasion is shown by the high rank of the French officials present ; they included, in addition to Picot, Jules Cambon, the Secretary-General of the Ministry of Foreign Affairs, and the Minister's Chef de Cabinet, de Margerie.[26]

Sokolow told Weizmann that the French representatives ' gave

[21] *Sledm.*, No. 42 (6 April 1917).

[22] *Sledm.*, No. 49 (7 April, 1917).

[23] Sokolow to Weizmann, 4 April 1917: copy in *N.S.P.*

[24] See above, p. 389.

[25] ' I understand that at the interview question of foreign suzerain Power in Palestine was avoided ': Sykes to F.O., 9 April 1917: *Sledm.*, No. 42.

[26] So reported by Alliance Israélite to Conjoint Foreign Committee, C.F.C. 1917/458. The A.I. would almost certainly have been well informed. The date, April 9th, is fixed by a telegram from Sykes to the Foreign Office (*Sledm.*, No. 42).

me most encouraging promises. I was told that they accept in principle the recognition of Jewish nationality in terms of a national home, local autonomy, etc.'[27] Exactly what assurances were given to Sokolow is uncertain, but the impression that it was desired to make is shown by the messages telegraphed, in Sokolow's name, through French official channels, to Brandeis and Tschlenow: 'After favourable results in London and Paris was received with goodwill by Ministry here. Have full confidence Allied victory will realise our Palestine Zionist aspirations.'[28] The words 'and Paris' were not in Sokolow's original draft and were inserted at the request of the French officials.[29] Their significance did not escape Weizmann, who was seriously disturbed by their implications. On April 28th he telegraphed to Sokolow, through Foreign Office channels, as follows[30]:

> 'Your work in France may be interpreted as negotiations on behalf of our Movement in favour of a French alternative. Such an impression is not admissible. You only went on the suggestion of Sir Mark Sykes to explain Zionist Movement *à titre d'information*. I shall only go to Egypt with distinct programme to support Jewish Palestine under British protectorate. . . .'

Writing to Sokolow on May 1st,[31] Weizmann pointed out that 'the impression conveyed to Washington and Moscow by these telegrams was that you are equally satisfied with the success in London and Paris and you consider the success in both places of

[27] Sokolow to Weizmann, 19 April 1917: copy in *N.S.P.* The ten days' interval is surprising, but no earlier reference by Sokolow to his reception at the Quai d'Orsay has come to light.

[28] Text given in Sykes' telegram to F.O. of 9 April 1917: *Sledm.*, No. 42.

[29] Sokolow to Weizmann, 12 May 1917: 'It is true that the additional words " and Paris " (" after the favourable results in London and Paris," etc.) have been suggested by the French Government, and you are quite right in saying that I could but accept it. . . .': *Ch.W.P.*

[30] Copy (undated) in *Ch.W.P.* marked: 'The following confidential telegram has been received from the Foreign Office.' The date, April 28th, is fixed by a reference to this message in Weizmann's letter to Sokolow of May 1st (*Ch.W.P.*): 'You are no doubt in possession of all my telegrams and especially of the message which I conveyed to you on Saturday last through the kindness of the Foreign Office.' ('Saturday last' would be April 28th.)

[31] Copy in *Ch.W.P.*

equal value. Whereas I am perfectly convinced that you may have put in the word " Paris " out of politeness—in fact, you were not in a position to refuse it—in Washington and Moscow they may think that you, as a representative of the Zionist Organisation, consider it possible to advocate a French protectorate or a joint Anglo-French control.'

Sykes, on the other hand, was not at all disturbed by the outcome of Sokolow's visit to the Quai d'Orsay; on the contrary, he was highly pleased. He had told the Foreign Office the day before that ' as regards Zionism . . . the French are beginning to realise that they are up against a big thing and cannot close their eyes to it. . . . At present it would be dangerous to moot the idea of a British Palestine,[32] but if the French agree to recognise Jewish Nationalism and all that [it] carries with it as a Palestinian political factor, I think that it will prove a step in the right direction and will tend to pave the way to Great Britain being appointed Patron of Palestine, that is, of the Brown Zone minus Jerusalem and Bethlehem and a small enclave, by the whole of the Entente Powers.'[33]

Sokolow has described how eagerly Sykes waited to hear what had happened at his interview with Cambon and de Margerie. ' We arranged,' he writes,[34] ' for him [Sykes] to wait for me at my hôtel. But as I was crossing the Quai d'Orsay on my return from the Foreign Office I came across Sykes. He had not had the patience to wait. . . . I gave him an outline of the proceedings. This did not satisfy him. . . . I had to give him full notes and he drew up a minute report. " That's a good day's work," he said, with shining eyes.'

Sykes immediately telegraphed a short report to London, incorporating the text of Sokolow's messages sent through French official channels to Brandeis and Tschlenow.[35] He followed this up with a letter in which he commented: ' The situation now is, therefore, that the Zionist aspirations are recognised as legitimate

32 Yet Sykes's letter of April 6th to the F.O. (*Sledm.*, No. 49— see above, p. 388) shows that by that date he had already mooted the idea in conversation with Picot.

33 *Sledm.*, No. 49 (8 April 1917).

34 *History of Zionism*, II, xxx.

35 *Sledm.*, No. 42 (9 April 1917).

by the French. . . . M. Sokolow assures me that the bulk of the Zionists desire British suzerainty only, but naturally the moment is not ripe for such a proposal at present, but provided things go well, the situation should be more favourable to British suzerainty with a recognised Jewish voice in favour of it.'[36]

Sokolow had known from the start that he could expect little help from the French Jews and would be fortunate if he did not have to contend with their active opposition. Zionism had not struck root in France, and though there was on paper a French Zionist Federation, it had only a shadowy existence. Both in England and the United States the Zionists were drawn mainly from the Jews who had flooded in from Eastern Europe. In France a much larger proportion of the 100,000 Jews were native-born, and the East European element was of nothing like the same importance. Conditioned to assimilation, and all the more sensitive about their status as Frenchmen because they were still living under the shadow of the Dreyfus affaire, the accredited representatives of French Jewry—the group corresponding roughly to the Conjoint Foreign Committee—were even more nervous about the Zionist heresy than were their counterparts in England. Emotional hostility to Zionism was particularly marked among the leading figures in the Alliance Israélite, which, as a spearhead of French culture in the East, was well known and favourably regarded in official circles.

There was one outstanding exception. Just as in England certain members of the Rothschild family had identified themselves with Zionism, so in France the Zionists could count upon the whole-hearted support of Baron Edmond. Realising from the start, as Sokolow did, that the Alliance might be a dangerous enemy, the Baron did what he could to strengthen Sokolow's hands. In a letter to Tschlenow (22 August 1917),[37] Sokolow recalls how, at a meeting at Baron Edmond's house, he had given battle to the anti-Zionists and congratulates himself on having more than held his own. It is clear that in the end there was some slackening of the tension between the Zionists and the Alliance.

[36] *Sledm.*, No. 49 (9 April 1917).
[37] Copy in Z.A.

This may have been due in part to the direct influence of Baron Edmond, but in the letter to Tschlenow already mentioned Sokolow remarks that the main reason why his Jewish adversaries had been at least temporarily disarmed was that the Zionists could count upon support in official quarters. Exactly what passed between the Government and the Alliance remains uncertain.[38] What we know is that both Baron Edmond and two of the Alliance leaders were kept informed about Sokolow's conversations with French officials,[39] and that on April 12th, three days after his meeting with Cambon and de Margerie, he was invited to a conference at the offices of the Alliance.[40]

Addressing a select group of members of that body on April 14th, Sokolow expounded the Zionist proposals,[41] taking special pains to explain what was meant by the recognition of a Jewish nationality in Palestine. The Zionists, he is reported to have said, did not desire to set up a State ; the Jews would form a nation in Palestine, but would be subjects of the protecting Power—Great Britain or France. The British Government had accepted the main features of the Zionist programme. Sir Mark Sykes, Sokolow went on, had put him in touch with M. Picot, who took the view that, should Palestine come within the French sphere of interest, the French Government would likewise be prepared to give the Zionists what they asked for, except as regards the proposed Chartered Company. He had received assurances to a similar effect from high officials of the Ministry of Foreign Affairs, who had authorised him to telegraph to Brandeis and to the Jewish leaders in Russia informing them that the French Government was favourably disposed. It will be noticed that Sokolow, who must have been acutely aware of the embarrassing position in which he found himself, was careful to leave it an open question whether the protecting Power would be Great Britain or France.

[38] The records of the Alliance Israélite were destroyed during the German occupation of Paris in the Second World War.
[39] Bigart (Secretary of the A.I.) to Lucien Wolf, 16 April 1917: *C.F.C.* 1917/454.
[40] Bigart to Sokolow, 12 April 1917: Z.A.
[41] The account of the meeting which follows is taken from a résumé of the proceedings received by the Conjoint Foreign Committee from the A.I. (Bigart to Wolf, 16 April 1917): *C.F.C.* 1917/455ff.

Two points not yet mentioned were raised by Cambon and de Margerie at their meeting with Sokolow on April 9th. In passing on to the Foreign Office what Sokolow had told him about the interview, Sykes reported[42] that the French had ' pressed the importance of Jewish interests in Russia being thrown into the scale against [the] Pacifists.' This, so far as is known, was the first suggestion that the Zionists might be useful instruments for that purpose. Sykes also reported that Sokolow would be visiting Italy, where the French thought that there was some useful work for him to do ' towards [the] consolidation of [the] Entente.' This was the origin of Sokolow's visit to Rome, which, as it turned out, was to bring him into contact, not only, as originally planned, with the Italian Government, but also with the Holy See.

The motives of the Quai d'Orsay in encouraging Sokolow to visit Italy can easily be surmised. Italian claims in the Eastern Mediterranean were now being strongly pressed, and Italy was insisting (among other things) on her right to send a military contingent to Palestine. ' Consolidation of the Entente' may be interpreted as a euphemism for the natural desire of the French to discover how Zionism was regarded by their Italian would-be rivals. A direct enquiry would imply an admission that Italy had a right to be consulted; soundings by Sokolow would avoid this embarrassment. If, without having made sure of the Italian attitude, the French were to come out openly in favour of Zionism, the Italians might possibly take advantage of the situation to pose as the protectors of Catholic interests against the Jewish peril. If, on the other hand, the Zionists received encouragement in Rome, this risk could be discounted and the French would have all the more reason for not being backward in bidding for Jewish goodwill.

Sykes, as we have seen, had taken the view that if a declaration of sympathy with Zionist aspirations could be extracted from the French, this would in the long run strengthen the British claim to suzerainty in Palestine. The same applied, in a minor degree, to the Italians. Immediately after Sokolow's interview with the French Foreign Office officials, Sykes reported to London that Sokolow ' is going to Italy to try and get the Italians to concur

[42] *Sledm.*, No. 42 (9 April 1917).

in Zionist aspirations, which would be advantageous to us,' and asked that the Italian Embassy should be requested to pave the way for him.[43]

But Sykes was looking beyond the Italian Government to the Vatican. After leaving Paris, his next stop on his way to the East was Rome, where on April 11th he saw Monsignor Pacelli[44] and on the 13th was received in audience by the Pope. He reported to the Foreign Office that Monsignor Pacelli 'let it be easy to see that the idea of British patronage of the Holy Places was not distasteful to Vatican policy. The French, I could see, did not strike him as ideal in any way. . . .' This was one point gained, but Sykes went further: 'I also,' he wrote, 'prepared the ground for Zionism by explaining what the purpose and ideals of the Zionists were and suggested that he [Monsignor Pacelli] should see M. Sokolow. . . . He was most interested and expressed a wish to see Sokolow. . . .'[45]

Before his departure from Paris, Sykes had told Sokolow that he would leave instructions for him in Rome, and on arriving there about April 23rd Sokolow found a letter from Sykes, dated April 14th, waiting for him at the British Embassy. Sykes wrote that he had spoken about Zionism both to Monsignor Pacelli and to the Pope and had pointed out to them that 'Zionist aims in no way clashed with Christian in general and Catholic desiderata in particular in regard to the Holy Places.' He advised Sokolow to call on Monsignor Pacelli and 'if you see fit, have an audience with His Holiness,' adding that the British representative at the Vatican, Count de Salis, would make the necessary arrangements.[46]

Sokolow was taken completely by surprise. 'The French Government,' he wrote to Weizmann (May 12th),[47] 'wished me to go to Italy and obviously I had to do it, the more so that this was also Sir Mark's opinion. . . . I arrived for the definite purpose of getting the most reliable information about the attitude and the intentions of the Italian Government with regard to Palestine and Zionism. . . . A new element entered my programme: the

[43] *Sledm.*, No. 49 (9 April 1917).
[44] Later, Pope Pius XII.
[45] *Sledm.*, No. 49 (15 April 1917).
[46] Orig. in *N.S.P.*
[47] *Ch.W.P.*

Vatican. It never crossed my mind before that I should approach the Vatican. . . .' He then refers to the letter left for him in Rome by Sykes and goes on: 'I was rather perplexed at this engagement. It was more than enough for me to inform myself about the Italian Government, but I was not prepared for the Vatican pourparlers . . . but I had no choice. . . . I had before me a *fait accompli*. . . .'

Not without misgivings, Sokolow braced himself to his task. Almost immediately after his arrival in Rome arrangements were made for him to be received at the Vatican, and on April 29th he had an interview with Monsignor Pacelli.[48] Pacelli let Sokolow do most of the talking but took the lead when it came to the question of the Holy Places, insisting that these would have to be clearly defined to the satisfaction of the Holy See, and hinting that the Zionists would be required to keep clear of an area extending well beyond the Holy Places themselves. Sokolow's comment on the conversation was that 'in spite of the extraordinary courtesy shown . . . the interview was somewhat strenuous.' So was his interview two days later with the Papal Secretary of State, Cardinal Gasparri,[49] who, like Monsignor Pacelli, dwelt on the question of the Holy Places and developed this theme to a point at which, Sokolow remarks, 'I felt a chill in my bones.' The Church, it appeared, would claim for the reserved area, not only Jerusalem and Bethlehem, but Nazareth and its surroundings, Tiberias and even Jericho. All the same, the Cardinal was by no means unfriendly. Reminding Sokolow that Catholics had likewise had much to endure under the Czarist régime, he spoke sympathetically about the sufferings of the Jews in Russia. He mentioned a memorandum submitted in 1916 to the Holy See by the American Jewish Committee and said that the Pope's reply had shown how strongly the Church condemned the persecution of the Jews. As to Zionism, Gasparri, having made his sweeping reservations about the Holy Places, went on to assure Sokolow that, subject to its being satisfied on

[48] The interview is described in a letter of the same date from Sokolow to Weizmann: copy in possession of Mr. Florian Sokolow, a copy of whose English translation of the original Russian is in *N.S.P.* The same applies to the document mentioned in Note 49.

[49] Described in a memorandum by Sokolow dated the day of the interview, May 1st: *N.S.P.* (orig. in Russian)—see Note 48.

this point, the Holy See wished the Zionists well in their attempt to build a Jewish State.[50] Sokolow's note continues:

'I did not wish this premature superlative to pass without comment. "We do not plan to create a State but only an autonomous home." To this he replied: "Do not worry. I only used that as a figure of speech. Call it what you will. I assure you that from the Church you will have no opposition. On the contrary, you may count on our sympathy. We shall be glad to see the land [sic] of Israel."'

In his note of the conversation Sokolow remarks that Gasparri gave the impression of preferring Great Britain to France.

On May 4th Sokolow was received in private audience by Pope Benedict XV.[51] Thirteen years before, Herzl had been received by Pius X, but had gone away discouraged. He was told, says his biographer, that the Church could not support the return of the infidel Jews to the Holy Land.[52] But times had changed. Zionism had now engaged the benevolent interest of a Great Power—the Power whose armies were challenging the Turks in Palestine and whose views as to its future might carry decisive weight. The Zionists could no longer be brushed aside, and the Church had nothing to lose by a friendly gesture.

The Pope dwelt, as was to be expected, on the concern of the Church for the inviolability of the Holy Places and for the maintenance of all its established rights and privileges in Palestine. Sokolow explained that Zionism had a two-fold purpose—to

[50] The word actually used by Sokolow in his account of the conversation is the Hebrew *Malkuth* = 'Kingdom.'

[51] The conversation is described at length in a report sent to Weizmann by Sokolow under cover of a letter dated 15 May 1917, in which he explains that this and other reports enclosed in the same letter were dictated by him in Italian because he wanted to write them while the interviews were fresh in his mind. The note of his audience of the Pope is in dialogue form but is not, of course, to be taken as a verbatim record. The quotations in the text are translations from the original Italian. A copy of the report is in Z.A. A copy of the covering letter to Weizmann is in the possession of Mr. Florian Sokolow.

[52] Bein, *Herzl*, p. 490 ; see also Christopher Sykes, *Two Studies in Virtue* (London, Collins, 1953), pp. 156ff. Mr. Josef Fraenkel has called the author's attention to the fact that a few weeks after Herzl's audience of the Pope, one of his supporters, York-Steiner, had a more friendly hearing at an interview with the then Secretary of State, Merry del Val—reported in *Die Welt,* 1 April 1904.

create in Palestine a centre of Jewish national life and Hebrew culture and to provide a refuge for Jewish victims of persecution. The Zionists, he declared, had no designs whatsoever on the Holy Places and would scrupulously respect whatever arrangements might be agreed upon between the Christian Powers. The Pope seems to have accepted these assurances as satisfactory and to have expressed as clearly as Gasparri had done, but rather more warmly, his approval of Zionist aspirations. The return of the Jews to Palestine, he declared, was a miraculous event. ' It is providential; God has willed it.' According to Sokolow's note, the interview closed as follows:

' His Holiness: " But what, then, can we do for you?"

'Sokolow: "We desire that Your Holiness accept the assurance of our loyalty and accord us your moral support. That is our aspiration."

'His Holiness: "Yes, yes—I believe that we shall be good neighbours." '

Like Cardinal Gasparri, the Pope had enquired about the position of the Jews in Eastern Europe and had referred, in this connection, to the American Jewish Committee's appeal to him and his reply. When Sokolow touched upon the British claim to suzerainty in Palestine, the Pope seems to have made no explicit comment, but Sokolow told Weizmann that he had spoken significantly of his admiration for Great Britain and his faith in British wisdom and justice.[53]

It was in the light of these conversations that Weizmann felt justified in assuring a London Zionist Conference on May 20th that no opposition need be feared from the Catholic Church: ' We have assurances from the highest Catholic circles that they will view with favour the establishment of a Jewish National Home in Palestine and from their religious point of view they see no objection to it and no reason why we should not be good neighbours.'[54] This seemed to be the position at the time, but it was not long before, disturbed by the protests which began to reach them from Palestine, and also, perhaps, by the suspicion that Sokolow had represented the aims of Zionism as more modest

---

[53] Sokolow to Weizmann, 12 May 1917: *Ch.W.P.*
[54] *Zionist Review*, June 1917, pp. 34ff.; Sokolow, II, 54ff.

than they really were, the Papal authorities began to have second thoughts. When Sykes revisited Rome in the winter of 1918, he found Gasparri unsympathetic.[55] Early in 1919 *The Tablet* published a denial of 'the story which is being circulated that the Holy Father is a supporter of Zionism,' explaining that, while he had offered his good wishes to 'any who desired to take part in the formation of a Jewish " Home " in Palestine,' there could be no question of his expressing approval of 'a sort of Jewish State.'[56] About the same time *The Times*[57] published a message from Rome to the effect that at a Consistory on March 10th the Pope had declared that 'it would be for us and for all Christians a bitter grief if unbelievers in Palestine were put into a superior or more privileged position.' In November 1919 Colonel Meinertz-hagen, reporting, as Chief Political Officer, on the situation in Palestine, told the Foreign Office that 'it is known that the Vatican is violently opposed to Zionism.'[58] When the Palestine Mandate came before the Council of the League of Nations in 1922, the Articles designed to give effect to the Balfour Declaration were severely criticised in a memorandum submitted to the Council by Cardinal Gasparri.[59]

But in the spring of 1917 the policy-makers at the Vatican had comprehensible reasons for showing a friendly interest in Zionism. Sokolow had been commended to the Vatican by the representative—himself a loyal and influential Catholic—of a Power whose goodwill it was clearly desirable to cultivate. Whether the War would end with the defeat of the Central Powers was still an open question, but, if it did, the future of Palestine was a matter on which the British view would carry weight and might be decisive. The changed situation in Russia, which tended to strengthen the position of the Holy See in resistance to Orthodox pretensions in the matter of the Holy Places, had also had the effect of making the future of Palestine an issue between the Western Allies. At a time when the British seemed to be in the

---

[55] See above, p. 281.

[56] *The Tablet*, 1 March 1919. About this time an attempt was being made to strengthen the Roman Catholic position in Palestine by representations to the British Government in favour of immigration from Malta.

[57] *The Times*, 12 March 1919.

[58] *B.F.P., First Series*, Vol. IV, No. 358, p. 526 (10 November 1919).

[59] See Cmd. 1708 (1922).

ascendant, the Church had nothing to gain by showing exclusive favour to the French. There was, moreover, at least a possibility that a future Peace Conference might be moved to consider the whole question of the international status of the Papacy, and in that event a good deal might turn on the attitude of Great Britain.

A case could even be made out for the view that the Jews were worth cultivating for their own sake. The Holy Synod had taken an active part in instigating the persecution of the Jews in Czarist Russia. The Jews could, therefore, be supposed to have a common interest with the Roman Catholics in undermining the position of the Orthodox Church both in Palestine and also in Eastern Europe. This, it may be conjectured, was part, at least, of the significance of Cardinal Gasparri's reminder, at his interview with Sokolow, that Catholics and Jews had alike suffered under the Czarist régime.

Though the Vatican had not, up to this time, been in contact with the Zionists during the War, there are indications of certain approaches having already been made to Jewish leaders in Great Britain and the United States.

In the summer of 1915 a certain François Deloncle, who had been for some years a member of the French Chamber of Deputies and had at one time edited *Le Siècle*,[60] called on Lucien Wolf on the introduction of the Chief Rabbi, Dr. Hertz. According to Wolf's report to the Conjoint Foreign Committee,[61] Deloncle told him that he had twice been received in audience by the Pope, who had ' expressed the most liberal intentions with regard to the Jews and offered to issue an Encyclical on their behalf.' Deloncle, Wolf reported, had gone on to point out that ' in order to be of effective use, it was necessary that [the Pope's] diplomatic position should be strengthened, and that the Holy See should take part with the belligerent States in the Congress of the Powers at which terms of peace will eventually be settled.' Accordingly, Deloncle had proposed that the British Jews should exert themselves in three directions: First, 'they should use their influence to secure the acquiescence of His Majesty's Government and the Allies in a proposal to be made by the

60 Presumably, the politician of that name whom Lord Bertie mentions in his diary (7 April 1915) as having spoken about ' the necessity of opposing the aims of the Holy Synod.' Bertie, I, 139.
61 *C.F.C.*, 1916/158ff. (16 July 1915).

United States that the Holy See shall be admitted to the [Peace] Congress as representing the neutral States and the cause of religious liberty, more especially the emancipation of the Jews and other oppressed dissenters in the Russian Empire.' Secondly, they were to support 'a proposal that the Pope be permitted to accredit a special mission to His Majesty's Government.' Lastly, they were to represent to the Foreign Office that the Russian Government should be advised to receive a similar mission. 'If this were done, the Pope would make the interests of the Russian and Polish Jews his special care.'

With what authority, if any, the proposals thus described by Wolf were put forward by Deloncle it is impossible to be sure. In support of them he was reported by Wolf to have argued that Jews and Catholics had a common interest 'in saving Europe from the Greek Orthodox Church and Slav barbarism,' and that they were also on common ground 'in desiring to preserve Palestine from Russian domination.' The Conjoint Committee found it impossible to take Deloncle's suggestions seriously and promptly rejected them.[62]

But that is not the end of the story. In the winter of 1915 Deloncle went back to Rome, where (if he is to be believed) he was again received by the Pope. He was accompanied by Hermann Bernstein, an American Jewish journalist, to whom he had been introduced by Leopold Greenberg. Soon afterwards Deloncle and Bernstein, together with Greenberg's son, Charles, set out for New York, where they got in touch with the American Jewish Committee, of which Bernstein had formerly been the Secretary.[63]

[62] Ibid.

[63] Except for the references to Leopold and Charles Greenberg, this paragraph is based on information given to the Conjoint Foreign Committee by the American Jewish Committee in a letter dated 15 May 1916: C.F.C., 1916/279ff. As to Leopold Greenberg, Lucien Wolf wrote to Louis Marshall (President of the American Jewish Committee), 31 August 1916 (C.F.C., 1916/439): '. . . We were under the impression that we had put an effectual end to [Deloncle's] enterprise. . . . It was only when it was too late, that we heard of Deloncle's introduction to Mr. Bernstein through the medium of Mr. Greenberg, and even then Mr. Greenberg assured us that his action had been taken with a view to controlling, and not helping, M. Deloncle.' As to Charles Greenberg, his sister, Mrs. Sholto, has informed the author that she remembers her father having arranged for Charles to accompany Deloncle.

411

Having been assured by Deloncle that the Pope would be prepared, if suitably approached, to state publicly that the Church deplored and reprobated the persecution of the Jews, the Committee submitted to him, through Deloncle, a petition drawing attention to the indignities and cruelties inflicted upon the Jews in the Eastern war zone, and appealing, on humanitarian grounds, for the intervention of the Holy See.[64] The Pope, through his Secretary of State, replied sympathetically,[65] and the Committee was subsequently informed that the Catholic clergy in Poland had, in fact, been directed to do their best to alleviate the sufferings of the Jews.[66]

That the Deloncle mission had something to do with the Palestine question can be inferred from an entry in Mrs. Weizmann's diary (25 March 1916)[67] recording a conversation between Weizmann and Leopold Greenberg about certain correspondence (copies of which Greenberg produced) between Deloncle and ' American financial Jewry' concerning the position of the Jews in Poland. As to this, ' Pope has written a most sympathetic reply to representations by the American Jewish Committee.' Mrs. Weizmann goes on to say that ' with regard to Palestine, it was proposed that it should be neutralised, with Pope's representative in the Government.'

Shortly after receiving the Pope's reply to its petition, the American Jewish Committee was presented by Deloncle with a document described as 'The Pact of Lugano.' This was a draft of an agreement to be entered into between representative Jews and Catholics in Poland, and to be countersigned by leading Jewish organisations in other countries. The Committee was told that the text had been submitted to the Vatican and approved by the Pope. At a time when the future of Poland was in doubt, the agreement would, in effect, have pledged, not only the Polish Jews, but world Jewry to work, under the auspices of the Roman Catholic Church, for Polish independence.[68] These proposals

---

[64] A.J.C. to C.F.C., 15 May 1916, cited above, Note 63. Text of petition (30 December 1915) set out in *C.F.C.*, 1916/284ff.

[65] Text of reply (9 February 1916), *C.F.C.*, 1916/286ff.

[66] A.J.C. press communiqué (7 April 1916): *C.F.C.*, 1916/283.

[67] *V.W.P.*

[68] A.J.C. to C.F.C., 15 May 1916: loc. cit. The text of the 'Pact of Lugano' is not in the C.F.C. papers, but that its purport was as described above

having come to the notice of the Conjoint Foreign Committee, that body, after consulting the Foreign Office,[69] pointed out to the American Jewish Committee that 'international Jewish support for the Polish Independence Party at this moment would be every-where regarded as an anti-Russian manifestation and consequently as an attempt to embarrass the Allies in the War.'[70] The American Committee had decided independently that it did not wish to be involved in the 'Pact' and had already declined to take the matter further.[71]

All this formed part of the background to Sokolow's reception at the Vatican in the spring of 1917. The instructions left for him by Sykes at the British Embassy had diverted him from the original purpose of his mission to Rome. His work at the Vatican completed, it still remained for him to sound the Italian Govern-ment. He had hoped to see the Foreign Minister, Baron Sonnino, but in this he was disappointed. In conversation with the British Ambassador, Sir Rennell Rodd, on May 10th, Sonnino said that Sokolow had asked for an interview but would have to be refused. From what he had heard of Sokolow's ideas he was inclined, he told the Ambassador, to be sympathetic, but he thought it better not to give the matter the importance it would have if he dealt with it personally.

Since Sokolow was received a few days later by the Prime Minister, Boselli, Sonnino's attitude is, at first sight, a little sur-prising. It may possibly have had something to do with the fact

[69] In the last-mentioned report Wolf writes that he found the Foreign Office 'very much perturbed' by the A.J.C.'s correspondence with Deloncle. In their letter of 15 May 1916 the A.J.C. told the C.F.C. that 'Professor Felix Frankfurter, one of our Committee, received a cablegram from Lord Eustace Percy warning us against committing our-selves to Rome in respect to matters other than those of a purely humani-tarian nature.'

[70] C.F.C. to A.J.C., 28 April 1916: *C.F.C.*, 1916/150ff.

[71] A.J.C. to C.F.C., 15 May 1916: *C.F.C.*, 1916/279ff.

can be inferred from references to the document in the above-mentioned letter; from the A.J.C.'s letter of 6 April 1916 to Deloncle and his associate in Paris, Lucien Perquel (*C.F.C.*, 1916/288ff.); from C.F.C.'s letter to A.J.C., 28 April 1916 (*C.F.C.*, 1916/150ff.); and from Lucien Wolf's report to the C.F.C. (17 May 1916)—*C.F.C.*, 1916/147ff.

that he was himself of Jewish extraction. He may have felt that it would be somewhat embarrassing to him to be personally involved in the Zionist question. There is another possible explanation. It so happened that Sokolow started his work in Rome at a moment when there was a certain strain in Anglo-Italian relations. On April 29th—soon after the Conference at St. Jean de Maurienne—the British Ambassador had handed to Sonnino a communication from his Government raising the whole question whether the Italian claims to large territorial gains in the partition of the Turkish Empire could be justified in the absence of an effective Italian contribution to the war with Turkey.[72] Sonnino's personal resentment at this rebuff may help to account for his disinclination to show a marked interest in a Zionist emissary sponsored by Great Britain. Whatever the explanation, Sonnino preferred to leave Sokolow to be received, in the first instance, by the Secretary-General of the Ministry of Foreign Affairs, Di Martino.

Accompanied by Angelo Sereni, the head of the Italian Jewish community, Sokolow saw Di Martino on May 8th.[73] In discussing the future status of Palestine he was less inhibited than he had been in Paris.[74] England, he declared, had most important interests to safeguard in Palestine and knew that she could count on the loyalty of the Jews. France, he told Di Martino, was well-disposed to the Zionists, recognising that she would have an interest in good neighbourly relations between Palestine and French Syria. Invited to define the Italian attitude, Di Martino replied with a cautiously worded declaration which he had, he said, been authorised to make in the name of the Minister of Foreign Affairs: Italy would not take the initiative in the matter of Zionism but was in sympathy with Zionist aspirations and would give them her moral support. Di Martino expressed pleasure at the satisfactory outcome of Sokolow's approach to the Holy See and ended by telling him that, after consultation with

[72] Toscano, op. cit., p. 301.
[73] The accounts which follow of Sokolow's conversations with Di Martino and Boselli are based on his own full notes of these interviews in N.S.P.
[74] Sokolow to Weizmann, 12 May 1917: W.P.: 'I am profoundly convinced that Great Britain will have Palestine if there is a strong wish for her having it. For this last solution I could not work in Paris: here [Rome] it was easier.'

Sonnino, arrangements had been made for him to see the Prime Minister.

The Prime Minister, Boselli, received Sokolow, again accompanied by Sereni, on May 12th. Either Boselli knew very little about Zionism or he was in no hurry to discuss the subject. He dwelt on the liberal treatment of the Jews in Italy, on the good relations between the Italian Jews and their fellow-citizens, and on their eminent services to the State. The conversation rambled on, and Sokolow evidently had to work hard to bring the Prime Minister to the point. In the end, Boselli reaffirmed what Sokolow had been told by Di Martino. The Zionist question, he said, was not one in which Italy could take the initiative, but should a move be made by other Allied Powers more closely concerned, the Zionists could count on Italy's moral support 'within the limits of the possible.' The one point in the Zionist programme on which Boselli seems to have had his doubts was the idea of a Chartered Company. Towards the close of the interview he repeated that, subject to the further examination of questions of detail, the Zionists could rely upon the sympathetic interest of the Italian Government. As a further mark of goodwill, the Italian Ambassador in London was instructed from Rome to give Sokolow a friendly hearing.

It was the French who had originally prompted Sokolow's visit to Italy, and the Quai d'Orsay had been kept well informed of his activities in Rome by the French Ambassador, Barrère.[75] The Ambassador's reports had cleared the way for further advances to the Zionists, and before leaving Rome on his return to London Sokolow was told that the French Government would like him to break his journey in Paris.[76] The few days he had meant to spend there lengthened out into nearly a month, and it was not until the middle of June that he was back in London.

Almost immediately after his arrival in Paris towards the end of May 1917, he had an interview with de Margerie. Having heard his account of his conversations with Di Martino and Boselli and of his audience of the Pope, de Margerie—he wrote

[75] Sokolow to Sereni, 27 May 1917: copy in Z.A.
[76] Ibid.

to Sereni—told him that by his work in Rome he had rendered an important service to the Zionist cause and congratulated him on a brilliant success.[77]

Reassured about the attitude of the Italians, the French Government had no hesitation in making further friendly gestures to the Zionists. On May 25th Sokolow was received by the Prime Minister, Ribot,[78] and on the same day he had a long and friendly conversation with Jules Cambon.[79] He saw Cambon again a few days later and pressed for the verbal assurances he had received to be confirmed in writing.[80] As he explained to his Russian colleague, Rosoff,[81] he wanted this because he feared that the French Government might weaken under renewed pressure from the anti-Zionist Alliance Israélite, whose opposition, though temporarily silenced, ' continues,' he said, ' irreconcilable regarding [the] question [of] nationality, on which I energetically refused to make [the] slightest concession.' In response to Sokolow's request, Cambon wrote to him on June 4th as follows:

> ' You were good enough to present the project to which you are devoting your efforts, which has for its object the development of Jewish colonisation in Palestine. You consider that, circumstances permitting, and the independence of the Holy Places being safeguarded on the other hand, it would be a deed of justice and of reparation to assist, by the protection of the Allied Powers, in the renaissance of the Jewish nationality in that Land from which the people of Israel were exiled so many centuries ago.
>
> ' The French Government, which entered this present war to defend a people wrongly attacked, and which continues the struggle to assure the victory of right over might, can

---

[77] Ibid.

[78] ' I have been received this morning by the Prime Minister, and I am exceedingly satisfied ': Sokolow (Paris) to Weizmann, 25 May 1917. (Transl. from Russian.) Copy in *N.S.P.* No details are given. The interview is mentioned also in Sokolow's letter of 26 May to Sereni (loc. cit.), but likewise without details.

[79] Sokolow to Sereni, 26 May 1917, loc. cit.

[80] This appears from a letter of 2 June 1917 from Sokolow to Cambon (copy in Z.A.) and from Cambon's reply of June 4th (*N.S.P.*).

[81] Telegram, Sokolow to Rosoff, 6 June 1917: *N.S.P.*

but feel sympathy for your cause, the triumph of which is bound up with that of the Allies.

' I am happy to give you herewith such assurance.'[82]

A copy of this document is known to have been handed by Sokolow to the Foreign Office on his return to London in the middle of June, but the Cambon letter was not made public. Cautiously though it was worded, the French may have felt that its publication would be inconvenient at a time when it was important for them to do nothing to offend their supporters in Syria. The Zionists, for their part, may have had no particular desire to let it appear that France, and not Great Britain, had been the first in the field with a formal declaration in their favour. Whatever the explanation, no public use was made of the Cambon letter. Its existence remained unknown to the Zionists outside a narrow circle, and some of Sokolow's own associates found him curiously secretive about its contents. Sacher was infuriated by his refusal to show it to the Zionist Political Committee. 'The only reason, I am convinced, for withholding it is,' he wrote, 'that it falls so miserably short and Sokolow is afraid of criticism.'[83] Sokolow's own view was that the Cambon letter was of value because, as he explained to Sacher, 'this is the first time that a Government committed itself to a statement that there exists a Jewish nationality in Palestine. Once this nationality is admitted, the rest follows of itself. . . . They [the French] at once agreed to admit all sorts of colonising on charity lines, but it was extremely difficult to get them to recognise the Jews as one of the small nations of this war, and happily we have overcome the difficulties there. . . .'[84]

The Cambon letter must be read in the context of the plans which were then being made for sending Sokolow to Russia. It was thought in Paris, and the same view was taken in London, that the Zionists could and should use their influence with the Russian Jews in the interests of the Allied cause. Both Governments were anxious for Sokolow to undertake this mission. He

---

[82] Orig. in Z.A. The translation from the French is Sokolow's (*History of Zionism*, II, 53).

[83] Sacher to Leon Simon, 10 July 1917: *Leon Simon Papers*.

[84] Sokolow to Sacher, 10 July 1917: copy in Z.A.

had agreed to do so and had told Cambon that he was sure he would have some success.[85] As we shall see later, this project came to nothing, but at the beginning of June 1917 it was still assumed that Sokolow would be going to Russia. With Cambon's letter of June 4th to Sokolow was enclosed a copy of a letter of the same date from Cambon to the French Ambassador in Petrograd.[86] The Ambassador was told that Sokolow

> 'has secured in London, Rome and Washington the support of the leading figures in public life, and the British Government is encouraging his efforts, which are aimed at the creation of Jewish colonies in Palestine. The French Government cannot but associate itself with its allies in their views on this great enterprise, and I have conveyed this to him in my letter.

> 'It is certain that Jewish influence can and should be exercised in Russia in favour of the Allies and for sustaining the forces of resistance on which the Provisional Government seeks to rely. The influence of M. Sokolow, which is considerable, will be used in this sense. I beg you to be good enough to advise M. Sokolow and to give him your support.'[87]

Sokolow remained in Paris another two weeks, but there is no record of his having had further contacts with the French Government. The Cambon letter marked the end of the chapter which began with his acceptance of the French invitation to Paris some two months earlier. He had obtained a vague assurance of French support, but, except for any hopes they may have staked on Zionist propaganda in Russia, the French had received nothing tangible in return. In the interests of their own claims in Palestine they had hoped to detach the Zionist Movement from its exclusive reliance on Great Britain. Once it had become clear that no assurances of theirs would induce the Zionists to favour French control of Palestine, or even to rest content with an Anglo-French condominium, they had no incentive to go further on a road that

[85] Sokolow to Jules Cambon, 2 June 1917: copy in Z.A.
[86] N.S.P. The letter begins: 'Mon cher ami: M. Sokolow se rend en Russie. . . .' 'Mon cher ami' must obviously be the Ambassador in Petrograd.
[87] Transl. from the French.

was leading nowhere. A few weeks after the Cambon letter, the Russian Chargé d'Affaires in Paris was reporting to his Government that French opinion seemed to have become noticeably cooler towards the idea of a Jewish State in Palestine.[88]

All the same, there was still a spark of life in the Cambon letter. From Balfour's statements on the subject[89] it can safely be inferred that the French Government was not consulted in advance about the Balfour Declaration, but when the question of a British assurance to the Zionists was under discussion by the War Cabinet on 4 October 1917, Balfour wished to satisfy his colleagues that the French could be expected to acquiesce. Accordingly, after dealing with the objections of the anti-Zionist Jews, ' Mr. Balfour,' it is recorded, ' then read a very sympathetic declaration by the French Government which had been conveyed to the Zionists.'[90] Thus, the Cambon letter, long forgotten after its burial in the Foreign Office files, was at a critical moment disinterred to weight the scales in favour of the Balfour Declaration.

This incident was referred to by Picot in a lecture given in Paris in 1918.[91] According to Picot, ' a qualified representative of the British Government ' had been heard to say, at a recent gathering in London, that had he not been able to produce the Cambon letter to the War Cabinet, it would never have been persuaded to agree to the Balfour Declaration. ' Thus, once more,' said Picot, ' and on a question of the first consequence, the liberal Governments of the *Entente* found themselves completely and ardently in accord.'

Speaking to a Jewish audience in Paris many years later,[92] Picot gave his version of the story in more colourful but not necessarily more accurate detail. He had, he said, arrived in London in October 1917 and had seen various Members of Parliament specially interested in the Eastern question.

' One day Sir Mark Sykes came to see me at the Embassy.

---

[88] Adamov, No. 323 (14 July 1917).

[89] See below, pp. 587-588.

[90] Lloyd George, *Treaties*, II, 1136, quoting from an unspecified but obviously authentic record of the proceedings: see below, p. 516.

[91] 29 August 1918. Text in *Une Renaissance juive en Judée* (Paris, Driay-Cohen, 1918). Quotations transl. from the French.

[92] 1 March 1939. Text in *La Terre Retrouvée* (Paris), 1 April 1939. Quotations transl. from the French.

"The discussion has taken a turn for the worse; there are growing doubts because the British Government is totally ignorant of the position taken up by the French Cabinet. Is it possible for you, without asking Paris for instructions, to come to-day to Downing Street and to tell our Ministers what your Government has done . . . ?" I replied: "I am prepared to go with you and to read our formula. . . ." I arrived and told the people I saw: "Here is what has been done. I have never been able to understand its having been kept secret. . . ." I must say that the British Ministers seemed exceedingly astonished that the French Government should have gone so far and that this should have been done so many months ago without their having any knowledge of it.'

Thus, Picot concluded, in this—as in so many matters—France could be seen to have played a decisive part.

In October 1917 the Cambon letter had been for months in the possession of the Foreign Office; a copy had been handed by Sokolow to Sir Ronald Graham on June 18th. Picot's story is, therefore, somewhat surprising, but it is not altogether incredible. Balfour might not have been told about the letter or he might have forgotten its existence. How much really turned on it is another question. In his anxiety to justify the paradox that the Jews owed the Balfour Declaration to France as much as to Great Britain, Picot naturally dramatised the introduction of the Cambon letter and magnified its importance. Whether it played as decisive a part as he invited his audience to believe is, to say the least, highly questionable. What is certain is that Balfour used it as part of his argument for the Declaration, and to this extent, at all events, Sokolow's exertions in Paris were not wholly unrewarded.

[*Note.*—In his study of 'The Palestine Question in Italian Diplomacy, 1917-20' (*Journal of Modern History*, Chicago, September 1955) Professor F. E. Manuel states (p. 265) that 'on May 21st, 1917, Angelo Sereni, President of the Community of Israelite Italians, had presented Dr. Nahum Sokolow to Sonnino. . . . During the conversation Sokolow reported to Sonnino on his talks with Ribot, the French Premier, and Balfour, who had both expressed their sym-

pathies with Zionism, and implied that his trip to Rome was related to British Foreign Office advice. . . .' The source is described by Professor Manuel as ' *Sionismo, Movimento Sionista*: memorandum on the conversation, signed Sonnino, May 21st 1917.'

There seems clearly to be some mistake: (1) Sonnino himself explained to the British Ambassador (see above, p. 413) why he did not propose to grant an interview to Sokolow. (2) Had such an interview, nevertheless, taken place, it is inconceivable that there would not have been a word about it in Sokolow's reports on his work in Rome, which include detailed accounts of his conversations with Di Martino and Boselli. (3) The *J.C.* printed on 10 August 1917 (p. 16) a belated report from Rome to the effect that Sokolow's efforts to obtain an interview with Sonnino had proved unsuccessful but that he had been received by the Secretary-General of the Ministry of Foreign Affairs. In the next issue (August 17th, p. 19) the *J.C.* writes, with reference to this report: ' We are desired to state that M. Sokolow's representations were made to the Italian Government as a whole and not to particular members of that Government.' If Sokolow had, in fact, seen Sonnino, the communiqué would obviously have said so. (4) Sokolow cannot possibly have reported, on May 21st, during his visit to Rome, on his interview with Ribot. After leaving Rome and returning to Paris, he saw Ribot for the first time on May 25th.]

CHAPTER 28

SOUNDINGS IN THE UNITED STATES

WHILE SOKOLOW WAS fighting his diplomatic battles in Paris and
Rome, Weizmann and his colleagues in London were concentrating their efforts on propaganda in Russia and the United States.

In communicating to Lord Rothschild the substance of
Sokolow's early reports from Paris, Weizmann drew the moral
that 'the most important point at present is to strengthen the
hands of the British Government . . . There can be no doubt at
all that the French have no claim [to Palestine], and it is incredible that they should press in such an aggressive form a case
for which there is no slightest justification.'[1]

What the Zionists could do to strengthen the hands of the
British Government, and their own claims upon it, was to persuade the Russian and American Jews, representing between them
by far the greater part of world Jewry, to come out openly and
unambiguously in favour of a Jewish National Home in Palestine
under the aegis of Great Britain as the protecting Power. Through
the Jews it might be possible to influence their Governments and
to bring home to them—so, at least, it was hoped—the clear distinction between an old-fashioned annexation of Palestine and a
British trusteeship designed to pave the way for a Jewish
Commonwealth.

Weizmann dwelt on this aspect of the matter at his interview
with Robert Cecil on April 25th.[2] 'A Jewish Palestine under a British
protectorate could not,' he pointed out, 'be interpreted simply as
an annexation of Palestine by Great Britain. In view of the relations of the Jews to Great Britain . . . it would be easily understood that Great Britain [was] keeping the country in trust for
the Jews.' A day or two earlier he had made the same point in
a letter to Brandeis. 'Both Russia and America,' he wrote, 'are at
present proclaiming anti-annexationist principles. . . . I need not
dwell on the fact that Jewish national democracy, and the Zionist

[1] 7th April 1917. Copy in *Ch.W.P.*
[2] The quotation is from Weizmann's note of the interview—see above, p. 391.

422

Organisation which essentially represents this democracy, trust implicitly to British rule, and they see in a British protectorate the only possibility for a normal development of a Jewish Commonwealth in Palestine. Whereas, in my opinion, Great Britain would not agree to a simple annexation of Palestine, it would certainly protect and support a Jewish Palestine.'[3]

In the spring and summer of 1917 Weizmann and his colleagues were doing everything in their power to popularise these ideas in Russia and the United States, but their efforts had only a partial success. In Russia the propaganda in favour of British sponsorship of Zionist aspirations elicited a feeble response from the Jews and none from the Government. In the United States its reception was more encouraging. Brandeis and most of the other leading American Zionists had been pro-British from the start and were pre-disposed to accept the view that Zionist interests would best be served by British suzerainty in Palestine. On the other hand, this consideration carried no weight with the State Department, nor did it greatly interest the President. Robert Lansing, the Secretary of State, was no friend of the Zionists, while Wilson, though vaguely sympathetic, shared no inclination to exert himself in favour of an Anglo-Zionist alliance.

On 8 April 1917 Weizmann wrote to Brandeis about his encouraging interviews with Balfour and Lloyd George and went on: 'We look forward here to a strengthening of our work by the American Government and the American Jews, and on that point I had a conversation with Mr. Hapgood in the presence of Mr. Herbert Samuel, Mr. Neil Primrose, Mr. James de Rothschild and Commander Wedgwood, M.P. An expression of opinion coming from yourself and perhaps from other gentlemen connected with the Government in favour of a Jewish Palestine under a British Protectorate would greatly strengthen our hands.'[4]

Norman Hapgood[5] was an intimate friend of Brandeis and, like him, stood high in President Wilson's esteem.[6] Josiah Wedg-

[3] 23 April 1917: copy in *Ch.W.P.*
[4] Copy in *Ch.W.P.*
[5] Editor of *Harper's Weekly*, 1913-16; later, U.S. Minister at Copenhagen.
[6] He had been an important link between Brandeis and the White House during the discussion of proposals for anti-trust legislation just before the War: A. S. Link, *Wilson, The New Freedom*, p. 437.

wood had first met Weizmann at one of Lloyd George's breakfast-parties in 1916.[7] During a visit to the United States later in that year he had made it his business to get in touch with the American Zionists and had discussed the Zionist question with Colonel House.[8] He had recently suggested that the United States should be invited to take control of Palestine on the understanding that the Jews would be given their chance to realise their national aspirations.[9] Similar proposals had been made by Hapgood, who had, in a widely syndicated article in the American press, come out with a scheme for the establishment in Palestine of a Jewish Republic under the protection of the United States.[10] At or before the meeting mentioned by Weizmann in his letter of April 8th both Hapgood and Wedgwood had evidently been brought round to the view that the Zionists would do best to work for a British protectorate.

Herbert Samuel was no longer in office but had all the prestige of an ex-Cabinet Minister. Neil Primrose, who had accompanied de Rothschild at his interview with C. P. Scott some two months earlier,[11] was still a member of the Government as Joint Chief Whip. Weizmann thus had the backing of an impressive group of advisers in urging Brandeis to secure the support of American Jewry, and, if possible, of the American Government, for 'a Jewish Palestine under a British Protectorate.'

In his letter of April 8th Weizmann explained to Brandeis that 'it is only owing to the kindness of the British Government that a possibility has been given to us to write fully to you on the situation here.' The next message to reach Brandeis from London had evidently been sent through British official channels, since he received it on April 25th from the British Embassy in Washington.[12] It was a telegram dated April 21st from James de Rothschild:

[7] C. V. Wedgwood, *The Last of the Radicals* (London, Cape, 1951), p. 183.

[8] Ibid.

[9] See *Palestine*, 31 March 1917.

[10] See *Zionism Conquers Public Opinion* (New York, 1917), a brochure published by the Provisional Zionist Committee, p. 3.

[11] 27 January 1917—see above, p. 365.

[12] A copy of this message in the *Brandeis papers* is marked: 'Above cable received in Washington from British Embassy, April 25th.'

'. . . After careful consideration of all leading Zionists and friends, Mr. Achad Ha'am, Rothschild and Herbert Samuel, and discussions with competent authorities, unanimous opinion only satisfactory solution Jewish Palestine under British protectorate. . . . Public opinion and competent authorities favourable. Only opponents Wolf and friends. This information strictly confidential. It would greatly help work if American Jews would support this scheme for [? before] their Government. We also rely upon immediate expression of opinion of yourself and other American prominent Jews. Most desirable if [sic] you should discuss the position with Mr. Balfour during his visit.[12a] Please telegraph.'

Before Brandeis had replied to this message, he received a further telegram from London. It was sent on April 30th and signed by de Rothschild, Weizmann and Joseph Cowen:

'. . . Press here reports American Administration favours Jewish Republic in Palestine. Consider existing circumstances against this. Such projects, if pressed, will only tend to complicate international position, raise fresh antagonisms and bring about joint control of Powers in Palestine, which would be disastrous. Claim that solution in Saturday's cable[13] only sound one. Support from you and Government would be invaluable. Information confidential. Please telegraph your views, what result of conversations and what action you are taking. . . . Imperative all Zionists agree to policy to strengthen hands of friends.'[14]

This telegram was dispatched a few days after Weizmann's interview with Robert Cecil on April 25th, when, having spoken of his anxiety about the arrangements in regard to Palestine which he understood to have been made between Great Britain and France, he had been told that it would strengthen the position very considerably if the Jews of the world would express themselves in favour of a British protectorate. Writing to Brandeis on

[12a] Balfour, with a group of advisers, had gone to the United States for conversations with the American Government.

[13] 'Saturday' = April 21st.

[14] *Brandeis papers.*

April 28th,[15] Weizmann enclosed a copy of Scott's letter of April 16th containing the information disclosed by de Caix about British commitments to the French concerning the future of Palestine.[16] 'We are,' he wrote, 'trying our utmost to clear up the matter, but we would certainly need all the help from America in order to strengthen our hands . . . I am sure you will agree with me that much can be done in America . . . and your support would, no doubt, strengthen the hands of our Government in this particular matter. . . . It is most certainly necessary in the interests of Zionism that America should support the plan of a British protectorate, which is the only guarantee for a future healthy Jewish development in Palestine.'

Any hopes there may have been of active American intervention in this sense were doomed to disappointment, but Brandeis' personal response was a whole-hearted acceptance of the London programme, and in this, as was to be made clear at the end of the War, he had behind him the whole body of organised Zionists in the United States.

Brandeis did not reply immediately to the message from London, but on May 1st de Haas, on behalf of the Provisional Zionist Committee, telegraphed to Weizmann: 'Inform Francis [sic] Rothschild that Brandeis received cable but withheld direct answer until interview with Balfour. In the meantime we wish to assure you that we will stand solidly with you in every respect and exert ourselves to the utmost . . .'[17] A few days later, Brandeis himself telegraphed his approval of the Zionist programme, adding, however, that it would not be prudent for him to say anything for publication at the moment.[18] On May 14th, in a letter to Norman Hapgood dealing mainly with other matters, Brandeis asked him to tell Weizmann and de Rothschild that 'my talks with Mr. Balfour, Eustace Percy and Sir Eric Drummond[19] on

[15] Copy in Z.A.

[16] Above, p. 391.

[17] Z.A 'Francis' must be a slip for 'James.' There may have been an error in transmission.

[18] 9 May 1917. A draft of this telegram in the *Brandeis papers* is dated May 6th.

[19] Lord Eustace Percy (later, Lord Percy of Newcastle) and Sir Eric Drummond (later, Earl of Perth) were members of Balfour's entourage during his visit to the United States and Canada.

Palestine are very encouraging. Likewise a talk I had with the President a week ago.'[20] On the 17th Brandeis telegraphed to de Rothschild: 'Have had satisfactory talk with Mr. Balfour, also with our President. This is not for publication.'[21] Professor Manuel, who has examined the State Department files on the subject, speaks of a copy of the Zionist programme having been sent to the Department by Brandeis in May 1917 with a covering note reading: 'I think you will be interested in enclosed formulation of the Zionist programme by Weizmann and his associates and which we approve.'[22]

Balfour had arrived in Washington on April 22nd, and Brandeis had been introduced to him soon afterwards at a White House luncheon.[23] Apart from this, Brandeis appears to have had two conversations with Balfour in Washington—one at breakfast with him at his hôtel[24] and the other, on May 10th, at the British Embassy.[25] No contemporary record of these talks has come to light, and for what passed at them we have to rely mainly on a memorandum prepared by Felix Frankfurter, some seventeen years later, for Balfour's biographer, Mrs. Dugdale.[26] 'Memory,' he writes, 'has had to be relied on, but the memory is that of

20 *Ch.W.P.*
21 Z.A. A draft in the *Brandeis papers* is dated May 15th. James de Rothschild's prominence in the interchanges between Brandeis and the London Zionists reflects Brandeis' estimate of the importance of the Rothschild backing for Zionism. At the end of 1916 a leading American Zionist wrote to Weizmann: '[Brandeis] was gratified to learn of the attitude of the leading families in Anglo-Jewry towards the Zionist Movement, and his pleasure in the report I brought him had led me to feel that I ought to write to you in order to indicate how heartening and helpful it would be if he might have a personal assurance from a representative of that family. . . .' Lewin-Epstein to Weizmann, 22 December 1916: *Ch.W.P.*
22 F. E. Manuel, op. cit., pp. 165-166. There is in the *Brandeis papers* a document setting out the Zionist programme and marked 'copied, 5/21/17' [i.e. 21 May 1917], but not accompanied by a covering letter.
23 Mason, *Brandeis*, p. 453.
24 Lord Percy of Newcastle (Lord Eustace Percy) to the author, 27 November 1951.
25 British Embassy to Brandeis, 8 May 1917, proposing appointment with Mr. Balfour at the Embassy 'on Thursday next' (i.e. May 10th): *Brandeis papers*.
26 *Dugdale papers*.

Brandeis' Zionist secretary at the time, as well as the memories of two or three of us who were in the Justice's confidence.' According to the Frankfurter memorandum, 'the two men did not enter upon detail because they found themselves so quickly in thorough accord with the ethical and political implications of Zionism.'

> 'The essential contributions of the talks between Brandeis and Balfour in Washington were the powerful impression left on Balfour's mind of the ethical purposes and practicalities of Zionism and the popular strength among Jewry in America of the desire for the Jewish Homeland. . . . Balfour was powerfully struck with the intellectual and moral distinction of Brandeis. Shortly after the meeting between the two men, Lord Eustace Percy quoted Balfour as saying that not only was he impressed with the high moral tone of Brandeis on the Palestinian question, but that in many ways he was probably the most remarkable man he had met on his visit to the United States. Brandeis, on his side, was equally won by Balfour. He was struck with Balfour's keen understanding of the Jewish problem and said that the whole long discussion with Balfour was pithily summed up by Balfour's quietly emphatic remark: "I am a Zionist."'

Balfour seems to have touched on the question of Anglo-American co-operation in Palestine and to have been told by Brandeis that American public opinion would fight shy of any such responsibility.[27] But, as appears from the Frankfurter memorandum, the discussions were concerned less with practical politics than with broad questions of principle. Their effect was to strengthen Brandeis in his confidence in British intentions and to make the Zionist cause still more attractive to Balfour.[28]

27 Mrs. Dugdale writes in her biography of Balfour, II, 231: '[Brandeis] gave no great encouragement to the idea of United States participation, observing that the bulk of American citizens were still opposed to the war and would not wish to take responsibilities outside it.' This is not in the Frankfurter memorandum. The source is not cited, but Mrs. Dugdale may have got this from Balfour himself in one of her conversations with him. The same statement is repeated, in substance, by Professor Manuel (*The Realities of American-Palestine Relations*, p. 78), but again without citation of the source.

28 During his visit to Canada after completing his work in the United States, Balfour took occasion to re-affirm his interest in Zionism. While in

CHAPTER 29

SOUNDINGS IN RUSSIA

ALMOST IMMEDIATELY AFTER their first approaches to Brandeis in the spring of 1917 the Zionist leaders in London launched a parallel campaign in Russia. But there their programme—a Jewish Commonwealth in Palestine under British protection—ran into obstacles which they had under-estimated. The climate was un-propitious, and the results of their efforts were not impressive.

They were, to begin with, under the disadvantage of having to start their propaganda at a time when Great Britain no longer commanded the respect and admiration of the Russian Jews to the same extent as in the past. By instinct and tradition the Jews of Eastern Europe had before the War been strongly pro-British. They had idealised Great Britain as a humane and liberal Power, which had not only set an example of civilised behaviour in its treatment of its own Jewish citizens but had, more than any other, shown an understanding of the Jewish problem and a genuine desire to see the Jews given their rightful place in the world. But in the spring of 1917 the prevailing mood among the Jewish masses was one of disenchantment. They had their grievances against Great Britain, and these were being exploited by left-wing propaganda designed to discredit Russia's war-time ally. Newly liberated by the collapse of the Czarist Government,

---

Ottawa, he expressed a desire to meet the President of the Canadian Zionist Federation, Clarence de Sola, and, at his request, arrangements were made for de Sola to call on him at Government House. De Sola told the Zionist Committee in New York that in the course of the conversation ‘there was scarcely a point of interest in connection with the Zionist Movement that was not thoroughly discussed, and the future of Palestine and of the Hebrews, as a nation, were, of course, among the important points taken up.’ An American Zionist Convention, meeting at Baltimore a few weeks later, was informed, in a message from de Sola, that Balfour had told him that the British Government was prepared to support the establishment of a Jewish homeland in Palestine: de Sola to Zionist Provisional Committee, New York, 29 May 1917: *Brandeis papers; J.C.*, 20 July 1917.

they looked coldly on those who had tried to shore it up. Had not Great Britain been the staunch friend and backer of a régime which had systematically oppressed the Jews and subjected them to brutal maltreatment in the Eastern war zone? Had she not stood firmly by the side of her Czarist friends and tamely acquiesced in their illiberal policies? The Jews could not be expected to take an indulgent view of the circumstances which forbade her to intervene; all they knew was that she had done nothing to help them. In this connection, it turned out to be unfortunate that, while in Russia on the eve of the Revolution, Milner had not concerned himself with the Jewish question and had made no attempt to see any of the Jewish leaders[1]. The Jews, moreover, were incensed by the anti-semitic bias shown by some of the British press correspondents in Russia in their accounts of the Revolution and its aftermath, and more particularly by what Lucien Wolf described, in one of his reports to his Committee, as 'the calumnies of *The Times*.'[2] Another grievance which played into the hands of anti-British propagandists was the British Government's decision to give unnaturalised residents of Russian origin, nearly all of them Jews, a choice between joining the British Army and being sent back to Russia.[3]

When the news of the Balfour Declaration reached Russian Jewry towards the end of November, it was welcomed by the Zionists, and not by Zionists only, with fervent demonstrations of gratitude to Great Britain. Amid the confusion which followed the Bolshevik *coup d'état* not only avowed Zionists, but many other Jews, dismayed by Lenin's seizure of power and uncertain of their future under a new and uncongenial régime, could see in the Declaration a gleam of light in a darkening sky. With the Declaration actually before them, large numbers of Russian Jews gratefully welcomed the promise of British sponsorship of Zionist aspirations in Palestine, but it was another matter, in mid-1917, to persuade them to demand it.

This would not have been easy even if Russian Jewry had been

[1] See above, p. 347, note 25.
[2] *C.F.C.*, 1917/328: see above, p. 323.
[3] All these points are brought out in reports on the situation in Russia received by the Conjoint Foreign Committee: *C.F.C.*, 1917/56 8ff. (10 May 1917); 596ff. (3 July 1917).

more overwhelmingly Zionist in its outlook than, in fact, it was. The Zionists were unquestionably a powerful force in Russo-Jewish life, but they by no means had it all their own way. The preparations which began to be made soon after the Revolution for an All-Russian Jewish Congress at once brought to a head the long-standing feud between the Zionists and the Bundists. The Zionists pressed for the Palestine question to be included in the agenda of the Congress; the Bundists insisted that the Congress should deal solely with Russo-Jewish affairs.[4] A representative Jewish conference in the Ukraine was reported in June to have resolved by a very large majority that the agenda ought to include a demand for an autonomous Jewish centre in Palestine.[5] Nevertheless, the Zionists had in the end to be content with a rather lame compromise; the last of four main items on the programme of the Congress (the first three being concerned with the position of the Jews in Russia) was to be 'the problem of guarantees for the civic and national rights of the Jews in (*a*) Poland, (*b*) Palestine, (*c*) Rumania.'[6]

The election of delegates did not take place until early in 1918. By that time the Zionists—thanks partly to the impact of the Balfour Declaration—had grown strong enough to secure for themselves, together with a small group of Zionist Socialists, some 60 per cent. of the seats. The Bundists, now evidently discredited, were in a small minority, the non-Zionist delegates being drawn mainly from other Parties.[7] Though the Zionists had not even then an overwhelming majority, they were much the largest single group, but in the spring and summer of 1917 their position must have been more precarious, or they would hardly have reconciled themselves to the relegation of the Palestine question to the not very conspicuous place assigned to it in the agreed agenda.

Not only were the Russian Jews divided on the Zionist question, but even the Zionists were in no hurry to respond to the appeal from London. The slogans of the day told against it. Whatever

---

4 The controversy is described in a message from Petrograd in *J.C.*, 20 July 1917. As to the Bundists, see above, p. 67.

5 *J.C.*, 8 June 1917.

6 *Zionist Review*, 1917, p. 119. This decision was taken at a preparatory conference in Petrograd in August 1917.

7 *J.C.*, 22 March 1918.

Weizmann and his friends might say, British suzerainty in Palestine, even if linked with the establishment of a Jewish Commonwealth, smacked uncomfortably of annexation. And did not the principles of democracy require that, in any case, no decisive move should be made by the Russian Zionist leaders until the whole subject had been exhaustively debated by the Jewish public and its views tested by a referendum? Neither from the Russian Zionists, nor, still less, from the Russian Government, was it found possible to elicit any declaration in favour of a settlement of the Palestine question on the lines of the London programme.

The Provisional Government seems first to have begun to interest itself in Zionism when Sokolow's arrival in Rome was reported, early in May, by the Russian Ambassador to the then Foreign Minister, Miliukow.[8] Sokolow had called on the Ambassador, who had told him that the Embassy had no instructions as to Russian policy on the Zionist question, had advised him to go slowly and had wanted to know why the Zionists had not approached the Russian Ambassadors in other capitals.[9] After the Ambassador had sent a further report on Sokolow's activities in Rome,[10] Terestschenko, who had succeeded Miliukow as Foreign Minister, told the Russian representatives in London and Paris that he wished to be informed about the various international Jewish organisations, 'and especially about those working for an independent Jewish State in Palestine.'[11] The exact significance of the enquiry is uncertain, but it can hardly be explained by mere curiosity. The inference seems to be that the Provisional Government was not prepared to write off Russian interests in Palestine and wished to consider how they might be affected by Zionist activities.

Both the Lwow and the Kerensky Governments made some

[8] Adamov, No. 299 (3 May 1917).

[9] Sokolow to Weizmann, 1 May 1917: copy in *N.S.P.*

[10] Adamov, No. 308 (19 May 1917).

[11] Adamov, p. 261(1) (22 May 1917). Replies were sent from London and Paris on May 26th and July 14th respectively (ibid., Nos. 310, 323). The report from London dealt solely with the Zionist Organisation; the report from Paris, on the other hand, described the Jewish Colonisation Association as the only body doing practical work for Zionism.

friendly gestures to the Zionists. In June a number of Jewish soldiers were given special leave to attend an All-Russian Zionist Conference at Petrograd, and the Conference received a message of good wishes from Terestchenko.[12] In August the Russian Consul-General at Salonica was reported to have assured a Jewish deputation that there was every hope that, on the day that the Jews demanded it, Russia would warmly support the creation of a Jewish Palestine.[13] The words 'on the day that the Jews demanded it' may be significant, for a few weeks later Tschlenow was reported by the Petrograd correspondent of *The Jewish Chronicle* to have been told on high authority that Kerensky and Terestchenko were ready to support the Zionist movement 'on condition that the Jewish people should determine among themselves whether they constitute a nation or a religious sect.'[14]

Writing to Sokolow in September, Tschlenow described the Russian attitude as most favourable. He had, he said, been promised that at the forthcoming Inter-Allied War Aims Conference the Russian delegate would consult representatives of the Zionist Organisation on all matters relating to Palestine.[15] Tschlenow was satisfied that the Provisional Government was thoroughly well-disposed towards Zionism; indeed, in the letter just quoted he went so far as to tell Sokolow that he had received much more definite assurances of support than had been given to the Zionists in England. But even supposing that Tschlenow had not over-estimated these assurances and that the Provisional Government was sincere in professing sympathy with Zionist aspirations in Palestine, it would have been surprising if it had been attracted by the idea of British sponsorship. Terestchenko's enquiries about Zionist activities suggest that he was not disposed wholly to disinterest himself in Palestine. It would, in any case, have been inconsistent with Russia's avowed policy for the Provisional Government to come out in favour of a Jewish Commonwealth in Palestine under British protection at a time when it was working for a peace settlement with Turkey on the footing

---

12 Sokolow, II, 28.
13 *J.C.*, 10 August 1917.
14 *J.C.*, 28 September 1917.
15 Tschlenov to Sokolow, 24 September 1917: *N.S.P.*

that the annexationist ideas underlying the Secret Treaties were discredited and obsolete.

Nor did the Russian Zionist leaders attempt to secure any such declaration. Though repeatedly appealed to by Weizmann to approach the Provisional Government in support of the London programme, they made no move in that direction. They themselves fought shy of the programme, and, to the end, Tschlenow, clinging to the principle of 'neutrality,' preferred to play for safety and to find reasons against irrevocably tying the Zionist Movement to Great Britain.

Cautious by nature, he had comprehensible reasons for moving warily. When he and Sokolow left for London at the end of 1914, it had been laid down by the Berlin Zionist Executive that there must be no 'negotiations' with the Government of any Power at war with Turkey.[16] In considering the London programme, he had to think of its possible effect on the position of the Jews in Palestine, who in the spring of 1917 were again being terrorised by the Turks, and of the two-and-a-half million East European Jews living in the occupied territories under German or Austrian administration. In Russian politics Tschlenow was known in Moscow as an active supporter of the Constitutional Democrats.[17] He may well have felt that his association with the Cadets made it all the more important for him to do nothing calculated to prejudice Zionism in the eyes of the Socialist elements which, under the leadership of Kerensky, were coming into the ascendant. He may also have been influenced by his contacts with the Berlin-dominated Zionist Bureau in Copenhagen, and especially by the views of its Director, Victor Jacobson, who, though not himself of German nationality, shared the outlook of his German colleagues in the Berlin Zionist Executive.

The first attempt to interest Tschlenow in the plans agreed upon in London was made by Weizmann in a telegram dated April 27th.[18] It was on the same lines as James de Rothschild's message of a few days earlier to Brandeis. Tschlenow was told

[16] See above, p. 102.
[17] Shm. Levin, *The Arena*, p. 302.
[18] Copy in *Ch.W.P.*

that, after discussions with leading English Zionists, with friends like Achad Ha'am, the Rothschilds and Herbert Samuel, and also with 'the competent authorities,' a unanimous decision had been reached in favour of a Jewish Palestine under British protection, and that it was most important that the Russian Jews and their organisations should approach their Government in support of this programme.

This was followed by a letter in which Weizmann explained to Tschlenow, as he had explained a few days before to Brandeis, that there was no question of an old-fashioned annexation: 'England is not yearning to annex Palestine, and were it not for the combination with us, she would hardly oppose the internationalisation of that country.'

> 'On the contrary,' he went on, 'one fears here that, in view of the present feelings in Russia and in America, it is difficult to work in favour of a British protectorate save on the condition that the Jews themselves wish it; in other words, Great Britain is ready to take Palestine under her protection in order to give the Jews the possibility of getting on their feet and living independently. It is, therefore, extremely important that Russian Jewry proclaim the importance of this question and bring it home to the Russian Government.'[19]

On May 1st Weizmann wrote to Sokolow (then in Rome) that he had telegraphed to Moscow and Washington that 'the only programme for which we are working here, and for which we expect them to work, is our old plan.'[20] Two weeks later a further telegram was sent to Moscow asking for a reply to the messages from London, and on the same day, May 16th, Tschlenow telegraphed that the Russian Zionist Committee welcomed the results obtained in England. This was encouraging as far as it went, and the Zionist leaders in London now looked hopefully to the All-Russian Zionist Conference which was to meet in Petrograd in about three weeks' time.

In a message to the Conference Weizmann telegraphed on June 4th:[21]

[19] Transl. from the original Russian: Copy in *Ch.W.P.*
[20] Copy in *Ch.W.P.*
[21] Copies in *Ch.W.P.* and *Z.A.*

Most important present juncture all great Zionist Federations co-ordinate unanimous effort. England, South Africa, Canada and America support plan integral Jewish Palestine under British trust with all necessary guarantees future national development to Commonwealth. Desire your support this plan before the Russian democracy and its Government. Consider this solution fully corresponding principles democratic settlement. We are for internationalisation Holy Places and decidedly opposed international or plural control or condominium rest of Palestine. . . . In addition to previous communications authorised state that in interview with His Majesty's Secretary of State for Foreign Affairs I received assurances of encouragement and support our plans.'[22]

Sokolow, now back in Paris after his visit to Rome, had made arrangements for travelling from France to Russia, and it had been hoped that he would arrive there in time to take part in the Petrograd Conference. A visit to Russia had first been suggested to him by Cambon and de Margerie when he met them in Paris early in April. Some four weeks later Weizmann told the Foreign Office that if Sokolow were given facilities for visiting Russia, he could do something to counteract the anti-British activities of certain elements among the Russian Jews. The Foreign Office agreed, and on May 18th Weizmann telegraphed to Sokolow: 'Authorities consider your visit to Russia most essential. Have wired Tschlenow request postpone Conference.'[23] The Conference, however, was not postponed, and by the time Sokolow felt free to leave Paris in the middle of June it was over.[24] Even though he would have to miss the Conference, he still hoped to carry out his Russian mission, but, as it turned out, he was needed in London, and the whole project had in the end to be abandoned.

Realising that, because of his commitments in Paris, he would not be able to address the Russian Conference in person, Sokolow

---

[22] This seems to refer to Weizmann's interview with Robert Cecil on April 25th—see above, p. 392. During Balfour's absence in the United States, Cecil was Acting Foreign Secretary. This message must have passed the British censorship and its transmission must almost certainly have been facilitated by the British authorities.

[23] N.S.P.

[24] It opened on June 6th and closed on the 13th: Sokolow, II, 27; *Zionist Review*. July 1917, p. 50.

telegraphed to Petrograd, on June 6th, a message of enormous length for the confidential information of the organisers.[25] In a reference to the telegram sent to the Conference a day or two earlier by Weizmann, he spoke of a British protectorate as the ideal solution, adding, however, that 'formally [the] phrase "Entente protection" is still current in diplomatic quarters. . . . The work outside Great Britain and the English-speaking countries, although being essentially of the same [pro-British] orientation, must be, in its form, more general.' He dwelt on the importance of the Cambon letter, describing it as 'the greatest moral victory our idea ever gained,' and urged that an effort be made 'to obtain from [the] Russian Government such approval as [has been] received from other Entente Powers.'

Weizmann's message from London had amounted to an invitation to the Conference to declare itself in favour of 'an integral Palestine under British trust,' with guarantees for the eventual emergence of a Jewish Commonwealth. Telegraphing from Paris with the Cambon letter fresh in his mind, and also, perhaps, with a fuller appreciation of the state of feeling in Russia, Sokolow did not go so far as to ask for an explicit endorsement of the London programme. He described British trusteeship as the ideal solution but at the same time reminded the Russian leaders that among Russia's Western allies there were other interested and friendly Powers—notably France—whose susceptibilities must be taken into account.

The resolutions adopted by the Petrograd Conference not only ignored the London programme but carefully avoided any reference at all to Great Britain or to any other foreign Power.[26] They demanded simply that in the peace settlement due weight should be given to 'the clearly stated will of the Jewish nation for the re-settlement and re-birth of Palestine as its national centre.' The resolution went on to declare that it was necessary to 'organise among the Jews a referendum on the [Palestine] question,' 'to lay before the All-Russian Jewish Congress the question of Jewish claims in Palestine,' and, lastly, 'to claim the admission of a representative of the Jewish nation at a future peace conference.' It is no wonder that in Zionist circles in England these resolutions

[25] Copy in N.S.P.
[26] Text, in Engl. translation, in Sokolow, II, 41-42.

had a chilly welcome. This verbiage was not what was wanted. 'I quite agree with you,' Sokolow told Sacher, 'about the resolutions of the Petrograd Conference; I was very much anoyed about them. . . . We must not lose heart because a cloud seems to hide for a time the proper course for our Russian brethren.'[27]

If the resolutions were a disappointment to the London Zionists, Tschlenow's presidential address was, from their point of view, no better.[28] Moving and impressive as it was in its exposition of the Zionist case, it steered clear of anything which could possibly be interpreted as an appeal for British sponsorship of Zionism or a plea for British suzerainty in Palestine. The best evidence of the impression produced by Tschlenow's speech is the use made of it by the Berlin Zionist Executive and the Copenhagen Bureau in their approaches to the German Government. A few weeks after it was delivered, the Berlin Executive brought it to the notice of the German Foreign Office with the comment that it showed how unreservedly the Russian Zionists accepted the fact that Palestine belonged to Turkey.[29] Three months later, the Copenhagen Bureau, in a letter to the German Legation,[30] dwelt on the successful efforts of the Berlin Executive to bind the Zionist Organisation to 'absolute neutrality' (in other words, to prevent it from gravitating towards the Entente), and cited Tschlenow's speech as an outstanding example.

The Zionist leaders in England were not disposed to accept Tschlenow's unhelpful attitude as final and took steps to open his eyes to the realities of the situation as they saw it. Writing to Sacher on July 10th,[31] Sokolow told him that 'our friend Boris left last week for Russia . . . and he will personally inform and encourage our brethren there in the spirit of our orientation.' Sokolow was referring to Boris Goldberg, a leading Russian Zionist, who, after visiting the United States, had spent some time in London and was well informed as to what had been going on there behind the scenes.

---

27 Sokolow to Sacher, 10 July 1917: Z.A.
28 French translation in *Le Sionisme et la Révolution Russe* (Paris, Hamoledeth, *n.d.*).
29 22 July 1917: Z.A.
30 23 October 1917: Z.A.
31 The letter of 10 July 1917 already quoted.

At the end of July, Goldberg and Tschlenow, together with Victor Jacobson and the two German members of the Zionist Executive, Warburg and Hantke, met in Copenhagen.[32] Goldberg reported on Zionist activities in England and on Sokolow's visit to Paris and Rome. He produced a full note[33] of the London Conference between Mark Sykes and the Zionist leaders on February 7th and explained that this had called for a formulation of the Zionist 'demands.'[34] Weizmann and Sokolow, he said, thought it essential that, before going further, they should be assured that the Russian and American Zionists were satisfied with the 'demands' and endorsed them. Tschlenow remarked that, before approving them he had felt that he must first discuss them in Copenhagen with other members of the Zionist Executive. As to Zionist policy generally, he said that the Russian Zionists believed that this was not the time for asking for a Jewish State— still less was it desirable to ask for a Jewish State under foreign protection.

The unanimous decisions with which the meeting ended implied disapproval of any attempt to tie the Movement to the Entente and were clearly designed to correct the balance. The aims of Zionism, as set out in the Basle programme, were, it was declared, in harmony with the principles proclaimed by the belligerents on both sides. Hence, parallel with the work to be carried on in the Entente countries, the Governments of the Central Powers must be pressed for an assurance that they would join at the proper time in bringing the Zionist question before the peace conference. With a view to preparing the ground, Warburg and Hantke were to do their best to establish a pro-Zionist Committee in Germany on the model of the British Palestine Committee. A few days after the meeting, Lichtheim told a German Foreign Office official that he had just returned from Copenhagen, where he had met Zionists from Russia and England. He had, he said, come back with the clear impression that Zionists abroad did not desire to prejudice the international

[32] Proceedings recorded in minutes of Copenhagen meeting of Zionist Executive, 29-31 July 1917: Z.A.

[33] ' Ein ausführliches Protokoll.'

[34] The programme shown to Sykes before the Conference was commonly referred to as the Zionist ' demands.'

character of the Movement by identifying it with the Entente.[35]

If Goldberg's mission had been designed—as Sokolow put it—'to encourage our brethren [in Russia] in the spirit of our orientation,' it had not been a marked success. Sokolow, now beginning to despair, wrote to Tschlenow at the end of August imploring him to be practical and realistic.[36] The Russian Zionists seemed, he said, to be the victims of too much talking in too many committees. It was time for them to come down to earth. Let them make up their minds to join forces with their fellow-Zionists in England and the United States and show some confidence in the English leadership, giving it the full powers without which it could do no effective work. Sokolow did not even now press Tschlenow to come out openly in favour of the British orientation, but he hinted plainly enough at what he wanted—a free hand for Weizmann and himself in their political work in London.

But Sokolow's appeal was of no avail. A few weeks later he got his answer. A copy of his letter had been sent by him to Victor Jacobson, the Director of the Copenhagen Zionist Bureau,[37] who was in close touch with the Berlin Zionist Executive and shared its outlook. Tschlenow had discussed the letter with Jacobson,[38] whose advice may have coloured his reply. 'For the last six months,' he wrote,[39] 'you have been demanding from us a public statement in favour of your conception . . . You will surely agree with us that before making such a statement we must have clear and positive promises. So far we have not got them even from England . . . In Russia we have been given much more definite pledges.' Was it true, he asked, as had recently been learnt 'from an absolutely trustworthy source,' that in 1915 Great Britain and Russia had conceded Palestine to France? Was

---

[35] Lichtheim to Dr. Goeppert, 5 August 1917: Z.A., Lichtheim, who had by this time left Constantinople and was working at the Zionist headquarters in Berlin, is not mentioned among those present in the minutes of the Copenhagen meeting, but he had evidently gone to Copenhagen with his chiefs, Hantke and Warburg. The reference to Zionists from England can only mean Boris Goldberg. There is no indication of anyone else having come from England.

[36] Sokolow to Tschlenow, 22 August 1917: Z.A.

[37] A copy, marked ' copy to Dr. V. Jacobson,' is in N.S.P.

[38] He says so in his letter of 24 September 1917 to Sokolow; N.S.P.

[39] The quotations in the text transl. from the original Russian.

it certain that Great Britain was going to persist in the Palestine campaign, and what would happen if she did not succeed in wresting Palestine from the Turks? These risks must be insured against: they did not appear, said Tschlenow, to have been taken into account.

Tschlenow remained unconvinced to the end. In October he decided to come to London. The British Government was informed and facilitated his journey from Bergen. On October 24th Sir Ronald Graham reported to Balfour that Tschlenow was on his way, pointing out that, since he was the leading figure among the Russian Zionists, it was desirable that the proposed pro-Zionist declaration should be approved before his arrival.[40] There was a few days' delay before the declaration was finally agreed to by the War Cabinet on October 31st, and by this time Tschlenow was already in London. He was less impressed than the Foreign Office had expected and still maintained a certain reserve. Mrs. Weizmann wrote in her diary (31 October 1917): 'Everybody is most enthusiastic except Tschlenow, who still advocates Jewish neutrality and [the] policy of sitting on the fence.'

Mrs. Weizmann was not, perhaps, quite fair to Tschlenow. His attitude is reflected in his comments on the Declaration in an article published in *The Zionist Review* a few weeks before his death early in 1918.[41] 'On the 2nd November,' he wrote, 'Great Britain spoke its word. The word of Britain is always weighty in the council of the nations . . . The other nations have not yet declared themselves openly, but so far as some of the Great Powers are concerned we are quite assured. 'The Jewish State is a world necessity,' said Herzl, 'and consequently must arise.' The World War has made clear to the nations and their Governments the truth of this idea. . . .' If Tschlenow shrank from leaning exclusively on Great Britain, it was not only because the outcome of the war was still uncertain, but because, in harmony with traditional Zionist thinking, he pictured the establishment of a Jewish national home in Palestine as part of a negotiated peace settlement to which both groups of belligerents would be parties.

[40] Below, p. 544.
[41] *Zionist Review*, December 1917, p. 125.

CHAPTER 30

THE DISCOMFITURE OF THE CONJOINT
FOREIGN COMMITTEE

WHILE WEIZMANN AND SOKOLOW were working for the acceptance of the London programme in Russia and the United States, British Jewry was moving towards a pitched battle between the Zionists and the influential group of British Jews represented by the Conjoint Foreign Committee.

Early in the War both the Zionist leaders and the Conjoint Committee had put out feelers towards some kind of accommodation. Meetings had taken place and memoranda had been exchanged, but all to no purpose. Neither side had been prepared to make the concessions demanded by the other, and the pourparlers had ended in a deadlock. After their breakdown in the early summer of 1915[1] there had been one or two half-hearted attempts at a rapprochement, but these had come to nothing, leaving the two sides as far apart as ever. The Conjoint Committee had realised that the Zionists stood to gain by the change of Government at the end of 1916, and that, with Lloyd George as Prime Minister and Balfour at the Foreign Office, they would be in a strong position for pressing their claims. By the spring of 1917 the Committee was scenting imminent danger and was exerting itself to make sure that its case should not go by default. By coming into the open with a reasoned statement of its views, it precipitated a controversy which was to end in its discomfiture and to bring about, to the advantage of the Zionists, drastic changes in the leadership of the Anglo-Jewish community.

After their abortive conversations in the middle of 1915 there was for more than a year no direct exchange of views between the Zionists and the Conjoint Committee. In the summer of 1916 James de Rothschild, in deference to the strongly expressed wishes of his father, Baron Edmond, tried to break the ice by

[1] Above, p. 181.

arranging an informal meeting at his house between Weizmann and Lucien Wolf. Baron Edmond was convinced that there was enough common ground for a working arrangement,[2] but his hopes—whether his son shared them is doubtful—were disappointed.

It was not that the moment was particularly ill-chosen. On the contrary, it so happened that in the summer of 1916 there was at least one subject on which Weizmann and Wolf were broadly in agreement. This was the handling of the awkward questions which were arising from the presence in England of considerable numbers of unnaturalised Russian Jews who were, as aliens, escaping military service.[3] Weizmann accepted the view, held by Wolf and strongly supported by Herbert Samuel,[4] who, as Home Secretary, had this embarrassing problem on his hands, that energetic efforts must be made to induce these Jews to volunteer for service in the British Army. In this matter Weizmann, together with some other Zionists, had found it possible to co-operate with Wolf,[5] but on the Palestine question the two men had nothing in common, and a single interview[6] was enough to show that there was no point in going further.

Nevertheless, neither side was in a hurry to put itself in the wrong with the Jewish public by provoking an open conflict. A point had been reached at which each was interested in testing the other's intentions, and not long after Weizmann's unfruitful conversation with Wolf, discussions began between the Zionists, with Sokolow as their spokesman, and the Conjoint Committee, represented by Wolf, with a view to the re-opening of the talks which had broken down in 1915. A lengthy and involved correspondence[7] in which each side tried to improve its tactical position by extracting preliminary assurances from the other, began

[2] In a description of his visit to Paris in July 1916 Lucien Wolf writes: '[Baron Edmond] read me extracts of a letter he was writing to his son, James, asking him to arrange an understanding between Weizmann and myself'; *C.F.C.*, 1916/486. A copy of this letter (undated) is in *Ch.W.P.*

[3] See below, pp. 488ff.

[4] Ibid.

[5] Ibid.

[6] On 17 August 1916. There is a note of the conversation in *C.F.C.*, 1916/400ff.

[7] Copies in *C.F.C.*, 1917/283, 285, 290, 291, 445, 449-453, 459.

in October 1916 and was brought to an end in the following April by Wolf's announcement that his Committee must now resume full liberty of action.[8]

While temporising adroitly so as to keep the correspondence alive, the Zionists appear at no stage to have been prepared to make any serious concessions to the Committee as the price of its co-operation or benevolent neutrality. They were still less disposed to do so after it had become clear, early in 1917, that they were on a flowing tide. Wolf, for his part, seems to have realised that the change of Government might be expected to tell in favour of the Zionists and that prompt action was required to neutralise their advantage. He made it his business to seek an early interview with the new Foreign Secretary, and at a meeting with Balfour at the end of January, 1917[9] he took occasion to raise the Palestine question in the course of a conversation concerned mainly with the position of the Jews in Eastern Europe.

He began by enlarging upon the importance of the Conjoint Committee and 'its essentially representative character.' He was at pains to make it clear that, though the Committee regarded Zionism as irrelevant to 'the main Jewish question'—the future of the Jewish masses in Russia and Rumania—it 'would rejoice if the Zionists made Palestine the seat of a flourishing and reputable Jewish community.' 'We should,' he told Balfour, 'have no objection if that Jewish community developed into a local Jewish nation and a Jewish State.' What the Committee insisted upon was, he explained, that in their propaganda and their activities in Palestine the Zionists should not imperil the rights and status of Jews elsewhere. A Jewish nation or State in Palestine must not 'claim the allegiance of the Jews of Western Europe, who are satisfied with their local nationalities,' nor must anything be done—as, for example, by demanding a privileged status for the Jews in Palestine—'to compromise the position and aims of Jews in other countries.' 'Outside these reservations,' Balfour was assured, 'we left a perfectly free hand to the Zionists, and

[8] Wolf to Sokolow, 26 April 1917: *C.F.C.*, 1917/459.

[9] 31 January 1917. A copy of Wolf's note of the conversation is in *C.F.C.*, 1917/56ff. A copy was sent to Balfour at his request and its receipt acknowledged without comment: ibid., 74-76.

we were even disposed, within certain limits, to co-operate with them in promoting their schemes.'

On all this it appears from Wolf's report that Balfour made no comment, except that 'he was disposed to think that we were right in arguing that Zionism offered no solution to the Jewish question in Eastern Europe.' Balfour expressed himself at some length on the situation in Russia, but on the Zionist question he was not to be drawn and left Wolf to do nearly all the talking.

What the Conjoint Committee conceived to be at stake was nothing less than the status of the Jews, and their integration in the national life, not only in England, but wherever they had been, or claimed to be, admitted to full equality of rights. It was no part of the Committee's case that Palestine had no special significance for the Jews. What concerned it was that on no account should there be any blurring of the distinction between a Jewish community, or a Jewish State, in Palestine and Palestine as the home—or, still worse, the national home—of the Jewish people. On this point there could be no compromise, for, once the Jews were proclaimed to be a people, with Palestine as their national home, then, as the Committee saw it, the anti-Semites would have won, since their case would have been conceded.[10] If the Conjoint Committee may be thought to have been hyper-sensitive, this was not unnatural at a time when everyone with a German or German-sounding name was to some extent under a cloud, when in the East End of London and in Leeds[11] there were signs of mounting indignation against the unnaturalised Jewish immigrants who were escaping military service, and when there was a widespread impression that Jews were somehow identified with the extreme left-wing element in Russia.

During the controversial exchanges preceding the final rupture

---

[10] 'I understand . . . that the Zionists do not merely propose to form and establish a Jewish nationality in Palestine, but that they claim *all* the Jews as forming at the present moment a separate and dispossessed nationality, for which it is necessary to form an organic political centre, because they are and must always be aliens in the lands in which they now dwell. . . . I have spent the larger part of my life in combating these doctrines, when presented to me in the form of anti-Semitism . . . They constitute a capitulation to our enemies. . . .' Wolf to de Rothschild, 31 August 1916: *C.F.C.*, 1916/411.

[11] As to anti-Jewish disturbances in Leeds see *J.C.*, 8 and 15 June 1917.

in the spring of 1917 the Zionists and the Conjoint Committee wrangled endlessly about the true construction of expressions like 'nation,' 'nationality,' and 'national home.' But neither side made any serious impression on the other, nor were these questions of semantics of much interest to the rank-and-file of the Zionists and their sympathisers. The ordinary Jews who were in growing numbers gravitating towards Zionism were none too clear in their own minds as to precisely what they wanted or expected to see happening in Palestine or as to how, if at all, it might affect their personal lives. They had little taste for refined thinking about the Zionist philosophy and its implications. They had simply an instinctive feeling that the Zionists were moving in the right direction and ought not to be obstructed. At a time when a new world order seemed to be in the making, the idea, however vaguely conceived, of a restoration of the Jews to Palestine had an emotional appeal which they found irresistible.

In expounding its views in the spring of 1917 the Conjoint Committee was careful to disclaim any lack of sympathy with Jewish aspirations in Palestine, insisting only that these should not exceed the limits of the carefully worded formula which Lucien Wolf had submitted to the Foreign Office some twelve months earlier. But in its approach to the Palestine question there was no such emotional impulse as inspired the Zionists. For the Conjoint Committee the whole matter was, in fact, of secondary importance, since that body was and had always been preoccupied with the position of the Jews in Eastern Europe and had never believed that anything that might be achieved in Palestine could help appreciably to improve it. It was no wonder that Wolf's rather dull and prosy formula,[12] however sensible and statesmanlike it may have appeared to his Committee, was unacceptable to Jews whose imagination had been fired by the prospect of a new flowering of Jewish life in Palestine.

The Conjoint Committee stated its case on grounds of principle and supported it with rational arguments. But behind these was the passionate conviction that for British Jews, who had not merely enjoyed the full fruits of equality of status but had, in their

[12] For text of the formula see above, p. 222. It had originally been communicated privately to the Foreign Office but was incorporated in the statement published by the Committee in May 1917—see below, p. 453.

own minds, identified themselves unreservedly with the national life, their Government's endorsement of Zionism would mean that they had suffered a kind of rejection and disinheritance—a *diminutio capitis* which, even though it left their legal rights unimpaired, would be painfully felt. The conflict between the Zionists and their opponents was all the more bitter because on the anti-Zionist as well as on the Zionist side it was tinged with emotion.

The battlefield was not substantially different from what it had been before the War, but whereas the Zionists had then been a struggling minority, they were now coming into the ascendant. Even in 1915 the Conjoint Committee had felt able to treat the Zionist leaders with a certain hauteur. Two years later its own position had become precarious. In the interval it had wearied and irritated the Foreign Office with its incessant prodding on the Russo-Jewish question, in which the British Government, having difficulties enough of its own with its touchy and unreliable Czarist ally, had been in no position to intervene. When the Russian Jews were relieved of their disabilities as a result of the March Revolution, the Committee's occupation was to that extent gone, and, though it continued to prepare the ground for the consideration of other Jewish questions[13] which might arise in the peace settlement, its main immediate concern was now to dissuade the Government from committing itself to the Zionists. But here also it was fighting on unfavourable ground. Not only did the Zionists command the personal sympathies of leading members of the Government, but there were important practical considerations which gave them an advantage over the Conjoint Committee. On a realistic view of British interests, the Committee had nothing attractive to offer. The Zionists, on the other hand, could be relied upon to work in support of the British claim to Palestine, to say nothing of the influence which they might—it was believed—be able to exert in counter-acting hostile propaganda in Russia and apathy about the War in certain circles in the United States. Not only had the Conjoint Committee no Lloyd George or Balfour on its side, but by the test of practical utility it was hopelessly outclassed.

[13] e.g., that of Jewish disabilities in Rumania.

For another reason the Committee's standing had deteriorated. Within Anglo-Jewry itself its authority was beginning to be challenged. For many years before the War the Anglo-Jewish community had, for all practical purposes, been governed by the members of a small and closely knit group of relatively old-established families. Their management of its affairs had been notably efficient and public-spirited, and, partly for this reason, partly because of the prestige attaching to wealth and social standing, it had come to be accepted as part of the natural order of things. It was from this circle that nearly all the leaders and most of the members of the Conjoint Foreign Committee had been drawn ever since the establishment of that body in 1878. But this oligarchical régime, benevolent as it was, could not last for ever, and, as the stratification of society became gradually less rigid in England, there emerged even in Anglo-Jewry, conservative as it was in its respect for tradition, some questioning of the established leadership. In the circumstances of the War, the activities of the Conjoint Committee assumed exceptional importance, and because of the mystery in which they were shrouded and the Committee's reluctance to acknowledge accountability even to its own parent bodies—the Board of Deputies of British Jews and the Anglo-Jewish Association—it was particularly exposed to attack. The Committee thus became the centre of a controversy behind which lay the desire of elements in Anglo-Jewry not belonging to the privileged inner circle to assert themselves and show who were the masters. Much the same thing was happening about the same time in the United States, where the movement, mainly but not exclusively inspired by the Zionists, for the setting up of a democratically elected American Jewish Congress signified an attempt to dethrone the select group represented by the American Jewish Committee.

Even before the spring of 1917, when the Conjoint Committee plunged into direct collision with the Zionists, there had already been rumblings of dissatisfaction both with its membership (broadened though this had been by some co-options) and with its autocratic methods. When the crisis came and in a close division the Committee's public exposition of its views on the Palestine question was repudiated by the Board of Deputies, Zionists and friends of Zionism joined forces with others whose

main purpose was to censure the Committee for its behaviour in publishing a statement of this character without having consulted its parent bodies. Commenting on the debate at the Board of Deputies, *The Jewish Chronicle,* itself strongly pro-Zionist, remarked that the result should not be regarded simply as a condemnation of the Conjoint Committee's statement. It marked a rebellion against 'the Grand Dukes'—'a revolt against the system of oligarchical repression. The great betrayal was only the immediate occasion of the resolution.'[14] The battle between Zionists and anti-Zionists was, in fact, mixed up with a struggle for power in the internal politics of Anglo-Jewry.

Realising that in its efforts to deflect the Government from a pro-Zionist policy it was now at a serious disadvantage, and knowing also that in the Anglo-Jewish community itself its position was none too strong, the Conjoint Committee had all the more reason to make sure that its case should at least not be allowed to go by default. Lucien Wolf's announcement to the Zionists on April 26th that the Committee must resume its full liberty of action followed closely on Sokolow's meeting in Paris with leading members of the Alliance Israélite. The Committee had received from the Alliance a report of Sokolow's statement, from which it appeared, if Sokolow was to be believed, that the British Government had already intimated its approval, in principle, of the Zionist programme.[15] Wolf at once sent the Foreign Office a copy of the report, asking to be told whether Sokolow's statements were correct and pointing out, that, in the view of his Committee, 'very serious mischief might result if an agreement on the Palestine question were concluded without their participation, more especially as the gentlemen with whom His Majesty's Government have so far been in negotiation are all foreign Jews having no quality to speak for the native Jews of the United Kingdom.'[16] Wolf was informed in reply that 'no new agreement on the Palestine question has been concluded. His Majesty's Government are sincerely anxious to act in all matters affecting the Jewish community, not only in its own best

[14] *J.C.,* 22 June 1917.
[15] See above, p. 403.
[16] Wolf to F.O., 21 April 1917: *C.F.C.,* 1917/462.

interests, but with a due regard to the wishes and opinions of all its sections, and they will not depart from these guiding principles.'[17]

Wolf sought further reassurance at an interview with Lord Robert Cecil on May 8th.[18] He was told, he reported to his Committee, that '[Cecil] quite understood our view and that Mr. Balfour had . . . shown him my memorandum of my conversation with him. . . . He added that it went without saying that we were to be consulted before any final engagements were entered into.' In the course of the conversation Cecil had referred to Herbert Samuel as a strong Zionist, whereupon 'I said I did not think he was a Zionist of the type of the official leaders of the Zionist Movement and that I had always found him quite reasonable.' Sokolow's statement to the Alliance Israélite was not expressly mentioned to Cecil, but Wolf told his Committee that it need have no anxiety 'so long as no agreement is concluded—and none will be concluded—without previous consultation with us.' A few days later, Claude Montefiore reported to his colleagues that he had seen Milner, who had 'said that there had been many conversations about Palestine but nothing more' and had 'confirmed the assurance of the Foreign Office that we would be consulted before anything final was done.'[19]

This was on May 16th. Only four days later, Weizmann, having outlined to a Zionist Conference in London the Zionist programme as he conceived it, assured his audience—and he was not contradicted—that it had the Government's approval:

> 'States,' he said, 'must be built up slowly, gradually, systematically and patiently. We, therefore, say that while the creation of a Jewish Commonwealth is our final ideal . . . the way to achieve it lies through a series of intermediary stages. And one of those intermediary stages, which I hope will come about as a result of this war, is that . . . Palestine will be protected by such a mighty and just Power as Great Britain. Under the wing of this Power Jews will be able to develop and to set up the administrative machinery which,

[17] F.O. to Wolf, 27 April 1917, ibid., 463.
[18] A copy of Wolf's note of the interview is in *C.F.C.*, 1917/472.
[19] *C.F.C.*, 1917/464 (16 May 1917).

while not interfering with the legitimate interests of the non-Jewish population, would enable us to carry out the Zionist scheme.

'I am entitled to state in this assembly that His Majesty's Government is ready to support our plans.'[20]

Before its suspicions had thus been confirmed, the Conjoint Committee had already seen the danger-signals and made up its mind to throw up such defences as it could. In spite of the assurances received from Cecil by Wolf and from Milner by Montefiore, the Committee was uneasy about the position. It had been kept in the dark about the half-promises, if no more, which had evidently been made by the Government to the Zionist leaders. It could, no doubt, rely upon being consulted before the Government committed itself irrevocably on the Palestine question, but it was felt to be important that its views should be precisely formulated and plainly heard before it was too late for them to make any impression.

The Committee was in an uncomfortable position because of plain hints from the Foreign Office that any public polemics on the Zionist question would be embarrassing to the Government and should be avoided. Early in May it had twice been intimated to Wolf, first by a Foreign Office official, Lancelot Oliphant, and then by Robert Cecil in person,[21] that Cecil would strongly deprecate any action by the Committee which would involve it in an open controversy with the Zionists. Cecil's anxiety is comprehensible. At a time when the British Government was encouraging the Zionist leaders to rally Jewish opinion in the United States and Russia in support of the British claim to suzerainty in Palestine, nothing could be more inopportune than that its own Jewish citizens should publicly advertise their differences on the Zionist question. The Conjoint Committee and the like-minded Jews for whom it spoke were in a painful dilemma. Did the loyalty which British Jews owed to their Government require those of them for whom Zionism meant, as it meant for Wolf, a threat of 'perpetual alienage'[22] to suppress their fears, and,

20 Sokolow, II, 56, *Zionist Review*, June 1917, p. 35.
21 Interviews with Oliphant and with Cecil, 1 and 8 May 1917: *C.F.C.*, 1917/202, 207.
22 Wolf's memorandum of April 1915: *C.F.C.*, 1915/109.

because British interests appeared to require it, to acquiesce in a policy repugnant to their own wishes and feelings?

The Committee sought a way out by framing a reasoned statement of its views in language which—so gravely had its effect been miscalculated—seems genuinely to have been meant to be unaggressive. Against the advice of the Chief Rabbi, Dr. Hertz,[23] the Committee, with two dissentients,[24] approved on May 17th a draft laid before it by its Joint Presidents—the heads of the two parent bodies—and authorised them to send it to the press. Under the headlines 'Palestine and Zionism'—'Views of Anglo-Jewry,' the Statement appeared in *The Times* of May 24th over the signatures of the Presidents of the Board of Deputies of British Jews and the Anglo-Jewish Association—D. L. Alexander, K.C., and Claude Montefiore.

Wolf had been anxious that, in deciding to issue a statement to the press, the Conjoint Committee should not be thought to have disregarded Cecil's admonitions against public polemics. On May 18th he had written to the Foreign Office explaining why it was felt that it had now become imperative for the Committee 'to give such guidance to the community as is in their power.' He had suggested that Cecil might like to see a copy of the Statement, which he described as 'a very conciliatory one,' before it was published, in which case 'I shall be very happy to show it to him and discuss it with him.'[25]

On May 24th—the very day on which the Statement appeared

---

[23] The Chief Rabbi, though not a member of the Committee, was present by invitation without a vote. His dissent is mentioned in the record of the proceedings in *C.F.C.*, 1917/223-224.

[24] The two dissentients were members of the A.J.A. delegation. Of the remaining five A.J.A. delegates, three voted for the Statement, one was absent and one was either absent or abstained—the records are not clear on the point. These last two appear subsequently to have expressed disapproval of the Statement; writing on 9 August 1917 to Sir P. Magnus, Claude Montefiore said, with reference to the A.J.A. representatives other than himself: 'Four of these six men were strong opponents of the Statement about Palestine.' (A copy of this letter, then in the possession of the late Dr. W. Mowshowitch, was shown by him to the author in 1952). Of the seven B. of D. delegates, three voted for the Statement and four were absent. Of the seven co-opted members, six voted for the Statement and one was absent.

[25] *C.F.C.*, 1917/530-531.

in *The Times*[26]—Sir Ronald Graham replied that Cecil would be glad to avail himself of Wolf's offer.[27] Wolf was now in the awkward position of having to explain that 'publication was a little hurried,' the Committee's hand having been forced by a leakage which had resulted in 'a most unscrupulous attempt to discredit the Conjoint Committee . . . in *The Jewish World* on Wednesday.'[28]

The Conjoint Committee's Statement made it clear that the Committee stood by 'a formula adopted by them in March 1916, in which they proposed to recommend to His Majesty's Government the formal recognition of the high historic interest Palestine possesses for the Jewish community, and a public declaration that at the close of the War "the Jewish population will be secured in the enjoyment of civil and religious liberty, equal political rights with the rest of the population, reasonable facilities for immigration and colonisation, and such municipal privileges in the towns

---

[26] Though dated May 24th, Sir R. Graham's letter had, presumably, been written and signed the day before.

[27] *C.F.C.*, 1917/532.

[28] Wolf to F.O., 25 May 1917: *C.F.C.*, 1917/533. 'Wednesday' was May 23rd. An explained in a letter from the Chief Rabbi, Dr. Hertz, to Claude Montefiore (30 May 1917: *C.F.C.*, 1917/549ff.), what happened was, briefly, as follows: The impending publication of the Statement was disclosed by Dr. Hertz to Leopold Greenberg, the Editor of *The Jewish Chronicle*, who was at this time also the Editor of the mid-weekly *Jewish World*, in the hope that Greenberg might induce the Zionist leaders to make some conciliatory move, as a result of which it might become possible ' to find a formula that would save the community from the manifesto and the dissensions consequent thereon.' The date of Dr. Hertz's meeting with Greenberg appears to have been May 18th. According to a memorandum by Lucien Wolf (*C.F.C.*, 1917/542ff.), Greenberg called on Wolf on May 22nd and told him that he had heard about the proposed Statement and that some strong comments on the subject would appear in next day's *Jewish World*. He urged that the Statement should not be sent to the general press. Wolf's reply was that ' [the Committee's] own constituents were becoming impatient . . . and, as there was no reason for withholding their views any longer, I could not see that it would be wrong of them to state to their constituents, and the public at large, what their attitude was . . . I must not be taken as for one moment assenting to the statement which had been made to him [Greenberg] with regard to the impending issue of a manifesto. I only desired to point out to him the circumstances which would probably justify . . . some public statement of the views of the Conjoint Committee . . .'

and colonies inhabited by them as may be shown to be necessary." [29]

This, it was declared, was still the policy of the Conjoint Committee, which was and had always been ready to co-operate with
the Zionists in a policy

'aimed primarily at making Palestine a Jewish spiritual
centre by securing for the local Jews, and the colonists who
might join them, such conditions of life as would best enable
them to develop the Jewish genius on lines of its own,'

leaving 'larger political questions . . . to be solved as need and
opportunity might render possible.'

But 'the Committee have learnt from the published statements
of Zionist leaders in this country that they now favour a much
larger scheme of an essentially political character.' The Committee 'would have no objections to urge against a local Jewish
nationality establishing itself' in Palestine. What it emphatically
rejected was the 'wider Zionist theory, which regards all the
Jewish communities of the world as constituting one homeless
nationality, incapable of complete social and political identification with the nations among whom they dwell,' and as needing,
therefore, 'a political centre and an always available homeland
in Palestine.' This, the Committee declared,

'must have the effect, throughout the world, of stamping the
Jews as strangers in their native lands, and of undermining
their hard-won position as citizens and nationals of those
lands.'

The Conjoint Committee might not have laboured this point
so strongly had it not been incensed by its reading of certain
contributions to the semi-official Zionist publication, *Zionism and
the Jewish Future.*[30] In his analysis of the Zionist case Lucien
Wolf had more than once indignantly drawn attention to Gaster's
statement[31] that 'the claim to be Englishmen of the Jewish persua-

---

[29] It was not mentioned in the Statement that the formula had not merely
been 'adopted by' the Conjoint Committee but had in March 1916 been
semi-officially communicated by Wolf to the Foreign Office (see above,
p. 222) and in October 1916 formally submitted to the Government in
the name of the Committee: *The Jews and the War, No. 1* (1917)
(London, Conjoint Foreign Committee, 1917), p. 25 and Enclosure III.

[30] See above, p. 299.

[31] *Zionism and the Jewish Future*, p. 93.

sion—that is, English by nationality and Jewish by faith—is an absolute self-delusion,' and to Weizmann's remark[32] that 'the efforts of the emancipated Jew to assimilate himself to his surroundings . . . deceive nobody but himself. The position of the emancipated Jew, though he does not realise it himself, is even more tragic than that of his oppressed brother . . . The facts of the Jewish position in the East and West alike . . . point to the same fatal source of weakness in the Jewish struggle for existence —the lack of a home . . . It is this central problem—the homelessness of the Jewish people—that Zionism attacks.' The same passage was quoted by Montefiore in explaining to the Council of the Anglo-Jewish Association why the Conjoint Committee had been unable to keep silent.[33] The Committee's resentment was all the stronger because the authors of these statements were, in its eyes, 'foreign' Jews, who had presumed to approach the British Government on the Palestine question over the heads of the accredited leaders of British Jewry.

After elaborating its objections to 'the national proposals of the Zionists,' the Committee turned to what the Statement described as

> 'the proposal to invest the Jewish settlers in Palestine with certain special rights in excess of those enjoyed by the rest of the population, these rights to be embodied in a Charter and administered by a Jewish Chartered Company.'

'Any such action,' it was declared, 'would prove a veritable calamity for the whole Jewish people. In all the countries in which they live the principle of equal rights for religious denominations is vital for them.'

The Statement ended with a peace offer: 'If the Conjoint Committee can be satisfied with regard to these points, they will be prepared to co-operate in securing for the Zionist organisations the united support of Jewry.' This seems genuinely to have been meant to be conciliatory, but it was possible to detect in it an irritating note of condescension.

The appearance of the Statement let loose the public controversy which the Foreign Office had tried so hard to discourage.

[32] pp. 6-7.
[33] J.C., 8 June 1917.

There were violent attacks on the Conjoint Committee in the Jewish press, letters on both sides in *The Times*,[34] a *Times* leader[35] giving judgment decisively in favour of the Zionists, a debate at the Council of the Anglo-Jewish Association and, finally, a trial of strength at the Jewish Board of Deputies, ending, though by a narrow margin, in the discomfiture of the Conjoint Committee, to be followed soon afterwards by its dissolution.

Why, it may be asked, should such strong feeling have been aroused by the Conjoint Committee's manifesto? After all, it may be said, all it asked was that the Zionists should disavow the idea that 'the Jewish communities of the world' constituted 'one homeless nationality, incapable of complete social and political identification with the nations among whom they dwell,' and that they should agree not to demand a privileged status for the Jews in Palestine. Many of those who objected to the statement would by no means have wished to argue that such ideas were sound and that such demands would be legitimate. In his letter to *The Times*,[36] which had been shown to Weizmann before being submitted for publication,[37] Lord Rothschild remarked that 'we Zionists cannot see how the establishment of an autonomous Jewish State under the aegis and protection of one of the Allied Powers can be considered in any way subversive to the position or loyalty of the very large part of the Jewish people who have identified themselves thoroughly with the citizenship of the countries in which they live.' Weizmann himself, in his letter to *The Times*, while insisting that the Jews did constitute a nationality, declared that 'the Zionists are not demanding in Palestine monopolies or exclusive privileges, nor are they asking that any part of Palestine should be administered by a Chartered Company to the detriment of others.'

But no Zionist or friend of Zionism could be expected to take the Statement at its face-value or to doubt that its real purpose, was not to heal wounds but to inflict them. It was, in fact, hopelessly prejudiced by its background and origins. At

[34] 25, 28 May and 1 June 1917.
[35] 29 May 1917.
[36] 28 May 1917.
[37] Rothschild to Weizmann, 24 May 1917: *Ch.W.P.*
[38] 28 May 1917.

no time had the Conjoint Committee shown any constructive interest in the Palstine question. Disliking Zionism but recognising that it could not be ignored, the Committee had all along concentrated its efforts on taking the sting out of the Movement and making it innocuous. Everyone knew that the brains of the Committee, and almost certainly the real inspiration of the Statement, were Claude Montefiore and Lucien Wolf, the most determined and the most formidable anti-Zionists in the Anglo-Jewish community. Some remembered that only a few weeks before the Statement appeared in *The Times, The Edinburgh Review*[39] had published an article by Wolf in which he disdainfully wrote off the Zionist Movement, telling his readers (inter alia) that '[the Zionists] declare that where emancipation does not exist it is not worth striving for and where it does exist it is no remedy.'

The manifesto might have aroused less indignation if the Committee had kept the controversy within the domestic arena by addressing itself to the Jewish public through the Jewish press. By choosing *The Times* as its forum the Committee scandalised many Jews who felt that this public advertisement of its differences with the Zionists, and the manner in which they were presented, could do the Jewish community no good. This was open to the rejoinder that the Committee was no less entitled to make its position generally understood than were the leading Zionists who had expressed their views, with as much publicity as was obtainable at the time, in *Zionism and the Jewish Future.*[40] But Jews incensed by the Committee's action were in no mood to listen to any such plea. Remembering Cecil's warnings against public polemics, Lucien Wolf told the Foreign Office that 'the Statement has been drawn up in the most conciliatory terms, and the Committee feel that it might well serve as a starting-point for fresh negotiations and as the basis for a compromise.'[41] If so, it was ill-devised for that purpose. It is not surprising that by the Zionists and their sympathisers it was interpreted as an insidious attempt to discredit the Movement, to present the British public with a

---

[39] April 1917.

[40] In his conversation with Greenberg on May 22nd (see above, p. 453, note 28) Wolf made the point that Zionist publicity 'was certainly not limited to the Jewish community': *C.F.C.*, 1917/546.

[41] Wolf to F.O., 25 May 1917: *C.F.C.*, 1917/533.

distorted picture of its aims and outlook, and to deter the Government from supporting it save to the extent of an emasculated programme to be approved by the Conjoint Committee.

Of the two parent bodies of the Conjoint Committee, the first to consider the Statement was the Anglo-Jewish Association. When the Council of the Association met on June 3rd, it had before it what amounted to a vote of censure on the Conjoint Committee. After some discussion, the mover of the resolution, Dr. Gaster, asked leave to withdraw it as a mark of personal respect for Claude Montefiore. This was agreed to, and the matter dropped.[42] Wolf at once wrote to the Foreign Office (June 4th) asking that Cecil should be informed of what had happened. 'My own impression,' he said, 'is that the Manifesto has done a great deal of good in the way of clearing the air, in abating the extreme pretensions of the Zionists, and in paving the way for a complete understanding. I always thought this would be its effect.'[43]

In the light of this letter, Wolf's position was all the more embarrassing when, two weeks later, he had to report to the Foreign Office the result of a debate on a similar motion at the Board of Deputies. By 56 votes to 51, the Board, on June 17th, adopted a resolution expressing 'profound disapproval' of 'the views of the Conjoint Committee as promulgated in the communication published in *The Times*' and 'dissatisfaction at the publication thereof,' and declaring that the Committee had lost the confidence of the Board.[44] The best that Wolf could do was to draw attention to the narrowness of the majority against the Conjoint Committee, observing that 'the net effect is to show that the parties are more evenly balanced in the Jewish community than was generally supposed . . . The decision really shows that not only are the English-born and well-to-do classes all on the side of the Conjoint Committee, but that a large portion of the foreign and poor elements are also on that side.'[45]

However persuasively Wolf might argue that the two sides were fairly evenly matched, there was no getting over the fact

[42] *J.C.*, 8 June 1917.
[43] *C.F.C.*, 1917/535.
[44] *J.C.*, 22 June 1917.
[45] Wolf to F.O., 18 June 1917: *C.F.C.*, 1917/538.

that the Board—a body considerably more representative than the Association of the rank-and-file of the Jewish community—had condemned the publication of the Statement and declared that the Conjoint Committee had lost its confidence. Soon afterwards the Committee was dissolved,[46] not to be revived until after the Balfour Declaration,[47] and then only on the footing that it was not to deal with the Zionist question unless expressly authorised to do so by both the parent bodies.

The vote at the Board of Deputies was not a resounding success for the critics of the Conjoint Committee, who only just scraped home, nor was the debate a straightforward trial of strength between Zionists and anti-Zionists. The mover of the vote of censure[48] explained that 'the whole purpose of the motion was that the Board should once again resume control of foreign affairs, which had been usurped by the Conjoint Foreign Committee.' The seconder[49] said that 'they had purposely left out the question of Zionism; the question was whether the Conjoint Committee had any right to send a document to *The Times*.' Though the resolution expressed disapproval of the Statement itself as well as 'dissatisfaction at the publication thereof,' its promoters were evidently relying on the support of members who, though antagonised by the behaviour of the Conjoint Committee, would not have described themselves as Zionists. The narrow majority by which the Conjoint Committee's action was condemned could not correctly be interpreted as an impressive Zionist victory. The fact remained that the Conjoint Committee had been censured by the Board of Deputies and to that extent discredited and disarmed.

This was the main but by no means the only advantage derived by the Zionists from the Conjoint Committee's ill-judged move.

---

46 By resolution adopted by the Board of Deputies on 15 June 1917 and by the Anglo-Jewish Association on September 9th.

47 The Committee was re-constituted, under the name of the Joint Foreign Committee, in February 1918.

48 Elsley Zeitlyn, who had framed the resolution. His account of the episode, and his part in it, can be read in a privately printed brochure, *A Paragraph of Anglo-Jewish History* (London, 1936). The debate is reported at length in *J.C.*, 22 June 1917, from which the quotations in the text are taken.

49 Nathan Laski. The words quoted are from an interposition in the course of the debate.

It had elicited from the Chief Rabbi, Dr. Hertz, a letter to *The Times*[50] in which, speaking with all the authority of his office, he asked leave to dispel 'the misconception that the [Conjoint Committee's] Statement represents in the least the views held either by Anglo-Jewry as a whole or by the Jewries of the Overseas Dominions.' Lord Rothschild had likewise publicly identified himself with the Zionists, first, in his letter to *The Times*,[51] and again in the debate at the Board of Deputies. Though he took no part in the affairs of the House of Rothschild (his interests were far removed from finance), and though he was not, and made no claim to be, the lay leader of the Anglo-Jewish community, the views of the holder of the Rothschild peerage carried weight both with Jews and with the general public. Lastly, the dissolution of the Conjoint Committee was accompanied by drastic changes in the leadership of the Board of Deputies. Herbert Samuel's brother, Sir Stuart Samuel, a Member of Parliament for an East London constituency, who was at least tepidly pro-Zionist, became President of the Board, with Lord Rothschild as one of the two Vice-Presidents. Thus, when the War Cabinet, in the autumn of 1917, asked the President of the Board of Deputies, among other Jewish leaders, for his views on the projected pro-Zionist declaration, the reply was very different from what it would have been had the old régime still been in power.

The repudiation of the Conjoint Committee by the Board of Deputies and its subsequent disappearance did not put an end to the activities of the anti-Zionists. They remained unshaken in their belief that there would, in the end, be a heavy price to be paid by the Jews if the British Government committed itself to the Zionists, and when, a few months later, the Balfour Declaration came before the War Cabinet for approval, they did their best to discourage any such move. But, though they had not been silenced by the collapse of the Conjoint Committee, they had suffered a severe setback. The personal standing of some of them still assured them of a hearing, but they no longer had as their mouthpiece an apparently authorititative body claiming, as had been claimed for the Committee by Lucien Wolf, in one of his communications to the Foreign Office, to speak for British Jews

[50] 28 May 1917.
[51] Ibid.

as their 'duly elected representatives for business of this kind.'[52]

For the Zionist leaders the fall of the Conjoint Committee came at just the right moment. They were doing their utmost to interest the Russian and American Jews in the idea of a Jewish Commonwealth in Palestine under British protection. Their efforts would have been seriously prejudiced, and their standing with the British Government impaired, if the anti-Zionists had gained the upper hand in England. They could now point to what had happened after the publication of the Conjoint Committee's statement as evidence that that body did not speak for Anglo-Jewry, and, with their position thus strengthened, they were emboldened to ask the Government whether the time had not come for it to identify itself formally and openly with the Zionist cause.

[52] 21 April 1917: *C.F.C.*, 1917/462.

CHAPTER 31

FIRST STEPS TOWARDS THE DECLARATION

THE OVERTHROW OF the Conjoint Committee removed a stumbling-block at a time when the Zionists were already beginning to press for a more precise British commitment. Writing to Sir Ronald Graham on 13 June 1917, Weizmann had represented that 'it appears desirable from every point of view that the British Government should give expression to its sympathy and support of the Zionist claims on Palestine. In fact, it need only confirm the view which eminent and representative members of the Government have many times expressed to us, and which have formed the basis of our negotiations throughout the long period of almost three years.'[1] The Foreign Office was inclined to agree. On the same date, June 13th, Balfour had before him a minute by one of his advisers in which it was suggested that the time had arrived 'when we might meet the wishes of the Zionists and give them an assurance that His Majesty's Government are in general sympathy with their aspirations.'[2]

Weizmann's move had, as usual, been well-timed. The atmosphere was propitious. Balfour had just returned from the United States greatly impressed by his conversations with Brandeis. There is no evidence of his having discussed the Zionist question with President Wilson,[3] but it would be surprising if he had not been informed of the 'very encouraging' interview with the President reported to London by Brandeis in the middle of May.[4] There was, therefore, good reason to suppose that in this quarter a British declaration in favour of Zionism would be well received. As to the French, they had formally expressed their sympathy with Zionist aspirations in the Cambon letter of June 4th. This

---

[1] Copy in *Ch.W.P.*
[2] Balfour's remark, 'Personally, I should still prefer to associate the U.S.A. in the protectorate, should we succeed in securing it' (quoted by Mrs. Dugdale, II, 232) refers to this minute.
[3] Dugdale, II, 232.
[4] Above, p. 427.

would make it difficult for them to object to a British gesture to the Zionists—a step, it could be argued, which the Cambon letter had made all the more necessary, since it was not desirable that Great Britain should seem to lag behind. Weizmann and his colleagues were being encouraged to impress upon the American and Russian Jews that if Great Britain gained control of Palestine, she could be relied upon to favour the building up of a Jewish Commonwealth. They had hinted, or more than hinted, that they were authorised to give this assurance, but it would be all the more convincing if a friendly interest in Zionism had been openly expressed by the British Government itself.

On these lines a persuasive case could be made out for a British declaration. A possible objection on the British side had been disposed of by the War Cabinet's decision, early in June, to persist in the Palestine offensive and to press it, even at the price of a still more costly effort, to a victorious conclusion. There was no longer any question of the campaign being suspended or petering out and the Zionists—as Sykes had feared for a moment[5] —left in the lurch. There was another consideration which the Foreign Office may have had in mind in recommending that the Zionists should now be given some further encouragement. The German Government was believed to be showing some interest in Zionism. Might not delay on the British side result in the Germans getting in first?

The Foreign Office had been given some reason to think that it might. When Weizmann, for the Zionists, together with Malcolm, for the Armenians, went on June 10th to protest to Ormsby-Gore against the British Government's supposed preparations for a soft peace with Turkey, he hinted that the Zionist leaders in Germany were being courted by their Government and mentioned, in particular, approaches made to them through the medium of Dr. Lepsius.[6] The Lepsius story must have reached Weizmann from some source in which he had confidence, but it

---

[5] Above, p. 332.
[6] This was reported by Ormsby-Gore in his note of the interview (as to which see above, p. 354: *Sledm.*, No. 54. Dr. Lepsius was a leading Evangelical divine, well known for his championship of the Armenian cause.

seems almost certain that he had been misinformed.[7] All the same, the Berlin Zionist Executive had, in fact, been in contact with the German Government. Quite apart from anything it had been told by Weizmann, the Foreign Office may well have had its own suspicions of what was going on in Berlin and have been ready to believe that, if it was seriously desired to anchor the Zionist Movement to Great Britain, the risk of German competition could not be left out of account. This line of argument certainly counted for something when the question of a pro-Zionist pronouncement came before the War Cabinet in the autumn of 1917 and may have had some weight when it was first considered by the Foreign Office in June.

With the Foreign Office already in a receptive mood, the collapse of the Conjoint Committee enabled the Zionists to press still more persuasively for a clear and, if possible, a public statement of British intentions.

The result of the Board of Deputies debate on June 17th was at once triumphantly reported to Weizmann by Rothschild:[8] 'I write to tell you that we beat them by 56-51 . . . I have written to Mr. Balfour asking him for an appointment for yourself and me for Tuesday or Wednesday, and I shall be able to show him that the majority of Jews are in favour of Zionism, as we have forced the authors of the manifesto to resign.' Balfour was agreeable, and Weizmann and Rothschild saw him a few days later[9] with encouraging results. No note of the conversation has come to light, but Weizman writes in his autobiography[10] that he and Rothschild 'put it to the Foreign Secretary that the time had come for the British Government to give us a definite declaration

[7] Mr. Lichtheim, who was closely concerned on the Zionist side with the relations between the German authorities and the Berlin Zionist Executive, has informed the author that he has no recollection of any overtures by Lepsius. Lepsius' name does not occur in the papers of the Berlin Executive examined by the author.

[8] Rothschild to Weizmann, 17 June 1917: *Ch.W.P.*

[9] Exact date uncertain. It must have been after June 17th and before Weizmann's departure for Gibraltar (see above, p. 356) at the end of the month. In *Trial and Error* (p. 255) Weizmann speaks of the interview having taken place a few days after his letter to Sir R. Graham of June 13th.

[10] *Trial and Error*, p. 256.

of support and encouragement. Mr Balfour promised to do so and asked me to submit to him a declaration which would be satisfactory to us, and which he would try and put before the War Cabinet.'

Weizmann left London on his mission to Gibraltar at the end of June 1917 and was not back until July 22nd. This prevented him from taking any part in the preparation of the Zionist draft, which was completed and submitted to Balfour a few days before his return. Before leaving, however, he had made certain arrangements with Rothschild. These are referred to by Sokolow in letters to colleagues who took part in the drafting. 'The first steps,' he told Sacher,[11] 'were taken by Chaim together with Lord R., and Lord R. will suggest the formula of this declaration in a private way. . . . The formula or formulas chosen will have to be given to Lord R. for his suggestions; this has been decided before Chaim left . . .' 'The declaration,' Sokolow wrote to Joseph Cowen,[12] 'is to be given by the Government and we are going to suggest it in a private way.' It was understood, in other words, that the draft should not be formally submitted by the Zionist Organisation to the Government but should be communicated to Balfour in a personal letter from Rothschild. This, as will be seen, is exactly what happened. Rothschild wrote to Balfour on July 18th enclosing a draft declaration, and on November 2nd Balfour replied by sending Rothschild the text—a very different text—of the declaration approved by the War Cabinet.

The draft sent to Balfour on July 18th had been approved by Rothschild, but in its preparation the main responsibility on the Zionist side had devolved, in Weizman's absence, on Sokolow. From his handling of the matter it can be inferred that he had been warned against expecting too much of the Government. In a message to the Zionist Conference in Petrograd early in June Weizmann had announced as the Zionist programme 'integral Jewish Palestine under British trust with all necessary guarantees development to Commonwealth,' and had told the Russian Zionists that this was what the British Government had in mind: 'Authorised state that in interview with His Majesty's Secretary of State for Foreign Affairs I received assurances of encourage-

[11] 10 July 1917: Z.A.
[12] 9 July 1917: Z.A.

ment and support our plans.'[13] But at no stage of the discussions about the proposed declaration did Sokolow suggest that it should say anything about a Jewish Commonwealth or Jewish State in Palestine. He had obviously been given to understand that the Government would not be prepared to enter publicly into any such commitment, and his more impetuous advisers, Sacher and Sidebotham,[14] had, therefore to be firmly overruled.

Before Weizmann left England some drafting had already been done, at his request, by Sacher, but, as it seemed to Sokolow, on the wrong lines. The nature of Sokolow's criticisms can be inferred from Sacher's comments. 'I am persuaded,' Sacher wrote (July 9th),[15] 'that . . . my original idea of asking for as much as possible is the right one. I think my own draft erred in not going far enough, not in going too far.' Sokolow's reply[16] was that 'if we want too much we shall get nothing; on the other hand, if we get some sympathetic declaration, I hope we will gradually get more and more.'

Sacher was not impressed. He proceeded to submit a fresh draft, in which Sokolow's plea for moderation had been deliberately ignored. The Government was to be invited to declare 'that one of its essential war aims is the reconstitution of Palestine as a Jewish State and as the national home of the Jewish people. . . . The definite form of such reconstitution must be an integral Palestine which is a self-governing State.' With his own draft Sacher sent Sokolow another by Sidebotham on similar lines, but amplified by an explanation of what was meant by a Jewish State—'not a State of which membership is restricted to Jews but a State whose dominant national character . . . will be Jewish in the same sense as the dominant national character of England is English, of Canada Canadian and of Australia Australian.'[17]

Sacher and Sidebotham appear to have been alone in insisting that the formula should raise the question of a Jewish State, and

13 Above, p. 436.
14 Others consulted were: Ahad Ha'am, J. Cowen, J. Ettinger, Simon Marks, I. M. Sieff, Leon Simon, S. Tolkowsky.
15 To Sokolow, 9 July 1917: Z.A.
16 10 July: ibid.
17 Texts of both drafts in *Ch.W.P.* and Z.A. Sacher's covering letter (11 July 1917) is in Z.A.

their drafts never had any chance of being adopted. But it was not only on this point that Sokolow had to restrain some of his advisers and reject their suggestions. He had to make it clear that there would at this stage be no point in submitting an elaborate programme on the lines of the proposals—commonly referred to as 'the demands'—which had been laid before Mark Sykes in anticipation of his meeting with the Zionist leaders in February, 'It is not here,' Sokolow told Cowen[18] 'a question of the "demands," which remain as they were. Our purpose . . . is to receive from the Government a *general* short approval of the same kind as that which I have been successful in getting from the French Government.' In explaining the position to Sacher, Sokolow wrote (July 10th):[19] 'A good deal of confusion arose with regard to this document. It is not an agreement, neither is it a full programme. Such agreement or programme we may get from H.M. Government after having presented our demands, but before having handed it over we cannot claim anything in the form of a programme. It has, therefore, been suggested that for the time being we should get a *general* approval of Zionist aims— very short and as pregnant as possible.'

The words 'it has been suggested' clearly refer to suggestions by the Foreign Office. Sokolow was not working in a vacuum. While he was consulting his advisers, he was at the same time in continuous contact with Mark Sykes, who, assisted by Harold Nicolson,[20] then a junior member of the diplomatic service, and by a Foreign Office official, Mr. Dunlop, was relied upon by Balfour for the production of a draft going far enough for the Zionists and not too far for the Government. From Harold Nicolson's reminiscences of those July days we learn that 'Dr. Sokolow would visit us daily, slow, solemn, patriarchal, intense.'[21] Nicolson speaks of the work done on the drafting of the declaration by himself and Dunlop, 'encouraged by the dynamic optimism of Mark Sykes, inspired by the dogged perseverance of Nahum Sokolow.'[22] 'Sokolow,' he remarks,[23] 'gave the impression,

---

[18] 9 July 1917: Z.A.
[19] Z.A.
[20] Later, Sir Harold Nicolson.
[21] *The Spectator*, 3 January 1947.
[22] *The Spectator*, 26 May 1939.
[23] *The Jerusalem Post*, 2 November 1954.

not of a prophet or a politician, but of a very industrious science student, who was interested, not in fantasies or irony, but in hard ascertainable facts. Mark Sykes' blustering, gay manner disconcerted him.'

When attempts at drafting began at the Foreign Office end, the key-words seem to have been 'asylum' or 'refuge.' The British Government was to declare itself in favour of the establishment in Palestine of a sanctuary for Jewish victims of persecution. Sokolow, as was natural, protested that this would by no means meet the case, and in the end he secured the acceptance of the view that, echoing the Basle programme, the declaration should speak of a home—a national home—for the Jewish people.[24] On this vital question of principle—for, from a Zionist point of view, such it was—the Foreign Office gave way, but on another point it was adamant. As Sokolow was at such pains to impress upon his advisers, what the Government was to be asked for was 'a *general* approval of Zionist aims' without elaboration. That a strong hint to this effect had come from the highest quarters may be inferred from Ahad Ha'am's allusion, in a letter to Sokolow (July 11th), to 'what you told me to-day in the name of the leader [sic] of Foreign Affairs,' from which, he said, it followed that 'the letter should contain nothing superfluous and no detailed 'conditions' but should be brief and in general terms.'[25]

The next day, July 12th, Sokolow and a group of his advisers agreed upon a formula which, surprising as it may appear, must have seemed to them to satisfy these requirements.

'His Majesty's Government, after considering the aims of the Zionist Organisation, accepts the principle of recognising Palestine as the National Home of the Jewish people and the

24 This passage is based on the recollections of Sir Harold Nicolson, kindly communicated by him to the author in conversation and correspondence. Cf. his reference to 'a gentle sanctuary' in his article on the subject in *The Spectator* of 16 May 1952. In the *Observer* (12 May 1959) he writes: 'In the first draft of the Balfour Declaration the words " asylum for the Jews " were used in place of the words " national home." We believed that we were founding a refuge for the disabled and did not foresee that it would become a nest of hornets.'

25 *Igrot*, V, 303-304. (Orig. in Hebrew.) The author is indebted to Sir Leon Simon for the translation and to the publishers, Bet Ahad-Ha'am, Tel Aviv, for permission to quote.

right of the Jewish people to build up its national life in Palestine under a protection to be established at the conclusion of peace following upon the successful issue of the War.

'His Majesty's Government regards as essential for the realisation of this principle the grant of internal autonomy to the Jewish nationality in Palestine, freedom of immigration for Jews, and the establishment of a Jewish National Colonising Corporation for the re-settlement and economic development of the country.

'The conditions and forms of the internal autonomy and a Charter for the Jewish National Colonising Corporation should, in the view of His Majesty's Government, be elaborated in detail and determined with the representatives of the Zionist Organisation.'[26]

In sending Lord Rothschild, on July 13th, some explanatory comments on this draft, Sokolow told him that it would have to be shown to Sir Mark Sykes and Sir Ronald Graham.[27] A day or two later he informed his advisers that something shorter was required,[28] and at a meeting on July 17th his informal drafting Committee did the necessary pruning.[29] Why re-drafting was called for appears clearly enough from Sokolow's explanation in sending the revised version to Rothschild:[30]

'It was feared,' he wrote, '[that] the first declaration was too long and contained matters of detail which it would be undesirable to raise at the present moment. It was thought that the declaration should contain two principles, (1) the recognition of Palestine as the national home of the Jewish people, (2) the recognition of the Zionist Organisation.'

This emaciated formula was agreed to by Rothschild, accepted

[26] Text enclosed with letter of 13 July 1917 from Sokolow to Leon Simon: 'I am sending you enclosed herewith copy of the formula as accepted at yesterday's meeting': Ch.W.P.

[27] Sokolow to Rothschild, 13 July 1917: Z.A.

[28] Leon Simon, The New Palestine, 28 October 1927, p. 318.

[29] A note taken at the time, now in Sir Leon Simon's papers, fixes the date as July 17th and shows that those present, in addition to Sokolow, were Cowen, Ettinger, Marks, Sacher, Sieff, Simon and Tolkowsky.

[30] 18 July 1917: Z.A.

by Sykes[31] and embodied in a letter from Rothschild to Balfour.

Balfour had not been easy to satisfy. A large number of versions had already been shown to him and rejected, and even now his advisers seem to have had some difficulty in inducing him to approve the draft. But finality had at length been reached, and about a month after Balfour had invited the Zionists to submit a draft declaration, Rothschild wrote to him as follows:[32]

July 18th, 1917.

'Dear Mr. Balfour,

At last I am able to send you the formula you asked me for. If His Majesty's Government will send me a message on the lines of the formula, if they and you approve of it, I will hand it on to the Zionist Federation and also announce it at a meeting called for that purpose. I am sorry to say that our opponents commenced their campaign by a most reprehensible manœuvre, namely to excite a disturbance by the cry of British Jews versus foreign Jews. They commenced this last Sunday, when at the Board of Deputies they challenged the newly elected officers as to whether they were all of English birth (myself among them).[33]

Yours sincerely,

ROTHSCHILD.'

'Draft Declaration

'1. His Majesty's Government accepts the principle that Palestine should be reconstituted as the National Home of the Jewish people.

'2. His Majesty's Government will use its best endeavours to secure the achievement of this object and will discuss the necessary methods and means with the Zionist Organisation.'

[31] 'I have pleasure in informing you that I showed to-day the amended draft to Sir Mark Sykes and he approves of it entirely'—Sokolow to Rothschild, 19 July 1917: Z.A. Since this was on July 19th, it looks as though Rothschild's letter to Balfour, set out below, though dated July 18th, must actually have been sent a day or two later.

[32] The text of the draft declaration is printed in Z.C. 1921 Rpts., 'Political Rpt.' App. 2. For a copy of Rothschild's covering letter the author is indebted to the late Leopold Amery.

[33] See, as to this incident, J.C., 15 July 1917.

More than three months were to pass before this draft was translated—and then in a drastically amended form—into the Balfour Declaration.

Appendix to Chapter 31

Sir Harold Nicolson has kindly permitted the publication of the following extracts from correspondence between the author and himself:

The author to Sir Harold Nicolson, 19 March 1952.

'. . . I wonder whether I am right in thinking, in the light of our conversation, that the course of events was, briefly, as follows: While the Zionist Committee were at work on a draft to be submitted by Rothschild to Balfour, you, on Sykes' instructions, were working on a draft reply to Rothschild, to be submitted to Balfour for approval. Sokolow was shown your successive drafts, the idea being, naturally, that the formula to be submitted by Rothschild should be one known in advance to be substantially acceptable to Sykes and Balfour.

'When your final draft had been completed and Sokolow knew what formula might be expected to be acceptable, he went back to his Committee and arranged for a draft on *your* (or Sykes') lines to be submitted. When Rothschild wrote on the 18th July, Balfour's approval of the formula had already been obtained, though in the end Balfour, on further reflection, made the slight amendment mentioned above.[34]

'I appreciate that you do not necessarily know what passed between Sokolow and his Committee, but the real object of my enquiry is to find out whether I am right in thinking that the Rothschild draft was, in fact, *your* (or Sykes') draft, and had been agreed in advance between Sykes and Sokolow, and was known, before being submitted, to be substantially in terms acceptable to Balfour.'

[34] This refers to the amendment mentioned below at p. 522.

THE BALFOUR DECLARATION

Sir Harold Nicolson to the author, 25 March 1952.

'I am afraid you attribute much more importance to my part in the Declaration than is really justified. I was only attached to Mark Sykes to see that he did not lose documents, etc. I certainly had something to do with the drafting but could not tell you for certain at what times, or by whom, alternative drafts were submitted. I think your version of the sequence of events is probably accurate, but I fear that from recollection only I could not assure you that that was precisely what occurred. All I can assure you with confidence is that "it was more or less like that."'

CHAPTER 32

GEORGE BARNES—SMUTS

LORD ROTHSCHILD'S LETTER to Balfour of 18 July 1917 was circulated to the Ministers concerned at the beginning of August.[1]
Three weeks later, the Foreign Office was informed by the Prime
Minister's Secretariat that a statement on Palestine was being
considered,[2] and at the beginning of September the question of
policy raised by Rothschild's letter came before the War Cabinet.

That body still included four of it five original members—Lloyd
George, Bonar Law, Curzon and Milner. The fifth, Arthur Hen-
derson, had been replaced as the representative of Labour by
George Barnes. During the summer the War Cabinet had been
enlarged by the inclusion of Sir Edward (later, Lord) Carson
and of General Smuts, who, after declining the Palestine Command, had agreed, instead of returning to South Africa, to share
in shaping the policy of the Imperial Government.

Bonar Law's views on the Zionist question are unknown.[3]
During the last stage of the discussions in the War Cabinet Weizmann was under the impression that he was responsible for the
holding up of the Declaration. After seeing Weizmann on
October 19th, Scott wrote in his Journal: 'W. hopeful as to
Government declaration of Zionist policy in relation to Palestine.
Bonar Law the difficulty—not hostile but pleading for delay.'
This would be consistent with what Bonar Law's biographer has
described as his 'instinctive scepticism and caution,'[4] but whether
the reports which had reached Weizmann were correct must
remain an open question. It so happened that it fell to Bonar
Law to receive Lord Rothschild and other leading Zionists when,

---

[1] Mentioned by Sir R. Graham in his memorandum of 24 October 1917, as
to which see below, p. 544.

[2] Memorandum by W. J. Childs, of the Foreign Office, in Dugdale papers.

[3] Lord Coleraine has told the author that he has been unable to find any
positive evidence as to his father's attitude to the Balfour Declaration.
An enquiry addressed to Bonar Law's biographer has elicited no information on the subject.

[4] Robert Blake, *The Unknown Prime Minister*, p. 343.

a few weeks after the Declaration, they waited upon the War Cabinet to express their gratitude,[5] but his polite acknowledgment tells us nothing about his personal opinions on the subject.

As appears from several entries in Scott's Journal,[6] Carson, who had been First Lord of the Admiralty, in succession to Balfour, from December 1916 until his promotion to the War Cabinet some seven months later, had in that capacity become familiar with Weizmann's name and his scientific work for the Government. Nothing is known about his views on Zionism except that, in response to the British Palestine Committee's appeal for support in the winter of 1916, he had, according to Sidebotham,[7] expressed 'general sympathy.'

In the early days of the War Cabinet, and before he had entered it himself, Carson told Scott in conversation what he thought of it. 'Speaking of George's eccentric War Cabinet,' Scott writes in his Journal (27 February 1917), '[Carson] said that of course Milner and Curzon were the only two, besides G. himself, who counted, and of these Milner was by far the more useful and influential. . . . As to Curzon, he was really imposible to work with because of his incurable . . . opinionativeness.' It was fortunate for the Zionists that this was so, for, while Milner was among their firmest supporters, Curzon—if not the most popular member of the War Cabinet, certainly the most knowledgeable on Middle Eastern affairs—by no means shared Milner's views. He had been present, and had not demurred, when Lloyd George told Sykes on April 3rd, that, as head of the Political Mission to the Egyptian Expeditionary Force, he was to work (among other objects) for the free development of Zionism under British auspices.[8] Nevertheless, when it came to the point, Curzon expressed serious misgivings about the proposed pro-Zionist declaration, believing that it involved too far-reaching a commitment. In October 1917, when the question was ripe for decision, he intervened at the last moment with a highly critical memorandum, and, even though

---

[5] 14 December 1917: Sokolow, II, 123; *J.C.*, 21 December 1917.

[6] 27 February, 19 April, 2 May 1917.

[7] *Great Britain and Palestine*, p. 42. He is not, however, mentioned in the report laid before the B.P.C. as to the response to its appeal—above, p. 304.

[8] Above, p. 384.

in the end he withdrew his objections, he made it clear that he did so without enthusiasm, still fearing that the Declaration would excite hopes which could never be realised.[9]

The Labour Party, represented in the War Cabinet by George Barnes, made a cautious reference to the Zionist question in a memorandum on war aims circulated to affiliated organisations in August 1917 and approved later in the year at a Special Conference of the Labour Movement:

> 'The British Labour Movement demands for the Jews in all countries the same elementary rights of tolerance, freedom of residence and trade, and equal citizenship that ought to be extended to all the inhabitants of every nation.
>
> 'It further expresses the opinion that Palestine should be set free from the harsh and oppressive government of the Turk, in order that this country may form a free State under international guarantee, to which such of the Jewish people as desire to do so may return and may work out their own salvation, free from interference by those of alien race or religion.'[10]

The Russo-Jewish Socialist Party, the Bund, had, in the summer of 1917, a representative in London,[11] and his anti-Zionist propaganda may have had some effect on the left wing element in the British Labour Movement. That Weizmann was not very sure of the Labour Party is suggested by a letter to Sykes in which he writes (22 September 1917): 'I beg to return the note which you so kindly sent me yesterday. The more I think of the documents which you read to me, the more I am convinced that they must be given to the L.P. to keep this party in order.'[12]

The Labour Party's rather cautious approach to the Zionist question is reflected in a reference to the Balfour Declaration in

[9] Below, pp. 545-546.

[10] Text in *British Labour Policy on Palestine* (London, 1938). See also S. Levenberg, 'Zionism in British Politics' (*The Jewish National Home, 1917-1942*, ed. P. Goodman, London, 1943), pp. 112-113.

[11] Moses Ehrlich. The *Morning Post* of 25 August 1917 refers to anti-Zionist views expressed by him in an interview published in the left wing Socialist paper, *The Call*.

[12] *Sledm.*, No. 66.

George Barnes' autobiography,[13] where he speaks of it as having been intended to give the Jews 'only a right of asylum and citizenship in a country which to them had a peculiar interest as a cradle of their race.' Barnes is here repudiating the idea that the Declaration was to be interpreted as 'giving the Jews a right to rule the country,' but there may be some significance in his choice of the word 'asylum' and in his omission of any reference to the conception of a national home for the Jews. Nevertheless, at the time of the Declaration Barnes was known both to the Zionists and to the anti-Zionists as one of its supporters. Writing to Brandeis on October 7th,[14] Weizmann mentions him, together with Milner and Smuts, among the Ministers who, in addition to Lloyd George and Balfour, 'have advocated our cause very strongly.' Just after the Declaration Weizmann told Rothschild how relentlessly the anti-Zionists had fought it to the last. 'For example,' he said, 'Sir Matthew Nathan had got at Mr. Barnes, who was friendly, and tried to persuade him of the danger of the Declaration, but I am happy to say that they all failed.'[15]

Barnes was not, however, one of the most influential members of the War Cabinet. Among the newcomers who had entered the inner circle in the summer of 1917 the Zionists had gained a much more powerful supporter.

Speaking on a Zionist occasion in London in 1949, Field-Marshal Smuts referred to the practical considerations which, added to other motives of a different order, had influenced the War Cabinet in favour of a promise to the Jews of a national home in Palestine. Among these he singled out in particular the expectation that 'it would rally Jewry on a world-wide scale to the Allied cause.'[16] In private as well as in public Smuts expressed views which explain why he believed it to be important for the Allies to have the Jews on their side, and why, even in 1949, after the British Mandate for Palestine had come to its melan-

[13] *From Workshop to War Cabinet* (London, Herbert Jenkins, 1923). In *An Eastern Tour* (London, n.d. — ? 1920) Barnes makes a friendly reference (p. 63) to Zionist colonisation in Palestine.

[14] *Ch.W.P.*

[15] Weizmann to Rothschild, 2 November 1917: Z.A. The author has not found any independent corroboration of this report.

[16] The Weizmann Forest Dinner, 22 November 1949; speeches reported at length in *J.C.*, 25 November 1949.

choly end, he still expressed the hope that Israel 'would never forget that it was Britain that first took Weizmann by the hand, and that that grip should never be relaxed.'[17] At a meeting of the War Cabinet Eastern Committee in December 1918, Lord Robert Cecil having remarked that the Palestine Mandate would be no great prize—'whoever goes there will have a poor time'— Smuts rejoined: 'It would affect Jewish national opinion, and nationally they are a great people.'[18] Colonel Meinertzhagen wrote in his diary in 1921: 'Smuts tells me he was influenced, when he agreed to the Declaration, by a desire to have the Jews on his [sic] side during the War. He appreciated their force in world politics and thought that by making such a Declaration he would enlist their help.'[19]

There is no evidence of Smuts' having begun to concern himself with Zionism before 1917, but in South African politics he had already had occasion to define his attitude towards the Jews in his sympathetic handling of various domestic questions affecting their interests—in some cases, notably in regard to the admission of Jewish immigrants from Eastern Europe, even at the risk of swimming against the stream. A picture of Smuts, as seen by the South African Jews, is to be found in a character-sketch in the Johannesburg *Zionist Record*; it appeared in February 1917,[20] when he was on his way to London to represent South Africa at the Imperial War Conference.

'He is racially and religiously tolerant to an exceptional degree. While it has fallen to his lot to take measures for the restriction of undesirable immigration, he has shown that he is not animated by any desire to differentiate against the Jews as such; the contrary, in fact, is the case, for it will be remembered that he once spoke (at Johannesburg) optimistically as to the contribution that was likely to be made to South African progress by 'the oft-despised Russian-Jewish immigrant'. . . In his Transvaal Education Act . . . he laid down conditions that must be considered distinctly favour-

[17] Ibid.
[18] Lloyd George, *Treaties*, II. 1150.
[19] 23 July, 1921. Meinertzhagen, *Middle East Diary*, p. 105.
[20] 15 February 1917.

able to the Jewish community . . . It is known that in politics he favours those Jewish influences which are exercised for the country's good.'

Smuts had, and had shown himself to have, a genuine esteem for the Jews, but from the Zionist organ's silence on the subject it can be inferred that he was not known to have expressed any decided views on Zionism. It was not, however, altogether strange to him. In view of his selection as the South African representative at the Imperial War Conference, the South African Jewish Congress was anxious to interest him in questions of Jewish concern likely to arise in the peace settlement—among them that of the future of Palestine. Just before his departure for London, the organisers of the Congress approached him through a Jewish journalist, Nathan Levi,[21] whom he received at his home at Irene on February 6th. 'I can assure you,' Levi reported to the Secretary of the Congress,[22] 'that he was not only au fait with the subject (for instance, he knew all about Russia and about Territorialism)[23] but that it required no argument to convince him. He wishes to see Palestine peopled with Jews and denuded of Turks, and he also wishes to prevent undue immigration into South Africa by making other countries fit to live in.' Smuts thought highly of Jews, but not so highly that he would not be glad to see some counter-attraction provided for Jews who might otherwise be drawn to South Africa. 'He asked me,' Levi went on, 'to send you the enclosed statement, and I believe he would like it published, so that everyone may know of his attitude.' It was published in the *Zionist Record* a few weeks later.[24] The gist of it was as follows:

21 Levi, who was on the editorial staff of the Afrikaans organ, *Die Volkstem*, was personally known to Smuts, having accompanied him on his election campaign in 1915—see J. C. Smuts, *Jan Christian Smuts* (London, Cassell, 1952), p. 159. A biography of Smuts by Levi was published in London by Longmans in 1917.

22 A copy of his report was enclosed with a letter (23 February 1917) from the S.A. Jewish Congress to the Conjoint Foreign Committee: C.F.C., 1917/385-386.

23 Zangwill's movement for the acquisition anywhere in the world—not necessarily in Palestine—of a territory available for the large-scale settlement of Jews, with a prospect of autonomy.

24 6 April 1917.

'[General Smuts] at once stated that he required no convincing on the subject of political and religious equality of Jews, as he deemed them fully worthy of them. Also, he assured the interviewer that the principle of Zionism appealed to him greatly from more than one standpoint. He promised to consider the Congress resolutions carefully and to give them his cordial support at the Conference as far as would seem possible to him after a thorough examination of all the circumstances.'

Smuts seems first to have become seriously interested in Zionism when, in the spring of 1917, he was studying the military situation in the Turkish theatre of war and making up his mind whether to accept the command in Palestine. 'You can readily understand,' he said at a Jewish meeting in Johannesburg in 1919, 'how an offer like that, pressed upon me repeatedly before I finally declined it, brought home to me more than ever before the consideration of Palestine and of the Jewish question generally.'[25] In his views on Zionism Smuts may, perhaps, have been influenced in some degree by Milner; in the War Cabinet, as Leopold Amery notes in his memoirs,[26] Smuts and Milner, in spite of the past which divided them, were natural allies. Soon after his entry into the War Cabinet we find Smuts showing some interest in Vladimir Jabotinsky's idea of a Jewish Legion for service in Palestine.[27] Jabotinsky saw him in the summer of 1917 and came away with the impression that he strongly favoured the proposal. In describing the conversation, Jabotinsky speaks of having been closely questioned on the situation in Russia[28]—a fairly clear indication that at this time Smuts was thinking, as Milner was, of what the

---

[25] 'Address delivered by General The Right Hon. J. C. Smuts on November 3rd 1919 in the Town Hall, Johannesburg, at a Reception given in his honour by the Jewish Community of South Africa.' This brochure, published (apparently) by the S.A. Zionist Federation jointly with the S.A. Jewish Board of Deputies, includes also the text of an Address presented to Smuts, who is told (inter alia): 'We shall never forget the valuable aid you rendered in the furtherance of our claim to national reconstitution in Palestine.'

[26] II, 99.

[27] Mr. J. C. Smuts, letter to the author, 9 January 1953; Jabotinsky, *Die Jüdische Legion im Weltkrieg*, pp. 96-97.

[28] Jabotinsky, loc. cit.

Zionists might be able to do to counter the pacifist propaganda which was driving Russia away from her allies.

At what stage Smuts first came into personal contact with Weizmann is not altogether clear. Weizmann writes in his autobiography that in the middle of the War he had his first interview with Lord Reading and that on the same day he first met Smuts.[29] It looks as if there must be some confusion, since there is no trace of any meeting between Weizmann and Reading before the Balfour Declaration except for an interview in July 1916,[30] when Smuts was not in England. It seems clear that Weizmann did not meet Smuts until, at the earliest, some time in June 1917, for Sacher wrote to him on June 14th: 'You will see that Smuts is joining the War Cabinet. If so, he won't go to Palestine, but we must try to win him for our cause.'[31]

Describing in his autobiography a conversation with Smuts on September 21st, Weizmann writes:[32] 'I had another talk with Smuts—a member of the War Cabinet—and obtained from him the expected reiteration of his loyalty.' This implies that he had seen Smuts before, but no record of any earlier meeting is discoverable. Of what passed at the interview on September 21st nothing is known except for what can be inferred from Sacher's letter to Weizmann of September 25th:[33] 'I am glad that you found Smuts so very understanding. I will send him as soon as possible the publications you suggest. We shall let him have a complete set of *Palestine*.' As time went on, an intimate personal relationship developed between Smuts and Weizmann, but no correspondence between them while the Declaration was in the making has come to light.[34]

In the post-War years no statesman of comparable stature fought more strongly than Smuts for the honouring of the

[29] *Trial and Error*, p. 202.

[30] Mentioned in *C.P.S. Journals*, 26 July 1916.

[31] Copy in *Sacher letters*, 14 June 1917.

[32] *Trial and Error*, p. 258.

[33] *Ch.W.P.*

[34] There is none in *Ch.W.P.* or Z.A. Sir Keith Hancock has informed the author that the Smuts Papers do not include any pre-Declaration correspondence between Smuts and Weizmann and 'have nothing to offer about the origins of the Balfour Declaration': to the author, 17 February 1959.

Declaration or proclaimed more emphatically his belief in its wisdom and justice. Addressing a deputation of South African Jewish M.P.s in 1921, he was reported[35] to have spoken of the Declaration as 'one of the most valuable historic results of the Great World War.' 'It will stand out,' he told a Zionist meeting in Johannesburg in 1926, 'as one of the great causes, and one of the principal achievements of the Great War.'[36] In 1930, when a White Paper issued by the Ramsay MacDonald Government[37] seemed to foreshadow a marked change in British policy in Palestine to the disadvantage of the Jews, he intervened with an indignant protest to the British Prime Minister, declaring that, 'as one of those responsible for the Balfour Declaration,' he felt bound to warn the British Government against defaulting on 'a debt of honour.'[38] In a memorandum submitted in 1946 to the Anglo-American Committee then enquiring into the situation in Palestine, he told the Committee that, 'as one who took an active part in the framing of the Declaration,' he looked upon it as 'a solemn and sacrosanct document,' giving assurances to the Jewish people which 'should not be abridged or tampered with more than is absolutely necessary under all the circumstances of the case.' He reminded the Committee that, reflecting on the fate which had befallen the Jews, the authors of the Declaration had been convinced that 'historic justice demanded a policy of their return to the ancient homeland.'[39] He struck the same note in his speech—one of his last public utterances—at the Weizmann Forest Dinner in London in 1949. 'As for me,' he said, 'a Boer with vivid memories of the recent past, the Jewish case appealed with peculiar force. I believed with all my heart in historic justice, however long delayed.'[40]

Smuts would not have expressed himself in such terms if he had not been much more than passively acquiescent in the Declaration. The Zionists knew at the time that he was on their

---

[35] *1921 Z.C. Rpts.*, 'Organisation Report,' South African Supplement, p. 2.
[36] *Zionist Record* (Johannesburg), 30 April 1926.
[37] Cmd. 3692 (1930).
[38] *The Times*, 27 October 1930.
[39] Full text of the memorandum (communicated by Smuts, though this is not stated) in *Zionist Record*, 19 April 1946.
[40] *J.C.*, 25 November 1949.

side; writing to Brandeis early in October 1917, Weizmann told
him that, besides Lloyd George and Balfour, 'other members of
the Cabinet, like General Smuts, Mr. Barnes, the representative
of Labour, and Lord Milner, have advocated our cause very
strongly.'[41] The part actually played by Smuts in helping to secure
the approval of the Declaration is, however, difficult to assess.
Weizmann's letter to Brandeis was written a few days after the
Zionist question had come before the War Cabinet, for the second
time, on October 4th, but in speaking of Smuts' advocacy of the
Zionist cause Weizmann cannot have been referring to anything
that he may have heard as to what had happened on that occasion, since Smuts had not been among the Ministers present.
There is, in fact, curiously little evidence from accessible sources
as to the exact nature and extent of Smuts' influence on the events
leading up to the Declaration. One who was well placed to observe them has described him.[42] in this connection, as 'a kind of
wing forward.' It seems tolerably clear that, though he must rank
among the architects of the Declaration, his contribution was not
of quite the same order as that of Balfour, Milner or Lloyd
George.

How is it, then, it may be asked, that we find Smuts, in the
post-war years, going out of his way to identify himself personally
with the Declaration, and how are we to account for the energy
with which, as one of those who must hold themselves responsible
for the assurances to the Zionists, he pressed for them to be
honoured? Part of the answer may be simply that we do not
know all that happened behind the scenes. Even if Smuts does
not seem to have played a particularly conspicuous part in the
proceedings of the War Cabinet when considering the Declaration, it may be that, if the whole story could be told, it would
be found (as a competent authority has suggested) that 'here,
as in most things, he exerted his influence in the background.'[43]
But it must also be borne in mind that at the time of the Declaration Smuts had no long-standing interest in Zionism, with which
he seems only recently to have come into contact, nor had he ever
been in Palestine. He went there early in 1918, at the request of

[41] To Brandeis, 7 October 1917: *Ch.W.P.*
[42] In conversation with the author.
[43] Mr. J. C. Smuts, in a letter to the author, 9 January 1953.

the War Cabinet, for consultations with Allenby and saw the Holy Land with the eyes of one belonging to a people steeped in the Hebrew scriptures. 'I need not remind you,' he told a Jewish audience in 1919,[44] 'that the white people of South Africa, and especially the older Dutch population, have been brought up almost entirely on the Jewish tradition'—a theme which he went on to develop in language curiously reminiscent of one of Lloyd George's speeches in a similar strain. 'The Old Testament, the most wonderful literature ever thought out by the brain of man— the Old Testament has been the very marrow of Dutch culture here in South Africa. I am sure that there are thousands, tens of thousands, of Dutch people in this country who know the Old Testament better than many Jews themselves . . .'

It looks as though Smuts' visit to Palestine must have fired his imagination and helped to raise his interest in Zionism to a plane on which it reflected, not merely an intellectual conviction, but an emotional experience. In the speech just quoted he referred to 'the time when I was in Palestine thinking over the problems connected with the Jewish people.' 'I could feel,' he said, 'how that apparently deserted country, so forbidding and grand, gave birth to the greatest religion on earth, the loftiest religious spirit in history. It required something rugged, something terrible, to have bred and to have created that literature and that spirit, which has been, perhaps, the most powerful influence in the history of the human race . . . Your people, your little people, has had a mission, a civilising mission, in the world second, perhaps, to none among the nations of the earth . . . and I do not see why they should not once more play a great part in the history of the world.'

---

[44] Speech at Johannesburg, 3 November 1919—see above, note 25.

CHAPTER 33

THE JEWISH LEGION CONTROVERSY— EDWIN MONTAGU

WHEN LORD ROTHSCHILD's letter came before the War Cabinet on 3 September 1917, more than two months had passed since the Zionists had been invited by Balfour to submit a draft declaration. In the interval the situation had changed in some respects to their disadvantage. Edwin Montagu[1] had become a Minister of Cabinet rank, though not a member of the War Cabinet, on joining the Lloyd George Administration, in the middle of July, as Secretary of State for India. Thus, the question of a pro-Zionist declaration reached the War Cabinet at a time when the only Jew with direct access to the inner circle was an implacable anti-Zionist. The Zionist cause had also suffered some damage from the flaring up of a controversy as to the proposed formation of a Jewish Regiment generally assumed to be destined for Palestine. A War Office announcement that a Jewish unit was to be raised had not only infuriated the anti-Zionists but had been a source of serious dissension amongst the Zionists themselves. Lastly, there was the understanding reached in the middle of August between Great Britain and France on the one hand and Italy on the other as a sequel to their conversations in April at St. Jean de Maurienne concerning the Italian claim to a share in the partition of the Turkish Empire.[2] As part of the tripartite arrangement, it had been agreed that the form of the international administration to be set up for the truncated Palestine forming the 'Brown Area' of the Sykes-Picot Agreement should be decided in accord with Italy. This meant, in effect, that both Great Britain and France re-affirmed their adherence to the prin-

---

[1] (1879-1924). His father, the first Lord Swaythling, and Herbert Samuel's father were brothers.

[2] Balfour to Italian Ambassador, London, 18 August 1917: Ribot to Italian Ambassador, Paris, 22 August 1917. (The 'yellow zone' mentioned in para. 3 of the memorandum setting out the agreement corresponds to the 'brown area' of the Sykes-Picot Agreement.)—B.F.P. *First Series*, Vol. IV, pp. 640-642. See also Pingaud, III, 247-249.

ciple of internationalisation and accepted Italy as a partner in the international régime.

It had been stipulated by Great Britain and France that the whole tripartite arrangement should be kept secret. So, indeed, it was, but the Zionists were disturbed by rumours from which they inferred that plans had been agreed upon which ruled out a British trusteeship for Palestine and ignored the claims of the Jews. This was the conclusion drawn by a writer in *Palestine*,[3] who was, indeed, under no misapprehension in thinking that Italy meant to insist upon a condominium in which she would have a share. In his valuable analysis of the relevant Italian State Papers,[4] Professor Manuel has shown how persistently the Italians, obsessed by their ambition to gain a foothold in Palestine, fought by every means at their disposal against a British monopoly, trying—among other moves—to detach the American Zionists from their exclusive reliance on Great Britain and doing their best, at a later stage, to embarrass the British authorities in Palestine by anti-Zionist propaganda.[5]

With France intent on ingratiating herself with the Syrian Arabs and Italy competing with her for the favour of the Catholic Church, nothing could be more unlikely than that a combination of which these Powers formed part would exert itself to promote the establishment in Palestine of a national home for the Jews. Still less did the tripartite arrangement leave room for a Jewish national home under British protection. If, therefore, the agreement, so far as it related to Palestine, was to be taken seriously, it was, on the face of it, difficult to reconcile with the assumptions on which the Zionists had been encouraged to build in their discussions with the British Government. The Government does not, however, seem to have seen in it any real obstacle to its plans for a British claim to Palestine, coupled with a British commitment to the Zionists. The Italians could be reminded, as in due course they were,[6] that the tripartite agreement had been provided with

[3] 15 September 1917.

[4] *Journal of Modern History* (Chicago), Sept. 1955, pp. 263ff.

[5] As to Italian anti-Zionist propaganda, see *B.F.P., First Series,* Vol. IV, Nos. 196, 358, 413.

[6] Balfour to Italian Ambassador, 26 November 1918, quoted *B.F.P., First Series,* Vol. VII, No. 29.

an escape clause. The whole arrangement was governed by the overriding condition, which had not been and would not be satisfied, that it was subject to the concurrence of Russia. At the end of 1918 Lloyd George extracted Clemenceau's assent to the proposal that Palestine should come under British administration, and, once the French had begun to give way, the Italian pinpricks were of little practical importance. Thus, in the event, the paper commitment to Italy in the tripartite agreement of August 1917 had no embarrassing consequences for the British Government and did the Zionists no harm.

A more direct threat to the Zionist position was the boiling up of the Jewish Legion dispute, which might easily have ended in a disastrous split in the Zionist ranks and the loss of Weizmann's leadership.

The question of a pro-Zionist declaration reached the agenda of the War Cabinet at a time when a confused and angry controversy was raging among the Jews in England as the result of a War Office announcement, at the end of July 1917, that arrangements were being made for the formation of a Jewish infantry regiment, with the Shield of David as its regimental badge.[7] No special rôle had been officially assigned to the Jewish regiment, but it was generally assumed to be intended for service in Palestine. The whole proposal was obnoxious to a large section of the Anglo-Jewish community, including many British Jews who could not be classed as anti-Zionists. It was disliked just as strongly, though on different grounds, by most of the Zionist leaders in England, the one outstanding exception being Weizmann, whose differences with his colleagues had become so acute that halfway through August he had threatened to retire and leave them to their own devices.

The idea of a Jewish fighting force for service in the Allied cause was not new. It was associated especially with the name of Vladimir Jabotinsky,[8] who, in the early days of the War, tried

[7] *The Times*, 28 July 1917.
[8] (1880-1940.) Born in Russia and started life as a journalist, serving as a foreign correspondent of one of the leading Russian newspapers. He became an ardent Zionist, and his brilliant literary and oratorical gifts brought him at an early age into prominence in the Movement. During

to interest some of the Zionist leaders in a rather nebulous scheme for the formation of a Jewish Legion to be placed at the service of one of the Allied Powers—preferably Great Britain—with a view to its being eventually used in Palestine.[9]

According to Jabotinsky,[10] Weizmann from the start showed some interest in his proposals, but neither Sokolow nor Tschlenow would have anything to do with them. Nor would the Zionist General Council, which, at a meeting in Copenhagen in the summer of 1915, adopted resolutions denouncing the propaganda in favour of 'the formation of a Jewish Legion for the conquest of Palestine,' and declaring that such proposals were inconsistent with the basic principles of Zionist policy.[11] Four of the eight members present were Germans, the other four being Russians. It is no wonder that the Council refused emphatically to countenance propaganda in favour of a Jewish declaration of war— for that was what it could be said to amount to—on Germany's Turkish ally.

This was in June 1915. By that time Jabotinsky had already achieved a partial success. In the winter of 1914-15 a considerable number of Jewish refugees from Palestine, most of them of Russian nationality and liable, therefore, to be treated by the Turks as enemy aliens, had found asylum in Egypt. Jabotinsky had gone to Egypt at the end of 1914, and by the spring the British authorities had been persuaded to sanction the voluntary recruitment of Jewish refugees for service with the British Army as an auxiliary unit on an as yet unspecified Turkish Front. The

---

[9] Since Palestine was not at this time a theatre of war and there was no certainty that it ever would be, the whole idea sounds somewhat unreal. It must, however, be borne in mind that it took shape soon after the British declaration of war on Turkey and at a time when there must have seemed to Jabotinsky and his friends to be at least a possibility of a rapid British advance into the heart of the Turkish Empire.

[10] *Die Jüdische Legion im Weltkrieg* (Berlin, 1930), pp. 41-42.

[11] Minutes of meeting 10-11 June 1915 : Z.A.

---

the latter part of the 1914-18 War he worked in close association with Weizmann. After the War the two drifted apart. Jabotinsky had no patience with Weizmann's *attentisme*, and in 1924 he founded the Zionist Revisionist Movement as a challenge to the established leadership. Impatient, tempestuous and distrusted by many as lacking in poise and judgment, he was generally recognised as a man of strong personality, high courage and lofty character.

first volunteers were sworn in at the end of March, and on April 26th, the day after the first British landing, the Zion Mule Corps went ashore on the Gallipoli Peninsula, where it served with credit under its British Commanding Officer, Colonel Patterson, until the evacuation. It was disbanded in March 1916, and all that survived of it was a group of some hundred-and-fifty ex-members who voluntarily enlisted in the British Army. These were sent to England for training and, after serving together in the home battalion of a London Territorial Regiment, were eventually to form the nucleus of a Jewish unit of The Royal Fusiliers.[12]

What was in the end to bring the Jewish Legion idea back to life was a fresh series of events starting in the spring of 1916.

Jabotinsky has left a vivid description of the Jewish East End of London as he saw it in the second year of the War. In this 'foreign island'—'a separate world, shut off, as by a thick wall, from embattled England'—they would tell you, he writes, that no one interfered with them while they went quietly about their own business; 'though we sit at home while the English boys fight, no one does us any harm.'[13] When compulsory military service came into force in England at the beginning of 1916, this state of affairs began to attract public notice. Many of the East European immigrants of recent years had not been naturalised, with the result that some 20,000[14] Russian Jews of military age were escaping conscription, which was applicable only to British subjects. That citizens of an Allied country resident in England should serve neither in the British Army nor in their own began to be resented as an intolerable anomaly, and by the summer of 1916 the Government had made up its mind that the matter could not be allowed to rest. It came within the purview of the Home Office, as the Department dealing with aliens, and Herbert

---

12 See Jabotinsky, op. cit.; J. H. Patterson, *With the Zionists in Gallipoli* (London, Hutchinson, 1916). The first British official in Egypt to interest himself in the project was Sir Ronald Graham, who was later, after being transferred to the Foreign Office, to be closely concerned with the events leading to the Balfour Declaration.

13 Jabotinsky, op. cit., p. 54.

14 The number is not precisely known. According to a statement by a Government spokesman in the House of Lords (27 July 1916: O.R. col. 991), the total number of Russians of military age resident in the U.K. was estimated at 25,000. Of these the great majority would certainly have been Jews.

Samuel was thus presented with as awkward and embarrassing a problem as any he had to handle as Home Secretary.

His personal feelings on the subject come out clearly in a letter to Lucien Wolf. 'If,' he wrote (30 August 1916),[15] 'the mass of the Russian Jews in this country refuse to lift a finger to help, when this country is making immeasurable sacrifices in a war with which the cause of liberty all over the world is bound up, the effect on the reputation of the Jewish name everywhere will be disastrous.' Some four weeks earlier Samuel had told the House of Commons that it had been decided that Russians of military age should be made to understand that they were 'expected either to offer their services to the British Army or to return to Russia to fulfil their military obligations there.'[16]

Early in 1916, when the agitation about the Russian Jews was beginning to gain momentum, Jabotinsky had seized the opportunity to bring his Jewish Legion idea to the notice of the War Office and the Foreign Office.[17] Weizmann supported him, and in July Scott tried to interest Lloyd George, then Secretary of State for War, in what he described in his Journal[18] as 'Weizmann's plan for forming a special Brigade for Russian Jews.' These proposals did not find favour with the Government, and, realising that for the time being it was useless to press them, both Weizmann and Jabotinsky, together with some other Zionists, joined in an organised effort, in which they found themselves in temporary alliance with (among others) Lucien Wolf, to persuade Russian Jews of military age to volunteer as individuals for service in the British Army.[19]

The response was negligible; up to the end of November 1916 the number of enlistments was less than four hundred.[20] The Government now decided that the time had come for stronger measures, and at the end of February 1917 Bonar Law, in a state-

---

15 Copy in *C.F.C.*, 1916/471. (Published by kind permission of Lord Samuel.)

16 H.C., 29 June 1916: O.R., col. 1084.

17 Lucien Wolf was informed of this by the Foreign Office, 4 April 1916: *C.F.C.*, 1916/410.

18 28 July 1916.

19 *J.C.*, 28 July, 22 September 1916; *C.F.C.*, 1916/472.

20 Bonar Law, H.C., 29 November 1916: O.R., col. 306.

ment in the House of Commons,[21] foreshadowed the legislation which eventually took shape as the Military Service (Conventions with Allies) Act.[22] So far as Russians resident in England were concerned, the effect of the Act, together with an Anglo-Russian Convention signed as soon as it had received the Royal Assent, was that men of military age were invited to choose between service in the British Army and the risk of deportation to Russia.

Legislation on these lines could not be laid before Parliament until there had been an exchange of views between the British and Russian Governments. The diplomatic preliminaries had delayed the introduction of the Act, and by the time it came into force in July 1917 the situation had changed. The Zionists had made a marked advance in their relations with the British Government; the British invasion of Palestine was now in full swing; the United States had ranged itself with the Allies, but a good many Americans, including a considerable section of the Jewish population, were known to be half-hearted about the War; it had become urgently necessary to appeal to every element in Russia which might exert a steadying influence in the situation seen to be developing as a sequel to the March Revolution. Some of the ideas current at the time are reflected in a memorandum summarised in *The Times* of September 3rd and stated to have been 'submitted to the War Cabinet after the Russian Revolution and the entry of the United States into the War.' It was pointed out,' *The Times* recalled, 'that the great majority of Jews in the world, could, in view of these two events, be considered as entirely pro-Entente, but that, at the same time, they had no special interest in the prosecution of the War to complete victory. The suggestion was made that, by inspiring the unassimilated millions of the Jewish people in America and Russia with an ideal of which the realisation would be essentially dependent on victory, a living link would be created between the Jews and the fortunes of the War. The suggested idea was the liberation of Palestine with the help of a combatant Jewish Legion . . .'

The authorship of the memorandum was not disclosed, but it clearly echoed the views of Jabotinsky, who, backed by Weizmann, had taken advantage of the changed situation to revive his propaganda and had, through the good offices of Colonel

21 H.C., 27 February 1917: O.R., col. 1853.   22 Royal Assent, 10 July 1917.

Patterson, gained an influential supporter in Leopold Amery.[23] Amery, besides being an Assistant-Secretary to the War Cabinet, was Assistant Military Secretary to the Secretary of State for War, Lord Derby, and was thus well placed for influencing the War Office. Early in April Derby saw Jabotinsky and his friend, Joseph Trumpeldor,[24] who had been associated with him in Egypt in the organisation of the Zion Mule Corps. Jabotinsky and Trumpeldor pressed upon Derby the case for the formation of a Jewish unit for service in Palestine and assured him that, if this were done, large numbers of Russian Jews could be relied upon to come forward. The proposal had the attraction that it pointed a way out of the disagreeable situation which would arise if the Russian Jews failed to enlist in the British Army, thus inviting deportation. Derby was favourably impressed by the interview and strongly disposed to go forward with Jabotinsky's proposal. By the end of April they were well on the way to being accepted, as is shown by Mark Sykes' remark, in telegraphing to the Foreign Office from Cairo on April 28th, that if there was not going to be a determined British advance in Palestine, then 'the Jabotinsky scheme should not be proceeded with.'[25]

Weizmann had been using his influence in the same direction. At his interview with Lloyd George on April 3rd he spoke—so Scott, who was present, records in his Journal—of 'the great change which the Russian Revolution had produced in the feeling of the Russian Jews in England . . . He did not dispute that the Russian Jews ought now to fight. They ought to be sent to Palestine. That would go far to reconcile them.' 'George,' Scott writes, 'agreed, but added that it would have the worst effect on public opinion on the Jewish claims to Palestine if they were not willing to fight for it. Weizmann said they will fight and fight well.'

The end of it was that on 28 July 1917, almost immediately after the coming into force of the new Act and the signature of the Anglo-Russian Convention, the press published a statement by the War Office to the effect that arrangements were nearing completion for the formation of a Jewish regiment of infantry.

[23] Jabotinsky, op. cit., p. 69; Amery, II, 117-118.
[24] 1880-1920. Served in the Russian Army in the war with Japan. Settled in Palestine in 1912.
[25] *Sledm.*, No. 42, quoted above, p. 332.

The regimental badge was to be 'a representation of King David's Shield.' Instructions had already been issued for the transfer to the new unit of Jewish soldiers with a knowledge of Yiddish or Russian.[26]

This announcement was received in the Anglo-Jewish community, and by no means only in anti-Zionist circles, with a cascade of disapproval. Why should there be a Jewish regiment any more than there was a Roman Catholic or a Methodist regiment? Thousands of British Jews, many of them pre-conscription volunteers, were already serving in the Army or other branches of the Armed Forces. Why should the public be given the impression that the Jewish contribution was represented by a single unit to be raised under pressure near the end of the third year of the War? Who could tell how the elements from which this regiment was mainly to be recruited would acquit themselves, and why should the reputation of the Jews have to be staked on its unpredictable performance?

In some quarters resentment was all the stronger because the formation of a Jewish regiment, assumed on all hands to be destined for Palestine, was interpreted as one more concession to Zionist propaganda. The anti-Zionists were incensed, but, though their protests were the loudest, there were serious misgivings in the Anglo-Jewish community as a whole. Sir Stuart Samuel, the newly elected President of the Jewish Board of Deputies, told the Board that there was widespread and determined opposition to the proposal, and that he had never known any question on which the community was so unanimous.[27] Looking back on what had happened, Lord Rothschild wrote to Weizmann early in September: 'I am strongly of the opinion that the origin of the whole misfortune arose from the fact that that the Jewish regiment and all its consequences were too hastily entered upon by the Government, and I fear Mr. Jabotinsky was the wrong man to advise on the subject owing to his fanatic enthusiasm.'[28] A Jewish deputation to Lord Derby to protest against the scheme was followed by a counter-deputation representing its supporters, and so confused did the situation

[26] *The Times*, 28 July 1917.
[27] *J.C.*, 17 August 1917.
[28] Rothschild to Weizmann, 2 September 1917: *Ch.W.P.*

become that Derby was driven to despair. When Scott called on
him at the end of August in the hope of persuading him to stand
firm, he made it clear that he had been shaken. 'I had not
realised,' Scott writes in his Journal,[29] 'that he was quite so
helpless. "Everything moves in a circle," he said, "and you come
back to where you started."'

In the end the idea of a Jewish regiment to be known by that
name was dropped. There was to be a *de facto* Jewish unit, but
it would form a battalion of The Royal Fusiliers and would have
no special Jewish emblem. A distinctive name and badge, it was
announced, would have to be earned.[30] Something having thus
been conceded to both sides, recruiting began but was not
notably brisk. Though there was a ready-made nucleus in the
shape of a group of ex-members of the Zion Mule Corps, it took
Colonel Patterson, who had been selected as the Commanding
Officer, some four months to raise one battalion.[31] By this time
Russia was almost out of the War, with the result that most of
the Russian Jews for whom the scheme had been primarily
designed succeeded, after all, in escaping military service. Nevertheless, a start had been made, and to the battalion raised in
England (the 38th Royal Fusiliers) there were later added two
more (the 39th and 40th), consisting mainly of American Jews,
together with locally recruited Palestinians. The 38th and 39th
saw active service in Palestine and in the late summer of 1918
took a creditable part in the operations in the Jordan Valley.[32] To
this extent, at least, Jabotinsky's dream was to come true.

Weizmann seems very early in the War to have been attracted
by Jabotinsky's ideas,[33] and it is not surprising to find him backing them when they began, in the spring of 1917, to have some
practical significance. Lloyd George had told him that if the
Jews wanted a national home in Palestine, public opinion would
expect them to be ready to fight for it.[33a] At a time when he was
pressing the Government for a pro-Zionist declaration he may

[29] 29 August 1917.
[30] Patterson, op. cit., p. 24; *The Times*, 13 September 1917.
[31] Patterson, op. cit., p. 25.
[32] See Allenby's Dispatch, 31 October 1918, quoted Patterson, op. cit.,
pp. 188-189.
[33] Jabotinsky, op. cit., pp. 41-42.
[33a] See above, p. 491.

well have felt that his plea would carry all the more weight if he could show that he was doing his best to raise a Jewish fighting force for service in Palestine. How closely he identified himself, in his own mind, with Jabotinsky's propaganda is shown by his remarks on the subject in addressing a Zionist Conference in London in 1919: 'Most of you,' he said, 'will have forgotten the fact that most of the Zionists have opposed the Legion. It was only my poor person that started that.'[34] Though his instinct told him to support the project, his views were unacceptable to the great majority of his colleagues, and at the time when the Zionist question came before the War Cabinet on September 3rd feeling was running so high against him that he was in a mood to throw up the leadership.

That the Jewish Legion idea should have been strongly disliked by many Zionists is comprehensible. Ahad Ha'am, to whom Weizmann had in the past so often turned for advice, wrote to him (August 17th):[35] 'You know my point of view in principle. Although it is highly advisable to have Jewish soldiers at the Palestine Front, they should be in British (or, if possible, American) units and not in a separate Jewish regiment. I consider the latter to be an empty demonstration, the result of which may prove disastrous both to Palestinian and, generally, Turkish Jewry and to our future work in Palestine, if, after all, it is not occupied.' Ahad Ha'am was expressing views firmly held by many other members of Weizmann's inner circle. So strained were the relations between Weizmann and his colleagues that on the same day, August 17th, he wrote to Sokolow:[36] 'I wish to inform you that . . . after having weighed all the consequences, I have come to the inevitable conclusion that it is impossible for me to continue to serve either on the Executive of the E.Z.F.[37] or on the Political Committee.[38] I have, accordingly, placed my resignation from the Presidency of the E.Z.F. in the hands of the Council and beg leave to sever my connection with the P.C. . . . I am deeply grieved that it will be impossible for me to co-operate

[34] 'Address by Dr. Ch. Weizmann, September 21st 1919' (London, British Federation).
[35] *Ch.W.P.* Printed in *Igrot*, V, 308-309. (Orig. in Russian.)
[36] *N.S.P.* (Orig. in Russian.)
[37] English Zionist Federation.
[38] An Advisory Committee set up by Weizmann and Sokolow in July 1917.

with you, and I take this opportunity to express my full admiration for you and your work.'

Weizmann did not persist in his resignation, but the storm did not abate. On September 3rd the War Cabinet, having considered a draft pro-Zionist declaration, decided, as we shall see, to temporise. Two days later, Weizmann, disappointed in his hopes, embittered by what he considered to be the rebellious attitude of his colleagues, and disturbed also by personal anxieties connected with his scientific work for the Government,[39] again let it be known that he was not prepared to go on. 'Will you kindly allow me,' he wrote to Sokolow,[40] 'to tell you for the last time that very serious reasons of a personal character compel me to discontinue the work in which I have been up to now associated with you? The surrounding atmosphere, full of mistrust, jealousy and fanaticism, makes any useful work unthinkable for me. Once again I thank you for all your friendship and loyalty . . .' On the same day, September 5th, he wrote to Leon Simon: [41] 'From now onwards you will not be troubled any longer by my interference with Zionist affairs. The field is clear for you and your friends to do as you think fit for the good of the cause.'

Ahad Ha'am told Weizmann that if he resigned at that juncture, this would be 'an act of treason' and 'from a personal point of view . . . would be moral suicide.'[42] Again Weizmann gave way, but the tension remained. There was still smouldering opposition to his views on the Jewish regiment and to what one member of the Political Committee had called 'the general policy of Imperialism and militarism of which [Weizmann] is enamoured,' and to this was added resentment at his having drifted into a close association with Jabotinsky, whom Rothschild was not alone in regarding as a dangerous adviser. On October 7th, less than three weeks before the Balfour Declaration, one of Weizmann's intimate friends wrote to another: 'In general I agree that this Declaration business is of no very great importance, and I do my best with my own little circle to keep the

[39] C.P.S. Jnls., 9 August 1917; Scott to Weizmann. 8 August, 14 September 1917: Ch.W.P.
[40] 5 September 1917: N.S.P. (Orig. in Russian.)
[41] Leon Simon papers.
[42] Ahad Ha'an to Weizmann, 5 September 1917: Ch.W.P. Printed in Igrot, V, 315-316. (Orig. in Russian.)

sense of proportion. It's not hard, because they take a pretty similar view. I'm inclined to think also that W. has outlived his usefulness as a Zionist leader. He has got to break with Jabotinsky or with us . . .'

Weizmann had to look outside his own circle for his firmest supporter. Scott wrote to him on September 12th about 'a rumour that . . . you were resigning your position as head of the Zionist Organisation in this country. That would be a real misfortune. So far as I can judge and my experience goes, you are the only statesman among them.'[43] In explaining the situation to Scott, Weizmann spoke his mind about his colleagues. 'The so-called Maximalist tendencies,' he wrote, 'have demoralised not only Russia but threaten to undermine the state of things even outside Russia. I feel that in a minor degree in my own organisation. Being constituted, as it is, chiefly of Russian Jews, they began to introduce Soviet tactics into the Zionist Movement, and my only answer to that was that, not desiring to take the responsibility for the consequences, I would leave them to continue the work, if they can. This had had the effect of sobering them down, and hence the rumours of my resignation. My hands would be very much strengthened if the Declaration . . . could be obtained as soon as possible. It would be of great value not only here but in Russia and America.'[44] 'I'm glad,' Scott replied,[45] 'that you are only keeping your people in order—à la Kerensky!—and not leaving them leaderless.'

This was the atmosphere in which Weizmann was moving near the final stage of his struggle for the Declaration.

Edwin Montagu's appointment as Secretary of State for India was announced in the press[46] just after the text of Rothschild's letter to Balfour, submitting a draft Declaration, had been finally agreed upon in the middle of July. The Zionists were disturbed, well knowing that in Montagu they had a dangerous enemy. 'Do you remember,' Rothschild wrote to Weizmann some weeks

[43] Ch.W.P.
[44] Weizmann to Scott, 13 September 1917: orig. in possession of The Manchester Guardian. Copy kindly sent to the author by the late A. P. Wadsworth.
[45] 14 September 1917: Ch.W.P.
[46] The Times, 18 July 1917.

later,[47] 'I said to you in London, as soon as I saw the announcement in the paper of Montagu's appointment, that I was afraid we were done?' Writing to Rothschild immediately after the announcement, Sokolow told him that he had spoken about it to Mark Sykes: 'I asked [Sykes] if he thought that the appointment of Mr. Montagu might affect our cause adversely (of course, without mentioning any source for these fears), to which question he answered in the negative. Let us hope, therefore, that there will be no difficulty in the way of getting the proposed Declaration.'[48]

Sykes was by nature an optimist, but on this point he had been over-confident. Though Montagu did not succeed, in the end, in wrecking the Declaration, some of his Ministerial colleagues were shaken by his vehement protests, and, but for the fixed determination of others, the delaying action he fought so stubbornly might well have achieved its purpose.

Montagu's father, the first Lord Swaythling, had been a strictly observant Jew of the old school, uncompromising in his adherence to the traditional forms and ceremonies, and neither permitting himself nor countenancing in others any deviation from the letter of the Law. Montagu had not entirely jettisoned the Jewish associations into which he had been born. Though, unlike his cousin, Herbert Samuel, he had retained only a tenuous connection with the Jewish community, he had not left it. When he married in 1915, it was a Jewish marriage, his wife, a daughter of Lord Sheffield, having before the ceremony been formally accepted as a proselyte.[49] He was a devoted son, and in this and other ways he did what filial piety required. But though he had thus identified himself as a Jew, he had never actively concerned himself either with the affairs of Anglo-Jewry or, until the shadow of a British alliance with the Zionists crossed his path, with the larger questions concerning Jewry as a whole which exercised the minds of many of his Jewish contemporaries. His early upbringing in a strictly Orthodox environment may have had something to do with the claustrophobia which made the Declaration so intolerable a threat to his peace of mind. He is said once to have told John

47 18 September 1917: *Ch.W.P.*
48 Sokolow to Rothschild, 19 July 1917: Z.A.
49 *J.C.*, 23 and 30 July 1915.

Morley that he had been striving all his life to escape from the ghetto.[51] His vehement rejection of Zionism reflected his fear of being forced back.

If he was sensitive on the point, this is not surprising at a time when offensive comments were being made upon him as a Jew by a certain section of the English press. When it was rumoured, in June 1917, that he had been selected as Chairman of a Committee on labour unrest, the *Morning Post* had enquired whether anyone would call him a typical Englishman. 'Will any-one suggest,' it asked, 'that he is the type to command the respect of the British working-man?' Just before entering the Lloyd George Government in July he had been attacked in the same paper as 'a politico-financial Jew,' who, like other Jews, was disqualified for public life by a dual allegiance.[52]

Such insults were all the more wounding at a moment when Montagu had special reasons for being concerned about his personal position and his political future. A parliamentary career of brilliant promise had been interrupted by Asquith's resignation at the end of 1916. Like many of the other Liberal Ministers, Montagu had followed Asquith out of office and had had for six months to content himself with such public activities as were open to him outside the charmed circle. Now at last, having made his peace with Lloyd George, he had found his way back to a position in which he could do justice to his powers, and, on succeeding Austen Chamberlain at the India Office, had staked his reputation on the mission to India which was later to bear fruit in the Montagu-Chelmsford reforms. Meeting him late in September, C. P. Scott found him still 'full of anxiety, first as to the success of his mission, and, secondly, as to his political future.'[53] It is no wonder that he was desperately anxious that a pro-Zionist pronouncement by the British Government should not embarrass him at the very moment when fresh pros-pects were opening before him. At this turning-point in his for-tunes nothing could, from his point of view, be more disastrous for him personally, nor could anything be better calculated to

[51] Lloyd George, *Treaties*, II, 1133. Lloyd George tells the same story, but without mentioning Montagu's name, in his *War Memoirs*, II, 1023-1024.
[52] The *Morning Post*, 5 June and 10 July 1917.
[53] *C.P.S. Jnls.*, 28 September 1917.

prejudice his work in India, than a British declaration which, as he saw it, would imply that he belonged, as a Jew, to a people apart, with its home—the real focus of its loyalties—in Palestine. Personal ambitions were at stake, but there was something more. Montagu had before the War been at the India Office as Under-Secretary of State. He had ever since been deeply interested in India and its people and anxious to serve them. The Balfour Declaration embittered him all the more because of his anxiety lest his hope of at last doing something for India should be frustrated.

For another reason, in no way connected with Zionism, Montagu was at this time under a severe emotional strain. In the days of the Asquith Administration he had been on more intimate terms with his leader than any other of the younger Liberal Ministers. He had not only been indebted to Asquith for rapid political advancement but had enjoyed his personal friendship.[54] When, within a few months after Asquith had been manœuvred into resignation in circumstances bitterly resented by his supporters, Montagu went over to Lloyd George and accepted office in his Government, this was looked upon as an act of desertion both by Asquith himself[55] and his friends. They did not disguise their disapproval and made Montagu painfully aware of it. Scott describes in his Journal[56] a meeting with Montagu at one of Lloyd George's breakfast-parties early in August. Lloyd George asked Montagu about the attitude of the Liberals since he had joined the Government. 'Absolutely cold,' Montagu replied. 'They don't speak to me. . . . They regard me as a deserter. . . . They say that Asquith made me, and it is true and I like and admire him, but is that any reason why I should not try to serve the nation . . . ?'

The nervous tension under which Montagu was labouring helps to explain why in his passionate protests against a British commitment to the Zionists there is a note of personal anguish and frustration. This comes out clearly in the closing passage of a personal letter to Lloyd George written just after a meeting of

[54] Spender and Asquith, *Life of Lord Oxford and Asquith* (London, Hutchinson, 1932), I, 202; II, 13, 254.
[55] See Asquith's letter to Montagu, quoted by F. Owen, *Tempestuous Journey*, p. 417.
[56] 10 August 1917.

the War Cabinet, at which the question of a pro-Zionist declaration had been considered, on October 4th. 'You are being misled,' he told Lloyd George, 'by a foreigner, a dreamer and idealist, who . . . sweeps aside all practical difficulties.' He speaks of the gravity of the matters at stake in his Indian mission and goes on:

> 'Judge of my consternation . . . when this Zionist business intrudes itself on the horizon. . . . If you make a statement about Palestine as the National Home for Jews, every anti-Semitic organisation and newspaper will ask what right a Jewish Englishman, with the status at best of a naturalised foreigner, has to take a foremost part in the government of the British Empire. . . . The country for which I have worked ever since I left the University—England, the country for which my family have fought, tells me that my national home, if I desire to go there, therefore my natural home, is Palestine. . . .'

By this time Montagu had realised that he was fighting a losing battle. Scott wrote to Weizmann on October 14th: [58] 'I think the thing will go through all right. Montagu, when I saw him last Sunday[59] at Alderley, seemed to have come to that conclusion. He said Lloyd George and Balfour were immovably favourable and, if I remember rightly, Milner is favourable too. . . . Bye-the-bye, Montagu sails next Saturday,[60] so he won't be in at the finish!'

Montagu was beaten but not reconciled. When the news of the Declaration reached him in India, he resented it, not only as an error of policy which would, he was convinced, make his task in India more difficult, but as a personal injury wantonly inflicted upon him at a critical moment in his career. 'I see from Reuter's telegram,' he wrote in his diary (November 11th), 'that Balfour has made the Zionist declaration against which I fought so hard. It seems strange to be a member of a Government which goes out of its way, as I think, for no conceivable purpose that I can see, to deal this blow at a colleague that is doing his

[58] Ch.W.P.
[59] October 7th.
[60] He sailed, in fact, on October 18th.

best to be loyal to them, despite his opposition. The Government
has dealt an irreparable blow at Jewish Britons and they have
endeavoured to set up a people which does not exist; they have
alarmed unnecessarily the whole Moslem world; and, in so far
as they are successful, they will have a Germanised Palestine on
the flank of Egypt. Why we should intern Mahomed Ali in India
for Pan-Mohammedanism when we encourage Pan-Judaism I
cannot for the life of me understand. It certainly puts the final
date to my political activities.'[61]

---

[61] *An Indian Diary* (London, Heinemann, 1930), p. 18. In the summer of
1922, however, he wrote to Herbert Samuel: ' As you know, I regarded
the Balfour Declaration with strong opposition and disapproval, and even
to-day would give anything that it should not have been made . . . But
it seems to me that conflict of opinion on the basis of the policy must
have ended when the Declaration was announced and endorsed. It is
almost a platitude to say that Great Britain's promises . . . ought to be
kept and honoured without hesitation . . .': quoted by Lord Samuel,
Memoirs, p. 170.

CHAPTER 34

THE ZIONIST QUESTION BEFORE THE WAR CABINET, SEPTEMBER 1917

IN HIS *Truth About the Peace Treaties*[1] Lloyd George tells us that 'it is recorded'—he does not say where, but it is possible to guess[2] —'that the War Cabinet on September 3rd 1917 "had under consideration correspondence which had passed between the Secretary of State for Foreign Affairs and Lord Rothschild on the question of the policy to be adopted towards the Zionist movement."'

By a curious accident, the matter came before the War Cabinet at a meeting in which neither Lloyd George nor Balfour could take part. Lloyd George had left London for a rest towards the end of August and was still away. Balfour was on holiday in Scotland and was not back at the Foreign Office until September 14th. Unfortunate as this was for the Zionists, they were not left friendless. Balfour was represented by Robert Cecil, and Milner and Smuts were among the Ministers present, but so also was Edwin Montagu, who, though not a member of the War Cabinet, had been invited to express his views.

He had already made them known in a memorandum characteristically entitled *The Anti-Semitism of the Present Government*. At the War Cabinet on September 3rd he 'expanded the argument contained in his memorandum,' insisting that 'the use of

---

[1] *Treaties*, II, 1117. In the references in this and succeeding chapters to the proceedings of the War Cabinet, the quotations are taken from Lloyd George's work, where they are printed in quotation-marks. Lloyd George's narrative covers three War Cabinet meetings (3 September, 4 October, 31 October 1917). He does not always indicate specifically the meeting to which a quotation refers, but the date can in all cases easily be identified.

[2] 'I can testify personally that my husband had an immense store of contemporary documents and relied mainly on these and on the Cabinet records which were at his disposal for his story of Passchendaele': Frances, Countess Lloyd George, letter to *The Times*, 15 March 1949. This refers to Lloyd George's *War Memoirs*, but there is no reason to doubt that the same material, including the Cabinet records, was at his disposal for the purposes of his work on the Peace Treaties.

the phrase "home of the Jewish people" would vitally prejudice the position of every Jew elsewhere.' To this it was rejoined that 'the existence of a Jewish State or autonomous community in Palestine would strengthen rather than weaken the situation of Jews in countries where they were not yet in possession of equal rights, and that in countries like England . . . their position would be unaffected by the existence of a national Jewish community elsewhere.' But Montagu's vehement protest had made an impression and was all the more effective because only a few days earlier the Secretary of State for War, Lord Derby, had felt compelled to give assurances which recognised the strength of the Anglo-Jewish opposition to the recruitment, *eo nomine,* of a Jewish regiment. The idea of a pro-Zionist declaration was not rejected by the War Cabinet out of hand, but Montagu had successfully obstructed a decision in its favour. The end of an inconclusive discussion was that it was thought best to temporise: 'it was decided to communicate with President Wilson, informing him that the Government were being pressed to make a declaration of sympathy with the Zionist movement and seeking his views as to the advisability of such a declaration being made.' It will be observed that it was not, apparently, decided to tell Wilson that the British Government favoured such a declaration.

There is nothing to suggest that it had been intended from the start to consult the President. This idea seems have emerged as an afterthought from the discussion on September 3rd, when the War Cabinet was shaken by Montagu's protest against a pro-Zionist declaration, but not to the point of being prepared to dispose of the matter there and then. As shown by Cecil's anxiety to be assured of Wilson's assent,[3] the Foreign Office was now convinced that the sooner a declaration was approved by the War Cabinet the better. It can certainly have desired no postponement, but, an immediate decision being unobtainable, it may well have believed that an appeal to Wilson would strengthen its hands. In this it turned out to be mistaken, but in the light of what was known at the time—or supposed to be known—about Wilson's attitude to Zionism, the supporters of a pro-Zionist policy had better reason than its opponents to favour a request for his views.

[3] See draft telegram with instructions for Sir W. Wiseman, below, p. 504.

It had been proposed at the War Cabinet that a draft declaration should be laid before Wilson, and that this should be a draft proposed by Milner as an alternative to the slightly amended version of the Rothschild formula recommended by Balfour.[4] In the end, however, the message to Washington set out neither the Milner draft nor any other form of words, but simply enquired whether a pro-Zionist declaration would be acceptable in principle. On September 4th Colonel House wrote to the President that Lord Robert Cecil had telegraphed to him as follows:

'We are being pressed here for a declaration of sympathy with the Zionist movement and I should be very grateful if you felt able to ascertain unofficially if the President favours such a declaration.'[5]

House's own advice to Wilson was to be cautious. He wrote to him on September 7th: 'Have you made up your mind regarding what answer you will make to Cecil concerning the Zionist movement? There are many dangers lurking in it, and if I were the British, I would be chary about going too definitely into that question.'[6]

A week after telegraphing to House, Cecil was still without a reply, and on September 11th the Foreign Office had ready for dispatch the following message for Sir William Wiseman:

'Has Colonel House been able to ascertain whether President favours declaration of sympathy with Zionist aspirations as asked in my telegram of September 3rd? We should be most grateful for early reply as September 17th is the Jewish New

---

[4] See Lloyd George, op. cit., II, 1133 (quotation): 'On the question of submitting Lord Milner's draft for the consideration of the United States Government, Mr. Montagu urged:' etc. As to the various drafts, see below, pp. 520ff.

[5] Quoted textually by Manuel, p. 167. A footnote to a paraphrase of this message in 'The Palestine Question in the Wilson Era,' by Professor Selig Adler (New York, 1948), p. 305) shows that the document is in the *Wilson papers*. Professor Adler's paper (reprinted from *Jewish Social Studies*, X.4) is based on a careful examination of the relevant documents in the *Wilson papers* and in the National Archives in Washington. Professor Adler has kindly given the author permission to draw freely on the results of his researches, as set out in this paper.

[6] Quoted in full by Manuel, p. 168, and in part (citing *Wilson papers*) by Adler, p. 305.

Year and announcement of sympathy by or on that date would have excellent effect.'[7]

This message, however, was not dispatched, for before it had gone off a telegram from House, dated September 11th, had reached the Foreign Office. It was clear and discouraging. Wilson had been approached as requested and had expressed the opinion that

'the time was not opportune for any definite statement further, perhaps, than one of sympathy, provided it can be made without conveying any real commitment.'

In the colourless language of the question put to Wilson, through House, on September 3rd there was nothing to suggest that the British Government attached importance to the matter or regarded it as urgent. That it did consider it important and urgent was implied in the instructions drafted a week later for transmission to Sir William Wiseman, but that message was never sent. When Wilson decided on his reply to Cecil's enquiry, he had had no clear lead from the British side, nor did he know precisely what kind of declaration the British Government had in mind.

In assenting rather half-heartedly to a declaration 'conveying no real commitment' Wilson did not specify his reasons for declining to go further, but some of them can be conjectured. As a matter of words, a declaration of sympathy with Zionist aspirations would not necessarily presuppose the expulsion of the Turks from Palestine, but it would plainly point that way. It had, therefore, to be borne in mind that, though diplomatic relations had been severed, the United States was not at war with Turkey. Wilson may also have been influenced by the idea, not yet wholly extinct, that it might be possible to coax Turkey out of the War, from which it would follow that the United States should not countenance any annexationist designs which might stand in the way. A simpler and, perhaps, just as likely an explanation would be that, in a matter in which he was not particularly interested, Wilson was content to be guided by House and to agree with him that Great Britain should not be encouraged

[7] *Dugdale papers.* As to Sir W. Wiseman, see below, p. 529.

to enter into what might turn out to be an embarrassing commitment. There is no evidence of Wilson's having taken counsel with anyone but House. Brandeis had either (as seems probable) not been consulted or, if he had, had been over-ruled, for it cannot be supposed that he would have advised the President to answer the British enquiry as frigidly as he did. Exactly what lay behind Wilson's discouraging message remains uncertain. That it was not based on any very firmly held conviction is suggested by the rather puzzling episode of Brandeis' intervention in the interval between House's telegram of September 11th and the reopening of the question by the British Government some four weeks later.

On September 18th Weizmann wrote to Sacher that he had heard that Wilson had been consulted, 'and to my great astonishment I hear that Wilson thinks the time not ripe for this declaration. . . . When I first heard of the telegram having been sent to Wilson (that was about last Thursday),[8] I wired to Brandeis requesting him to use his influence in our favour. . . . But up to the present I have heard nothing from Brandeis.'[9] The next day, September 19th, Weizmann telegraphed to Brandeis: 'Following text declaration has been approved by Foreign Office and Prime Minister and submitted to War Cabinet.' Then follows the text of the formula submitted to Balfour by Rothschild on July 18th.[10] The message ends: 'May expect opposition from assimilationist quarters. Would greatly help if President Wilson and yourself would support text. Matter most urgent.'[11] Weizmann followed this up with a telegram to two leading New York Zionists, asking them to 'see Brandeis and Frankfurter immediately discuss my last two telegrams with them,' and suggesting that it might be necessary for him to go to the United States himself.[12]

On September 23rd Brandeis saw House and consulted him

8 September 13th.
9 Copy in *Ch.W.P.* No copy of the telegram to Brandeis mentioned in this letter has come to light.
10 The Rothschild formula, with a minor amendment, had been approved by Balfour. It is not clear whether it had, in fact, been approved by Lloyd George.
11 *Brandeis papers.*
12 To de Haas and Lewin-Epstein, 20 September 1917: ibid.

as to the reply to be sent to Weizmann. The next day, September 24th, he wrote to House, 'pursuant to yesterday's conference,' sending him a copy of a message to Weizmann 'as agreed upon and sent by wire to-day through the British War Office.' It read as follows:

> 'From talks I have had with President and from expressions of opinion given to closest advisers I feel that I can answer that he is in entire sympathy with declaration quoted in yours of 19th as approved by Foreign Office and Prime Minister. I of course heartily agree.—Brandeis.'[13]

The 'declaration quoted in yours of the 19th' was the Rothschild draft. It could hardly be suggested that this did not imply 'any real commitment.' What it involved was not only the British Government's acceptance of the 'principle that Palestine should be reconstituted as the National Home of the Jewish people,' but its promise to 'use its best endeavours to secure the achievement of this object,' coupled with an undertaking to 'discuss the necessary methods and means with the Zionist Organisation.' If on September 11th Wilson was satisfied that the time was not opportune for a pro-Zionist declaration unless it could be made without 'conveying any real commitment,' how did it come to pass that, less than two weeks later, Brandeis was able to report that the President 'was in entire sympathy with' the Rothschild formula?

The obvious explanation is that, Weizmann's appeals having made him aware of what had happened, Brandeis had used his personal influence with the President to undo the harm that had been done. He had either persuaded Wilson that there was nothing in the Rothschild formula which could be interpreted as 'conveying any real commitment' or he had induced the President to change his mind about the kind of declaration he could approve. It looks, however, as though this may not be quite the whole story. In assuring Weizmann, on September 24th, that the President was in entire sympathy with 'the declaration quoted in yours of 19th,' Brandeis referred to 'talks I have had with the President.' Was he referring to recent talks or only to conversations he had had with the President in the past? If he had Wilson's direct authority for his message to Weizmann, why

[13] Brandeis to House, 24 September 1917: ibid.

should he have troubled to refer also to 'expressions of opinion given to [the President's] close advisers'?[14] These 'close advisers' would certainly include Colonel House, and there must surely be some significance in the fact that, before telegraphing to London on September 24th, Brandeis had seen House and discussed with him what Weizmann was to be told. It seems probable, though it is only a matter of inference, that, having been convinced by Brandeis that a declaration on the lines of the Rothschild formula ought to command American support, House had advised the President in the same sense and got him to agree. This would fit in with what is known of the background to Wilson's favourable reply when he was again consulted by the British Government early in October. There is, as we shall see, good reason to believe that it was on House's advice that he approved the proposed declaration.

At the time of the first British enquiry early in September, House had plainly hinted to Wilson that it would be unwise to rush into any commitment to the Zionists. When, as seems to have happened, he had second thoughts, what lay behind them? On the evidence at present available this question does not admit of any confident answer. Whatever the explanation, it seems unlikely that House had conceived a burning enthusiasm for the Zionist cause on its merits. His approach to the question appears to have been what might be expected of a man moving, as he did, in circles in which anti-semitism was a matter of course. The atmosphere prevailing in Washington at the time is illustrated by the frigid reception given to Lord Reading when he arrived there in September on a special mission from the British Government. 'Reading's first task,' Sir Arthur Willert tells us,[15] 'was . . . to smash the whispering campaign which . . . had been launched against him. . . . He was a Jew and would, therefore, not go down well in Washington . . .' Just about the same time House was writing to Wilson (September 20th): 'The objection to Lippmann is that he is a Jew, but, unlike other Jews, he is a

---

[14] Manuel, p. 168, assumes that Brandeis was referring to earlier talks with Wilson and says that his message was 'only a description, not specifically authorised, of what Wilson thought.'

[15] *The Road to Safety* (London, Verschoyle, 1952), p. 120. Sir Arthur was during the War the Washington correspondent of *The Times*.

silent one.'[16] This is quoted by Professor Selig Adler from the *Wilson papers,* where he has found evidence which satisfies him that, contrary to the conventional Jewish picture of House, 'actually he was ... deeply anti-semitic. His little notes to Wilson so frequently reflect this feeling that one is convinced that the attitude formed an essential part of his make-up.'[17]

Though it seems clear that at heart House shared the anti-semitic prejudices of his environment, he gave the Zionists the impression that he was their friend. Stephen Wise speaks in his memoirs[18] of 'warm and heartening help from House,' who 'not only made our cause his very special concern but served as liaison officer between the Wilson Administration and the Zionist Movement.' In February 1917 Wise wrote to Brandeis: 'I sent the memorandum to Colonel House covering our question, and he writes: "I hope the dream you have may soon become a reality." '[19] In October, after seeing House together with Wise, de Haas reported to Brandeis: 'He has told us that he was as much interested in our success as ourselves.'[20] Only three days before (October 13th), House had been confiding to Wilson what he really thought of the Zionists and their propaganda: 'The Jews from every tribe descended in force, and they seemed determined to break in with a jimmy, if they are not let in.'[21]

House clearly disliked Jews and was irritated by the Zionists. But there was at least one Zionist for whom he had genuine respect. After a meeting with Brandeis in November 1912 he had written to Wilson: 'His mind and mine are in accord concerning most of the questions that are now to the fore ... Norman Hapgood lunched with us and I found in him an enthusiastic admirer of Brandeis.'[22] Since then Brandeis had grown in stature and reputation. His nomination for the Supreme Court showed how high he stood in the President's esteem, and when he saw House on the Zionist question in September 1917, he could be sure of a respectful hearing. There are no means of telling how Brandeis

[16] Adler, p. 306.
[17] Ibid.
[18] *Challenging Years* (New York, 1949), p. 187.
[19] 7 February 1917: *Brandeis papers.*
[20] 16 October 1917: ibid.
[21] Adler, p. 306, citing *Wilson papers.*
[22] House, *Intimate Papers,* I, 194 (22 November 1912).

put the Zionist case or what arguments he used that carried weight with House. What can reasonably be inferred from the known facts is that it was as a result of his personal intervention with House that Brandeis found himself in a position to send Weizmann his re-assuring message of September 24th.

By sending that message through British official channels Brandeis had made sure that it would go direct to the British Government. As was doubtless the intention, it encouraged the advocates of a pro-Zionist declaration to believe that a further approach to Wilson would have a more satisfactory result. The fact remained that Wilson had already spoken for himself. House's chilling message of September 11th to Robert Cecil still held the field, and the damage it had done was not easily to be repaired. If the Zionists had not had powerful friends and, thanks to Scott and Weizmann, direct personal access to the Prime Minister, Wilson's cold douche might still have been the end of the Declaration. Describing an interview with Balfour on September 21st, Rothschild reported to Weizmann: 'Mr. Balfour began, before I could open my lips, by saying that he had seen you[23] and that he had told you that in his and the Prime Minister's absence the Cabinet had discussed the matter and had concluded that the moment was not opportune for a declaration.'[24] Commenting on a suggestion from his Department that an effort should be made to expedite a pro-Zionist pronouncement, Balfour minuted on September 24th: 'Yes. But as this question was (in my absence) decided by the Cabinet against the Zionists, I cannot do anything until that decision is reversed.'[25]

In telling Weizmann and Rothschild that the Cabinet had concluded that the moment was not opportune, Balfour was clearly echoing the language of House's discouraging telegram of September 11th, but there is no reason to think that there was any formal Cabinet decision to that effect. Balfour seems likewise to have been over-stating the case when he minuted that the question had been 'decided against the Zionists.' What appears to

[23] A letter of September 20th from Weizmann to Scott mentions an interview with Balfour on the 19th but gives no details. (A copy of this letter, which is in the possession of the *Manchester Guardian*, was kindly sent to the author by the late A. P. Wadsworth.)
[24] *Ch.W.P.*
[25] Quoted by Mrs. Dugdale, *Balfour*, II, 233.

have happened—it came to much the same thing—was that, without having been formally disposed of by the War Cabinet, the question of a pro-Zionist declaration had simply disappeared from its agenda, not to be brought back until the end of September, and then only by the express direction of the Prime Minister.

Discouraged though he was, Weizmann did not accept defeat, nor did Mark Sykes. Both assumed that the declaration was not dead, and towards the end of September they were discussing Sykes' draft of an elaborate memorandum designed to clarify the issues when the Palestine question came to be reconsidered.[26]

Sykes begins his memorandum by observing that 'this area is necessarily excluded from the zones in which the Arab question is regarded as the dominant one . . . It is to be noticed at once that the interests involved in Palestine do not affect any one nation but certain international forces which are common to many nations.' First among these Sykes mentions the various Christian Churches. He goes on to draw attention to the special significance of Jerusalem for the Moslem world and then turns to the Jews. After describing the background to the Zionist Movement, he sets out very fairly what he calls 'the assimilated Jewish case' and the Zionist reply. Up to this point there is no very notable difference between the final text of the memorandum and the draft on which Sykes had invited Weizmann's views. In the revised version certain of Weizmann's comments are reflected in some amplification and some re-phrasing, but there is no marked divergence from the draft. It is when he comes to his description of the Zionist programme that Sykes does depart significantly from his draft by inserting a passage not included in the document shown to Weizmann—a passage in which the paragraph negativing the idea of a Jewish State reads a little curiously when it is remembered that only a few months earlier Weizmann was being encouraged to popularise the idea of British sponsorship of a Jewish Commonwealth in Palestine:

[26] *Sledm.*, No. 66. Both the draft and the revised version are undated, but to the draft is attached a letter from Weizmann, dated 22 September 1917, in which he thanks Sykes for 'the note which you kindly gave me yesterday . . . I have made a few remarks, which you may, perhaps, find acceptable.' Copies of the draft and of Weizmann's letter are in *Ch.W.P.*

'It would be as well,' Sykes writes, 'to rehearse precisely what the Zionists desire and what they do not desire.

'What the Zionists do not want is:

'I. To have any special political hold on the old city of Jerusalem itself or any control over the Christian or Moslem Holy Places.

'II. To set up a Jewish Republic or other form of State in Palestine or any part of Palestine.

'III. To enjoy any special rights not enjoyed by other inhabitants of Palestine.

'On the other hand, the Zionists do want:

'I. Recognition of the Jewish inhabitants of Palestine as a national unit, federated with [? other] national units in Palestine.[27]

'II. The recognition of [the] right of bonâ fide Jewish settlers to be included in the Jewish national unit in Palestine.'

Sykes goes on to say that 'there can be no doubt that Zionism is a permanent and positive force in world Jewry . . . It may be assumed safely that so long as there are large unassimilated masses of Jews in East Europe, Zionism will be a positive force, with supporters in all Jewish communities throughout the world. . . . The Palestinian problem, as will be seen, is exceedingly complicated. We have to consider the question of the Holy Places, the local population and Zionist aspirations. If the world fails to take into consideration any one of these matters, trouble must ensue. . . .'

This memorandum is of interest because it may have had some influence on the War Cabinet in deciding whether, and in what form, a pro-Zionist declaration should be approved. Sykes, for his part, took it for granted that the question had not been dis-

[27] The 'national unit' idea seems to have been adopted by the author of the volume on 'Syria and Palestine' in the series of handbooks prepared by the Historical Section of the Foreign Office for the use of the British Delegation to the Paris Peace Conference: 'They [the Zionists] seek to have in Palestine cultural and local autonomy, together with commercial (sic —— ? communal) representation, such as has been granted to the Mohammedans in India.'—*F. O. Handbooks*, No. 60, pp. 63ff. As to whether Sykes was justified in denying that the Zionists wanted a Jewish State, see below, p. 523.

posed of it by its disappearance from the War Cabinet's agenda as a result of Montagu's protest and Wilson's discouragement. He was not mistaken. From the moment Weizmann heard of Wilson's message he had been anxious to make a personal appeal to the Prime Minister. He had asked Scott to help him,[28] but until near the end of September Lloyd George was inaccessible. During the greater part of the month he was unwell and away from London, and he was not back at work until September 23rd. A few days later Scott contrived the meeting so urgently desired by Weizmann. He describes in his Journal (September 28th) a breakfast with Lloyd George, 'who seemed quite himself again after his recent illness,' and goes on: 'After that we went for a walk in the Park, Kerr joining us. I had asked Weizmann to come in case George should like to see him and they had a few words downstairs, and George, on Weizmann's representation of urgency, told Sutherland[29] to put down "Palestine" for the next War Cabinet.' 'I saw George for two or three minutes only,' Weizmann told Sokolow, 'but he immediately ordered that our case be placed on the agenda of the next meeting of the Cabinet.'[30]

---

[28] Weizmann to Sacher and Sacher's reply, 18 and (?)19 September 1917: *Ch.W.P.*

[29] Later, Sir William Sutherland; a member of Lloyd George's personal secretariat.

[30] 30 September 1917: *Ch.W.P.*

CHAPTER 35

FURTHER CONSIDERATION BY THE WAR CABINET, OCTOBER 1917

HAVING BEEN ASSURED that the Zionist question would be re-considered by the War Cabinet, Weizmann was determined that Montagu should not again succeed in getting it shelved. Realising that another setback would be dangerous, and might be fatal, for the Zionists, he turned at once to the preparation of a memorandum pressing for a decision, and a prompt decision, in their favour.

The salient passages are as follows:

> 'We cannot ignore rumours which seem to foreshadow that the anti-Zionist view will be urged at the meeting of the War Cabinet by a prominent Englishman of the Jewish faith who does not belong to the War Cabinet. . . . We must res-pectfully point out that in submitting our resolution [sic] we entrusted our national and Zionist destiny to the Foreign Office and the Imperial War Cabinet in the hope that the problem would be considered in the light of Imperial in-terests and the principles for which the Entente stands. We are reluctant to believe that the War Cabinet would allow the divergence of views on Zionism existing in Jewry to be presented to them in a strikingly one-sided manner. . . . We have submitted the text of the declaration on behalf of an organisation which claims to represent the will of a great and ancient, though scattered, people. We have submitted it after three years of negotiations and conversations with prominent representatives of the British nation. We there-fore humbly pray that this declaration may be granted to us. This would enable us still further to counteract the demoralis-ing influence which the enemy press is endeavouring to exercise by holding out vague promises to the Jews, and finally to make the necessary preparations for the construc-

tive work which would have to begin as soon as Palestine is liberated.'[1]

This appeal to the War Cabinet, signed by Weizmann and Rothschild, was sent to the Foreign Office on October 3rd. When the War Cabinet met the next day, both Lloyd George and Balfour were present, and, with the exception of Smuts, the supporters of a pro-Zionist policy were this time assembled in full strength. Since the abortive discussion on September 3rd their hands had been strengthened by reports from various sources which suggested that, if the British Government hesitated much longer about a pro-Zionist declaration, it might find itself forestalled by the Germans. The weight of authority and argument behind the proposal was thus considerably greater than it had been on September 3rd.

Nevertheless, even now no final conclusion was reached. Weizmann's 'prominent Englishman of the Jewish faith' was again in attendance and, having already circulated a second memorandum in support of his anti-Zionist views, developed them with the same passionate conviction as before. Montagu's argument was on much the same lines as on September 3rd, but this time he referred explicitly to his mission to India. 'How,' he demanded, 'would he negotiate with the people of India on behalf of His Majesty's Government if the world had just been told that His Majesty's Government regarded his national home as being in Turkish territory?'[2] The vehemence of his attack can be inferred from a personal letter written just after the Cabinet on October 4th, in which he explains his position to Lloyd George: 'Please do not resent my expression with all the vigour of which I was capable of views which I cannot but hold. . . .' Then follows the passage already quoted,[3] in which he recapitulates the reasons for his uncompromising resistance. Though, as he himself was compelled to recognise, Lloyd George and Balfour were immovable, and the same could be said of Milner, Montagu held his ground stubbornly and secured enough support—probably from Curzon, who is known to have disliked the proposal, though on

[1] Copies in *Ch.W.P.* and Z.A.
[2] Lloyd George, *Treaties, II*, 1134.
[3] Above, p. 500.

different grounds—to succeed once more in staving off an irrevocable decision.

In stating the case for a pro-Zionist declaration, Balfour dealt at some length with Montagu's argument on behalf of the anti-Zionist Jews. 'This Movement,' he said,[4]

> 'though opposed by a number of wealthy Jews in this country, had behind it the support of a majority of Jews, at all events in Russian and America, and probably in other countries. He saw nothing inconsistent between the establishment of a Jewish national focus in Palestine and the complete assimilation and absorption of Jews into the nationality of other countries. . . . What was at the back of the Zionist Movement was the intense national consciousness held (sic) by certain members of the Jewish race. They regarded themselves as one of the great historic races of the world, whose original home was Palestine, and these Jews had a passionate longing to regain once more this ancient national home . . .'

The unspecified but, presumably, authentic record from which this passage is extracted by Lloyd George in his *Truth About the Peace Treaties* is quoted by him as continuing: 'Mr. Balfour then read a very sympathetic declaration by the French Government which had been conveyed to the Zionists, and he stated that he knew that President Wilson was extremely favourable to the Movement.' Balfour is quoted, further, as having informed the War Cabinet that 'the German Government were making great efforts to capture the sympathy of the Zionist Movement.'

This last point was important. The Foreign Office was more anxious than it need have been about an imminent German move, but in the autumn of 1917 it was firmly under the impression that the Germans were courting the Zionists and might at any moment publicly identify themselves with the Zionist cause, thus providing themselves, particularly in Russia, with a useful instrument of political warfare. Importance was attached to articles in the German press demanding a pro-Zionist policy; indeed, surprising as it may appear, there is good reason to believe that Balfour's warning about German intentions was based largely on a summary of such articles, drawing attention to their significance, in

[4] Lloyd George, *Treaties*, II, 1135ff.

The Jewish Chronicle of 21 September 1917. Almost at the same moment *Palestine*[5] devoted its main leading article to the same theme, pointing out that Zionism was now being discussed as a matter of consequence 'in almost every variety of German newspaper, High Junker, Clerical, Liberal and even Socialist,' and that Germany was becoming 'the home of a powerful propaganda, stimulated by the German Government itself, in favour of including in the Peace Settlement provision for a Jewish national centre in Palestine.' Nor was it only in Jewish or Zionist organs that this question was raised. The War Office Daily Review of the Foreign Press noted (September 8th) an article in a leading Munich newspaper showing a marked interest in Zionism. An editorial in *The Times* of September 13th remarked that from the comments of the enemy press on the Zionist question it could be seen 'how desirous it is to prove that Palestine can only be regained for Jewry under German auspices.' Urging the British Government not to delay in showing sympathy with the aspirations of 'the best part of Jewry,' a writer in *The New Europe* (September 29th) warned the Government against letting the Germans get in first.

Misleading as they can now be seen to have been, the reports current at the time as to the German Government's intentions were taken seriously by the Foreign Office and to the long-term case for a pro-Zionist policy added a cogent argument for a speedy decision in its favour. When it was resolved, on October 4th, again to consult President Wilson, it was explained to him that the question of a pro-Zionist declaration had been re-opened because of the danger of a forestalling move by the Germans.[6]

In commending the declaration to the War Cabinet, Balfour, as we have seen, gave it to be understood that no opposition need be expected either from the Americans or the French. The 'sympathetic declaration by the French Government which had been conveyed to the Zionists' is clearly the letter received by Sokolow from Jules Cambon on 4 June 1917.[7] Balfour's assurance that 'President Wilson was extremely favourable to the Movement' was evidently an allusion to Brandeis' telegram of September 24th,

[5] 22 September 1917.
[6] See below, p. 528.
[7] Above, p. 416.

in which he told Weizmann that he was satisfied that the President was 'in entire sympathy with' the formula submitted to Balfour by Rothschild in July. But Brandeis' message was, on the face of it, difficult to reconcile with the President's reply to the British enquiry early in September. The only direct intimation that there had been of Wilson's views was that the time was, in his opinion, not opportune for a declaration conveying any real commitment. The question having been re-opened, ought he not to be asked whether he would now approve of such a declaration as the War Cabinet was considering?

This was agreed to, and, in the light of Montagu's stubborn resistance to the proposed declaration as a threat to the vital interests of British Jews, it was also agreed to give both sides a final hearing by inviting the views of the Zionist leaders and of representative British anti-Zionists.

When Weizmann heard of this concession to Montagu, he did not conceal his indignation.

'It seems,' he wrote to Philip Kerr (October 7th),[8] 'as if the Cabinet, and even yourself, attach undue importance to the opinions held by so-called "British Jewry." If it is a question of the Jews who have settled in Great Britain, well, the majority of such Jews are in favour of Zionism. If, on the other hand, by British Jews one understands the minority of wealthy half-assimilated Jews who have been in this country for the last three or four generations, then of course it is true that these people are dead against Zionism, but . . . Zionism is not meant for these people, who have cut themselves adrift from Jewry; it is meant for those masses who have a will to live a life of their own, and these masses have a right to claim the recognition of Palestine as a Jewish National Home. The second category of British Jews, I believe, will fall into line quickly enough when this declaration is given to us. I still expect a time, and I do so not without apprehension, when they will even claim to be Zionists themselves. Some Jews and some non-Jews do not seem to realise the fundamental fact that, whatever happens, we shall get to Palestine.

[8] Copy in *Ch.W.P.*

... No amount of talk by Mr. Montagu or people like him will stem the tide. ...'

The Zionist memorandum of October 3rd had alluded to the 'Imperial interests' at stake in the Palestine question. Weizmann ended his letter to Philip Kerr on the same note: 'It is true that British help, if it comes now, will be invaluable to us, but it is equally true that a reconstructed Palestine will become a very great asset to the British Empire.'

The Zionists had already complained of 'the strikingly one-sided manner' in which 'the divergence of views on Zionism existing in Jewry' was being presented to the War Cabinet as a result of Montagu's direct access to the inner circle. It seemed to Weizmann that there was no warrant for still further concessions to the anti-Zionist elements in British Jewry. But Montagu played no part in the life of the Anglo-Jewish community, to which he was but lightly attached, and there was something to be said for the view that the War Cabinet was under a certain moral obligation to give a hearing to British Jews of the type represented by members of the now extinct Conjoint Foreign Committee. Lucien Wolf had a few months earlier been told by the Foreign Office that the Conjoint Committee could count upon being consulted before the question of a British commitment to the Zionists was finally decided,[9] and, after seeing Milner in the middle of May, Montefiore had reported to his colleagues that 'he confirmed the assurance of the Foreign Office that we should be consulted before anything final was done.'[10] Though in October 1917 the Conjoint Committee was no longer in being, it was in the spirit of these undertakings that men like Montefiore should be invited to state their case and not be left with the grievance that anti-Zionist British Jews had been over-ridden without the hearing they had been promised.

In view of the War Cabinet's sensitiveness to the protests of the anti-Zionists, Weizmann made up his mind that there must be a vigorous counter-offensive. The Council of the English Zionist Federation, Weizmann presiding, decided on October 11th that 'in view of certain circumstances, an immediate series of

[9] See above, p. 450.
[10] See above, p. 450.

meetings be held in order to pass resolutions stating the desire of the Jews for the reconstitution of Palestine as the national home of the Jewish people and urging the British Government to use its best endeavours to facilitate the achievement of this object.'[11] Resolutions in these terms were passed, on October 21st, by some three hundred Zionist and other Jewish bodies all over the country and forwarded to the Foreign Office.[12] So concerned was Weizmann about the situation which seemed to be developing that he considered the possibility of some understanding behind the scenes which would avert a head-on collision with the anti-Zionists. 'I wonder,' he wrote to Herbert Samuel (October 18th),[13] 'whether it would be possible for you to see Sir Philip Magnus and Sir Stuart Samuel. I am quite sure that with these two gentlemen a satisfactory arrangement could be arrived at so as to avoid a somewhat humiliating fight at the last moment.' This suggestion was not followed up and no more was heard of it.

What was submitted both to President Wilson and to the Zionist and anti-Zionist Jews was not an abstract question of principle but a draft declaration which had been laid before the War Cabinet on October 4th by Milner—an amended and amplified version of a formula he had put forward in August as an alternative to the slightly amended version of the Zionist draft recommended by Balfour.

Leopold Amery records in his memoirs[14] that about half-an-hour before the War Cabinet met on October 4th, he was asked by Milner whether he could draft 'something which would go a reasonable distance to meeting the objections both Jewish and pro-Arab without impairing the substance of the proposed declaration.' What Amery produced was a formula (it may conveniently be referred to as the Milner-Amery formula) which, with certain amendments, was to be finally approved by the War

---

11 *J.C.*, 19 October 1917.
12 Some of these meetings are reported in *J.C.*, 26 October 1917. The figure of three hundred is given by Sir Ronald Graham in his memorandum of October 24th—below, p. 544.
13 Copy in *Ch.W.P.*
14 II, 116. (He does not actually mention October 4th but says 'early in October.')

Cabinet on October 31st and to emerge as the Balfour Declaration:

> 'His Majesty's Government views with favour the establishment in Palestine of a national home for the Jewish race and will use its best endeavours to facilitate the achievement of this object, it being clearly understood that nothing shall be done which may prejudice the civil and religious rights of existing non-Jewish communities in Palestine, or the rights and political status enjoyed in any other country by such Jews who are fully contented with their existing nationality.'

The opening words, down to 'the achievement of this object,' were based on Milner's August draft—a considerably watered-down version of Balfour's formula, which was itself slightly more cautious, though only on a minor point,[15] than that submitted in July by the Zionists.[16] The Milner draft began: 'His Majesty's Government accepts the principle that every opportunity should be afforded for the establishment of a home for the Jewish people in Palestine and will use its best endeavours to facilitate [not, as in the Balfour draft, 'to secure'] the achievement of this object.' The Milner-Amery formula substituted 'Jewish race' for 'Jewish people' and—a more important amendment—altered 'a home' to 'a national home.' But the main substance of the British undertaking, as expressed in Milner's August draft, remained unchanged. The British Government was to declare that it favoured the establishment in Palestine of a national home for the Jewish race, and not, as Rothschild had proposed and Balfour had agreed, its acceptance of 'the principle that Palestine should be reconstituted as the national home' of the Jews. Amery remarks in his memoirs that one merit of the Milner-Amery formula was that it 'conveyed no suggestion that Jews, as such, belonged to Palestine.' He might have added that it likewise avoided any suggestion that Palestine belonged to the Jews.

The Zionist draft would have engaged the British Government to 'discuss the necessary methods and means with the

---

15 See below, p. 522.
16 The text of the Rothschild draft is set out at p. 470 above. For full text of successive versions see Appendix, p. 664.

Zionist Organisation.' Balfour had proposed to substitute an undertaking 'to consider any suggestions which the Zionist Organisation may desire to lay before' the Government, and on this point Balfour's wording had been adopted by Milner. In the Milner-Amery formula this feature of the proposed declaration disappeared altogether, and the Zionist Organisation was no longer mentioned.

Amery completed his work—and this appears to have been his main contribution—by tacking on to the declaration the two limiting provisos already quoted as part of the Milner-Amery draft—the first probably intended (but this is not certain) to satisfy Curzon[17] and the second put in for the benefit of Montagu. It will be remembered that Amery speaks in his memoirs of Milner's request for a draft meeting the objections 'both Jewish and pro-Arab.' It is not quite clear whether the rather curious expression 'existing non-Jewish communities in Palestine' was meant to refer to the Arabs or whether this part of the proposed declaration was directed primarily to the position of the various Christian communities, whose traditional rights were of special concern to the French and Italian Governments and to the Roman Catholic and Orthodox Churches[18] However that may be, the progressive watering down of the formula submitted by Roth-schild in July, and in substance accepted at the time by Balfour, was clearly a response, not only to the pressure of the Jewish anti-Zionists, but also to reminders that in dealing with the Palestine question there were other claims and interests to be considered besides those of the Jews. Of the Arab aspect of the matter more will be said later. Here it need only be mentioned that during the summer of 1917 some warning notes had already been sounded in messages reaching Mark Sykes from a trusted informant in Egypt, Albina,[19] and from General Clayton,[20] who on

---

[17] 'The reference to Jews outside Palestine was, of course, to satisfy Montagu. The provision about non-Jewish communities in Palestine was, no doubt, Curzon's, but I cannot remember definitely': Mr. Amery to the author, 1 July 1952.

[18] In the Italian paraphrase of the Declaration (see below, p. 592) 'non-Jewish communities' appears as 'religious communities.'

[19] *Sledm.*, No. 44 (10 August 1917). As to Albina, see Shane Leslie, pp. 241, 276.

[20] Allenby's Chief Political Officer.

August 20th telegraphed from Cairo: 'I am not sure that it is not as well to refrain from any public pronouncement just at present. It will not help matters if the Arabs . . . are given yet another bone of contention in the shape of Zionism in Palestine as against the interests of the Moslems resident there.'[21]

It is not, perhaps, fanciful to see a reflection of Sykes' anxiety in his September memorandum. In a passage already quoted,[22] he explained that the Zionists had no desire to set up a Jewish State in Palestine or any part of it, and that what they demanded was simply the recognition of the Jewish population of Palestine, including Jews who might settle there, as 'a national unit federated with national units in Palestine.' At Sykes' conference with leading Zionists on 7 February 1917 Rothschild had said that 'he sympathised fully with the development of a Jewish State under the British Crown,' and Sacher had likewise spoken, in terms, of a Jewish State.[23] In his speech at the London Zionist Conference in May Weizmann had hinted at the eventual emergence of a Jewish State, though he had spoken of this as a distant dream and had been careful to emphasise that 'the conditions are not yet ripe for the setting up of a State *ad hoc*: States must be built up slowly, gradually, systematically and patiently.'[24] In his letter to *The Times* (May 28th) Rothschild had referred to 'the establishment of an autonomous Jewish State under the aegis and protection of one of the Allied Powers.'[25] On the other hand, in affirming that the Zionists had no desire to set up a Jewish State Sykes was saying no more than had been said by Sokolow in Paris, when he addressed the representatives of the Alliance Israélite in April 1917[26] and again in Rome, not long afterwards, at his interview with Cardinal Gasparri.[27] In a pamphlet published a few months later Leon Simon pointed out that 'even Herzl, whose use of the term "Judenstaat" has given rise to so much misunderstanding on this point, did not demand

---

[21] *Sledm.*, No. 44 (20 August 1917).
[22] Above, p. 512.
[23] Above, p. 372.
[24] Above, p. 450.
[25] Above, p. 456.
[26] Above, p. 403.
[27] Above, p. 407.

such conditions as are suggested to English minds by the phrase
"Jewish State."[28] When, in July, Sokolow and his Committee had
been working on a formula for the proposed British declaration,
Sacher and Sidebotham had advised that the Government should
be invited to commit itself to 'the reconstitution of Palestine as
a Jewish State,' but their drafts had been rejected in favour of a
much less forthright form of words.[29] After the Balfour Declaration, Sokolow still insisted that the Zionists were not trying to
build up a Jewish State. 'It has been said,' he wrote, 'and is still
being obstinately repeated by anti-Zionists again and again, that
Zionism aims at the creation of an independent "Jewish State."
But this is wholly fallacious. The "Jewish State" was never a
part of the Zionist programme.'[30] Sykes was not, therefore, without respectable authority for what he said on the subject in his
September memorandum.

The truth seems to be that the Zionists themselves would
not have found it easy to agree upon a precise formulation
of their ultimate objectives. Even Zionists who were at heart
convinced that the Jews needed a State of their own might
well have preferred to leave this to the future and to keep their
dreams to themselves—*y parler jamais, y songer toujours*. On the
question of what the Zionists really wanted it was possible to
point to evidence either of a relatively modest programme or of
more ambitious hopes. The significance of Sykes' September
Memorandum is that it shows what he wanted them to want.

The War Cabinet Secretariat had now to give effect to the
decision to invite comments on the proposed declaration from
Zionist leaders and from representative British Jews. Identical
letters in the following terms were sent on October 6th to the
Chief Rabbi (Dr. Hertz), Rothschild, Sokolow and Weizmann, and
to Leonard (later, Sir Leonard) Cohen (President of the Jewish
Board of Guardians), Sir Philip Magnus, M.P., Claude Montefiore
(President of the Anglo-Jewish Association) and Sir Stuart Samuel,
M.P. (President of the Board of Deputies of British Jews):

'I am directed by the Prime Minister to inform you that,

[28] For a fuller quotation see below, p. 624.
[29] Above, pp. 466ff.
[30] *History of Zionism* (publ. 1919), I, xxiv-xxv.

at the instance of the Secretary of State for Foreign Affairs, the question of drawing up a formula setting forth the attitude of His Majesty's Government towards the Zionist movement in general and to the future of Palestine in particular has been under preliminary discussion by the War Cabinet. In view of the apparent divergence of opinion expressed on the subject by Jews themselves, the War Cabinet decided that they would like to receive in writing the views of representative Jewish leaders, both Zionist and anti-Zionist, upon the form and words of the proposed draft declaration that has been submitted to the War Cabinet for consideration.'

The letter then sets out the text (with one slight variation)[31] of the Milner-Amery formula, followed by a request for comments in writing within a week.[32]

As was to be expected, the most impressive statement of the anti-Zionist case came from Claude Montefiore. He had nothing against Jews being encouraged to settle in Palestine and, 'when their numbers permit it, ultimately obtaining the power which any large majority may justly claim.' What he objected to was the conception of a national home in Palestine for the Jewish race.

'The phrase "a national home for the Jewish race" appears,' he wrote, 'to assume and imply that Jews generally constitute a nationality. Such an implication is extremely prejudicial to Jewish interests, as it is intensely obnoxious to an enormous number of Jews. . . . A national home for the Jews on the score of the oppressed condition of the Jews is no longer necessary. . . . The Polish-Jewish question will, with the co-operation of the Allies, be doubtless settled as favourably as the larger Russian Jewish problem has already been settled. The Rumanian Government will also not be able to resist the pressure of events. . . . For the true well-being of the Jewish race emancipation and liberty in the countries of the world are a thousand times more important than a

[31] The concluding words, 'Jews who are fully contented with their existing nationality' now read: 'Jews who are fully contented with their existing nationality and citizenship.'

[32] The author is indebted to Lord Cohen for the original letter addressed to Sir Leonard Cohen. The letter (in identical terms) addressed to Dr. Hertz is preserved among his papers.

"home.". . . . It is very significant that anti-Semites are always very sympathetic to Zionism. It is no wonder. . . . I and my friends do not desire to impede colonisation and immigration into Palestine. . . . Whoever the suzerain Power of Palestine may be, we are in favour of the Jews, when their numbers permit it, ultimately obtaining the power which any large majority may justly claim. . . . The words "who are fully contented with" ill express the facts. When thousands of Jews are fighting with passion and ardour for their respective countries, they are not merely *contented* with their nationality. It is bone of their bone and spirit of their spirit. . . . If the present words of the draft declaration are, for some reason or reasons unknown to me, believed by His Majesty's Government to be in the interest of British policy, and if His Majesty's Government is anxious to publish this formula for the sake of *this* country as well as for the Jews, I would of course, subordinate my Jewish feelings, wishes and interests to the interests of England and the Empire. . . .'[33]

Leonard Cohen stated the anti-Zionist case on much the same lines as Montefiore. So did Philip Magnus, adding that, while he would welcome a proposal for the establishment in Palestine of a centre of Jewish culture, he feared that such a declaration as was now contemplated would antagonise other sections of the population of Palestine and might result in the Turks dealing with the Jews as they had dealt with the Armenians. Sir Stuart Samuel, without expressing any decided opinion of his own, told the War Cabinet that he thought that Jews resident in Great Britain (he was careful not to say 'British Jews') were by a large majority favourable to the establishment of a national home for Jews in Palestine under proper safeguards. There were, he added, many English Jews who had been aloof from the Zionist Movement but would agree that those Jews who wished to go to Palestine should be enabled to do so, provided that it was made clear that, should a Jewish State be set up, it would have no claim to the allegiance of Jews outside Palestine. He thought that German and Austrian Jews should be excluded from Palestine for twenty years.

[33] Published by kind permission of Mr. L. G. Montefiore.

Weizmann, Sokolow and Rothschild, while proposing some verbal changes in the Milner-Amery formula, welcomed the proposed declaration without attempting any elaborate re-statement of the Zionist case.[34] They were unequivocally supported by Dr. Hertz, who re-affirmed the views he had already expressed publicly in *The Times*.[35] It was fortunate for the Zionists that they had the Chief Rabbi on their side. If what was in question was the attitude of Anglo-Jewry, no one could speak for it more impressively than its ecclesiastical head.

> ' It is,' he wrote, ' with feelings of the profoundest gratification that I learn of the intention of His Majesty's Government to lend its powerful support to the re-establishment in Palestine of a National Home for the Jewish people. The proposed declaration . . . will mark an epoch in Jewish history. . . . I must, as Chief Rabbi, thank the Prime Minister, the Secretary of State for Foreign Affairs and the members of the War Cabinet for their striking sympathy with Jewish aspirations and assure them that the overwhelming majority of Anglo-Jewry, as well as of the Jewries of His Majesty's Overseas Dominions, will rejoice with me at this broad humanity and far-sighted statesmanship of the men who guide the destinies of the Empire.'[36]

On October 9th the text of the proposed declaration was sent to Herbert Samuel, with a covering letter giving the names of the persons already consulted and explaining that it was felt that ' your opinion should also be ascertained, the more so as the War Cabinet has already received two memoranda on the subject from Mr. Montagu.'[37] In his reply[38] Samuel took as his starting-point the reasoning of the memorandum which, nearly three years

---

[34] Weizmann did, however, deal at some length with the divergence of opinion among Jews referred to in the War Cabinet letter, pointing out that the anti-Zionists ' are almost exclusively to be found amongst those Jews who by education and social connections have lost touch with the real spirit animating the Jewish people as a whole.' Copy in *Ch.W.P.*

[35] Above, p. 460.

[36] Printed in *The Jewish National Home, 1917-1942*, ed. P. Goodman (London, Dent, 1943), pp. XX-XXI.

[37] *H.S.P.*

[38] Ibid. Published by kind permission of Lord Samuel.

before, when he himself was in the Cabinet, he had circulated to his colleagues:

> 'The policy embodied in the draft declaration . . . seems to me to be right. If the Turks are left ostensibly in control of Palestine, the country is likely to fall in course of time under German influence. If Germany or any other Continental Power is dominant there, Egypt would be exposed to constant menace. The best safeguard would be the establishment of a large Jewish population, preferably under British protection. I feel no doubt that the policy expressed in the declaration is that which is desired by the mass of the Jewish people both in this country and throughout the world. . . . If the policy were carried into effect through British influence, it would be calculated to win for the British Empire the gratitude of Jews throughout the world, and, wherever the interests of the country of which they are citizens were not involved, to create among them a bias favourable to the Empire. I presume that such a declaration would not be made public until a favourable military situation had been brought about in Palestine. . . . But the adoption of the declaration now, and its confidential communication to those who are interested, would clear the air, and would be, I think, a wise step.'

The Jewish leaders had now been duly consulted, but it was not until October 16th that the War Cabinet learnt the result of its second approach to President Wilson.

The text of the Milner-Amery formula was telegraphed by Balfour to Colonel House on October 6th, with a request for its submission to the President. On the same day the United States Embassy in London telegraphed direct to Wilson, by-passing the State Department, in the same sense, explaining that the 'question of a message of sympathy with the [Zionist] Movement' was being re-considered by the British Cabinet 'in view of reports that [the] German Government are making great efforts to capture [the] Zionist Movement.'[39]

---

[39] Adler, 'The Palestine Question in the Wilson Era,' pp. 305, 306, citing *Wilson papers*.

With House's knowledge and approval, Brandeis had already assured Weizmann that he had good reason to believe that the President was 'in entire sympathy with' the Rothschild draft. If this did not involve too precise a commitment to be acceptable to Wilson, he might have been expected to agree without hesitation to the more cautiously worded formula which had now been submitted to him. If, as seems to have happened, House had to persuade him to assent, what was the difficulty? A clue to the answer is possibly to be found in a message sent to Weizmann by Brandeis after his conversation with House on September 23rd. Having assured Weizmann, on September 24th, that the President could be relied upon to support a pro-Zionist declaration, Brandeis told him, in a separate telegram of the same date, that 'it would be wise for you to get French and Italians to enquire what attitude President is on declaration referred to in yours of 19th.'[40] House had encouraged Wilson—if, indeed, he needed any encouragement—to be suspicious of British intentions. 'The English,' he told him (September 18th), 'naturally want the road to Egypt and India blocked, and Lloyd George is not above using us to further this plan.'[41] It may be that, while not objecting to the Milner-Amery formula itself, Wilson was unenthusiastic about an exclusively British declaration, not wishing to help the British, in the contentious matter of Palestine, to steal a march on their French and Italian allies and competitors.

Whatever the explanation, it seems clear that it was not without some prompting by House that Wilson eventually authorised a favourable reply to the British enquiry. Sir William Wiseman,[42] who was *persona grata* both with the President and with House, was relied upon by the Foreign Office for dealing with the declaration at the American end. Sir William's recollection is that 'Colonel House was influential in bringing the matter to the President's attention and persuading him to approve' the formula.[43]

---

[40] *Brandeis papers.*

[41] Adler, p. 306, citing *Wilson papers.*

[42] Head of the British Military Intelligence Service in the U.S.A.

[43] Sir William Wiseman to the author, 7 November 1952, referring to his telegram of October 16th to Sir E. Drummond (see below).

House's intervention is evidenced by a note sent to him by Wilson on October 13th: 'I find in my pocket the memorandum you gave me about the Zionist Movement. I am afraid I did not say to you that I concurred in the formula suggested by the other side. I do and would be obliged if you would let them know it.'[44] It appears, therefore, that Wilson had had some advice from House but had forgotten to take any action in the matter—a lapse of memory which suggests that he was not greatly interested. The contents of House's memorandum are not known, but he had probably been convinced by Wiseman that the matter was important and urgent and had advised the President accordingly. Having been told by Wilson on October 13th that the formula was approved, House passed this on to Wiseman, who on the 16th telegraphed to Sir Eric Drummond[45] in London:

'Colonel House put formula before President, who approves of it but asks that no mention of his approval shall be made when His Majesty's Government makes formula public, as he has arranged that American Jews shall then ask him for his approval, which he will give publicly here.'[46]

These last words imply that the Zionists had been informed of Wilson's approval of the formula, but it is somewhat surprising to find that Brandeis does not seem to have been consulted while it was under consideration in Washington. 'I cannot help feeling,' Wise wrote to him on October 17th, 'that it would have been better if the Colonel or Cyrus had consulted you prior to assenting to the declarations [sic] submitted.'[47]

Wise seems here to be referring to certain changes in the Milner-Amery formula which he and his friends would have wished to propose. The text of the formula had been telegraphed by Weizmann to Brandeis on October 9th.[48] On looking at it,

---

[44] Paraphrase in Adler, p. 307, citing *Wilson papers*: text in Manuel, p. 168.

[45] Private Secretary to the Foreign Secretary; later, Earl of Perth.

[46] In a dispatch dated 19 May 1919 from Balfour to Curzon, 'the correspondence with Sir William Wiseman in October 1917' is mentioned as evidence of American endorsement of the Balfour Declaration: *B.F.P.*, *First Series*, Vol. IV, No. 196, note 4, p. 281.

[47] *Brandeis* papers. 'Cyrus' was a code-name for the President.

[48] Copy in Z.A.

the American Zionist leaders found it unsatisfactory in two respects. They disliked the words, 'the rights and political status enjoyed in any other country by such Jews who are fully contented with their existing nationality and citizenship,' and wished to substitute: 'the rights and civil political status enjoyed by Jews in any other country.'[49] Brandeis appears to have proposed, further, the alteration of 'Jewish race' to 'Jewish people.'[50] 'The two corrections we desired to make' were mentioned by Wise at an interview with House on October 16th.[51] On both points the declaration was amended in the sense desired by the American Zionists before its final approval by the War Cabinet on October 31st, and they were not unnaturally under the impression that this was the result of their representations to House.[52] In this, however, they were mistaken. Precisely similar points had been raised independently by some of the Zionist and other Jewish leaders in England who had been asked by the War Cabinet for their views on the draft declaration, and there is good reason for believing that the amendments in question were, in fact, approved in response to suggestions by the Chief Rabbi,

---

[49] De Haas to Brandeis, 15 October 1917: *Brandeis papers*.

[50] In *Trial and Error* Weizmann says (p. 261) that this suggestion 'actually came from Brandeis.' It may well be that Brandeis did propose this change, but it was suggested by Sokolow as early as October 12th (Sokolow to Rothschild, 12 October 1917: Z.A.), and there is no reason to think that it had by this time already been suggested to Sokolow or his colleagues by Brandeis.

[51] Wise to Brandeis, 17 October 1917: *Brandeis papers*. In his above-mentioned letter to Rothschild of October 12th (Z.A.) Sokolow also wrote: 'Where it says "or the rights and political status enjoyed in any other country by such Jews who are fully contented with their existing nationality and citizenship," I would suggest to limit this sentence to: "or the rights and political status enjoyed by Jews in any other country."' This was three days before de Haas wrote to Brandeis (October 15th— *Brandeis papers*): 'I telephoned to you to-day that the Weizmann message came to hand and we went into immediate session about it. Both Wise, Levin and myself feel that the third sentence could well be amended . . . We would favour the following: "or the rights and civil political status enjoyed by Jews in any other country."' (There is no reference in the letter to the substitution of 'people' for 'race.')

[52] See de Haas, *Brandeis*, p. 92; de Haas in *The New Palestine* (New York), 28 October 1927, pp. 321, 343. The same suggestion is conveyed in a passage at pp. 34-35 of the 'Statement to the delegates of the Twelfth Zionist Congress on behalf of the former Administration of the Zionist Organisation of America' (New York, 1921).

Weizmann, Sokolow and Rothschild. Wise reported to Brandeis on October 17th that House had told him the day before that 'it [the formula] had gone through just as it is.' 'I pointed out,' Wise continued, 'the two corrections we desire to make and I believe he will find it possible to make those suggestions, although, on the other hand, he did not definitely promise this and may feel that it is not worth while making the changes.'[53] Wise guessed correctly. No representations in favour of these or any other amendments of the formula reached the Foreign Office from Washington.

[53] Wise to Brandeis, 17 October 1917: *Brandeis papers.*

CHAPTER 36

CONTACTS BETWEEN GERMAN ZIONIST
LEADERS AND THE GERMAN GOVERNMENT

WHEN BALFOUR SPOKE, on October 4th, of German efforts to capture the Zionist Movement, he was warning the War Cabinet
that if it delayed much longer in authorising a pro-Zionist
declaration, it would be playing the enemy's game. German competition for Zionist sympathies was a theme of which much was
to be heard during October, and the belief that a German move
might be imminent was to play an important part in expediting
the War Cabinet's approval of the Balfour Declaration on
October 31st.

President Wilson, as we have seen, was told on October 6th
that it was because of reports that they were being courted by
the Germans that the question of a British assurance to the
Zionists was being re-considered by the War Cabinet. When,
towards the end of the month, the Declaration was still hanging
fire, the Foreign Office, in pressing for a prompt decision, pointed
out that 'delay may throw the Zionists into the hands of the
Germans.'[1] In a memorandum of which more will be said later,
even Curzon, sceptical though he was about the practicability of
the Zionist programme, conceded that the proposed declaration
might well serve a useful purpose as a check on 'the sinister
political designs of the Germans.'[2] *The Times*[3] insisted that further
procrastination would be disastrous, since Germany appreciated
the importance of an understanding with the Zionists, 'and she
has not been idle in attempting to forestall us.' How far were
these anxieties well-founded?

The German Government's intentions seem to have been
deduced mainly from articles in German newspapers of almost

[1] The Graham memorandum—see below, p. 544.
[2] Below, p. 545.
[3] 26 October 1917.

all political colourings[4] pointing out the solid advantages to be expected by Germany, and likewise by her Turkish ally, from an understanding with the Zionists, and urging the Government not to let the enemy monopolise them. The leading exponent of these ideas was Major Franz Karl Endres, a former General Staff Officer, who had served under von der Goltz in Turkey and was now the military correspondent of the *Muenchener Neueste Nachrichten*. Endres—the German Sidebotham—was the most persistent advocate of a pro-Zionist policy, but similar views were expressed, though usually from a rather different standpoint (for Endres had some appreciation of the idealist element in Zionism), by other writers in the German press—notably the influential Junker publicist, von Döbbeler. All this, it could be argued, could not have happened without the assent, if not the prompting, of the German Government, from which the inference could be drawn that the press campaign might well reflect a policy soon to be translated into action. Had it been a serious embarrassment to the Government, it would, no doubt, have been suppressed, but the deduction that Germany was on the point of aligning herself publicly with the Zionists can now be seen to have been erroneous.[5]

Something has already been said about the cordial relations, in the earlier part of the War, between the Berlin Zionist Executive and the German Foreign Office, and between the Zionist Agency in Constantinople and the German Embassy. In the middle of 1916, Richard Lichtheim, writing from Constantinople, still felt able to report to the Zionist Committee in New York that the Zionists had firm assurances, supported by a good deal of practical evidence, of German goodwill.[6] But these assurances had never been translated into a precise undertaking—still less into a public commitment. In the days of American neutrality and divided sympathies the Germans had assiduously courted the American Jews but had even then stopped short of an open pro-

---

[4] A notable exception was *Germania*, the organ of the Roman Catholic Centre Party.

[5] What follows is based mainly on the Berlin and Copenhagen material in the Zionist Archives and on information for which the author is indebted to Mr. Richard Lichtheim. (As to Mr. Lichtheim's co-operation, see above, p. 206).

[6] 10 July 1916: Z.A.

Zionist declaration. Useful as this might have been to them in their political warfare, it would have cost them in Turkish irritation a higher price than they had been prepared to pay, and the Berlin Zionist Executive had pressed for such a declaration in vain.

By the spring of 1917 the incentive had become weaker and the objections more serious. The Turks were unreliable allies, and it was more important than ever that nothing should be done to antagonise them. On the other hand, once the United States had entered the War, the Zionist leaders in Berlin had lost their trump card in their relations with the German Government, and on the German side there was a perceptible cooling off.[7]

Not that all was lost. In the German-occupied parts of Eastern Europe—notably in Russian Poland—there was a large Jewish population which, both during the War and in the peace settlement, might be useful to the Germans, if it could be educated to regard them as its friends. An effective appeal to the Zionists might strengthen the pro-German elements in Russia. In the United States there were among the unassimilated Jewish masses many who had little interest in the War and might be impressed by German promises of sympathy with Zionist aspirations. Even though German hopes of total victory had not yet been finally extinguished, the War might end with a negotiated peace, and the Germans, with much at stake in the settlement of the Turkish question, had something to lose by standing by in silence while the Zionists moved into the enemy's orbit.

Hence, though its main motive for gratifying the Zionists had evaporated with the American declaration of war, the German Government still maintained friendly relations with the Zionist leaders with whom it had been so long in contact. It was always ready to give them a hearing and seems to have paid some attention to the case they made out for a public assurance of German sympathy with their cause. They had reason to believe that on this subject there was a sharp difference of opinion between the Information and the Political Branches of the German Foreign Office, the Information Branch—it was reported—favouring the proposal but being strongly opposed by the Political Branch on

---

[7] Mr. Lichtheim to the author, 16 April 1952.

the ground that Germany was in no position to invite a quarrel with the Turks.[8]

The propagandists may well have been attracted by the idea, but it is easy to understand why the Political Branch should have thought the objections insuperable. In deference to Turkish susceptibilities, the German Government had from the start had to move warily in its dealings with the Zionsts. It had good reason to be still more cautious at a time when the Turks could no longer be counted upon as subservient and dependable allies, and when some of their leaders—notably Djemal Pasha—were in sharp disagreement with the German General Staff about the handling of the combined force assembled under von Falkenhayn for the re-capture of Baghdad.[9]

In their hostility to Zionism and their veto on any encouragement of Zionist aspirations the Turks were as obdurate as ever. They had been incensed by Morgenthau's Cincinnati speech in May 1916,[10] when he had announced that arrangements could be made after the War for the sale of Palestine by Turkey to the Jews. They had been still further antagonised by press reports that this had been agreed to by Turkey under German pressure.[11] Lichtheim had done his best to appease the Turks and his explanations seem to have had some effect,[12] but Turkish suspicions of the Zionists had not been allayed. When, at the suggestion of the German Foreign Office, Hantke and Lichtheim saw Djemal Pasha during his visit to Berlin in the summer of 1917, they came away empty-handed.[13] They were told that the existing Jewish population of Palestine would be fairly treated but that no further

8 Memorandum by Lichtheim, 10 August 1917, reporting confidential information which had reached him (apparently from inside the Foreign Office) concerning divisions of opinion as to the action to be taken in the light of a dispatch from the German Minister in Berne drawing attention to the growing importance of the Zionist Movement and its success in engaging the interest of the Entente Governments : Z.A.

9 Wavell: *The Palestine Campaign*, pp. 108-109; Djemal Pasha, *Memories of a Turkish Statesman* (London, Hutchinson, n.d.), pp. 189-190.

10 Above, p. 289.

11 These reports are referred to in a letter of 26 July 1916 from the Copenhagen Zionist Bureau to the Zionist Committee in New York: Z.A.

12 This appears from a report to Berlin, dated 10 September 1916, from the German Ambassador in Constantinople: *D.G.F.O.*, K962/177837.

13 Note of the interview, stated to have been arranged by the Foreign Office, in memorandum dated 28 August 1917: Z.A.

Jewish immigrants would be allowed. The Jews could settle anywhere else in Turkey they liked, but not in Palestine. The Turkish Government, Djemal declared, wanted no new nationality questions, nor was it prepared to get into trouble with the Palestine Arabs, who formed the majority of the population and were to a man opposed to Zionism. The one grain of comfort that Hantke and Lichtheim carried away was Djemal's rather curious remark that it was conceivable that some future Turkish Government might take a different view or even that he himself might one day change his mind. The point of these cryptic observations was not very clear. For the present, at all events, it was evident that the Turks were not prepared to make any concessions to the Zionists—much less to be parties to a public pronouncement in their favour.

This discouraging interview took place at the end of August 1917. A few weeks later the Berlin Zionists found themselves in a still worse position when the Turks stumbled upon the Jewish spy-ring working in Palestine for the British under the direction of the Aaronsohns. At a time when the Turks were in no mood to show indulgence to the Zionists, and when Turco-German relations were by no means cordial, it is no wonder that the Germans, tempted as they may have been by its advantages, shrank from committing themselves to a pro-Zionist declaration.

If the Berlin Zionist Executive failed to pin them down, it was not because it was backward in pressing its case. A memorandum handed to the German Foreign Office towards the end of June 1917 was followed a month later by a more elaborate document setting out at length the reasons why it was submitted that both Germany and Turkey would be well advised to give the Zionists some encouragement.[14] It was pointed out that Great Britain was showing a marked interest in the Movement in the hope of using it to her own advantage. The French, competing with the British for the mastery of Palestine, had lately begun to make friendly gestures to the Zionists. The Morgenthau mission, whose purpose, it was said, was to sound the European Powers on the Palestine question, was evidence of the extraordinarily favourable attitude

---

[14] Copy of the memorandum, dated 22 July 1917, in Z.A. There is a reference to an earlier memorandum, dated 24 June 1917.

of the American Government. The memorandum continued: 'We think it desirable to draw the special attention of the Foreign Office to the fact that the Entente Governments are exerting themselves in this manner to gain, for their own purposes, the sympathies and material resources of Jewry. In our capacity as the supreme governing body of the Zionist Movement we can give a most positive assurance that our adherents throughout the world never were, and are not now, willing to put the Zionist Movement at the service of any one Power or group of Powers. . . . The efforts of all Zionists in all countries are directed to one end only—that, with the aid of the European Powers, a sure foundation may be laid for the realisation of Zionism.'

The Berlin Executive went on to explain that, in approaching their respective Governments, 'the Jews of the Entente countries . . . are guided exclusively by Jewish interests. . . . Indeed, Zionist circles in England, America and Russia attach the greatest importance to its being shown by the Central Powers that they, too, view the Jewish effort with favour.' The Foreign Office was reminded that the Berlin Executive 'has throughout the war done its best to calm Jewish public opinion when Turkey has taken action against the Jews, and so to guide the Zionist Movement as to prevent it from following in the wake of the Entente and keep it true to its original character.' It would surely be appreciated that in this the Executive could only hope to succeed if it could show that its decision to remain in Berlin was being justified by visible results.

All this led up to an appeal to the German Government to recognise that the time had come for Germany, in her own interests, to define her position on the Zionist question and to advise Turkey to do the same. 'We are well aware,' the Foreign Office was assured, 'of the difficulties standing in the way, but we believe that, in view of the public discussion of the question, this is the moment to work for the solution desired by us, by which Germany will gain an important measure of goodwill and Turkey economic advantages of the greatest value.'

This was the burden of the memorandum submitted to the German Foreign Office on 22 July 1917. A few days later came the curious incident of Boris Goldberg's visit to Copenhagen,[15]

[15] See above, p. 439.

where, together with Tschlenow, he discussed the situation with the three members of the Berlin Zionist Executive—Warburg, Hantke, and Jacobson. What was understood in London to be the purpose of Goldberg's mission was, as we have seen, to explain to Tschlenow the case for the London programme—a Jewish Commonwealth in Palestine under British protection—and to bring him and his Russian colleagues into line. What actually happened was that, after Goldberg had explained in some detail what had been going on in London, Paris and Washington, and Tschlenow had reported on the situation in Russia, it was agreed that, side by side with what was being done in the Entente countries, a parallel effort must be made to enlist the support of the Central Powers both by direct approaches to their Governments and also by propaganda modelled on that of the British Palestine Committee.[16]

Whatever reports may have been reaching Downing Street, it is clear that at this stage it was, in fact, the British and not the Germans who were making the pace in overtures to the Zionists, and that, as between the German Government and the Berlin Zionist Executive, the courtship was on the Zionist side. The Germans were keeping clear of any positive commitments and were not responding to the representations of the Berlin Executive, which, out of concern for the international character of the Zionist Organisation, for the security of the Yishuv, and for its own status and prestige, and also, perhaps, for patriotic reasons, was desperately anxious that Germany should not stand aside while the Movement was being captured by the Entente.

The Berlin Executive was persistent. Soon after the Copenhagen meeting at the end of July, Lichtheim saw Dr. Goeppert, who was handling these matters at the German Foreign Office, and re-stated the case for a German move.[17] By demonstrating its goodwill, the German Government, Goeppert was assured, could strengthen the influence of the German-Jewish element in the Zionist Organisation and so do something to ensure the protection of German interests when the time came for the resumption of Zionist activities in Palestine. At the end of August, Hantke and Lichtheim had an interview in Berlin with Count

16 Ibid.
17 Note of the interview, 5 August 1917, in Z.A.

Bernstorff,[18] who, after leaving Washington on the American declaration of war, had been appointed German Ambassador in Constantinople. The Zionist spokesmen impressed on him how strongly the tide was flowing in favour of Zionism in the Allied countries and how anxious they were for some counter-demonstration on the German side, and, in particular, for a more helpful attitude on the part of the German Embassy in Constantinople. In Washington Bernstorff had, as in duty bound, interested himself in the Zionist question, but he was in no position to give any assurances about the present policy of the German Government, and his attitude, though friendly, was non-committal.

It was now becoming evident that no active German encouragement was to be expected. Major Endres had been induced to take an interest in the idea of a German-Palestine Committee and the starting of a German publication on the lines of *Palestine*. At an interview with Dr. Goeppert towards the end of September Lichtheim was told that the Foreign Office did not favour this scheme because the Turks would suspect that the German Government was behind it.[19] A few days later, the Foreign Office, while making it clear that no official support would be forthcoming, relented to the extent of agreeing not to veto the project on the clear understanding that it would be carried out on the sole responsibility of the promoters.[20] The embargo had been lifted, but, killed by so much discouragement, the whole plan was dropped, not to be heard of again until, in the spring of 1918, it was revived as part of Germany's rather feeble riposte to the Balfour Declaration.

At the time of the Declaration the German Government was still holding back from any commitment to the Zionists. On 23 October 1917, a week before the Declaration was approved by the British War Cabinet, the German Minister to Denmark, Count Brockdorff-Rantzau, received a representative of the Copenhagen Zionist Bureau, which had for some time been on

[18] Note of the interview, 28 August 1917, in Z.A.

[19] Note of the interview, 20 September 1917, in Z.A. On September 26th Endres wrote to the Zionist Central Office in Berlin that he understood that, having regard to its relations with the Turks, the German Government was not in a position to associate itself with pro-Zionist propaganda: Z.A.

[20] Lichtheim to Endres, 28 September 1917: Z.A.

friendly terms with the Legation. The Minister had just returned from Berlin, where the Foreign Office had discussed with him a memorandum in which Victor Jacobson, on behalf of the Berlin Zionist Executive, had once more pressed for a pro-Zionist pronouncement by the German Government. Brockdorff-Rantzau informed the Zionist spokesman, Martin Rosenblüth, that he had been told in Berlin that such a move would not at present be in German interests.[21]

It was not that the Germans no longer attached any importance to Jewish goodwill. On taking charge of the Constantinople Embassy in the summer of 1917 Bernstorff did his best to protect the Jews in Palestine from further maltreatment by the Turks. In reply to an invitation from Von Papen, then a General Staff Officer on the Turkish Front, to visit him in Jerusalem, Bernstorff wrote (21 October):[22] 'I should much like to view the situation there at close quarters, and more especially to study the Jewish question, which so often gives us trouble.' He assured Georg Bernhard,[23] who had written to him about the perilous position of the Jews in Palestine, that 'these questions are part of our daily bread here.'[24] Bernstorff records in his memoirs[25] a discussion with Talaat Pasha[26]—apparently just before the Balfour Declaration—about 'the establishment of a Jewish home in Palestine.' 'Talaat,' he writes, 'was ready to promise all I wanted, provided Palestine remained Turkish after the War, but he took every opportunity of saying: "I will gladly establish a national home for the Jews to please you, but, mark my words, the Arabs will destroy the Jews."' That Bernstorff should have tried to interest Talaat in the Zionist question is not surprising, but, if Talaat did give the impression that he would be prepared to gratify the Germans on

---

[21] Note by Rosenblüth of interview with Brockdorff-Rantzau, 23 October 1917: Z.A. Brockdorff-Rantzau said that, against the advice of certain Jewish friends of his, including, in particular, Max Warburg, he had done his best for the Zionists but had been plainly told at the Foreign Office that this was not the time for a pro-Zionist move. No record of Brockdorff-Rantzau's discussion with the Foreign Office has, up to the present (June 1959), come to light in *D.G.F.O.*

[22] *The Memoirs of Count Bernstorff* (London, Heinemann, 1936), p. 171.

[23] Editor of the *Vossische Zeitung*.

[24] 3 November 1917: *Memoirs*, p. 172.

[25] p. 171.

[26] The Turkish Grand Vizier.

this point, either he was not serious or he soon changed his mind. There was no sign of any weakening on the Zionist issue in the unhelpful statement which was the best that could be extracted from him when, disturbed by the British Declaration, the Germans were casting about at the end of 1917 for some means of neutralising its effect.[27] In January 1918 a spokesman of the German Foreign Office made a statement about Palestine to a representative German Jewish deputation. He went as far as he could, but his guarded and inhibited language showed that this was a matter on which the Germans still felt obliged to take their cue from the Turks.[28]

From what Brockdorff-Rantzau was told in Berlin on the eve of the Balfour Declaration it is evident that, whatever Talaat may have said half-seriously in conversation with Bernstorff, the German Foreign Office knew well enough what was the real attitude of the Turks and was satisfied that any open pro-Zionist announcement would be damaging to German interests. Left to themselves, the Germans might well have been responsive to the arguments so persistently pressed upon them by the Berlin Zionist Executive. With the Turks in the mood in which they were in the autumn of 1917, such a move would have cost Germany more than it was considered to be worth.[29]

[27] Below, p. 602.
[28] Ibid.
[29] On 12 November 1917 the Berlin Zionist Executive wrote to the Foreign Office drawing attention to the Balfour Declaration and asking for an interview with the Foreign Minister. The reply was that Kuhlmann was too busy to grant such an interview: *D.G.F.O.*, K 692/K179794-95 and 179796. In reply to a telegram, dated 30 December 1917, in which the German Minister at Berne asked for instructions in the light of a Havas Agency report that Germany would not oppose the creation of an independent Jewish State, the Minister was informed that the report was a complete fabrication; Germany was not in a position to agree to plans which would rob Turkey of a province: *D.G.F.O.* K692/180051 and 180052.

CHAPTER 37

THE WAR CABINET APPROVES THE DECLARATION, 31 OCTOBER 1917

WHEN THE War Cabinet discussed the draft declaration on 4 October 1917, the question of an explicit British undertaking to the Zionists had already been under consideration by the Foreign Office and, at a later stage, at Cabinet level, for something like four months. Towards the end of October it looked as though at last the way was clear. In spite of the discouraging advice he had given when first approached, President Wilson had now agreed to a declaration on the lines of the Milner-Amery draft. The anti-Zionist British Jews had had their say and could not complain of not having been heard. Edwin Montagu had fired his last shot and was on his way to India. The only other Jewish member of the Government, Sir Alfred Mond, though sceptical about the possibility of a Jewish State, had publicly expressed some sympathy with Zionism and admiration for what the Jews had achieved in Palestine.[1] The War Cabinet had been assured by the Chief Rabbi that the proposed declaration would be welcomed by the overwhelming majority of Anglo-Jewry, and much the same view had been expressed, in slightly more guarded language, by the President of the Board of Deputies of British Jews. As a result of the campaign set on foot by the English Zionist Federation, resolutions in support of the Zionist programme had poured into the Foreign Office from hundreds of Jewish bodies in various parts of the country.

All the obstacles, as it seemed, having fallen, the Foreign Office was anxious that the declaration should be approved by the War Cabinet without further delay. How impatiently it now awaited

[1] Later, Lord Melchett; article in *The Weekly Dispatch*, 8 April 1917. He had been appointed First Commissioner of Works, without a seat in the Cabinet, on the formation of the Lloyd George Government at the end of 1916. After the Declaration he sent a warmly worded message to a Zionist thanksgiving meeting at Swansea (*J.C.*, 23 Nov. 1917), and he subsequently became an active supporter of the Zionist cause.

a decision, and for what reasons, can be seen from a memorandum submitted to Balfour on October 24th by Sir Ronald Graham.[2]

Balfour was reminded that the Zionists had been kept waiting more than three months for a reply to Lord Rothschild's letter of July 18th. On no account, it was urged, should there be any further procrastination, since the result might be to throw the Zionists into the arms of the Germans and to put an end to the prospect of attracting valuable support for the Allied cause from the Zionist forces in Russia and the United States. The German press was taking up the Zionist question, and the British Government might at any moment find itself confronted with a German move. Graham went on to speak of the situation in Russia, in which, he said, the Jews were playing an important rôle. They were now certainly against the Allies and in favour of Germany, but almost every Jew in Russia was a Zionist, and if the Jews could be made to realise that the achievement of Zionist aims depended on an Allied victory, a powerful element in Russian life would be enlisted on the side of the Entente. Balfour was asked to bear in mind that the Russian Zionist leader, Tschlenow, was on his way to England, that it was important that the declaration should be approved before his arrival, and that the moment they received it the Zionists would be prepared to start active propaganda in the interests of the Allies in all parts of the world. Graham dwelt particularly on the work which the Zionists, with Weizmann's personal co-operation, would be prepared to do in Russia, adding, however, that propaganda was likewise greatly needed in the United States.

Balfour can hardly have needed to be convinced that there should be no further delay in the approval of the declaration. Graham's memorandum of October 24th was intended, presumably, to strengthen his hands in pressing the War Cabinet to accept this view. But at this point a new obstacle appeared. A final decision was delayed—though, as it turned out, only for a few days—by Curzon's announcement that he proposed to circulate a memorandum on the subject. His views would clearly have to be weighed before the debate could be closed. The Zionists knew that Curzon was no friend of theirs and was standing in the way

---

[2] Sir R. Graham was the head of the Eastern Department of the Foreign Office.

of the declaration. The reports which were reaching them are echoed in an entry in Mrs. Weizmann's diary: 'For the third time the War Cabinet has had on the agenda the Palestinian Declaration, and for the third time it was put off owing to our Jewish enemies. On the eve, Lord Curzon came in to say that the question is too important and he would like to postpone it in order to present a memorandum on the subject. Sir Mark Sykes, Ormsby-Gore and Sir Ronald Graham were furious and saw in it nothing but obstruction . . .'[3]

Curzon's memorandum, dated October 26th,[4] was an elaborate and closely reasoned document in his best magisterial style. He did not concern himself with the dispute between Zionist and anti-Zionist Jews. The question he raised was whether the proposed declaration might not embarrass the British Government by encouraging hopes incapable of being realised. Palestine, he pointed out, was a poor country, devoid of natural resources—'a country calling for prolonged and patient toil from a people inured to agriculture, and even so only admitting after generations of a relatively small population.' It was already inhabited by some half-a-million Arabs, who 'will not be content either to be expropriated for Jewish immigrants or to act merely as hewers of wood and drawers of water for the latter.' 'Is it not obvious,' Curzon asked, 'that a country which cannot within any approximate period contain anything but a small population, which has already an indigenous population of its own of a different race . . . cannot, save by a very elastic use of the term, be designated as the national home of the Jewish people?' On a realistic view, the most that could be done, so far as the Jews were concerned, would be 'to secure to the Jews (but not to the Jews alone) equal civil and religious rights with the other elements of the population, and to arrange, as far as possible, for land purchase and settlement of returning Jews.' 'I would,' Curzon continued, 'gladly give my adhesion to such a policy, all the more that it appears . . . to be urgently demanded as a check or counterblast to the scarcely concealed and sinister designs of the Germans.

---

[3] This diary note is dated October 18th, but this may be a slip for the 28th. The preceding and succeeding entries are dated respectively July 13th and October 31st.

[4] Full text in Lloyd George, *Treaties*, II, 1123ff.

But in my judgment it is a policy very widely removed from the romantic and idealistic aspirations of many of the Zionist leaders whose literature I have studied.'

Curzon did not, however, persist in his objections. When the question came before the War Cabinet, for the last time, on October 31st, he recognised the strength of the case for the declaration and was prepared, not without some misgivings, to support it. For what passed at this meeting we have again to rely on Lloyd George's quotations from an unspecified record.[5] From these it appears that while Curzon 'could not share the optimistic views held regarding the future of Palestine' and 'feared that by the suggested declaration we should be raising false expectations which could never be realised,' he acknowledged that he was impressed by 'the diplomatic arguments' in favour of the declaration and 'recognised that some expression of sympathy with Jewish aspirations would be a valuable adjunct to our propaganda, though he thought that we should be guarded in the language used in giving expression to such sympathy.'

What the War Cabinet was considering was not whether, in the eventual peace settlement, Great Britain should try to do something for the Jews in Palestine, but whether the British Government should there and then enter into a public undertaking to the Zionists. According to the source drawn upon by Lloyd George,[6] Balfour did not think it necessary to dwell on the larger aspects of the Zionist question, nor did he say anything about strengthening the resistance to French pretensions in Palestine or about any long-term advantages to be expected from a British association with the Zionists. He chose to rest the case for the declaration mainly on its value as propaganda.

'He stated,' we are told, 'that he gathered that everyone was now agreed that, from a purely diplomatic and political point of view, it was desirable that some declaration favourable to the aspirations of the Jewish nationalists should now be made. The vast majority of Jews in Russia and America,

---

[5] *Treaties*, II, 1136ff.

[6] Referring to the quotation which follows, Lloyd George writes (*Treaties*, II, 1137): 'I have already quoted the words actually used by Mr. Balfour when he submitted the Declaration to the Cabinet for its approval.'

as, indeed, all over the world, now appeared to be favourable to Zionism. If we could make a declaration favourable to such an ideal, we should be able to carry on extremely useful propaganda both in Russia and America. He gathered that the main arguments still put forward against Zionism were twofold:

'(a) That Palestine was inedaquate to form a home for either the Jewish or any other people.

'(b) The difficulty felt with regard to the future position of Jews in Western countries.[7]

'As to the meaning of the words "national home,"[8] to which the Zionists attach so much importance, he understood it to mean some form of British, American, or other protectorate, under which full facilities would be given to the Jews to work out their own salvation and to build up, by means of education, agriculture, and industry, a real centre of national culture and focus of national life. It did not necessarily involve the early establishment of an independent Jewish State, which was a matter for gradual development in accordance with the ordinary laws of political evolution.'

This time the War Cabinet came at last to a decision. The next day, November 1st, Sir Ronald Graham sent privately to Weizmann the text of a declaration—a slightly amended version of the Milner-Amery formula[9]—authorised to be made by the Foreign Secretary. It would be embodied, Graham explained, 'in

---

[7] It might have been expected that, having raised these points, Balfour would deal with them, but Lloyd George's quotation contains nothing more than is printed here.

[8] The expression 'a national home for the Jewish people' echoed the words of the Basle programme, 'the creation in Palestine of a home for the Jewish people,' with the insertion of what had now come to be considered the indispensable word 'national.' It is an expansion of the expression 'Jewish national home' coined by Sokolow in 1916: see his letter of 3 November 1916 to members of the Committee then drafting a Zionist programme: N.S.P.

[9] 'a national home for the Jewish race' had been altered to 'a national home for the Jewish people' and, at the end of the Declaration, 'the rights and political status enjoyed in any other country by such Jews who are fully contented with their existing nationality and citizenship' had been altered to 'the rights and political status enjoyed by Jews in any other country.'

a letter which Mr. Balfour is addressing to Lord Rothschild, with a request to communicate it to your Organisation.'[10]

Why, it may be asked, was the letter to be addressed to Rothschild? Weizmann was the President of the English Zionist Federation, whereas Rothschild held no office either in the Federation or in the World Zionist Organisation, of which it was the English branch. It was, however, through Rothschild that the Zionists had submitted their formula in July, and in transmitting it to Balfour he had suggested that the Declaration he was asking for should be addressed, in the first instance, to himself: 'If His Majesty's Government will send me a message on the lines of the formula . . . I will hand it on to the Zionist Federation.'[11] There is no difficulty in understanding why this arrangement was favoured. Sokolow, the titular representative of the World Zionist Organisation in England, was a foreigner and a member of the Executive of an international movement having its headquarters, at least nominally, in Berlin. Weizmann, though a British subject and the head of the English Zionist Federation, would have been an awkward choice, for, eminent as was his personal standing, Sokolow was his senior in rank in the Zionist hierarchy. The selection of Rothschild not only avoided all these embarrassments but had the decisive advantage of associating the Declaration with the most potent name in Jewry.

On November 2nd Balfour wrote to Rothschild:

'Dear Lord Rothschild,

I have much pleasure in conveying to you, on behalf of His Majesty's Government, the following declaration of sympathy with Jewish Zionist aspirations which has been submitted to, and approved by, the Cabinet.

"His Majesty's Government view with favour the establishment in Palestine of a national home for the Jewish people, and will use their best endeavours to facilitate the achievement of this object, it being clearly understood that nothing shall be done which may prejudice the civil and religious rights of existing non-Jewish communities in Palestine, or the rights and political status enjoyed by Jews in any other country."

[10] *Ch.W.P.*
[11] Above, p. 470.

'I should be grateful if you would bring this declaration to the knowledge of the Zionist Federation.'[12]

What was it that brought the War Cabinet, after two false starts, to the point of decision?

During the first half of 1917 the British Government's active encouragement of the Zionists had been directly related to the idea that they could help, in some measure, to extricate it, so far as Palestine was concerned, from the encumbrance of the Sykes-Picot Agreement. The main practical purpose of the plan of campaign worked out and set in motion by Mark Sykes had been to impress upon the French, first, that in any settlement of the Palestine question the Zionists must be taken seriously into account, and, secondly, that they were immovable in their desire for a British trusteeship and would regard French predominance, or even an Anglo-French condominium, as wholly unacceptable.

But by the time the Declaration came before the War Cabinet in the early autumn, the situation had changed. From what is known of the grounds on which the War Cabinet was invited to approve a pro-Zionist pronouncement it does not look as though pressure on the French played any part in them. That the French should, if possible, be kept out of Palestine remained axiomatic, but it seems no longer to have been felt, as it had earlier been so strongly felt by Sykes, that this was, of itself, a conclusive reason for a close understanding with the Zionists. With a large-scale campaign in Palestine under way and a British military occupation in prospect, it may well have been assumed that, for all practical purposes, the French were already out of the running, so that there was no compelling need for the Zionists to be brought in as a makeweight. Nor was it now quite as obvious as it had seemed a few months before that the Zionists ought to be encouraged to press for a British trusteeship. However clear it might be that there could be no room in Palestine for the French, did it necessarily follow that Great Britain must claim exclusive control for herself? Was it certain that this would be to her advantage? Might not American control, or at least an Anglo-American combination, be worth considering as a possible

[12] Original deposited by Lord Rothschild in British Museum: *Addl. Ms.* 41178, folios 1 and 3.

549

alternative? These questions, as we shall see, were to be looked at more closely after the end of the War, but at the time of the Declaration they were already being raised. The ideas which had, in the spring and summer, played so large a part in British relations with the Zionists may not have been entirely extinct, but, unless there is some deliberate suppression in Lloyd George's account of the proceedings, they were not discussed or even mentioned at any of the three Cabinets at which the Declaration was debated.

Thus, the Declaration came before the War Cabinet at a time when the practical considerations which had at first told most strongly in favour of an understanding with the Zionists had lost some of their urgency. But, while they were receding into the background, others had been emerging. These centred mainly round the Russian Revolution and its aftermath. By the spring of 1917 the British Government had already begun to interest itself in the suggestion that the Zionists might be able to exert a steadying influence in Russia and to strengthen the forces opposed to a breach with the Allies and a separate peace. By the autumn, events in Russia had taken a sharp turn for the worse, and there was a strong case for a public commitment to the Zionists, if there was any chance, however slender, of its helping to avert the impending catastrophe. To this was added anxiety about the response of the American Jews, and especially of those having ties with Russia, to pacifist propaganda calculated to impede the American war effort. What was uppermost in the War Cabinet's mind in approving the Balfour Declaration is evident from its discussions, as described by Lloyd George, on October 4th and 31st. It was thinking of the rapidly deteriorating situation in Russia, of the apathy towards the War of a considerable section of American Jewry, of the propagandist value of a pro-Zionist declaration, and of the urgency of the matter in the light of reports suggesting that, if such a declaration were further delayed, the Germans might blunt its edge by forestalling it.

This is the simple answer to the question why it was decided, at this particular point of time, to give the Zionists an assurance of British support in the terms of the Balfour Declaration. It is not an answer to the question why the Zionists were taken seriously enough to make such an assurance worth considering,

nor does it explain how it came to pass that the British Government was prepared to accept the long- term moral obligations implicit in a pro-Zionist policy publicly announced. Though the Declaration had a strictly practical purpose related to the war situation at the time, it is not to be accounted for merely as an eleventh-hour device for dealing with a problem of political warfare. Behind it lay the long story already told in full—the links forged between Great Britain and the Zionists by their early pre-war contacts; the instinctive sympathy with Zionist aspirations shown by leading British statesmen from the moment Turkey entered the War; the impression made by Weizmann and Samuel in their sustained effort to convince the British Government that the Zionists were a powerful force in Jewry and that Jewish good-will was an intangible asset worth acquiring; the response of some imaginative minds to the suggestion that a large-scale Jewish settlement in Palestine might not only have a stabilising influence in an area in which important British interests were at stake, but might contribute to the regeneration of the Middle East as a whole; the strengthening of the Zionist case by the conception of Zionism as a rallying-point for the healthy and creative elements in Jewish life and an antidote to the subversive movements in which Jews in rebellion against their lot were finding an outlet for their frustrated energies; Mark Sykes' conversion to Zionism and his growing enthusiasm for a cause which he found more interesting and attractive the more closely he looked at it; his interview with Lloyd George in the spring of 1917, when he was told that the Prime Minister wanted Palestine to be brought within the British sphere and the Zionists helped to achieve their aims under British auspices; the encouragement of Zionist propaganda designed to popularise the idea of a Jewish Commonwealth in Palestine sponsored by Great Britain, and to convince the Russians and the Americans that a British trustee-ship would not be a cloak for an old-fashioned annexation; the half-promise to the Zionists, four months before the Declaration was approved, of a public assurance that Great Britain was on their side. Though the emphasis varied with changing circumstances, there were at every stage strictly rational arguments, related to a realistic assessment of British interests, in favour of a pro-Zionist policy. But, when these have been given full weight,

something still remains to be added. At a private gathering a few weeks after the Declaration, Balfour was asked whether it represented a bid for Jewish support in the War. According to a description of the incident in Colonel Meinertzhagen's diary,[12a] he at once replied: 'Certainly not. Both the Prime Minister and myself have been influenced by a desire to give the Jews their rightful place in the world; a great nation without a home is not right.' This bears no resemblance to what is known of Balfour's argument in commending the Declaration to the War Cabinet on 31 October 1917, but it is none the less true that his approach to the whole question of British relations with the Zionists—and, though his interest was more superficial, the same would seem to apply to Lloyd George—was coloured by a genuine desire 'to give the Jews their rightful place in the world.' All this may have little to do with the War Cabinet's conscious motives for approving the Declaration, but without this background neither its origins nor its significance can be understood.

What, then, were the Zionists being promised? The language of the Declaration was studiously vague, and neither on the British nor on the Zionist side was there any disposition, at the time, to probe deeply into its meaning—still less was there any agreed interpretation.

On one point which Weizmann and his colleagues had from the start regarded as fundamental the Declaration was, of necessity, silent. It did not give the Zionists, nor did they expect it to give them, any assurance that the British Government would make itself directly responsible for the establishment of the Jewish national home. In the circumstances of the time, it would plainly have been impossible for Great Britain openly to designate herself as the Protecting Power. But the question was not merely one of propriety. In commending the Declaration to the War Cabinet, Balfour had not only said nothing about a British trusteeship for Palestine but had, on the contrary, made it clear that on this point Great Britain remained uncommitted.

What the British Government did undertake was to use its best endeavours to 'facilitate' (no more) 'the establishment in Palestine of a national home for the Jewish people'—not, as it had

[12a] *Middle East Diary*, pp. 8-9 (7 February 1918).

been put in the Zionist draft and as Balfour would, apparently, have been prepared to concede, the reconstitution of Palestine as the national home of the Jews.[13] The Declaration was a political and not a legal document, and the crucial words did not lend themselves to close analysis. As to what, precisely, was to be facilitated, the public utterances of the Zionist leaders at the time suggest that this was a question which they were not anxious to press. Tschlenow, it is true, in an article in *The Zionist Review*,[14] spoke of the Declaration as foreshadowing 'a Jewish Palestine,' but a 'Manifesto to the Jewish People,' published at the end of 1917 and signed by Sokolow, Tschlenow and Weizmann, confined itself to rhetorical allusions to the realisation of 'the aspirations of 1897' and of 'our ideal of liberty in Palestine.'[15] At the thanksgiving meeting at the London Opera House on 2 December 1917[16] only one—Dr. Gaster—of the seven Jewish speakers said anything about a Jewish State or Commonwealth. All the others, including Weizmann and Sokolow, were content to acclaim the Declaration without attempting to interpret it. But, though they did not publicly associate themselves with Gaster's demand for 'an autonomous Jewish Commonwealth in the fullest sense of the word,' this does not mean that they were not at heart in agreement with him. How the Declaration was, in fact, understood by Weizmann comes out clearly enough in the record of his interview with Balfour some twelve months later:[17]

> '. . . The Englishness of England,' he said, 'is determined by the fact that the preponderant influence in this country . . . is English. This state of affairs does not preclude the development of non-Jewish [*sic*] [? non-English] individuals. Any law-abiding citizen of Great Britain, whether he is of English extraction or not, can . . . take part in the life of the country without any hindrance. In a Jewish Commonwealth there would be many non-Jewish citizens . . . but the preponderant influence would be Jewish. . . .'

There can be no doubt as to the underlying assumption. Jews

13 See above, p. 521, and Appendix, p. 664.
14 December 1917, p. 123.
15 Text in Sokolow, II, 124ff.; *J.C.*, 21 December 1917.
16 As to this meeting, see below, p. 565.
17 Z.A. As to this interview, see further below, p. 637.

would wish, and would be encouraged, to settle in Palestine in numbers large enough to ensure their predominance. If, when this point had been reached, Palestine was given self-government, the result would be a Jewish Commonwealth according full equality of rights to what would by that time have become an Arab minority.

On the British side, it was not until the drafting of the Mandate for Palestine was taken in hand after the War that it became necessary to look closely at the nature and extent of the British commitment to the Jews. British interpretations at the time ranged from Lord Robert Cecil's 'Judaea for the Jews,' speech at the London Opera House meeting a month after the Declaration[18] to his reply, a few weeks later, to an enquiry from the State Department as reported to Washington by the American Ambassador: 'The British Government pledges itself to put the Jews in Palestine on the same footing as other nationalities. No discrimination shall be made against them. This is as far as the British Government has gone.'[19] At the end of the War the idea that the Declaration pointed to the eventual emergence of a Jewish State was by no means extinct. On the contrary, as late as December 1919 Eric Forbes-Adam, the Foreign Office official then specialising in the Palestine question, expressed the view that this was what was intended: 'The British Government,' he wrote, 'by their acceptance of Zionism have to a much greater degree [than the French] accepted the natural implications which Zionists give to the declaration of a national home, i.e., an attempt to make Palestine a State . . . and . . . to turn the State into a Jewish State.'[20] Forbes-Adam's memorandum was minuted, without any expression of dissent on this point, by Vansittart and Curzon.

As to what Balfour personally had in mind, there is a sharp contrast between the views of two authorities, both of whom can be said to have assisted at the birth of the Declaration. Sir Harold Nicolson writes[21] that Balfour 'did not foresee that Zionism would entail the creation of an independent sovereign State, throbbing with the young pulse of fervent nationalism. He believed that it

18 See below, p. 565.
19 See below, p. 599.
20 B.F.P., First Series, Vol. IV, No. 409, p. 608 (30 December 1919).
21 The Spectator, 16 May 1952.

would lead to the establishment . . . of a gentle sanctuary, in which the despised Jews of Eastern Europe would find peace and religion.' On the other hand, Lord Harlech (then Mr. Ormsby-Gore), representing the British Government at a meeting of the League of Nations Permanent Mandates Commission in 1937, told the Commission that the partition scheme at that time favoured by his Government 'transformed the Balfour Declaration from a declaration regarding the beginning of a policy into a policy of which they could see the end, namely the establishment of an independent sovereign Jewish State. That, certainly, was the conception in Lord Balfour's mind.'[22] This accords with a record in Colonel Meinertzhagen's diary[23] of a conversation with Balfour early in 1918. Balfour is quoted as saying: 'My personal hope is that the Jews will make good in Palestine and eventually found a Jewish State.' This is not inconsistent with Lord Hankey's impression[24] that Balfour was not prepared to predict precisely where the Declaration would lead. Lord Hankey's recollection of a good many conversations with Balfour is that, when asked privately what he understood by a Jewish national home in Palestine, his answer would be, in effect, that he could give no exact definition—it might turn out to be anything from a religious and cultural centre, a kind of Jewish Vatican, to a Jewish State; time alone would show.

Whatever may have been Balfour's personal hopes and expectations, once the terms of the Mandate began to be seriously considered in 1919 the British Government moved progressively further away from any commitment to the idea of a Jewish State or Commonwealth in Palestine. An influential group of members of the Zionist General Council insisted that the Government should be urged to insert in the draft Mandate some reference to the eventual establishment of a Jewish Commonwealth. Weizmann was warned that the Zionists must desist from pressing this point if they wanted a British Mandate.[25] It was not, however,

[22] Minutes of 32nd Session of the P.M.C., p. 180.
[23] Meinertzhagen, op. cit., pp. 8-9 (7 February 1918).
[24] Mentioned to the author in conversation and quoted with Lord Hankey's permission.
[25] Reports submitted to 12th Zionist Congress (1921): Political Report, p. 30.

until the summer of 1922 that, under the pressure of the situation which had developed since 1917, the British Government publicly rejected the view that the Balfour Declaration entitled the Jews to look forward to the emergence of a Jewish State. The British promise, it was pointed out, had been to facilitate the establishment of a Jewish national home *in Palestine*; 'the terms of the Declaration . . . do not contemplate that Palestine as a whole should be converted into a Jewish national home.' No such purpose, it was declared, could be read into the Declaration, nor was there anything in it to warrant the suggestion that Palestine was destined to become 'as Jewish as England is English.'[26] More than that, 'His Majesty's Government regard any such expectation as impracticable and have no such aim in view.'[27]

This was the central feature of the Statement of British Policy in Palestine contained in the White Paper of June 1922. A year later, the Statement was rounded off by a still more explicit repudiation of the idea of a Jewish State. Speaking in the House of Lords on 27 June 1923, the Colonial Secretary, the Duke of Devonshire, used language designed to remove any lingering doubt:

> 'Again and again it has been stated that the intention from the beginning has been to make a National Home for the Jews, but every provision has been made to prevent it from becoming in any sense a Jewish State or a State under Jewish domination.'[28]

[26] An allusion to a phrase used by Weizmann in his statement to the Council of Ten at the Peace Conference, February 1919: see below, pp. 616, 625.
[27] Statement of Policy published in Cmd. 1700 (1922).
[28] H.L., 27 June 1923: O.R., Col. 676.

Part IV

Epilogue

THE DECLARATION, NOVEMBER 1917 – TO SAN REMO, APRIL 1920

CHAPTER 38

THE RESPONSE TO THE DECLARATION, I

WITHIN TWO OR three days of its reaching Lord Rothschild the Declaration was made known by Weizmann to his colleagues on the Council of the English Zionist Federation, who, on November 5th, passed a resolution congratulating their President 'on having, in conjunction with Mr. Sokolow, brought about this most momentous achievement towards the realisation of the national aspirations of the Jewish people.'[1]

It was not, however, until November 9th that the Declaration was published in the press. In his reply to the War Cabinet's request for his views early in October, Herbert Samuel, while strongly supporting the proposed declaration, had assumed that it would not be made public 'until a favourable military situation had been brought about in Palestine.' The timing of the press release seems clearly to have been related to the success, at the third attempt, of the British attack on the Turkish stronghold at Gaza. On October 31st, when the War Cabinet approved the Declaration, these operations were known to be imminent, but they were not finally completed until the morning of November 7th. On that day Scott, who had evidently only just learnt of the Declaration, wrote to Weizmann congratulating him on 'a success for which the Movement owes almost everything to you . . . We are at liberty, I gather, to publish the important news in to-morrow's paper.'[2] 'To-morrow' would have been Thursday, November 8th, the day after the fall of Gaza, but in the end— almost certainly in order that *The Jewish Chronicle,* which

---

[1] *Ch.W.P.* The Declaration was formally communicated to the English Zionist Federation by Rothschild on 18 November 1917 : Sokolow, II, 99.
[2] Ibid.

appeared weekly on Fridays, should not be anticipated by the dailies—publication was delayed until the 9th.[3]

In one respect, as it turned out, the timing was not altogether fortunate. November 8th was the day on which the Bolsheviks made good their coup d'état in Petrograd, and the next day the Balfour Declaration had to compete for publicity, not only with the British advance in Palestine and the important Inter-Allied Conference which had just opened at Rapallo, but with the ominous messages coming in from Russia. The English dailies varied widely in their estimates of its news-value. The *Manchester Guardian* not only treated it as first-class news but gave it a full-dress leading article. In *The Times* the text of Balfour's letter appeared on the leader page side by side with a report of Lenin's seizure of power, but without editorial comment. In the other London dailies the Declaration had a less prominent place; for the average man in the street, if he was not a Jew, it would have been no more than one item of news among others, to be glanced at and soon forgotten as the tide of events swept on. It is an instructive fact that no reference to the Declaration is to be found in *The Annual Register*.[4] According to Sir Ronald Storrs, even on Englishmen specially interested in Middle Eastern affairs the

[3] Greenberg, the Editor of *The Jewish Chronicle*, heard about the Declaration from Weizmann on November 2nd. This was a Friday, and the next issue of the paper would not appear until the following Friday, November 9th. Greenberg at once wrote to Weizmann (November 2nd: *Ch.W.P.*) suggesting that publication 'should not be till Friday next.' Greenberg's daughter, Mrs. Sholto, has informed the author that publication 'was held up from Tuesday that week [i.e., November 6th] until Friday so that the J.C. could be first with the news,' and that 'both Weizmann and Sokolow were put out over the delay' (to the author, 20 September 1951). In an article in *The Jewish Annual* (London), 1951-52, the Rev. S. Levy writes (p. 78) that 'on November 6th [Tuesday] Greenberg told him that he had that day 'succeeded in ensuring that the date of release for publication of the Declaration should be the following Friday, November 9th.' Exactly what happened is not quite clear, but it seems tolerably certain that the press release would have been a little earlier than it was but for Greenberg's successful plea for *The Jewish Chronicle*.

[4] It is curious that neither is the Declaration mentioned in 'Principal Events, 1914-1918,' published in 1922 by the Historical Section of the Committee of Imperial Defence, though under 'Palestine' there is an entry (p. 350) reading: 'British Government in message to King of Hedjaz declare intentions with regard to the future of [Palestine], Jan. 4th 1918.'

Declaration made little or no impression. 'With ninety-five per cent. of my friends in Egypt and Palestine (as in England) the Balfour Declaration,' he writes, '. . . passed without notice.'[5]

Nevertheless, though several of the most widely read newspapers expressed no opinion on the merits of the Declaration, its reception in the English press generally was friendly and in many cases warmly sympathetic.[6] The *Manchester Guardian* (November 9th) saw in it 'at once the fulfilment of an aspiration and the signpost of a destiny.' 'Epoch-making' was the *Daily Chronicle's* description (November 9th). The *Daily News* (November 10th) believed that the Declaration 'may prove to be an event of the first importance in the history of the world.' The *Observer* wrote: 'There could not have been at this juncture a stroke of statesmanship more just or more wise.' Among the leading weeklies, both *The Nation* and *The Spectator* welcomed the Declaration, and so did *The New Statesman*, which, recalling the article it had published on the subject in the early days of the War,[7] remarked that the reasons then given for a pro-Zionist policy had lost none of their force.

From the friendly—in many cases enthusiastically friendly— comments of the press, and the messages of warm approval elicited by the English Zionist Federation from a considerable number of well-known public men,[8] it might be inferred that the Balfour Declaration was launched on a strong tide of pro-Jewish sentiment. This was not the case. It was published at a time when British public opinion was not notably well-disposed towards the Jews. Writing to Tschlenow some two months before the Declaration, Sokolow warned him of a marked falling off in 'le philo-sémitisme d'autrefois.'[9] This was ascribed by Sokolow to the unpleasant controversy, then in full swing, concerning the military obligations of unnaturalised Jewish immigrants. But there were other reasons. There was the vague impression that the Russian Jews were the mainspring of Bolshevism.

[5] *Orientations* (London, Nicholson and Watson, 1937), p. 398.
[6] Press references are assembled in Sokolow II, 88ff, and in *The Zionist Review*, December 1917, pp. 144ff. They have not been independently verified.
[7] 21 November 1914: see above, p. 137.
[8] *Zionist Review*, Dec. 1917, pp. 130ff., 155ff., Sokolow, II, 113ff.
[9] 22 Aug. 1917: Z.A.

There was the backwash of the xenophobia reflecting the anxiety neurosis which developed as the War dragged endlessly on. Even when the war situation was at its worst there was never any danger of anti-semitism becoming an obsession with the British public, but an undercurrent of ill-feeling was perceptible and was exploited by certain newspapers to a point at which the Jews began to feel themselves on the defensive. On the very day on which the Balfour Declaration was communicated to Lord Roth-schild, *The Jewish Chronicle* wrote (November 2nd): 'None too soon the Board of Deputies is giving attention to the antisemitic campaign which a section of the press in this country, shamelessly indifferent to the national interests, is sedulously conducting.' On the day the Declaration was published, a leading London Rabbi, addressing a Christian audience, was reported in *The Jewish Chronicle* (November 9th) to have protested against 'reactionary newspapers which made daily aspersions upon the members of the Jewish faith of a kind that would have been impossible in normal times.' A few months later, the Jewish Board of Deputies found it necessary to set up a special committee 'for dealing with the constant press attacks on the Jews.'[10]

Nevertheless, it is impossible to read what was said and written about the Declaration at the time without being convinced that the welcome accorded to it in many influential quarters was sincere. Whatever the man in the street may have thought of it, if he thought about it at all, there were clearly many educated Englishmen who, responding instinctively to the idea of the restoration of the Jews to Palestine, felt genuine pride and satisfaction at the prospect of the future Jewish State being founded with the encouragement and under the aegis of Great Britain. That the Declaration paved the way for a Jewish State seems, to judge from the press, to have been taken for granted. The headlines in the London newspapers—'A State for the Jews' (*Daily Express*)—'Palestine for the Jews' (*The Times, Morning Post, Daily News*)—speak for themselves. *The Spectator* wrote of 'the proposal for the establishment of a Jewish State in Palestine.' The *Manchester Guardian* saw the Declaration as leading to 'the ultimate establishment of a Jewish State.' *The Observer* wrote: 'It is no idle dream that by the close of another generation the new

[10] *J.C.*, 26 April 1918.

Zion may become a State.' Little notice was taken of the difficulties which might attend the establishment of a Jewish State in
a country in which, in 1917, Jews were only a small minority of
the population. The emphasis was on such themes as the enrich-
ment of the family of nations 'by the return of one of its oldest
and most gifted members to a normal place within the circle,'[11]
or 'the simple and humane instinct of reparation'[12] which prompted the British assurance to the Jews, or the part which could
be played by a Jewish State in Palestine as a 'rallying-point for
Jews all over the world'[13] and 'a unique link between East and
West.'[14] The strategic importance of Palestine and the British
stake in its future were by no means overlooked, but the reader
was not usually reminded that serious responsibilities might be
involved in administering the country in the spirit of the Balfour
Declaration, nor invited, on the other hand, to accept the view
that a pro-Zionist policy would, nevertheless, be in harmony with
important British interests. That these matters should have been
touched upon lightly or not at all is not surprising, but it is likewise not surprising that, when difficulties arose, the British public
was ill-prepared for them and inclined to murmur at what it felt
to be an unnecessary burden.[15]

As for the Jews, the Zionists and their sympathisers, now representing a very substantial section of the Anglo-Jewish community,
acclaimed the Declaration with the jubilant enthusiasm that was
to be expected. By other sections of Anglo-Jewry it was received
with a certain reserve, and by some with dismay. Leading British
Jews who had fought actively against any such pronouncement
did not conceal their consternation. On the other hand, among
those who had simply stood aloof from the Zionist Movement
there were some who, even though faintly embarrassed by the
Declaration, were prepared to make the best of it and, if some

[11] The *Daily Chronicle.*
[12] The *Nation.*
[13] *The Spectator.*
[14] The *Observer.*
[15] Writing in 1937, Sidebotham speaks of 'the persistent argument against
the British Mandate in Palestine that it was a sentimental fad or a luxury,
to indulge which was to be less than fair to the welfare of our own
people,' and recalls his efforts in *Palestine* to emphasise 'the argument to
British interests': *Great Britain and Palestine*, p. 52.

common ground could be found, to co-operate with the Zionists in giving effect to what had now been announced as the settled policy of the British Government.[16]

The first representative Jewish body to make itself heard was the Board of Deputies of British Jews, which, on 18 November 1917, passed a resolution thanking the Government for their 'sympathetic interest in the Jews as manifested by' the Declaration, but rather pointedly avoiding any explicit endorsement of its contents.[17] An identical resolution was adopted soon afterwards by the Council of the Anglo-Jewish Association. The President, Claude Montefiore, though he did not oppose the motion, said plainly that he viewed the Declaration 'with grave and serious misgivings.'[18]

Their rather gingerly approach to the Declaration suggests that both bodies had to have regard to a fairly strong undercurrent of doubt, if not of positive disapproval. Their restraint did not, however, reflect the mood of what were usually known as 'the Jewish masses.' The Chief Rabbi may have been putting it rather too high when he told the War Cabinet that the Declaration would be received with rejoicing by 'the overwhelming majority of Anglo-Jewry,' but there were certainly large numbers of Jews from whom it evoked a strong emotional response and many others who, if not so deeply moved, found that it had somehow stirred their imagination. Among these were a fair number of anglicised middle-class Jews, but it was an audience drawn

[16] The prime mover was Sir Lionel Abrahams, K.C.B. After a meeting, on 17 December 1917, with some leading Zionists, including Weizmann and Sokolow, Abrahams and his friends decided to promote an Anglo-Jewish conference for the purpose of reconciling differences of opinion on the Palestine question. The same group also had some meetings with Lionel de Rothschild and certain of his anti-Zionist friends in the hope of getting agreement on a generally acceptable formula. It may have been partly because of Abrahams' premature death that nothing came, at the time, of either of these moves. The above is based on records kindly placed at the author's disposal by the late Albert Hyamson, who was active in seconding Abrahams' efforts.

[17] 'This Board desires to convey its heartfelt thanks to His Majesty's Government for its sympathetic interest in the Jews, as manifested by the letter addressed to Lord Rothschild by the Right Hon. Arthur J. Balfour dated 2nd November 1917, which has been published in the press': *J.C.*, 23 November 1917.

[18] *J.C.*, 7 December 1917.

mainly from the East End of London which, on December 2nd, packed the London Opera House at a thanksgiving meeting organised by the English Zionist Federation and presided over by Lord Rothschild.[19] For such an audience it was a revelation to see Herbert Samuel—a man from a different world—on a Zionist platform and to hear him speak, in Hebrew, the consecrated words, 'Next year in Jerusalem.' The Government was represented by the Assistant Foreign Secretary, Lord Robert Cecil, who, echoing some of the ideas of Mark Sykes but going, possibly, a little beyond his brief, summed up the Government's intentions in a loudly applauded sentence:

'Our wish is that Arabian countries shall be for the Arabs, Armenia for the Armenians, and Judaea for the Jews.'

Besides Lord Rothschild and Herbert Samuel, the Jewish speakers included Weizmann and Sokolow, James de Rothschild, Israel Zangwill and the ecclesiastical heads of both sections of the Jewish community the Chief Rabbi, Dr. Hertz and the Haham, Dr. Gaster.

It was an impressive but not a representative platform. Unless Rothschild who had recently become a Vice-President of the Jewish Board of Deputies, can be counted as an exception, none of the recognised lay leaders of Anglo-Jewry took part in the proceedings.[20] Some of them, including three of the four whose views had been requested by the War Cabinet,[21] had already replied to the Declaration by organising the League of British Jews—a body formed, as it was put by one of its founders, Sir Philip Magnus, to be a standing protest against 'the tendency . . . to fix upon the Jews the acceptance of a nationality other than, and in addition to, that of the country of our birth or where we have lived and worked.'[22] The League tried hard, but in vain, to

19 Fully reported in *J.C.*, 7 December 1917; see also Sokolow, II, 100ff.
20 Sir Stuart Samuel, however, the President of the Board of Deputies, had already expressed approval of the Declaration and on December 9th presided at a thanksgiving meeting in Manchester: *J.C.*, 16 November and 14 December 1917.
21 Claude Montefiore, Leonard Cohen and Sir P. Magnus. The exception was Sir S. Samuel.
22 'League of British Jews: Report of First General Meeting, March 14th, 1918,' p. 6. The foundation of the League was reported in *J.C.*, 14 November 1917.

impress its views on the influential circles to which the standing of its members gave it access. Some months after the Declaration, its President, Lionel de Rothschild, accompanied by Sir Charles Henry, M.P.,[23] one of Lloyd George's Jewish personal friends, called on Lord Beaverbrook, then Minister of Information, to urge him to do nothing to encourage the idea of a Jewish national home. Henry, together with Lord Swaythling, had seen Lloyd George and told Beaverbrook that the Prime Minister was on his side. 'I asked the Prime Minister,' Lord Beaverbrook writes, 'for a clear ruling. He would not answer "yes" or "no."' Having become aware of what was going on, Balfour, on 22 August 1918, wrote to Lloyd George pointing out with some asperity that the Zionist and anti-Zionist arguments had been fully considered by the War Cabinet before authorising his Declaration. Lloyd George is quoted by Lord Beaverbrook as having replied (27 August 1918) '. . . I gather from your letter that [Henry] must have given a false impression of my conversation with him and Lord Swaythling . . . I have always been a strong supporter of your policy on the question of Zionism, and nothing that was said by Henry, Swaythling or Philip Magnus in the least affected my opinions.'[24]

The militant anti-Zionists remained irreconcilable, but by the time the Peace Conference opened at the beginning of 1919 the Anglo-Jewish community as a whole had begun to adjust itself to the new situation. In April 1919 Lucien Wolf brought to the notice of the Peace Conference a statement on Palestine agreed to both by the Board of Deputies of British Jews and the Anglo-Jewish Association. Cautious though they had been at the beginning, both the representative Anglo-Jewish bodies now identified themselves with the Declaration, subject only to one proviso— that it must not 'be held to imply that Jews constitute a separate political nationality all over the world, or that the Jewish citizens of countries outside Palestine owe political allegiance to the Government of that country.'[25] A petition submitted a few weeks

---

[23] Treasurer of the League of British Jews.

[24] Lord Beaverbrook, *Men and Power* (London, Hutchinson, 1956), pp. 291-294. The Lord Swaythling referred to is the second Lord Swaythling, Edwin Montagu's elder brother.

[25] *The Peace Conference, Paris, 1919* (London Joint Foreign Committee, 1920), pp. 112-113.

later by the English Zionist Federation, and stated to have been signed by more than 77,000 Jews in the United Kingdom,[26] appealed to the Peace Conference to give effect to the Balfour Declaration and 'to make such provision regarding Palestine as shall secure to the Jewish people the fullest rights and the opportunity to re-constitute Palestine as its national home.'[27]

It is not to be inferred that the Zionists had now captured the Anglo-Jewish community. There were still some implacable anti-Zionists. There were many other British Jews who, though they might be prepared to interest themselves in the rebuilding of Jewish life in Palestine, shrank from what seemed to them to be the embarrassing and even dangerous implications of the Zionist philosophy and from what they perceived to be the real objective of the Zionist Movement—the establishment of a Jewish State. The old dividing-lines had by no means been obliterated, but now that the British Government was fully committed to a pro-Zionist policy, the conflict was no longer as bitter nor the differences as clear-cut as they had been while the Balfour Declaration was in the making or at the moment of its first impact on Anglo-Jewry.

As material for propaganda the Declaration was aimed more particularly at the Russian and American Jews, but this did not mean that the Government was not interested in the response of its own Jewish citizens. It had been disturbed and embarrassed by their divided views and had been anxious that their differences should not flare up into open conflict. But, though the Declaration was nominally addressed, through Rothschild, to the English Zionist Federation,[28] England was only the launching-platform. Its main short term purpose was to create a favourable current of opinion in other parts of the Jewish world. Sir Ronald Graham's memorandum of 24 October 1917 shows how strongly it was felt at the Foreign Office that there was no time to be lost, and how

26 Out of a Jewish population of the order of 300,000.
27 Loc. cit., pp. 114-115.
28 In his letter of 2 November 1917 Balfour asked him to communicate the Declaration to 'the Zionist Federation,' obviously echoing Rothschild's words in his letter to Balfour of July 18th: 'If His Majesty's Government will send me a message . . . I will hand it on to the Zionist Federation,' meaning, it seems clear, the English Zionist Federation.

impatiently the War Cabinet's *nihil obstat* was awaited. As soon as it was forthcoming, preparations at once began to be made for giving publicity to the Declaration and driving home its significance, not only in Russia and the United States, but also, as far as possible, in the enemy-occupied parts of Eastern Europe and even in the enemy countries themselves.

This propaganda was thought important enough to warrant the strengthening of the Department of Information—at that time a Branch of the Foreign Office but soon to be raised to the status of a separate Ministry—by the formation, in November 1917, of a Jewish Section. This was staffed mainly by Zionists and directed by Albert Hyamson, who had all through the War been closely associated with Weizmann and his inner circle. 'Our work,' Hyamson writes,[29] 'was principally to popularise the Balfour Declaration and to advertise and explain the general attitude of Britain and of the British Government towards matters of interest to Jewry among Jews of all countries except Britain. The Zionist Organisation had a similar programme directed towards the non-Jewish world. We worked in close co-operation.' Literature in all the principal languages spoken by Jews was prepared by the Jewish Section for distribution, through local Zionist Societies or through other channels at the disposal of the Ministry of Information, to Jewish communities in all parts of the world. Special measures were taken to see that it reached the Jews of Central and Eastern Europe. Leaflets giving the news of the Declaration were widely circulated in Poland and the neighbouring territories and were dropped from the air over Jewish centres in Austria and Germany.[30] When Lord Beaverbrook became

---

[29] To the author, 4 December 1951. See also Israel Cohen's article in *The New Palestine* (New York), 28 October 1927, p. 319.

[30] Report of the Palestine Royal Commission. (Cmd. 5479; 1937), p. 23; Lloyd George, *Treaties*, II, 1130-1140. The literature prepared by the Jewish Section appears to have included translations into various languages of a Zionist brochure entitled 'Great Britain, Palestine and the Jews,' and reprints of the Balfour Declaration issue of *The Zionist Review*. The author has not been able to find any specimens of the leaflets dropped from the air. He understands that there are none in the possession of the Imperial War Museum, of the Psywar Society, or of the Zionist Archives. In this connection, he desires to express his thanks to Mr. Rigby and Miss Coombes (I.W.M.), Mr. P. H. Robbs (Psywar Society), and Mr. R. S. Auckland.

Minister of Information in February 1918, he recognised the propaganda value of the Declaration and, as he recalls in his reminiscences, did not fail to make the most of it.[31]

In the enemy and enemy-occupied parts of Eastern Europe, and especially in Poland, the Jews were strongly moved by the Declaration. An eye-witness recalls that in Cracow 'the Jews received the Balfour Declaration with indescribable joy. It would be no exaggeration to say that they ran amok with joy.'[32] A Jewish writer describes as follows the response to the Declaration in his native Galicia: 'The Balfour Declaration not only gave courage to the Jews at a time when they were in need of such encouragement . . . It gained a new ally for England. The hearts of the Jewish people began to beat for England, and we, Zionists, were happier with the victories of the Allies than the victories of the Germans.'[33] In Lemberg the local Jewish organ came out openly in praise of England: 'The leading European Great Power has extended a hand to the Jewish people in order to lift it up once more into the ranks of the independent self-governing races.'[34]

The impact of the Declaration was felt even in Germany itself. The Zionist leaders in Berlin had tried to persuade their Government that Germany would serve her own interests by taking the Zionist Movement under her protection. But when Great Britain gave the Zionists the encouragement which Germany had withheld, the German Zionists openly acclaimed the British Declaration and made no attempt to minimise its significance. How greatly it impressed them is shown by the surprisingly uninhibited comments of their principal organ, the *Jüdische Rundschau*:[35] 'This declaration of the English Government is an event of extraordinary significance. It is the first occasion on which a Great Power has officially declared itself in relation to Zionism . . . The

---

[31] Op cit., p. 291.

[32] Dr. I. Schwarzbart to the author, 13 February 1953.

[33] J. Tenenbaum, *Galitzie, Mein Alte Heim* (Buenos Aires, 1952), pp. 213-215. The author is indebted to Dr. Schwarzbart for the quotation and the translation from the original Yiddish.

[34] *Lemberger Tageblatt*, 16 November 1917 (in English translation), *Zionist Review*, January 1918, p. 181.

[35] 16 November 1917, qtd. (in Engl. translation) *Zionist Review*, December 1917, pp. 166-167.

recognition of [the Zionist] claim by the British Government is an event of world historic importance.'

Anything calculated to weaken, however slightly, the war-will even of a small section of the enemy peoples would be so much gained. But this could yield no immediate dividend. On the propagandist plane the really urgent question was whether the Declaration could be turned to account in Russia. Could the Russian Jews be made to feel that they must use whatever influence they might have to keep Russia in the War, or, if it was too late for this, that they must make it their business to obstruct German exploitation of Russian resources, and especially of the produce of the Ukraine?

In retrospect such ideas may well sound naïve, but it is evident that the illusions underlying them were seriously entertained. According to Sir Ronald Graham's memorandum of 24 October 1917,[36] the Jews were playing an important part in the situation in Russia. Almost every Russian Jew, he said, was a Zionist, and a pro-Zionist declaration by the British Government would enlist a powerful element in Russian life on the side of the Entente. Writing some three months after the Declaration, a War Office expert expressed the view that it was 'even possible that, had the Declaration come sooner, the course of the Revolution might have been affected,' and went on: 'Even now, in the question of economic control the support of the Jews of South Russia is of fundamental importance . . . The connection between Russian and German Jews makes the Jew the natural channel for the exploitation of Russian resources by the Central Powers. This channel has now been to some extent interrupted . . .'

There was, in fact, a twofold miscalculation. The Jews who were playing a significant part in the situation in Russia were those associated with the extreme left-wing elements now coming into the ascendant. Jews of this type, so far from being likely to be impressed by a pro-Zionist declaration, were violently hostile to Zionism. And if the Zionists were in no position to deflect the forces which were sweeping Russia out of the War, neither was it within the power of the Jewish grain and cattle dealers in the Ukraine, even if all of them had been Zionists, to offer any serious

[36] Above, p. 544.

obstruction to the Germans in their search for supplies. How confused was the British picture of the situation in Russia can be inferred from a passage in Lloyd George's book on the Peace Treaties. Speaking of the practical value of the Balfour Declaration, 'I could point out,' he writes, 'substantial . . . advantages derived from this propaganda among the Jews. In Russia the Bolsheviks baffled all the efforts of the Germans to benefit by the harvests of the Ukraine and the Don.'[37] The Bolsheviks had their own motives for obstructing the Germans, but the Jews among them were the last people likely to be moved by the Balfour Declaration. But at the time of the Declaration the realities of the situation had not been fully grasped. False hopes still lingered, and, clutching at a straw, the Foreign Office thought it possible that an appeal to Zionist sentiment among the Jews might somehow help to avert the impending disaster.

At a meeting at the Foreign Office immediately after the Declaration it was decided that a Zionist mission should leave for Russia forthwith. A few days later the Bolshevik *coup d'état* put an end to these plans, and no more was heard of them. Weizmann did his best to get in touch with the Russian Zionist leaders, but communications were difficult, and the Declaration did not become widely known among the Russian Jews until three weeks after its publication. The response was immediate and impressive. An address presented to the British Ambassador in Petrograd, in the name of the Russian Zionist leaders, on 20 November 1917 asked him, in emotional language, to assure his Government that the Jews would never forget what they owed to Great Britain for her sympathy with their national aspirations.[38] In a dispatch forwarded to London by the Ambassador on December 13th the British Consul-General in Moscow reported that a Zionist deputation had waited upon him a few days earlier 'to express their thanks to the British Government for its declaration on the subject of Palestine' and to invite him to be present and speak at a pro-British demonstration.[39] *The Times* of December 12th published a message from its Odessa correspondent describing a Jewish thanksgiving meeting attended by a vast

---

[37] *Treaties*, II, 1140.
[38] *J.C.*, 28 December 1917.
[39] Copy (presumably furnished by F.O. to London Zionist Bureau) in Z.A.

crowd, which later marched in procession first to the British and then to the United States Consulate. Similar public demonstrations were reported to have taken place in Petrograd, Moscow, Kieff and Minsk.[40] The Petrograd correspondent of *The Jewish Chronicle* summed up his impressions as follows:

> 'The Jewish resolutions of appreciation of the Balfour Declaration on Zionism, the demonstrations of joy and praise of England, the articles in the Jewish press with the heading "Long Live England," and, finally the greetings of the young Zionist Workmen's Organisation to the British democracy . . . were unmistakable signs of the warm sympathy of the Jews towards England.'[41]

There were some discordant voices among the Jews, and that not only among the left-wing extremists but also among the assimilationists at the opposite end of the social scale. Their views were reflected in a report, dated 4 December 1917, in which the situation as seen through anti-Zionist eyes was described to the Foreign Affairs Committee of the Anglo-Jewish Association by its Petrograd correspondent, Rubin Blank:[42] 'Your work, like ours, is much embarrassed by the Zionist agitation, which has gained a fresh impetus since the British Government's declaration of sympathy. This declaration has made a great noise here, its political significance having been enormously exaggerated.' But even Blank had to admit that the Zionist Movement had received a powerful impetus from the Declaration—how powerful is shown by the energetic measures taken by the Bolsheviks to check it. *The Jewish Chronicle* reported (1 March 1918) that the newly appointed Commissar for Jewish affairs, S. M. Dimantschew, had declared that his task would be to combat Zionism, especially among the Jewish soldiers. In the same issue *The Jewish Chronicle* also reported that the Petrograd Zionist organ had already been suppressed and its editors sent to prison. At the elections held early in 1918 for a Russo-Jewish Congress the Zionists and their associates emerged as much the largest single group. The Russian

[40] Russian Central Zionist Committee to Weizmann, 18 December 1917: *Ch.W.P.*

[41] *J.C.*, 25 January 1918.

[42] For a copy of this document the author is indebted to the late Dr. D. Mowskowitch. (Orig. in French.)

authorities made it clear that, because of its unmistakably anti-Bolshevik complexion, the Congress would not be allowed to meet.[43]

But the spectacular growth of the Zionist Movement amongst the Russian Jews, the pro-British sentiments so fervently expressed by the Russian Zionists, their long-standing feud with the Bolsheviks—all this was powerless to exert the slightest influence on the balance of forces in Russia. In terms of a change in the political climate, the propaganda directed to the Russian Zionists did not yield, and was incapable of yielding, any practical result. But one hope remained. There was still, it was believed, at least an off-chance that the Russian Jews might be moved by the Balfour Declaration to use the economic power with which they were optimistically credited to obstruct the enemy's designs on Russian resources, and especially on the food supplies so urgently needed by the Germans and still more urgently by their starving Austrian allies. Strongly worded messages in this sense were sent to the Russian Zionist leaders both from London and from New York. On 21 December 1917 Weizmann telegraphed to Brandeis:

'Information received that Germans contemplate during armistice to establish purchasing committees South Russia . . . and to obtain produce and petrol which would render our blockade ineffective . . . We think that Jews of South Russia who control trade could effectively counteract German and Bolshevik manœuvres in alliance with Ukraine. We have telegraphed to our friends Petrograd, Rostoff, Kieff, Odessa, and beg you to do the same, appealing to them on behalf of Allied and Palestinian cause . . . Jews have now splendid opportunity to show their gratitude England and America.'[44]

Three weeks later the British Ambassador in Washington telegraphed to the Foreign Office the text of a similar appeal by Stephen Wise and other well-known American Zionists to Zionist leaders in Petrograd, Odessa and Kieff. After referring to the German proposals at Brest-Litovsk, 'which leave no doubt as to their Imperialistic aims,' the message went on:

[43] *J.C.*, 22 March 1918.
[44] Copy in Z.A.

' We have learnt with grave apprehension that Imperialistic Government is seeking to provision its army through south-west Russian and is seeking to accomplish this purpose through Russian Jews. We refuse to believe the Jews of Russia will allow themselves thus to be used as catspaws by Imperialistic Germany. It would greatly imperil cause of Jews and particularly in Palestine. Please leave no effort untried to prevent this propaganda movement of Imperialistic Germany from succeeding.'[45]

Weizmann and his American colleagues had done their best, but their hopes of effective anti-German action by the Jews were not and could not be realised. They were based, to begin with, on an exaggerated estimate of the economic power of the Jews in South Russia. Though Jewish middlemen played a significant part in South Russian trade, they were not indispensable to the Germans, who preferred other methods of procuring supplies. The Germans did encounter obstruction, but this was mainly because of the passive resistance of the Ukrainian peasants, who disliked the requisitioning and hid their stores for fear of confiscation.[46] No doubt Bolshevik agents were at work in the Ukraine, and among them some Jews. Even so, the Jews generally do not seem to have been regarded by the Germans as particularly hostile; if they had, they would not have been allowed to handle most of the authorised trade in food parcels for Germany,[47] nor would the German Commander in the Ukraine, General Hoffmann, have suggested that the disappointing deliveries of grain might have turned out better if Jewish dealers had been engaged to buy in the open market.[48] There is, in fact, no evidence of any widespread anti-German activity on the part of the Jews, and

[45] Copy encl. in Foreign Office letter, 17 January 1918, to Weizmann: Ch.W.P.

[46] Sources: W. E. D. Allen. *The Ukraine* (C.U.P., 1940); Sir J. Wheeler-Bennett, *Brest-Litovsk* (London, 1938). Both writers discuss the German procurement of supplies in South Russia and the difficulties which it encountered, but neither of them refers to any organised obstruction by the Jews or mentions them as an important factor in the situation. The author's personal enquiries among Jews well acquainted with Russian affairs at the time have failed to elicit any evidence that the Zionist appeals to the South Russian Jewish traders had a perceptible effect.

[47] Allen, op. cit., p. 297.

[48] Wheeler-Bennett, op. cit., p. 317.

it is tolerably certain that such Jews as did try to embarrass the Germans were inspired much less (if at all) by the Balfour Declaration than by sympathy with the new régime in Russia.

Though the British Government's most urgent preoccupation was the crisis in Russia, it was hoped that the Balfour Declaration might also be turned to good account in the United States.

In his work on the Peace Treaties Lloyd George discusses the Government's reasons for believing that 'the support of the Zionists for the cause of the Entente would mean a good deal as a war measure.' After referring to the situation in Russia, he goes on:

> 'It was believed also that such a Declaration would have a potent influence upon world Jewry outside Russia and secure for the Entente the aid of Jewish financial interests. In America their aid would have a special value when the Allies had almost exhausted the gold and marketable securities available for American purchases.'[49]

The whole passage bears a striking resemblance to a summary of the motives for the Declaration in the History of the Peace Conference published fourteen years earlier under the auspices of the Royal Institute of International Affairs. After referring to the situation in Russia in language precisely identical, save for a few trifling verbal variations, with that used by Lloyd George, the Chatham House History continues:

> 'It was believed also that such a declaration would have a potent influence upon world Jewry in the same way, and secure for the Entente the aid of Jewish financial interests. It was believed, further, that it would greatly influence American opinion in favour of the Allies.'[50]

It is quite credible, though on the evidence at present available there is no positive proof of it, that at an earlier stage—as, for example, at the time of Grey's proposal, in the spring of 1916, for a pro-Zionist declaration by Great Britain jointly with her

---

[49] *Treaties*, II, 1122.
[50] *A History of the Peace Conference*, VI, 173. The parallelism suggests a common source, but efforts to identify it have been unsuccessful.

allies—there may have been a vague idea that there were financial as well as political advantages to be gained from an appeal
to the Jewish feeling for Palestine. What is hard to believe is
that at the time of the Balfour Declaration the British Government was angling for the support of American Jewish bankers
and expected the Declaration to warm their hearts. Mark Sykes,
the Government's principal adviser on the Zionist question, was
well aware that everywhere the Jewish financial magnates had,
almost to a man, fought shy of Zionism and shown themselves
nervously suspicious of Zionist propaganda. Unless the Government was much worse served by its sources of information than
there is any reason to suppose it to have been, this elementary
fact must have been perfectly well known to it at the time of the
Declaration. Even if it had been urgently necessary to enlist the
support of American Jewish bankers, it would have been naïve
to suppose that the Declaration would be helpful. But in fact
there was no such necessity. By the time of the Declaration there
was no longer any question of direct approaches by the British
Government to the American money-market. The financing of
Great Britain and other Associated Powers had been taken by
the United States Government into its own hands. Any war loans
now to be raised in the United States would be American loans,
which the Jewish financial houses could be relied upon to support
at least as zealously as other American bankers.

What was it, then, that caused Sir Ronald Graham, in pressing
for the speedy approval of the Declaration, to represent to Balfour
that, besides the results to be hoped for in Russia, propaganda
was also urgently needed in the United States?

In the light of the Russian collapse and the certainty that its
effect would soon be felt in dangerous pressure on the Western
Front, American preparations for active intervention in the War
seemed to anxious and impatient observers in the Allied countries
to be gaining momentum much too slowly. What was in Graham's
mind was probably no more than an impression that the Jews
as a whole were among those sections of the American public
which were lukewarm about the War and needed some special
stimulus to induce them to throw themselves wholeheartedly
into the American war effort. If the Foreign Office was thinking
of any particular category of American Jews, this would almost

certainly have been, not the upper stratum of American Jewish society, but the unassimilated masses, whose general attitude towards the War was reflected in their drift in large numbers into the ranks of the pacifists.

How strong this pacifist movement had become is shown by one of Stephen Wise's letters to Brandeis. The Zionists had been trying since 1915 to wrest the leadership of American Jewry from the conservatively-minded and, on the whole, anti-Zionist American Jewish Committee, which was objected to as a self-appointed oligarchy. Confident that the result would be a striking demonstration of the strength of Zionist sentiment among the Jewish masses, both Brandeis and Wise, together with other prominent Zionists, had been actively associated with a movement for the organisation of a representative and democratically elected American Jewish Congress. Recognising that the agitation for a Congress had become irresistible, the American Jewish Committee had felt obliged to come to terms with it and had agreed, in the end, to be represented on the Organising Committee. But in the autumn of 1917 Wise himself was becoming nervous as to what would happen if such a Congress were convened. Writing to Brandeis on 29 September 1917,[51] he drew attention to the impression which was being made on the Jewish proletariat by the pacifist propaganda of the People's Council for Democracy and Peace. In its appeal to the Jews that propaganda was all the more persuasive because the Council had at its disposal a Jewish leader of the standing and moral stature of Dr. J. L. Magnes.[52] Wise was convinced, he told Brandeis, that until there had been more time to counteract the activities of the Council, an American Jewish Congress could not safely be allowed to meet. This being the prevailing atmosphere, it is not difficult to understand why it was believed in London that, with their hands strengthened by the Balfour Declaration, there was useful work to be done by the Zionists in the United States. Among the Jewish workers and intellectuals there were some who still clung to the Bundist ideas which they had brought with them from Russia. These were, on principle,

[51] *Brandeis papers.*
[52] See N. Bentwich, *Judah L. Magnes* (London, East and West Library, n.d.), pp. 103-104.

opposed to Zionism, but there were many others—almost certainly a majority—who, whether they called themselves Zionists or not, were Zionists at heart. If, then, the Jewish masses were to be made less susceptible to pacifist propaganda, the Balfour Declaration might well help to provide an effective antidote.

There was a hint of this in a message to American Jewry issued by Lord Reading a few months after succeeding Spring-Rice, at the beginning of 1918, as British Ambassador in Washington. Before leaving London Reading had seen Weizmann and Sokolow. Writing to Brandeis on 16 January 1918,[53] Weizmann described the conversation as 'quite satisfactory,' but to Reading personally the Declaration made little appeal. When it was first suggested to him by his press adviser, Arthur Willert, that he should make a statement on Zionism, he showed some embarrassment.

> 'To my surprise,' Willert writes, 'he hung back and, instead of having ready what he wanted to say, asked me to draft something. "You see," he explained, in effect, "I have no great personal sympathy with Zionism. Why should I have? Here I am, Ambassador, Lord Chief Justice, Peer, and I started from nothing. I owe it all to England. I am English. How can I help it if I do not feel strongly about a national home for the Jews?"'[54]

All the same, Reading agreed, in the end, to the publication of a statement in which he identified himself with the Balfour Declaration ('I warmly support the Declaration in both my public and private capacity') and was careful to make a complimentary reference to the American Zionists and their contribution to the War effort:

> 'I have been profoundly impressed by the splendid energy of the American Zionists and by the wholehearted way in which, to no small extent under their leadership, the Jewish people of the United States have thrown themselves into the War.'[55]

[53] *Ch.W.P.*
[54] Sir Arthur Willert, *The Road to Safety*, p. 123.
[55] *The Maccabean* (New York), May 1918.

Propaganda apart, the new turn of events clearly called for close co-operation between the Zionist leaders in London and their American colleagues. Immediately after the Declaration it was decided to send a Zionist liaison officer to the United States, and, after consultation with the Foreign Office, the choice fell on Aaron Aaronsohn, who was personally known to Brandeis and enjoyed his confidence.

Ten days after the Declaration Weizmann wrote to Brandeis: 'In order to discuss the various plans, and also in order to prepare the way for a more intimate co-operation, we have decided, with the consent of H.M. Government, to send over Mr. Aaronsohn to America. I will send you . . . [a] copy of the instructions he is carrying with him.'[56] Aaronsohn's instructions, based on a draft by Sykes,[57] were 'to keep [the British and American Zionist Organisations] in touch with one another, to help the United States Organisation to appreciate the actual significance of the various political and military developments, to act as the channel of communication between the United States Organisation, through the medium of Mr. Brandeis, and the British Organisation, through that of Dr. Weizmann. Subject to the above, to further to the utmost of his power the rousing of Zionist enthusiasm, the stimulating of pro-Entente propaganda and the consolidation and alliance of the Zionist forces with those of Arabs and Armenians.' Aaronsohn was told to make no public speeches and give no interviews to the press and was expressly enjoined to take no action of any kind save through the medium of Brandeis.

In the event, Aaronsohn spent only about two months in the United States, returning to London early in 1918. He had done some useful work, but the results of his mission fell far short of the ambitious programme which had been sketched for him. This is not surprising, but his instructions, inspired by Sykes, are of interest as reflecting some of the ideas current at the time. The 'rousing of Zionist enthusiasm' was to go hand in hand with 'the stimulating of pro-Entente propaganda.' Aaronsohn was to work for a union of forces between Zionists, Arabs and Armenians—the triple alliance which had long been one of Mark Sykes' favourite dreams. The American Zionists were to be made to understand

56 Weizmann to Brandeis, 12 November 1917: *Brandeis papers.*
57 The original of Sykes' draft, in his own hand, is in *Ch.W.P.*

the actual significance of the various political and military developments,' probably meaning, among other things, that they were to be made to realise that British policy in the Middle East was as fully in harmony with American as with British interests. That this was in the minds of those who framed the instructions may be inferred from a letter of 14 January 1918 from Weizmann to Brandeis.

> 'A Jewish Palestine,' Weizmann writes, 'initiated by Great Britain and supported by America, a Palestine which stands in friendly contact with a free Armenia and an independent Arabia, means a death-blow to the combination of Islamo-Prussian-Turanian domination in the East . . . America may begin to realise this danger later than we do in Europe, but it will have to face it all the same. For it must be abundantly clear that there is a complete coincidence of American-British-Judean interests as against Prusso-Turkish interests. . . .'[58]

In interpreting Aaronsohn's instructions, it must be borne in mind that he was accredited to Brandeis personally. The British estimate of Brandeis' standing is illustrated by a passage in a letter from Colonel Arthur Murray to Sir William Wiseman. Writing privately from London to Wiseman in October 1918, Murray, who had served as Military Attaché at the British Embassy in Washington, speaks of the imperative need for close co-operation between London and Washington in preparations for the Peace Conference. There must, he says, 'be here some sort of check on the actions of Lloyd George. This can only be achieved by the constant presence on the spot of someone who can really speak authoritatively as from the President. Who else is there besides House who can act in this capacity? It has been suggested that Brandeis might be such a person and that he and House should take it in turns to be over here . . .'[59]

This suggestion came to nothing, but it would not have been made if Brandeis had not been known to be in close touch with what was going on behind the scenes in Washington. From a British point of view this made it all the more desirable to enlist his active personal interest in the working out of the Balfour

[58] Copy in *Ch.W.P.*
[59] Arthur Murray, *At Close Quarters* (London, John Murray, 1946), p. 59.

Declaration. On the other hand, Brandeis himself seems to have felt that, as a responsible citizen of a country which was not at war with Turkey, he must exercise a certain restraint. His co-operation with the Zionist leaders in England was not as close as had been expected, and he was felt in London to be holding himself somewhat aloof.

Weizmann's disappointment comes out in a telegram to Brandeis dated 28 January 1918:[60] '. . . Our work this critical time rendered extremely difficult through lack of information from you. Your apparently changed attitude quite inexplicable . . .' This appears to refer particularly to the question of American representation on the Zionist Commission then preparing to go to Palestine under Weizmann's leadership. Such representation had been strongly desired, and Brandeis had been relied upon to arrange it. There was, however, no sign of its being forthcoming, and in the end Weizmann was given to understand that it was out of the question, since it was regarded as inconsistent with the neutral position of the United States in the war with Turkey.[61] On this point the State Department was not to be moved, and Brandeis could do nothing but conform loyally to the settled policy of his Government.

In the irritated tone of Weizmann's protest against Brandeis' 'changed attitude' it is possible to discern a first faint warning of the conflict which was later to develop between them and to lead, in the end, to an open breach. Incompatibility of temperament, contrasting origins and backgrounds, and—as it turned out—irreconcilable differences on questions of principle were to drive them gradually apart until it was no longer possible for them to make a pretence of working together. Those American Zionists who took their lead from Brandeis insisted to the end that 'we have always steadily adhered to the national idea . . . we do not desire to build Palestine as a mere refuge for the oppressed,'[62] but they were charged by their opponents with

[60] Z.A.
[61] This was made clear in a telegram from Brandeis dated 1 May 1918: Z.A. In the end, an American Jew, Walter Meyer, was attached to the Commission, but not as a member: Manuel, p. 175.
[62] ' Statement to the Delegates of the Twelfth Zionist Congress on behalf of the former Administration of the Zionist Organisation of America' (New York, 1921), p. 33.

seeking to make a mere colonising agency out of a Movement designed to express the national aspirations of the whole Jewish people. How acute the tension was to become can be seen from an allusion to 'the struggle in America' in one of the reports of the Zionist Executive to the first post-war Zionist Congress (1921): [63] 'The event proved that many of the best elements in American Zionism, and the overwhelming majority of the Jewish masses of America, have adopted the national conception of Zionism . . . The former American leaders obviously were at variance with the majority regarding the essential character of Zionism.'

But it was not until 1921 that the latent differences of outlook came to a head, and even then, though his breach with Weizmann was never healed, Brandeis did not cease to serve the Zionist cause according to his own conception of what was needed. Still less is there any question of his having lost interest after the Balfour Declaration. As has already been suggested, the 'changed attitude,' of which Weizmann complained was not quite as inexplicable as he thought. That it signified no cooling off is shown by an interview with Brandeis described by the British Ambassador, Sir Cecil Spring-Rice, in a report to Balfour dated 4 January 1918: [64]

'Justice Brandeis . . . called on me yesterday . . . He explained the situation among the Jewish community. He regarded the Zionist problem from the point of view, not of the territorial question, but of idealism. He thought that it served as a rallying-point to the Jewish race, especially on its idealistic side . . . For himself and his friends he could say that the hope of the Jewish race for their elevation and their conservation depends on the prosecution of Zionism. His friends knew by experience that under German control the idea could never be realised and that under English control their idea could be realised. It was for this reason that Jews everywhere, he believed, would be deaf to German blandishment. I reminded him of the attitude of the Jews and crypto-Jews in Turkey at the time of the Young Turk Revolution

[63] 'Organisation Report,' pp. 10, 11.
[64] *Spring-Rice*, II, 421.

and of a similar attitude of the Jews now in control of the Russian Revolution. He said that the alliance between England and Imperialistic Russia has caused a breach between the Jewish race and England which was rapidly being healed.'

Spring-Rice himself had from the start been sceptical about the Jewish response to the Balfour Declaration. He reported to the Foreign Office (28 November 1917) that the American Zionists were only a small minority and that, though it was important to maintain friendly relations with them, yet it was necessary not to alienate the opposing faction. A few weeks later he explained his views more fully in a letter to Balfour (21 December 1917):[65]

'How far you can build on re-establishing really good and friendly relations with the large Jewish population in this country by a friendly attitude to the Zionist Movement is not very certain. You would not conciliate all the Irish by making Carson a Viscount, and the situation is rather similar. The great masses of Jews appear to be bitterly opposed to the Zionist leaders, and the rich Jews are divided among themselves.'

Like the United States Ambassador in London,[66] the British Ambassador in Washington was evidently inclined to think that the Zionists were not to be taken very seriously. At his interview with Spring-Rice on 3 January 1918 Brandeis did his best to correct this impression. 'I asked him,' Spring-Rice reported, 'how much influence the Zionists possessed with the Jewish community. He said they were violently opposed by the great capitalists and by the Socialists, for different reasons, but on a poll it appeared that the Zionists were in a large majority or at any rate controlled a majority of votes.'[67]

A message from Washington published in The Times of 10 November 1917 agreed with Brandeis' view and put it still more strongly: 'The Balfour Declaration . . . fills the American Jews with enthusiasm and strengthens their determination to

[65] Spring-Rice, II, 420.
[66] For Walter Page's view see above, p. 358, note 29.
[67] Brandeis was probably referring to the results of the American Jewish Congress elections in June 1917.

prosecute the war to a victorious conclusion. To-day the Zionist Movement represents nearly ninety per cent. of all American Jewry, indeed, all Jews, except Socialists of the Hillquit type and an extremely small minority of wealthy financiers.'

This observer was nearer the mark than Spring-Rice, but his picture was over-simplified. By no means all the American Jews who were embarrassed, rather than elated, by the Balfour Declaration were either Socialists or wealthy financiers. The native-born middle-class element was more noticeable among the American than among the English Zionists, but, as in England, the assimilated Jewish bourgeoisie had tended, on the whole, to stand aloof from the Movement. To many Jews of this type the Declaration seemed, at first sight, to arouse awkward questions of dual allegiance, and it was some time before they found their bearings. Some of them—a small but vocal and influential group—proclaimed themselves out-and-out anti-Zionists, and, like the founders of the League of British Jews, remained to the end irreconcilable.[68] A much larger number hesitated for a time but found themselves in the end impelled to seek an accommodation with the Zionists, if they could achieve this without compromising their principles. A statement of their position can be found in a resolution adopted in April 1918 by the American Jewish Committee. After declaring it to be axiomatic that 'the Jews of the United States have here established a permanent home for themselves and their children . . . and recognise their unqualified allegiance to this country,' the resolution went on to acknowledge that 'there are Jews everywhere, who, moved by traditional sentiment, yearn for a home in the Holy Land for the Jewish people . . . This hope, nurtured for centuries, has our wholehearted sympathy.' Accordingly, 'the [British] announcement was received by this Committee with profound appreciation,' and 'the opportunity will be welcomed by this Committee to aid in the realisation of the British Declaration.'[69]

The pattern was, in fact, much the same as in England, but with one important distinction. In England immigration from

[68] For text of an anti-Zionist petition submitted by this group to President Wilson in March 1919 see M. Jastrow, *Zionism and the Future of Palestine* (New York, 1919), Appendix.
[69] Text in *Jewish Post-War Problems* (New York, American Jewish Committee, n.d.), VI, 66-67.

Eastern Europe during the thirty years before 1917 accounted for only about one-half of the Jewish population. In the United States the proportion was vastly greater, and the Declaration had, therefore, a much larger ready-made audience.

A statement issued on 14 November 1917 by the Provisional Executive Committee for General Zionist Affairs reflects in its exuberant head-lines the natural elation of the Zionists: 'British Declaration favouring Jewish State'—'Not only a Jewish homeland in Palestine but protection of the status of Jews throughout the world guaranteed by Great Britain.'[70] In a message to the London Opera House meeting on 2 December 1917 the Provisional Committee telegraphed: 'The hearts of millions of our people are filled with joy. . . . The wise and high-minded purpose of His Majesty's Government . . . is in consonance with the policy of the British nation respecting the Jews and the liberation and protection of small nationalities . . .'[71] A Zionist Convention which met at Baltimore on December 16th adopted a resolution asking the Zionist leaders in London

> 'to convey to His Majesty's Government expressions of gratitude from the Jewish people for the Declaration, which is in consonance with the traditions of the British people . . . Deeply we rejoice in the triumph of British arms in Palestine . . . another step in the march of the Allied Forces, who are to establish throughout the world the principle of the invincible integrity of smaller nationalities.'[72]

The American Zionists responded to the Declaration with exultant rejoicing and an outpouring of gratitude to Great Britain. They spoke already for a large proportion of American Jewry, but they had not yet fully established their ascendancy. But though there were still cross-currents, the main stream was flowing strongly in their direction—how strongly is shown by the proceedings of the American Jewish Congress when, after several postponements, it met at Philadelphia a month after the end of the War. The Congress consisted partly of delegates directly

[70] Press release dated 14 November [1917]. Copy in Z.A.
[71] *Zionist Review*, January 1918, p. 171.
[72] *J.C.*, 4 January 1918.

elected by popular vote and partly of representatives of various Jewish bodies with an aggregate membership estimated at about one million. One of the organisations represented was the American Jewish Committee. Though the Congress was not formally qualified to speak for the whole of American Jewry, it had behind it an impressive body of support. It resolved by an overwhelming majority to send a delegation to the Peace Conference and to instruct its delegates to

> 'co-operate with the representatives of other Jewish organisations, and specifically with the World Zionist Organisation, to the end that the Peace Conference may declare that, in accordance with the British Government's Declaration of November 2nd, 1917 . . . there shall be established such political, administrative and economic conditions in Palestine as will assure, under the trusteeship of Great Britain, acting on behalf of such League of Nations as may be formed, the development of Palestine into a Jewish Commonwealth, it being clearly understood that nothing shall be done which shall prejudice the civil and religious rights of existing non-Jewish communities in Palestine or the rights and political status enjoyed by Jews in any other country.'[73]

With an enthusiasm as fervent as that with which they acclaimed the Balfour Declaration the American Jews were, eighteen months later, to express their gratitude to Great Britain on her acceptance at San Remo of the Palestine Mandate. The strength of their emotional response to the Declaration was the measure of their indignant reaction when things started to go wrong in Palestine and of their almost hysterical denunciation of Great Britain as the Mandate drifted to its melancholy end.

[73] 16 December 1918: *Z.C. 1921 Rpts.*—'Political Rpt.,' p. 78.

CHAPTER 39

THE RESPONSE TO THE DECLARATION, II

NEITHER IN PARIS nor in Rome was the Declaration received with any pleasure. Both the French and the Italians claimed a voice in the future of Palestine—the French under the Sykes-Picot Agreement and the Italians by virtue of the assurances given to them by their allies as a sequel to the Conference of St. Jean de Maurienne. That neither Government had been consulted in advance is plain from Balfour's replies to questions in Parliament. That both disliked the Declaration is shown by the efforts needed to induce them to endorse it. In each case it fell to the Zionists or their friends to extract the endorsement, and in each case it was communicated, not to the British Government, but to the Zionists.

A parliamentary question addressed to the Foreign Secretary on 19 November 1917 enquired 'whether the desire of the Government to re-establish a Jewish Zionist nationality in Palestine has been communicated to the Allied Powers, especially to France, Russia, Italy and the United States; and whether it is one of the allied war aims, or only a British war-aim, to set up a Zionist community in the Holy Land.' Balfour replied:

'No official communication has been made to the Allies on the subject, but His Majesty's Government believe that the declaration referred to would meet with their approval.'[1]

On December 12th Balfour was asked whether 'in all the steps hitherto taken [in regard to Palestine] and in the promises made, such as that of the restoration of the Jews to Jerusalem, he is acting in complete accord with the representatives of the French Republic.' The reply was:

'The honourable gentleman need be under no apprehension

[1] H.C., 19 November 1917: O.R., Col. 838.

that in our policy in Palestine we shall fail to show the fullest consideration for the opinions of our allies.'

The official report continues:

> 'Mr. Lynch: "While recognising that, has an accord already been established so that the Allies are working together in this matter?"
> 'Mr. Balfour: "Yes; we are working in the fullest accord."'[2]

In the spring of 1919, Balfour, writing from Paris to Curzon, who had taken charge of the Foreign Office during his absence at the Peace Conference, suggested that it might be useful to remind the British military authorities in Cairo that 'both the French, United States and Italian Governments have approved the policy set forth in my letter to Lord Rothschild.' So far as France and Italy were concerned, the evidence, and the only evidence, mentioned by Balfour in support of this statement consisted of 'M. Jules Cambon's letter to M. Sokolow of June 4th [1917] and M. Pichon's letter to M. Sokolow of February 14th 1918,' and, as to Italy, 'the Marquis Imperiali's letter to M. Sokolow of the 9th May 1918.'[3] It is obvious that Balfour was not in a position to point to any expression of approval by the French or the Italians as between themselves and the British Government.

In the light of Picot's account[4] of what happened when the Balfour Declaration was being considered by the British War Cabinet, his Government might have been expected to lose no time in endorsing it. Picot's story need not be believed in its entirety, but it is difficult to suppose that it is a pure invention. The whole point of it is that he went out of his way to remove a possible obstacle to the War Cabinet's approval of the Declaration by reminding it that Cambon's letter to Sokolow of 4 June 1917 was already on record as evidence of his own Government's sympathy with the Zionist Movement. Why, then, after the Declaration had been approved and published, did the French so long preserve a sulky silence?

[2] H.C., 12 December 1917: O.R., Col. 1151.
[3] Balfour to Curzon, 19 May 1919: *B.F.P., First Series,* Vol. IV, note 4 to No. 196, p. 281. (The date of the Cambon letter is printed as 'June 4th, 1914 [1918]'—a slip for June 4th, 1917.)
[4] Above, p. 420.

Picot's calculation seems to have been that, if there was going to be a British declaration, France could not afford to be a passive onlooker. She must be in a position to claim that she had at least indirectly had a hand in the decision. A simple explanation of the apparent discrepancy between Picot's intervention and the subsequent behaviour of his Government would be that, acting— as he says himself—without waiting for instructions from Paris, Picot had simply misjudged the situation as seen at the Quai d'Orsay. An alternative view would be that the inconsistency is more apparent than real. France was not prepared to be rushed into open approval of the British Declaration because she shrank from anything which might tend to strengthen the British claim to Palestine. On the other hand, Picot's production of the Cambon letter was designed to give her a card up her sleeve by enabling her to contend, in pressing for the internationalisation of Palestine, that there would and could have been no such declaration without her assent as an interested party.

Within a few weeks of the Declaration the French Foreign Minister, Pichon, addressing the Chamber of Deputies after the capitulation of Jerusalem, pointedly declared that Palestine was to be internationalised. Turkish rule would be replaced, he said, neither by a French nor by a British administration, but by 'an international régime based on justice and liberty.'[5] A few days before, Pichon had carefully steered clear of any reference to the British Declaration in giving the French Zionists an assurance of their Government's goodwill; they were simply told that France could be relied upon to favour every effort to ameliorate the condition of the Jews in the land of their ancestors.[6] In a report laid before the French Senate on December 31st on a petition concerning French relations with the Arabs, Zionism was described by the Rapporteur as 'une utopie dangereuse.'[7]

It was not until three months after the Declaration that the French Government was induced to take notice of the Declaration. At the end of January 1918 Sokolow went to Paris at the head of a Zionist mission. He could expect no help from the

[5] *Journal Officiel:* Chamber, second sitting, 27 December 1917.

[6] A. Spire, *Le Mouvement Sioniste* (Paris, 1918), p. 19.

[7] Jung, II, 211-213, quoting from Senate proceedings, *Journal Officiel,* 31 December 1917, pp. 1244-45.

official leaders of French Jewry, who had let their Government know that they were no friends of Zionism,[8] but he could count, as before, upon the active interest of Baron Edmond de Roth-schild. The Prime Minister, Clemenceau, had as one of his private secretaries a young friend of the Baron's, Georges Wormser,[9] who, from his personal recollection, has given the following account of what happened behind the scenes.[10]

Through Wormser, the Baron, who had long been on friendly terms with Clemenceau, suggested to him that France would do well to match the British commitment to the Zionists with a similar assurance. Wormser's impression was that Clemenceau did not take the British move very seriously, discounting it as mere propaganda. Clemenceau wrote to the Baron politely advising him to broach the subject with the Foreign Minister, Pichon, who, in turn, appeared, when approached, to be only mildly interested. Wormser reported this to Clemenceau, who thereupon told Pichon that it was his personal wish that a statement should be made, adding that the whole matter was, after all, of no great consequence. Taking the hint, Pichon, without thinking it necessary to consult the Cabinet, invited Sokolow to call at the Ministry[11] and, after receiving him on February 9th, authorised the following communiqué for publication:

> 'Monsieur Sokolow, representing the Zionist Organisations [sic] was this morning received at the Ministry of Foreign Affairs by Monsieur Stephen Pichon, who was happy to confirm that there is complete agreement between the French and British Governments in matters concerning the question of a Jewish establishment in Palestine.'[12]

---

[8] This was what Sokolow was told at the Quai d'Orsay: see entries for 31 January and 9 February 1918 in his 1918 Paris diary, publ. *Zion* (Jerusalem), November 1952, pp. 44, 47.

[9] Later, President of the Central Consistory of French Jewry.

[10] What follows is taken from a note kindly furnished to the author by M. Wormser. He has told the author that he has a perfectly clear recollection of the incident.

[11] Sokolow's interview with Pichon on February 9th is described in the entry under that date in his Paris diary: loc. cit., pp. 46-47.

[12] French text, with not quite accurate English translation (e.g., 'un établissement juif' appears as 'a Jewish national home'), in Sokolow, II, 128.

This was followed a few days later by a letter, dated 14 February 1918, from Pichon to Sokolow:[13]

> 'As arranged at our meeting on Saturday, the 9th of this month, the Government of the Republic, with a view to defining its attitude towards Zionist aspirations looking to the creation of a national home for the Jews in Palestine, has published a communiqué in the press.
>
> 'In sending you this text, I am particularly glad to take this opportunity to congratulate you on the generous devotion with which you are working for the realisation of the hopes of your co-religionists, and to thank you for your zeal in making known to them the sympathy aroused by their efforts in the countries of the Entente, and especially in France.'

The Zionists naturally made the most of Pichon's assurances, but two years later, at the London and San Remo Conferences, they were to be brushed aside by the French representatives, who stoutly maintained that there had never been any official French endorsement of the Balfour Declaration.[14]

For an insight into the Italian Government's response to the Declaration we are indebted to the valuable researches of Professor F. E. Manuel in the Italian State archives.[15] From these it appears that the Italians were in two minds as to how to handle the situation. Like the French, they had given Sokolow some vague assurances of sympathy in the spring of 1917,[16] but, like them, did not now consider that they were under any obligation to follow the British lead. They attached some importance to Jewish goodwill but a good deal more to the maintenance of their own claim to a share in the future administration of an internationalised Palestine. In no circumstances were they prepared, if they could help it, to see Palestine monopolised by the

---

13 French text, with English translation, again not quite accurate, ibid.

14 See below, pp. 660-661.

15 F. E. Manuel, ' The Palestine Question in Italian Diplomacy, 1917-1920':
Journal of Modern History (Chicago), September 1955, pp. 263ff.

16 Above, pp. 414-415.

591

British. How, then, could they endorse a British move which seemed to point plainly in that direction? Or was it possible, on the other hand, that their own Jews, who, unlike the French Jews, were disposed to be in sympathy with Zionism, might somehow help to advance their ambitions in Palestine?

The Italian Foreign Office began, as we learn from Professor Manuel, by trying to get the best of both worlds. Italian representatives in various capitals were put up to make friendly references to the Declaration, but a formal endorsement by the Government in Rome was withheld. The Zionists were not satisfied, and after the French Government had been persuaded to make its gesture in February 1918, Sokolow, who was handling the matter on the Zionist side, felt that he was in a strong position for pressing the Italians not to lag behind. They were not, however, prepared to be rushed. By the end of April Sokolow was becoming impatient and showed it in what is described by Professor Manuel as an almost peremptory letter (22 April 1918) to the Italian Ambassador in London, the Marquis Imperiali. The Foreign Minister, Sonnino, decided in the end that it would be as well to gratify the Zionists. It seems to have been felt in some Foreign Office circles in Rome that any expression of sympathy with Zionist aspirations should be communicated by the Italian Government to its own Jews and not to Sokolow. Sonnino did not accept this view, and at his direction Imperiali wrote to Sokolow on 9 May 1918—six months after the Balfour Declaration—as follows:

'On the instructions of His Excellency Baron Sonnino, His Majesty's Minister of Foreign Affairs, I have the honour to inform you that, with reference to representations which have been addressed to them, His Majesty's Government are pleased to confirm the declarations already made through their representatives at Washington, The Hague and Salonica to the effect that they will gladly be prepared to use their best endeavours to facilitate the establishment in Palestine of a Hebrew national centre, it being understood that nothing shall be done to prejudice the existing juridical and political status of the existing religious communities or the civil and

political rights enjoyed by Israelites in any other country.'[17]

Like the French and the Italians, the Americans were slow to identify themselves with the Balfour Declaration, but for different reasons. France and Italy were at war with Turkey. France had been from the start, and Italy had lately become, a party to the secret Treaties concerning the partition of the Turkish Empire. Basing themselves on those Treaties, both were competing for a share in the future control of Palestine. The United States was not involved in that competition. The partition of the Turkish Empire formed no part of its war aims, and it had abstained from declaring war on Turkey. But this very fact was in itself an obstacle to an American endorsement of the Declaration. The Secretary of State, Robert Lansing, seems to have disliked the Declaration on other grounds, but in persuading the President to keep silent on the subject his main, though not his only, argument was that Palestine was Turkish territory and the United States and Turkey were not at war.

This point was strongly made by Lansing in his letter of 13 December 1917,[18] in which he advised Wilson to resist the pressure of the American Zionists for a public expression of American approval.

'First,' he reminded the President, 'we are not at war with Turkey, and therefore should avoid any appearance of taking territory from that Empire by force. Second, the Jews are by no means a unit in the desire to re-establish their race as an independent people. . . . Third, many Christian sects and individuals would undoubtedly resent turning the Holy Land over to the absolute control of the race credited with the

---

[17] Italian text, with English translation, in Sokolow, II, 129. The translation is not quite accurate—e.g. the words 'stato giuridico e politico delle già esistenti comunite religiose' appear as 'the civil and religious rights of existing non-Jewish communities,' and, in the reference to the position of Jews in countries other than Palestine, the words 'diritti civili e politici' appear as 'the legal or political status.' Professor Manuel states (loc. cit.) that, in transmitting to Sokolow the text drafted in Rome, Imperiali inadvertently omitted the words safeguarding the position of 'existing religious communities' and corrected the omission in a further letter to Sokolow dated 18 June 1918.

[18] *For. Rns. U.S., Lansing Papers* (Washington, 1940), II, 71.

death of Christ. For practical purposes, I do not think that we need go further than the first reason given, since that is ample ground for declining to announce any policy in regard to the final disposition of Palestine.'

Attached to the original document, now in the Archives of the State Department, is a note by Lansing, reading as follows: 'The President returned me this letter at Cabinet meeting December 14th, 1917, saying that very unwillingly he was forced to agree with me, but said that he had an impression that we had assented to the British Declaration regarding returning Palestine to the Jews.'[19]

According to a competent American authority,[20] there is reason to doubt whether Lansing's note is a strictly truthful account of what passed between Wilson and himself. On this point the evidence seems inconclusive. What is clear is that Wilson was headed off from his original intention and, for the time being at least, dropped the idea of making it publicly known that he approved the Declaration. It was not only the American Zionists who were disappointed and embarrassed by his silence. Its depressing effect was felt even in Russia, where, in February 1918, a Zionist deputation was reported to have protested to the United States Embassy in Petrograd against the President's noticeable failure to identify himself publicly with the Zionist cause.

It was not until some ten months after the Declaration that Wilson was at length persuaded to give the Zionists some open encouragement. He did so in response to the urgent representations of Rabbi Stephen Wise, who, after Brandeis' elevation to the Supreme Court, had succeeded him as Chairman of the American Provisional Committee for General Zionist Affairs.[21] According to Wise's own account of the matter,[22] the immediate occasion of his approach to the President was a rumour (it proved to be well-founded) that an anti-Zionist agitation was being worked up by Morgenthau in conjunction with other like-minded American Jews. After an interview with the President on 27 August 1918, Wise remembered an important point he had overlooked and, in

19 Ibid.
20 Professor S. Adler, op. cit., p. 308.
21 Brandeis became Honorary President.
22 *Challenging Years* (New York, 1949), p. 192.

a letter to Wilson,[23] reminded him that in the Basle programme 'no reference is made to the character of the suzerainty which might obtain over such homeland. The Balfour Declaration, likewise silent on this subject, involves no challenge to the present suzerainty and leaves that for determination at the peace table.' Wilson responded with a letter to Wise, dated 31 August 1918, in which, avoiding any formal statement of American policy, he assured the Zionists of his personal goodwill.[24] After an allusion to 'the reconstructive work which the Weizmann Commission[25] has done in Palestine at the instance of the British Government,' 'I welcome,' he wrote, 'an opportunity to express the satisfaction I have felt in the progress of the Zionist Movement in the United States and in the Allied countries since the declaration by Mr. Balfour on behalf of the British Government . . .' Then followed a paraphrase of the Declaration, the letter being rounded off by a further reference to the work of the Zionist Commission: 'I think that all Americans will be deeply moved by the report that even in this time of stress the Weizmann Commission has been able to lay the foundations of the Hebrew University at Jerusalem, with the promise that bears of spiritual truth.'[26]

Nothing more was heard from Wilson during the War, but just before the opening of the Peace Conference in January 1919 he was seen by Weizmann and gave him to understand that the Zionists could count upon his personal support.[27] A few weeks afterwards he went further. On the eve of his departure from New York, early in March, on his return to Paris after his flying visit to the United States, he received a deputation representing the strongly pro-Zionist American Jewish Congress. Without formally authorising any official statement, Wilson allowed him-

[23] Text in Manuel, p. 176.
[24] Text in Sokolow, II, 130-131. This letter, together with ' the correspondence with Sir William Wiseman in October 1917,' is the only evidence of American endorsement of the Declaration mentioned by Balfour in his letter of 19 May 1919 to Curzon: B.F.P., First Series, Vol. IV., note 4 to No. 196, p. 281—see above, p. 531, note 46.
[25] A Zionist Commission, headed by Weizmann, had arrived in Palestine in April 1918.
[26] Professor Manuel suggests (op. cit., p. 177) that ' the Zionist leaders had to compose their own congratulations,' the style, he says, not being Wilson's.
[27] J.C., 17 January 1919; see also The Times, January 16th.

self to be quoted as favouring even larger promises to the Zionists than those contained in the Balfour Declaration:

> 'I am persuaded that the Allied nations, with the fullest concurrence of our Government and people, are agreed that in Palestine shall be laid the foundations of a Jewish Commonwealth.'[28]

Wilson himself seems to have felt that he might have gone a little too far. Lansing asked him whether the statement was authentic and pressed, if it was not, for a denial.[29] None was forthcoming, but Wilson was sufficiently embarrassed to write privately on the subject to House, explaining, rather lamely, 'that while he did not use the direct words quoted, he did in substance say what was quoted, though the expression "foundations of a Jewish Commonwealth" went a little further than his idea at the time. All that he meant was to corroborate his expressed acquiescence in the position of the British Government with regard to the future of Palestine.'[30] This rather curious incident suggests that Wilson was not giving the Zionist question much serious thought. The obvious explanation is that, pre-occupied with other matters which interested him more, he had been ready to allow words to be put into his mouth.

Strongly as he was reported to have expressed himself at his meeting with the Jewish deputation, it was not long before the Zionists felt obliged to approach him again. In May 1919 Wilson was known to be favouring a proposal for the appointment of an Inter-Allied Commission—it was reduced in the end to an American Commission—to report on the situation in the area

28 *The Times*, 4 March 1919; *J.C.*, 7 March 1919.

29 Lansing to Wilson, 13 April 1919: S. Adler, citing State Department Archives, op. cit., p. 323. The time-lag after the publication of the statement is not fully explained.

30 Wilson to House, 16 April 1919: S. Adler, op. cit., p. 323, citing State Department Archives. The words in quotation-marks are Professor Adler's. It is not clear whether they are a paraphrase or the words actually used by Wilson. In spite of his having admitted to House that he had gone a little too far, Wilson soon afterwards, at a meeting of the inner circle of the Peace Conference (3 May 1919), said that the Palestine problem was difficult because the British and American Governments had promised the Jews a State, to which the Arabs strongly objected: P. Mantoux, *Les Délibérations du Conseil des Quatre* (Paris, 1955), I, 482.

broadly known as Syria after an enquiry on the spot. Alarmed at the prospect of indefinite delay in a decision as to the future of Palestine, Felix Frankfurter, on behalf of the Zionist Delegation in Paris, appealed to the President to use his influence in favour of an early settlement in harmony with the Balfour Declaration.[31] Wilson wrote in reply (May 16th): 'I never dreamed that it was necessary to give you any renewed assurance of my adhesion to the Balfour Declaration, and so far I have found no one who is seriously opposing the purpose which it embodies.'

Wilson's 'adhesion' to the Declaration is not in doubt, but there is nothing to suggest he was at any time particularly interested in Zionism. There was here no American Balfour. Once Wilson had been induced to assent to the Declaration, he never changed his mind, but what seems to be reflected in his handling of the Zionist question is a certain vague benevolence rather than any strong feeling or serious thought.[32]

But even this was more than was to be hoped for from the Secretary of State. As was to happen again some forty years later under the Truman régime,[33] Zionism was a subject on which there was a marked divergence of views between the State Department and the White House. Anti-Semitism and anglophobia, both endemic in the United States, were by no means unknown in official circles in Washington and formed in combination an unpropitious background for their approach to a pro-Zionist policy sponsored by Great Britain. The State Department was all the less inclined to favour such a policy because it was sensitive to the anti-Zionist views of the American missionaries in the Levant,[34] who, through the Syrian Protestant College at Beirut, had done much to foster the Arab national movement and had educated a good proportion of its intellectual élite. When the question of an American endorsement of the Balfour Declaration first arose in the winter of 1917, the main objection pressed upon

---

[31] The Wilson-Frankfurter correspondence (May 8, 13, 14, 16, 20) is printed in B.F.P., First Series, Vol. IV, No. 180, pp. 260-262.

[32] The author has been told by Sir Arthur Willert and by the late Lord Percy of Newcastle that their impression was that Wilson was not seriously interested in Zionism.

[33] See Harry S. Truman, Years of Hope and Trial (London, Hodder and Stoughton, 1956), II, 148, 163, 168, 170, 175.

[34] S. Adler, op. cit., p. 317.

Wilson by Lansing was, as has been seen, that the United States was not at war with Turkey. But this was not the whole story. It seems to have been, not merely Lansing's personal view, but the settled conviction of the State Department that the United States, having enough on its hands already, had nothing to gain by involving itself gratuitously in a somewhat dubious enterprise with which it had no direct concern. Even after the end of the War, and after Lansing had ceased to be Secretary of State, the State Department still did its best to keep clear of Zionism. The first formal American endorsement of the Balfour Declaration took the form of a Joint Resolution of both Houses of Congress, signed by President Harding in September 1922.[35] But the State Department shrugged its shoulders at the Joint Resolution and remained as anxious as ever to avoid any Zionist entanglement.[36] In the same year, 1922, a start was made with the negotiations leading up to the Anglo-American Convention of 1924, by which the United States secured the safeguards it had insisted upon for American commercial and other interests in Palestine (prominent among them were the Standard Oil Company's exploration rights in the Negev), and, in return, formally 'consented' to the exercise of the Mandate by Great Britain.[37] When the Convention began to be drafted, the question arose whether the Balfour Declaration should be introduced into the preamble. It was recited in the preamble to the first British draft, but the State Department asked (12 July 1922) that this recital should be struck out. On the British side it was argued that there should be some specific reference to the establishment in Palestine of a national home for the Jewish people, 'having regard to the interest taken in this policy in the United States . . . of which the recent resolutions of both Houses of Congress have offered striking evidence.'[38] If the State Department had had its way, the Convention would have been silent on the subject. In the end the Americans conceded that the preamble to the Convention should recite the full text of the Palestine

[35] Public No. 73, 67th Congress.
[36] An incident described by Professor Manuel, op. cit., p. 280, illustrates what he describes as ' the cynical attitude of the State Department.'
[37] The relevant diplomatic correspondence is printed in *Mandate for Palestine* (Washington, Government Printing Office, 1927). For text of the Convention see Treaty Series, No. 54 (Cmd., 2559 : 1925) H.M.S.O.
[38] Curzon to the United States Ambassador, 2 October 1922.

Mandate, including its preamble.[39] This, in turn, recited the Balfour Declaration, which was thus enabled to be unobtrusively introduced into the Convention.

It looks as if at the time of the Declaration the Foreign Office was under no illusions as to Lansing's lack of enthusiasm. From its explanations of British policy in Palestine for the benefit of the State Department it may be inferred that it realised that what would appeal to Lansing and his colleagues was an assurance that no far-reaching promise to the Jews was to be read into the Declaration. There is a striking contrast between what Colonel House was told by Lloyd George a few weeks after the Declaration and the impression gained by the United States Ambassador in London, Walter Page, from a conversation a month later with Lord Robert Cecil. On 20 November 1917 House wrote in his diary: 'P.M. and Lord Chief Justice took dinner with us . . . What Great Britain desires are [various gains in Africa and elsewhere] . . . Palestine to be given to the Zionists under British or, if desired by us, under American control.'[40] This rather exuberant description of British policy in Palestine fits in better with Cecil's 'Judaea for the Jews' speech at the London Opera House on 2 December 1917 than with the results of Page's enquiries about British intentions as he reported them to Lansing some three weeks later.

The London Embassy had been instructed by the State Department to 'investigate discreetly and report fully to Department reasons for Balfour's recent statement relative to Jewish State in Palestine.'[41] Page replied:[42] 'Lord Robert Cecil, in charge of Foreign Office while Balfour is ill, informed us that the British Government has an understanding with the French Government that Palestine shall be internationalised. Mr. Balfour's letter printed in *The Times* of November 9th merely [stated] that the British Government pledges itself to put [apparent omission] the Jews in Palestine on the same footing as other nationalities. No

---

[39] United States Ambassador to Ramsay MacDonald, 30 April 1924. (The negotiations had been interrupted by the Lausanne Conference on the Turkish Peace Treaty.)

[40] House, *I.P.*, III, 240.

[41] 15 December 1917: *For. Rns., U.S.*, 1917, Suppl. 2, I, 473.

[42] 21 December 1917: ibid., p. 483. The words in brackets—'stated,' 'apparent omission'—are so printed in the official American text.

discrimination shall be made against them. This is as far as the British Government has gone.' Then followed an account of 'an informal conversation,' in which Cecil is stated to have expressed the hope that the United States would consent to be the protecting Power. A desire to make this suggestion more attractive in American eyes may possibly help to account for Cecil's evident anxiety—if he was correctly understood by Page—to minimise the significance of the Declaration.

Commenting on Page's telegram, the Assistant Secretary of State, Phillips, told Lansing that he had found it particularly interesting because Balfour had given the impression that he was committing his Government 'to a policy of Palestine for the Zionists.'[43] If, as would be comprehensible, the State Department found Page's report somewhat bewildering, Page himself was convinced that his assessment of the Declaration was substantially correct. Discussing British policy in the Middle East, he wrote privately to Arthur Page in January 1918:[44] 'Their idea of the future of Palestine is that, whoever shall manage the country, or however it shall be managed, the Jews shall have the same chance as anybody else. Of course that is quite an advance for the Jews there, but their idea is not that the Jews should have command of other populations there or control over them—not in the least. My guess at the English wish, which I have every reason to believe is the right guess, is that they would wish to have Palestine internationalised, whatever that means. That is to say that it should have control of its own local affairs . . . but that some Great Power, or number of Powers, should see to it that none of the races that live there should be allowed to impose upon the other races . . .' Then follows a passage in which Page explains 'why I have never been able to consider the Zionist movement seriously.'

A few weeks after this letter was written, the British Ambassador in Washington was instructed to apprise the United States Government of the principles on which Palestine would be

---

[43] Phillips to Lansing, 24 December 1917: S. Adler, op. cit., p. 310, citing State Department Archives. Phillips may have read Cecil's 'Judaea for the Jews' speech.

[44] *Life and Letters of Walter Page*, ed. Burton J. Hendrick (London, Heinemann, 1930), II, 349-350 (19 January 1918).

administered under British military occupation. A Note handed to the State Department on 12 February 1918 could be read, and was, presumably, meant to be read, as an assurance that, though the Zionists could not be ignored, they would be kept in check and not unduly favoured. The State Department was informed that the British authorities would do their best to ensure free exercise of all religions, the protection of all sacred sites, and the employment, wherever possible, of locally recruited officials, 'no special community being favoured,' together with 'the maintenance of Zionism on right lines' and 'the establishment of a régime of religious equality, justice and fair play for all.'[45] It is not, perhaps, fanciful to see some significance in the guarded allusion to Zionism, coupled with the strong hint that the British authorities could be relied upon not to give the Jews any undue encouragement. Though the language of the Note was in itself unexceptionable, it seems clearly to have been designed to relegate the Balfour Declaration to the background, on the assumption that the more narrowly it was interpreted the better the State Department would be pleased.

Great Britain's undertaking to the Zionists elicited somewhat half-hearted applause from her allies, but so far as its purpose was to embarrass the Central Powers, it had some success. That they were troubled by the Declaration is shown by their rather feeble attempts at a counterblast. The first move came, a little surprisingly, from Vienna. On 17 November 1917 the Austro-Hungarian Foreign Minister, Count Czernin, received a member of the Berlin Zionist Executive and—according to an official communiqué[46]—pledged his Government's support to the Zionists in their efforts to reach an understanding with the Turks. The Berlin Zionist organ duly applauded this assurance and dutifully made the most of it. But at this stage of the War Austria-Hungary carried little weight, and if anything was to be done to counteract

---

[45] S. Adler, op. cit., p. 310, citing State Department Archives: Manuel, p. 174.

[46] Printed in *Jüdische Rundschau* (Berlin), 30 November 1917. It has been suggested to the author by Dr. Robert Weltsch that Czernin's move was probably made at the instance of a Jewish commercial magnate, Nathan Eidinger, who had managed to make himself influential in Austro-Hungarian Foreign Office circles.

the effect of the British Declaration, it could not be done effectively by Czernin. The Germans, however, were not free to say anything worth saying about Palestine. They were still inhibited by their uneasy relations with the Turks, and the Turks were in no mood to be helpful.

This became clear when the Grand Vizier, Talaat Pasha, allowed himself to be interviewed in Constantinople by a representative of the *Vossische Zeitung*, Julius Becker. Becker, who was a Jew and a Zionist, had been introduced to Talaat by the German Embassy.[47] He did his best to extract a reassuring statement on the Zionist question, but with no marked success. His report of the interview, published in the *Vossische Zeitung* of 31 December 1917,[48] showed how skilfully Talaat, while vaguely foreshadowing some concessions to the Jews, had hedged on every important point.[49] Hard as he had tried, Becker had achieved very little, but this was as far as it was possible to get with the Turks, and the German propagandists had to make the best of it. On 5 January 1918 two members of the Berlin Zionist Executive, together with some other Jewish leaders representing the Komité für den Osten[50] were invited to the Foreign Office, where a prepared statement was read to them by the Under-Secretary of State, von der Bussche-Haddenhausen. After speaking of the German Government's benevolent intentions towards the Jews in its policy in Eastern Europe, the statement continued:

'As regards the aspirations in Palestine of Jewry, especially Zionists, we welcome the recent statement of the Grand Vizier, Talaat Pasha, expressing the Turkish Government's intention, in accordance with the friendly attitude they have always adopted towards the Jews, to promote a flourishing Jewish settlement within the limits of the capacity of the

[47] Becker's confidential report (undated) to the Berlin Zionist Executive is in the Zionist Archives. The interview underwent some editing before being published.

[48] Reprinted in *Jüdische Presse* (Berlin), 4 January 1918.

[49] There is a full account of the interview in *The Zionist Review*, February 1918, p. 198.

[50] See above, p. 98.

country, local self-government corresponding to the country's laws, and the free development of their civilisation.'[51]

The German Jewish press acclaimed these assurances with the appropriate comments, but this anaemic and inelegantly drafted formula could hardly be regarded as a stirring clarion-call to the Jewish world.

The Germans were, in fact, in no position to compete with the Balfour Declaration, but they followed up the Foreign Office statement with such counter-propaganda as was open to them. The Jewish Section of the British Ministry of Information was matched by a Jewish Section of the Berlin Foreign Office set up, early in 1918, under the direction of a Jewish specialist in Eastern affairs.[52] With official approval, a German Committee was organised as a counterpart, on a more imposing scale, of the British Palestine Committee and was joined by several eminent German politicians and publicists.[53] Efforts were made to obliterate divisions among the German Jews on the Zionist question. This was the main *raison d'être* of a newly constituted body, the *Vereinigung Jüdischer Organisationen Deutschlands*, in which all sections of German Jewry agreed to be represented. Responding to what was certainly the desire of the German Government, the *Vereinigung* showed an active interest in Jewish aspirations in Palestine, and, when Talaat Pasha visited Berlin in the spring of 1918, steps were taken to bring that body into contact with his entourage.[54]

The main representative organ of German Jewry, the *Central-verein* ('The Central Union of German Citizens of the Jewish Faith'), had before the War shown no enthusiasm for Zionism and had been extremely circumspect in its pronouncements on that delicate topic. But the Balfour Declaration caused it to have second thoughts. In a statement published in its organ, *Im Deutscher Reich*, in February 1918, the *Centralverein* explained why, at this juncture, the anti-Zionist campaign which was being called for by some of its members would be injurious to German

---

51 *Jüdische Presse* (Berlin), 11 January 1918. The English translation is that published in *The Zionist Review*, February 1918, p. 198.

52 Lichtheim, *Memoirs*, Chapt. 20; Böhm, I, 675.

53 Lichtheim, *Geschichte*, p. 216; Böhm, I, 675.

54 Lichtheim, *Gechichte*, p. 216; *Zionist Review*, April 1918, p. 218.

interests. Germany, it was pointed out, could not afford to let the Balfour Declaration hold the field. The British were trying to represent themselves as the Jews' only friends; 'Germany can and must take the wind out of their sails.'

It was in this spirit that all the leading Jewish organisations, though many of their members had been detached from or even hostile to Zionism, associated themselves with the *Vereinigung* and assented to its taking up the Palestine question with the Turkish delegation in Berlin. What emerged from the conversations was a rather vague but grandiose scheme for the establishment of autonomous Jewish settlements in various parts of Asiatic Turkey, including Palestine, under the auspices of a Jewish Chartered Company to be formed with headquarters in Constantinople.[55]

This was in the spring of 1918. The Chartered Company project fizzled out, but a fresh series of pourparlers opened in July, when a number of German and Austrian Jewish leaders, both Zionists and non-Zionists (they included two members of the Berlin Zionist Executive), received and accepted an invitation from Talaat to meet him in Constantinople. In September Talaat was reported to have announced that the exchange of views had been fruitful. He would favour the creation of a Jewish religious centre in Palestine under Turkish protection. It had been decided, he said, to do away with the regulations restricting Jewish immigration and settlement, and a special Commission had been set up to work out proposals for submission to the Turkish Parliament.[56]

Talaat's motives for all this make-believe are obscure. He may have been responding to strong pressure by the Germans, or it may be that, realising that Turkey was at her last gasp, he thought that it might somehow pay his Government to ingratiate itself with the Jews. His eleventh-hour offer of sweeping concessions to the Zionists had no practical significance; by the end of October Turkey had been driven out of the War.

[55] *Zionist Review*, April 1918, p. 218.
[56] J.C., 19 July, 6 September, 30 September 1918.

CHAPTER 40

THE IDEA OF AN AMERICAN MANDATE
FOR PALESTINE

IT WILL HAVE been noticed that, in commending the Declaration to the War Cabinet on 31 October 1917, Balfour carefully refrained from linking it with a British claim to the permanent control of Palestine. He touched lightly and ambiguously on the choice of a protecting Power. Treating this as an open question which need not now be decided, he spoke vaguely of 'some form of British, American or other protectorate'—the French were tacitly brushed aside—and left it at that.

The Zionists had been actively encouraged to demonstrate their desire for a British trusteeship. Mark Sykes had invited them to do so at his meeting with the Zionist leaders in February 1917. The strengthening of the British claim to Palestine had been accepted both on the British and the Zionist side as the underlying purpose of Sokolow's conversations with Picot and of his subsequent activities in Paris and Rome. These moves, inspired by Sykes, had been followed by a series of messages, many of them sent through British channels, in which the Zionist leaders in London urged their friends in Russia and the United States to work for a Jewish Commonwealth in Palestine under British protection, and assured them that this programme commanded British support. That such appeals would be welcome to the British Government had been strongly hinted to Weizmann by Lord Robert Cecil at their interview at the end of April 1917. A few weeks earlier Lloyd George had personally told Mark Sykes that he wanted Palestine brought within the British sphere and the door left open for the development of the Zionist Movement under British auspices. It had, in fact, been assumed on both sides, throughout the British Government's discussions with the Zionists, that both were equally interested in a post-war settlement which would leave Great Britain firmly installed in Palestine.

Balfour's personal view had been from the start that the United States ought, if possible, to be induced to interest itself in the

Palestine question. In informal conversation with Weizmann in 1916[1] he seems to have gone so far as to say that, if something was to be done for the Jews in Palestine, he would like it to be done under American rather than under British auspices, explaining that he did not want Great Britain to be suspected of using the Zionists in furtherance of Imperialist designs of her own. This, however, was before he had gone to the Foreign Office and before a British undertaking to the Zionists had begun to be seriously considered. By the summer of 1917 Balfour appears to have accepted a British claim to Palestine as *chose jugée*, though still hankering after some kind of American co-operation. 'Personally,' he wrote in a minute already quoted (13 June 1917), 'I would still prefer to associate the U.S.A. in the protectorate, should we succeed in securing it.' He had already broached the idea of a joint trusteeship at his interview with Weizmann earlier in the the year, and the same theme had been touched upon by Lloyd George, possibly at Balfour's prompting, when he saw Weizmann at the beginning of April.[2] But there had even then been no question of the United States being brought in otherwise than as a partner in an Anglo-American combination. At no time during the discussions in 1917 had it been suggested to Weizmann either by Balfour or Lloyd George that Great Britain might prefer to withdraw altogether, leaving Palestine to the United States as sole trustee.

This, however, was what was plainly contemplated as at least a possibility in Balfour's reference, on 31 October 1917, to 'some form of British, American or other protectorate.' He was not using empty words but propounding genuine alternatives. Possibly it was already beginning to be felt that, combined with a commitment to the Zionists, a Mandate for Palestine might prove burdensome and embarrassing. It may have been thought that an American Mandate could be as effective as a British Mandate in keeping out the French and would irritate them less. Perhaps it was desired, on wider grounds of policy, to draw the United States into the Turkish peace settlement, while at the same time demonstrating that Great Britain was not seeking, under cover of the Balfour Declaration, to secure Palestine for

[1] See Weizmann's account of the conversation, summarised above, p. 150.
[2] Above, pp. 381, 383.

herself, thus clearing her, in American eyes, of the hideous charge of Imperialism.

Whatever the reasons—on the evidence at present available they can only be conjectured—the idea of an American protectorate was seen to have its attractions, and within a few weeks of the Declaration the Americans were being invited to consider it. Whether Lloyd George ever genuinely favoured the proposal seems, to say the least, very doubtful. It looks as though, in his own mind, he meant all along to secure Palestine for Great Britain to the exclusion of any other Power. The fact remains that he personally appears to have given the Americans, through Colonel House, the impression that, if they were prepared to become responsible for Palestine, Great Britain would willingly stand aside. In an entry in his diary already quoted[3] on another point House describes a meeting with Lloyd George and Reading on 20 November 1917, when there was some informal talk about British war-aims. After mentioning British desiderata in other parts of the world, he goes on: 'Palestine to be given to the Zionists under British or, if desired by us, under American control.' House took this conversation seriously enough to incorporate his diary note, including the reference to Palestine, in his formal report to his Government on the Inter-Allied Conference which opened in London at the end of November 1917.[4] In the report, however, the material words read: 'if desired by us, *also* [author's italics] under American control,' from which it is, perhaps, to be inferred that what Lloyd George really suggested as a possibility was an Anglo-American partnership. However that may be, there was no ambiguity about the views of Lord Robert Cecil, as reported to Washington a few weeks later by Walter Page.[5] Lord Robert, then temporarily in charge of the Foreign Office, had been seen by Page as a result of Lansing's enquiry as to the real meaning of the Balfour Declaration. Telegraphing to Lansing on December 21st, the Ambassador, having explained how he understood from Cecil that the Declaration was to be interpreted,[6] went on:

[3] House, I.P., III, 240. See above, p. 599.
[4] *For. Rns. U.S.*, 1917, Suppl. 2, I, 344.
[5] Ibid., I, 483: see above, p. 599.
[6] See above, p. 599.

'Then followed an informal conversation. An internationalised Palestine must be under the protection of some Great Power.[7] Lord Robert, speaking only for himself, feared that the Continental Powers would not agree that any one of them should hold the protectorate, and some of them would object even to England holding it. Still speaking informally and only for himself, he hoped that the United States would consent to be the Protecting Power when the time comes, and he felt sure that all the Powers would gladly agree.'

Earlier in the conversation Cecil, as we have seen, had explained, according to Page, that what was meant by the Balfour Declaration was simply that the Jews in Palestine should be put 'on the same footing as other nationalities.' 'No discrimination shall be made against them.' If on this point Page understood him correctly, what Cecil was now proposing was, in effect, that the United States should become the protecting Power on the understanding that, so far as the Jews were concerned, all that had to be done was to see that they were not at a disadvantage as compared with other elements of the population.

There the matter seems to have rested for the time being, but at the end of the War the idea of an American protectorate was revived. Unreal though it was, for there never was any likelihood of its commending itself to the Americans, it was seriously discussed, and on the eve of the Peace Conference there was in some British circles a decided feeling that the United States should be invited, and, indeed, pressed, to become responsible for Palestine.

The ideas current in these quarters at the time are brought out in an article on 'America's Place in World Government' in *The Round Table* of December 1918. The views expressed are instructive because they reflect the opinions of a group of well-informed students of affairs on the fringe of the inner circle. The burden of the article was that the United States must somehow be persuaded to take a hand in dealing with the intractable problems arising from the rivalries of the European Powers in

[7] Cecil was tacitly setting aside the idea of a condominium implicit in the reference, in paragraph 3 of the Sykes-Picot Agreement, to the establishment in Palestine of 'an international administration.'

the Middle East. 'Her very detachment,' it was urged, 'renders her an ideal custodian of the Dardanelles. For exactly similar reasons, her task in preserving the autonomy of Armenia, Arabia and Persia will be easier than if it were to rest in our hands. Her vast Jewish population pre-eminently fits her to protect Palestine. Her position between India and Europe removes all our objections to the railway development which these regions require.'

Eighteen months earlier *The Round Table*[8] had referred with manifest approval to those Zionists 'who would like to see Palestine a British protectorate' and, after quoting what had been written by a German Zionist about the potential advantages to Germany of 'a protectorate over the Jews,' had commented that 'other Powers than Germany may take those possibilities to heart.' What was then being hinted at was plain enough, but in the interval there had clearly been some cooling off. Far from seeking the advantages of 'a protectorate over the Jews,' Great Britain, having issued her pro-Zionist Declaration, would, it was now suggested, do well to leave the rest to the United States.

Almost at the moment when this article appeared in December 1918 the question of a protecting Power for Palestine was being discussed by the Eastern Committee of the War Cabinet.[9] The Chairman, Lord Curzon, told the Committee that when the Palestine question had come before the Imperial War Cabinet (this would have been in July 1918), 'a good many of us,' including Curzon himself (though he had since changed his mind), had favoured an American protectorate, feeling that Great Britain would do well to limit her commitments in that part of the world, and agreeing with the Canadian Prime Minister, Sir Robert Borden, that an effort ought to be made to interest the United States in responsibilities outside the American Continent.

Lloyd George, obviously drawing on an authentic record, sets out verbatim part of the proceedings of the Eastern Committee. The balance of opinion was now in favour of a British claim to the Palestine Mandate, but the idea, once so vigorously canvassed, that Great Britain stood to gain by a permanent associa-

[8] June 1917: see above, p. 321.
[9] What follows is based on Lloyd George's quotations from the record of the Committee's proceedings, *Treaties* II, 1142, pp.

tion with the Jewish national home hardly figured in the argument.

It did emerge at one point, as is shown by the following instructive exchanges:

> 'General Wilson . . . It lies between us and the Americans.
> Lord Robert Cecil: There is not going to be any great catch about it.
> General Wilson: No.
> Lord Robert Cecil: Because we shall simply keep the peace between the Arabs and the Jews. We are not going to get anything out of it. Whoever goes there will have a poor time.
> General Smuts: It would affect Jewish national opinion, and nationally they are a great people.
> Lord Robert Cecil: They are likely to quarrel with the protecting Powers.
> General Wilson: If well-handled, I do not think so.
> General Macdonogh: I suggest the most important thing in the consideration of the position of Palestine is . . . its being, as Mr. Balfour says, the home of the Jewish people and, therefore, interesting the whole of the Jews all over the world.'

Though, to judge from Lord Robert Cecil's intervention, they did not now make any strong appeal to the Foreign Office, the ideas which had been so much alive a few months earlier had not become entirely obsolete. But they were not in the forefront of the discussion. The view that Great Britain would do best, on the whole, to secure the Mandate, if she could, for herself, rather than renounce it in favour of the United States, was based mainly on arguments in which the Zionist aspect of the matter played little part.

It was common ground that the choice lay between Great Britain and the United States, and that no third alternative need be considered. That the mandate for Palestine should go to France was agreed to be out of the question. 'Her presence there,' Curzon told his Committee, 'would be quite intolerable to ourselves, and it is clear that it would be equally unwelcome to the

people.' On the other hand, the idea of an American Mandate was by no means brushed aside, and Curzon took it seriously enough to explain at considerable length why he had now come round to the opinion that it was not, on the whole, to be desired. He pointed out that 'the Americans have no experience of this sort of work or this kind of people.' 'I suggest,' he said, 'that the Americans in Palestine might be a source, not of assistance, but very much the reverse, to ourselves in Egypt.' He reminded the Committee that 'Palestine is really the strategical buffer of Egypt,' and that the time might come when 'the Canal will have to be defended—as it has been in this war—from the Palestine side.' He invited the Committee 'to contemplate the position of the Americans, placed as they would be, if the French ambitions as regards Syria are fulfilled, midway between the French and ourselves. It would be a position which would almost certainly result in friction with both parties.'

Another argument advanced by Curzon in favour of a British rather than an American Mandate was directed to British relations with the Arabs. 'Ought we not,' he asked, 'to try and keep the Arabs of Palestine in close touch with the Arabs of the country both to the east and to the north? If you, so to speak, segregate them under the charge of a separate Power which has no interest in those regions, you will really sterilise them and arrest their growth.' Curzon went on to say that it was a material considera-tion that 'from all the evidence we have so far, the Arabs and the Zionists in Palestine want us.' He did not, however, pretend that the relations between them were harmonious. In an earlier part of his statement he had referred to 'an increasing friction between the two communities,' and to the awkward situation to which this might give rise at a time when Great Britain was already embarrassed in that part of the world by 'difficulties with our European allies.' His conclusion, in which he can hardly be said to have expressed himself with his usual lucidity, was that Great Britain should, nevertheless, not be deterred from seeking the Mandate. 'If it becomes a question of America and ourselves, believing in our own mind that it is best for the in-terests of the people of both parties that we and not America should be the [protecting] Power, we should give every en-couragement to this view which I have put forward, namely, that

under the principle of self-determination both the Zionists and the Arabs should be left to speak for themselves.'

After Robert Cecil had declared himself rather half-heartedly in favour of a British Mandate, the Committee agreed on its recommendations. A single Great Power should be selected to administer Palestine as 'representative of the nations.' That Power should be neither France nor Italy; the choice lay between the United States and Great Britain, and 'while we would not object to the selection of the United States of America, yet, if the offer were made to Great Britain, we ought not to decline.' To this it was added that 'the choice, whatever form it may take, should be, as far as possible, in accordance with the expressed desires (a) of the Arab population and (b) of the Zionist community in Palestine.'

What echoes of these discussions had reached the Zionists is uncertain. That they had heard rumours of a possible offer of the Palestine Mandate to the United States can be inferred from a pamphlet by Harry Sacher published early in 1919 by the London Bureau of the Zionist Organisation.[10] Taking seriatim all the conceivable alternatives to a British Mandate, Sacher explained at length why each of them was, from a Zionist point of view, unacceptable. An American Mandate would be no exception, and that for three main reasons. First, 'the average American has a natural belief in the superiority of the American type; and in the limited experience of America as a colonial Power the tendency of the American Government is to give the American image to the subject peoples.' Secondly, 'democracy in America too commonly means majority rule without regard to diversities of type or stages of civilisation or differences of quality . . . If the crude arithmetical conception of democracy were to be applied now, or at some early stage in the future, to Palestinian conditions, the majority which would rule would be the Arab majority. No Jew doubts the sincerity with which America would assume the trusteeship over a Jewish Palestine, but the dangers here indicated are dangers inherent in American conditions.' Thirdly, 'it would not be to the advantage of a Jewish Palestine

[10] H. Sacher, A Jewish Palestine: The Jewish Case for a British Trusteeship.

to compel Jews to intervene on its account in American domestic politics in order to avert the dangers that might arise out of American internal tendencies.'

The purpose of Sacher's pamphlet was indicated by its title— *A Jewish Palestine: The Jewish Case for a British Trusteeship.* The whole elaborate argument led up to the conclusion that 'Great Britain is the best fitted of all the Powers to conduct a Jewish Palestine through all the stages of its evolution to a free and full Jewish State. The only two possible candidates from the Jewish point of view are England and America, and the overwhelming choice of the Jews is for Great Britain.' At a time when other ideas seemed to be in the air, the Zionists thought it necessary to demonstrate how firmly, and for what reasons, they adhered to Weizmann's original conception of a Jewish national home to be built up under the aegis of the one Power on which he believed that the Jews could rely.

It is no wonder that the Zionists were disturbed by the suggestions which had evidently reached them that there might be alternatives, or at least one alternative, to a British Mandate. But they were more anxious than they need have been. Even if the British Government had finally made up its mind that it would prefer the United States, rather than Great Britain, to be responsible for Palestine, there is nothing to suggest that the Americans would have been prepared to entertain the proposal. The King-Crane Commission, in a report submitted to President Wilson in September 1919,[11] advocated an American Mandate for a Greater Syria to include Palestine, but its recommendations fell flat and it never looked as though anything would come of them. In the early days of the Peace Conference the American Delegation, though the United States had not been at war with Turkey, was interesting itself in the Turkish peace settlement. Before the whole conception of American Mandates had become meaningless as a result of the American decision to stay outside the League of Nations, it seemed possible or even likely that the United States would agree to become the protecting Power for

[11] Text in *For. Rns. U.S.*, 'Paris Peace Conference, 1919' (Washington, 1947), XII, 751ff.

certain of the ex-Turkish territories.[12] But President Wilson and his advisers were thinking of Armenia, parts of Asia Minor and Constantinople, and it was here that there seemed, for a time, to be a prospect of American co-operation in giving effect to the projected Peace Treaty. Whatever Dr. King and Mr. Crane might think, the Americans had at no time any intention of plunging their hands into the Syrian cauldron, nor is there anything to suggest that they would, at any stage, have been prepared to get entangled with Palestine.

Nor is there any reason to suppose that Lloyd George, for his part, ever seriously contemplated relinquishing the fruits of the British victory in Palestine, which had helped him to clear the ground for a British claim to the Mandate by breaking down the barrier of the Sykes-Picot Agreement. This he had achieved by a bargain made privately with Clemenceau during his visit to London at the end of 1918. Though its terms are still not precisely known, a bargain there must have been, for even if Clemenceau personally cared less about the Middle East than about problems nearer home, he was not the man to give something for nothing. Whatever may have been the consideration promised by Lloyd George, what he extracted from the French Prime Minister was an assurance that France would assent to a British instead of an international administration for Palestine, as well as to the transfer of Mosul from the French sphere in Syria to the British sphere in Mesopotamia.[13] According to Clemenceau, these sub-

---

[12] Clemenceau had his own suspicions as to why the British Government favoured this proposal: ' Si l'idée vient à notre peuple que les Anglais ont mis les Américains en Asie pour en chasser les Français, cela créera un état d'esprit que, pour ma part, je rédouterais'—Council of Four 21 May 1919: Mantoux, *Les Délibérations du Conseil des Quatre,* II, 139.

[13] *B.F.P., First Series,* Vol. IV, P. 251. The agreement was not reduced to writing: Lloyd George, *Treaties,* I, 1038; Gontaut-Biron, p. 156, quoting Briand in the Chamber of Deputies, 25 June 1920: ' Une conversation en décembre 1918 entre les deux ministres, sans procès-verbal et sans secrétaire.' Clemenceau said, at the Council of Four (21 May 1919), that he had expected compensation, on which Lloyd George commented that if Clemenceau had consented to sacrifice certain claims, it was because Great Britain had promised to come to the help of France if she were attacked: Mantoux, op. cit., II, 138, 140. A French memorandum on the Syrian question (10 October 1919) argues that ' contre-parties ' were implicit in the Lloyd George-Clemenceau agreement, which without them would be null and void: *B.F.P., First Series,* Vol. IV, encl. to No. 314, p. 452. Temperley (A *History of the Peace Conference,* VI, 82)

stantial departures from the Sykes-Picot Agreement were agreed to, so far as Palestine was concerned, subject to the reservation that the Holy Places question must be settled to the satisfaction of France[14]—a point to which the French were to return at the London and San Remo Conferences in 1920. Whether Clemenceau was right or not, the substantial effect of his understanding with Lloyd George was that France, having started in 1914 by claiming Palestine for herself, and having then been driven back to the condominium envisaged by the Sykes-Picot Agreement, had now abandoned the contest in favour of Great Britain.

There is nothing to suggest that the case for a British Palestine, as pressed upon Clemenceau by Lloyd George, rested to any significant degree on the Balfour Declaration or on the pro-British bias of the Zionists. To judge from Lloyd George's subsequent allusions to his interview with Clemenceau, the Jewish aspect of the Palestine question was but lightly touched upon. Writing to Clemenceau about the Syrian situation in October 1919,[15] he gives his version of the reasons for 'the understanding arrived at between yourself and myself in December last year in regard to Palestine and Mesopotamia.' 'The British Empire,' he points out 'had practically alone overthrown Turkey. . . . The French Government . . . had been unable to participate in the Turkish campaign in more than a small degree and had even opposed its prosecution.' As to Palestine, 'international Government had proverbially proved a failure and . . . the sentiments

---

14 'Sous réserve que les conditions relatives aux Lieux Saints nous donneraient satisfaction': Mantoux, op. cit., II, 159 (Council of Four, 22 May 1919).

15 Lloyd George to Clemenceau, 18 October 1919: B.F.P., First Series, Vol. IV, encl. to No. 334, p. 483.

---

quotes a magazine article by Tardieu (June 1920) in which he writes that it was part of the arrangement that in any allocation of Mandates France should be allotted a Mandate including Damascus and Aleppo, Alexandretta and Beirut. According to Renouvin (Histoire des Relations Internationales, Paris, 1957, VII, 200-201), the consideration was British assent to French control, not only of the coastal strip of Syria, but of Aleppo, Homs and Damascus. According to The Zionist Review, February 1919, p. 171, 'a careful study of the inspired French press suggests that the French Foreign Office is anxious to deal with the British on the following lines: Great Britain to have Palestine, Mesopotamia (including Mosul) and Arabia, France to have all Syria, including Damascus and Aleppo.'

of the inhabitants of Palestine, whether Arab or Zionist, appeared to favour a British Mandate.' This is the only reference to the Jews. They do not figure at all in Lloyd George's statement on the same subject in 1920 at San Remo.[16] What he says is simply that 'both he [Lloyd George] and M. Clemenceau had agreed that any régime of an international character would almost certainly lead to trouble, and that it was preferable that the Mandate for Palestine should be committed to a single Power, and that that Power should appropriately be Great Britain, as the conqueror of Palestine.'

Though in Lloyd George's conversation with Clemenceau on the eve of the Peace Conference the Balfour Declaration does not seem to have figured prominently, if at all, it moved into the foreground when, a few weeks after the opening of the Conference at the beginning of 1919, arrangements were made for a Zionist delegation to be heard by the Council of Ten. The principal Zionist spokesmen, Sokolow and Weizmann, were followed by the Russian Zionist leader, Ussishkin and by two representative French Jews of contrasting types, the Zionist André Spire and the non-Zionist Sylvain Lévi. The delegation left with the Council a memorandum in which, after inviting the Peace Conference to 'recognise the historic title of the Jewish people to Palestine and the right of the Jews to re-constitute in Palestine their national home,' the Zionist Organisation proposed that 'the sovereign possession of Palestine shall be vested in the League of Nations and the government entrusted to Great Britain as Mandatory of the League.'[17] It was reported to the Zionist Conference then meeting in London that, after the hearing, André Tardieu, who had sat as one of the French representatives on the Council of Ten, had made a statement to the effect that the Zionist proposals had been sympathetically received and that France would not

---

[16] B.F.P., First Series, Vol. VIII, p. 164.

[17] For Weizmann's account of the proceedings see Reports submitted to the Twelfth Zionist Congress (1921), Political Report, pp. 21ff. They are briefly described in Lloyd George's Treaties, II, 1155. The only full note is that printed in For. Rns. U.S., ' The Paris Peace Conference,' IV, 161ff. (Washington, 1943).

oppose a League of Nations Mandate for Palestine, with Great Britain as the Mandatory.[18]

This was on 27 February 1919. A week later, Lloyd George, Clemenceau and Colonel House met privately to discuss (among other matters) the allocation of Mandates for the territories to be detached from Turkey. According to Lloyd George's note of the conversation, House said that he thought that the United States would be prepared to take Mandates for Armenia and Constantinople. It having been agreed that Syria would go to France, 'I [Lloyd George] then said that America would accept a Mandate for Constantinople [and] Armenia and supervision for Anatolia, France would be Mandatory for Syria and such part of Cilicia as would be agreed upon between the Americans and the French; we would take Palestine and Mesopotamia, which includes Mosul.'[19]

Lloyd George's firm resolve to bring Palestine within the British sphere, and his reasons, come out clearly in Milner's account of a conversation with Clemenceau early in March. Milner had been deputed to deal with the Syrian question when, immediately after the end of the War, it was causing serious friction between Great Britain and France. He wrote to Lloyd George (5 March 1919):

'I told [Clemenceau] frankly that we had no desire to . . . try to get Syria for ourselves. Our interest was confined to an extended Mesopotamia, to Palestine and to a good connection between them.'[20]

Whatever doubts may have been felt about a British Mandate for Palestine by some of Lloyd George's colleagues, this represented the British Government's policy as laid down by the Prime Minister. What it meant was that, for the security of what was once described by Lawrence[21] as 'our Monroe area' in the East, there must be a solid block of British-controlled territory from the Mediterranean to the Persian Gulf, with communications not

---

[18] J.C., 7 March 1919.
[19] 7 March 1919: Lloyd George, *Treaties*, I, 288.
[20] Ibid., II, 1046.
[21] *The Letters of T. E. Lawrence*, ed. David Garnett (London, 1938), p. 265.

dependent at any point on the goodwill of another Power. For this purpose control of Palestine was indispensable.

These were Lloyd George's views about the future of Palestine. They were not Balfour's. Writing to Curzon on 1 July 1919, Balfour approved a suggestion by Herbert Samuel that the Government should inform the Palestine Military Administration that 'their policy contemplates the concession to Great Britain of the Mandate for Palestine.'[22] But if Balfour agreed, it must have been with the mental reservation that the policy was one about which he, personally, had his doubts. Only a few days earlier he had sent Lloyd George a memorandum setting out his own ideas as to the form to be given to the Turkish peace settlement.[23] He proposed, as to the allocation of Mandates, that the Mandate for Palestine should go to 'the American[s] or English.' A month later, Colonel Meinertzhagen, who had just been appointed Chief Political Officer on Allenby's Staff, saw Balfour in Paris and wrote in his diary (30 July 1919): '. . . Balfour went on to say that he himself was not in favour of a British Mandate over Palestine but that he would not oppose it. The P.M. was very anxious to secure a British mandate for purely sentimental reasons.' Not long afterwards Balfour had before him a minute on the Palestine question by a senior Foreign Office official, Robert Vansittart,[24] who wrote (6 August 1919): 'Not only has the Mandate not been given: is it *certain* that we should accept it, if offered? Considerations are beginning to emerge which might conceivably make it wiser for us, while supporting Zionism to the extent of our power, not to be the mandated Power.' On this Balfour commented: 'I am an ardent Zionist— but I agree with Mr. Vansittart that if only our own convenience is to be consulted, I should personally like someone else to take the Mandate. I do not, however, think this will happen.'[25] In a memorandum written a few days later[26] Balfour set out at length

22 *B.F.P.*, *First Series*, Vol. IV, No. 210, pp. 300-301.

23 Memorandum dated 26 June 1919: ibid., encl. to No. 211, pp. 301ff.

24 Later, Lord Vansittart.

25 *B.F.P.*, *First Series*, Vol. IV, No. 237, p. 330.

26 Ibid., No. 244, p. 346 (11 August 1919). For a further reference to this memorandum see below, p. 649.

his views on the future of Syria, Mesopotamia and Palestine. He accepted without question the idea of 'a British sphere centring round the Euphrates and the Tigris,' but as to Palestine, while laying it down that there must be 'a home for the Jews in the Valley of the Jordan,' he pointedly refrained from prosposing Great Britain as the protecting Power. In January 1922, when Balfour was in the United States for the Washington Naval Conference, we find him writing to the Secretary of State, C. E. Hughes: 'The task which the British Government have undertaken in Palestine is one of extreme difficulty and delicacy. At Paris I always warmly advocated that it should be undertaken, not by Great Britain, but by the United States.'[27]

But all this was beating the air. The whole idea of an American Mandate turned out to be a chimera and was soon cast aside, not to be revived until in 1945 Winston Churchill, in a moment of understandable exasperation, suggested that the time had come for Great Britain's position in Palestine to be re-examined. 'I do not think,' he wrote to the Colonial Secretary and the Chiefs of Staff, 'that we should take the responsibility upon ourselves of managing this very difficult place while the Americans sit back and criticise. Have you ever addressed yourselves to the idea that we should ask them to take it over?. . . At any rate, the fact that we show no desire to keep the mandate will be a great help.'[28]

It is not surprising that Churchill should have been tempted, in 1945, to look for some way of getting rid of the Mandate. Nevertheless, it was fortunate for Great Britain, as well as for the Jews, that in the distribution of responsibility in 1919-1920 Balfour's dream of an American Mandate for Palestine did not come true. No great effort of the imagination is needed to picture the situation in which Great Britain would have found herself in 1940-41 if, with Syria looking to Vichy and the Germans thrusting towards Egypt, her shaky position in the Middle East had been still further complicated by the presence in Palestine of the then neutral United States. As for the Jews, there is not the least

---

[27] 13 January 1922: *Mandate for Palestine*, p. 58.
[28] 6 July 1945: *The Second World War* (London, Cassell, 1954), VI, 654. He goes on: 'I am not aware of the slightest advantage which has ever accrued to Great Britain from this painful and thankless task. Somebody else should have their turn now.'

reason to suppose that the Americans would have been more skilful or more successful than the British were in dealing with the difficulties inherent in the Palestine Mandate. Though it gradually grew tired, discouraged and resentful and in the end abandoned the task in despair, the British Government, once having chosen to accept the exacting duties imposed upon it by the Mandate, made an honest attempt, over a long period of years, to muddle its way through. The Americans would have found the problem no less intractable, and they might well have been less patient and quicker to tire of their frustrations. For the American Jews, the backbone of the Zionist Movement outside Palestine, an American Mandate might have proved a serious embarrassment. In England the Jews suffered surprisingly little from the backwash of the tension between Jews and British in Palestine. It may be doubted whether the American Jews, a much larger and more conspicuous section of a less tolerant society, would not, in like circumstances, have found themselves in an unenviable position. Weizmann's instinct was sound when he showed his unwillingness to contemplate any alternative to a British Mandate, just as Curzon's was when, at the end of 1918, he invited the War Cabinet Eastern Committee to consider the position which might arise under an American Mandate, with 'the Americans, placed as they would be, if French ambitions in Syria are fulfilled, midway between the French and ourselves.'

CHAPTER 41

THE ARAB QUESTION

THOUGH WELL BEFORE the end of the opening phase of the Peace Conference a British claim to the Palestine Mandate had been firmly asserted by Lloyd George, Vansittart's minute of 6 August 1919, and Balfour's comment, show how serious were the doubts entertained in some influential British quarters and how long they persisted. Vansittart did not specify the 'considerations . . . which might conceivably make it wiser for us . . . not to be the mandated Power,' but some of them, at least, are self-evident.

Writing to Weizmann in January 1915 about the points that he must be prepared to deal with on meeting Lloyd George, C. P. Scott warned him that among these were almost sure to be 'the present strength of the Jewish element in Palestine and the possibility of its rapid expansion in relation to the local Arab population, which so greatly outnumbers it.'[1] A few weeks later, when Grey vaguely suggested to Herbert Samuel that the government of Palestine might be vested 'in some kind of Council to be established by the Jews,' Samuel 'expressed a doubt whether the Arab population, who number five-sixths of the inhabitants would accept such a government.'[2] Grey himself alluded to the numerical preponderance of the Arabs in Palestine when, in March 1916, he proposed an Allied declaration in favour of Zionism. What would attract the Jews, he pointed out, was the prospect of gaining control of 'the internal affairs of Palestine' 'when in course of time the Jewish colonists . . . have grown strong enough to cope with the Arab population.'[3] At Sykes' first meeting with the Zionist leaders in February 1917 he told them that 'one would have to go carefully with the Arabs.'[4]

The Zionists, for their part, or at least the more thoughtful among them, recognised from the start that the Arabs could not

[1] Scott to Weizmann, 14 January 1915: *Ch.W.P.*, quoted above, p. 140.
[2] Samuel, *Memoirs*, p. 144.
[3] Above, p. 224.
[4] Above, p. 373.

be brushed aside. Writing in 1916 in *Zionism and The Jewish Future*,[5] Norman Bentwich pointed out that 'it is not to be expected that the Jews will be able to occupy and appropriate the whole country.' This, he explained, presented no real problem, since 'there is ample room for the children of Esau and of Jacob to live together in harmony on the land,' and a just Administration should be well able 'to secure a good understanding . . . between the two elements that are in origin akin and stand in material need of each other.' Replying in October 1916 to the anti-Zionist case, as set out by Lucien Wolf in correspondence with James de Rothschild, the authors of a Zionist memorandum were emphatic on the point that the Zionists claimed no monopoly of Palestine for the Jews. 'Palestine,' they wrote, 'will contain one or more national and religious groups besides the Jews . . . Whatever be the national or religious group to which a man may belong . . . his position as a citizen of Palestine will be exactly the same.'[6] In March 1917 Weizmann told Scott that he was anxious to go to the East as soon as possible and 'enter there into negotiations with the leading Arabs from Palestine.'[7] A few weeks later, Lord Rothschild, in his letter to *The Times*,[8] declared that 'we Zionists . . . only desire to be allowed to work out our destinies [in Palestine] side by side with other nationalities in an autonomous State under the suzerainty of one of the Allied Powers.'

How heavily the problem of relations with the Arabs was weighing upon some, at least, of the more sophisticated Zionists is shown by one of Harry Sacher's letters to Leon Simon.[9] 'At the back of my mind,' he wrote in June 1917, 'there is firmly fixed the recognition that, even if all our political schemings turn out in the way we desire, the Arabs will remain our most tremendous problem. I don't want us in Palestine to deal with the Arabs as the Poles deal with the Jews, and with the lesser excuse that belongs to a numerical minority. That kind of chauvinism might poison the whole Yishuv. It it our business to fight against it . . . It is going to be extraordinarily difficult and it will give us unhappy years, but it has to be done.' Sacher is here thinking less

[5] pp. 203-204.
[6] *C.F.C.*, 1917/253-254 (11 October 1916).
[7] Above, p. 379.
[8] 28 May 1917.
[9] *Sacher Letters* (14 June 1917).

of anything that the Jews might have to fear from the Arabs than
of what the Arabs might have to fear from the Jews. There is
clearly an underlying assumption of Jewish predominance. But
there is still a recognition of the difficulties inherent in the
presence in Palestine of an Arab population greatly outnumbering
the Jews.

It was precisely on this question of predominance that Sykes,
anxious from the start that the Zionists should not run into
collision with his Arab protégés, tried to moderate their expectations. It had been suggested to him by Gaster, early in 1917, that
Palestine should be organised broadly on the lines of the Turkish
Millet system. Gaster gave him to understand that Zionist aspirations would be satisfied if the Jews were recognised as a 'nation'
within such a system and granted the same internal autonomy
as would be enjoyed by one or more other *Millets* or 'nations.'
Sykes was favourably impressed; 'the idea,' Gaster wrote in his
diary, 'pleased him [Sykes] very much.'[10] There was nothing
obviously inconsistent with that idea in the statement of Zionist
aims submitted to Sykes just before his meeting with the Zionist
leaders in February 1917.[11] Building on this proposal, Sykes invited the Zionists to accept the view that the essence of their
requirements would be met if the Jews were recognised in Palestine as a 'national unit.' He seems to have pressed this point when
Rothschild's letter to Balfour was in process of being drafted in
the summer of 1917,[12] and he returned to it in September, when,
in the final version of his *Note on Palestine*, he placed first among
the Zionist aims 'recognition of the Jewish inhabitants of Palestine as a national unit federated with [other] national units in
Palestine.' But, the Zionists had been allowed, and, indeed, encouraged, to speak of a Jewish Commonwealth in Palestine and
to think of Palestine in terms of 'Judaea for the Jews.' How the
two conceptions were to be reconciled it was not sought to explain, unless, indeed, it could be suggested, a little disingenuously,

[10] *Gaster diaries*, 30 January 1917.
[11] Above, p. 369.
[12] Referring to the proposed wording of a draft (subsequently superseded)
of the Zionist formula for a declaration, Ahad Ha'am wrote to Sokolow
(11 July 1917): 'I understood from what you said that you added these
words on the advice of Sykes so that there should be an opportunity of
introducing " national unit " ': *Igrot.*, V, 303-304.

that a Jewish 'national unit' enjoying internal autonomy side by side with other 'national units' would, in fact, answer to the description of 'a Jewish Commonwealth.'

The Zionists' own picture of a Jewish Commonwealth was, perhaps, a little vague. Some Zionists, at least, would probably have said that they preferred to speak of a Jewish Commonwealth rather than of a Jewish State because they were not thinking in terms of sovereign independence. As one of Weizmann's inner circle wrote in 1917, 'even Herzl, whose use of the term *Judenstaat* has given rise to so much misunderstanding on this point, did not demand such conditions as are suggested to English minds by the phrase "Jewish State" . . . Zionism needs and values [gentile] sympathy, not because it holds out the promise of some fifth-rate "Jewish State," but because it foreshadows the possibility of resuming . . . the interrupted work of building up in Palestine the foundations of the Jewish Commonwealth—that Commonwealth which will become in time the nerve-centre of Jewry and the visible embodiment of the Jewish attitude to life.'[13]

If a 'Jewish Commonwealth' was not, or was not necessarily, merely another name for a Jewish State, neither were the Zionists thinking of a Palestine to be cleared of Arabs and monopolised by Jews. They could truthfully affirm their conviction that there was and would always be room in Palestine for both. What was, however, implicit in the aims of Zionism, as commonly conceived at the time of the Declaration, was the idea of Jewish predominance—not, indeed, as Sacher was at such pains to emphasise, the predominance of a Herrenvolk, but a weight of numbers which would mean that the Jews would set the pace and give the country its tone and colour.

From a Zionist point of view, how could it have been otherwise? Everywhere the Jews had had to accept the status of a minority, sometimes enjoying tolerant or even generous treatment, more often oppressed, if not actively persecuted, but even where, as in the United States, they were wholly free from disabilities,

[13] Leon Simon, *The Case of the Anti-Zionists—A Reply* (Zionist Organisation, London Bureau, 1917), pp. 18, 24. Sokolow, in his Introduction to his *History of Zionism* (publ. 1919), writes (Vol. I, pp. xxiv-xxv): 'It has been said, and is still being obstinately repeated by anti-Zionists again and again, that Zionism aims at the creation of an independent "Jewish State." But this is wholly fallacious.' See also pp. 523-524.

even where, as in England, their legal status was as secure as it was in America and their social status a good deal better, never quite certain of themselves and perpetually seeking reassurance. For most Zionists—perhaps for nearly all but the relatively few who thought in terms of a spiritual centre—the real attraction of the Movement was that, if it achieved its purpose, there would be one country in the world, and that their own historic home, in which the Jews would not need to rely on the forbearance of others, since they would be the unchallengeable masters of a house built by themselves. This was what Weizmann meant when at the Peace Conference he told the Council of Ten that the Zionists hoped 'to build up gradually a nationality which would be as Jewish as the French nation was French and the British nation British. Later on, when the Jews formed the large majority, they would be ripe to establish such a government as would answer to the state of the development of the country and to their own ideals.'[14] There was no beating about the bush when, speaking on the second anniversary of the Balfour Declaration, Herbert Samuel declared that the object in view was that 'with the minimum of delay [Palestine] may become a purely self-governing Commonwealth under the auspices of an established Jewish majority.'[15]

Nor was Balfour, for his part, in any doubt as to what the Declaration implied. 'We are consciously seeking,' he said to Brandeis in 1919, 'to reconstitute a new community and definitely building for a numerical majority in the future.'[16] From a purely British point of view, it had often been argued in favour of a pro-Zionist policy that a large-scale settlement of Jews in Palestine under the auspices of Great Britain would strengthen her position in a part of the world in which she would need reliable

---

14 *For. Rns. U.S.*, 'The Paris Peace Conference,' IV, 169-170. This is not quite the same as Weizmann's own version of what he said: '. . . that there should ultimately be such conditions that Palestine should be just as Jewish as America is American and England is English': 12 Z.C. Reports (London, 1921), Political Report, p. 22. Sidebotham's rejected draft of a formula to be submitted to Balfour (July 1917—above, p. 466) spoke of 'a State whose dominant national character . . . will be Jewish in the same sense as the dominant national character of England is English, of Canada Candian and of Australia Australian.'
15 London Opera House, 2 November 1919: *J.C.*, 7 November 1919.
16 24 June 1919: *B.F.P., First Series*, Vol. IV, p. 1277.

friends. A weak Jewish settlement could make little difference one way or the other. There was no force in the argument unless it pre-supposed a predominantly Jewish Palestine.

That this was what was contemplated had come to be regarded by the Zionists as axiomatic. But the Arabs were in possession, and the British Government was aware of that elementary fact. How were the realities of the situation to be squared with the hopes which the Zionists had been permitted and, indeed, invited, to entertain?

From the noticeable watering down of the formula originally proposed for the Balfour Declaration by the Zionists and, in substance, approved by Balfour it may be inferred that at the time of the Declaration the War Cabinet had the Arab aspect of the matter in mind. On the other hand, it seems to have been believed that, in the form in which it was finally approved, the Declaration need not be expected to give rise to any serious difficulties with the Arabs. How much attention the whole question had received is uncertain. Amery speaks in his memoirs of having been asked by Milner, on 4 October 1917, to draft something which would meet the objections 'both Jewish and pro-Arab.'[17] Smuts had something to say on the subject in his speech at Cape Town in April 1926:[18]

> 'I remember when in the War Cabinet [the Balfour Declaration] was discussed many a week, many a month . . . One side was the people who argued: Why should we declare in favour of a national home; why should we go against the Arabs? . . . They went further and said: "Why antagonise the Mahommedans?' . . . Then we had the opposition of the Jews themselves . . . Those who remember the formula . . . will remember how both these lines of opposition were smitten, because . . . the formula of the national home was declared in favour of Palestine, and that formula tries to save the face of the Mahommedan world and other nationalities living in Palestine. It saved the fleshpots of all those living in Palestine . . .'

In a memorandum submitted by Smuts to the Anglo-American

17 Above, p. 520.
18 *The Zionist Record* (Johannesburg), 30 April 1926.

Committee of Enquiry in 1946,[19] he explained that at the time of the Declaration 'it was naturally assumed that large-scale immigration of Jews into their historic homeland could not and would not be looked upon as a hostile gesture to the highly favoured Arab people,' who, he says, 'largely as a result of British action, came better out of the Great War than any other people.'

Smuts, like Amery, was looking back over a long period of years. His recollections are not conclusive evidence of what passed in the War Cabinet in the autumn of 1917, but both he and Amery are clearly under the impression that the Arabs were by no means overlooked.

On the other hand, Lloyd George's account of the proceedings of the War Cabinet—not necessarily exhaustive but obviously authentic as far as it goes—suggests that the possibility of trouble with the Arabs did not figure prominently at any of the three meetings at which the Declaration was considered. It seems clear that on all three occasions much more attention was paid to the objections of the anti-Zionist Jews than to any which might be encountered on the Arab side. Only one member of the War Cabinet is on record as having mentioned the presence of an Arab majority in Palestine as a serious obstacle to the proposed assurance to the Zionists. This was Curzon, whose views on the subject, as set out in his memorandum of 26 October 1917, have been mentioned already and need not here be repeated. In the end, as has been seen, even Curzon did not press his objections. In addressing the War Cabinet in support of the Declaration on 31 October 1917, Balfour is quoted by Lloyd George as having alluded to certain arguments which had been used against him.[20] He does not, however, appear to have thought it necessary to deal with the question whether the Declaration might lead to trouble with the Arabs in Palestine or prejudice British relations with the Arab world generally. These were matters which he would hardly have passed over in silence if serious concern had been felt about them at the time either at the Foreign Office or in the War Cabinet.

Least of all do they appear to have troubled Lloyd George. A few weeks after instructing Sykes, in April 1917, to work for the

[19] Printed in *The Zionist Record*, 19 April 1946.
[20] Above, p. 547.

development of Zionism under British auspices, he was in Paris on his way home from St. Jean de Maurienne. The British Ambassador, Bertie, talked to him about Palestine, pointing out that the Jews would not be able to hold their own without extraneous support and asking what effect this would have on the Arabs. Bertie also expressed anxiety about French intransigence on the Palestine question. Lloyd George, he writes in his diary (20 April 1917),[21] 'said . . . we shall be there by conquest and shall remain, we being of no particular faith and the only Power fit to rule Mohammedans, Jews, Roman Catholics and all religions . . .' There is nothing to suggest that Lloyd George ever wavered in his robust belief that Great Britain could take all the difficulties in her stride.

In Cairo the British authorities saw the situation rather differently.

Zionism seems first to have engaged the interest of the Arab Bureau after Aaron Aaronsohn's arrival in Egypt at the end of 1916. The earliest reference to the subject in *The Arab Bulletin* is a by no means unsympathetic account of the Movement in the issue of 19 January 1917. Against this must be set a paper by T. E. Lawrence, written in 1915 and disinterred for publication in the *Bulletin* two years later,[22] in which some not unfriendly remarks about the Jewish colonists in Northern Palestine were followed by a highly uncomplimentary description of the 'German Zionist Jews' further south—'the most foreign, most uncharitable part of its whole population. Behind these Jews is their enemy, the Palestine peasant.' Up to the time of the Balfour Declaration the only other items of Zionist interest to be found in the *Bulletin* are two contributions by leading Palestinian Jews setting out opposing views as to the impact of Jewish colonisation on the Arab cultivator.[23] It is not possible to infer from the *Bulletin* whether the Arab Bureau had any collective view on the Zionist question or was invited to express one.

But, as the Balfour Declaration came nearer, the Political

[21] Bertie, II, 122.
[22] 12 March, 1917: printed also in *Secret Dispatches from Arabia*, by T. E. Lawrence (London, n.d.), pp. 70ff. As to *The Arab Bulletin*, see list of sources, p. 667.
[23] 27 September 1917.

Branch of the General Staff in Cairo knew what was on foot and was perturbed. Some two months before the Declaration, Allenby's Chief Political Officer, General Clayton, suggested to Mark Sykes that, for the time being at least, the British Government should refrain from any public pronouncement in favour of Zionism, since there was nothing to be gained by giving the Arabs 'yet another bone of contention.'[24] Soon after the Declaration had been published, Clayton telegraphed to Sykes: 'Recent announcement by His Majesty's Government on Jewish question has made profound impression on both Moslems and Christians, who view with little short of dismay prospect of seeing Palestine, and eventually Syria, in hands of Jews, whose superior intelligence and commercial abilities feared by all alike.'[25] The state of feeling in those parts of Palestine already under British occupation was described by the writer of a Palestine Letter published in *The Arab Bulletin* of 18 March 1918. 'There is no doubt,' he reported, 'that nothing hampers so greatly our local relations with the existing non-Jewish inhabitants of Palestine as the vagueness of our declaration in favour of Zionism. It is idle to suppose that anyone in possession can feel at ease in a Promised Land.' How the situation was viewed at the British Residency in Cairo can be inferred from a passage in the biography of Sir Reginald Wingate, who was High Commissioner in Egypt at the time of the arrival in Palestine of the Zionist Commission. 'The Zionists, led by Dr. Chaim Weizmann, Wingate found reasonable but woefully uninformed as to conditions in Arab countries. "I, therefore, recommended them," he wrote to Lord Hardinge,[26] to feel their way carefully and to do all in their power to show sympathy and goodwill to the Arab and Moslem peoples, with whom their future must lie." '[27]

The reports from Cairo and Jerusalem made their mark in London. From the moment the Balfour Declaration was published Sykes impressed upon the Zionist leaders his conviction that the success of their cause depended upon an understanding with the

---

[24] Clayton to Sykes, 20 August 1917: *Sledm.*, No. 44.
[25] 28 November 1917: *Sledm.*, No. 75.
[26] Permanent Under-Secretary of State at the Foreign Office.
[27] R. Wingate, *Wingate of the Sudan* (London, John Murray, 1955), pp. 225-226.

Arabs, whose national aspirations must—he insisted—be reconciled and linked with their own. Addressing a Zionist meeting in Manchester soon after receiving Clayton's disturbing message of November 28th about Arab unrest, he warned the Zionists 'to look through Arab glasses,'[28] and telegrams drawing attention to his speech were sent after the meeting to Brandeis and to the Zionist Committee in Egypt. By the end of 1917 Sykes was becoming seriously uneasy. In a general survey of the situation in the East, written in January 1918,[29] he describes the Declaration as a valuable asset giving Great Britain, and the Entente as a whole, 'a hold on the vital forces of Jewry,' but goes on, nevertheless, to express concern about 'a whole crop of weeds growing up around us,' and among them 'Arab unrest in regard to Zionism.' In a memorandum on British relations with the Zionists prepared about the same time by a War Office expert, the writer, though clearly a convinced believer in a pro-Zionist policy, speaks of 'the natural hostility of the Arabs' and describes some of the measures taken 'to minimise one of the great disadvantages of the Declaration from a British point of view.'

Weizmann was aware of the British Government's embarrassments in Palestine but believed that to explain them it was necessary to look beyond the local Arab agitation to more dangerous forces working in the background. Writing to Brandeis on 14 January 1918, he analysed the situation in Palestine as follows:[30]

'The French are making themselves as disagreeable as possible there. They pose as the conquerors of Palestine, as the protectors of the Christians, as the modern Crusaders. M. Picot ... is at present the soul of this French propaganda ... The British naturally resent all that, but they are extremely anxious not to create more friction between them and the French than is absolutely necessary ... A further complication are the Arabs, Moslem and Christian. The Moslems are friendly to Great Britain, and their political centre of gravity is shifting towards the Hedjaz ... But the Christian Arabs, or so-called Syrians, are broken up into fractions and factions swayed by influences over which nobody

[28] 9 December 1917: *J.C.*, 14 December 1917.
[29] 1 January 1918: *Milner papers* ('Palestine' file).
[30] Copy in *Ch.W.P.*

can have any definite control . . . The Syrians are a hetero-
geneous group and they are worked—sometimes without
themselves knowing it—by obscure French financiers desirous
of clinging to the concessions which they obtained from
Turkey . . . They are further worked by the Jesuits (not by
the Vatican!) and, last but not least, by the anti-Zionists like
Reinach and his friends . . . They dare not work openly
against Great Britain, but they preach a crusade against us
. . . You therefore have to face a very widespread coalition . . . consisting of Jesuits with branches stretched across
Austria—South Germany . . . Syrians with Syrian-French
financiers . . . their Jewish associates . . . and this so-called
"Jewish" influence stretches across to Salonica and to the
pseudo-Jewish members of the Committee of Union and
Progress . . .

'Much will depend upon our activity and achievements
in Palestine between now and the Peace Conference. We
must, therefore, work with great intensity and clearness of
purpose. But we must also remember that, while Great
Britain will welcome our activities in Palestine now, it will
certainly not allow us to do such things which might lead
to an increase of jealousy on the part of France and all the
forces which centre round it, or which might be construed
by the world as a hidden desire of Great Britain to annex
Palestine by simply using the Jews as a blind . . . Our activities must, therefore, be of such a nature as to meet these
objections . . .'

Weizmann's immediate purpose was to impress upon Brandeis
the extreme importance of American participation in the Zionist
Commission then preparing to leave for Palestine. This may help
to account for the rather melodramatic picture of the situation in
terms of a far-flung combination of sinister forces conspiring to
embarrass Great Britain and to wreck the hopes of the Zionists.
Some of the ideas sound a little like echoes of Mark Sykes, but
Sykes did not, in fact, entirely approve of the letter. Two days
later Weizmann wrote to Brandeis that Sykes had seen 'the part
of my letter . . . which refers to France and the Syrians' and
thought it too pessimistic. He himself, he said, did not agree; 'in

my opinion, the difficulties with the French are much more serious than they appear to Sir Mark.'[31]

Besides urging the Zionists to be conciliatory, the British authorities made some effort on their own account to allay Arab suspicions. Soon after the Declaration, an American 'special agent' in Cairo, William Yale, reported to Washington that British political officers—he mentioned in particular, Colonel Symes[32]—were doing their best to make the Declaration acceptable to the Syrian nationalist leaders then in exile in Egypt.[33] Early in January 1918 Commander D. G. Hogarth[34] was sent to Jeddah bearing a carefully formulated message from the British Government to King Hussein.[35] It began by re-affirming the determination of the Entente Powers to ensure that 'the Arab race shall be given full opportunity of once again forming a nation in the world.' The message then went on to deal with the Palestine question. 'So far as Palestine is concerned,' Hussein was told, 'we are determined that no people shall be subject to another,' but because that country contained shrines and Holy Places sacred to Moslems, Jews and Christians (mentioned in that order), 'there must be a special régime to deal with these places approved of by the world.' In other words, the protection of the Holy Places of all three religions must be treated as a matter of international concern.

Up to this point the message was explaining the policies of the Entente Powers as a whole. Then followed a passage in which the British Government spoke in its own name:

> 'Since the Jewish opinion of the world is in favour of a return of Jews to Palestine, and inasmuch as this opinion must remain a constant factor, and, further, as His Majesty's Government view with favour the realisation of this aspiration, His Majesty's Government are determined that, in so far

[31] 16 January 1918: copy in *Ch.W.P.*

[32] Later, Chief Secretary to Government of Palestine (1925-28) and Governor-General of the Sudan.

[33] Manuel, p. 184.

[34] Hogarth, a distinguished archæologist with special knowledge of the Near and Middle East, served during the War as head of the Arab Bureau.

[35] Printed in Cmd., 5964, 1939.

as is compatible with the freedom of the existing population, both economic and political, no obstacle should be put in the way of the realisation of this ideal.

'In this connection, the friendship of world Jewry to the Arab cause is equivalent to support in all States where Jews have a political influence. The leaders of the Movement are determined to bring about the success of Zionism by friendship and co-operation with the Arabs, and such an offer is not one to be lightly thrown aside.'

This last paragraph reads like an echo of the language in which, some eighty years earlier, Palmerston instructed the British Ambassador in Constantinople to impress upon the Sublime Porte how much Turkey stood to gain by encouraging the return of the Jews to Palestine: 'The Turkish Government must at once see how advantageous it would be to the Sultan's cause thus to create useful friends in many countries . . .'[36]

Hogarth reported to Cairo that on the Palestine question Hussein was accommodating: 'King seemed quite prepared for formula and agreed enthusiastically, saying he welcomed Jews to all Arab lands. Explained that His Majesty's Government's resolve safeguarded existing local population.' The words 'Arab lands' should be noted. Hogarth told the British High Commissioner in Cairo that 'the King would not accept an independent Jew State in Palestine, nor was I instructed to warn him that such a State was contemplated by Great Britain. He probably knows little or nothing of the actual or possible economy of Palestine, and his ready assent to Jewish settlement there is not worth very much.' The Zionists seem to have had no knowledge, at the time, of the Hogarth mission, but had they been aware of it, they would probably have objected that its effect, so far as Palestine was concerned, was to put it into Hussein's head that the settlement of Jews in Palestine was a matter on which he was entitled to have a say. All the same, the British Government had told Hussein that it was 'determined' (a strong word) that the return of the Jews to Palestine should be encouraged and had tried to make this announcement more palatable by the injection of the idea— one of Sykes' favourite themes—that the Jews had it in their

[36] Above, p. 6.

power to be of material assistance to the Arabs in realising their larger aspirations.

In Palestine itself advantage was taken of Weizmann's arrival in Jerusalem at the head of the Zionist Commission in April 1918 to bring him into personal contact with the local Arab leaders. Handling the situation with the address to be expected of him, Weizmann did his best to reassure the Arabs.

'Zionists,' he told them 'desire to create conditions under which the moral and national development of those of the Jewish people who have freely chosen to come to Palestine would be rendered possible; this development would not and must not be to the detriment of any of the great communities already established in the country, but must, on the contrary, be to their advantage . . . All the fears expressed openly or secretly by the Arabs that they are to be ousted from their present position were due either to a fundamental misconception of Zionist aims and intentions or to the malicious activities of their common enemies.'[37]

Commenting on the state of feeling in Palestine at the end of April, *The Arab Bulletin* reported[38] that Weizmann's explanations of Zionist aims had had a gratifying affect and had produced a better atmosphere.

But the improvement did not last. By the end of 1918 tension had again become acute, and when the Palestine question was discussed in December by the Middle Eastern Committee of the War Cabinet, Curzon's account of the local situation was decidedly discouraging. 'The Zionist programme,' he told the Committee, 'and the energy with which it is being carried out, have not unnaturally had the consequence of arousing the keen suspicion of the Arabs. By 'the Arabs' I do not merely mean Feisal and his followers at Damascus but the so-called Arabs who inhabit the country. There seems, from the telegrams we receive, to be growing up an increasing friction between the two communities . . . and altogether a situation which is becoming rather

[37] Speech at Jerusalem Governorate, 27 April 1918: *Zionist Review*, June 1918, p. 27.
[38] 30 April 1918.

critical.'[39] A Foreign Office memorandum of about the same date remarked that 'in the Zionist talk of a Jewish State the Arab portion of the population is well-nigh forgotten.'[40] Weizmann's studied moderation in expounding the Zionist programme had produced, for the moment, a certain détente, but its effect had soon worn off. By the end of the year the pendulum had swung back and a peaceful settlement of the Palestine question in harmony with the British assurances to the Zionists seemed further off than ever.

British war-time policy in the Middle East required that the Arabs should be encouraged in their national aspirations. Since the British Government was at the same time encouraging the national aspirations of the Jews, it had somehow to isolate Palestine, if it could, from the impact of the forces which it had itself helped to set in motion in the Arab world. But as the tide rose in other parts of the Middle East, it could not be prevented from overflowing into Palestine. First, there was the backwash of the impetus given to the Arab national movement by the fall of Damascus at the beginning of October 1918, when the occupation of the city was deliberately staged so as to lay the foundations of the myth that it had been liberated by Feisal at the head of an invincible Arab army.[41] Secondly, there was the bombastically worded declaration in which, soon after the capitulation of Damascus and the end of the war with Turkey, the British joined with the French in the surprising announcement that 'in prosecuting in the East the war let loose by German ambition' the two Governments had had as their object 'the complete and definite emancipation of the peoples so long oppressed by the Turks and the establishment of National Governments and administrations deriving their authority from the initiative and free choice of the indigenous populations.'[42] Syria and Mesopotamia were expressly mentioned in the declaration; Palestine was not. But it was part of the Arab nationalist creed that Palestine was an integral part

---

[39] Lloyd George, *Treaties*, II, 1143.
[40] Ibid., II, 1152.
[41] See Elie Kedourie, *England and the Middle East* (Cambridge, Bowes and Bowes, 1956), pp. 117-122, and sources there cited.
[42] 7 November 1918. Text in Report of Palestine Royal Commission: Cmd., 5479 (1937), p. 25.

of Syria, and had not Syria been promised a Government drawing its authority from the free choice of the indigenous population? How, then, it could be asked, could there be room in Palestine for a national home for the Jews? If, on the other hand, the omission of any reference to Palestine meant that it was to be separated from Syria and reserved for separate treatment, was it to be inferred that, for the sake of the Jews, the Palestine Arabs were to be deprived of the benefits to be enjoyed by the rest of the Arab world? Even if the Anglo-French declaration was not addressed to Palestine, it was audible there, and its echoes were bound to have a disturbing effect—all the more so because of the approaching Peace Conference.

Some of the half-thought-out ideas which, so long as it was only a matter of words, had been easy to clothe in sonorous generalisations were now casting lengthening shadows as the Conference came near and the Covenant of the League of Nations began to take shape. Among them was the idea of self-determination. Though in the framing of the League Covenant the word was not used nor the principle unreservedly affirmed, the draft Article on Mandates submitted to the League of Nations Commission of the Peace Conference early in 1919, and in substance adopted in the final text of the Covenant,[43] declared that 'certain communities formerly belonging to the Turkish Empire have reached a stage of development where their existence as independent nations can be provisionally recognised . . .' These 'communities' were not identified, and the place of Palestine in the new order in the East was left, at least on paper, an open question.

All this was not calculated to lighten the task of those with whom it rested to reconcile the Palestine Arabs to the Balfour Declaration and what it was seen, or suspected, to imply. How hard they tried depended to some extent on their personal sympathies. What was visible in Palestine was an overwhelming Arab majority, and the day-to-day impact of its presence was not easy to withstand. For many of the members of the British Military Administration in Palestine the reasons for the Declaration were a mystery. Even though few of them—it might be an overstatement to say none—would consciously have obstructed the

[43] Article 22—originally Article 19.

declared policy of their Government, their approach to the problem with which it presented them in their contacts with the local population was bound, whether they knew it or not, to be coloured by their personal views as to its wisdom and justice.

Weizmann was aware that the situation in Palestine was deteriorating, and, as the Peace Conference drew near, he began to press for some action which would show that the British Government's intentions remained unchanged. At an interview with Balfour on 4 December 1918 he explained why he sought re-assurance. According to a note of the interview in the Weizmann Archives,

> 'Dr. Weizmann submitted . . . that the Jewish position at present was critical . . . The Jews, he said, are falling between the wheels of the new political machine which is being set up in the East of Europe . . . This state of affairs . . . accounts for the great tension and anxiety which is felt in the Jewish communities all over the world with regard to the fate of Palestine, or, better, with regard to the interpretation given to the Declaration of the British Government . . . Zionism is not a solution for all the evils which oppress the Jewish people now, but it is a great hope and comfort, like a bright light showing in the distance . . . Moreover, a community of four or five million Jews in Palestine would be a sufficiently sound economic basis from which the Jews could radiate out into the Near East and so contribute mightily to the reconstruction of countries which were once flourishing . . . But all this pre-supposes free and unfettered development of the Jewish National Home in Palestine . . . so that we should be able to settle in Palestine about four to five million Jews within a generation and so make Palestine a Jewish country . . .
>
> 'At this stage Mr. Balfour asked whether such a policy would be consistent with the statement made in his Declaration that the interests of non-Jewish communities in Palestine would be safeguarded. Dr. Weizmann replied in the affirmative . . . In a Jewish Commonwealth there would be many non-Jewish citizens, who would enjoy all the rights and

privileges of citizenship, but the preponderant influence would be Jewish . . .

'Mr. Balfour agreed that the Arab problem could not be regarded as a serious hindrance in the way of the development of a Jewish National Home in Dr. Weizmann's sense, but he thought that it would be very helpful indeed if the Zionists and Feisal would act unitedly and reach an agreement on certain points of possible conflict.

'Dr. Weizmann replied that he had every confidence in the possibility of reaching such an agreement . . .'

Six months earlier, the British military authorities in Cairo had brought Weizmann and Feisal together in the hope that they might reach some understanding which would help to relieve the tension in Palestine. They had met on 4 June 1918 at Feisal's headquarters near Aqaba and, with Colonel Joyce, a British officer attached to the Sharifian forces, as interpreter, they had had an amicable but inconclusive exchange of views. According to a report in *The Arab Bulletin*, 'Dr.Weizmann told [Feisal] that the Jews do not propose to set up any government of their own but wish to work under British protection to colonise and develop Palestine, with all consideration for legitimate vested interests.' Feisal replied that, in view of the use which could be made by hostile propagandists of any pronouncement by him in favour of Arab territory coming under non-Arab control, he could only express his personal opinion that Weizmann's hopes were not incapable of realisation. *The Arab Bulletin* commented that what the meeting had produced was 'some mutual esteem,' which would be helpful 'when the time for bargaining comes.'[44]

When Balfour advised Weizmann, six months later, to seek an agreement with Feisal, he evidently believed that the time for bargaining had arrived. In the meantime, there had been some further indications of Feisal's views. Weizmann had spoken to Balfour of the urgent need for free immigration into Palestine. In advising him to come to an understanding with Feisal Balfour may have been thinking of a memorandum which had been submitted to the War Office a few weeks earlier by Colonel Lawrence. According to Lawrence, the Arabs 'will not approve Jewish in-

[44] *Arab Bull.*, 18 June 1918.

dependence for Palestine but [will] support, as far as they can, Jewish infiltration, if it is behind a British as opposed to an international façade.'[45]

But infiltration was not what the Zionists wanted or had been led to expect. The Palestine of which they had been encouraged to dream was not an Arab country which allowed some Jews to trickle in. Was there, then, no hope of bridging the gulf between what Feisal had let it be known that he was prepared to offer and the least that the Zionists could accept? Was it not at least conceivable that by an agreement with the Arab nationalists on a broader basis the Zionists might be able to turn the flank of the local opposition in Palestine? If the British Government's wishes were what Robert Cecil had declared them to be—'Arabia for the Arabs, Judaea for the Jews'—might it not be expected to favour and promote such an agreement?

Palestine contained, after all, only a trifling fraction—not much over five per cent.—of the ten million or more Arabs in the former Turkish Empire. The real driving-force of the Arab national movement was not in Jerusalem but in Damascus and Baghdad. Because of its special significance for Christians as well as for Jews, there was in any case no real likelihood of Palestine being at any time handed over unconditionally to a Moslem Arab State. What really interested Feisal was a settlement which would give the Arab nationalists what they wanted in the remainder of the Arab world, and more particularly in Syria, where they were drifting towards a collision with the French. It so happened, moreover, that the most implacable enemies of Zionism had been precisely those elements among the Syrian Christians which, swimming against the stream, favoured a French protectorate for Syria. To this extent, at least, there could be supposed to be common ground between the Arab nationalists and the Zionists. Might there not, then, be room for a bargain by which, Jewish predominance in Palestine being conceded, the Jews would undertake, in return, to support the Arabs in their larger national aspirations?

The idea that the Jews had it in their power to be helpful to the Arabs was not new. After a conversation with Mark Sykes in

---

[45] Memorandum dated 4 November 1918: *The Letters of T. E. Lawrence*, ed. David Garnett, p. 268.

April 1917 Aaronsohn wrote in his diary: 'Si les Arabes ont pour
eux les Juifs et l'Angleterre, ils peuvent défier la France.'[46] Soon
after the Balfour Declaration, Sykes sent Clayton a letter to be
read to the Arab Committee in Cairo. 'Jewry,' he wrote, 'is scattered throughout the world. If Zionism and Arab nationalism join
forces, I am convinced that the liberation of the Arabs is certain.
. . . Zionists, owing to my insistence and education, are now ready
to co-operate with the Arabs in freeing Syria and the remaining
parts under Turkish thrall.'[47] In the message from the British
Government brought by Hogarth to the Sherif Hussein in January
1918 it was impressed upon the Sherif that 'the friendship of
world Jewry to the Arab cause is equivalent to support in all
States where Jews have a political influence.'

What might be expected to appeal particularly to Feisal was
the idea that the Jews might somehow strengthen his hands in
resisting French domination of Syria. How strongly it did appeal
to him and how long he clung to it may be inferred from a Foreign
Office minute dated 30 December 1919, in which the writer—Eric
Forbes-Adam—remarks: 'Although some of Feisal's entourage
dislike Zionism, Feisal himself and his most influential supporters
are understood to realise that they can look to Zionism for sound
advice with both men and especially money as an offset to the
French.'[48] Forbes-Adam may have been thinking of a Note in
which a British Political Officer, Colonel Cornwallis, writing from
Damascus on 25 September 1919, had reported on recent conversations with Feisal. The relevant passage is as follows:

'Dr. Weizmann has approached him [Feisal] and two long
discussions have already taken place. I understand that Dr.
Weizmann, in return for the Emir's help in Palestine towards
the realization of Zionist aspirations, proposes to give money
and advisers, if required, to the Arab Government and claims
that the Zionists can persuade the French Government to

[46] 28 April 1917. It is not clear whether Aaronsohn is echoing something
said to him by Sykes.
[47] 16 November 1917: *Sledm.*, No. 71.
[48] *B.F.P., First Series*, Vol. IV, No. 409, p. 608. At the Anglo-French Conference at the end of 1919 Curzon remarked that the Zionists were difficult to deal with and might even, by some understanding with Feisal,
make trouble for the French: ibid., p. 598 (23 December 1919).

640

waive their claims of influence in the interior. The Emir is strongly inclined to come to an agreement but matters are at present at a deadlock since the Emir asks the Zionists to throw in their lot definitely with the Arabs against the French, while Dr. Weizmann is in favour of allowing the French to occupy the coastal districts, saying that they can be squeezed out later.'[49]

Early in January 1919, a month after Balfour had advised Weizmann to seek an understanding with Feisal and just before the opening of the Peace Conference, Feisal, having met Weizmann in London, was persuaded to join with him in executing a formal Agreement designed, as stated in the preamble, to provide for the 'closest possible collaboration' between the Arab and Jewish peoples 'in the development of the Arab State and Palestine.' The Agreement begins by declaring (Article I) that 'the Arab State and Palestine in all their relations and undertakings shall be controlled by the most cordial goodwill and understanding.' It is laid down (Article III) that the Constitution of Palestine shall 'afford the fullest guarantees for carrying into effect the British Government's Declaration of the 2nd November 1917,' and (Article IV) that 'all necessary measures shall be taken to encourage and stimulate immigration of Jews into Palestine on a large scale.' Provision was to be made (Articles IV, V) for the protection of Arab peasants and tenant farmers in Palestine and for Moslem custody of the Moslem Holy Places. The Zionist Organisation undertook, on its part (Article VII) to 'use its best efforts to assist the Arab State in providing the means for developing the natural resources and economic possibilities thereof.' Finally, the parties agreed (Article VIII) 'to act in complete accord . . . before the Peace Congress.'

To the Agreement Feisal appended (in Arabic) a proviso which Antonius translates as follows:

'Provided the Arabs obtain their independence as demanded in my Memorandum dated the 4th of January, 1919 to the Foreign Office of the Government of Great Britain, I shall concur in the above Articles. But if the slightest modification

[49] Ibid., No. 295, pp. 421-422.

or departure were to be made [sc. in relation to the demands in the Memorandum] I shall not then be bound by a single word of the present Agreement, which shall be deemed void and of no account or validity, and I shall not be answerable in any way whatsoever.'

The document signed by both parties included this proviso, to which, therefore, Weizmann must be taken to have assented, though what he had before him was not an exact English translation of Feisal's Arabic but a condensed paraphrase. This appeared in the document in handwriting. The writing is that of T. E. Lawrence, from which it may be inferred that he was the intermediary.[50]

Subject to Feisal's escape clause, the Arabs, so far as Feisal could speak for them, had now conceded—at least on paper—all that the Zionists required. In return for an undertaking by the Zionists to do their best for the welfare of the future Arab State, Palestine, unincumbered by any Arab claim, had, in effect, been set apart for the Jews. What Feisal had primarily in mind in his proviso was the achievement of genuine Arab independence in Syria. It would, however, be naïve to suppose that all would have gone smoothly if only that condition had been satisfied. In the resolutions of the Syrian Congress which met at Damascus in July 1919 the Feisal-Weizmann agreement was completely

---

[50] Text, with English translation of Feisal's proviso (which, unlike the rest of the document, was in Arabic) in Antonius, pp. 437-439. The document included a condensed English version of the proviso, reading: ' If the Arabs are established as I have asked in my manifesto of January 4th addressed to the British Secretary of State for Foreign Affairs, I will carry out what is written in this agreement. If changes are made, I cannot be answerable for failing to carry out this agreement.' This was in Lawrence's handwriting: see, on this point, statement by the Colonial Secretary, Ormsby-Gore, in H.C., 19 June 1936—O.R., Col. 1395. The Agreement is dated 3 January 1919, but Feisal refers in his proviso to a memorandum submitted by him under date January 4th. The explanation may be that January 3rd was inserted as the date of the agreement before signature but it was actually signed a day or two later. According to Antonius (p. 284), Feisal was strongly advised by Lawrence to enter into the agreement. An entry in Colonel Meinertzhagen's diary (12 February 1919, *Middle East Diary*, pp. 14-15) records his personal conviction that the Zionists should ' go all out for independence in Palestine.' ' I got Lawrence to agree,' he writes, ' and he promised Feisal's support.'

ignored. 'We reject,' the Congress declared, 'the claims of the
Zionists for the establishment of a Jewish Commonwealth in that
part of Southern Syria which is known as Palestine, and we are
opposed to Jewish immigration into any part of the country.'[51]
The Agreement was still-born, but for the Zionists it had at least
the advantage that they could point to it as evidence that the
national aspirations of the Arabs and the Jews were, as Feisal
saw it, not incapable of being reconciled.

Within a few weeks of his signature of the agreement it looked
as though Feisal might be having second thoughts. The Zionists
were disturbed when they saw him reported in a Paris newspaper
as having stated in an interview that he was opposed to the setting up of a Jewish Commonwealth in Palestine.[52] Weizmann
pressed for a denial and was supported in his protest by an influential American member of the Zionist Delegation in Paris,
Felix Frankfurter. Feisal must have been advised that the Zionists,
and especially the American Zionists, might be useful friends and
had better be appeased. He addressed himself to Frankfurter,
and in a lengthy letter, dated 1 March 1919,[53] emphatically re-
affirmed his belief that the Arab and Jewish national movements
had common interests pointing to friendly co-operation. 'Our
deputation here in Paris,' he wrote, 'is fully acquainted with the
proposals submitted yesterday by the Zionist Organisation to the
Peace Conference, and we regard them as moderate and proper.
We will wish the Jews a hearty welcome home.' The Feisal-
Weizmann Agreement is not mentioned or alluded to, but Feisal
speaks warmly of his close and friendly relations with Weizmann
—'a great helper of our cause.' 'I look forward,' he concludes,

---

51 Para. 7 of Resolutions of the General Syrian Congress, Damascus, 2 July
1919: Antonius, p. 441.
52 Z.C., 1921 Rpts., Political Report, p. 23.
53 Ibid., pp. 23-24; full text also in J.C., 7 March 1919. At the Shaw Enquiry in 1929 the authenticity of the letter was called in question by
counsel for the Palestine Arab Executive (Minutes of Evidence, I, 486,
492, and II, 847 (Colonial, No. 48: 1930)). This was, however, the first
occasion on which any such suggestion had been made after the letter,
which was widely published at the time, had been on public record for
more than ten years. Frankfurter himself sent a copy, on 23 March 1919,
to Professor Westermann of the American Peace Delegation: Manuel,
p. 234. Referring to Feisal's letter, Colonel Meinertzhagen writes (Middle
East Diary, pp. 15-16): 'This letter was drafted by Lawrence, Weizmann, Frankfurter, and myself.'

' and my people with me look forward, to a future in which we will
help you and you will help us, so that the countries in which we
are mutually interested may once again take their place in the
community of civilised peoples of the world.'

The Zionists had hoped, and so also—it would seem—had the
British Government, that by a broad understanding with the
Arab leadership at a higher level they might succeed in blunting
the edge of the anti-Zionist agitation in Palestine. Feisal, for his
part, by no means dismissed out of hand the idea of a bargain
with the Zionists; there is no reason to suppose that he was simply
playing with them. But he, like Weizmann, had to reckon with
his extremists. In dealing with the dual problem of French
pressure in Syria and Zionist pressure in Palestine he was not
entirely the master of the situation, nor was he always clear in
his own mind as to where his duty and his interest lay. His
dilemma was described in a dispatch sent to London in August
1919 by the Acting Chief Political Officer in Cairo: [54] ' The situation is exceedingly difficult for the Emir Feisal, whom I believe
to have made honest attempts to hold the balance between the
moderate and extreme sections of the Arabs and who desires to
fulfil his promises both to His Majesty's Government and to the
Zionists; and this very honesty has to a certain extent under-
mined his influence.' A report forwarded to London by the Chief
Political Officer some three months earlier had drawn attention
to Feisal's inability to control the situation in Palestine: ' Feisal
is beginning to realise the difficulties which he will have in reconciling the Palestinians and the Zionists and no longer treats the
question as a minor one. He has abandoned his idea of having a
Conference here [Damascus], but intends to ask various notables
to visit him separately and endeavour to convert them. He will
also try to induce the Zionist Commission to moderate its demands
and will probably propose a conference to the Peace Commission.' [55]

Neither Feisal's pact with Weizmann nor his letter to Felix
Frankfurter had, in fact, been followed by any perceptible im-

---

54 Colonel French to Lord Curzon, 30 August 1919: *B.F.P.*, *First Series*,
Vol. IV, No. 257, p. 368.

55 *B.F.P.*, *First Series*, Vol. IV, encl. 1 (dated 16 May 1919) to No. 182,
p. 265. ' The Peace Commission '—i.e., the King-Crane Commission.

provement in the situation in Palestine. In the spring of 1919 the anti-Zionist agitation was showing no sign of abatement and seemed, indeed, to be gaining momentum. Both the French and the Italian Governments had uttered words which sounded like an endorsement of the Balfour Declaration, but their local representatives were evidently satisfied that they would not be sorry to see the British in difficulties in Palestine and would not disapprove of some quiet fishing in troubled waters.[56] To add to the unrest, there was the excitement caused by the news that the American Commission of Enquiry sponsored by President Wilson would soon be coming to Palestine with terms of reference from which it might be inferred that the future of that country could still be regarded as an open question. The impending arrival of the Commission had precisely the unsettling effect which the Zionists had feared when, through Felix Frankfurter, they appealed to the President to re-affirm his approval of the Balfour Declaration.[57]

The reports now beginning to come in from British representatives on the spot show that the situation was getting on their nerves. On 2 May 1919 General Clayton telegraphed to London the text of a memorandum in which the head of the British Military Administration in Palestine, General Money, advised the Government, in effect, to drop the Balfour Declaration. 'In the present state of political feeling,' General Money wrote, 'there is no doubt that if Zionist's [sic] programme is a necessary adjunct to a mandatory, the people of Palestine will select in preference the United States or France as the mandatory Power . . . If a Mandate for Great Britain is desired by His Majesty's Government, it will be necessary to make an authoritative announcement that the Zionist programme will not be enforced in opposition to the wishes of the majority. . . . The idea that Great Britain is the main upholder of the Zionist programme will preclude any local request for a British Mandate . . .'[58] Clayton expressed his

---

56 As to the behaviour of French and Italian representatives, see *B.F.P.*, *First Series*, Vol. IV, note 1 to No. 183, p. 272 (2 May 1919); No. 196, p. 282 (19 June 1919); No. 358, p. 526 (10 November 1919); No. 413, p. 616 (13 January 1920).

57 Above, p. 597.

58 *B.F.P., First Series*, Vol. IV, note 1 to No. 183, p. 272. The further *B.F.P.* citations in this chapter refer to this volume.

agreement: 'I consider above a true appreciation of the situation. Fear and distrust of Zionist aims grows daily and no amount of persuasion or propaganda will dispel it.'[59]

Balfour, as was to be expected, would have nothing to do with General Money's proposal. 'There can, of course,' he wrote to Curzon on May 19th, 'be no question of making any such announcement as that suggested in . . . General Clayton's telegram.' He thought that Clayton should be reminded that the policy embodied in the British Declaration of 2 November 1917 had been approved by France, Italy and the United States and should be invited to take every opportunity 'of emphasising the general unity of opinion among the Allies on this matter in responsible quarters in Palestine.'[60] This was duly brought to Clayton's notice, only to elicit the rejoinder that 'unity of opinion among the Allied Governments on the subject of Palestine is not a factor which tends to alleviate the dislike of non-Jewish Palestinians to the Zionist policy.'[61]

In the meantime, the gist of General Money's memorandum had been communicated by the Foreign Office to Herbert Samuel, with an invitation to put forward any suggestions he might have to offer 'as to how the present hostility to Zionism in Palestine can best be allayed by the administrative authorities on the spot.'[62] The main point made by Samuel in his reply[63] was that 'the attitude of the administrative authorities in Palestine does not appear to be fully in harmony with that of H.M. Government,' and that, accordingly, the Government should make it clear to the Administration that 'their policy contemplates the concession to Great Britain of the Mandate to Palestine,' and 'that the terms of the Mandate will certainly embody the substance of the Declaration of November 2nd 1917.' It should also, he suggested, be made clear to the Administration 'that in no circumstances will the Arabs be despoiled of their land or required to leave the country; that there can be no question of the majority being subjected to the rule of the minority, and that the Zionist programme does not include any such ideas.' The Administration

[59] Ibid.
[60] Ibid., note 4 to No. 196, p. 281.
[61] Ibid., No. 196, p. 282 (19 June 1919).
[62] Ibid., encl. 1 to No. 197, p. 282 (31 May 1919).
[63] Ibid., encl. 3, p. 284 (5 June 1919).

should be instructed 'to bring these facts to the attention of the Arab leaders . . . and to impress upon them that the matter is a *chose jugée* and that continued agitation could only be to the detriment of the country and would certainly be without result.'

Unimpressed by Clayton's warnings, Balfour approved these proposals,[64] but it was some time before he gave effect to them. On July 30th he saw Colonel Meinertzhagen on his appointment as Chief Political Officer in succession to Clayton, who was now replaced by a convinced pro-Zionist. According to Meinertzhagen's record of the interview in his diary,[64a] he told Balfour that, in his opinion, Arab opposition to Zionism would not last in any obstructive form once it had been made clear that the Jews were to have their National Home in Palestine and that His Majesty's Government were determined to see it through. Balfour, he writes, promised to telegraph in this sense to Cairo. It would seem to have been at Meinertzhagen's prompting that on 4 August 1919 instructions on precisely the lines suggested by Herbert Samuel, and echoing the language of his letter to the Foreign Office, were sent to the Acting Chief Political Officer, Colonel French, for his information and guidance 'and for that of all heads of administration and their local representatives.'[65]

Even then it was thought advisable to move cautiously. When Weizmann, who knew of the instructions sent to Cairo, asked for the substance of them to be made public, Balfour firmly declined. 'I consider,' he wrote to Curzon (11 September 1919), 'that there are considerable and obvious objections to the publication at the present moment of such a statement as that desired by Dr. Weizmann.'[66] The reasons, or some of them, were mentioned by Meinertzhagen in his first report as Chief Political Officer on the situation in Palestine.[67] Having explained that the contents of the message to Colonel French had been duly made known to the Arab leaders, he discussed the question of publication. Receding

---

64 Ibid., No. 210, p. 301; Balfour (Paris) to Curzon, 1 July 1919.
64a *Middle East Diary*, pp. 24-27.
65 Ibid., No. 236, p. 329.
66 Ibid., No. 249, p. 355; No. 273, p. 381.
67 Ibid., No. 298, pp. 425-428 (26 September 1919). In an earlier part of the dispatch Meinertzhagen writes: 'My views on Zionism are those of an ardent Zionist. . . . I do not . . . approach Zionism in Palestine with an open mind, but as one strongly prejudiced in its favour.'

a little from the view he had expressed at his interview with Balfour on July 30th, 'the people of Palestine,' he wrote, 'are not at present in a fit state to be told openly that the establishment of Zionism in Palestine is the policy to which H.M.G., America and France are committed . . . It has, therefore, been thought advisable to withhold for the present your telegram of August 4th, 1919 from general publication.' After speaking of the need for 'a statement giving in the most moderate language what Zionism means,' he went on: 'It is only by a gradual education in Zionism, by a closer acquaintance with Zionists of the more tolerant and moderate school and by a clear definition of H.M.G.'s determination to prevent unfairness towards other creeds and races, that Zionism can be imposed upon Palestine without violent opposition. At the same time I am losing no opportunity to impress on Zionists the necessity of patience and the certainty of eventual success.'

The instructions sent on 4 August 1919 for the guidance of the British authorities in Cairo and Jerusalem were clear enough. They had been told in the plainest terms that the British Government intended to become the Mandatory for Palestine, that the Balfour Declaration was to be carried into effect, and that it should be impressed upon the Arab leaders in Palestine that this must be accepted as *chose jugée*. But for Balfour the situation was not quite so simple. In his own mind he was by no means enthusiastic about the assumption by Great Britain of responsibilities which he would have preferred to see accepted by the United States. He was not comfortable about a British Mandate, nor could he close his eyes to the fact that the Declaration, firmly though he stood by it, was not easy to reconcile with some of the principles—notably the principle of self-determination—which, as many were insisting with almost religious zeal, must govern the making of the new world order.

When Balfour met Brandeis in Paris in June 1919, he remarked, according to Frankfurter's note of the conversation,[68] that 'Palestine presented a unique situation. We are dealing not with the wishes of an existing community but are consciously seeking to re-constitute a new community and definitely building for a

[68] *B.F.P.*, pp. 1277-1278 (24 June 1919).

numerical majority in the future.' He had, he went on, great difficulty in seeing how President Wilson could reconcile his adherence to Zionism with the doctrine of self-determination, to which Brandeis replied that 'the whole conception of Zionism as a Jewish homeland was a definite building up for the future as the means of dealing with a world problem and not merely with the disposition of an existing community.' Balfour gave the argument a slightly different turn at his interview with Meinertzhagen a few weeks later. 'He agreed . . . in principle,' Meinertzhagen wrote in his diary (30 July 1919), 'to the creed of self-determination, but it could not be indiscriminately applied to the whole world, and Palestine was a case in point . . . In any Palestinian plebiscite the Jews of the world must be consulted, in which case he sincerely believed that an overwhelming majority would declare for Zionism under a British Mandate.'

Balfour's memorandum of 11 August 1919 on the future of Syria, Palestine and Mesopotamia[69] has already been referred to as evidence of his tepid interest in the idea of a British Mandate for Palestine. It opens with some pungent observations on the Syrian question, leading up to the conclusion that the Powers concerned have 'got themselves into a position so inextricably confused that no really neat and satisfactory issue is now possible for any of them.' Having spoken of the contradiction between the letter of the League Covenant and the policies of the Allies, he remarks that this 'is even more flagrant in the case of Palestine than in that of Syria. For in Palestine we do not propose even to go through the form of consulting the wishes of the present inhabitants of the country, though the American Commission[70] has been going through the form of asking what they are . . . I do not think that Zionism will hurt the Arabs, but they will never say they want it . . . So far as Palestine is concerned, the Powers have made no statement of fact which is not admittedly wrong and no declaration of policy which, at least in the letter, they have not always intended to violate.'[71]

Balfour is far from drawing the inference that the Declaration should be thrown overboard. He re-affirms his faith in Zionism

[69] Ibid., No. 242, pp. 340-349.
[70] i.e., the King-Crane Commission.
[71] Loc. cit., p. 345.

but at the same time expresses his distaste for cant, suggesting, in effect, that, having lost their way in a maze of words, the Allies would do well to drop pretences and come down to realities.

> 'The four Great Powers,' he writes, 'are committed to Zionism. And Zionism, be it right or wrong, good or bad, is rooted in age-long traditions, in present needs, in future hopes, of far profounder import than the desires and prejudices of the 700,000 Arabs who now inhabit that ancient land. In my opinion, that is right. What I have never been able to understand is how it can be harmonised with the declaration,[72] the Covenant or the instructions to the Commission of Enquiry.'[73]

Since, not only as regards Palestine, but also as regards Syria and Mesopotamia 'the literal fulfilment of all our declarations is impossible,' what, Balfour asks, would be 'the next best thing'? Ought not an attempt to be made, in a spirit of realism, to devise a settlement which, 'shall, as far as possible, further not merely the material interests but the hopes and habits of the native population,' while taking into account 'the legitimate aspirations of other peoples and races, in particular of the French, the British and the Jews,' and harmonising as fully as might be with 'the essential spirit of the various international pronouncements whose literal provisions it seems impossible in all cases to fulfil'? Balfour then goes on to outline his programme. Palestine is mentioned rather vaguely in the opening paragraph, which reads as follows:

> 'The fundamental conception underlying the Sykes-Picot Agreement should be maintained—namely, a French sphere centring round Syria, a British sphere centring around the Euphrates and the Tigris, and a home for the Jews in the valley of the Jordan.'[74]

Why 'a home for the Jews in the Valley of the Jordan' should have been referred to as part of the fundamental conception underlying the Sykes-Picot Agreement it is difficult to understand. Balfour must have forgotten that in dealing with Palestine the

[72] i.e., the Anglo-French declaration of 7 November 1918—above, p. 635.
[73] Loc. cit., p. 345.
[74] Loc. cit., p. 346.

Agreement did not make, and was never intended to make, any provision for the Jews. But he does, at all events, propose to set apart 'the Valley of the Jordan' as a home for the Jews, and in a later part of his memorandum he makes it clear that he is thinking of an area east as well as west of the Jordan, giving as his reason that 'if Zionism is to influence the Jewish problem throughout the world, Palestine must be available for the largest number of Jewish immigrants.'[75] But, while he speaks, in terms, of a British sphere in Mesopotamia, he is significantly silent as to the choice of a protecting Power for Palestine.

Forced to recognise that responsibility for Palestine was bound, in the end, to devolve upon Great Britain, Balfour came to accept this as an inescapable fact. He was compelled to acknowledge that there was no practicable and acceptable alternative, but it was without enthusiasm that he acquiesced in the policy favoured all along by Lloyd George and brought to fruition in April 1920, when at the San Remo Conference a British Mandate for Palestine, already agreed to in principle at the London Conference a few weeks earlier, was formally approved.

[75] Loc. cit., p. 347.

CHAPTER 42

THE LONDON AND SAN REMO
CONFERENCES

THE ZIONISTS HAD had their hearing at the Peace Conference as
early as February 1919, but more than a year was to pass before
a final decision was reached as to the future of Palestine. The
delay was due to the holding up of the Peace Treaty with Turkey
because of the ambiguous attitude of the United States.

Though the United States had not been at war with Turkey,
President Wilson and his advisers had in the early stages of
the Conference shown an active interest in the peace settlement in the East. It had been assumed that the United States
would take part in the framing of the Turkish Treaty and would
be prepared to accept Mandates for certain of the ex-Turkish
territories.[1] By the early autumn of 1919 this was becoming doubtful. American opinion was hardening against it and, indeed,
against Wilson's whole conception of the part to be played by
the United States in the new world order. The Turkish Treaty
had to wait until the Americans had made up their minds, and
uncertainty as to what they wanted, and as to what they were
themselves prepared to do, was a serious embarrassment to the
Powers more directly interested in the winding up of the war
with Turkey. The irritation it was causing in London is illustrated by Curzon's telegram of 18 October 1919 to the British
Ambassador in Washington: '. . . Existing delay in settlement
caused by American exigencies is already producing lamentable
consequences and may gravely imperil chances of Peace Treaty
with Turkey. Moreover, behind American scheme lie projects, at
any rate in some minds, with which we have not much sympathy. . . .'[2] It was not until towards the end of 1919 that it

---

[1] See above, pp. 613-614.

[2] *B.F.P., First Series*, Vol. IV, No. 550, pp. 826-827. Curzon's illustration
of these ' projects ' has a bearing, as it happens, on the Palestine question. In the telegram quoted above he goes on to refer to messages from

became clear to the other Powers concerned that the United States intended to wash its hands of the Turkish Peace Treaty and that there was no longer any serious prospect of American co-operation.

The delay in dealing with the Turkish question had had a demoralising effect throughout the Middle East and had to be brought to an end if the situation was not to deteriorate still further. It was agreed between Great Britain, France and Italy that they must now go forward without the United States, and at an Inter-Allied Conference which opened in London on 12 February 1920 the Turkish Peace Treaty began at last to take shape.[3]

By this time Balfour had left the Foreign Office for the less burdensome duties of Lord President of the Council, and both at the London Conference and, later, at San Remo the Foreign Office was represented by Balfour's successor, Lord Curzon.[4] Whatever may have been his personal views on the Zionist question, Curzon fought no less stoutly than Lloyd George for what had now become the settled policy of the British Government. Great Britain was to claim the Mandate for Palestine, to accept responsibility for giving effect to the Balfour Declaration, and to press for its formal endorsement by the Principal Allied Powers in the formulation of the Turkish Peace Treaty.

Since the Lloyd George-Clemenceau compact of December 1918 there had been a change of Government in France. The Millerand Administration held strong views about French interests in the Levant and was determined to fight every inch of the ground in their defence. The mood in which it approached the London Conference can be well understood. Without any tangible compensation, France had given way to Great Britain on the Palestine question and also as regards Mosul. This was

---

[3] The British Secretary's notes of the proceedings of the London Conference are printed in *B.F.P., First Series*, Vol. VII.

[4] Curzon succeeded Balfour as Foreign Secretary on 24 October 1919.

Paris and Constantinople reporting that Morgenthau was inviting the Turkish Grand Rabbi to come to Paris and wanted to put him in touch with the British Peace Delegation, and describing the Grand Rabbi as '[a] strong anti-Zionist,' as having been 'in close touch with the Committee [of Union and Progress],' and as being 'unreliable and anti-British.'

mortifying enough, but to these frustrations others were being added. There was the British pressure for a rectification of the Sykes-Picot line in favour of Palestine. There was the angry controversy between the two Powers as to the extent to which France was entitled to make her presence felt in the Syrian interior. What would be left of the Sykes-Picot Agreement if, in the end, Great Britain emerged with a solid block of British-controlled territory from the Persian Gulf to the Mediterranean, while the French were, for all practical purposes, left to content themselves with a precarious foothold on the coastal strip of Syria? Having manœuvred France out of her Grand Design in the East, Great Britain would be well on the way towards achieving her own.

Seen through French eyes, this was a realistic picture of the situation. It is no wonder that in the matter of Palestine the French were not in a notably co-operative frame of mind. If the British were not going to be helpful about Syria, why should the French be helpful about Palestine? In spite of the Lloyd George-Clemenceau agreement, they had never reconciled themselves to their complete exclusion from Palestine and had gone on dreaming of some kind of condominium. Within a few weeks of Lloyd George's meeting with Clemenceau Pichon spoke out in the Chamber about the secular rights of France in Syria, the Lebanon and Palestine and said that no doubt Great Britain would honourably act up to her engagements to France.'[5] At the Peace Conference, Pichon said, in March 1919, that ' the French Government . . . did not want to have the responsibility of administering Palestine,' but added that 'they would prefer to see it under an international administration.'[6] In a letter to Sokolow, printed in his *History of Zionism,* Pichon speaks of the just régime to be established in Palestine ' under the collective control of the European Powers.'[7] Only a few weeks before the opening of the London Conference in February 1920, Berthelot, the Secretary-General

---

[5] Bertie, II, 312 (diary, 2 January 1919): see *J.O.*, Chamber, second sitting, 29 December 1918.

[6] 20 March 1919: *For. Rns. U.S.*, ' Paris Peace Conference,' V, 1-14; Lloyd George, *Treaties*, II, 1058-1059.

[7] ' cette Palestine où un contrôle collectif des Puissances Européennes assurera désormais à chacun le respect de ses droits les plus sacrés ': Sokolow, II, ix. The letter is undated but was evidently written in 1919.

of the French Ministry of Foreign Affairs, was telling the British Peace Delegation in Paris that, while the French Government would be prepared, if a definitive agreement were reached, to support the British Government's views as to the future of Palestine, it must be remembered that there were a number of obstacles in the way, such as the movement for internationalisation and the demands of Italy, to say nothing of the claims of the Arabs.[8]

Berthelot's hint that France would be prepared, on terms, to refrain from embarrassing Great Britain in the matter of Palestine must be read in the light of the Anglo-French dispute about the future of Syria. Writing to Clemenceau on 18 October 1919, Lloyd George had reminded him that by the Sykes-Picot Agreement France had undertaken to uphold an independent Arab State in an area including Damascus, Homs, Hama and Aleppo. Lloyd George had pressed for the spirit of that undertaking, and of the Anglo-French declaration of November 1918, to be honoured: 'As it is the desire of the British Government that France shall exercise the mandatory power, it is clearly of the utmost importance that the French Government should spare no pains to establish a friendly understanding with the Emir Feisal and the Arab population of Syria.'[9] Two months later, at an Anglo-French Conference in London, Berthelot contended that, by virtue of the understanding reached in December 1918 between Clemenceau and Lloyd George, the French were entitled to be 'satisfied with regard to their Syrian Mandate,'[10] meaning that France must be at liberty to make her presence felt throughout the whole of the mandated territory, and not merely in the coastal zone, as distinct from the interior. On this point the French were to get their way. So far as Syria was concerned, the final result of the Inter-Allied discussions which began at the end of 1919 and ended, four months later, at San Remo was that Great Britain washed her hands of the Syrian question, and France, relieved of any further

---

8 *B.F.P., First Series*, Vol. IV, No. 398, p. 585 (12 December 1919). In a comment (December 18th) not communicated to Berthelot, Vansittart and Forbes-Adam observed: 'Nor would the internationalisation of Palestine seem at this stage a contingency to be contemplated, since the Zionists, who are primarily interested, are known to be strongly opposed to it.': ibid.

9 *B.F.P. First Series*, Vol. IV, No. 334, pp. 482, 488.

10 Ibid., p. 596 (23 December 1919).

British pressure in favour of the Arabs, was left with a Mandate which she could interpret as she thought fit. 'At San Remo,' Curzon told the Hythe Conference in August 1920, 'a Mandate for Syria had been accepted by France and a Mandate for Palestine and Mesopotamia had been accepted by Great Britain. Each country had left the other with a free hand to proceed with those Mandates, and this decision had been pursued with equal loyalty by both sides.'[11]

In the matter of Syria the French made good their claim, but they had hoped for still more. Even in regard to Palestine they had not despaired of salvaging something from the ruins of paragraph 3 of the Sykes-Picot Agreement. At the London Conference, when it opened in February 1920, they offered no resistance to a British Mandate, but they were not prepared to submit without a struggle to their total exclusion from Palestine. They were still feeling their way towards some kind of *de facto* condominium and tried to insert an opening wedge by insisting that the question of the Holy Places must be reserved for separate consideration outside the Turkish Peace Treaty. 'The Holy Places,' Cambon told the Conference, 'had been in the hands of the French since the fifteenth century. The Vatican had always recognised that fact . . . Should a Mandate for Palestine be granted to Great Britain, France would be bound to make certain reservations in regard to the Holy Places.'[12] Lloyd George would have none of it; it would be impossible, he declared, 'to create an empire within an empire.'[13] The French were to raise this question again at San Remo, where they fought hard for some concession, but in the end with little success.

At the London Conference the question of incorporating the

---

[11] *B.F.P., First Series*, Vol. VIII, No. 83, p. 716. Curzon was referring to the French occupation of Damascus and the expulsion of Feisal. 'The action of the French,' he said, 'had been accepted by the British, who had made no representations at all to the French in regard to that action.' He went on, however, to reject the French contention that, after what had happened in Syria, Great Britain could not properly allow Feisal to be a candidate for the throne of Mesopotamia, insisting that 'Great Britain must carry out its pledges to the Arabs—the pledges that they had given in regard to the setting up of an independent Arab State.'

[12] *B.F.P., First Series*, Vol. VII, No. 11, p. 109 (17 February 1920). Further *B.F.P.* citations relating to the London Conference refer to this Volume.

[13] Ibid., p. 111.

Balfour Declaration in the Turkish Peace Treaty was not discussed. The French view, later to be strongly pressed, was that there could be no reference to the Declaration, since this was merely a unilateral announcement by Great Britain and did not bind her allies. On this point the French were to fight their main battle two months later at San Remo, where the British delegation insisted that the Declaration should be incorporated in the Treaty —partly, perhaps, because the British Government wished to underline as emphatically as possible the joint responsibility of the Allies as a whole for the policy to which it was pledged to give effect. At the London Conference there was only some preliminary skirmishing, in the course of which Berthelot politely threw cold water on the Balfour Declaration:

' As regards the declaration of Mr. Balfour, when he said that it could not be held to amount to a formal Allied declaration and a binding engagement on the part of the Allies, he trusted that this would not be construed as intending any disparagement of Mr. Balfour, who was a man who was beloved by all.'[14]

Berthelot had shown his hand in a barbed reference to the Declaration a few days earlier: 'The French . . . would do their best to favour the development of a Jewish home in Palestine, so long as this development did not run counter to the wishes of the original inhabitants.'[15]

In the course of a confused and rambling discussion at the San Remo Conference two months later, the French eventually explained that they would be prepared, as Berthelot put it, ' to accept the terms of the Declaration in substance . . . All the Powers could do was to concede the substance of the Declaration—that is, to subscribe to the establishment of a national home for the Jews.'[16] What they still objected to, as they had objected to it all along, was any reference in the Treaty to the Declaration itself. Their attitude was not, perhaps, quite as irrational as it may at first sight appear. At the time of the Declaration the French had, by virtue of the Sykes-Picot Agreement, an undeniable interest in

[14] Ibid., No. 20, p. 184 (21 February 1920).
[15] Ibid., No. 11, p. 103 (17 February 1920).
[16] B.F.P., First Series, Vol. VIII, No. 15, p. 168 (24 April 1920).

Palestine. The position, as they saw it, was that Great Britain had chosen, without consulting them, to make a spectacular announcement on a matter closely concerning themselves. Their sneers at the Declaration at the London Conference and their curiously obstructive behaviour at San Remo may be explained by their not incomprehensible resentment.

As to their handling of the Holy Places question, their motives are self-evident. Once installed as the guardian of the Holy Places and the protector of Christian interests, or even as the principal member of some international body charged with these functions, France would have gone some way towards re-entering Palestine by a back-door. The prospect was, from a French point of view, all the more inviting because, as a result of events in Russia, the Orthodox Church had been left in a weak position and, with France in control, could be disarmed and pushed into the background.

At the London Conference there was no firm decision about Palestine except for an understanding that the Mandate should be assigned to Great Britain. As part of a synopsis of a draft Treaty of Peace with Turkey the following paragraph was approved by the Conference on February 21st: [17]

> 'Palestine, the boundaries to be defined in accordance with its ancient limits of Dan to Beersheba, to be under British Mandate.'

The outline of the Treaty contained, at this stage, no reference to the Balfour Declaration nor to any other conditions to be attached to the projected Mandates for the ex-Turkish territories.

The final consideration of the Turkish Treaty was reserved for a further Conference, to be held in Italy. The choice fell upon San Remo, where a full-dress meeting of the Allied Supreme Council opened on 18 April 1920.[18]

As at the London Conference, the British Delegation was headed by Lloyd George and Curzon. Balfour was not a member,

---

[17] B.F.P., No. 20, p. 182.
[18] The British Secretary's notes of the proceedings of the San Remo Conference are printed in B.F.P., First Series, Vol. VIII. Citations in the footnotes relating to the San Remo Conference refer to this Volume.

but while the Conference was in progress he was invited to San Remo for consultation[19] and on April 22nd was reported in *The Times* to have had a long interview with Lloyd George. Weizmann and Sokolow also travelled to San Remo, and so did Herbert Samuel, who, on April 18th, submitted to the British Delegation a memorandum[20] setting out his proposals for a Middle Eastern settlement. There should be, first, a completely independent Arab Syria, with Feisal as its sovereign. Next, Western Syria should be administered by France under a League Mandate, Feisal's sovereignty being recognised in this area if, but only if, the French consented. Thirdly, Palestine should be administered by Great Britain under a League Mandate—'the Mandate to embody provisions relating to the Jewish National Home which should be satisfactory to the Zionists.' Fourthly, there should be an independent Hedjaz, under the sovereignty of King Hussein. Lastly, Mesopotamia should be 'under British administration and, if desired, under an Arab sovereign.' (There might possibly be a sixth unit, consisting of 'a more purely British State at Basra and the neighbourhood.') The five 'States' (Samuel's word) 'should form a loose confederation.' So far as Palestine was concerned, the notable feature of the scheme was that it would link the Jewish National Home with a group of Arab 'States.' The memorandum was submitted by Samuel in his own name and makes no reference to the views of the Zionist leaders.

The San Remo Conference was mainly occupied with matters other than the Palestine question, which was not reached until April 24th. Once more battle was joined on the French demand for a special régime for the custody of the Holy Places and the protection of the rights of religious communities. The French pressed for these matters to be reserved for an Inter-Allied Commission to be appointed by the League of Nations and to consist of representatives of the religious bodies concerned.[21] They appealed to their allies 'to consider what was the moral situation in France created by centuries of sacrifice,' and pointed out that 'in regard to this question, for historical reasons extending over a number of years, there was a keen sensibility on the part of

[19] *The Times*, 21 April 1920.
[20] H.S.P.
[21] B.F.P., No. 15, p. 165 (24 April 1920).

the French nation.' Lloyd George's rejoinder was that there was no room for dual control. 'To have two Mandatories in Palestine would make it quite impossible for Great Britain to administer the country, and it might even easily raise difficulties in regard to her relations with France. In any case, the task of governing Palestine would not be an easy one, and it would not be rendered less difficult by the fact that it was to be the national home of the Jews, who were an extraordinarily intelligent race but not easy to govern.'[22]

The discussion ended in a compromise. On the understanding that France would not press for any special privileges for herself, Lloyd George agreed that the Mandatory (not the League) should appoint a Special Commission, with a Chairman to be nominated by the League Council, to deal with 'all questions and claims concerning the different religious communities.' In return for this concession, with which the French had in the end to content themselves, Lloyd George invited them to agree that the Treaty should incorporate the Balfour Declaration.[23]

On this point the French Delegation had at first been adamant. Curzon pointed out that 'the Jews attached a passionate importance to the terms of this Declaration, and that they would be . . . deeply incensed if the pledges given in Mr. Balfour's Declaration were not renewed in the terms of the Treaty.'[24] The French delegation was not impressed. 'All the Jews in France,' Berthelot said, 'were anti-Zionists and had no desire at all to go to Palestine.'[25] 'As regards Mr. Balfour's Declaration on behalf of the Zionists, had it,' he asked, 'been generally accepted by the Allied Powers?'[26] 'The Declaration,' he insisted, 'had never been officially accepted by the French Government,'[27] and as for Pichon's letter to Sokolow of 14 February 1918, 'Monsieur Pichon's connection with the Declaration was, he submitted somewhat vague. . . . It was not in any way evident that Monsieur Pichon had accepted the whole Declaration in its entirety . . . He [Berthelot]

[22] *Ibid.*, pp. 164, 166.
[23] p. 167.
[24] p. 159.
[25] p. 167.
[26] p. 160.
[27] p. 168.

disputed the necessity of referring to Mr. Balfour's Declaration, which had long been a dead letter.'[28]

Later in the proceedings, Berthelot, in a statement already quoted,[29] conceded the acceptance of the Declaration in substance, though not its incorporation in the Treaty. But the French still had a card to play. Berthelot 'attached great importance to the question of political rights.' Was it not essential, Millerand asked, that the 'political' as well as the 'civil' rights of non-Jewish communities should be expressly safeguarded?[30] This last diversionary move led nowhere. All that came out of it was an agreement to insert in the *procès-verbal* an undertaking by the Mandatory Power to the effect that nothing in the Mandate would 'involve the surrender of the rights hitherto enjoyed by the non-Jewish communities in Palestine.' Even then the formula was, from a French point of view, two-edged, for it continued:

'This undertaking not to refer to the question of the religious protectorate of France, which had been settled . . . by the undertaking given by the French Government that they recognised this protectorate as being at an end.'[31]

Without eating their words, the French quietly desisted from their efforts to keep the Balfour Declaration out of the Turkish Peace Treaty. Stubbornly as they had fought, their resistance had at last been worn down, and they abandoned a struggle in which they had been under strong pressure from the British and had had no support from the Italians.

On April 25th the Supreme Council agreed upon the terms of the Article relating to Mandates to be inserted in the Turkish Treaty. So far as Palestine was concerned, it provided that the Mandatory should be responsible

'for putting into effect the declaration originally made on the 8th [*sic*] November 1917 by the British Government, and adopted by the other Allied Powers, in favour of the establishment in Palestine of a national home for the Jewish people, it being clearly understood that nothing should be

[28] pp. 162-163.
[29] See note 16.
[30] *B.F.P.*, pp. 168-169.
[31] Ibid., p. 176.

done which may prejudice the civil and religious rights of existing non-Jewish communities in Palestine, or the rights and political status enjoyed by Jews in any other country.'

The resolution ended by declaring that the Mandatories selected by the Principal Allied Powers were France for Syria, and Great Britain for Mesopotamia and Palestine.[32]

In November 1919 General Smuts had told a Jewish meeting in South Africa that 'you will yet see an ever-increasing stream of emigration towards Palestine; in generations to come you will see a great Jewish State rising there once more.'[33] In a newspaper article published some three months before the San Remo decision, a British Cabinet Minister, Winston Churchill, had pictured the emergence of 'a Jewish State under the protection of a British Crown which might comprise three or four millions of Jews.'[34]

A different and more subdued note was struck by the Chief Administrator of Palestine, General Bols, when, on April 28th, he explained what had happened at San Remo in a statement read to a gathering of representatives of the Moslem, Christian and Jewish communities:[35]

'The Supreme Council has decided upon the Mandate for Palestine and that Mr. Balfour's Declaration regarding a Jewish National Home in Palestine is to be included in the Turkish Peace Treaty . . .

[32] B.F.P., pp. 176-177. The Palestine portion of the Mandates Article agreed upon by the Supreme Council appeared as Article 95 of the still-born Treaty of Sèvres. The Balfour Declaration was recited in substantially the same terms in the Mandate for Palestine as approved by the Council of the League of Nations in July 1922.

[33] Johannesburg, 3 November 1919: text in brochure published by the S.A. Zionist Federation jointly with the S.A. Jewish Board of Deputies.

[34] Illustrated Sunday Herald, 8 February 1920.

[35] Text in J.C., 7 May 1920: see also The Times 1 May 1920. The statement was an adaptation of a draft sent to Cairo by the Foreign Office on 7 November 1919 (B.F.P., First Series, Vol. IV, No. 353, p. 508). This draft was in substitution for one previously submitted by Colonel Meinertzhagen but rejected as going too far in endorsing Zionist aspirations, as well as pre-judging the decision of the Peace Conference as to the Mandate (ibid., No. 328, p. 470, and No. 353, pp. 507-508).

'I will now read you Mr. Balfour's Declaration, the inclusion of which in the Treaty means that there will be no interference with religious customs or the Holy Places or any curtailment whatever of the religious liberty of the subject, but only the maintenance of public order and security. Immigrants will be allowed to enter only as required for the development of the country, and immigration will be controlled by the British Government of the country. . . . The British Government will govern and in no sense will a minority be allowed to control the majority of the population when the time arrives for any form of representative government . . . The decision has at last been given and henceforward there must be an end to political strife and unrest. All true Palestinians must now strive with one another in healthy rivalry to the good of Palestine and the welfare of future generations . . .'

APPENDIX

SUCCESSIVE DRAFTS AND FINAL TEXT OF THE BALFOUR DECLARATION

ZIONIST DRAFT JULY 1917 (see p. 470)	BALFOUR DRAFT AUGUST 1917 (see p. 520)	MILNER DRAFT AUGUST 1917 (see p. 520)	MILNER-AMERY DRAFT 4 OCTOBER 1917 (see p. 521)	FINAL TEXT 31 OCTOBER 1917 (see p. 548)
1. His Majesty's Government accepts the principle that Palestine should be reconstituted as the national home of the Jewish people. 2. His Majesty's Government will use its best endeavours to secure the achievement of this object and will discuss the necessary methods and means with the Zionist Organisation.	His Majesty's Government accept the principle that Palestine should be reconstituted as the national home of the Jewish people and will use their best endeavours to secure the achievement of this object and will be ready to consider any suggestions on the subject which the Zionist Organisation may desire to lay before them.	His Majesty's Government accepts the principle that every opportunity should be afforded for the establishment of a home for the Jewish people in Palestine and will use its best endeavours to facilitate the achievement of this object and will be ready to consider any suggestions on the subject which the Zionist organisations may desire to lay before them.	His Majesty's Government views with favour the establishment in Palestine of a national home for the Jewish race and will use its best endeavours to facilitate the achievement of this object, it being clearly understood that nothing shall be done which may prejudice the civil and religious rights of existing non-Jewish communities in Palestine or the rights and political status enjoyed in any other country by such Jews who are fully contented with their existing nationality (and citizenship). (*Note*: words in brackets added subsequently—see p. 525	His Majesty's Government view with favour the establishment in Palestine of a national home for the Jewish people and will use their best endeavours to facilitate the achievement of this object, it being clearly understood that nothing shall be done which may prejudice the civil and religious rights of existing non-Jewish communities in Palestine or the rights and political status enjoyed by Jews in any other country.

SOURCES

1. Unpublished Material

SHORT CITATION	PARTICULARS AND REMARKS

A.A. Diaries

Diaries of Aaron Aaronsohn, in the possession of the Aaronsohn Memorial Foundation, Zikhron Ya'akov, Israel.
By the courtesy of Miss Rifka Aaronsohn, and through the good offices of Mr. Yoran Ephrati, the author has been furnished with copies of the entries for parts of 1916-1917.
In a number of cases the accuracy of the diaries can be tested by reference to the Sledmere *papers. In each case it is confirmed.*

Arab. Bull.

The *Arab Bulletin* (1915-1919)—a series of reports prepared for official use by the Arab Bureau set up in Cairo by the British High Command.
The author is indebted to the Librarian of the Foreign Office for permission to peruse and quote from the Bulletin.

Bentwich papers

Papers of Herbert Bentwich in the possession of Professor Norman Bentwich, who has kindly made them available to the author.

Brandeis papers

Papers of Justice L. D. Brandeis deposited at the University of Louisville, Louisville, Ky., U.S.A.
The author is indebted to the President of the University, Dr. Philip Davidson, and to the Dean of the Faculty of Law, Dr. A. C. Russell, for their ready help in arranging for him to be provided with photostats of the relevant papers, and to Mr. R. C. Carter for valuable assistance in this connection. The author's thanks are due to Justice Felix Frankfurter, Mrs. Paul Raushenbush and Mrs. Adèle Brandeis for their good offices in the matter.

C.F.C.

The records (1915-1917) of the war-time 'Special Branch' (directed by Lucien Wolf) of the Conjoint Foreign Committee of the Board of Deputies of British Jews and the Anglo-Jewish Association.
For permission to use this material the author is indebted to the Board and the Association.
Each of these annual volumes consists of a large number of self-contained sets of documents. For convenience of reference, the pages of each volume of the set used by the author—that belonging to the Anglo-Jewish Association—have been numbered consecutively throughout the volume, and citations in footnotes refer to this numbering. All documents in C.F.C. are copies.

SHORT CITATION	PARTICULARS AND REMARKS
Ch.W.P.	Papers of Dr. Chaim Weizmann in the Weizmann Archives, Rehovoth, Israel. *The author is indebted to Mrs. Weizmann for kindly arranging for him to be provided with microfilms of the relevant papers. The invaluable services, in this connection, of Mr. Boris Guriel have already been gratefully acknowledged.*
C.P.S. Jnls.	C. P. Scott's notes of interviews with persons in public life during his weekly visits to London. Deposited in the British Museum (no Addl. MS. number). *The author is indebted to the executors of the late J. R. Scott and to the Trustees of the British Museum for access to the relevant portions of these papers.*
Dugdale papers	Material collected by Mrs. Dugdale for her biography of Arthur Balfour and now in the possession of Mr. Michael Dugdale, who has kindly made it available to the author.
Gaster papers *Gaster diaries*	Diaries of, and copies of letters written by, Dr. Moses Gaster. *The author is indebted to Mr. Vivian Gaster for kindly furnishing him with copies of extracts from these papers, and to the Gaster Trustees for permission to use them.*
H.S.P.	Papers kindly made available to the author by Viscount Samuel.
Leon Simon papers	Papers kindly made available to the author by Sir Leon Simon, C.B.
L.S.P.	A small collection of papers in the author's personal possession. *These papers will, in due course, be deposited either in the Weizmann Archives or, as may be appropriate, in the Zionist Archives.*
N.S.P.	Papers of Nahum Sokolow, the property of Vallentine, Mitchell, Ltd., and temporarily in the possession of the author. *These papers will, in due course, be disposed of in the same manner as the L.S. papers (see above). They have been extracted by Mr. Florian Sokolow from a vast mass of documents left by the late Nahum Sokolow. The author is indebted to Dr. Celina Sokolow and Mr. Florian Sokolow for permission to use this material.*

SOURCES

SHORT CITATION	PARTICULARS AND REMARKS
Sacher letters	Extracts from the correspondence of Mr. Harry Sacher, who has kindly made copies available to the author.
Sledm.	Papers of Sir Mark Sykes in the possession of Sir Richard Sykes, Bart., at Sledmere, Yorks. *The author is indebted to Sir Richard Sykes for kindly making these papers available to him and to Mr. Christopher Sykes for his good offices in the matter.*
V.W.P.	Copies kindly made available to the author by Mrs. Weizmann of extracts from her diaries and correspondence.
Z.A.	The Zionist Archives, Jerusalem. *The author has been furnished with microfilms of a large number of relevant documents selected from the Zionist Archives by the Director, Dr. Alex Bein, assisted by Mr. H. F. Frischwasser-Ra'anan.* *File numbers are not quoted in the footnotes, but it is understood that there will be no difficulty in identifying and producing any document cited with a Z.A. reference which it may be desired to inspect in the Archives.*

Note: The author has not seen the Balfour papers deposited in the British Museum but has reason to believe that they contain nothing throwing light on the origins of the Balfour Declaration.

° P. 151, note 20. In his letter to Mrs. Weizmann, dated 9 January 1906, Weizmann writes: ' I saw Balfour to-day and had quite a long conversation with him about Zionism. He said he saw no political difficulty about obtaining Palestine, only economic ones. We also talked about Territorialism—I tried to show him how impossible it is and promised to send him a memorandum.'

2. *Published Works*

ABBREVIATIONS USED FOR CERTAIN TITLES

(This is not a bibliography)

SHORT CITATION	PARTICULARS AND REMARKS
Adamov	E. Adamov (ed.), *Die Europäische Mächte und die Türkei Während des Weltkrieges—Die Aufteilung des Asiätischen Türkei,* translated from the Russian by Kerstein and Mironow, Dresden, 1932. *German translation of Vol. VI of the series of documents from the archives of the Russian Foreign Office, publ. Moscow, 1924.*
Amery	L. S. Amery, *My Political Life,* London, Hutchinson, 1953.
Antonius	G. Antonius, *The Arab Awakening,* London, Hamish Hamilton, 1938.
Bein, *Herzl*	A. Bein, *Theodor Herzl,* trans. by M. Samuel, Philadelphia, J.P.S., 1945.
Bein, *Return to the Soil*	A. Bein, *The Return to the Soil,* Jerusalem, Z.O., 1952.
Bertie	*The Diary of Lord Bertie of Thame,* ed. Lady Algernon Gordon-Lennox, London, Hodder & Stoughton, 1924.
B.F.P.	*Documents on British Foreign Policy, 1918-1939, First Series,* London, H.M.S.O.: No. IV (1952), Nos. VII & VIII (1958).
Böhm	A. Böhm, *Die Zionistische Bewegung,* Berlin, Jüdischer Verlag, 1935.
Dugdale, *Balfour*	Blanche Dugdale, *Arthur James Balfour,* London, Hutchinson, 1936.
F.O. Handbooks	Handbooks prepared under the direction of the Historical Section of the Foreign Office, No. 60 ('Syria and Palestine'), London, H.M.S.O., 1920. *Originally prepared for the use of the British Delegation at the Paris Peace Conference and subsequently published substantially as issued to the Delegation.*
For.Rns.U.S.	*Foreign Relations of the United States,* Washington, Government Printing Office.

SOURCES

SHORT CITATION	PARTICULARS AND REMARKS
Gontaut-Biron	R. de Gontaut-Biron, *Comment la France s'est installée en Syrie*, Paris, Plon, 1923.
Goodman's *Jewish National Home*	*The Jewish National Home, 1917-1942*, ed. P. Goodman, London, Dent, 1943.
Gooch & Temperley	G. P. Gooch & H. W. V. Temperley (ed.) *British Documents on the Origins of the War, 1898-1914*, London, H.M.S.O., Vols. IX and X.
Ig'rot	Letters of Ahad Ha'am, pub. in *Pirke Zichronot ve Ig'rot*, Tel Aviv, Bet Ahad Ha'am, 1931.
J.C.	*The Jewish Chronicle* (London weekly).
Lichtheim, *Memoirs*	Richard Lichtheim, *Ein Rest ist Zurückgekert* (unpublished in the orig. German—published in Hebrew version as *She'ar Yashoov*, Tel Aviv, Newman, 1953. See note at page 206).
Lichtheim, *Geschichte*	Richard Lichtheim, *Die Geschichte des Deutschen Zionismus*, Jerusalem, R. Mass, 1954.
Lloyd George, *Memoirs*	*War Memoirs of David Lloyd George*, London, Nicolson & Watson, 1933-36.
Lloyd George, *Treaties*	D. Lloyd George, *The Truth About the Peace Treaties*, London, Gollancz, 1938.
Manuel	F. E. Manuel, *The Realities of American-Palestine Relations*, Washington, Public Affairs Press, 1949.
Pingaud	A. Pingaud, *Histoire Diplomatique de la France pendant la Grande Guerre*, Paris, Vol. I, n.d.; Vol. III, 1940. *It is generally accepted that the author of this work had access to the archives of the French Ministry of Foreign Affairs.*
Poincaré	R. Poincaré, *Au Service de la France*, Paris, Plon, 1926.
Samuel, *Memoirs*	Viscount Samuel, *Memoirs*, London Cresset Press, 1945.
Shane Leslie	Shane Leslie, *Mark Sykes*, London, Cassell, 1923.
Sokolow	N. Sokolow, *History of Zionism*, London, Longmans, 1919.

SHORT CITATION	PARTICULARS AND REMARKS
Spring-Rice	*Letters and Friendships of Sir Cecil Spring-Rice*, ed. Stephen Gwynn, London, Constable, 1929.
Trial and Error	Chaim Weizmann, *Trial and Error*, London, Hamish Hamilton, 1949.
Temperley, *H.P.C.*	H. W. V. Temperley (ed.), *A History of the Peace Conference*, publ. under the auspices of the British (later, Royal) Institute of International Affairs, London, Henry Frowde and Hodder & Stoughton, 1924.
Z.C. 1921 Rpts.	Reports submitted by the Executive of the Zionist Organisation to the Twelfth Zionist Congress, London, 1921.
Z.C. *Prot.*	Protocols of Zionist Congresses (*XI. Z.C. Prot.* = Protocol of the Eleventh Zionist Congress).

Note: The author regrets that he has not been able to consult Dr. N. N. Gelber's *Hatzharath Balfour Vetoldoteha* ('The Balfour Declaration and its History'), which is available only in Hebrew.

INDEX

INDEX

W

Warburg, Professor Otto, 61, 65, 97, 206

War Cabinet (British), and Palestine, 331–8; and Declaration, 337, 543–56, 588

War Office Daily Review of the Foreign Press, and Zionism, 517

Webster, Sir Charles, 125

Wedgwood, Josiah, 162–3; and American Zionists, 423–4

Weizmann, Chaim, 59, 60, 63, 97, 99, 117–30; and Zionist Central Office, Berlin, 117; and Lloyd George, 119, 139–40, 378–85, 423, 513; Smuts' tribute to, 120n; and Zionist Movement, 121, 162; and Jewish University, 121–2, 184; and Gaster, 124; and Balfour, 126, 147–8; 154–5, 423; and Samuel, 127, 134–46; and James de Rothschild, 127; and Ussishkin, 147; and Kerr, 319; and British rule in Palestine, 335; and Jewish Commonwealth in Palestine, 336; and Council of Ten, 348; and Morgenthau mission, 356–60; and Sykes-Picot Agreement, 379; and Russia, 422–3; and United States, 422–8; and French claim to Palestine, and Cecil, 422–3; and Russian Jews, 443–4; and Zionist Conference in London, 450–1; and Zionist claims on Palestine, 462–70; mission to Gibraltar, 465; and Labour Party, 475; and English Zionist Federation, 494–5; and Zionist Organisation, 496; and War Cabinet, 514–5; and British Jewry, 518–9; and anti-Zionists, 520; and Jewish State, 523; and Milner-Amery formula, 527; and Arab question, 630–2; and Zionism, 637–8; and Feisal, 638.

Whishaw, James, 170

Willert, Sir Arthur, and Reading's mission to Washington, 508–9; and Reading's statement on Zionism, 578

Wilson, President Woodrow, 195–6; and Brandeis, 196; and House, 196; and Declaration, 197, 510, 529–32, 595–601; and Turkey, 355; and draft declaration, 503–13, 517; and Zionist Movement, 517–8, 530; and Milner-Amery draft, 543; and Inter-Allied Commission, 596; and American Commission of Enquiry, 645

Wingate, Sir Reginald, and Arab question, 629

Wise, Rabbi Stephen, 197; and House, 509; and Milner-Amery formula, 530; and Wilson's attitude to Declaration, 594–5

Wiseman, Sir William, 529

Wolf, Lucien ('Diplomaticus'), and Conjoint Foreign Committee, 164, 171, 218, 444–5, 519; and *The Fortnightly*, 173; and Jewish opinion in United States, 218; and Jewish population in United States, 220; and formula for Palestine, 222–4; and Cecil, 450; and Peace Conference, 566

Wolffsohn, David, 34, 36–7, 40, 92, 314; and Ottoman State, 64; and support of Churchill, 150–1

Woolley, Leonard, 291

Wormser, Georges, and France's attitude to Declaration, 590.

Z

Zangwill, Israel, 122

Zionism and the Jewish Future (1916), 299, 300, 301, 454, 457, 622

Zionist Agency, Constantinople, 207; and German Embassy, 534

Zionist Bureau, Copenhagen, 101, 207, 438

Zionist Commission of Enquiry, 32

Zionist Executive, Berlin, and German Foreign Office, 216, 438, 534, 537–8

Zionist General Council, and Arab problem, 93; Weizmann and 121, 166; and Berlin headquarters, 191; and Jewish Legion, 487; and Jewish Commonwealth, 555

Zionist Movement, Germany and, 21; (1914), 59–94; diplomatic position of, 60; strength of, 66; Basle Programme and, 86; Tschlenow and, 167; von Kühlmann and, 211; Cromer and, 300; and United States,